Innovation, Technology, and Knowledge Management

Series Editor

Elias G. Carayannis, George Washington University, Washington D.C., USA

For further volumes:
http://www.springer.com/series/8124

Nagy K. Hanna

e-Transformation: Enabling
New Development Strategies

 Springer

Nagy K. Hanna
5852 Marbury Road
Bethesda MD 20817
USA
nagyhanna@comcast.net

ISBN 978-1-4419-1184-1   e-ISBN 978-1-4419-1185-8
DOI 10.1007/978-1-4419-1185-8
Springer New York Dordrecht Heidelberg London

Library of Congress Control Number: 2009938216

Printed on acid-free paper

Springer is part of Springer Science+Business Media (www.springer.com)

Preface

This book draws on my long journey during more than 35 years in international development assistance, mostly while working at the World Bank. It is motivated above all not only by my passion for meeting development challenges but also by revolutionary advances in information and communication technologies that offer powerful new tools for addressing these challenges.

This journey convinced me that taking a holistic approach that would strategically integrate the new technologies into development would be a long-term challenge. Even a premier development institution like the World Bank has been having a difficult time integrating the new technologies into development strategies and processes. Despite superior payoffs from such integration, most of the incentives within aid agencies and developing countries reinforce a divide between development practitioners and technology or innovation policy specialists. The fact that the advances in information and communication technologies represent a techno-economic paradigm shift demanding strategic responses does not make the integration challenges any easier.

This journey started with my early fascination with how technical assistance to developing countries has been using conceptual and quantitative models as tools for policy analysis, investment planning, knowledge management, and institutional learning.[1] I soon realized how prevalent is information poverty and its consequences on limiting choices for all actors in development—managers, investors, producers, and policy makers. I also realized that much of the massive technical assistance dedicated to building and using these models did not produce the desired results, namely developing local capacity and improving decision making. These technologies for decision making were not adapted to or appropriated by the local actors. The transfer of intangible technologies, like tangible ones, depended on complementary factors to make knowledge and innovation work for development.[2]

---

[1] These were the days (early 1970s) when planners put much faith in models. These models sprang not only from advances in econometrics but also new computing and software languages that permitted optimization and the simulation of complex systems with multiple feedbacks.

[2] I had the opportunity to testify to the US Congress on the potential for using satellite technologies to share knowledge and technology with developing countries (hearings before US House

My early experience at the World Bank covered several development sectors—public sector management, small enterprise development, technical education, and rural development. I was struck by the central role of institutional and technological change in development. Yet, mainstream development economics had a blind spot for such issues. Working day-to-day with policy and decision makers in the Bank's Resident Mission in Indonesia during 1978–1983, I realized that these factors matter more for development than financial resources. I then launched the first economy-wide management and institutional development assessment conducted by the Bank (Hanna, 1985a).

Later I assumed a variety of corporate staff functions at the Bank, including corporate strategy and knowledge management, and gained much insight into the role of information and communication in the effectiveness of institutions. In an increasingly turbulent and competitive external environment, public and private organizations have to shift from slow evolution and inward orientation to agility, strategic adaptation, and accelerated innovation and learning (Hanna, 1985b). The information technology revolution was being increasingly felt at all levels and was initially resisted due to concerns about information sharing, skills and role changes, bureaucratic and information power, and inability to measure quick improvements in quality and productivity. As a new president of the World Bank, James Wolfensohn, aimed to transform the institution into a "Knowledge Bank," I had the opportunity to help and gain a deeper appreciation of the new technologies and of the institutional change processes that must support them.

Shifting perspectives again, in a corporate evaluation function, I gained further appreciation of the ubiquitous and critical role of knowledge and communication in development processes and in pursuing effective assistance and holistic development (Hanna, 2000). Integration of development programs and ownership of policy reforms relied on information and communication processes among all stakeholders and on empowering the weak and disadvantaged partners with knowledge (Hanna and Picciotto, 2002).

In my next position, in the operations part of the Bank, I tried to build bridges between two distinct camps: ICT specialists and mainstream development practitioners. The new language of ICT specialists was incomprehensible to mainstream development researchers and practitioners. ICT specialists were true believers in technological determinism and the power of their specialized tools and knowledge. Hybrid staff who could bridge the two camps faced major disincentives. As there was no natural home to bring about a shared understanding of this new dimension of development, I organized a Bank-wide ICT Task Force, with practitioners from the main sectors of development. We drew a "manifesto" for the *Role of the Bank in Information Age* (Hanna, 1990) that was widely disseminated to senior management and staff. The basic response of top management was that, given competing

---

of Representatives, International Science and Technology Transfer Act of 1974). These were pre-Internet days, and yet there was much hope that knowledge and technology "transfer" could quickly impact global development. Much of attention then, as it is now, was focused on the power of the new technologies, regardless of institutional context.

priorities and the claims established by better understood sectors, this new challenge may have to be isolated or "outsourced" to other specialized aid agencies or wait for a better time. However, some progress was made. A unit was created in 1991 to manage ICT components in investment projects.

This "grassroots" initiative was complemented by publishing two reports: *Information Technology Revolution and Economic Development* (Hanna, 1991) and *Information Technology in World Bank Lending* (Hanna and Boyson, 1993). A key finding was that the value of ICT components had been rising in Bank lending ahead of other investments and already reached $1 billion annually by 1991—representing a significant 10% of investment lending. They are also present as components in almost 90% of development projects. But the quality of design and implementation of these components has lagged behind the rest of Bank lending portfolio, with serious consequences for overall development assistance.[3] The implications for development assistance were clear: ICT is already claiming a large share of development financing, is a significant factor in development and project performance, and aid agencies are challenged to design strategic responses to deal with this neglected dimension of development.

To reinforce this advocacy for mainstreaming ICT in development, I studied the experience of industrial countries with policies and programs for the *Diffusion of Information Technology* (Hanna et al., 1995) and the links between the *East Asian Miracle and Information Technology* (Hanna et al., 1996). These and other studies have shown that learning about technology can be accelerated through concerted public–private partnerships. Through these partnerships, countries discover promising new sources of growth and diversification and ensure that promotion initiatives are strategically coordinated. However, it was difficult in the 1990s to advocate assistance for technology, innovation, or industrial policies as development economics was then captive to market fundamentalism.[4]

In parallel, I initiated a dialogue with senior officials in several developing countries to help them build on their initial success in the ICT sector and to adopt a strategic approach to ICT mainstreaming across key sectors of the economy. India presented a promising case. An initial success was to finance a study of India's strategy for exporting software services, around 1990, when the industry was in its infancy. The study was fully owned by NASSCOM[5] and the Indian Government and subsequently disseminated widely within India and abroad. It led to much visibility for India's potential in this new field. A follow-up work was to propose a national strategy for information technology development and diffusion in support of poverty reduction and economy-wide competitiveness (Hanna, 1994).

---

[3] This finding was subsequently confirmed and reinforced by several independent evaluations conducted by the Bank's Internal Audit Department, Operations Evaluation Department, and Quality Assurance Group.

[4] See, for example, Yusuf (2009).

[5] The Indian National Association of Software and Services Companies.

Building on this momentum, I worked with local stakeholders in India on a proposal for Bank assistance to finance a comprehensive strategy and investment program for integrating ICT into India's development strategy. Senior Bank management declined to support such assistance on the grounds that India was not ready for such an advanced strategy.[6] Other proposals for Bank assistance in designing and financing national ICT strategies met a similar fate, including one for Sri Lanka that was to be revived a decade later.[7]

In 2002, an opportunity arose to develop a holistic approach to leveraging ICT for Sri Lanka's development strategy and to finance an integrated policy and investment program to implement e-Sri Lanka. The experience was documented in two volumes (Hanna, 2007a, 2008). The proposal was initially resisted within the Bank, since it was cross-sectoral in coverage and could intrude on departmental turfs. It took much persistence from the client country and task team leader to overcome resistance and onerous reviews before approval by the Bank's Board of Directors. The program is still under implementation, but much has been learned. A key lesson from design and early implementation is that developing visions, leaders, and new institutions is essential to success. A few countries have since adopted similar integrated approaches to ICT, with Bank assistance.

My experience with such approaches has since included a range of other countries, such as Russia, India, Philippines, Thailand, Brazil, Mexico, Armenia, Turkey, Jordan, and Ghana. I founded a global community of practice on e-development to promote dialogue among practitioners and to mainstream ICT for development. The ICT agenda is increasingly visible in national development strategies and aid programs, even though not well integrated into development thinking and practice.

But inserting ICT into development thinking and practice still requires overcoming major challenges. The gap is wide, as ICT specialists fail to speak the mainstream development language, while policy makers, macroeconomists, and other development specialists in more established sectors still view ICT as an add-on or marginal technical fix to development. This gap is shared across developing countries, aid agencies, think tanks, and academia. The perspectives of development studies and ICT science need to be integrated. Development practitioners and ICT specialists are increasingly challenged to communicate across this divide and to fashion the multi-disciplinary approaches necessary to manage the transformations made possible by this techno-economic paradigm.

A World Bank conference, held in January 2009, involving leading academics such as Jeffery Sachs as well as top industry leaders and development practitioners has reached similar conclusions on enabling development with ICT. The emerging consensus is that ICT is a transformational tool for development and must be

---

[6] In a World Bank decision meeting on the proposed project, the country manager in chair concluded that ICT is a luxury and that Indian decision makers do not use information for decision making.

[7] The Bank, like most aid agencies, was not ready then to accept that the information technology revolution would require more strategic responses at the Bank and country levels.

both mainstreamed in all sectors and integrated as the enabler in a core package for empowering the poor and reaching the Millennium Development Goals.

Development theory and practice cannot afford to miss on the most powerful and transformative technology of our time. The new information and communication technology can be central to development and can provide a sense of excitement and hope about development. But ICT is not a magic bullet to be pursued by the technology specialists in isolation of development thinking and practice. The ongoing technological revolution must lead to a new conception of development that integrates ICT into all development options, processes, and solutions.

These experiences and concerns led me to write this book. Its intended audience includes both mainstream development practitioners and ICT strategists. Bridging the gap requires mutual understanding and movement by both groups. For academics and students of ICT and development policy, it can be used as a textbook that bridges theory and practice. It offers an integrated framework to guide our inquiry into the future of development, enriched by lessons of experience.

This book was inspired by the former President of the World bank, James Wolfensohn, who advocated a comprehensive approach to development where ICT can be a powerful enabler. It draws on the insights and contributions of many colleagues in developing countries I worked with, independent international consultants and academics, and colleagues at the World Bank. I owe special thanks to Peter Knight, independent consultant and a former colleague at the World Bank, for his reviews of the full draft of the book. I would also like to acknowledge the insightful comments of Richard Heeks, Professor, University of Manchester; J.-P. Auffret, Professor, George Mason University; Sandor Boyson, Professor, University of Maryland; Elias Carayannis, Professor, George Washington University; Peter Scherer, former World Bank manager; and Silvana Rubino-Hallman, Inter-American Development Bank. Among World Bank colleagues, I would like to acknowledge the contributions of Philippe Dongier, Manju Haththotuwa, Samia Melhem, Alexy Volyents, Oleg Petrov, Arsala Deane, and Christine Qiang.

A final thanks is to the editorial staff of Springer, the continuous support of Elias Carayannis and Nicholas Philipson, and Sasikala Rajesh of Integra, India. It is my hope that this book will provide the impetus for a more active dialogue and partnerships among development strategists and practitioners on the one hand, and ICT for development, knowledge economy, and information society specialists who are concerned with using the new technologies to transform economies, governments, enterprises, and communities, on the other.

Contents

Section IV   Implementing e-Development Strategies

Chapter 1
Introduction

The ongoing ICT revolution, combined with the forces of globalization, has provoked the hopes and fears of countries at all levels of development. Rapid advances in information and communication technologies have been the driving forces of globalization. These advances have transformed logistics and created global, real-time demand-driven supply chains. They have created a new playing field for worldwide competition with increasing premium for agility and business intelligence. They made it possible to capture and leverage information and knowledge into all kinds of economic activity. Knowledge, learning, and the ability to harness ICT are now more than ever at the heart of development.

Could ICT make globalization more inclusive? Would developing countries be able to harness this technological revolution and integrate themselves into the knowledge-based global economy, or would they be left out of the loop? Could we harness the transformative power of the ICT revolution to generate sustainable growth, empower the poor, and extend public, health, and educational services beyond the richest markets? Could ICT help countries innovate new development models or do development differently? Could ICT become the platform for a new style of development?

Debate continues about the potential nature and scale of impact of ICT on productivity, growth, and poverty reduction in developing as well as developed countries. Skepticism prevailed for a decade or more about the impact of ICT on advanced economies, including the United States. Solow's famous productivity paradox summed it up: "you see computers everywhere except in productivity statistics" (Solow, 1987). Since the mid-1990s, studies began to show evidence of significant impact on productivity and growth in OECD countries, particularly in the United States and Canada (Brynolfsson and Hitt, 2000). Although productivity is the most critical factor in accelerating growth, productivity measures do not capture improvements in quality, variety, timeliness, and customer service.

Information technology is expected to be the catalyst for an unprecedented productivity surge, provided that investment in the technology is complemented by investment in organizational capital, processes, practices, and culture (Brynolfsson, 2009). Skepticism is giving way to enthusiasm. Some leading development economists like Jeffery Sacks are moving ahead of the pack to affirm that "information technology has been the single most important development tool of our

N.K. Hanna, *e-Transformation: Enabling New Development Strategies*, Innovation, Technology, and Knowledge Management, DOI 10.1007/978-1-4419-1185-8_1, © Springer Science+Business Media, LLC 2010

generation".[1] This is a dramatic shift for some, but for the majority of main-stream development practitioners, ICT remains a specialist domain with very limited influence on development thinking and narrow applicability to development practice.

Understandably, there is a yearning for a "magic bullet" for development. Much of progressive thinking about ICT for development is based on the slowly emerging but clear evidence of ICT impact in OECD countries and some dramatic results from a narrow range of pilot projects in developing countries (OECD, 2004a; World Bank, 2009b). But the magic bullet approach carries as much risks as ignoring the potential of the ICT revolution.

Many developing countries are inspired by the success stories of fast-growing exports of ICT services from a diverse group of countries such as Singapore, India, China, Taiwan, Korea, Malaysia, Ireland, Israel, and Finland. Similarly, the EU countries were inspired by the dynamism and productivity increases of the US economy in the 1990s and the emergence of the so-called new economy or knowledge economy. The ongoing ICT revolution, combined with the forces of globalization, has provoked intense hopes and fears in countries at all levels of development. The hope is to leapfrog to a fast-paced, knowledge-based, innovation-driven, and net-worked economy. The fear is to be kept out of the knowledge and learning loop, fail to surf the wave of change and perhaps to be left irremediably behind, unable to catch the next wave. Others remain skeptical or concerned but have not adopted any coherent response, perhaps overwhelmed by daytoday development challenges.

This chapter first identifies several disconnects between ICT specialists and other development practitioners and their consequences for missed development opportunities and wasted ICT investments. Next, it raises the issue of whether development practitioners would miss this techno-economic paradigm shift or respond by harnessing it for development. The ICT revolution demands a fundamental rethinking of development, without abandoning the lessons learned for the new global context. Next, the chapter outlines key characteristics of network knowledge-based economies, of innovation clusters and innovation networks, and of the role of ICT in this context. It argues for integrating ICT into development at a strategic and holistic level.

The remaining part of this chapter conceputualizies ICT integration into development as a process. It outlines the potential interactions and phases of this process, which will be elaborated in the rest of the book. This process should be thought of and led in strategic and creative ways so as to open up new development possibilities and leverage ICT as the most powerful and transformative technology of our time. It is a process of development innovation and self- discovery. The chapter concludes with a brief outline of the structure of the book and the main cross-cutting themes.

---

[1] Jeffrey Sachs, January 28, 2009, speaking at the World Bank's conference: "Enabling a Better World: The Impact of ICT" as part of the IT sector week, 2009.

Disconnects and Their Implications

There are four basic disconnects between ICT specialists and: (1) the providers of complementary assets; (2) public sector reformers and governance specialists; (3) community developers and their grassroots organizations; and (4) science and technology and business policy makers. Such disconnects and communication gaps have serious consequences for realizing the potential benefits from ICT investment and for opening up options for governance reform and broad-based development.

The first disconnect is between ICT managers and those managing other factors that are essential to transformation, such as human and organizational capital. The potential contribution of ICT will be determined by factors such as leadership, human capital, local institutions, supporting mechanisms for innovation and diffusion, complementary investments, spillovers, and learning. Investments in human resources, business process innovation and reengineering, and organizational change are necessary to realize the benefits from ICT. The prevailing disconnect ignores the interdependencies between ICT and other factors, in favor of a technocratic approach. A holistic approach would integrate and invest in complementary factors, promote adaptation and innovation, and align ICT to institutional reforms and development strategies.

The root of many ICT for development projects is due to their techno-centric approach, poor understanding of the socio-institutional context, and consequently, neglect of complementary investments in human resources and organizational change (Heeks, 2006; Mansell et al., 2007; Fountain, 2001). A holistic approach implies adaptation and optimization of various complementary factors to fit the context. ICT project managers have to connect with stakeholders, the providers of complementary change factors, and the context and process of development. The potential of ICT must be tested and deployed in diverse contexts, and such testing must lead to adapting the human, technical, and institutional factors to ensure that ICT investment contributes to development. Models for mainstreaming ICT in government and communities are not yet clearly established in most developing societies. Those models or best practices are unlikely to be universal as much of the nature and scale of ICT's impact is influenced by these complementary investments and contextual factors.

Concerning the second disconnect, the current status quo in which mainstream development practitioners and governance specialists continue to ignore the potential roles of ICT poses serious risks to reform and development efforts. The complexity and expense of some ICTs and poor understanding of the political economy that governs their use have led some to doubt the relevance and priority of these technologies for public sector reform and poverty reduction. Others have hailed these technologies as the great hope for improved governance and social inclusion in developed and developing countries. Neither posture is effective.

Currently, there is a big communication gap between ICT and technology policy specialists, who understand the requirements and potential of these new technologies, on the one hand, and policy makers and governance reformers, who understand the context and imperative for reform, on the other hand. The latter do not see the importance of this technological revolution. Yet, their awareness and ownership are critical to marshal complementary policy and institutional measures for ICT to induce change. This gap remains remarkably difficult to bridge despite two decades of profound global and local changes brought about by ICT.

This disconnect is reinforced by the current isolation of the disciplines of information systems and computer sciences from development economics and development studies. Information and computer studies tend to ignore the ideas of development economics and development studies (Heeks, 2009). Even though science and technology and innovation policy are moving back to the mainstream development agenda, ICT concerns are not considered a part of the innovation or science and technology agenda or the larger development paradigms and processes.[2]

Another form of this disconnect between public reformers and ICT providers is when policy makers delegate investment decisions in ICT systems and operations to the specialists, Aaccordingly, public managers rely on powerful global ICT providers to define their needs, without adequate ICT policy or in-house competency to hold powerful providers accountable (Dunleavy et al., 2008). Government information and communication systems have become big business in modern economies. Investment in ICT is increasing faster than most other elements of government budgets in developed and developing countries. Developing countries spend about 6% of their GDP on ICT, including ICT in government. This amounts to US $1 one trillion annually (2009). Public sector managers need to understand ICT as a critical aspect of the modern state and as a force for reform and transformation. They need to develop some basic expertise within government to exploit the new technologies and maintain well-contested markets for ICT services.

The third disconnect is between ICT policy makers and specialists, on the one hand, and community development practitioners and poverty specialists, on the other hand. Poverty in all forms is perpetuated by lack of access to information, knowledge, and skills, and by institutions of exploitation. Sen articulated a conception of "development as freedom" (Sen, 2000). And ICT has been viewed by some as a "technology of freedom" and empowerment. Yet integrating these perspectives has not materialized. A few community development leaders and NGOs have taken the initiative to integrate ICT among their tools to empower their communities, practice community-driven development, and enhance the livelihood strategies of the poor. But ICT and community development practitioners are not yet engaged in exploring what role information and communication play in poverty reduction and social learning processes and where digital technologies fit into these processes.

The fourth and final disconnect is between ICT specialists and innovation and business policy makers. In advanced economies, public policy and business literature have increasingly recognized the central role of ICT in competitiveness and business strategy. Over the last two decades, many leading corporations have

---

[2]This separation is most evident in the publications of the World Bank and the OECD Development Centre that are concerned with either innovation (science and technology) or ICT (e-government, e-business, e-society).

leveraged ICT for product, process, and business model innovation. They have also created the new and powerful role of chief information officer (CIO) and developed institutional mechanisms to secure top management governance of enterprise-wide knowledge, information, and ICT. This has been a two-decade journey; the role of CIO and the mechanisms for integrating ICT and business strategy and process are still evolving. But among developing countries, this disconnect still looms large. The communication gap is even larger between ICT specialists and development practitioners dealing with private sector and small enterprise development. The powerful role of ICT in promoting competitiveness, innovation, and entrepreneurship, and in creating and sharing knowledge does not appear in the debates on innovation policies, growth strategies, or SME programs of aid agencies.

These disconnects led to highly polarized attitudes to the impact of ICT on government, business, and society. At one end of the spectrum is the e-utopiainist or technological determinist literature, supported by ICT specialists, ICT suppliers, and ICT consultants and even uninformed policy makers and politicians. At the other end is economic development and public management and administration literature, written in often strongly backwards-looking vein, with a blind spot about the importance of information and communication to growth and public and private sector performance. ICT developments are assigned a footnote to history (Dunleavy, in Mansel, 2007, pp. 404–425). A few researchers, such as Fountain (2002), have transcended this divide to stress the Internet as a revolutionary lever for institutional change and, at the same time, the importance of institutional and political processes in shaping the use and diffusion of ICT.

Missing a Techno-economic Paradigm Shift?

Taking a macroperspective or long-term perspective, technological revolutions are associated with socio-institutional transformations or techno-economic paradigms (Perez, 2002). Each technological revolution leads to a surge in productivity development. We are living through one of these technological revolutions, perhaps one more profound than any other in history (Hanna, 1991, 2009). The impact of the ongoing revolution extends beyond the developed countries to countries at various levels of development. It extends from industry to services and from business to public agencies, communities and civil society organizations.

There is a significant risk that development practice will fail to appreciate the profound implications of the new techno-economic paradigm and the need to respond in real time to the consequent challenges. An incremental and narrow perspective of development misses viewing development as a process of transformation, as a non-incremental paradigm shift, and as a discovery of new sources of growth and innovation. As Meier (2005, p. 183) has rightly noted and Yusuf (2009, pp. 45–46) reinforced in reviews of development economics, development economists tend to think incrementally and short term. Meier states that "much of the evolution of development economics has been based on the reductionist model of analysis... failing to focus on development as a dynamic process with attention to the interrelation

of the parts" (Meier 2005, p. 185). This tendency and the consequent failure to prepare developing countries to master the new paradigm would constitute a strategic
failure in development thinking and practice.

A backward-looking development strategy misses the new possibilities opened
by the ICT revolution. Development strategies tend to be based on "me too," global
"best practice" or a "Washington consensus" mentality. The east Asia "miracle" presented an anomaly to the consensus of development strategies of the last two decades
of the 20th century, as it took a long time to interpret and absorb its lessons. To avoid
being left behind, developing countries must be active innovators and agile followers
in order to ride this technological wave. They should build the necessary experience
for the digital age, as they cannot afford to rely only on the "tried and proven" development strategies of the industrial age. This forward-looking posture is particularly
pertinent to reforming government and building the information society.

Responses to the Emerging Transformation Challenge

An increasing number of governments are responding to this technological
"tsunami." Two international summits of the United Nations have been convened
in 2003 and 2005: the World Summits on Information Society (WSIS)—with over
20,000 participants in each, including many heads of states, top policy makers, business leaders, international aid agencies, the media, and thousands of NGOs. The
dominant thrust of these summits and many follow-up conferences and working
committees has been to capture and refine a global commitment on leveraging ICT
as a critical ingredient of development. Policy makers in developing countries hear
the hype from such conferences and ICT multinationals, hear of the progress made
by some leading nations like Korea and Singapore, see the impact from pilot and
demonstration projects and are infused with a sense of urgency.

The response of many governments has been to formulate national ICT policies and strategies, where ICT is treated mainly as a sector or industry. Donors and
aid agencies have responded by piloting a variety of ICT applications for specific
sectors or target groups, by including ICT components in development projects,
by dealing with telecommunications infrastructure as a free-standing sector, and
most recently, by carrying out assessments of e-readiness. But how effective are
such responses? Are the core ministries and top policy makers engaged in shaping
development policies to harness ICT in all economic sectors?

The current status quo whereby mainstream development practitioners continue
to ignore the potential roles of ICT poses serious risks to development. The complexity and expense of some ICTs and the urgent needs of the poor have led some
to doubt the relevance and priority of ICT for development. Others have hailed
the promises of these technologies as the greatest hope for developing countries.
Currently, there is a big communication gap between ICT and technology policy
specialists who understand the potential benefits and implications of these new
technologies, on the one hand, and mainstream development economists, other
sector specialists, and policy makers who do not see the importance of this technological revolution, but whose awareness and ownership are critical to marshal

complementary policy and institutional measures for ICT to enable development. This gap remains remarkably difficult to bridge despite two decades of profound changes brought about by ICT, in the global marketplace and particularly among developed countries.

With few exceptions, almost all countries did not start with a comprehensive strategy for ICT in development or e-Transformation. They often started with isolated pilots to explore or demonstrate the role and relevance of ICT in development. Aid agencies, NGOs, and/or private businesses often took the lead in financing pilot initiatives. Government agencies usually operate in silos and few have the leadership and institutions to develop a holistic vision or program of e-development. Some governments partnered with the private sector to invest in a segment or another of e-development such as the telecommunications infrastructure, the IT sector, or IT-enabled services. Few progressive policy makers led e-strategies for their sectors, in education, health, or other priority e-sectors.

Some pioneering countries have adopted progressively more comprehensive approaches to their national ICT strategies and developed their economic growth and information society strategies around ICT as an enabler as in Korea, Singapore, Ireland, Taiwan, Finland, and Chile. In the last decade or so, the UNDP supported a large number of national ICT strategies that were more comprehensive in coverage than a sectoral ICT strategy. These strategy documents were seldom implemented for lack of resources, implementing mechanisms, and/or local ownership. Only recently governments have begun to adopt clear steps toward designing and implementing national ICT strategies and integrated e-development programs.

Countries have to fashion their own responses. The ongoing technological, institutional, and economic transformations are a rather recent and complex phenomenon, and poorly understood at present. What must be done to enable a country to take advantage of the opportunities and avoid the risks of this global change? What are the common elements and emerging best practices of e-enabled development strategies? What approaches to strategy formulation proved successful? How could strategies be turned into results?

Countries may take one of three postures. They may surf the Schumpeterian wave to gain relative position in global competitiveness. Alternatively, they may strive to just keep up with this technological wave, to maintain their current competitive position, and avoid getting crushed in the undertow. The third posture is for a country to ignore this ongoing revolution and take a wait-and-see attitude, in the hope that this technological paradigm will become more predictable, best practices would be established at a global scale, and learning costs would be minimized. Opting for the third option, these countries would risk losing their competitive position in many key industries, perhaps dramatically.

Given the magnitude and pace of this technological wave of creative destruction, passive postures and ad hoc responses are likely to lead to erosion in competitiveness and even marginalization.

The potential of ICTs must be tested and deployed in the context of developing countries. Models for mainstreaming ICT in government, business, and communities are not yet clearly established. These models or best practices are unlikely to be universal as much of the nature and scale of ICT impact are influenced by complementary and contextual factors. The potential contribution of ICT will be determined by factors such as political economy, human capital, local institutions, supporting mechanisms for innovation and diffusion, complementary investments and innovations, and externalities, spillovers, and learning. A proactive posture would integrate and invest in these complementary factors, promote innovation in support of e-Transformation, and use ICT to make the greatest development impact.

A Development Paradigm for the ICT Revolution

Technological revolutions and the associated socio-institutional transformations or techno-economic paradigms have been studied from the perspective and in the context of the early adopters (Perez, 2002; Chapter 2). Each technological revolution is unique, with its set of opportunities to deploy and problems to overcome, its set of solutions and techno-economic paradigm, and its set of best practice. Each leads to a surge of productivity, a surge of development. We are living through one of these technological revolutions, perhaps one more profound than any other in history. To take advantage of the information and communication revolution for development, it should be also viewed from the perspective of the fast followers among developing countries.

In past revolutions, the diffusion of the techno-economic paradigm was sequential, and as paradigms matured in the core countries, investment opportunities moved further and further out to the periphery, stretching and spreading across the world in successive waves or frontiers. However, in a highly globalized and networked world, the ongoing ICT revolution and its paradigm are likely to be worldwide in character, from its early phases. The spread of trade and production networks across developed and developing countries began from early phases of this revolution, as in the case of mobile phone and Internet penetration. Global competition demands ICT adoption among all participants. Some of the periphery countries have been leaping ahead and catching up during the early phases in the core countries, such as Korea, Singapore, Taiwan.

I argue for development strategies that would harness the potential of, and be responsive to the ongoing information and communication revolution. Prevailing development theories and practices have been conditioned and shaped by the industrial age and its techno-economic paradigm—emphasis on centralization, mass production, physical infrastructures, tangible investment, energy intensity, hierarchical organizations, isolated R&D functions, etc. Information, knowledge, innovation, networks, lifelong learning, knowledge institutions, and new technologies play limited roles in such development strategies. We need to understand the potential of the ongoing technological revolution, its requirements, and its techno-economic paradigm so we can define the new best practice frontiers for development.

There is a significant risk that development practice would fail to understand the profound implications of the new techno-economic paradigm and to respond in real time to the consequent challenges. As Meier (2005, p. 183) has rightly noted, and

Yusuf (2009, pp. 45–46) reinforced in reviews of development economics, development economists tend to think small, incrementally, and short term. Meier states that "much of the evolution of development economics has been based on the reductionist model of analysis…failing to focus on development as a dynamic process with attention to the interrelation of the parts" (Meier, 2005; p. 185). Similarly, Yusuf, in reviewing the history of World Development Reports of the World Bank over 30 years, states that "Economists remain highly specialized, and most view development from extremely narrow perspectives" (Yusuf, 2009, p. 103).

This incremental and narrow view of development has led to ignoring issues of technological and institutional innovation by mainstream economists for most of the six decades of development aid. It could miss viewing development as a process of transformation, non-incremental paradigm shift, and discovery of new sources of growth. Riding the waves of paradigm shifts or creative destruction is a highrisk, high-impact business. And aid agencies are usually risk averse, less attuned to such opportunities.

Building on Emerging Lessons of Development

Leveraging ICT for development, e-development or e-Transformation, should build on the broader lessons learned about development, growth, and poverty reduction. It draws on the hardwon lessons of development, that is, the centrality of knowledge, technological change, institutions, governance, investment climate, inclusion, and sustainability (Yusuf, 2009; Stiglitz, 1998; Rodrik, 2007).

e-Transformation is not just about particular sectors—knowledge industries or high-tech or the ICT sector—however important these may be as new sources for growth. e-Transformation is not about a newfound single factor or magic bullet that would substitute for capital investment, human development, effective governance, or institutional development as a source of growth and poverty reduction. Rather, e-development is about leveraging technology, innovation, and entrepreneurship for smart development (Carayannis and Caroline, 2006; Hanna, 2007b). It is about harnessing a new techno-economic paradigm that is relevant to developed and developing countries alike.

As the focus on development broadened, and became most holistic, incorporating such issues as governance and institutions, development rules, and policy recipes become less certain and less universal, hence the growing emphasis on experimentation, participatory development, and learning processes. E-development draws on the broad lessons of economic and social development as process of transformation that requires holistic and long-term visions, societal ownership, partnerships across stakeholders, and enhanced experimentation, learning, accountability, and evaluation of results (Hanna and Picciotto, 2002).

Development is increasingly viewed as a process of change and learning (Rodrik, 2004, 2007; Stiglitz, 1998, 1999b). It is a nonlinear, discontinuous, and uncertain process. Innovation, technological change, institutional transformation, and capability development are at the heart of this process (Rodrik, 2007; Dosi et al.,

1988; Freeman and Soete, 1997). Technology is much more than an ingredient in development strategies; it is an enabling tool and conditioning element of their viability. As technology changes, it opens new frontiers and sets conditions that generate development opportunities. Development becomes one of learning to benefit from opportunities arising from technological breakthroughs. A new technological revolution would constitute major discontinuities and shifts in the direction of change, providing new paths to development and opportunities for learning and catching up (Perez and Soete, 1988; Perez, 2001).

There is a growing recognition of the contribution of knowledge for development (Stiglitz, 1999a; World Bank, 1999). Development thinking has shifted over time from considering investment as the primary source of growth to one that gives due consideration to raising total factor productivity, with the help of upgrading technology, developing institutions, and deploying knowledge. There is also growing awareness of the enormous disparities in access to knowledge and communication and their implications for development. A strategy to take maximum advantage of the ICT revolution would thus respond to this belated recognition of the role of knowledge in development.

The context of development has been also changing. In a globalizing and connected world, ICT, the Internet, and institutions that are governing and transforming the sharing of information and knowledge had become integral to growth and poverty reduction. The digitalization of information flows is enabling massive knowledge transfers. Developing countries could move closer to the knowledge frontiers in health and educational standards, public sector management, and business models. Smart growth could be pursued through "inspiration," not just "perspiration" (Krugman, 1994). Growth could be generated from intangible resources, putting knowledge to work, adopting networked forms of organization, outsourcing business processes, and practicing new ways of doing business.

As will be explored in later chapters, new technology tools are also raising fresh issues concerning training in new skills, building of innovation systems, developing ICT governance systems, protection of intellectual property, and transacting, working, and living in a digital fast-moving world. Increasingly, policy makers will have to put knowledge and technology to work, and identify those enabling technologies with the greatest long-run potential for growth and poverty reduction. Learning to manage and deal effectively with these issues will make a significant difference to development outcomes. Smart policies will have to target areas for technology and capacity development, and to steer resources to these areas and over long periods to realize their full potential. This targeting will not be limited to ICT as an industry, but also as a core competency to apply ICT as a general-purpose technology.

The ICT revolution offers an avenue for shortening or leapfrogging some early stages of low-level adding industrialization for some countries and that route has been in part taken by some inspiring examples like Korea, Finland, Singapore, Ireland, and Mauritius, among others. This route is still open to other larger countries as India and the Philippines are demonstrating (Chapter 8 on the ICT industries).

But e-Transformation is not the domain of the few who moved fast ahead or of some privileged sectors. It is not just about knowledge-intensive development, "weightless" growth, or IT-based services. It is not be limited to ICT as a sector or to high-tech and knowledge-based sectors. Much of the gains in Total Factor Productivity (TFP) come from technology-embodied imports, of which ICT is an integral part. They also come from institutional and business process innovations, increasingly enabled by ICT. E-development is about enabling transformation and enhancing competitiveness of sources of growth across all key sectors of the economy (Chapters 11–14 on ICT applications in government, business, and community). e-Transformation is about ICT-enabled, broad-based, holistic development.

e-Transformation is broader than that of *high technology* or the *new economy*. It is more linked to knowledge, innovation, and competitive economy and inclusive, learning, and information society. But unlike the knowledge economy, which deals with the intangible resource of knowledge and the outcome of knowledge economy, it focuses on ICT as an entry point and takes a holistic approach to harness this technological revolution to transform the economy and society. This means acting on all elements of the e-development process, including policies, institutions, and capabilities to leverage the new technologies, and not just promoting the ICT industry or ICT investments.

Development experience also points to the centrality of institutions, leadership, and governance. Structural adjustment programs since the 1980s proved inadequate to spur growth without getting the institutions right. Deliberate and broadly owned strategy, strong government leadership and commitment, functioning market institutions, transparency and accountability, and a long-time horizon are also necessary for sustained growth and poverty reduction (World Bank, 2002). e-Transformation therefore builds on these lessons to realize the new ends of development. It further provides powerful tools for accelerating the development of institutions and governance. Later chapters—covering e-government, e-business, and e-society applications—will show how ICT can promote governance and effective regulation as well as strategic, institutional and grassroots learning.

The new technologies are potentially powerful tools for addressing the long-standing issues of institutional development, as they enable advanced forms of transparency, accountability, interactions, organization, and institutions in an economy. The impact of ICT is not limited to information sharing or knowledge transfer. It is a potentially powerful tool to transform the institutional structure for the organization of production and society. The reorganization that results from digital coordination brings about new and more advanced forms of organization, ways of doing business, and rules of the game. Advanced tools of information and communication can enhance speed and reduce costs of transactions, reduce uncertainties, promote effective interactivity, and enable enforcement of new rules of the game. They can facilitate experimentation with institutional forms and enable institutional flexibility and diversity.

Improved understanding of development in general and the microeconomics of growth in particular led to placing heavy emphasis on institutions that affect market functioning, investment climate, and the entry, growth, and innovativeness of enterprises (World Bank, World Development Reports of 2002 and 2005; Yusuf, 2009). Information gaps and asymmetries are major causes of market failures and inequities. Also high transaction costs, high regulatory burden, and many other aspects of poor investment climate exert major barriers to the entry, functioning and growth of firms. Advanced ICT application in government, business, and the media holds major promises in removing impediments to the free flow of information and reducing information gaps. Similarly, e-government and e-business applications can lower transaction costs, simplify procedures, shorten the time needed to fulfill them, facilitate trade, and create greater transparency and internal labor market flexibility. Already, some municipalities are demonstrating the dramatic impact of such applications on speeding transactions and reducing their costs (Chapter 13).

Development economics has long neglected leadership and managerial development and innovation as key determinants of development. Political leadership and managerial cadres are assumed to be given, not developed. Yet, experience demonstrates clearly that leadership, particularly political leadership, is essential to policy reform and institutional transformation. The quality and determination of the political leadership make a deep imprint on economic performance, as demonstrated by the superior economic performance of several East Asian and Nordic countries. Recently, some leading development economists have challenged this neglect. Rodrik, for example, writes "An attitudinal change on the part of the top political leadership...often plays as large role as the scope of policy reform itself" (Rodrik, 2007, pp. 38–39). Attitudinal changes on the part of leadership can mend the investment environment, shift e-government applications from window dressing to true transformation, and help build an inclusive information society.

e-Transformation, as explored in this book, emphasizes the role of leadership— political, managerial, social, and technical—in leading the necessary policy reforms and ICT-enabled process and service innovation. It also gives due attention to developing e-leadership institutions, e-policy frameworks, and effective regulatory bodies for the information infrastructure and the digital economy (Chapters 6 and 9). e-Transformation invests in new leadership and managerial skills—including new cadres of information, innovation, and ICT leaders—to facilitate business innovation, build a dynamic ICT industry, and enact the necessary policy reforms for an innovation economy (Chapters 6–8). Leaders are essential to promote innovation, cross-agency coordination, and government and enterprise transformation (Chapters 11–13). Leaders are also needed at the grassroots, to integrate telecenters into local development (Chapter 10), and to use ICT to empower communities and promote pro-poor innovation at the bottom of the pyramid (Chapter 14).

In a more widely distributed information environment and knowledge-enabled competitive world, inclusive and pro-poor growth strategies will have to harness the collective knowledge of society and the potential inherent in communities and participatory development. Recognizing the limits of the state and the market, development thinking turned to catalyzing and leveraging community knowledge, innovation and capital to promote grassroots development. Sustainable development at the local level depends on local participation, community empowerment, village networking, and NGO partnership.

e-Transformation is a "secondgeneration" development strategy for a smart, holistic, inclusive and participatory development. The growing challenges of development can now be more feasible to manage and development goals more realistic to realize with the tools made available by the ICT revolution. New tools like mobile phones and collaborative technologies enable more targeted and strategic communications and broad participation and ownership of development programs. They also facilitate cross-sectoral partnerships, peer production, enhanced experimentation, learning, accountability, and evaluation of results. e-Transformation aims to use ICT to support digital and social inclusion, community learning and knowledge sharing, public–private partnerships, network-based innovation, and grassroots building of institutions. It can help promote rural livelihood, agricultural innovation, access to health information and learning resources, and local monitoring of development programs and the environment (Chapters 14–16).

A Networked, Knowledge-Based Economy

Information, knowledge, and innovation are increasingly the main inputs and outputs of modern economies. It has become a core competency for enterprises and nations to produce, select, and interpret new information and knowledge and to turn it into productive activities (Dahlman et al., 2006; Castells, 1996; Castells and Cardoso, 2006). The speed of diffusion of information and knowledge has increased dramatically, due to ICT and globalization. Markets and technologies are changing rapidly. Companies can grow very quickly, but also decline quickly. With this volatility, cities and regions must guard against dependence on a single company or industry. In such an economy, high premium is placed on innovation, diversification, entrepreneurship, strategic adaptation, and fast learning.

The world is becoming increasingly networked—interconnections among individuals, businesses, governments, universities, and civil societies. Flat, networked, adaptive, and open structures are more aligned with knowledge-based and innovation-driven economies than bureaucratic, hierarchical, and closed organizations. There is also increased recognition of connectivity as a key component of public and social infrastructure in general. "New definitions portray high bandwidth connectivity as a necessity, perhaps even a public utility on the order of drinking water" (Dutta and Mia, 2008).

In the network economy, the technology infrastructure makes information more accessible and hence more valuable. Improved information infrastructure has vastly increased our ability to capture, retrieve, filter, organize, and distribute information. A networked economy is dynamically driven by network externalities, positive feedback cycles, creating a critical mass of demand, and the demand-side economies of scale (Shapiro and Varian, 1999). The old industrial economy was driven by economies of scale of production; the knowledge economy is driven by network economics, network externalities, and positive feedback. The value of a network, real or virtual, depends on the number of other people connected to it.[3] Positive feedback and learning loops are more potent forces in the network economy than ever before.

---

[3] According to Metcalf's law, the value of a network goes up as the square of the number of users.

The knowledge economy is a network economy. For companies, it is increasingly crucial to engage in strategic partnership and knowledge networks to tap into complementary knowledge resources and to respond quickly to rapidly changing markets and technologies. They are increasingly integrated into global supply chains and networked with customers and suppliers. Knowledge cities are developing high-quality electronic infrastructure for swift local and global communication. Each node—a company or city—has to develop its own flexible specialization within the network. Public agencies are also leaning to govern and deliver services by networks—by engaging public, private, and civil society partners in information, knowledge, and innovation networks. As will be further shown, information and communication technologies are providing the foundational blocks and tools for establishing, facilitating, and managing these networks. They are also enhancing the capacity of public and private organizations to restructure, remain flexible and agile, and learn quickly.

Innovation Systems, Innovative Clusters, and ICT

In today's intensely competitive world, a necessary condition for rapid growth is the ability to harness technology creatively, and this is particularly apt to the general-purpose technology of our time, ICT. Innovation is becoming central to growth and sustained development for middle-income developing countries in particular. For higher income countries in East Asia and Latin America, it is necessary to stay close to the technological frontiers and to produce a continuous stream of commercially successful innovations to sustain high levels of income (Yusuf, 2003). For those in middle- and low-income developing countries everywhere, it is necessary to compete harder on the basis of productivity, quality, and speed of delivery. They also need to develop innovative capability in their mainstay industries and services to sustain their competitive edge and growth. Innovation is also necessary to diversify into new industries and services, and ICT products and services industries are primary examples of successful diversification for low- and middle-income countries such as India and China.

An innovation system is a "set of institutions whose interactions determine innovative performance" (Nelson, 2000, p. 12). National innovation systems have been identified as the primary engine for innovative capacity and fast growth (Nelson, 2000; Freeman, 1997). Such systems are becoming increasingly open to innovation systems of other countries, as their efficacy increasingly depends not only on local institutions but also on global connectedness. These systems direct technological leaning and the cumulative process of building innovative capability. Countries must continuously invest in building skills, institutions, experience, tacit knowledge, local networks, and international partnerships.

The supply of innovation must be translated into products and process changes. Highly innovative firms must also have the ability to introduce new business models and to devise organizational forms that are open, flexible, efficient, and supportive of innovation, information diffusion, and technological advance (Chapter 2). In many developing countries, however, governments have discouraged organizational change, organizational diversity, and entrepreneurship. Hierarchical, family-controlled organizations and patriarchal management practices have remained the norm. Moreover, new business models are needed that induce R&D collaboration across the enterprise, among local enterprises and transnationally. Conservatism in organizing for innovation is reinforced by the scarcity professional managers and management consultants. As will be discussed later, ICT can foster more flexible and effective organizational forms, cross-functional learning, managerial innovations, knowledge management, and open and collaborative innovation.

Competition, information, and learning that induce innovation can be stimulated by the clustering of firms in urban areas (Porter, 1990). When competitiveness is keyed to technological advance that shortens product cycles, clustering offers several advantages (Yusuf, 2003). They provide thick labor market for specialized skills, thus reducing the search, hiring, and screening costs. They also socialize labor into cluster-specific aptitudes, thus reducing training costs. With the proximity of many specialized firms, clusters also reduce the risks arising from fluid and uncertain inter-firm re-adjustments. They induce firms to engage in reciprocal exchanges beyond market relations—information and knowledge spillovers, trust-based collaboration, learning, and innovation. They also facilitate the formation of business alliances and associations and help build social capital that supports innovation.

When clusters are networked, demand for innovation is further reinforced as leading firms pull others through learning networks. But only certain clusters spur innovation. These are the clusters that face continued and fresh competition from new entrants with fresh ideas. Innovative clusters are a local phenomenon, but their long-term dynamism depends on becoming part of a global network of similar clusters. Openness to ideas and human capital and the ability to tap the diaspora are critical to innovative clusters.

Having a world-class ICT infrastructure, information technology service centers, and ICT-enabled business support services are increasingly a prerequisite to the circulation of ideas and knowledge workers, technological interaction between local and foreign firms, and access to foreign markets. The demands for instant interaction and coordination, and emphasis on lean manufacturing and minimum inventory, are reinforcing the need for e-business solutions, first-class logistics, and broadband connectivity. ICT has caused a significant change in the management of supply chains with applications such as Enterprise Resource Planning (ERP), Internet-based mega portals, and business-to-business e-commerce marketplace (Chapters 2 and 13). Similarly, ICT continues to cause changes in the design of products and components. Computer-aided design, computer-aided engineering, computer-aided manufacturing, and many other digital tools are enabling international collaboration among researchers and designers and fully integrated manufacturing systems that shorten design and production cycles.

Making clusters innovative is both feasible and critical to innovation and dynamic growth—some of the key lessons in creating clusters are discussed in the context of the ICT industry (Chapter 8).

Integrating ICT into Development Strategy

Given the profound promises and pervasive impacts of ICT on national economies and global competition, this book argues that countries at all levels of development should embed ICT into their overall national development strategies. Enterprises have learned to use ICT to transform their business strategies. Much can be learned from the business sector about aligning ICT and business strategies. The integration of national development and ICT strategies would constitute advanced strategies for development—a new type of development strategy that is adaptive and responsive to the challenges and opportunities of our times. Integrating ICT into development thinking and action would leverage the central role of information and knowledge in competition and development and open new promising paths to development. Harnessing the potential benefits and managing the risks and impacts of ICT for development are challenging tasks in view of the complexity and uncertainty of the interaction between ICT, economic growth, and poverty reduction.

E-development strategy aims to use ICT to address urgent and perennial development problems in smart ways. E-development seeks to capture the opportunities opened by the new technologies and to use ICT to exploit current and develop potential comparative advantages. Development strategists should ask: how can we leverage ICT to help solve the food crisis? To address the energy and environmental crises? To accelerate the development of skills for the new economy? To support new sources of growth and employment? To enhance the competitiveness of small enterprises in a networked economy? To transform public services? To improve health delivery? To address the growing income inequality and development divides? Public policy makers must think simultaneously through the specific development challenges at hand and the potential of ICT as a general-purpose technology that can, with other complementary measures, address these challenges.

The business literature and surveys amply demonstrate that enterprises that were able to realize the benefits of the ongoing productivity revolution have been those enterprises that systematically integrated ICT into their business strategy, business innovation, and business practices. A 2009 survey by the consulting firm, Bain and Company, found that companies grew faster and lowered costs by making their IT departments effective: Respondents reported that 3-year compound annual growth was boosted by 17% and IT spending was cut by 8%. Furthermore, those firms achieving both ICT effectiveness and ICT strategy alignment with business strategy saw their annual growth rate jump 37%, while ICT spending rates dropped by more than 10%. Some enterprises like Wall-Mart owe their business model innovation to become the globally competitive trade enterprise by using ICT strategically for a highly efficient and responsive global supply chain. Lee & Fung company accounted for more than US $8 billion in garments and consumer goods in 2006, growing at an annual rate of 23% over the last 14 years (Fung, Fung and Wind, 2008). At the heart of its business strategy and success is the use of ICT to become a network orchestrator that builds and manages a robust universe of suppliers, and a network integrator that builds and leverages the company's value and intellectual property across the network.

To various degrees, countries that were able to advance most in producing and diffusing ICT and realizing the benefits of the ongoing productivity revolution have been those who have pursued an explicit and holistic ICT strategy and systematically integrated ICT into their overall development thinking and strategic options. Countries like Ireland, Singapore, Korea, Finland, and Taiwan have been formulating coherent and comprehensive national ICT strategies and integrating these strategies with their growth strategies, government transformation, community-driven development, and enterprise development and innovation. Others are beginning to follow similar approaches, as in China and India. Even poor countries and communities can reap significant benefits from integrating ICT into local development and livelihood strategies.

e-Development as a Process

A number of developing and transition countries have explicit and comprehensive national strategies on paper, but struggle to deliver any meaningful results. Remarkably, the list of "offenders" is not limited to the poorest and most resource-strapped countries. For example, some middle-income countries such as Romania, Bulgaria, and Russia have struggling, if not stillborn, national ICT strategies, or e-strategies. The main lesson learned from this comparison is that successful countries perceive e-development strategy not only as a policy document but also as *a dynamic and evolving process*. The core challenge of e-strategies is to build capacity for agile learning, adaptive implementation, and transformative leadership. In this context, focusing on a blueprint—the strategy *document*—may even hurt the country more it would help.

Integration of ICT into development is a highly complex process and requires much experimentation, adaptation, social learning, and agile coordinating. "We are not dealing only with the implementation of new information and communication technologies or with the creation of new economic activities or job opportunities. We are rather dealing with an overall societal, political and cultural change process in which various kinds of technical, institutional and social innovations interact with each other." (Kasvio, 2000). A holistic approach to ICT for development goes beyond the issues of digital divide and ICT industry promotion and toward building broad-based momentum for effective deployment of ICT throughout government, society, and economy. It provides developing countries with the tools to create dynamic comparative advantage by utilizing technological and institutional changes as the driving forces of development, while harnessing intangibles such as knowledge, and organizational and social capital.

Harnessing ICT for development requires a holistic framework that secures complementary investments. It requires a strategic framework that takes advantage of the multiple roles of ICT and helps integrate the options made possible by this technological revolution into the design of country development strategies. As such, ICT is not just a sector or pillar of the global knowledge economy, but a powerful engine and enabler with which new possibilities and modalities of development strategies can be pursued. ICT is viewed not only as a sector in competition with others for scarce resources but also as a cost-effective tool to enable all sectors to meet human needs better than through traditional means alone. The second part of the book defines this holistic framework and the key issues in designing an integrated ICT-enabled development strategy. It focuses on how to go about developing holistic e-development programs and integrate them into the country's overall development strategy.

A holistic approach will inevitably involve building the pillars or common foundations for applying ICT in various key sectors and across sectors or common functions (Fig. 1.1). It also involves taking account of the many interactions and interdependencies among these pillars (Chapters 4, 7–10, and 16). Some of these interdependencies are strong, others are moderate or low. Some of these interdependencies are known and should be taken in account upfront; others will emerge or become stronger and should be integrated into the programs, over time. E-development strategies take a holistic view in analyzing these interdependencies. However, they should remain strategic and focused by selecting and phasing investments to address these interdependencies over time, in line with the political economy and the dynamics of local learning.

Use/application	Cross-sector						Sectoral			
	e-Government			e-Business & finance			e-Society	e-Education	e-Health	e-Agri	e-Sectors
Pillars of e-Dev.	Central services	Local services	Public finance	SME	Large corp.	Banks					
Information infrastructure	■	▪	▪	■	▪	■	■	■	▪	■	▪
ICT Education & literacy	■	■	▪	■	▪	▪	■	■	▪	■	▪
ICT industry & services	■	▪	▪	■	▪	▪	▪	■	▪	▪	▪
Content development	■	■	▪	■	▪	▪	■	■	■	■	■
e-Policies	■	▪	■	■	▪	■	▪	■	▪	▪	▪
Leadership & institutions	■	■	■	■	▪	▪	■	■	■	■	■

Fig. 1.1 Orchestrating the e-development process (■, strong interaction; ▪, modest interaction)

This process must encompass many stakeholders. Governments play several critical roles: creating the enabling policy environment, correcting coordination failures, promoting technological learning, providing the institutional infrastructure for a market economy, and alerting other institutions through collective action. But governments cannot do it alone. In some countries, the private sector took the initiative or leading role, as in India. But even in this case, the Indian government has moved over time to assume a strategic leadership role and to become a better prepared partner for other stakeholders. Civil society participation is also essential to mobilize social entrepreneurship and social learning and to overcome the digital and development divides. Prospects for success substantially increase when governments work in close partnerships with business, civil society, and academia.

The e-development process may start with a broad assessment of national e-readiness and the opportunities and threats present in global environment (Fig. 1.2). An equally important starting point is an in-depth appreciation of the country development strategy and the role of information, communication, knowledge, and learning in realizing this strategy. These inputs should guide the creation of a shared vision of ICT-enabled transformation, the identification of the key stakeholders, and the development and engagement of e-leadership (ICT governance) institutions. Subsequently, a shared vision and engaged stakeholders and leaders should set the broad directions for national e-policies and e-strategies. In turn, these strategic thrusts should help identify and prioritize national e-development initiatives.

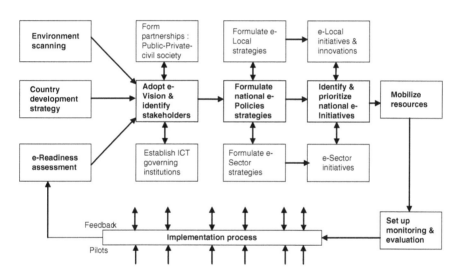

Fig. 1.2 e-development design and implementation process

This process should be carried out also at the sectoral and local levels and these processes should communicate and interact with the national process, to ensure bottom-up initiative, broad ownership, and deep integration across sectors and levels. Striking the right balance between local and national initiatives is a continuous challenge. The next step in this process is to mobilize the necessary resources from all partners and stakeholders. This may take many forms of public–private financing and innovative funding mechanisms to sustain the transformation process.

Integrated e-development faces many implementation challenges. Many developing countries have experienced significant vision-implementation or aspiration-reality gaps. These gaps need to be understood and systematically addressed if ICT-enabled transformation were to become a development practice. Moreover, as explored in Chapter 2 and illustrated throughout this book, ICT is a versatile tech-nology, with many possibilities to be discovered and diverse contexts within which it would be tested and adapted. Key to implementation success, therefore, is estab-lishing monitoring, evaluation, and learning systems as early as possible during the e-development process design. Monitoring and evaluation results should feedback into continuous assessment of progress, e-readiness, and development outcomes (Fig. 1.2). As true transformation takes time, measuring progress and demonstrat-ing benefits are critical to building and sustaining commitment to transformation. Integrating lessons of experience is also critical to speedup learning and reduce the costs of ICT-enabled development. This is the focus of the last section of the book.

Thinking Strategically About ICT-Enabled Development

The e-development strategy process is not primarily about developing detailed planning documents or conducting exhaustive analyses and measurements. It is first and foremost about thinking strategically about the fundamental options and opportunities made possible by the information technology revolution in the con-text of development and globalization. *Dirigist* and bureaucratic planning processes have been discredited in both the business and public sectors. Leading practition-ers in strategic planning have increasingly relied on agile processes and tools to engender creative and strategic thinking about options and opportunities (Mintzberg et al., 1998; Hanna and Picciotto, 2002; Hanna, 1985b). A creative, agile, and adaptive learning process is particularly necessary when dealing with fast-moving technologies and highly dynamic and interdependent global economy.

But from where should we start to think strategically about e-development? Should we start from a comprehensive national development strategy, based on analysis of comparative advantage? Or should we start with formulating a com-prehensive ICT sector strategy, based on ICT trends and their implications for development? Or should we first focus on partial ICT interventions in the context of a fully articulated national development plans? Is there an optimal sequence to follow in order to maximize the benefits from the fast-evolving ICTs?

To promote strategic thinking about the options, we simplify the potential range of country conditions and describe it along two dimensions that yield four scenarios (Fig. 1.3). Many countries neither have a comprehensive development strategy nor have a holistic ICT strategy (Scenario 1). Promoting a holistic approach to ICT for development may be an attractive entry point to induce more holistic thinking about development strategy itself. But adopting a major thrust in ICT in the context of unclear development strategy and poor enabling environment would be constrained by the lack of complementary inputs and would lead to modest payoffs (Scenario 2). It would become even counterproductive, if national and sectoral priorities remain unclear and thus investment in ICT becomes an end in itself. Under these conditions, it would be prudent to focus only on partial interventions in those sectors where there are relatively clear development priorities and strategies.

Fig. 1.3 Thinking
strategically about integrating
ICT and development

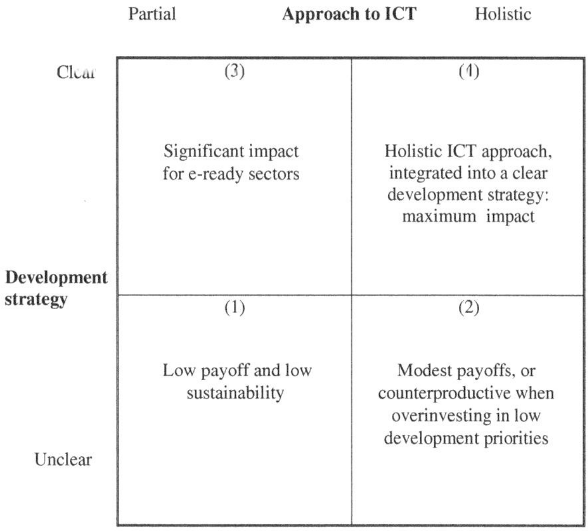

	Partial	**Approach to ICT**	Holistic
Clear	(3) Significant impact for e-ready sectors		(4) Holistic ICT approach, integrated into a clear development strategy: maximum impact
Development strategy	(1) Low payoff and low sustainability		(2) Modest payoffs, or counterproductive when overinvesting in low development priorities
Unclear			

A partial approach to leveraging ICT in the context of a clear and comprehensive development strategy would yield significant benefits but limited to sectors where ICT is deployed (Scenario 3). Finally, the evidence from leading countries suggests that the development impact of ICT is highest where the development strategy is clear and ICT is approached in a holistic fashion as the platform for that development strategy (Scenario 4). Countries may strive to move to this last scenario to maximize the development impact of ICT investments. This demands thinking holistically and simultaneously about ICT and development possibilities and then planning and experimenting to align and integrate both strategies.

The interactions between strategies for ICT and for economic development are not a one-time project or a single consultation or event. These interactions help shape and are shaped by a shared vision of transformation and the role of ICT in the transformation process. They should evolve over time, in response to mutual adjustments, experimentation, learning, and discovery. They are not the product of a single leader or institution. Rather, they should be nurtured and sustained by networks of institutions and champions who represent the demand for transformation and the supply of ICT-enabled innovations and solutions. They should be based on continuous dialogue among government reformers and business leaders on the one hand and the ICT suppliers and strategists on the other. Such interactions and creative thinking should be institutionalized and embodied in e-leadership institutions and policy making mechanisms.

Thinking Creatively About ICT-Enabled Transformation

Transformation or "creative destruction" demands creativity and innovation, and these in turn involve exploration, idea generation, discovery, experimentation, and a culture supportive of innovation and learning. As suggested earlier, lessons of development point to the failure of applying a single recipe or "Washington Consensus" to economic policies and institutions in diverse contexts (Rodrik, 2008; Stiglitz et al., 2000). They also suggest that development is a process of change, innovation, experimentation, learning, and ultimately, social and institutional transformation. But globalization and accelerated technological change, brought about by the information and communication revolution, can help accelerate this process and open up new options for development and innovation. Thus, creativity takes an even more important role than in the past in aiding the transformation process. Creative thinking about ICT deployment to enable transformation becomes an imperative. In the business sector, innovation has become a matter of survival.

Fortunately, we are learning more about the tools and conditions that could stimulate creativity; they apply equally to government agencies, enterprises, and grassroots organizations. Techniques used by large but creative corporations as well as individuals include, among others, creating innovation marketplaces, creating competitive grants for innovation, engaging external partners and users, creating customers or citizen feedback loops, and engaging stakeholders with diverse perspectives. For promoting creativity in using ICT in communities and SMEs, the participation of both development and ICT specialists would be necessary. The challenge for public agencies is higher as they tend to approach innovation as a "one-off" change using a big bang, instead of a series of tools and approaches that systematize the innovation process and develop a culture of innovation.

In this book, I argue for a holistic approach to e-development, including e-government, e-business, and e-society (Chapter 4). Such holistic approaches and integrating visions help present ICT strategies and applications in challenging and broadening terms. Recent studies of creativity suggest that broadening techniques challenge us to seek diverse ideas and help us capture interconnections and thus boost creativity, learning, and problem solving (Scientific American Mind, June/July, 2008, pp. 24–31). Such approaches may be institutionalized so as to systematize and sustain the innovation process at all levels where ICT is harnessed for transformation.

I also explore ways to promote grassroots innovation and tap community knowledge and creativity, since innovation and creativity cannot rely solely on topdown mechanisms (Chapter 14). Systems and institutions may be developed to generate and maintain the flow of good ideas and to enhance the capacity for innovation of organizations and communities. This is particularly important for ICT-enabled innovation and transformation as ICT is a versatile technology whose impact is conditioned by contextual factors. Generation and diffusion of creative solutions would emerge from the interplay of locally driven initiatives and nationally set enabling policies and scaling up mechanisms.

A Process of Self-Discovery

Thinking strategically and creatively about integrating ICT into economic and social development strategy is necessary not only at the front end of the transformation process, but also throughout implementation. Such integration involves using ICT in new ways and in new contexts. It is a process of technological and organizational innovation. Its success depends crucially on the specific context. Instruments and incentives used to promote ICT-enabled innovation and transformation work differently in countries with different levels of institutional maturity and technological capabilities. Governments, enterprises, and communities have to discover their own best practices, including exploration and adaptation of internationally promising practices. They must engage in experimentation and pragmatic innovation and search for solutions that work in the local context. In the economic literature, this is called a process of self-discovery (Rodrik, 2007). In the business literature, this is called an emergent strategy (Mintzberg et al., 1998).

ICT-enabled transformation (as innovation more broadly) is a process of self-discovery. At the country level, it involves identifying "first movers" and facilitating pockets of dynamism, then scaling up and learning from experience of the pioneers to build a critical mass for reform and transformation, then moving towards widening the transformation process beyond existing clusters or islands of excellence, in search of new innovation domains and diversified innovation-driven economy. At the enterprise or public agency level, similar processes are at work: first to identify promising innovation platforms, develop a portfolio of ICT-enabled transformation projects, then scale up successes into new services and practices, then institutionalize the process of government-wide or enterprise-wide restructuring and transformation. Leadership, vision, and top-down strategy play critical roles in enabling first movers, pilots, and bottom-up initiatives; in scaling up successes and building critical mass; and in institutionalizing the transformation process.

Structure

In the first section of the book, I address the basic question of why countries should be concerned with the impact of information and communication technology on their competitiveness and growth prospects, and why they should fashion national strategies that harness and integrate ICT into development. I discuss the profound opportunities, risks, and impacts of the ongoing ICT revolution. I explore why e-development is an opportunity and an imperative for competing in a global, networked, and innovation-driven economy.

Although awareness of ICT roles and impacts has increased substantially over the last decade, their holistic integration and systematic harnessing for development are lagging far behind. Understanding the diverse roles of ICT and the potential of the ongoing technological revolution is critical to effective integration of ICT into development thinking and practice. Moreover, the substantial risks and common failures to realize the benefits from ICT investments are often ignored or underestimated during strategy formulation and implementation. In this section I argue that national and holistic ICT-enabled development strategies are necessary to tap synergies, take account of externalities, secure the benefits, and minimize the risks.

My aim in this first section is to provide a big picture view for policy makers, strategists, and students of development. It touches on, but does not do justice to the most recent technological advances of ICT, such as the wireless revolution, collaboration and networking tools, open-source innovation models, and the revolutionary potential of switching information processing into utilities (Carr, 2008; Tapscott and Williams, 2006). This section does not aim to provide in-depth treatment of the technology for ICT specialists, but to offer a broad appreciation of the potential of current information and communication technologies for development strategists, and a strategic understanding of development trends for technology policy makers and specialists. It is a bridging effort.

The second section deals with the pillars of e-development. I propose e-development as a holistic framework for thinking about and acting on integrating ICT into development strategies. This framework helps create an ecosystem that harnesses ICT for sustainable and accelerated development. It takes account of interdependencies among policies, human resources, information infrastructure, local technological capabilities, institutional reforms, and investment priorities to make ICT work for economic and social development. I examine each key element or pillar of this ecosystem and the issues, options, and synergies that may be considered in developing a coherent ICT-enabled development strategy. This section is most relevant to ICT strategists and policy developers who are interested in understanding the foundations and building blocks for using and diffusing ICT through an economy.

The third section deals with usage and applications of ICT for governments, businesses, and local communities. Building on the pillars or foundational elements of e-development, this section outlines the strategic policy options and design issues involved in leveraging ICT to maximize developmental impact—transforming government institutions and services, networking businesses for innovation and competitiveness, and empowering communities for social inclusion and poverty reduction. It draws lessons from diverse developing country experience to guide countries as they design and implement their own national strategies for e-government, e-business, and e-society. This section may therefore appeal most to development practitioners who are interested in reforming governments, improving competitiveness of the private sector, and promoting social inclusion and innovation across the economy.

The second and third sections, together, explore some of the key synergies and interdependencies involved in e-Transformation, including the potential virtuous cycles arising from developing content, services, and applications on the one hand, and building the necessary leadership institutions, human resources, technological competencies, and information infrastructure, on the other. These two sections are the core of this book. They illustrate the key options and possibilities to tap synergies and pursue an integrated approach across all elements of e-Transformation, guided by a proposed e-development framework. They show that payoffs from ICT are ultimately determined by political will, managerial leadership, and social entrepreneurship.

The fourth and final section deals with implementation issues, the reasons for the current gap between the potential and actual performance of ICT for development, the need for tailoring e-development to diverse country conditions, and the role of leadership, consultation, monitoring, and evaluation. The concluding chapter draws on lessons of experience arising from designing and implementing e-development strategies in diverse country conditions. This section is likely to attract ICT leaders, strategists, and program mangers and practitioners.

Themes

This book is not about technology. It is about development as a socio-economic innovation and transformation process and the role of ICT as a catalyst and enabler of this process. Hence, the following themes are addressed throughout:

- e-Transformation is about integrating ICT strategically and organically into development processes, not ICT as a sector per se. Our thinking about development has not caught up with the new tools of the information revolution. The transformative power of ICT will not be tapped without new thinking that integrates ICT as enabler of all aspects of development. It is urgent to think strategically about how to make the ICT revolution work for development, with emphasis on development opportunities (Chapters 1–3, in particular).
- Holistic approaches are needed to exploit the synergies, externalities, and network effects of ICT, to secure co-investment in complementary resources, and to facilitate the necessary institutional and regulatory adjustments to realize ICT benefits. E-development is essentially about thinking holistically and long term, to capture key interdependencies and maximize development impact, yet acting strategically and selectively, to maintain focus, leverage entry points, and harness learning dynamics (Chapters 4 and 5).
- Policy frameworks and institutions are central to build an enabling ecosystem for ICT innovation and diffusion, secure effective implementation, capture the potential benefits, and sustain the diffusion and transformation processes. Understanding the political economy of development is essential to reform the enabling policies and build an ICT governance framework. Understanding the stakeholders and power structures is important to induce change and sustain the transformation. Leadership, vision, and incentives are also needed to bring about the potential innovation and transformation (Chapters 5, 6, 11, and 12).
- A premium should be placed on partnership, including cross-sectoral collaboration, to share common infrastructures, tap synergies and economies of scale, harness network effects, exploit comparative advantages, and promote open innovation and mutual learning. Government has to take a proactive posture and a leading role in promoting collaboration and innovation for e-Transformation (Chapters 7, 8, and 12–16).
- Experimentation, entrepreneurship, and learning are at the heart of e-Transformation. ICT-enabled development is a complex phenomenon that involves profound changes and substantial learning. Pursued in a changing

global and technological environment, the ICT agenda is still new and in flux, with no recipe or easy answers (Chapters 10–16).

- Much of this change and learning occurs at the local level. A national ICT-enabled development strategy should therefore emphasize bottom-up initiatives and multi-sectoral participatory approaches to promote change and learning. Central agencies should act as enablers, facilitators, and aggregators as well as strategists and inducers of collaboration, innovation, and change (Chapters 10–16).

Section I
Why an e-Transformation Strategy?

This section aims to improve understanding of the opportunities and challenges of the information and communication technology (ICT) revolution and their implications for development policy and strategies.[4] It also outlines the rationale for designing national strategies for e-Transformation or e-enabled development. It provides a context and appreciation for why new development strategies are necessary and possible to deploy with the support of ICT. The following sections (2–4) will examine the constraints and critical success factors to realizing the possibilities and managing the transformation.

Chapter 2 examines why developing countries should look ahead and try to harness ICT in support of economic and social development. It identifies the broad opportunities and promises of the ICT revolution as well as the risks and impacts and their implications for developing countries. It examines the pervasive and increasing impact of ICT on productivity, markets, organizations, innovation, finance, education, and many other economic activities. The outcomes are not predetermined—they will depend in large part on public policies and choices. But the opportunity costs of failing to respond are high. Harnessing the ICT revolution to work for development must become central to development policy and strategy.

Chapter 3 analyzes the role of ICT in development from three perspectives: accessing and processing information and knowledge; speeding up and reducing the costs of *production and transactions* throughout the economy; and making *connections* among people, NGOs, enterprises, and communities for empowerment, participation, co-ordination, decentralization, and social learning. It presents the basic options or objectives available to countries for deploying ICT for development: as an industry or sector in its own right; as a general-purpose technology to be harnessed and diffused across sectors; and as an enabling infrastructure for empowerment and service delivery. These options may complement or conflict with each other. The balance and mix among these objectives should be tailored to the level of economic development, available skills, and domestic technological capabilities.

---

[4]ICTs are defined as technologies that facilitate communication and the capture, processing and, transmission of information by electronic means. This definition encompasses the full range of ICTs from radio, television, and telephones to computers and the Internet.

They should also reflect the size and structure of the domestic market and social demand for participation and learning. This balance is an ongoing process and is ultimately shaped by local coalitions, political leadership, and overall development strategy of the country.

This chapter makes the case for a holistic approach to ensure that complementary inputs are integrated with ICT investments to realize the promised productivity, growth, and poverty reduction outcomes—even while minimizing the risks this revolution poses for countries at different levels of development. A holistic framework is subsequently proposed in Chapter 4.

Chapter 2
Promises and Implications of the Revolution

In this chapter, I explore the many ways ICT is likely to impact social and economic development and points to the strategic significance of ICT for enabling national development and poverty reduction strategies. Most evidence comes from OECD countries or is slowly emerging from a few advanced developing countries. Based on this evidence, I believe that ICT offers many promises and opportunities, even while posing serious risks and uncertainties. Its impact is likely to be pervasive. Countries must fashion their own responses. Ad hoc or passive postures are likely to lead to eroding competitiveness, increasing divides and marginalization.

First, I explore some of the promises and manifestations of the ICT revolution. Next, I suggest that we are still in an early phase of a technological wave and productivity revolution. Promising paradigm shifts within computing and communication point to that continuing dramatic decline in prices and increases in performance and intelligence of ICT systems. Moreover, long adjustment periods are needed for an economy to fully benefit from a revolutionary new technology. The ICT revolution and the accompanying socio-economic adjustments constitute a techno-economic paradigm shift with profound implications for the renewal of the productive and institutional structures in developed and developing countries alike.

Next, the pervasive and increasing impact of ICT examined. This impact encompasses organizations, markets, competitive strategies, innovation, financial services, employment, media and cultural development, regional and urban development, intelligent infrastructures and global supply chains, and energy and environment. Impact further extends to governance and participatory democracy, education and health, and poverty reduction.

The impact of ICT is accompanied by downside risks. I examine a few of these risks: wasting scarce development resources; exacerbating inequalities; reinforcing existing power distributions; and controlling, rather than empowering the individual. None of the promises or risks is pre-determined by the technology. They are the outcomes of complementary economic polices and socio-political choices. This argues for integrating the ICT agenda into the development strategy agenda, in creative and dynamic ways.

N.K. Hanna, *e-Transformation: Enabling New Development Strategies*, Innovation, Technology, and Knowledge Management, DOI 10.1007/978-1-4419-1185-8_2, © Springer Science+Business Media, LLC 2010

Promises of the ICT Revolution

With the beginning of the 21st century, a consensus has emerged among economists and policy makers that the world is in the midst of a general-purpose technological revolution with profound implications for developed and developing countries alike (UNDP, 2001; IMF, 2001). It is a technological revolution brought about by a set of new information and communication technologies. As a general-purpose technology (GPT), ICT represents a radical innovation and a major discontinuity. It facilitates and enhances process and product innovations. It has led to a general acceleration of economic processes and intensification of the use of information, knowledge, and communication in these processes.

The information and communication technology revolution has several striking differences from past general-purpose technological revolutions. Past revolutions like steam power, electricity, and the railroads have clearly yielded major benefits, although their diffusion took several decades, sometimes extended to a century. The fall in the relative prices of ICT goods has been sharper and sustained over a longer period than earlier technological revolutions. The benefits seem to be coming much faster than those of past revolutions. ICT is also closely linked to knowledge, communication, and human intelligence and thus enabling new types of innovation in management, organization, and business models. ICT impact will not be limited to manufacturing and transport—this GPT may have at least as much impact on public and business services, on educational and learning processes, and on individual and community empowerment. Finally, the production of goods embodying the new technology is much more globalized. This rapid innovation in the ICT sector, and the consequent rapid reduction in the cost of access, is democratizing ICT usage. Poor people can afford to use ICT tools like mobile phones to support their livelihood.

The ICT revolution has taken many attributes, reflecting many promises: productivity revolution, knowledge-based economy, information society, learning society, innovation-driven economy, and networked economy, among others.

It is a productivity revolution, impacting new ICT industries, ICT-using industries and services, and overall total factor productivity (TFP). Evidence is derived from advanced economies, particularly from the United States (Onliner and Sichel, 2000; Jorgensen and Stirah, 2000; Gordon, 2000).

It is a knowledge revolution that is giving rise to an information society or knowledge economy, whereby knowledge creation, codification, diffusion, and effective use are driving growth and competitiveness, and whereby lack of access to connectivity and knowledge tools is giving rise to digital and knowledge divides and pervasive exclusion (Kirkman et al., 2002).

It is a learning revolution that has given rise to the learning economy, learning organizations, lifelong learning (World Bank, 2002; ILO, 2001; UN, 1998). Accordingly, individuals, firms, and countries are able to create wealth and obtain access to wealth in proportion to their capacity to learn (Lundvall, 1996; Drucker 1993). Not only does this technological change crea new demands for learning and rai the bar for skills to function in the new workplace, but it also offers novel and powerful new pedagogies for learning and creativity. It empowers the students becoming more active and independent learners (Resnick, 2002).

It is an innovation-driven economy, whereby national innovation systems and regional clusters (bringing together research institutions, business startups, venture capital, and related services) would spark, speed, and sustain growth (OECD, 1998, 2001). The transition from resource-based and investment-driven growth to innovation-based development requires a government role in fostering a high rate of innovation (Kirkman, Cornelius, Sachs, Schwab, 2002).

Other names suggest various promises: fast-paced or "now" economy, networked economy, mobile economy, new economy, agile economy, and smart growth (Fine, 1998; Ranadive, 1999; Castells, 1996). These attributes highlight different but complementary aspects of the ongoing technological revolution:

- Speeding up all types of transactions throughout the economy, reducing all types of leads and lags, tightening supply chains, cutting time to market, and at times bringing response time close to zero.
- Networking organizations, overcoming distance, extending supply chains across cities and regions, and increasing economic relations between core and peripheral areas.
- Enabling mobility through wireless communication, mobile telephone, telework, teleservices, and e-learning.
- Generating substantial new opportunities for economic activity, new products, and services such as high-tech products, multimedia services, and knowledge industries.
- Enabling real-time control and remote monitoring of all types of processes, flows, and distribution systems, thus optimizing all kinds of logistics and reducing the material and energy intensities of almost all industrial processes and service activities.
- Enabling flat, agile, lean, extended, client-focused, flexible, learning organizations. The Internet itself is inherently based on horizontal communication among peers. It is profoundly anti-hierarchal. It enables networking, co-learning, co-producing knowledge, and combining producers and consumers.

Early Phase of a Technological Revolution

Before assessing the revolutionary potential of information and communication technologies, we need to appreciate the phase we are in and the lead time needed for the full impact to be realized. The ICT revolution is in its infancy, since ICT is still undergoing revolutionary change, and many of these technologies have yet to diffuse to the majority of mankind. Technical advances in many ICT areas continue apace and could level or change the playing field for developing countries, provided policy and institutional changes are made to capitalize on these advances. These include mobile devices, wireless communications, open-source software, low-cost access devices, and the coming paradigm shift to utility computing. The recent explosive growth of mobile phones in developing countries opens up massive possibilities for delivering services to rural and remote areas of the world, as will be illustrated later.

A paradigm shift is underway to deliver Internet-based software service (cloud computing) and to have computing power made available as a utility (utility computing), much like electrical utilities (Carr, 2008). This shift will have profound impact on ICT investment and diffusion: reducing the cost of ICT ownership, emphasizing the importance of shared infrastructures and broadband communications to realize economies of scale, and accelerating the diffusion of ICT as a general-purpose technology (Box 2.1).

Box 2.1 The Big Switch to Cloud Computing

Electrification, like computerization, led to complex and farreaching changes for companies and entire industries, and, as households began to connect to the grid, for all of society. Because they are general-purpose technologies and can thus be applied so broadly, they offer huge economies of scale, if their supply can be consolidated into utilities. They can be delivered efficiently from a great distance over a network and thus achieve the scale economies of central supply. Just as the economics of mechanical power changed in the early years of last century with the electric utility, the information utility will dramatically change the nature and economics of computing. The consequences for society—for the way we work, learn, communicate, entertain, and live—promise to be equally profound. Just as electrification extended man's physical powers a century ago, we are arriving at a moment with ICTs that is extending our intellectual powers in unprecedented ways.

Carr explores the potential impact of information and computing utility—and the rewiring of the world with the Internet—on the ICT industry, on user industries and on society at large (Carr, 2008). Computing applications will benefit from the economies of scale that utilities achieve, but unlike electrical appliances, computing applications have no physical form and can be made modular, and thus can be supplied from different sources and be delivered as digital services over a network to anywhere. So, the public computing grid will not be only a transmission channel as the electric grid is, but also a means for assembling a virtually unlimited array of options and computing components into unified and tailored services. The different components that used to be isolated—the PCs and other devices that are now dispersed throughout the world—are merging on the Internet into a World Wide Computer or "the computer in the cloud." With various programs and search engines, the World Wide Computer can automatically deliver customized services and "mash-up" various databases and software services for companies of all sizes.

Source: Carr, 2008

Advances in Internet technology are likely to provide the interactivity and real-world awareness needed to support business-to-business transactions, even while demanding limited communication capacity (by optimizing use of bandwidth). It will exploit sensors and smart tagging and tracing technologies to enable manufacturers to track every product they make from inception to phase out, and thus help manufacturers optimize their sensor-enabled supply chain assets country wide. The promise of next generation Internet is already being realized by early adopters in developing countries, for logistics by companies such as Cemex in Mexico and for enhanced customer service by Carrier China (Colony, Radjou, Howard, 2002).

Early Phase of a Productivity Revolution

New growth theorists and economic historians have characterized general purpose technologies (GPTs) by (i) wide scope for improvement and elaboration; (ii) applicability across a broad range of uses; (iii) potential for use in a wide variety of products and processes; and (iv) strong complementarities with existing or potential new technologies (Bresnahan and Trajtenberg, 1995; Helpman, 1998). General-purpose technologies are engines of growth. They play the role of "enabling technologies," opening up new opportunities rather than offering complete solutions. They act as catalysts, inducing complementary innovations in other sectors. While the steam engine is widely accepted as the GPT of the first industrial revolution, the electric dynamo is viewed as the GPT for the second industrial revolution.

In assessing the productivity impact of ICT, it is important to take account of the fact that long adjustment periods are needed for an economy to fully benefit from a revolutionary new technology (David, 1990, 2000). It is instructive to understand the dynamics of the productivity surge of the 1920s arising from electrification. In the case of the electric dynamo, the great productivity gains came not from the fact that electrical engines were faster and stronger than steam engines, but that they facilitated more efficient organization of work. It took decades for factories to be reorganized and for the full gains to be realized, but there were overall surge in productivity growth once a certain critical mass was reached. There are Paralels between the interconnection of electric motors through grids—and the associated transformation in manufacturing practices—and the interconnection of computers via communication networks. The Internet, diffusing much faster in the United States than electricity did during 1880–1920s, is a major step in this interconnection throughout local and global economies.

The ongoing technological revolution is so profound and pervasive that it challenges many traditional economic concepts that are rooted in incremental thinking. The transformative role of ICT has been difficult to capture in national statistics, due to several kinds of measurement problems and time lags (IMF, 2001; David 2000). However, the evidence in terms of economy-wide productivity has become most clear in the case of the United States, as a range of studies have measured a contribution of about 1% in labor productivity in the 1990s (Gordon, 2000; Oliner and

Sichel, 2000; Jorgenson and Stiroh, 2000; Council of Economic Advisors, 2001). Other studies have suggested significant (0.8%) increase in total factor productivity (TFP) growth, particularly driven by both ICT-producing and intensive ICT-using sectors (Kenny and Motta, 2002; Gordon, 2000; David, 2000).

Relatively more recent research suggests that ICT has driven the post 1995 revival of the productivity of US economy, almost doubling TFP (Brynolfsson, 2003); US productivity growth continued even during the economic downturns of 2000 and 2008 (Brynjolfsson, 2009). The evidence of impact on productivity is even more compelling and persuasive across countries at the microeconomic, firm and industry sector levels. Evidence from recent research provides a compelling case for ICT as a driver of productivity growth across many sectors of the United States, EU, and emerging economies.

The relatively recent adoption and low usage of ICT in many developing countries suggest that this revolution had not yet had a significant impact on economy-wide productivity, except among the Asian tigers and perhaps a very few emerging economies. In order to have significant impact on growth, a country needs to have a significant stock of ICT or users in place, and perhaps be more advanced in using that stock for economic transformation. But even in the context of a number of middle-income developing countries, studies indicate significant ICT contribution to firm productivity. In Korea, a comprehensive ICT strategy has been a key driver in the fast rebound of its economy from the financial crisis; the ICT industry's contribution to GDP growth rose from a mere 4.5% in 1990 to an astounding 50.5% in 2000 (www.mic.go.kr). Most recent evidence on ICT contribution to growth comes from large countries such as India and China, best reflected in terms of their substantial exports in IT services or hardware.

Economic history, the cumulative learning, and transformation process involved in using ICT, and the pace of this wave of technological change suggest that a "wait and see attitude" would keep many developing countries out of a technological revolution no less profound than the last industrial revolution (David, 2000; Perez, 2001; Freeman, 1994). Countries that adopt an inactive or reactive posture, rather than a proactive one, are likely to lose windows of opportunities to leapfrog or fail to exploit a structural change to gain or maintain competitive advantage in many of their industries and services. These countries may be simply locked out and marginalized. The Millennium Development Goals of halving global poverty, among others, are also unlikely to be met without these technologies.

Raising productivity through ICT use is essentially a developmental task that requires cumulative socio-technical learning and orchestrated investments in a combination of technological and social capabilities. Applying ICT to increase employment opportunities for the poor and empower them with information and learning also requires strategic intent, substantial experimentation, grassroots participation, social learning, and strategies for scaling up and sustainability.

ICT is the GPT of our age. As in earlier GPTs, the short-term impact (reflected in economy-wide productivity surge) may be uncertain, but the long-term impact will be profound and has been typically underestimated. The lead time for ICT to have its full impact may be shorter and more transformative than for earlier GPTs.

But advances in the technology are running far ahead of potential applications and the capacity of institutions and society to absorb and adjust to take full advantage of these technological capabilities. Moreover, the institutional changes and complementary innovations necessary for ICT diffusion and effective use in the public and educational sectors are likely to come at a slower pace than in business.

A Techno-economic Paradigm

Each technological revolution provides a new set of general-purpose, pervasive technologies, and a corresponding set of new organizational practices for a significant increase in productivity in existing sectors and this combined best practice is referred to as a techno-economic paradigm (Box 2.2; Perez, 2002). A techno-economic paradigm provides the means for modernizing all existing industries, activities, and infrastructures. This was the case with the deployment of the mass production paradigm in the mid20th century, and currently, the early phases of the ICT paradigm. A techno-economic paradigm articulates the technical and organizational model for taking the best advantage of the technological revolution and results in the rejuvenation of the whole productive structure.

Box 2.2 Technological Revolutions and Techno-economic Paradigms

Drawing on Kuhn, Dosi, and Freeman and other leading economic, development, and technology historians, Perez has articulated the overarching concept of techno-economic paradigm, as a best practice model made up of a set of all-pervasive generic technological and organizational principles (Perez, 2002, p. 15). It represents the most effective way of applying a particular technological revolution and of using this revolution for transforming a whole economy. When broadly accepted and adopted, these principles or generic tools become the common sense basis for innovation and investment, for organizing activities, and for structuring institutions. A techno-economic paradigm gradually defines the new best practice frontier.

Technological revolutions are defined by a powerful cluster of new dynamic technologies, industries, and products, plus associated infrastructures and together are capable of bringing about a long-term upsurge of productivity and development. Each of these sets of technological breakthroughs or sets of interrelated generic technologies spreads far beyond the sectors where they originally developed.

It is observed that these technological revolutions occur with some regularity, every 40–60 years, starting with the first industrial revolution around 1770, combining cotton industries, canals, and water power. The second, the age of steam and railways, started from 1830, using steam engines and steam-powered railways. The third, the age of steel and electricity, combines heavy engineering industries with rapid steel-steam ships and railways, electric networks and the telegraph. The fourth, starting early 20th century, started the age of oil, automobile, and mass production, combined with roads, ports, airports, universal electricity, and analog telephones. The fifth, starting around 1970, is the age of information and telecommunications, combining cheap microelectronics, control instruments, software, computers, combined with a new kind of infrastructure: digital communications and the Internet (Perez, 2002).

With each technological revolution, a set of dynamic new industries are accompanied by a facilitating infrastructure. Each technological revolution induces a techno-economic paradigm shift, as it demands new organizational models and practices to take advantage of the new potential. The new possibilities and associated requirements unleash transformation in the way of doing things across the economy. This transformation reaches beyond the economic sphere or the organization of production, to involve the socio-institutional sphere and to become the shared organizational common sense of the period. For example, in the era of car and mass production, the paradigm principles were mass production/mass markets, economies of scale, standardization, centralization, and hierarchies. In contrast, the guiding principles of the information age are decentralized integration, network structures, adaptability, agility, customization, knowledge as capital, clusters, and economies of scope.

Without subscribing to the details of regularity of this techno-economic paradigm, this model offers a powerful lens through which to view the ongoing information technology revolution, its dynamics, and its requirements, to unleash and harness its potential. Societies are shaped and shaken by each technology revolution, and in turn, the technological potential is steered by social, political, and policy choices, compromises, and adjustments. Each technological revolution encounters powerful resistance from established institutions and vested interests. Matching and realigning the social and institutional environment to assimilate fully a technological revolution and its techno-economic paradigm involve painful changes, and at times disruptions and destructions. Similarly, realizing the potential of the information and communication revolution requires revamping the productive structure, the building of new networks of institutions, the transformation of regulatory frameworks and governance, and even deep changes in ideas and culture.

Each techno-economic paradigm or surge involves a period of installation, during which a critical mass of investments in the new technologies and infrastructures are put in place against the resistance of the established paradigm. At about middle of the surge, there is a turning point when the built-up tensions are surmounted, creating the conditions for the deployment and wide diffusion. Such evolution by long leaps and massive economic transformations involves radical changes in production, consumption, management, organization, skills, communication, and transportation. It involves learning at all levels of society.

The transition to the new practices is not easy and takes decades. It is best described by Schumpeter (1942) as a process of "creative destruction" where the established leaders are unlearning much of the old and inventing or adapting to the new. Despite the challenges of transition and transformation, the process of diffusion of the technological revolution and its paradigm generates a great surge of development.

Understanding the dynamics of techno-economic paradigms and the necessary investments and changeover in governance and institutions is most critical to the information and communication revolution—perhaps the most pervasive and global technological revolution in recent human history. For the modern knowledge-based economy, the information and communication technology revolution combines the innovative and transformative powers of the earlier revolutions of the printing press, railways, electricity, and telephone. It further combines the new powers of microelectronics and the computing grid with those of biotechnology (bioinformatics) and nanotechnology. For slow-moving economies, this techno-economic paradigm shift may present a tsunami rather than a new technological wave.

Newcomers who understand the dynamics of the techno-economic paradigm shift can direct their efforts toward learning the new practices and may even find a route to leaping forward and catching up (Perez, 2001). The four "Asian tigers" took the leap forward with the microelectronics revolution, rejuvenated mature industries, and entered new and fast-growing industries. This involved intense learning and substantial investments in human capital and active absorption of technology. Similarly, development under the current techno-economic paradigm requires proactive and sustained efforts. According to this new paradigm, capacity to handle information, knowledge, and innovation will be more central than ever. This paradigm also calls for radical transformation in education and training systems, science and technology policies, and more broadly, in conceiving development strategies.

Pervasive and Increasing Impact

Early evidence from advanced economies and some new industrializing countries suggests a pervasive impact of ICT on

- Organizations and markets
- Competitive strategies
- Innovation
- Financial services
- Employment
- Media and cultural development
- Regional and urban development
- Intelligent infrastructures and global supply chains
- Energy and environment
- Governance and participatory democracy

- Education and health
- Poverty

Impact on Organizations and Markets

New forms of organizations have become possible or even necessary to leverage ICT: flat, agile, lean, extended, and client focused. The reorganization of production and distribution around ICT has enabled the adoption of new processes, procedures, and organizational structures, which in turn have led to sustainable gains in productivity, quality, and responsiveness. Early evidence started to emerge in the late 1990s in advanced countries (Brynjolfsson and Hitt, 2000; Litan and Rivlin, 2000). ICT has made it possible to have very large-scale organizations that are at the same time flexible, agile, and focused. Latest advances in areas such as mobile, broadband, and collaborative technologies (Web 2.0) have further intensified the transformative impact of ICT on organizations.

The forces of globalization and increased competition, combined with the ICT revolution, have spurred organizations to focus on their core competencies while outsourcing increasing amounts of activities and services. These organizations are also designing their supply chains ever more tightly and strategically (Fine, 1998). Multinational corporations have become dense communication networks, with vast extended boundaries. For example, Microsoft is engaged with over 300,000 partners across the globe. General Electric is innovating new ways to manage their enormous supply chain of 500,000 suppliers from more than 100 countries, using 14 languages (Box 2.3). These changes are providing opportunities for developing countries to insert themselves into the global supply chains and to their production activities and exports.

Box 2.3 General Electric Supply Chain Management: Using Software As a Service

General Electric supply chain includes 500,000 suppliers in more than 100 countries that cut across 14 languages. GE spends some $55 billion annually (2008) among this web of suppliers.

GE faces major challenges in managing this supply chain: accurately tracking interactions with these suppliers—the contracts, compliance, certifications, and other critical data that must be globally stored, managed, and made accessible to thousands across the globe and in real time. GE sought a supplier information system that was easy to use and install, united sourcing into a central repository, multi-language capabilities, and offered a self-service functionality so each supplier could manage its own data. Its goal was to achieve one view of the supplier base and one version of the truth in all that massive data.

Rather than investing in developing and hosting its own system on-premise, GE opted to purchase a supplier information management (SIM) product in what is considered one of the largest software-as-a-service (SaaS) deployment. The system now supports 100,000 users and 500,000 suppliers. Data transparency and quality have improved now that suppliers use the self-service capabilities of the system to manage their own data. This is just one example of advances in software technology and services being deployed by multinationals with major implications for participation by suppliers in many developing countries.

Source: CIO Magazine, March 1, 2009, pp. 24–25.

The ICT revolution had given rise to network-centric enterprises, virtual organizations, and business ecosystems. This involves establishing a network-centric enterprise that connects the different partners in a company's business ecosystem to support different value creation processes. There are many examples of such enterprises, and the wellknown pioneers include Wal-Mart, Cisco, and Toyota. The customer is put at the center of the value chain and significant infrastructure, process, and data standardization enable real-time communications, agility, and synchronization across boundaries. In the supply chain management context, this means establishing dynamic connections between the enterprise, suppliers, customers, and other partners to maximum value. It involves integrating enterprise information systems with external partners' systems and processes to enhance "sense and response" capabilities (Nambisan and Sawhney, 2008).

Network-centricity is being further extended to diverse domains. For example, it is being applied by social advocacy groups to enhance the reach, speed, and overall effectiveness of social movements. Another contrasting example comes from the US Department of Defense (DoD). In contrast to the traditional chain-of-command model, which epitomized military organizations for centuries, the network-centric model is flatter, less hierarchal, and aims at "total information awareness." The goal is to give everyone, from soldiers to commanders, access to the same data, so they react and interact in real time. Radio frequency identification (RFID) and satellite tags allowed DoD to have total asset visibility of every item in every container as it moved across the world to field operations. Sensors and Internet-based communications systems, seamlessly linked, gave forces "situational awareness"—enabling widely disbursed units to fight with real-time knowledge of each other's movements and those of the enemy (Eggers, 2005, p. 6). The promise of transition from an industrial age to information age government extends to all domains (Chapter 11).

Information technology is also changing the workplace in fundamental ways, with important implications for human resources. Firms in industrial countries are restructuring from segmented (hierarchical, compartmentalized) organizations to holistic organizations, characterized by job rotation, integration of tasks, and learning across tasks (Lindbeck and Snower, 2000). Studies suggest increasing returns to worker characteristics such as people skills, capacity to work in teams, multi-task, work without supervision, take initiative, and be entrepreneurial (Levy and Murnane, 1996). A variety of managerial innovations like total quality management (TQM) are designed to exploit these changes. Simple tasks are automated, while the premium on complex tasks increases dramatically. The demand is for both human capital deepening and widening and for workers able to adapt to rapidly changing environments.

Together, ICT and complementary organizational innovations are enhancing access to information resources and management of knowledge assets. It is also accelerating product innovation, empowering project-based teams, and enriching learning and knowledge sharing at all levels of the extended enterprise. A new breed of event-driven organizations is emerging to exploit and tailor real-time information for decision making and service delivery (Ranadive, 1999). Consequently, companies are giving increasing attention to their information infrastructure, knowledge management, and communication competencies. Investment in such intangibles in advanced economies now exceeds 35% of total corporate investment.

ICT is also transforming global and local markets. Electronically mediated markets are profoundly affecting the cost, speed, and transparency of market-based transactions. For example, available evidence shows that electronic markets are more transparent and efficient. Through lower transaction cost and increased reach, they result in up to 15% lower costs to consumers and up to 20% lower costs in business procurement (ILO, 2001). But the potential gains from e-commerce are likely to differ by industry and country. Countries that are more fully integrated into the global market or have high shares of trade in sectors where e-commerce used intensively, such as apparel in Sri Lanka, must position themselves to adopt e-commerce practices, or otherwise risk losing their position in the value chain. Taiwan, with 80% of exports in sectors such as electronics that are intensive users of e-commerce, is very exposed to e-commerce (Mann, 2002).

E-commerce transforms traditional transactions and creates new marketplaces in three ways (Chapter 14):

- Altering the process by which transactions takes place (e.g., putting the supply chain online to improve inventory control and quality management)
- Innovating new products and services (e.g., personally tailored products such as garments)
- Creating new markets in time, space, and information that did not previously exist (e.g., global auction markets, sales of artisanship products from the Andes)

Business-to-business (B2B) net-based transactions are transforming supply chains across the globe, leading to the rise of new channels or net-based inter-mediaries, and enabling small and medium enterprises (SMEs) to pool resources and auction or collectively supply large multinationals. In the United States, over 80% of transactions are estimated to be e-commerce transactions. The trade net of Singapore helped to link and process transactions among many players including customs, banks, ports, shipping agents, freight forwarders, cargo handlers, and various authorities. The savings in transaction costs and time were dramatic: 1% of Singapore's GDP; clearance time reduction from 3 days to 15 min.

Net-based business-to-consumer (B2C) transactions and point-of-sale scanners are providing producers, particularly multinationals, with detailed and instant information on local and distant buyers and markets. For consumers, C2B transactions are cutting consumer search costs, reducing lead time wait, and broadening choices. Increased information on both sides helps align supply and demand ever more tightly. Evidence also suggests that inventory-to-sales ratios have declined in countries and industries that have adopted ICT more quickly (IMF, 2001). In turn, better timing of inventory changes is helping to reduce economy-wide output volatility.

Most organizations today were designed for the world of high transaction and interaction costs of the 20th century, but a sudden fall in these costs is now underway due to the Internet and advances in ICT. This sea change opens the possibility of remaking these organizations to mobilize their intangible assets and the knowledge and creativity of their 21st century workforces (Bryan and Joyce, 2007). In a low-transaction cost world, issues of trading off hierarchy vs. collaboration and centralization vs. decentralization are resolved in ways that can mobilize knowledge, innovation, and minds. ICT enables efficient and effective large-scale collaboration, greatly increases the relative value of intangible assets relative to tangible assets, reduces organizational complexity, and simultaneously increases the economies scale, scope, and specialization. It has opened new frontiers to organizational and managerial innovation, beyond current best practices.

At a more basic level, information and communication are the lifeblood of efficient markets, and ICT could develop markets and alleviate poverty, even without advanced ICT applications like e-commerce. Market prices act as coordinating signals for producers and consumers. But in isolated villages in developing countries there are virtually no sources of information regarding market prices and other production-related information. Studies suggest the pervasiveness of poor and late information on prices, work, and income opportunities in rural areas, with heavy toll on the rural poor in developing countries (Eggleston et al., 2002; Hanna, 1991). Under these conditions, even basic communications technologies could play a major role in creating efficient markets, improving producer practices, and speeding innovation. The Grameen's program to lease mobile phones to low-income women in Bangladesh indicates that close to half of all calls involved economic purposes such as discussing market prices, employment opportunities, land transactions, among others. Rather than creating a "digital divide," ICT could be used to create "digital provide."

Competitive Strategies

These ICT-induced changes are transforming the rules of competition and giving rise to new types of competitive strategies: innovation-driven competition, time-based competition; mass customization; lean manufacturing, and demand-driven, built-to-order products (Fine, 1998). ICT has drastically cut long-standing obsta-cles to communication: time and distance. New communication technologies allow companies to source inputs independent of location. With costs of transport and information diminishing, countries are forced into the same competitive arena. The "new competition" entails flexible response, customization, networking, and new forms of inter-firm organization (clustering), rather than classic price competition dominated by vertically integrated firms (Best, 1990).

The life cycles of products, processes, and supply chains have become signifi-cantly shorter. In particular, the ICT and information-content industries' products, processes, and supply chains are outdated in few months, not years. To cope with such clock speeds, leading firms are developing the ultimate core capability: the ability to anticipate, invest in, assemble and manage global chains of capabili-ties (Fine, 1998). Dell Company takes orders for customized computers over the Internet, builds the machines to the orders, and ships the completed products often within 24 h. This is the product of an ICT-enabled competitive strategy that relies on tight and lean links between the corporation, customers, suppliers, distributors, and alliance networks. Buil-to-order, demand-driven supply chains have become a key competitive advantage in such fast-moving industries. Similarly, in fashion indus-tries like garments, time required from producing fiber to cloth has been cut to 10% of what it was a few years ago.

Competitive strategies of companies in advanced countries rely on intangible investments and intellectual assets. Investments in intangibles—software, databases, communication infrastructures, process re-engineering, training, and innovative potential, among others—are more important than investments in capital goods. Economic success is increasingly based on the effective use of such intangible assets as the key resource for competitive advantage.

Information and communication technology is also reshaping national economies and competitive strategies. The share of knowledge-intensive and high-technology production in trade has increased steadily. Trade represented about 30% of world GDP in 1970 and reached almost 50% in 2000. ICT is enabling offshore outsourc-ing and an increasing share of services in global trade. This represents significant opportunities for developing economies since services in advanced countries occupy some 70% of GDP and the labor force, and outsourcing even a small share of such services would have major developmental and employment impacts on developing countries.

Most recent, and closely associated with globalization and diffusion of the Internet, is the emergence of network-based competition (Fung et al., 2008). As global logistics, communications and coordination have improved, manufacturing is dispersed around the world and a virtual factory can be built from a global network of suppliers, in response to demand. A network orchestrator builds and manages this broad network and designs the best supply chain from it to meet a specific customer need. Such networks are emerging across diverse industries and services, from garments and car manufacturing to R&D, services, and open-source software development. Opportunities for network-based competition are not limited to the large multinationals. The Internet makes it easier for SMEs to participate in networks and to engage in network orchestration. For example, in Hong Kong alone, at least 50,000 small trading companies manage global and regional supply chains (Fung et al., 2008).

Competition is no longer just company against company, but also supply chain against supply chain or network against network. Partners in the chain are all members of the same team trying to optimize value. Competing network against network means that companies with access to the best networks can outperform competitors. Orchestration of such networks calls for new roles and competencies, apart from the ICT infrastructure. It calls for a shift in management from focus on the firm to the network and ecosystem, from control to empowerment and trust among partners, and from maintaining turf and specialization to bridging boundaries and capturing value and intellectual assets across the network. Network orchestration becomes a core competency for competing in a flat world, a multiplier that increases the reach and effectiveness of the organization.

Innovation

No industries had greater impact on work and everyday life since the second half of the 20th century that the information and communication technology (Chandler, 2001). Less recognized but equally profound is that ICT, and particularly the Internet, has become a powerful enabler of innovation—perhaps the most influential technology in powering the wave of innovation since the last quarter of the 20th century. Its application to finance, research, design, manufacturing, logistics, marketing, knowledge management, and customer service has enabled enterprises to become more efficient, flexible, and innovative—through process innovation, product and service innovation, and the creation of new business models. Even governments are now considering the use of ICT to improve not only the way public services are delivered but also the way they are created. Governments are beginning to set a service innovation agenda.

Information and communication activities are at the heart of the innovation process, and ICT has become a tool for amplifying brainpower and for innovation. ICT is transforming the way researchers conduct their research, communicate with other researchers and potential users, and instantaneously access relevant knowledge from a vast and growing global knowledge. For example, bio-informatics has emerged as a field arising from the essential role of ICT in enabling biomedical research. ICT is further accelerating the codification of knowledge and thus knowledge sharing. Science and industry are more closely integrated with ever shorter product life cycles.

Innovation practices are changing. Why? Various forces are pressuring companies to open up their innovation process (Chesbrough, 2006). The perennial quest for growth is increasingly challenging in the era of global competition, fast commoditization, and shrinking product life cycles. In such an environment, process and product innovation have become crucial for sustained growth, competitiveness, and moving up the value ladder. The combination of fast-changing demand patterns, shortening market windows and product life cycles (as in mobile phone), and the rising costs of product development (as in new drugs) compresses the economics of investing in innovation and depresses the returns to the "closed" model or internally focused innovation. How can firms compete effectively? By looking outside.

Innovation is increasingly diffused and global, multidisciplinary, collaborative, open, and driven by the ecosystem. Successful organizations will increasingly tap into a global marketplace of innovators, experts and collaborators—the global brain (Nambisan and Sawhney, 2008). New types of innovation intermediaries, the Internet and related global platforms for the digital economy have made tapping into such global networks of inventors, scientists, and innovative firms easier than ever before. Network-centric innovation relies on harnessing the resources and capabilities of external innovators, networks, and communities to amplify innovation reach, innovation speed, and the quality of innovation outcomes. Examples include open-source software, open-source journalism, electronic R&D networks such as InnoCentives, and the community-based encyclopedia Wikipedia.

Multinational corporations are increasingly carrying out R&D on a global basis. A new cyber infrastructure is emerging in OECD countries. It combines content, processing, and interactivity to build "grid communities" and conduct e-science and engineering. Through databases, networks, and computing, ICT is increasing the scope and scale of R&D. More recently, ICT is also changing the way scientists, including social scientists, do research through the use of massive simulations, "adaptive agents," and "artificial" societies.

In OECD countries, ICT is bringing about changes within and among institutions of a national innovation system—changes that are accelerating the rate of innovation and tightening the links between universities, research institutions, industry, and consumers. In addition to accelerating managerial and organizational innovations, ICT helps accelerate scientific and technological innovation. Enabled by electronic networks, linkages between universities and industries, as well as among firms, are allowing firms to access local and global knowledge, to improve their technological capabilities, and to facilitate their joint learning and innovation. Thus, ICT is enabling the creation and evolution of innovation clusters, knowledge networks, and learning communities.

ICT is profoundly changing the context within which innovation takes place. Past innovation revolved around mass production, economies of scale, and centrally driven R&D. Increasingly, there is a profound shift to flexible production, diversification, networked and open innovation, sourcing talents globally, integration of disparate technologies, interconnectedness and collaboration in R&D among many actors, and economies of scale. ICT is enabling these processes and practices. ICT is also enabling faster cross-border knowledge sharing, within multinationals and through R&D partnering with smaller actors. However, studies of the relationship between ICT and innovation suggest that ICT influences innovation in different ways for high- and low-income countries (Box 2.4).

Box 2.4 Does ICT Matter for Innovation: Complementary Perspectives

Studies of the relationship between ICT and innovation suggest that ICT does matter for innovation, but it matters in different ways for high- and low-income countries. Nations with the highest Networked Readiness Index are also characterized by innovation-based growth and competitiveness (Rodriguez, 2008; Dutta and Mia 2008). ICT is changing the speed and economics of innovation by several channels: decreasing the costs of experimentation; speeding design-test cycles; improving logistics; enabling firms to benefit from lead-user innovation; improving timely access and analysis of information; and enabling networked and collaborative innovation among firms and the formation of clusters. ICT is enhancing the competencies of firms to identify sources of information, to identify patterns, to segment markets; to mine data from transactions, to develop creative and exploration capacity through simulation and prototyping, to reduce the cost of failure through rapid prototyping and testing, and to improve capacity to execute, adapt, and monitor implementation.

A study by Orsorio-Urzua (in Dutta and Mia 2008) indicates that higher levels of networked readiness, particularly the use of ICT, are associated with higher levels of innovation. But this relationship between ICT use and innovation is stronger in developed nations. Contextual factors influence this relationship. This study advances some reasons for the stronger relationship in the developed world such as absorptive capacity and organizational capabilities, more sophisticated use of ICT and high awareness among enterprises about the role of product and process innovation in sustaining competitiveness. High-income countries have also gone through the phases of investing in information infrastructure and basic efficiency-enhancing uses of ICT and now have shifted the focus toward innovation. Access to broadband will increasingly become important for collaborative and distributed innovation practices.

The study suggests, however, that government strategy for ICT does matter significantly for innovation among low-income countries. Higher levels of coordination and integration could significantly enhance the effectiveness of both ICT use and innovation in developing economies. Firms are able to innovate and generate the new organizational capabilities only in the context of sound government strategies for using ICT for long-term competitiveness—going beyond access to ICT.

This analysis may be extended by taking a broad definition of innovation and identifying three types of innovations: creating and commercializing new knowledge and technology; acquiring and adapting global knowledge and technology; and using and diffusing knowledge and technology that is

already in-country. Because developing countries are behind the technological curve in most sectors, innovation should focus less on invention or the
first use (globally) of a new technology and more about the first application
of a product or process in a specific setting and thus about doing things differently with available technology. Accordingly, the last two types of innovations
are more important for developing countries—and typically neglected in the
analysis of innovation policies.

Understanding the roles of ICT in creating new knowledge, accessing best
practices, and enabling and diffusing innovation still at an early stage. But the
few studies available suggest that ICT can play varying roles in these different
types of innovation. The last two types of innovation may not require the same
level of ICT sophistication and the use of ICT for acquiring and diffusing
knowledge/technology may yield more payoffs for developing countries. The
last type in particular suggests that broad access to ICT can lead to grassroots
innovation and empower the poor to find their own ways meet their needs and
enable their livelihood strategies.

Sources: Carlos A. Osorio-Urzua, Chapter 13 in Dutta and Mia 2008; also
Rodriguez, 2008; and Hanna, 2008.

New tools for communication and collaboration are enabling networked and
grassroots innovation. ICT is reducing coordination and learning costs, enriching relationships with clients, enabling a shift in responsibility for adaptation and
customization to users, harnessing knowledge from multiple experiments, and creating user communities and new forms of user-led innovations or user-producer
co-invention. Global enterprises like Proctor & Gamble now draw more than 50%
of new product innovations from outside the corporation's own R&D—from users
and partners.[1] IBM has subscribed to the open-source model and invested substantial resources to align many of its product and process innovation initiatives with the
open-source model.

In addition to connecting the traditional actors of a national innovation system,
collaborative technologies are engaging users, communities, small enterprises, and
grassroots organizations in product innovation and adaptation. These actors practice
new styles of innovation: being open, peering, sharing, and acting globally (Tapscott
and Williams, 2006).

Collaborative ICT tools have given rise to new models of sharing knowledge
and collective production of ideas and innovations, which often bypass proprietary
systems. The power of these tools is reflected in many massively produced knowledge products and infrastructures: the Linux ecosystem, Wikipedia, and open-source

---

[1]This "connect and develop" innovation strategy led to R&D productivity increase by nearly 60%,
innovation success rate more than doubled, and the cost of innovation significantly fell (Huston
and Sakkab, 2006).

software. They draw on collective intelligence and mass collaboration. These tools can be also harnessed to promote inclusive, pro-poor innovation that would address the needs of the bottom of the pyramid and help share indigenous knowledge and empower local innovators.

Financial Services

Finance is one of the most information-intensive services, and thus is at the forefront in using ICT to achieve efficiency gains across the financial supply chain, including Internet banking or e-banking and e-payment. Electronic financial services have spread quickly in recent years among developed countries. Internet banking is becoming one of the main delivery channels as it dramatically decreases transaction costs and speeds them up. E-finance allows for establishing financial systems without first building a fully functioning financial infrastructure. It lowers processing costs for providers and search and switching costs for consumers. Most affected are brokerage markets where online trading is becoming the norm. Increased connectivity has accelerated the migration of securities trading and capital raising from emerging markets to a few global financial centers, with capital raised offshore by emerging markets increasing many folds in the past decade.

ICT-enabled transformation of finance has been driving deeper consolidations in key middle and back office functions. It is expected to lead to much lower costs and greater competition in financial services in developing countries as providing e-finance is much cheaper than providing financial services with existing technologies and physical infrastructure investment, especially in rural areas. In fact, online financial transactions are estimated to cost about 10% of face-to-face financial transactions.

E-finance reduces the need for government intervention as now the private sector can provide financial services even when a country's financial sector is weak. New technology makes better information more easily available. For countries with underdeveloped financial systems, e-finance offers an opportunity to leapfrog. The financial systems of these countries are unsophisticated and limited to small elite groups: urban customers with high net worth, state enterprises, and large agribusinesses rather than small and medium size firms, farmers, or microenterprises. Such systems have high intermediation costs and are plagued with problems of supervision and re-capitalization.

Branchless banking offers an opportunity to dramatically cut transaction costs and expand geographic coverage of financial services. New models of microfinancing and partnerships are emerging to serve the poor and SMEs, enabled by ICT (Mas, 2008). For example, SKS Microfinance in India has relied on ICT to lower the transaction costs so radically that microloans could be handled profitably and at scale—targeting the 800 million people at the base of the pyramid in India (IFC and WRI, 2007). Another example is the partnership formed between the Grameen Foundation USA and India's largest private bank, ICICI, to assist microfinance institutions in raising funds. Another ICICI venture in the pipeline is to partner with microfinance institutions and technology provider *n*-longue to harness thousands of entrepreneur-run Internet kiosks as a first entry point for savings accounts, insurance, microcredit, etc. (IFC and WRI, 2007). In Kenya, South Africa, and the Philippines, among others, multi-purpose pre-paid phone cards and electronic cash offer services to customers who did not even have formal bank accounts.

A relatively recent development is bill payment services via mobile phones. This is a relatively important application in the context of developing countries where access to a "payments utility" is a major enabler for achieving universal access to finance and where mobile phones have spread faster than in mature economies. Being able to make payments conveniently and securely is essential in modern life and commerce. It enables economic livelihood, supports remittances and social relationships, communal joint actions, and payments to needy families.

New players such as non-bank money transfer operators, m-phone operators, and e-payment technology vendors are developing niches and value-added operations in many countries. Retail or small-volume financial transfers destined for households and small enterprises are of particular relevance to poverty alleviation and remittances. These are increasingly relying on online money transfer systems, which are cost-saving for both originators and end users.

Mobile phones are increasingly used to mobilize substantial remittances and provide a new source for financing growth—with particular relevance to those at the base of the pyramid. The substantial and growing size of remittances has drawn the attention of both development and commercial banks. This flow of funds provides a large share of income for many at the bottom of the pyramid and financing mechanism for new businesses, new houses, and children's education. Recognizing the potential in transferring remittances, businesses are launching new services. One example is the formation of a consortium of 19 mobile operators in 2007 to serve more than 600 million customers in 100 countries by transferring remittances through their mobile phones, thus radically reducing cost. The consortium anticipates global remittances of more than $1 trillion annually by 2012 (IFC and WRI, 2007).

Poor people in developing countries are more likely than the rich to use mobile phones to do financial transactions (Mas, 2008). The poor in developing countries have less options for accessing bank services because of lack of physical banking infrastructure and low Internet penetration. A branchless banking, using mobile phones, could be far more preferable than the limited available options: traveling and queuing at distant branches or saving in cash and physical assets. Moreover, the potential of mobile phones for microfinance institutions is greater. These institutions face higher cost-of-service delivery due to the small transaction values they handle and the likely more remote and dispersed location of their customers.

However, using mobile phone as front-end part of growth or outreach strategy must be accompanied by adequate regulatory frameworks and by building adequate back-office systems and internal controls for the financing institutions. A lack of openness to new models of financial provision and a lack of policy certainty limit the realization of the potential of ICT-enabled new models. Branchless banking therefore raises novel issues for governments: what role should governments play in causing low-cost retail payment and banking infrastructures to spread? What is the right balance of priorities between fostering ICT-enabled innovation and ensuring system stability; between competition and interoperability; between creating financial choices and protecting consumers (Mas, 2008). Lessons for the road are emerging (Mas and Kumar, 2008).

Employment

Evidence shows that countries where ICT was used most widely were also where total factor productivity and employment have grown the most (ILO, 2001; IMF, 2001). Use of ICT is also associated with new patterns of job creation, destruction, and switching. Despite the hopeful signs of job creation, jobs are also lost through several channels: obsolescence, automation, and disintermediation. In labor markets at the forefront of the knowledge economy, diversity of employment and the share of self-employed and temporary workers are increasing.

Labor markets have become more demanding and turbulent. Most of this instability is being internalized within the enterprise, where jobs are continuously changing (ILO, 2001). With accelerated obsolescence of skills and jobs, attention is now shifting to mobility, employability, lifelong learning, and learning to learn. Beyond such foundation skills as the ability to learn and exchange knowledge, the need for ICT-related technical skills is increasing throughout the economy.

ICT impact on jobs is likely to have profound implications for quality of work and life, for income distribution, and for international division of labor. ICT-induced changes in jobs and employment opportunities are leading to labor migration and global competition for knowledge workers, particularly in the ICT industries. A new international division of labor is emerging. The Internet is reshaping the global distribution of employment in the vast majority of services.

As the informational and ICT-related content of jobs growing, the possibility of polarization in the demand and rewards between the unskilled and the knowledge workers is also increasing. These changes and potential risks are challenging the arrangements and institutions of an earlier industrial era, including trade unions and employers' organizations. Labor market policies as well as the right to lifelong learning have become central to ICT and knowledge diffusion. Conversely, e-learning facilitates lifelong learning.

The new technology tools for information and communication are leveraging education and knowledge workers. As electronic devices accomplish more and more routine tasks, demand for expertise and communication skills is rapidly rising. Similarly the demand for analytical skills is increasing. Human capital is taking an increasingly dominant position in national competitive strategies. Applications in knowledge management, business intelligence, data mining, distance education, telemedicine, and the strategic use of information (made available from transactions systems like e-tax and e-procurement) can all further leverage knowledge workers and expert professionals.

Media and Cultural Development

It has long been recognized that media and communications play a key role in development—social, cultural, and economic. The media plays diverse roles in development: (i) improving governance, public decision making, transparency, accountability, and responsiveness; (ii) promoting behavioral and social change in support of reforms and development (through social marketing and policy reform campaigns); and (iii) generating new sources of growth and employment, mainly through content creation by SMEs and significant multiplier effects (World Bank, 2007a; EU, 2007). These influences depend on the availability of relevant content that can educate and inform as well as entertain, the plurality and independence of media, enabling legislation and support for community-level broadcasting, and access to infrastructure and communication platforms.

The media is undergoing massive transformation, as a result of digitalization of content, platforms, and devices. The digital transformation is significantly enhancing the fluidity of media content and producing an abundance of sharable content. It is also introducing two-way, bottom-up, and lateral content production, distribution, and services. The top-down nature of traditional mass media is being challenged by the changing nature of choice from "on offer" to "on demand," from mass to individually tailored, and from corporate created to user created (Locksley, forthcoming).

User-created content, enabled by widespread access to broadband Internet and social networking tools, is emerging as a major force in shaping media, communication, and culture (Vincent and Vickery, 2008). User-created content has exploded into major bottom-up and lateral trends (OECD, 2007). The Internet has altered the economics of content production and information sharing. With lower access barriers, increased demand for content, lower entry barriers in upstream supply, and advances in collaboratively developed platforms and news aggregators, media and cultural content are advanced and increasingly shaped by broad user participation. The Internet is increasingly influenced by intelligent web services with technologies enabling users to be growing contributors to developing, collaborating, and distributing Internet content and developing and customizing Internet applications. A participative web is emerging and is providing a testing ground for low-cost production of content and low-cost experimentation of services, with social change implications.

Apart from technological factors, user-created content is driven by economic factors such as lower entry barriers to content creators, increased interest to user-created content by mobile operators and search engines, and growing availability of new business models to monetize content, such as advertizing-based models. Social drivers for user-created content include the young "digital natives," the growing desire to express oneself and be more interactive than possible on traditional media platforms, and the growth of community-driven projects. This is leading to increased user autonomy, diversity of users and content, and a shift from passive consumption of broadcasting to interactive and participative web.

The rise of effective, large-scale cooperative efforts—peer production of information, knowledge, media, and culture—Paralels those of business applications. The impacts of user-created content are wider than enabling network-centric innovation and competition in the business sector. They can help influence the traditional media, create alternative information and communication channels, help change government politics and civic life, and enable mass collaboration and community-driven programs.

User-created content and the growing wealth of networks raise many legal, institutional, and governance challenges (Benkler, 2006). Among the key immediate issues are copyright infringement, privacy concerns, content quality, and cyber-attacks making user data vulnerable. They also led increased urgency to issues of media literacy, e-literacy, strengthening capacities for local content production, and widening access to broadband infrastructure, and digital tools—issues of special relevance to developing countries.

But they also raise societal issues and choices that are fundamental to long-term social, political, and economic development. For more than 150 years, communication technologies have tended to concentrate and commercialize the production and exchange of information. The recent ICT developments present the possibility of a radical reversal of this long trend—a reversal toward mass participation and radical sharing of information and intelligence. Depending on societal choices, we may also witness the mergence of a substantial component of non-market production and exchange of information and of information-based tools, services, goods, and capabilities. This may lead to substantial redistribution of power and wealth from the 20th century industrial producers of information, media, and culture. This raises the central issue of whether public polices will promote a core infrastructure that is governed as common and therefore made available to anyone who wishes to participate in the networked information environment outside the market-based proprietary framework (Benkler, 2006). Or, will new business models emerge to appropriate and commercialize these bottom-up contributions?

How will the technological and economic forces that are shaping the media play out in the developing world? Will the Internet, digitization, and collaborative tools reduce inequalities and promote diversity in the media and communication environment at the local and global levels? Will this transformation allow more people to participate in knowledge creation and cultural sharing on a global basis? Will the economies of scale and scope of digital content production further reinforce the imbalance in trade and further displace local with global media? Unencumbered by legacy assets, will developing countries be able to leverage newly available and affordable technology platforms (mobile phone, wireless) to deliver relevant content?

Global debates on the need to foster a development-friendly Information and Communication Order, raged during the 1970s and 1980s at UNESCO and other UN organizations — including how developing countries might use the media and communication networks to become more economically, politically, and culturally self-reliant. Since, progress has been slow. The recent World Summits on

Information Society of 2003 and 2005 have revisited many of the issues of inequalities but in very different technological, economic, and political contexts. Today, equally strongly contested are the need to expand the opportunities for open access to media content and the Internet, to limit intellectual property rights protection on digital information resources, and to finance literacy and other capabilities necessary for people to participate in information societies (Mansel and Nordenstreng, 2007). The outcomes are likely to be shaped as much by geopolitics and globalization as by technological advances. They are also likely to be significantly influenced by mobilizing local NGOs, building social capacity to appropriate the new tools, promoting user and community-created content, and pursuing national media and telecommunications reforms within an inclusive e-development strategy.

Regional and Urban Development

The spatial implications of the communication revolution are profound and directions are uncertain. Lower transaction and communication costs, combined with goods production that is increasingly based on flexible specialization, tend to favor the dispersion of economic activities (IMF, 2001). Yet, real-time information about consumers, easier sharing of tacit knowledge, and the proliferation of producer-support services tend to favor the location of knowledge-intensive production near to large markets and urban centers. Concerning services, the ICT revolution has been promoting the dispersal of services that can be delivered remotely and effectively, based on codified knowledge. Meantime, it is inducing clustering and concentration of services that are driven by innovation, tacit knowledge, and face-to-face interactions. Electronic communications complement and even reinforce rather than substitute for face-to-face communications.

Governments have many reasons to worry about disparities in welfare among regions and to help lagging ones. When today's rich countries were developing during the 19th century, the growth of their leading areas was constrained to the rate of growth of their domestic markets and the world technological frontiers. Since technological progress and globalization have increased market potential in leading areas of developing countries, intensifying concentration of economic activities and amplifying spatial disparities. Governments cannot stop or ignore these forces, but can help lagging regions most by strengthening their economic integration with the leading areas. Economic development experience indicates that the key to help promote development in lagging regions, without undercutting overall economic growth of the country, is to shift from traditional spatial targeting to spatial integration (World Bank, 2009a).

Governments have many policy instruments for promoting economic integration to reduce those disparities: (1) policies and institutions such as land and labor regulations, and social services such as health and education; (2) incentives and investments in spatially connective infrastructure that facilitate movement of goods, services, people, and ideas; and (3) spatially targeted programs to help the lagging regions directly. Can ICT enable these three instruments and promote spatial integration? Yes, in various ways, as explored in Box 2.5.

Box 2.5 Can ICT Help Lagging Regions?

Set against this faster rise in disparities among leading and lagging regions in the developing world, is the opportunity for faster convergence—because ICT tools offer a wider range of methods and more affordable access to services and knowledge to bridge the economic distance between leading and lagging areas.

ICT can be an enabler of improving coverage of social services to lagging and remote regions as well as a cost-effective tool for delivering and managing spatially targeted programs. Telecenters can help deliver much needed e-government services, as well as e-education and e-health services and in the process equalize access and quality to these regions.

The diffusion of mobile services, even in remote areas, opens new opportunities to provide financial services over a mobile phone network. Many people in lagging regions have limited access to financial services. With the rise of remittances, better access to financial services help people in these areas overcome credit constraints. In the Philippines, 3.5 million people (out of 20 million mobile phone subscribers) have access to mobile phones that can transfer money (Mas, 2008).

Producers in lagging areas can access better information on prices they can get for their products. Small enterprises can also market their handicrafts through web sites. Communities can attract tourists to their unique cultural heritage and ecological diversity. With coordinated efforts, locally relevant content and solutions can be widely disseminated within and among lagging regions.

ICT is an increasingly critical spatially connective infrastructure in its own right as well as modernizer of other integrative infrastructures. ICT can modernize transport, facilitate international trade, and dramatically increase quality and speed of logistics, even for remote and lagging regions. Moreover, low communication costs make it possible to control production processes over long distances and reduce the need to co-locate management and experts with unskilled workers. This allows vertically integrated companies to outsource production to low-wage countries. It also facilitates the breakup of production processes into supply chains of companies distributed across countries. Low communication costs are particularly important for offshoring services.

Although leading regions in developing countries are likely to benefit most from these processes, rural and lagging areas can participate in this offshoring through various measures, including telecenters combined with specialized training, as demonstrated by pilots in rural India. The biggest outsourcers, in relation to local value added of these services, have been small countries in Africa like Angola and Mozambique.

Countries such as China are giving special attention to ICT as a tool for spatial economic integration. Empirical evidence confirms the link. For 29 areas in China, between 1986 and 2002, telecommunication infrastructure was strongly associated with subnational GDP growth (Lei and Haynes, 2004). Efforts to promote rural informatization in China are growing through a variety of central and local initiatives such as developing local content, Internet-enabled rural services, and shared access centers. Rather than resisting the forces of unbalanced growth, policy makers are using some of the growing resources from fast growth to balance development outcomes across regions. ICT is viewed as a critical tool in doing so.

Traditional regional policies focus on attracting individual firms to lagging regions through taxes, subsidies, and regulations by central and regional governments. Many countries have offered incentives to create economic mass in lagging areas and offset the higher transport and logistics costs and lower levels of public services. European countries have a long history with such spatially targeted policies and interventions. But even these countries now focus on "soft" interventions such as investing in innovation and supporting science and technology institutions, parks, and infrastructures. Investing in ICT infrastructure, including broadband, and research and innovation networks is a critical part of such soft interventions.

Source: World Bank, 2009.

How is the role of cities changing, and what role is ICT playing in this change? Globalization, far from undermining localization, actually intensifies local agglomeration by extending markets for regional products to the world. Globalization simultaneously frames and induces localization and locational specialization (Yusuf et al., 2000). It tends to heighten locational specialization and reinforces the advantages of large urban centers.

Cities have been always the engines of growth in regional economies and no country has achieved sustained growth without accompanying urban growth. Enabled by advanced communications in knowledge-based economies, cities are increasingly becoming the focal points for global and national economies. Cities are best endowed with knowledge infrastructure and educational institutions, higher shares of educated people, advanced communication infrastructure, and access to the global economy. Further, the scale of cities and the diversity of inhabitants create the interactions that generate new ideas. Urban regions also attract talent, as talent attracts talent, creating dynamic clusters (Florida, 2005). Cities are emerging as platforms or gateways to services, learning, innovation, creativity, and entrepreneurship, more than ever in history.

Cities are also differentiating and competing on a global scale, giving rise to global urban networks (Scott, 2000; Florida, 2005). They are seeking to secure and enhance their competitive advantage in a globalizing economy. They seek to combine both rich local knowledge spillovers and international best practices. They are the arenas of synergies, externalities, and agglomeration. Local governing coalitions therefore seek to harness these synergies, upgrade local human resources, promote incubators and risk capital, build advanced information infrastructures and information services, promote information flows, cultivate collaborative relationships among firms, and promote export markets for local products. Singapore envisioned its future role as an intelligent island or a regional hub for information-intensive services. The "walled" cities of China are opening up to all kinds of information flows.

The concentration of economic power and knowledge-based services in cities is strengthening demands for decentralization. Modern communications and greater openness to trade and ideas have circumscribed the authority of central government and enlarged the freedoms of subnational entities.[2] Many developing countries are acceding to diverse pressures to increase democratic participation and devolve authority to lower levels. Heightened awareness of ethnic or regional identities, combined with increasing inequalities and diverse responses to globalization, are contributing to the trend of placing greater responsibilities on local authorities. Municipalities are facing greater challenges in delivering an increasing array of services and satisfying demanding and diverse clients. For this, they have to partner with private sector and civil society.

Political and economic dynamics are favoring decentralization from national to city level. More and more national development business moves through subnational levels of government. In China, for example, local government budgets are more than 70% of total government spending. Cities are recognizing that they have more scope to act, more leverage to effect change, more prospects for trade, and more opportunities to shape their futures. Technological changes are favoring local agglomeration. The new emerging paradigm of flexible production systems is able to achieve considerable variety and significant scale of production by exploiting ICT. It relies on external networks and intensive transactions, complementarities, and specialization.

Information and communication technologies are thus inducing or reinforcing these trends, and when appropriately harnessed, can facilitate effective decentralization and efficient and sustainable urbanization. Service-sector jobs in industrial countries are increasingly contestable by developing countries. Beyond enabling global trade in services, advanced information infrastructures are increasingly important to attracting foreign direct investment, facilitating technology diffusion, and developing innovation clusters. ICT is contributing to the growth of highly dynamic, knowledge-based, and creative services, clustered in cities. In turn, cities must compete for highly mobile creative talent and knowledge workers and for innovative and income-elastic economic activities. They have to develop skilled human resources, attract global capital flows, address quality of life issues, and develop the software as well as the infrastructure of livable cities. Shanghai drew a "smart"

---

[2]Naisbitt and Barber, among others, show how sub-national and global or regional institutions are gaining relative power vis-à-vis nation states.

growth strategy to attract knowledge-based and information services industries, enhance access to information infrastructure, and enrich learning opportunities. The "digital cities" movement aims to enable relatively small cities to have many of the advantages of larger ones, without some of the agglomeration costs.

Cities are not just economic engines—they are centers for culture, innovation, and learning. They are also social communities. They are bearers of significant informal knowledge and repositories of tacit know-how. Regional agglomerations of producers are sites of accumulated cultural conventions, trust-based relationships, and social capital—a key factor in economic development. Cities that facilitate active participation in local affairs and collaboration among local institutions are nourishing not only a healthy community, but also a local competitive advantage. A rich cultural environment and a vibrant local community are increasingly important for attracting knowledge workers and sustaining knowledge industries.

The cultural-generating capabilities of cities can be harnessed into productive use with the help of ICT. Cities have always played a privileged role as centers of cultural activities such as tourism, arts, crafts, entertainment, fashion, advertising, publishing. That is unlikely to change. What is new is the likely impact of ICT on both the renewal of local cultures and the dissemination and use of cultural products on a global basis. ICT is leading to urban cultural synergies—strong interdependencies and spillovers in localized cultural production. Meantime, media companies are engaged in developing electronic platforms for use of cultural products on a global scale—projecting the cultural products of cities like Los Angles and Paris. Johannesburg is undergoing radical transformation in post-apartheid period, not only by modernizing its services but also by tapping its cultural origins in music, tourism, and performing arts.

It is projected that by 2020, over 4 billion people (55% of the world's population) will live in urban areas, and almost 94% of this increase will be in developing countries. It is therefore important to create the capacity to produce and diffuse technologies that support efficient and sustainable urbanization and favor local development processes. Some examples of the roles of ICT in facilitating effective decentralization and local management are explored in the chapters concerned with e-government and e-society. ICT applications can be targeted to strengthen local government management, revenue and expenditure management, citizen participation, and monitoring and accountability. Successful decentralization is contingent upon effective local governance, resource management, and accountability.

Intelligent Infrastructures and Global Supply Chains

Infrastructures shape businesses and whole economies. Past technological revolutions brought forth powerful new infrastructures: steamships, railways, roads, electricity, and telephones. These infrastructures then transformed industry and commerce. Eventually, these revolutions stabilized once businesses learned to harness their capabilities. The new information and communication infrastructure is still evolving rapidly and forcefully shaping the global economy and all kinds of industries and services. It is being built on the sustained exponential improvements in microelectronics, computing, digital communications, and information storage. Institutions are racing to catch up. But perhaps least visible and most pervasive is how microelectronics, sensory capabilities, memory, communications, information processing and control (intelligence capabilities) are being built into all kinds of physical infrastructures and products.

The range of applications is almost endless and this book does not focus on these types of applications as being integrated into e-development strategies, mainly because these applications are often embedded into hardware systems and are therefore driven more by technological imperatives than by institutional or human factors. However, appreciation of ICT uses in infrastructure and energy systems is warranted since these applications have implications for developing the enabling policies and human resources to take advantage of these technological advances. Moreover, these applications can be extremely relevant to the challenges of developing countries: improving transportation and public transit systems, reducing pollution and congestion, conserving energy, increasing safety and reliability of networks, and managing the fast growing urban systems.

Smart infrastructure includes an increasing array of applications, ranging from intelligent transportation systems, smart structures, to water distribution and irrigation systems, to real-time logistics, and smart energy grids. Its common feature is that it has built-in components that are able to collect and transmit information about the state of the infrastructure to a central processing facility and to receive back instructions which triggers controlling devices. ICT is enabling real-time control and remote monitoring of all types of flows and distribution systems, thus optimizing all kinds of logistics and reducing the material- and energy-intensities of almost all transport and distribution systems, industrial processes, and service activities.

Take the example of using ICT in the Indian railways, one of the largest and busiest networks in the world with a major developmental role throughout the economy. One of the earliest applications has been the computerized reservation and ticketing system, currently (2008) enabling passengers to book accommodation on any train from more than 1400 locations across the country and involving more than 1 million passenger transaction per day. Impact of the early phase was substantial, including savings in time and elimination of corruption associated with manual train reservations (Hanna, 1994). More recent ICT applications to the railways infrastructure management are contributing to operational efficiency, revenue management, and asset management for both freight and passenger transport and overall improvement of passenger services and safety (e-gov Magazine, April 2008, pp. 39–45).

Another example is the port of Singapore, perhaps the busiest seaport and which has the fastest turnaround time in the world. To a great extent, such efficiencies have been the result of long-term strategic investments in information technology, made since the 1970 s. Applications aimed to increase productivity, optimize investment in infrastructure, and improve port operations and management. Computer-integrated terminal operations and marine operations systems automate container terminal operations to maximize equipment and space use and apply expert systems and real-time databases to port navigation management (Hanna et al., 1996, pp. 163–164).

Such improvements, and more recent advances, have provided Singapore with real competitive advantages, for the port, and more widely, for the whole export-oriented Singaporean industries.

Many east Asian countries and trade hubs, such as Singapore, Taipei, and Hong Kong, have been investing in intelligent infrastructures to facilitate exports and imports and improve their overall competitiveness. One example is in integrating all modes of transport at sea and airports. Another is through cargo clearance systems such as the automated warehouse and distribution center of Taipei (Hanna et al., 1996, pp. 130). Automated warehouses at the Hong Kong air cargo terminal integrate various cargo handling through IT-enhanced physical infrastructure and services, leading to high speed and reliability.

Global supply chains are increasing the demand for intelligent infrastructure and for having an agile, lean, adaptable, and speedy response to demand (Boyson et al., 2004). Supply chains are expanding in reach and increasing in complexity, intermodal coordination, and performance requirements. With more global manufacturing and cargo traffic, efficiency of this physical Internet is at a premium. Large and leading companies are using their supply chains to compete and create sustainable advantages through responsiveness to customer demand. These chains are rendered efficient and intelligent with advanced uses of ICT. Shining examples include Wal-Mart, Dell computers, FedEx, and UPS (The Economist, June 17, 2006).

Such global supply chain requirements call for more intelligent local infrastructures and efficient local supply chains in developing countries. For example, the cost of logistics in China has been reduced from 25% of GDP in 1991 to 21% in 2006. India's cost of logistics represents about 13% of GDP. Meantime, America shows just how much cost can be saved: in 1982, logistics represented 14.5% of the America's GDP, but now (2006) the share is down to about 8%, and the inventory costs have fallen by 60% for the same period (The Economist, June 17, 2006, The Physical Internet, p. 12).

Logistics centers are shaping the landscape and the new centers of commerce. Historically, transport technology has always made physical impact on centers of commerce. Companies are moving some or all their operations to be near advanced logistics centers, especially airports and integrated transport systems. Some countries and cities are building on this trend to become global hubs or logistics cities. Dubai aspires to become such a hub or logistics city.

Information technology applications in infrastructure are also enabling local governments to exercise intelligent management of scarce local resources and develop more adaptive and responsive infrastructures. Information systems and real-time monitoring and control could optimize the use of urban infrastructures and resources such as land, water, electricity, urban transport, and financial resources. As many urban economies become more information- and knowledge-based, and mobile and broadband networks become ubiquitous in urban centers, telework or telecommuting becomes a more attractive alternative for some and part of reducing urban transport requirements and energy consumption. In Malaysia and many other local governments, government departments have collaborated on networked, Geographic

Information Systems (GIS) to facilitate land resource management and optimize infrastructure investments and usage. As urban infrastructure is being rapidly developed in many developing countries, like China, the opportunities to incorporate intelligent transport and advanced public transit systems are substantial.

Energy and Environment

Information technology promises a new growth paradigm that is less material based and energy intensive. This paradigm started with rapid advances in microelectronics (Freeman, 1987; Hanna, 1991). These advances are coalescing into new best-practice manufacturing systems that integrate flexible automation, process and product innovation, and organizational innovation. With the increasing concern about global warming and polluting manufacturing, the pressures are on to integrate ICT solutions to manufacturing processes, to optimize the use of raw materials, monitor processes, and reduce their energy consumption. Fortunately, ICT is expected to continue to drive energy-efficiency improvements, and several studies indicate that the potential for improvements substantial (Box 2.6).

Box 2.6 ICT as a Key Enabler of Energy-Efficient Practices

A McKinsey report estimates that cost-effective investments in existing energy productivity technologies (ranging from more efficient lightening, to more efficient home appliances, to advanced power plant technologies) could improve energy production and use in the United States by 25% over the next 20 years (Bressand et al., 2007). ICT would clearly contribute significantly to all these improvements. Another study of the United States estimated that ICT can reduce the growth of carbon emissions by one-third over a decade, as a result of continued ICT diffusion in e-commerce, supply chain management, telecommuting, reduced paper and materials consumption, shift in growth to less energy-intensive sectors, and ICT-driven efficiency improvements in a wide range of equipment (Laitner and Ehrhard-Martinez, 2008). A more recent (February 2008) study also by McKinsey's Global Institute concluded that the world could cut projected global energy demand growth between now and 2020 by at least half by capturing opportunities to increase energy productivity.

A similar study in Japan projects that widespread use of ICT could reduce carbon emissions by over 40% by 2050 (cited in Laitner and Ehrhard-Martinez, 2008; Atkinson and Castro, 2008). The reductions would come from intelligent transportation systems, widespread teleworking, and ubiquitous home energy management systems (cited in Laitner and Ehrhard-Martinez, 2008). These studies offer a picture of what is possible in a digitally enabled society.

These studies are based on a future where ICT can substitute energy-efficient digital connections for physical travel, and enable more energy-efficient practices and processes (Atkinson and Castro, 2008). Telecommuting is estimated to reduce energy use and carbon emissions quite significantly, as well as time and money. As travel is reduced largely at peak times of rush hours, telecommuting allows remaining cars to flow freely, thereby saving additional energy. Telecommuting also saves office space, and thus the need to build, heat, and cool. Similarly, videoconferencing can save on expensive and energy-intensive air travel. With advances in videoconferencing technologies, enabling real-time virtual meetings with high-definition audio and video, the potential for substitution and energy savings are significant. With the emergence of high-speed broadband, ICT is also enabling the "dematerialization" of the economy. Digital movies and music, web-based news, and electronic banking, all digitally distributed or transacted over the Internet, are among the many examples of relying less on paper and other energy-intensive vehicles.

Similarly, ICT can drive energy-efficient practices in business. ICT-enabled advances in supply chain technologies and production management help firms track inventory and engage in just-in-time production. With lean manufacturing, energy can be saved at every step of production and supply chain. ICT is also allowing more effective utilization of transport systems—using ICT to better schedule flights and raise seat utilization in air transport, for example. And as discussed earlier, similar gains are realized in rail and other modes of transport. New e-enabled business practices like Amazon.com's centralized warehousing are less energy consuming than brick-and-mortar retail operations.

Source: Atkinson and Castro, 2008; Author.

Applied to energy management, ICT is used to achieve more efficient and reliable control of electric grids—transmission and distribution of electric energy. Sensors in transformers and substations allow rapid detection of outages and other malfunctions and prompt dispatch for repairs. Smart meters installed in the premises of final users (businesses, factories, homes) permit two-way communication that can be used to implement smart marginal-cost pricing policies that encourage load leveling and thereby save on investment costs in generation and emissions associated with coal, gas, and other non-renewable sources. This includes the ability to turn off or reduce consumption of appliances in consumer premises—using plug-in hybrids and intelligent home appliances. Smart grids also help monitor and control energy theft, which are very significant in many developing countries. Transmission and distribution losses in India's power sector, for example, could be reduced by 30%, if ICT-enabled smart-grid technology were used to monitor and manage electricity grids.

Two-way communication in the grid can also favor co-generation from renewable sources owned by consumers (solar, wind, small hydro). Accordingly, the prosumer gets credit for contributions to the grid. Another use is for plug-in-electric vehicles, whose batteries can also be used as a source to store energy generated or acquired at non-peak periods and resell it to the grid at peak periods if plugged in. Under appropriate regulation, this allows sale of broadband Internet connections as well as power to consumers. In short, smart-grid technology, which is being tested on a large scale in Europe and the United States and some developing countries in pilots, promises significant economic, environmental, and digital inclusion benefits (Knight, 2008a,b).

Energy and environmental management also depends on strategic planning, monitoring, knowledge networks, and adaptation strategies. For example, ICT underpins advanced modeling to optimize the selection of sites for wind farms and the design of wind turbines. ICT enables monitoring of all aspects of environment and broad sharing of such information to all stakeholders. E-enabled green policy networks as well as e-enabled carbon markets are emerging to help formulate energy and environmental policies and adaptation strategies. Adaptation strategies are further supported by ICT-enabled knowledge building and connecting to those on the frontline.

Will the growing reliance on the ICT infrastructure lead to fast growing use of power by the infrastructure itself? ICT's energy costs are rising. Fortunately, the fast advances in ICT is leading to significantly more output per unit of energy: Whereas cars get around 40% more miles to the gallon than they did 30 years ago, ICT devices get 2.6 million % more instructions per watt than in 1978. Researchers have estimated that for every unit of energy consumed by ICT, there are corresponding savings of 6–14 units of energy (Atkinson and Castro, 2008).

In sum, ICT has catalyzed important innovations in energy efficiency. It is also revolutionizing electricity production, distribution, and consumption. Moreover, new energy production technologies, including solar and wind power, rely heavily on ICT for their design and management. The trend toward ICT-driven improvements in energy efficiency is expected to continue as the most promising ICT-enabled innovations are still in early stages of implementation even among advanced countries. The net impact on energy and the environment can be significant, but will depend on how quickly and fully society adopts not only the available ICT capabilities, but also the policies to spur adoption of ICT-enabled energy-conserving practices.

Governance and Participatory Democracy

The information revolution is changing the institutions of governance and participatory democracy. It is enabling more access to information for all, and thus transparency, accountability, and citizen empowerment. This potential presents many promises and daunting challenges for governance. Power over information is being decentralized, fostering new types of community and different roles for government (Kamarck and Nye, 2002; Eggers, 2005). Timely information on results is enabling governments to improve performance management and adopt more outcome-oriented and client-focused approaches. The information technology revolution is also enabling new forms of democratic input and citizen feedback (Chapter 11).

Accountability and trust in government rely on easy and free access to public information. Transparency keeps government accountable to citizens. In most developing countries, and until a decade or two ago, in developed countries, citizens have to go to great investigative lengths to find public information on budgets, services, and comparative performance of basic public services. Today, the Internet has become one of the most important tools in achieving a more transparent state in developed countries. In the United States, public officials are moving from a reactive stance of simply responding to freedom of information requests to proactively putting all kinds of public information online (Egger, 2005). Beyond displaying government documents, transparency is giving citizens access to government databases.

Increasing transparency in government also increases citizen involvement in government, boosts government credibility, reduces corruption, and raises performance. Transparency generates accountability, which in turn generates pressure for improved performance. For example, Colorado, Texas, and some other states in the United States started posting comparative public school test results online, and this helped parents make more informed choices about their children's educational alternatives. Publication of state "school report cards" correlated with improvements in the National Assessment of Educational Progress. Three years after Colorado's publishing of test results online, the percentage of elementary students meeting state reading standards went from 12 to 74%, while writing went from 2 to 47% (Egger, 2005, p. 129).

Another powerful example of digital accountability and links to improved performance is New York City Police Department's *Compstat* system, which tracks crime on a real-time basis. Keys to its success in improving performance are measuring results, timely intelligence, swift resource deployment, sustained follow-up, and assessment and accountability. Real-time statistics and performance information are shown on digital maps. *Compstat* has become an accountability tool, information-gathering and information-sharing forum, and an educational forum. Overall crime in New York City went down by over 50% and auto crime by 70% (Egger, 2005, pp. 130–131).

Applied to government, ICT and the Internet allow citizens to scrutinize the political process. Corruption flourishes in darkness and thrives on ignorance. In Latin America, Chile is the most corruption-free country as well as the leader in electronic government. All areas where corruption thrives in developing countries—permits, licenses, fees, taxes, and procurement—are now web enabled. In South Korea, Seoul's municipal government anticorruption web site (OPEN) has subjected key administrative processes to public tracking and scrutiny. Customs is also another area rife with corruption in developing countries. In the Philippines, where customs is fingered as the most corrupt office in the country, web enabling the customs process has not only reduced fraud but cut the time to release cargo by about 50–80% (Egger, 2005, pp. 134–136).

Government practices in information sharing have wide ramifications for the whole economy. Governments are the largest collectors, users, and disseminators of information resources on individuals and the economy. Their information sharing infrastructures and knowledge management practices have major consequences for individuals, businesses, and civil society, well beyond the functioning of government institutions.

Information technology is also being applied to the legislative branch of government, to enhance citizen participation in policy formulation and monitoring, and to promote democracy and the rule of law. E-government enables a more honest dialogue with the governed. Timely access to information, knowledge, and feedback is crucial to the policy making process and the identification of policy impacts and dissemination of good policy practices. It is critical to the practice of pragmatic and evidence-based policy formulation. Creating information-rich environments means not only assuring transparency, but also assuring that multiple voices (including those of the disadvantaged) are heard.

But ICT is not a silver bullet. Local realties matter. Corruption and accountability involve complex economic, cultural, and governance issues. It usually takes intense and prolonged pressures from outside stakeholders and citizens for governments to let the e-sunshine in. Citizens can be provided with the ability to comment online on all laws and rules before they are voted or finalized. But, will citizens use e-democracy forums to influence policy debates? Will public officials be able to manage the growing number of citizen comments on rules? Can elected officials use digital tools to enhance their ability to represent their citizens? Engaging stakeholders, building reform coalitions, and reaching more citizens by partnering with media are among the necessary measures to translate the enabling potential of ICT into improvements in governance and participatory democracy. These measures will be discussed in Chapter 12.

Education and Health

Technology and skills play critical and complementary roles in increasing productivity. Economic growth theory (Goldin and Katz 1998) shows that during the industrial revolution of the 18th century, mechanization of industrial process was profoundly deskilling. During the first half of the 20th century, by contrast, technical change slowed and became skill intensive. Since the last decades of the 20th century technological change has increased both in pace and skill bias. It may be the first case during which technical change has been simultaneously rapid and skill intensive (De Ferranti et al., 2002).

Globalization and the ICT revolution combined, are raising the level and changing the nature of demand for education and skills, at a fast pace. New competencies are in increasing demand for participating in the information society and knowledge economy: e-literacy, technological literacy, communication skills, problem solving, critical thinking, self-learning, team work, network management, change management, creativity, and initiative. Understanding this interplay at a relatively detailed level is critical to enable firms to adopt and adapt this general-purpose technology in developing countries and to focus reforms and content in education and training to those critical to participating in this revolution.

With accelerated technological change, growing premium for educated and skilled manpower, and new channels for knowledge and learning, learning has become a lifelong imperative. A culture of openness and continuous learning is necessary for inclusive information society and knowledge economy. Educational systems have to shift from established textbook knowledge to teaching how to learn and enabling individuals and organizations to become agile learners and problem solvers. A lifelong learning system covers learning from all sources: formal and informal. Much of this learning has to occur through networks that cut across academic, business, and local and global communities. Digital communication and the recent tools of social networking and collaboration technologies further enable the creation and dynamism of these learning systems.

Unlike earlier technological changes, this one is impacting the supply as well as the demand of education and training. The expectations are high that this technological revolution is central to learning and will change how education services are delivered. Current research and pilots suggest that ICT has the potential to fundamentally transform how and what people learn throughout their lives (www.techknowlogia.org; Resnick, 2002).

Learning is an active process in which people construct new understandings of the world around them through exploration, experimentation, and discussion. ICT is more than a tool to access and transmit information, but more broadly, a new medium through which people can simulate, create, express, and interact. Computers can be seen as a universal construction material, greatly expanding what children and adults can create and what they can learn in the process (Resnick, 1998). For example, children can now use computer simulations to explore the workings of systems of the world, from ecosystems to economic systems to immune systems. The Internet and distance learning are expanding the learning ecosystem beyond schools, enabling new types of "knowledge building communities" in which children and adults around the world collaborate on projects and learn from each other (Resnick, 2002). The school of tomorrow is likely to be fundamentally different (Box 2.7).

Box 2.7 The School of Tomorrow

The possibilities for using ICT to transform learning and schooling are enormous. Teaching and learning can be shaped in various ways to promote personalization, individualization, and localization. Teaching will increasingly involve teaching learners how to locate relevant information, judge the credibility of their sources, engage in collaborative problem solving, and take responsibility for how and what they learn. Young learners want to think for themselves and come up with their own complex questions. Giving students the space to do this in school time is motivating and should prepare them for real-life complex problems. Text no longer has to be the main medium for conveying meaning, as multimedia can more effectively demonstrate and develop understanding. Curricula can incorporate projects that call for teams with mixed sets of skills and backgrounds, enabling networked learning and learning communities.

In the school of tomorrow, teachers would become learning companions; they would accompany students on part of their learning journey. The borders between home and school will increasingly disappear. Schools will become community learning hubs. Knowledge will be increasingly constructed in collaborations among learners. A flexible, rich, and dynamic learning environment will emerge. The school of tomorrow will be integrated into its local and global environment and open to the world.

Source: Slinger, 2004.

The role of ICT is increasingly evident in higher education, mainly in response to the crucial role of higher education in the transformation toward a knowledge economy. Countries are pressed to reform their higher education systems, to develop open systems that recognize prior experience and exchange schemes and establish lifelong learning framework. Universities are called upon to collaborate with public and private sectors to contribute to innovation and tap global and local knowledge. New competition, modes of operation, and forms of delivery are emerging in higher education and corporate training, including distance education, mixed-mode teaching, open online universities, mega and virtual universities, corporate universities, and various forms of private sector participation and borderless educational services. Connectivity, knowledge management, education technology, and partnership are keys to these new forms of higher education. In turn, these forms raise new demands for governance and management of educational systems including flexibility, quality assurance, industry linkages, and intellectual property rights.

At a more basic level, ICT is critical to containing the fast increasing costs of education. Without the redesign of education systems to make greater use of ICT (and e-learning), whose relative price is falling, the price of conventional education will continue to rise and perhaps become prohibitive to many in the developing world. With traditional educational technologies, there may have been some qualitative improvements. But productivity in the educational sector is diminishing, stagnant, or at best increases at only a glacial pace (Knight, 1998). As a consequence, the relative price of educational services tends to rise. Educational systems in many developing countries are in organizational and financial crisis. Public officials, businesspeople, families, and workers are having difficulty restructuring expenditures to finance needed increases in the coverage, quality, and duration of education. But, to gain or maintain competitiveness in a knowledge-based economy, achieving these increases is a strategic priority.

Technology-enhanced learning will require substantial innovation or re-invention of the education sector. Competition among providers of education and training services is crucial. The private sector has a comparative advantage in introducing technology to train existing members of the labor force who require just-in-time knowledge. The private sector has the flexibility, agility, competitive environment, and market responsiveness necessary to provide just-in-time training. It could also partner with governments and engage in "education on demand" and help spur productivity increases in the provision of timely learning for business and government.

In the health sector, ICT applications span health education and training, diagnostics, telemedicine and telecare, medical records and information management, patient administration, and almost all aspects of health policy, research, and delivery. Health services delivery is essentially a knowledge transfer activity that is highly dependent on communications, knowledge management, and information support systems. The health sector is changing rapidly due to ICT-enabled technological advances—but the potential for transformation remains huge. Advances in telecommunications are enabling health professionals in rural areas to receive information and specialized knowledge and to keep track of disease outbreaks. The explosion of mobile phone usage in developing countries also has the potential to improve health service delivery on a massive scale, support increasingly inclusive health systems, and provide real-time health information and diagnosis in rural areas (Box 2.8). But m-health programs must be viewed and aligned within the broader contexts of national health care, e-government, and e-development programs—the sustainability and scalability of m-health programs ultimately depend on common building blocks.

Box 2.8 m-Health for Development

Developing countries face enormous challenges in meeting the health-related millennium development goals. The ability of developing countries to overcome these challenges is hindered by several core challenges, among them a global shortage of health-care workers. There is a growing recognition among governments, businesses, and NGO of the importance of leveraging new tools and solutions to address these interrelated challenges. The range of m-health applications in developing countries is fast expanding to include education and awareness, remote data collection, remote monitoring, communication and training of care workers, disease and epidemic outbreak tracking, and diagnostic and treatment support.

Here are some examples of m-health programs and applications from a few developing countries.

Short message service (SMS) now offers cost-effective, efficient, and scalable method of providing outreach services in awareness and education applications. Pilots in India, South Africa, and Uganda have shown that interactive message campaigns have greater ability to influence behavior than traditional means, offering information about testing and treatment methods, available health services, and disease management in areas such as AIDS, TB, maternal and reproductive health. SMS messages offer recipients confidentiality in environments where diseases such as AIDS are often taboo. And they have proven effective in targeting remote and rural populations.

Gathering data where patients live, keeping them updated and accessible on a real-time basis can be more effectively and reliably done via smart phones, PDAs, or mobile phones rather than paper-based surveys. Various initiatives in multiple developing countries are closing the information gap for patient data and in turn enabling public officials to gauge the effectiveness of health-care programs, allocate resources more efficiently, and adjust programs and policies accordingly. Similarly, the use of mobiles for remote monitoring of patients may become a crucial capability in developing countries where access to hospital beds and clinics are very limited. In Thailand, for example, TB patients were given mobiles so that health-care workers can remind them daily of their medication, which increased the medicine compliance rate to 90% as a result.

Disease and epidemic outbreak tracking m-health are being used in Peru, Rwanda, and India as an early warning system. Deployment of mobiles, with their ability to quickly capture and transmit data on disease incidence can be decisive in prevention and containment of outbreaks, as in cholera, TB, and SARS. Real-time tracking of incidents of encephalitis in Andhra Pradesh, India, helped government prioritize vaccinations, based on evidence of clusters of outbreaks.

Finally, the mobile phone is being equipped with specialized software applications for use in some African countries for diagnostic and treatment support. The phone is sued as a point-of-care device. The health-care worker is led through a step-by-step diagnostic process. Once data are entered (image and symptoms of patient captured on phone), remote medical professionals can diagnose and prescribe. These applications have the potential of dramatically increased access to care.

For middle-income countries, these applications will be also increasingly relevant for the prevention and early treatment of non-communicable diseases such as diabetes, and for health-care needs of the aging population.

Source: Vital Wave Consulting, 2009.

In advanced countries, the explosion of public access to health information on the Internet is changing the relationship of patients and the organizations that care for them throughout their illness. E-learning enables people to adopt behaviors and lifestyles that keep them healthy and productive as well as improving their quality of life. Information management support for health care can bring immense value—from shorter hospital stays and waiting times for operations to radically lower costs for health care over a patient's life. Policy makers, health-care professionals, and patients need to understand the full power and associated responsibilities that integrated information systems bring to care delivery as e-health does not simply automate paperwork but changes the way people work and relate

Poverty Reduction

Much of the literature and practice of ICT in development have focused on pilots and proof of concept about applying ICT for poverty reduction, and much of the impact on poverty has thus been anecdotal. The impact of ICT on the poor is at an early stage, even in developed countries. The potential is being demonstrated at the micro, intermediate, and macro levels. Donors and development practitioner have sought quick, off-the-shelf solutions that could be replicated in the poor communities of developing countries. However, experience has shown that such ready-made solutions could not be transferred and integrated into development context without raising issues of affordability, sustainability, scalability, and impact.

The impact of earlier information and communication technologies, particularly radio and television is better known, although their use as tools for informing and educating the poor is still relatively unexploited and disconnected from poverty reduction programs. The new ICTs do not replace the older technologies but can blend with them and extend their reach, enrich, and tailor their content and add new forms of "many-to-many" communication and action that bypass traditional power relations. For example, in Kothmale, Sri Lanka, a live radio program uses a panel of resource persons to browse the Internet at the request of listeners and thus add value by interpreting Internet information into a local context, in local languages, and by providing a platform for feedback and local discussion (http://www.kirana.lk).

ICT can open up new opportunities for the poor and small enterprises, even in remote areas. In Brazil's urban slums, the Committee to Democratize Information Technology (CDI) has created self-managed community-based "Computer Science and Citizenship Schools" using recycled ICT and volunteer assistance. As of July 2008, there were almost 840 such schools located in all of Brazil's major regions and six other Latin American countries: Argentina, Chile, Colombia, Ecuador, Mexico, and Uruguay. CDI schools train students for better opportunities for jobs, education, and life changes. Many other examples are available at www.Infodev.org.

ICT also offers the opportunity to provide investment resources to groups to which previously it was denied. In South Africa, for example, "AutoBank E" has developed an automated savings system using ATMs and aimed at the poorest depositors. The system proved to be highly popular, with 2.6 million depositors and 50,000 added each month (Economist, 3/25/2000, p. 81). More recently, the mobile phone has become an "electronic wallet," enabling all kinds of small funds transfer and financial transactions, and as a result, in a year or so, enabling 7 million

Kenyans (for a country with 38 million population; Economist, September 26, 2009) to have accounts with the mobile phone operator, that is, more than the total established accounts the population have with the local banks. Small retailers act like Bank branches. Similar schemes have become popular in the Philippines and South Africa. This can be a stepping stone to access to formal the billions of people who lack access to savings accounts, credit and insurance. ICT can also help intermediary institutions and local agents to work more efficiently and responsively and to target interventions to the needs of the poor: intermediaries such as health workers, agricultural extension agents, teachers, local planners, and local NGOs.

ICT may be also used to empower women, as both producers and consumers. For example, in the Philippines women account for about 65% of total workers in IT services and ITES. They account for 30% in India—a much higher rate of female participation in services than in the general economy. Given the higher wages in IT services, this participation may contribute to improving the status of women. The potential to access relevant public services, at less cost and time, at home or at a local center can be also a source of empowerment. Having access to relevant information such as rights, benefits, inheritance laws, health care, municipal services, and education should enable women and marginalized groups to access services and make informed decisions to meet their basic needs.

Various ICT tools are also used to assess and reduce vulnerability to natural disasters, where the poor are the most vulnerable—especially in cyclone warning, communication and response, awareness raising, and community involvement in hazardous reduction activities. ICT is increasingly used to improve disaster risk management at the global, national, and local levels. It can enable monitoring and enforcement of environmental quality. In Indonesia, for example, with weak enforcement of water pollution standards, government developed a public access information database rating firm compliance, and within the first 15 months of the program, about a third of the unsatisfactory performers came into compliance (World Bank, 1999).

The real challenge in all such applications is not the management of technology, but the institutional capacity and coordination processes to capture and share disaster risk management information that should go hand in hand to make effective use of the technology. As will be discussed later (Chapters 11–14), the technology enables but does not substitute for complementary investments in institutional capacity and process innovation.

Making ICT work for the poor will require new conceptions of development, a new view of the world's poor, and a new approach to innovation with ICT (Heeks, 2008). Rural telecenters and shared access have been the focus of much of ICT for development programs targeted to poor and rural communities. But these programs have raised issues of sustainability and scalability and the search is on to address these issues (Chapter 10). We still confront the challenge of how to connect the remaining 5 billion people who still lack access to the Internet. Low-cost terminals will remain central to ICT for poverty reduction. But efforts to develop "people's PC" and One Laptop per Child (OLPC) are still struggling to deliver on their promise. Wireless technologies such as WiMax also offer major promises to leapfrog and connect poor communities.

Deploying ICT for poverty reduction will inevitably require engaging poor communities in grassroots innovation and in co-producing relevant content and applications. A major challenge for using ICT for poverty reduction will continue to be the development of relevant content, services, and applications on increasingly affordable platforms. Countries are experimenting with new approaches and mechanisms for developing relevant content for poverty reduction and innovating applications for community empowerment (Chapter 14).

While focusing on ICT use for opening opportunities and delivering services to the poor, we must also monitor and address the impact of ICT on equity and income distribution within and among countries. The ongoing revolution is likely to be a driving force in processes of restructuring economies, generating wealth, and concentrating or distributing the new wealth. Would it inevitably lead to exacerbating the income disparities within developing countries? What role should the state play in these processes? This leads us to the next topic, managing risks.

Managing Risks

This is not purely a world of opportunity, but one of intense competition and uncertainty. The rapid advance of ICT is leading to pervasive and irreversible changes in information and communication among people. As the uses of information in daily life and work are unpredictable, so is the likely course of this revolution. There is a legitimate worry that ICT may be promoted as a development fad, not dissimilar to earlier ones, disregarding the risks (Wade, 2002; Kraemer and King, 2005; Carr, 2008). The main risks are

- Wasting resources: unrealized benefits at substantial costs
- Exacerbating inequalities and exclusion within and across countries
- Reinforcing existing power distributions and hierarchical structures
- Controlling, not empowering
- Polluting, not greening

Wasting Scarce Development Resources

In essence, the benefits from ICT investments are not automatic. To be realized, they require complementary investments in human capital and much organizational and social learning (Brynjolfsson and Saunders, 2009). Widespread adoption and effective use of new technologies require organizational flexibility and the willingness to take risks and adapt. Even when success is demonstrated at the pilot level, attention must be given to scaling up and sustainability challenges. These risks are real and do argue for coherent and realistic policies to integrate ICT into development and corporate strategies, not for abandoning technological change. ICT investments must also be subjected to cost–benefit analysis and placed in the context of other priorities or possibilities for development. New tools and motivating visions can help development if they are used to channel energy and commitment into action and institutional transformation. Enthusiasm about the possibilities being opened by the ICT revolution should not detract from the need to introduce the new set of tools and possibilities in sequential and learning-oriented ways and in complementary ways with investments in human and organizational capital.

Experience even among industrial countries suggests that ICT-enabled restructuring is fraught with difficulties and risks, including outright failure to deliver the promised benefits. A growing literature has documented these difficulties, particularly concerning the introduction of complex and integrated software infrastructures that require extensive process reengineering and behavioral changes in large organizations. Even large multinationals found that rather than realizing major gains in control and productivity, the ICT restructuring programs caused "drift" or loss of control (Ciborra, 2000). The use of ICT in the public sector, as in e-government, is fraught with even more risks and frequent failures than the private sector (Heeks, 2006, 2002; Rubino-Hallman and Hanna, 2006).

Exacerbating Inequalities

Technological change always favors the prepared, and in this case, ICT has been the fastest technological change in history, thus exacerbating adjustment problems. While as far reaching the agricultural and industrial revolutions of the past, the current technology revolution is unique in its pace of change and diffusion: it took a century for the printing press to reach 50 million people, 40 years for the radio, and 4 years for the Internet. Driven by "Moore's law," ICT advances are proceeding at enormous speed.[3] By the time developing countries have rolled out one generation of ICT or network infrastructure, advanced countries would have rolled out the next generation. The signpost for technological advance is constantly moving. Some developing countries may take advantage of their late start and leapfrog intermediate technological stages, as in wireless communication technologies. But, for reasons of financial and human resources and other complementary factors, and the presence of "network externalities," the majority of poor developing countries are likely to face the risk of a widening digital divide.[4]

This fast-paced technological revolution is also divisive within countries as individuals are in different positions to adapt. For example, the ICT revolution has propelled some Indians to become billionaires and a few software engineers to be more handsomely rewarded, but hardly touched the life of the majority who are not on the Internet, do not speak English, or find any relevant local content on the Net, those 40% who are illiterate, and the hundreds of millions who go to bed hungry. The

---

[3]Moore observed an exponential growth in the number of transistors per integrated circuit and predicted a continuation of this trend. This has been generalized into a continued exponential growth in ICT capacity.

[4]Network externalities are derived from the fact that the value of a telephone line increases with each new subscriber by the number of potential connections between users. This indicates substantial externalities and there may be a threshold effect through which ICT begins to have substantial impact only when at a certain penetration level in the economy.

digital divide may merely Paralel similar disparities in income and access to other development services such as education and health. But it does matter as it reinforces the divide in access to services across all sectors, and unless systematically addressed, it is likely to grow over time.

In breaking barriers to communications, ICT is accelerating globalization at a time of increasing world inequality. Differences in speed of ICT diffusion, and in access to complementary skills and institutions, are likely to widen the digital and knowledge divide among countries and enterprises. Despite the many examples of dramatic impact of specific ICT applications in developing countries, the aggregate impact has thus far been limited. The diffusion of ICT has been less extensive among SMEs than larger ones, and this digital divide is even much more significant within developing countries. As ICT induces product innovation and shorter life cycles, the speed of change is disrupting established supply relationships. The emergence of net-enabled global supply chains could further empower the multinationals to squeeze out more from their SME suppliers in developing countries.

The irruption of technological revolutions is typically accompanied by cleavages and polarizing trends and unless effectively managed can lead to crises and breakdowns of economies, financial markets, and institutions. Cleavages occur along many lines: new and matured industries, regionally, those trained to participate in the new technologies and those with obsolete skills, and internationally, between those countries ready to ride the wave and those left behind. In the early days of industrialization, these cleavages led to highly polarized income distributions and social revolts. A vast social learning process, cultural adaptation, and institutional adjustments must occur to ride the transition.

A number of factors point to the threat of exclusion of the poor in the current information revolution. With the exception of mobile phones, the gap in the provision of new ICTs is much larger within and among countries than income disparities. Benefiting from ICT requires complementary investments and skills, including literacy. Threshold effects are also at work: network externalities, scale economies, lack of local content in local languages, fragmented markets for software applications, and high cost of access for remote areas—factors that lead to or reinforce poverty traps and economic isolation for poor communities and poor countries. Poor and disadvantaged groups, particularly women, often face special constraints in accessing ICT and using them for their specific needs. Unequal access can worsen existing inequities. The risks of economic exclusion suggest that countries should be concerned with the level of connectivity and ICT provision—and with enabling access and deploying ICT and content in ways that expand relevant information for the poor, increase their voice in decision making, and address bottlenecks to their trade.

Will the ICT revolution exacerbate the wealth gap that it has up to now help widen, or begin to close it? The economics of information production and the global reach of the Internet combined can be a boon for consumers. But it can also thin out the professional work force in various information industries, ranging from newspapers, to publishing and media companies, to banking and other financial services, to middle management in many industries and services. Because ICT can perform symbolic processing, they augment or supplant humans in many information processing tasks that historically were not amenable to mechanization. With the rise of social networking, companies are also finding ways to leverage the global pool of free or cut-rate labor. World wide computing may provide a powerful tool for harvesting the economic value of labor provided by the many and concentrating it in the hands of the few (Carr, 2008, p. 183). The pressures on wages have become relentless in developed countries.

How will this impact the already highly skewed income distribution in developing countries? Will outsourcing compensate for the concentration of wealth within developing countries, or further exacerbate this trend? There is a natural desire to view the Internet as a leveling force, one that creates a fairer, more open, more egalitarian, and more democratic society, where economic opportunities are widely distributed. But the experience so far in developed countries–where substantial investments in ICT have been made—point to the replacement of both skilled and unskilled labor with software. The erosion of the middle class may accelerate as the divide widens between the digital elite and a large pool of labor force who face eroding incomes. The already highly skewed access to literacy and ICT may well deepen all other divides.

Reinforcing Existing Power Structures and Hierarchies

Finally, there is the risk of ICT becoming a tool for reinforcing current hierarchies and power structures, rather than reform and empowerment (Kraemer and King, 2005). The potential for ICT to produce reforms and broaden participation, in government and society, can be thwarted because public administrators and local elites will instead use ICT to serve their own interests and maintain the status quo. There is a long history of literature and empirical evidence that suggest ICT has been used most often to reinforce existing structural arrangements and power distributions rather than change them (Kraemer and King, 2005). Top managers use ICT to enhance the information available to them, to increase their control over resources, and in general to serve their own interests. Research has shown that the use of IT in the US government typically works at the surface of operations, is readily accepted because it leaves the deep structure of political relationships intact and is not associated with reforms (Fountain, 2001).

However, most of this evidence comes from the three decades of pre-Internet computerization programs in the United States. The facts of yesterday do not necessarily dictate the realities or possibilities of tomorrow. With the Internet and major advances in distributed access to ICT since the 1990 s, it has become increasingly possible to use ICT for shared control, organizational innovations, and democratized access to information. The power of these advances are by now demonstrated by the emergence of wholly new forms of organizations, industries, and supply chains, such as Dell Computer, Wal-Mart, Amazon.com, e-Bay, Google, and the transformation of the whole computer industry, among others.

Although business and government organizations exhibit fundamental differences that influence the outcomes of ICT use, political and societal organizations are under increasing social and global pressures to perform and open up, and they can learn a great deal from the lessons of business organizations. Many political and public leaders are expressing interest in using ICT to improve government operations and enable new services. They are increasingly aware of the rising demands of businesses and citizens and of the shrinking public resources. The most recent US Presidential elections (of 2008) have sho the potential of ICT use in political mobilization, including the Internet-based fund raising, weblogs, and Internet-based news sites, mobile messaging. There is no reason that government cannot learn to take advantage of ICT for mobilization of public opinion and reform.

What is increasingly clear, however, is that ICT can be an enabler and facilitator but not the primary driver and cause of reform. The benefits of ICT have not been evenly distributed within government or society. In less liberal and more unequal societies, they are even less likely to do so, unless political will and social values push for applying ICT for empowerment and public sector reforms. In later chapters on transforming government and empowering communities we will explore how ICT can be an integral part and enabler of reforming governments and building an information society.

Controlling, Not Empowering

In other places of this book, I explore the potential of ICT for empowerment and freedom for individuals and communities (this chapter, above; Chapter 12 on promoting transparent and accountable government; Chapter 14 on applying ICT for empowering poor communities). The nascent explosion of social production is viewed as sign of a new and liberating economy, where the Internet and collaborative technologies are enabling people to express themselves, to create and reproduce, distribute their work to broad audiences, and collaborate to produce various gods and services (Benkler, 2006).

But the Internet (and associated utility computing) is a disruptive force with uncertain impacts and many contradictions. It can be a tool of bureaucratic control or of personal liberation. It can be a conduit of communal ideals and of corporate profit. It can help build communities of interest as well as social tensions. As search engines and data mining algorithms are refined and made more powerful, they will enable individuals and corporations to discover hidden relationships among the various information we place on the web. Analyzing these relationships can unlock substantial confidential information about Internet users. While these capabilities put enormous power into the hands of individuals, they put even more power into the hands of companies, governments, and other institutions whose business is to control individuals (Carr, 2008, p. 191).

The technology's ultimate impact will be determined by how the tension of its dual nature—liberating and controlling—will be resolved. Although ICT as a tool for personal empowerment has been shaping modern society in recent years, institutions have been adept at re-establishing control, and ICT continues to be applied at higher levels of control (Carr, 2008, pp. 196–209). While the Internet offers people a new medium for voicing opinion and discovering information, it also provides institutions with a powerful tool for monitoring speech, identifying dissidents, disseminating propaganda, and conducting domestic surveillance. Similarly, corporations have found ways to use the Net to extend their influence over the lives and thoughts of their workers. The Net is also enabling companies to collect more information on consumers, analyzing their behavior, and targeting them with tailored products and messages. Online advertizing is now tightly tied to search engines and search results. "As we go about our increasingly digitized life, the threads that radiate from us are multiplying. . .We accept greater control for greater convenience" (Carr, 2008, p. 209).

Polluting, Not Greening

ICT may become a major source of pollution and energy consumption, rather than a greening technology. A major challenge of the 21st century is catastrophic climate change and the growing pollution of the environment of most urban areas of developing countries. A key promise of ICT is to provide less energy and less material consuming solutions to all kinds of manufacturing, services, and entertainment. This promise is particularly important to meeting the challenge of climate change as well as urban pollution, with the emergence of smart transportation and urban systems, smart energy networks, lean supply chains, telecommuting, telemedicine, distance education, and other energy-efficient practices. Yet ICT products, such as televisions, mobiles, and computers may become a major source of e-waste or dumping and pollution in developing countries. The energy consumption of data centers is also rising rapidly. Chip production is a growing and intensive user of water. Without a deliberate strategy, strong incentives, and political commitment, the promise of the "green IT" may not materialize.

Productivity, Growth, and Technological Determinism

Will the ICT revolution lead to a soft transformation or to an upheaval as traumatic as that of the first industrial revolution? Would it lead to new divides, break up of neighborhoods, increased job insecurity, financial volatility, and concentrated wealth, or lean and green production, revitalized and connected small-scale communities, and more inclusive societies? Will ICT lead to further centralization and control by a small group of elite, or fulfill the promise of becoming a tool for reform and empowerment?

I do not subscribe to technological determinism and the inevitability of the promises or risks of ICT. The role of technology is neither deterministic nor wholly malleable. The printing press, for example, has been an agent of change, but its impact varied across societies (Einstein, 1979). Different technologies make different kinds of human action and interaction easier or harder to perform. So, there is no guarantee that ICT will lead to improvements in productivity, growth, employment, and poverty reduction—or even more ambitiously, advances in innovation, empowerment, decentralization, human freedom, organizational transformation, cultural diversity, and social production of information (Benkler 2006). These are societal choices. They depend on many crosscutting social and economic policies.

Consider the potential impact of ICT on growth and productivity. We need to assess the prospects and conditions for ICT contribution to productivity, growth, and poverty reduction in developing countries. The "productivity paradox" and the slow emergence of ICT impact on productivity even in OECD countries can be explained among others by the considerable time needed for the diffusion of new technologies and for institutions to adjust or transform—changing from hierarchical to networked organizations, upgrading the workforce, or reengineering and inventing business processes. It takes time to build networks within and across firms and to enable new forms of interactions throughout the economy. Understanding this time lag is important in the development of ICT-enabled development strategy.

OECD research (2004) shows that several conditions or complementary factors influence the extent of diffusion and use of ICT and thus its impact on firms and economies: the extent of competition and nature of the regulatory environment, the availability of appropriate human capital, the ability and willingness of organizations to restructure and change work practices, the relative total costs of ICT deployment, and of course, the nature of the business or structure of the economy. While complementary factors are important to payoff from all kinds of investments, they are most critical in the case of ICT investment since ICT transforms the intellectual content and human interaction as well as the physical aspects of work.

Significant differences between OECD and developing countries are likely to influence the extent and speed of impact of ICT on growth and productivity. Relatively few developing countries have sizable ICT production sector and their ICT sectors have fewer backward and forward linkages into their domestic economy than in OECD countries. With the exception of a few large developing countries, most lack mass markets for ICT goods and services, resulting in higher costs and less efficient use.[5] ICT investments are generally higher in developing countries where equipment is imported and telecommunications user charges are much higher than in OECD countries. Most developing countries also have poor communication infrastructures, mostly limited to the urban centers, and with poor quality international connectivity. The most critical difference is in the absence of complementary factors: enabling legal and regulatory environment to reward innovation and entrepreneurship, competitive regulatory telecommunications framework, extensive human capital to use ICT, and access to high-quality business advice and venture capital.

These differences are not insurmountable. Rather, they point to ways in which governments, businesses, and aid agencies can act to increase the pace of ICT diffusion and the rate at which contributions to economic growth can be realized. The

---

[5]This could change with strategies to develop and produce low-cost ICT products that are adapted to local markets in poor countries.

benefits and risks associated with this revolution are not predetermined. They are a product of social and political choices. A passive public policy stance that leaves to market alone the direction of change will reinforce divides (ILO, 2001; UNDP, 2001). Passivity will also lead to economic marginalization and increasing social stress. The unprecedented advances in ICT and decline in prices imply a faster rate of diffusion than in previous technological revolutions. The constraints and risks to realizing the full benefits are significant, but a vigorous and coherent effort to harness the potential of ICT and synergize with complementary factors is likely to be critical to future growth and poverty reduction.

In a similar vein, whether the ICT revolution would exacerbate inequalities and reinforce existing power distributions, or promote more equitable and inclusive societies would ultimately depend on socio-political and economic policy choices. These choices cover the whole gamut: trade policies, tax policies, safety-net policies, training and education policies, competition and innovation policies, capital and labor market laws, and civil service and governance systems, among others. These policy choices encompass a broad spectrum of development issues and actors. They shape and can be shaped by the strategic options for leveraging ICT for development.

In sum, the ICT revolution will have profound impact on all aspects of growth, equity, and governance for countries at all levels of development. It provides a profoundly changing global context for development. It presents unprecedented opportunities, risks, and strategic options. Neither the benefits nor the downside risks are pre-determined. The opportunity costs of failure to respond are high. These prospects argue for integrating the ICT agenda into the economic policy and development strategy agenda. Leveraging ICT for socio-economic transformation can no longer be left to the technologists or ignored by mainstream development economists and other development practitioners.

Chapter 3
Options for ICT-Enabled Development

Business experience and literature suggests that mastering the use of ICT has become a core competency for pursuing competitive advantage and sustained growth in many industries and services (many to list, but for example, Fung et al., 2008). It is also likely to become a core competency in national development and in delivering public services, education, and training, and even microcredit and poverty reduction programs. In fact, "the innovation that is crucial to the future of well-being of the (east Asia and other developing countries) region is unthinkable without ICT" (Yusuf, 2003, p. 326). To realize this potential, the current focus on investment in physical infrastructure and hardware and on isolated experimentation and piecemeal implementation must be broadened and scaled up to address the enabling policies, institutions, infrastructures, and skills and to devise national strategies that are capable of agile adaptation and participatory social learning.

In this chapter, I argue for adopting coherent national e-Transformation strategies, guided by strategic options for using ICT for development. Countries such as Korea, Taiwan, and Singapore have pursued an explicit strategy and systematically integrated ICT into their overall visions and plans for development. These countries were able to advance most in harnessing the benefits of the ongoing ICT-enabled productivity revolution.

First, three fundamental roles of ICT and the corresponding strategic options the ICT revolution presents to developing countries are defined. The aim is to sharpen the options, not as mutually exclusive ones but to help policymakers balance and match these options for their country conditions, aspirations, and capabilities. These perspectives should also help development strategists to seek synergies and complementarities among ICT roles and development options. The chapter concludes with examining the possible roles of a national ICT strategy harnessing the ICT revolution for growth and poverty reduction. In the next chapter, I propose a holistic framework to help shape a national ICT strategy and capture the synergies among various elements of e-development.

N.K. Hanna, *e-Transformation: Enabling New Development Strategies*, Innovation, Technology, and Knowledge Management, DOI 10.1007/978-1-4419-1185-8_3,

Three Fundamental Roles

The promises and attributes of the ongoing revolution (in Chapter 2) suggest three fundamental and interdependent roles of ICT:

- Accessing and processing *information and knowledge*, with dramatic increase in the power and speed to access, process, adapt, and organize information. This, in turn, has accelerated learning, innovation, and knowledge creation and dissemination. In this sense, ICT may have at least the same profound impact of the invention of the printing press and mass media.
- Speeding up and reducing the costs of *production and transactions* throughout the economy. ICT is increasingly embedded into all types of production, processes, and transactions, giving rise to intelligent products, real-time control processes, facilitating trade, outsourcing business support and back-office services, and enabling complementary organizational innovations. In this sense, ICT may have similar implications as the steam engine, the electricity, and the railways in transforming production and transportation systems.
- Making *connections* among people, NGOs, enterprises, and communities. This gives rise to empowerment, participation, coordination, decentralization, social learning, connecting communities of practice, mobilizing social capital, and globalizing civil society concerns. ICTs have been increasingly described as "technologies of freedom" (Ithiel de Sola, 1983). There may not be a historical parallel to the enabling role of ICT to coordinate, collaborate, and empower.

A national development strategy that attempts to position an economy to take advantage of the ongoing revolution should take a comprehensive view of the three enabling roles of ICT. Often, proponents of one framework or another tend to focus on one of the roles of ICT, at the expense of others. For example, the "knowledge economy" framework, developed by OECD, has tended to focus on the role of knowledge in the economy, and thus view the role of ICT mainly in terms of access to knowledge.

But the knowledge lens neglects other equally important roles of ICT: in speeding up and reducing the costs of production and transactions and in empowering people to connect, mobilize, organize, overcome their isolation, and share their experiences and idiosyncratic information. Yet developing countries are characterized by high transactions and logistics costs and by the isolation and disempowerment of large parts of the population. An analysis of the correlation of ICT and knowledge with development (GDP per capita) suggests a positive and nonlinear relationship, but the fit of regression is much higher for the ICT index ($R^2 = 0.8$) than for the knowledge index ($R^2 = 0.6$), perhaps indicating a broader role of ICT than access to knowledge (de Ferranti et al., 2001).

The potential significance of e-government and e-commerce might be gauged from the work of Douglas C. North who determined that for a modern economy

45% of GDP can be accounted for by the cost of transactions.[1] A key strength of ICT is its ability to substantially reduce the cost of transactions. Even conservative estimates of the productivity benefits from ICT, if extended economy wide, could be expected, a priori, result in large gains in the productivity and competitiveness of the whole economy.

Rather than treating ICT as an isolated sector on its own, ICT should be used as a lens to rethink development strategies, as a tool to enable all sectors and as a new and powerful means to empower the poor. This does not mean that we believe in ICT as a technology fix, but that an understanding of the full potential and implications of the ongoing technological revolution is necessary to realize its potential for development—far beyond its contribution as a sector. It is also essential to understand what makes ICT different from other technologies or from earlier technological revolutions in order to marshal the specific policies, institutions, and capabilities (and their complementarities) that must accompany the effective use of ICT as an enabler for development.

On the demand side, it is critical to understand how information and communication are vital to the lives and livelihoods of the poor and how ICT could enhance their access to markets, institutions, services, education, and skills. Lack of efficient information and communication processes makes public institutions slow and unresponsive and shifts much of the burden of transactions onto citizens, particularly the poor. Poverty has multiple and mutually reinforcing causes, and lack of access to information and communication exacerbates all of them. The poor lack access to information about income-earning opportunities, market prices for goods they produce, about health, about their rights, and about public and welfare services. They lack access to knowledge, education, and skills to improve their livelihood. They lack voice in the political and development processes that shape their lives. If they can have access to relevant information and the tools to communicate with others, the poor can make their choices, articulate their interests, engage in social learning, and have more power over their lives. Understanding the information and communication aspects of poverty is therefore critical to exploit the three fundamental roles of ICT for poverty reduction.

Three Strategic Options for Development

The ICT revolution presents three fundamental options or perspectives for developing countries that parallel the three fundamental roles of ICT. These options are to harness ICT: as an industry or sector in its own right, as a general-purpose technology to be applied across sectors, and as an enabling infrastructure for empowerment

---

[1] Wallis, John J and Douglas C. North (1986) "Measuring the Transaction Sector in the American Economy" in SL Engerman and RE Gallman (eds.), Long Term Factors in American Economic Growth, Chicago, University of Chicago Press. See also Nobel Economics Prize speech, Douglas North, 1993.

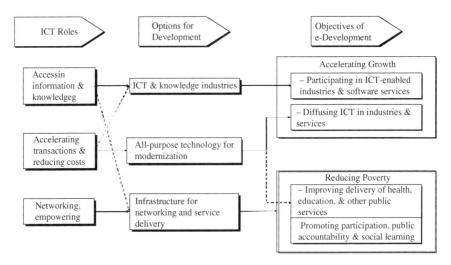

Fig. 3.1 ICT roles, options, objectives for development

and service delivery. Countries at different levels of development have tried to harness the ongoing ICT revolution in three ways that correspond to these three basic roles of ICT (Fig. 3.1):

- Promoting the ICT industries.
- Deploying ICT across sectors, as a general-purpose technology.
- Investing in ICT as an enabling and networking infrastructure.

Promoting the ICT Industries

Many countries have targeted *the ICT (hardware, software products, and services) industry* as one of the fastest growing, most dynamic, and highest value-added global industry. For many, this industry and related capabilities have been associated with new wealth, new economy, new entrepreneurship, new source of growth and competitiveness, and new innovation-driven culture. The global market (revenue) for ICT, including telecommunications, is about $3 trillion and for software and software products and services alone was estimated at US $1.5 trillion (Gregory et al., 2009). The compound annual rate of growth for the worldwide software industry during 1997–2007, at 15%, exceeds the rate of growth of the world economy by a wide margin. Developing countries' software industries are growing even faster, and for India and China, at two to three times faster than the world industry overall (Gregory et al., 2009).

   Globally, ICT sector value added continues to grow as a share of total business value added. ICT services account for about two-thirds of ICT sector value added in

OECD countries. Employment impact of the ICT-producing sector is also increasing. The share of the sector in total business workforce reached more than 10% in Korea. South–South trade in ICT is also increasing fast: it has equaled the North–North trade in 2004 ($410 billion) and has since exceeded it (UNCTAD, Information Economy Report, 2007–2008). It demonstrates the potential of the ICT market in developing countries, where the potential for ICT uptake is considerable—although this is still concentrated in a few Asian countries.

Much of the growth of the ICT sector in developing countries relied on heavy foreign direct investment (FDI) inflow since the 1990s. Multinational companies adopted global strategies that relied on locating hardware production in emerging markets and particularly in countries that built local ICT skills and manufacturing capabilities. This was later followed by outsourcing software and computer-related services. Such investments have positive spillover effects on the local manufacturing and services sectors. ICT multinationals are leaders and intensive users in the use of ICT and e-commerce themselves and engage their subsidiaries in developing countries and across the global supply chain in similar practices.

The trend in the international diffusion of ICT production is likely to continue, with significant potential for hosting this production in developing countries. Over 50 nations currently export software and ICT-enabled services in 2008. Capabilities in producing these services play an important role in facilitating growth and competitiveness in other domestic industries that increasingly depend on software as a core component in their design, production, and distribution processes.

Competition for attracting FDI and business process outsourcing (BPO) has been fierce. Differentiation and innovation strategies play increasing roles. Apart from global powerhouses like India and China, most developing countries will need to identify and pursue niche strategies. New aspiring countries are emerging as significant players: Egypt export revenue of IT-enabled services (ITES) has grown in a few years at 34% annual growth rate to US $1 billion (Economist Intelligent Unit, 2009). More and more countries are now aspiring to participate in this wealth creating industry and to leapfrog into information- and skill-intensive services—the Philippines, Brazil, Mexico, Ghana, Bangladesh, Cambodia, Vietnam, Malaysia, Singapore, Russia, and Romania, among others. Aspiring countries will need to invest in the enabling pillars: technical and language skills, telecommunications and connectivity infrastructure, and improving business climate and enabling environment.

The focus of this book is on software services and products, where participation in global production is very promising for developing countries for several reasons. In contrast to hardware manufacturing, software industry presents low entry barriers for developing countries. In the software industry, many firms are small and less capital intensive, requiring less fixed physical assets in plant and equipment. Moreover, the hardware industry relies on a longer supply chain and higher intensity of use of intermediate inputs than the software industry. In the software industry, the labor force is by far the most important input, accounting for up to 70% of the total cost of software production. Physical infrastructure requirements for software production are also modest—broadband telecommunications and modest power supply, but no heavy transport infrastructure. I also argue (in Chapter 8) that local competency in software services is also emerging a core competency for competitiveness in many other user sectors where local user–producer interactions and software adaptation are critical to leveraging ICT for competitiveness.

The focus of developing countries has been on the short-term benefits of wealth creation from exporting IT services and ITES, but the long-term societal benefits from deploying ICT services, innovations and culture are likely to be substantial. These industries are providing incentives for governments to improve the overall business environment, thus benefiting all sectors of the economy. Even within the same country, the promise of the industry is promoting competition among states to provide incentives and improve the investment climate for FDI, as in the case of Indian states. These dynamic industries are heightening the importance of education quality and reform, particularly technical and engineering education, and the need for partnerships between educational and business institutions. They are encouraging knowledge transfer of international best practices in IT usage, standards, outsourcing, IT-based businesses, and managerial and business innovation. They have increased the visibility of developing countries like India, among MNCs, as a destination for investment and innovation across many services and industries. They have induced the diaspora to establish links or return to home countries, thus augmenting human capital and tap risk capital.

What about leapfrogging? Can the ICT sector present a new route for economic development or a significant potential source of growth? In 2008, South Africa, Mauritius, Malta, Tunisia, Morocco, Egypt, Jordan, and many others were beginning to develop IT services and ITES as promising sources of economic growth. Finland, Ireland, and Israel present interesting cases of transformation to an information or innovation economy. Ireland's Industrial Development Authority launched an inward investment program that has been a driving force for the growth of Irish IT and ITES. The program included financial incentives, technology parks, marketing campaigns, investment promotion, human resources development, and linkages with SMEs, among others. It helped investors get started and worked closely with them to maximize their contributions to the local economy. Finland's profound transformation within a short period of a decade or two presents an interesting case (Box 3.1).

Box 3.1 Finland: A Case of Leapfrogging and Accelerated Transformation?

The Finish experience since 1991 is an example of how ICT can become a driving force in economic transformation and how institutions can play a critical role in forging national consensus, flexible response, and concerted action to guide this transformation. Until the 1970s Finland relied on resource-intensive industries. Since the beginning of the 21st century it has become the most ICT-specialized economy in the world and has ranked as number 1 in the World Economic Forum's competitiveness index.[2]

How did Finland become an ICT-enabled, innovation-driven economy? This transformation is the outcome of strategic focus and intent, applied in a coherent way and over time to various elements of e-development. Electronics, ICT, and related high-tech industries were targeted though a coherent industrial and innovation policies that encouraged competition and technological learning. This was complemented by creating public and private R&D institutions, venture capital funds, partnerships and associations that supported innovation, diffusion, and clustering of ICT industries. The Science and Technology Council is chaired by the prime minister and is responsible for the strategic directions of the national innovation system. The Finish National Fund for Research and Development was the public instrument to experiment and commercialize innovations on a broad front, without budgetary and political delays; since 1991 it has operated as a public foundation under the parliament. Many other institutions and institutional innovations have also contributed to promoting the policies, enabling environment and knowledge sharing necessary for a thriving ICT industry and fast technological learning.

The Finish Nokia has grown from a diversified conglomerate into a specialized, innovation-driven world leader in ICT and mobile communications and in 2008 accounted for 35% of the mobile phone market. Nokia became an engine for the ICT industry and by 2003 accounted for 25% of Finland's R&D expenditure.

The information infrastructure has also played a critical role. Finland is a relatively sparsely populated and geographically isolated country. Its early focus on competition in the telecommunication services and the wide access to the Internet helped lay the basis for a dynamic sector, facilitate collaboration on the national level, and establish presence on a global scale. This has accelerated the adoption of managerial innovations and tools for all types of user industries and for service sectors such as finance. Systematic efforts were made to reduce the digital divide.

Another key component of the Finish success is the education system and the development of necessary human resources for a technologically driven economy. Apart from securing broad literacy, educational institutions have been sufficiently flexible and responsive to technological change to produce the specialized skills for an ICT-driven economy.

What about the role of government in using ICT in the public sector and society at large? Finland has formulated information society strategies spanning 20 years (1995–2015). The national information society strategy was drawn up in close cooperation with actors in many areas of society, including

[2]Dahlman et al. (2006); and Hanna and Knight (forthcoming).

about 400 expert participants from central and local government, institutes of higher education, business, and industry and various organizations. Strategy preparation was preceded by an online questionnaire aimed at information society actors and a preliminary debate in the steering and monitoring group of the information society program.

For the 2003–2007 information society program, implementation was headed by the prime minister and shared by a ministerial group, including finance, communications, interior, trade, and education. In June 2007, the new Finnish government passed a resolution adopted the term "ubiquitous information society," specified the most important aims and priorities for speeding up e-development, and announced a decision to develop an action plan for the years 2008–2011, within the framework of the strategy for 2007–2015. This resolution also announced the formation of a new Ubiquitous Information Society Advisory Board, chaired by the minister of communications, and charged it with developing the action plan. The board was expected to provide insight on the identification of priorities for the national information society policy as well as on the setting of ambitious but realistic goal.

E-government was introduced as a tool of competitiveness and public sector reform. It has been embedded into Finland's information society since early 1990s and it is backed by broad citizen acceptance and participation. The stress is on quality and relevance of public information, transparency, e-engagement, and e-democracy. Wide Internet use and e-literacy have been enabling factors for the adoption of e-services. The prime minister's award is used to promote awareness, innovation, and best practices in e-government. An IT Strategy Committee is organized under the ministry of finance and led by a national CIO to promote technical interoperability, common platforms, information security, and digital TV.

Finland created several political and administrative institutions to build national consensus, guide, and lead the ICT-driven information society. The committee for the future is one such institution. It is one of the Finish parliament's standing committees. It conducts active and initiative-generating dialogue with the government to build long-term orientation and consensus on the future. Another agency is the Information Society Advisory Board, whose goal is to monitor and analyze the development of information society in the country. This is an independent advisory body with broad representation from relevant government agencies, parliament, private sector associations, and civil society. It is chaired by the minister of communications. Another body is the Association of Finish Local Authorities, charged with promoting the information society and bridging the digital divide at the local level.

These and many other institutions helped build trust, shared vision, and public–private partnerships. It helped Finland undergo a wrenching restructuring process to redeploy people from declining sectors in the old economy to the new ICT sectors and to position the country to take advantage of the forces of globalization.

Some of the key enabling conditions for success of Finland are trust in government and in technology, trust in government use of private information, good governance, openness to the outside world, shared vision, and enthusiasm about information society. A decentralized system of public administration, combined with national consensus and cohesiveness among the senior public service leaders helped the development and continued innovation of ICT use at all levels of government and society.

The challenge is to continue leadership in ICT production and yet further master ICT use. It is the use of ICT—not necessarily its production—that is the decisive factor for long-term economic growth. In the public sector, the challenge is to deepen cross-agency coordination and collaboration and back-office process innovation. These challenges will require continued institutional innovation and renewal.

In Chapter 8, we explore some of the strategic options and best practices in relaxing the binding constraints to IT services and ITES by aspiring developing countries.

Deploying ICT to Transform User Industries and Services

A second option or perspective is to exploit *ICT as a general-purpose technology* that can increase the productivity and competitiveness of the local economy, and particularly among the potentially information- and transaction-intensive industries and services. As ICT impact organizations, competitive strategies, and all kinds of transactions, ICT adoption and integration by all types of industries are fast becoming a requisite for survival and adaptation (Chapter 2). The payoffs of applying these new technologies to all types of processes can be dramatic—mainly derived from the associated organizational changes and business process innovations.

A unique aspect of ICT as a technology is that its impact also spans beyond manufacturing to all types of information-based and business support services. ICT-enabled productivity improvements in such services are often dramatic. These services are now a key to the competitiveness of any advanced economy. There is growing awareness among advanced and poor countries alike that this ICT deployment option is where most of the economy-wide benefits are likely to be. This is therefore the focus of Chapters 11–14, in terms of transforming government services, providing business support services, and empowering communities with IT-enabled solutions to local development problems.

Enterprises in developing countries, particularly SMEs, face serious difficulties in ICT-based competitiveness, innovation, and linkages to supply chain. Engaging in ICT-enabled transformation is a high-risk activity for small enterprises with limited access to financial and human capital. Policy makers need to address these general difficulties to enable speedy diffusion and effective use of ICT to transform local industries and services. Much can be learned from the decades of OECD programs to diffuse new technologies to SMEs (Hanna et al., 1996). In Chapter 13, we explore some of the options and lessons learned in promoting ICT adoption among SMEs.

The first option, the focus on ICT as a sector or source of export growth, tends to attract the attention of political leaders and the local ICT industry—often at the expense of attending to local user industries and service sectors. The political economy often favors the relatively influential and committed advocates of the ICT industry, and particularly those who would benefit the most from exporting ICT services, as in India. The potential benefits from adopting ICT throughout the economy are widely distributed. The potential beneficiaries, especially SMEs, are poorly organized to push for policies and programs to promote ICT adoption and diffusion.

Leveraging ICT as a Communication and Delivery Infrastructure

The third option is to view *ICT as an enabling or networking infrastructure* that would connect government agencies, NGOs, SMEs, and even the poor to participate in development. Many NGOs in Latin America are assisting microenterprises such as artisans to integrate into the global economy by using web sites for retail and wholesale buyers in industrialized countries, providing timely information on markets and buyers, and delivering a variety of training and business support services (Sanchez, 2001). In Chapters 10–14, we explore the issues surrounding the use and diffusion of ICT as a networking and delivery infrastructure for governments, businesses, and communities.

Access to information and communication is central to empowerment and to building human capabilities. Accordingly, this new infrastructure would enable local economic and social agents to network, mobilize, and share local information, access global knowledge and markets, coordinate local action, share local experiences and innovations, and accelerate social learning. It enables real-time information sharing among change agents, communities of practice, and otherwise isolated communities. No wonder that the Internet has powered global civil society movements for causes such as debt relief, banning land mines, and providing HIV drugs in poor countries. The Internet was just as powerful in mobilizing people locally in campaigns against corruption (Korea), for democracy (the Philippines), and to protect the environment (Brazil).

Strategic applications, or strategic information systems, are those of central importance to economic competitiveness and functioning in an increasingly integrated global economy, and hence should be essential to any national ICT strategy. For example, one of the most strategic and early applications of ICT in the merging economies was the modernization of the port of Singapore and establishing a electronic trade facilitation network—key steps in positioning Singapore as a global hub for logistics and regional hub for services. Another example is financial payments clearance and settlement system—a necessity for economic management and financial transaction in any globally integrated economy. In general, such systems represent new forms of national infrastructure because, like roads or utilities, they have major economies of scale, require substantial investments, and underpin other economic activities. These are the new infrastructures of the knowledge economy.

Which systems have this strategic importance is determined by country conditions and development priorities. Increasingly, globalization and international agreements are enforcing performance standards that can be met only with the aid of modern information and communication systems, as is the case with trade facilitation networks and customs modernization. Experience also suggests that there is a core group of information infrastructure and applications that all countries should put in place for the functioning of a modern economy. Included in this group are those concerning the modernization and integration of public finance and trade systems (planning and budgeting, debt management, expenditure management), tax administration, and trade facilitation.

Integrated financial information systems, for example, are being adopted to support control of aggregate spending, to prioritize expenditures across programs for allocation efficiency and equity, and to achieve outcomes and produce outputs at the lowest possible cost. For example, an integrated tax administration system for Jamaica has reduced the processing of some types of taxes from 4 weeks to 1 h or less. Critical systems also include those enabling the functioning of financial and other markets such as payment clearance and settlement systems, financial institution oversight systems, and land and business registry systems. Others are critical to the functioning of basic infrastructures such as air transport control, port operations, and utility management. Yet others may be critical to managing natural resources such as environmental monitoring, early warning, and geographic information systems.

Past experience indicates that governments in developing countries are rather quick, comparatively speaking, to realize the benefits of the systems that improve their own internal efficiency, oversight, and control mechanisms in finance-related areas, as described above. At the same time, ICT applications and services that improve interaction of the public sector with citizens and businesses, as well as those promoting ICT use in small businesses and social applications often get limited attention. They are mistakenly perceived as "luxury" that developing countries could not afford.

E-government services, for example, are capable of delivering both significant short-term benefits and long-lasting impact for developing countries. They can promote transparency and improved government responsiveness to the needs of citizens and businesses. ICT-enabled services can also bring about a number of important spillover effects, such as improve competitiveness of the private sector, decrease the brain drain of knowledge workers, and promote use of ICT among citizens and businesses. Last but not the least, e-services can transcend geographical, ethnical, and administrative divisions and thus can benefit economic and social development of countries with a legacy of civil wars, ethnic or regional unrest.

ICT use in government can also facilitate effective decentralization, more transparent and accountable governance, delivery of responsive public services, making public information resources available to all, and improving the quality and reach of health, education, and other basic services. This role is still in its infancy, but results of various pilots in many developing countries, particularly in Latin America, are encouraging. It is fast taking a central stage with e-government, e-commerce, e-learning, and other Internet-enabled activities.

Mobile telephony is serving as a digital bridge to the majority of mankind. For the short to medium term and for the vast majority of low-income population, mobile telephony is likely to be the sole tool connecting them to the information society. Among ICTs, mobile phones are most widely spread in developing countries. In the last 5 years (2003–2008), mobile subscribers in developing countries almost tripled and now account for about 60% worldwide. It has quadrupled in Africa. Mobiles do not require much complementary investment in infrastructure or skills. The cost of access has declined dramatically. Moreover, mobile telephony is growing in sophistication and functionalities. It provides a gateway to digital literacy and once it is appropriated on a large scale, the adoption of subsequent higher level technologies may become less intimidating.

Mobile telephony is offering a growing and distributed platform for delivering services to the poor and generating income by them. With existing functionality, SMS can be used for tasks ranging from seeking market prices for farmers and fishermen, to monitoring elections, to alerts in case of natural disasters. Mobiles can transform how distributed organizations operate. For example, ministries of agriculture and health, with many rural extension and health workers distributed across the country, suffer from slow reporting and feedback and much field time wasted on reporting and filling forms or awaiting information. In a pilot in Uganda, mobile phones are being used to diagnose and treat crop diseases that cause massive losses to farmers, presenting an opportunity to increase yields as location-specific information about disease threats is made available.

With smart phones or increased functionalities to more affordable phones, mobiles could also be used to deliver financial and banking services to those currently excluded. They are already playing a significant role in the receipt of remittances from distant relatives. New business models are also being created by the poor themselves, starting with the use of air time as currency, turning the mobile phones into mobile wallets (Heeks, 2008). The potential of mobiles is primarily constrained by user capabilities and present limited attention to applications for those at the bottom of the pyramid.

In particular, mobiles hold great potential for small- and medium-sized enterprises in all types of uses ranging from communicating with clients, ordering of supplies, receiving daily price quotes for agricultural exports and local fish markets, buying and selling of goods and services through e-commerce, as well as e-payment and e-banking. The use of mobile phone services by the small-scale fishing enterprises in Kerala, India, demonstrate the dramatic effects of simple ICT applications for poverty reduction (Box 3.2).

Box 3.2 Mobile Phone Impact on Small-Scale Fishing in Kerala

The fishing industry in Kerala is important as 70% of its population eat fish daily and over a million people work in fisheries. Fishing is done primarily by small enterprises. There is little storage of fish and little transportation between markets. Fishermen are traditionally unable to observe prices in other markets. Thus the quantity and prices of fish in any local market is determined by the local catch. This results in significant differences in prices, daily and across markets, as well as wasted catches.

As mobile phone was introduced in Kerala in 1997, fishermen adopted it quickly, reaching a penetration rate of 70%. Fishermen use the phones while at sea to find out the prices of different markets and to decide where to land their catches, conducting auctions by phone. After phone adoption, 30–40% of fishermen began selling fish outside their home markets. This significantly reduced the dispersion in prices among markets, from Rs. 10/kg before adoption to a few rupees after adoption. It also reduced wastage. The profits of fishermen jumped by Rs. 133 a day—a 9% increase. Impact on consumer is relatively modest—4% price reduction (Jensen and Trenholm, 2007).

Balancing and Matching Options to Countries

These perspectives on ICT present different options for development that may complement or conflict with each other. In many countries, the vocal and relatively well-placed ICT producers and their associations, like the national association of software companies (NASSCOM) of India, or the computer industries in Brazil and Mexico in the 1980s and 1990s, have played a major role in focusing national policy debates and strategies on the option of promoting and protecting ICT as an industry, often at the expense of local diffusion or broader application to development. But these local actors can be allies to support the other options and to build synergies between them. The development of local software capabilities can serve all three options.

The balance between these perspectives in formulating national ICT strategies should be timed and tailored to the level of economic development, available skills and domestic technological capabilities (ICT supply side), and the size and structure of the domestic market and social demand for reforms, participation, and learning (ICT demand side). This balance is an ongoing process and is ultimately shaped by local coalitions, political leadership, and overall development strategy of the country. Figure 3.2 presents the generic strategic options available for countries with differing demand and supply conditions (Hanna et al., 1996).

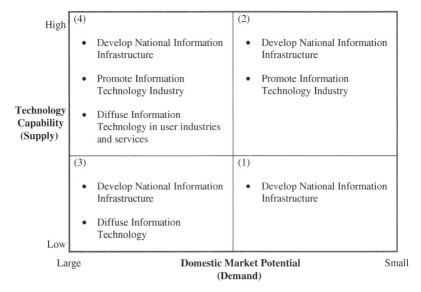

Fig. 3.2 Tailoring strategies to countries.
Source: Hanna et al. (1996). The East Asia Miracle and Information Technology

Roles of a National e-Development Strategy

Given the profound promises and pervasive impacts of ICT on national economies and global competition, countries need to embed ICT into their overall development strategies, as much as businesses have learned to integrate ICT into their core business strategies. Managing the benefits, risks, and impacts of ICT is a challenging task in view of the complexity and uncertainty of the interaction between ICT, economic growth, and poverty reduction.

Designing a national strategy for e-development should serve several pragmatic roles:

- Harness ICT contribution for growth and poverty reduction: address coordination failures, exploit network effects, secure complementary investments, and accelerate national learning.
- Raise awareness, mobilize resources, and build broad coalitions for policy and institutional reforms.
- Clarify roles, build public–private partnerships, and facilitate participation by all stakeholders, including NGOs.
- Focus scarce resources on exploiting ICT for national priorities and help sequence and phase complementary investments.
- Complement market forces, promote societal applications, enable bottom-up efforts, and ensure shared learning and scaling up of successful pilots.

- Leverage the potential of the ICT industry: address the special needs and dynamics of promising segments of the ICT industry for export and economy-wide competitiveness.
- Re-orient the national innovation system to meet the substantial and cumulative technological learning requirements of ICT as a general-purpose technology and the catalyst for productivity surge in business and government.

Harnessing ICT for Growth and Poverty Reduction

A national ICT strategy should be integrated into the overall development strategy of the country. It should assess the prospects and options for promoting the ICT industry, for using ICT in key sectors of the economy, and for empowering and networking all stakeholders in development. It should also systematically address how to use ICT as an enabling tool, in combination with complementary factors, to address the two overarching goals of development: sustainable growth and poverty reduction.

The prospects of ICT-enabled growth and poverty reduction in developing countries can be significantly enhanced by coherent strategies that support linkages among ICT infrastructure, production and domestic deployment, and improvements in critical complementary factors. These include policy and regulatory environments in support of private investment in ICT infrastructure and applications, ICT-enabled innovation and entrepreneurship, and more broadly, a favorable environment for private sector development and public sector reform. Human resources are a key complementary factor. A national ICT-enabled development strategy must therefore integrate ICT education, literacy, and capacity building into all aspects of development.

E-development should aim at harnessing the ongoing technological revolution to achieve the ambitious Millennium Development Goals. The massive backlog of educational, health, extension, and social needs of developing countries, including those of the rural and isolated communities, is unlikely to be met in a timely and effective manner without the innovative and strategic use of these new technologies. For example, the target of reducing poverty by half by 2015 in the context of a globalizing economy is unlikely to be met without addressing the implications of ICT for the competitiveness of developing economies, revitalizing threatened industries such as textiles, and diversifying into new ones such as call centers and business process outsourcing. E-development would systematically address the opportunities to use ICT to expand employment and earning opportunities, to access market information, and to lower transaction costs for the poor, women, marginalized communities, small farmers, traders, and artisans.

Easier access to global and local knowledge, enabled by ICT, can be decisive in helping developing countries reach the Millennium Development Goals at a very affordable and sustainable cost. ICT may be used in health and education, for example, by enhancing the delivery of basic training for health workers and teachers,

by increasing information sharing about diseases and famine, by increasing access
to family planning and AIDS prevention information and services, and by increasing access of extension workers and caregivers to specialist knowledge. Sustainable
development goals can be promoted by applying ICT for clean technologies, econ-
omizing on the use of energy and materials in production, using remote sensing for
resource and environmental risk management, and local monitoring by NGOs of
environmental abuses.

Information and communications technologies are characterized by strong interdependencies and significant externalities (Chapter 4). For example, coordinated
public decision making is necessary to effective public investment in common databases and networks and to set ICT policies and standards to promote
government-wide information sharing and one-stop access to public information
and services. As governments are typically the largest information providers and
ICT users, coordinated actions reduce duplication in data collection and ICT investments and training by various agencies, and at the same time focus resources on
improving the relevance, quality, and use of information (Chapter 12). National
ICT strategies should therefore address coordination failures, help exploit scale and
network effects, secure complementary investments in human capital, and create
synergies among programs (Chapter 16).

The risks of unrealized benefits from ICT investments are particularly high in the
context of poverty due to the mutually reinforcing causes of poverty and the scarcity
for complementary assets. The role of ICT in poverty reduction is through their
catalytic and leveraging effects on income opportunities, educational and health services, and welfare provision. ICT benefits can be realized mainly through a holistic
approach. A pro-poor ICT agenda should be pursued in line with a pro-poor agenda
in other sectors like education, health, and rural development.

Raising Awareness and Building Coalitions

National e-development strategies aim at raising awareness, promoting national
dialogue, generating consensus, and inspiring commitment to action. This was a
key function of Singapore's successive IT plans. National strategies should help
mobilize public and private resources and rally the energies of all stakeholders.
Through incentives and motivating visions, such strategies signaled to local and
foreign investors and civil society agents to participate in realizing opportunities
made possible by the ICT revolution. They helped engage investors, entrepreneurs,
and ICT users and industrialists in mutually reinforcing processes to tap synergies
and network effects (Chapter 4).

E-development strategies should harness hopes and inspirations and thus build
sustainable coalition for policy reforms and institutional change. They should clarify
the ICT options available for development, and those that should be taken, and thus
set and communicate strategic directions for all potential actors. They should set
nationally owned priorities for donors and international organizations to support.

This is particularly important for small and low-income countries where donors are often the major financiers of ad hoc applications.

E-development strategies can be critical to building coalitions for reforms. For example, NASSCOM in India has worked with reform-minded leaders in government and business to introduce reforms in many public policy spheres that hindered software exports, data communications, venture capital. A motivating vision could help overcome monopolies of telecommunications, bureaucratic inertia, and resistance to change. The threat of being left out of the loop, unable to participate in the knowledge-based global economy could help initiate overdue educational reforms. Providing success models and early demonstration effects—through well-timed pilot projects that are conceived within national strategies—could also alley fears and build a broader base for reform.

To play this role, e-development strategies must be meaningfully articulated and strategically communicated to various stakeholders. Moreover, e-strategy formulation should be led and supported by a guiding coalition. Leaders engaged in e-strategy design should deploy the necessary tools and processes to conduct stakeholder analysis, engage various stakeholders, build coalitions, and communicate through effective channels to raise awareness and build sustaining coalitions (Chapters 12 and 16).

Clarifying Roles and Responsibilities

A national strategy should help clarify roles and responsibilities and facilitate broad-based participation in the design and implementation of priority programs. It should not be viewed as a government-only strategy. In particular, it should define the role of government in setting the policy and institutional environment, in promoting ICT industry development, in targeting business segments or SMEs for ICT diffusion, and in supporting private and civil society initiatives. It should clarify the roles of government, private sector, and civil society, and who leads when and where.

An expanded vision of ICT in transforming economies and governments implies a corresponding need to engage a growing number of stakeholders and institutions and to promote clearer roles and extended networks among them. These roles and networks are bound to change over time as the transformation process deepens. A national strategy should anticipate such changes or at least facilitate the evolution of these roles, networks, and institutions in line with the requirements of the ongoing economic and social transformation.

Focusing and Prioritizing

A national e-development strategy process can help policy makers and other stakeholders focus, prioritize, sequence, and phase investments and complementary efforts. It should stimulate partnerships for investments and complementary actions. This is particularly critical for e-government, strategic or nationally shared systems, and other public sector applications that require major investments, institutional reforms, public–private partnerships, and long-term commitments. Similarly, choices will have to be made about the priorities for promoting access to information infrastructures for businesses, citizens, schools, government agencies, civil society, and the scientific community. Absence of such national strategies often contributed to donor-led, ad hoc and fragmented investments in information systems, with consequent distortions in priorities, enclave activities, duplication in investments, diffusion of efforts, unrealized or unsustainable benefits, poor demonstration effects, and little chances for scaling up.

Mobilizing and Complementing Market Forces

National strategies are needed to mobilize and complement market forces, promote societal applications, enable bottom-up efforts, and ensure shared learning and scaling up. National planners face two fallacies: the complacent view that "the private sector will take care of it" and the false dichotomy that top-down macroscale initiatives are doomed and only bottom-up approaches can work for the poor. Evidence suggests that the private sector does not invest in rural communication and societal applications to optimal levels without significant support and partnership from the government, in terms of subsidies, R&D, and other incentives. Countries with proactive programs and effective partnerships with the private sector and NGOs have been able to significantly reduce the digital divide as well as promote economy-wide competitiveness.

Scaling Up

Similarly, most pilots and bottom-up efforts do not scale up without sustained support from national institutions with the requisite resources, scope, and scale. Bottom-up efforts and pilots play an essential role in reducing uncertainties about the applicability of ICT to the problems of the poor and contribute to the knowledge required to apply ICT most effectively to these problems. However, propagation of these efforts involves more than mere replication on a larger scale. While focused efforts and intensive support can make it easy to adapt ICT to local opportunities, application on a large scale require broad policy and institutional reforms and changes in management practices—all likely to encounter resistance and to require national commitment and knowledge about processes to diffuse and scale up best practices.

Leveraging the Local ICT Industry

The ICT industry, particularly the most promising segment, the software industry, is characterized by fast growth and technological change, low entry barriers, high global outsourcing, dominance of small enterprises particularly in developing countries, intensive producer–user interaction, importance of local user base or domestic market, strong network or cluster effects, and high intensity of R&D. These features call for national strategies that focus attention and target resources, stimulate the development of enabling polices and infrastructures, provide shared facilities for small software houses and incubators for innovative start ups, set standards and procurement practices to develop the domestic market, support export promotion programs to build country image and ICT brand, and provide incentives for foreign direct investment, finance, entrepreneurship, and innovation (Tessler et al., 2003). Governments also play an important role through outsourcing their ICT requirements through competitive bidding and bootstrapping ICT use in the private sector.

Would this mean that the government would be "picking winners"? Not in terms of picking single companies or national champions. But, yes in terms of targeting this sector for its special characteristics and promises, and where there is a presumption of comparative advantage. Countries can no longer rely on selling generic skills such as low-cost labor as a source of comparative advantage (Porter, 1990). East Asian countries have taken the lead in implementing national ICT strategy processes and actively targeted segments of the ICT industry for systematic technological deepening, diffusion, and exports (Hanna et al., 1996). These countries with active targeting strategies in this sector had the most outstanding economic performance (Lall, 2003). To reduce the risks and improve the impact of targeting the ICT industry for promotion and focused efforts, governments should work with the private sector and other stakeholders to identify target market opportunities, match specific niches to comparative advantage, systematically assess current constraints, and jointly devise the policies and programs to develop the industry and exploit market niches.

What is the role of a national strategy in leveraging ICT as a general-purpose technology?

E-development strategies may target ICT as a core technological competency, in view of its requirements and its potential as a tool for competitiveness. Technologies differ in their learning requirements. Targeting technologies with substantial potential and spillover effects is shown to have greater dynamic benefits on economies (Lall, 2003). ICT is distinguished by the need for substantial and cumulative technological learning to realize its potential. It involves, among others, localization and adaptation, linkages among suppliers and customers, joint learning and standard setting, innovation intensity, and co-investment in complementary institutional resources.

Organizations go through several phases to leverage ICT—these phases ultimately lead to organizational and enterprise transformations. E-development strategies must also address the learning requirements for governments to use this technology for managing the public sector. Unfortunately, national innovation systems in developing countries are poorly equipped to deal with the technological learning requirements of this fast and pervasive technological revolution. A vibrant local ICT industry—particularly in the software services and ITES segments—can help accelerate the adoption and sustain the learning of local users—particularly public sector agencies, SMEs, and NGOs.

Reforming the National Innovation System

A special focus of a national ICT strategy should be to reform the national innova-tion system to promote the diffusion of ICT as a general-purpose technology (GPT) in user sectors with high developmental potential. Developing countries in particu-lar cannot afford wasteful and uncoordinated R&D and innovation efforts. Countries should devote their scarce R&D resources to a limited number of fields so as to cre-ate critical masses of research and innovation talent and generate useable findings that give rise to spillovers for both the ICT industry and leading user sectors.

A special target group for ICT diffusion is the SMEs. Industries and services in developing countries are predominantly SMEs. But ICT diffusion to SMEs is typically constrained by lack of common infrastructures, low awareness, and weak adoption capabilities, underdeveloped regulatory environment, among others. These SMEs also suffer from isolation, low productivity, and limited access to markets, finance, and information. So, the paradox is that these enterprises have the least access to ICT, yet can benefit the most from ICT deployment and diffusion.

Experience from national ICT diffusion program suggests that such programs can be effective in accelerating the diffusion process and in linking SMEs to the national and global supply chains (Hanna, 1995). Coordination among private sec-tor users is necessary to set cooperative standards for doing business and thus to establish common networks, databases, and value-added services. Similarly, gov-ernments may work with private sector associations and NGOs to identify priority business segments for promoting ICT diffusion and for partnering to modernize public services.

Conclusions

By developing a solid national ICT strategy, many countries can position their economies for competitive advantage within a global knowledge-driven economy. Those who understand the process can direct their efforts toward learning the new practices and may find a route to leaping forward and catching up. This will involve a great degree of learning and understanding of ICT impacts on markets, organi-zations, competitive strategies, innovation, as well as the implications for services, employment, education, regional and spatial development, and poverty reduction.

Furthermore, a successful ICT strategy requires substantial investment in human capital, active absorption of technology, ability to raise awareness, build coalitions, clarify roles and responsibilities, mobilize and complement market forces, and scale up. A special focus of a national ICT strategy should be to reform the national innovation system to promote the diffusion of ICT as a GPT.

Yet, enabling the use of ICT as a strategic tool provides many challenges. For most countries, the capacity to handle information remains a dilemma, especially since knowledge and innovation are becoming more central than ever. This paradigm calls for radical transformation in education and training systems, in science and technology policies, and even in conceiving development strategies.

The massive backlog of educational, health, extension, and social needs of developing countries will pose great difficulties in catching up, much less "leapfrogging." However, an innovative and strategic harnessing of the new technologies could be crucial to meeting the Millennium Development Goals in a timely and effective fashion. The digital technologies have supplied a new tool for development while the MDGs have set new targets in search of tools for delivery.

Harnessing the ICT revolution is essential for fast and high-quality growth. Macroeconomic management and liberalization are no longer sufficient to sustain high-quality growth and poverty reduction. Countries face strategic options in formulating their ICT-enabled development strategies. Balancing and matching these options to country aspirations and capabilities are of the essence in designing these strategies. The next section of the book proposes an integrated framework within which such strategic choices are pursued.

Section II
Designing e-Development Strategies

The ICT revolution is opening up new sources of growth and new opportunities to solve long-standing development problems. ICT is driving a technological revolution that is sweeping entire economies and transforming institutions, learning processes, and innovation systems. Yet, much of current research, education, and development assistance practice has focused on single elements of this transformation. Much of the documented failures of ICT applications in e-government, e-business, or poverty reduction can be traced to fragmented approaches that missed key enablers or operated within the current silos of the ICT paradigm.

Researchers and practitioners alike lament the lack of an integrated view of ICT4D as a part of the larger puzzle of development. Some suggest ways for framing ICT issues in broader contexts, by understanding the dynamics of ICT as a process (Wilson, 2005). But most researchers and ICT practitioners remain comfortable within their sectoral or disciplinary perspectives. Much like the fable of blind men and the elephant, each discipline or practice area remains focused on one element of the complex and interdependent process of e-development to the exclusion of the whole.

In response, I advance the framework of *e-development* as a holistic approach to leveraging ICT for development (ICT4D)—pursuing mutually reinforcing ICT-enabled development initiatives. It is about creating a knowledge economy "ecosystem"—an integrated approach that defines a vision, coordinates the work of stakeholders, and maps the connections and shapes the relationships among diverse players. Accordingly, ICT4D is defined most holistically so as to facilitate a way of systematically thinking about ICT as enabler of development, of strategically managing integrated ICT4D programs, of tapping synergies among interdependent elements and complementary factors to ICT, and of communicating to a broad community of practice.

The following two sections are the main body of the book, covering the design of all key elements of an e-development strategy: vision, policies, and institutions; information infrastructure and shared access; human resources; ICT industry development; and the crosscutting application and diffusion of ICT in government, business, and society. We start with defining a holistic view of e-development. This view must be kept in mind as we proceed to examine the key issues and best practices concerning the design of the key pillars of ICT-enabled development and the major sectoral and cross-sectoral applications of ICT for development. Unlike the traditional treatment of each pillar or sector application, we focus on the potential linkages and synergies among key elements of e-development and the options to the possibilities that should be explored, considered, and exploited to manage an integrated and effective ICT-enabled development.

Chapter 4
Holistic e-Development

E-development, or e-Transformation, can be conceived as composed of key, inter-dependent elements: an enabling policy and institutional environment; an affordable and competitive information infrastructure; a dynamic and innovative ICT industry: broad ICT literacy, education, and entrepreneurship; a coherent investment program to apply ICT to modernizing the public sector; and incentives to promote the effective use of ICT for developing the private sector and empowering civil society (Fig. 4.1).[1] The first four elements are the pillars or enablers to the effective use and mainstreaming of ICT in government, business, and grassroots community organizations (e-government, e-business, and e-society).

Elements of e-Development

The e-development process can be conceptualized in terms of key elements (Fig. 4.1):

(a) *Vision, Policies, Institutions, and Leadership.* Stakeholder participation and effective leadership have to be manifested in the well-defined vision and functional institutional framework and supporting policies for ICT use and production. Policies and institutions constitute the enabling environment which either enhance or obstruct the interactions among all other elements of e-development.
(b) *Human Resources.* Skilled human resources are at the heart of the ICT revolution, both as users and producers. Designing effective human development programs for fueling this revolution is at the heart of successful e-development;
(c) *ICT Sector Development or Production.* ICT is a global, dynamic, and high value-added industry, and thus often targeted for promotion. Moreover, the key segment of application software represents a core competency that can serve both ICT production (and exports) and its wide and effective domestic use.

---

[1] The figure is a highly simplified representation of the key enablers and application areas of ICT and the many possible interdependencies among them.

N.K. Hanna, *e-Transformation: Enabling New Development Strategies*, Innovation, Technology, and Knowledge Management, DOI 10.1007/978-1-4419-1185-8_4, © Springer Science+Business Media, LLC 2010

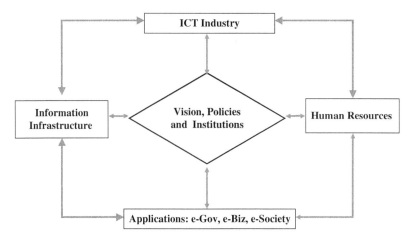

Fig. 4.1 Elements of e-development process

(d) *Information Infrastructure*. Without nationwide telecom infrastructure and affordable access to the Internet and ICT tools, e-development will benefit only a small fraction of the population, most likely urban, affluent, and educated. This element covers policies and innovative interventions to insure connectivity and access to the vast majority of population in developing countries.

(e) *Application or Usage of ICT in Government, Business, and Society*. National strategies should set priorities and broad directions for the use of ICT in key sectors of the economy, for public sector modernization and strategic applications that cut across sectors, for promoting e-commerce, for priority user sectors, and for programs to target and diffuse ICT to SMEs, NGOs, disadvantaged groups, and lagging regions.

These elements are closely interdependent. The scope of each element and the nature of such interdependencies are likely to vary across countries and over time. For example, introduction of e-government services is impossible without accessible infrastructure, while sustainable demand for information infrastructure, in turn, depends on the availability of relevant local content and e-government services.

Collectively, these elements or pillars of e-development cover the package of policies, investments, and institutions that enable an economy to apply and leverage ICT for social and economic development. At the heart of e-development is e-leaders and e-leadership institutions—individuals, networks, and institutions that develop a vision of a knowledge society, set policies, and priorities, forge national consensus on reforms, and coordinate and create synergies among the elements of e-development. To succeed, leaders should rethink and act simultaneously on the ICT infrastructure, human resources, ICT innovation system, policy and institutional regime, and ICT use and diffusion throughout the economy.

Role of an Integrative Framework

Adopting a holistic e-development approach is a key to establishing a balance between investment in the right technology, information, and connectivity infrastructure (the hard infrastructure), on the one hand, and the human resources and institutional capabilities, policy and regulatory environment, R&D, and technological learning and innovation (the soft infrastructure), on the other hand. The soft infrastructure constitutes the ecosystem that allows ICT investment to yield its transformative power. Experience suggests that many countries tend to overinvest in the hard infrastructure and underinvest in the soft infrastructure. Experience also shows that the greatest payoff will come from balanced improvements to both the soft and hard dimensions. E-development is about embedding issues of information infrastructure within a coherent and dynamic ecosystem. Understanding the interactions and interdependencies among key elements of e-development can help in diagnosing imbalances and gaps on ICT-enabled development and in managing a balanced course between the hard and soft infrastructure.[2]

The proposed e-development framework can be mapped on conceptual models of growth. Accordingly, growth is the result of interaction among several components: physical capital (investment in telecommunications and ICT application), human capital (technical education, e-literacy, flexible labor), total factor productivity growth (ICT-driven innovation and entrepreneurship, the use and mainstreaming of ICT in all sectors, and associated organizational innovation and transformation), and the overarching enabling environment (which shapes labor and capital markets and the diffusion of new technologies). Interaction among these components of growth is strongly defined by this enabling environment, which can either enhance or hinder it. Ultimately, leadership shapes the shared vision, policies, and institutions that advance these interactions and thus growth.

The e-development framework can explain the role of ICT as a sector and a cross-sector enabler. It can also be used as a guide the design and implementation of integrated ICT4D programs at the national levels, much is the same vein as Porter's system of competitive advantage (Porter, 1990; Heeks, 2006) is used to both explain sector development and guide the design of programs to enhance national competitive advantage. Porter's competitive advantage theory takes a holistic and systemic view of four elements or determinants of competitiveness: factor conditions, demand conditions, related and supporting industries, and firm or industry

---

[2]A two-dimensional approach to ICT in development is advanced in Chapter 12 of the GITR 2007–2008. It covers some key elements of the e-development framework and shows how useful this would be as a diagnostic approach to secure a balanced course between the ICT infrastructure (including capabilities to support infrastructure) and ICT ecosystem (policies and institutions). Our proposed framework is more comprehensive and detailed and includes ICT systems as part of the hard infrastructure, and human resources and technological capabilities as part of the ecosystem or soft infrastructure. Yet, the GITR shows that the two-dimensional model can help manage a balanced course and take account of interactions among these composite dimensions.

strategy, structure, and rivalry. It views these elements together as a mutually reinforcing system and their inter-relationships are continually evolving.

The e-development framework functions in the same fashion as a way to explain the dynamics of ICT-enabled development and to guide the design and strategic management of ICT4D programs. Appropriately coordinated and sequenced, programs covering these pillars can exploit the synergies, transforming the economy and accelerating development.

Underlying Cluster for the Knowledge Economy

One way of appreciating the e-development approach—of securing balanced progress and tapping synergies across the key elements of e-development—is to reinterpret this framework in terms of the microeconomic foundations of competitiveness.[3] Since many of the traditional sources of comparative advantage have been nullified by globalization, there is a growing recognition that competitiveness and prosperity are increasingly based on competitive advantage. Macroeconomic conditions, while necessary, are not sufficient. Accordingly, internal sources of advantage must be cultivated and assembled to create valuable products and services. More sophisticated sources of competitive advantage have emerged; these are based on knowledge, innovation, and investment in advanced skills. Competitiveness is also increasingly based on local interactions and synergies: relationships with suppliers and customers, insights about market needs gleaned from local partners and users, special access to technology and best practices from other local institutions, production flexibility arising from using nearby suppliers, business climate with low transactions costs, openness and access to advanced knowledge from local anchors of global players, etc.

More specifically the microeconomic foundations of national competitive advantage have been conceptualized in terms of factor or input conditions, demand conditions, strategy and rivalry, and related and supporting industries. Successful economic development requires sustained improvements in the quality and specialization of a nation's inputs: labor, capital, infrastructure, knowledge, and natural resources. Demanding customers educate local firms about how to improve products and services and force them to high value activities. Local demand thus provides a laboratory for successive upgrading. Vigorous local rivalry shifts over time from minimizing costs and process efficiency to innovation and differentiation. Healthy rivalry depends on policies that support competition, entrepreneurship, and new business development. The final determinant of the strength of a country's competitiveness is the extent and quality of local suppliers and related industries—that is, the formation of a cluster of dense networks of supporting industries and institutions. Cross-industry linkages, complementarities, and positive externalities are essential sources of competitive advantage.

---

[3]Much has been written on the cluster approach, in both the business and economic literature. Among the leading and pioneering writers is Porter (1980, 1985, 1990).

These four determinants constitute a mutually reinforcing system (Porter, 1990). The effect of one determinant is contingent on the state of others. Favorable demand conditions, for example, will not lead to competitive advantage unless the states of competition and support institutions are sufficient to respond. And while competitive advantage may be possible in natural resource-dependent or little sophisticated industries, such advantage is usually unsustainable. Government and business leadership play key roles in promoting policies and institutions that influence each of these determinants and the synergies and dynamics of the entire system.

The development of the ICT sector or cluster may be readily conceptualized along this framework of four determinants or diamond. The promotion of the ICT cluster may also be viewed in terms of e-development (Fig. 4.1): the human resources and information infrastructure represent the factor conditions, the use or application of ICT in public institutions and local businesses represent demand conditions (foreign outsourcers may be included as part of demand conditions for IT-enabled services); competition conditions may include the policies and regulatory frameworks for telecommunication, media, electronic transactions, information sharing, and content development as well as the general business environment; and other tools to promote supporting institutions and cluster formation may include incubators, IT parks, venture capital, and business support and research institutions.

But ICT is more than just another cluster that a country may choose to promote and successively upgrade as an industry. It may be argued that all clusters can contribute a nation's prosperity. It may also be argued that promoting ICT as an industry would be similar to the historical approach of an industrial policy, with the associated promises and pitfalls. In Section I, we argued that ICT, apart from being a promising industry, is a general-purpose technology for transforming all kinds of industries and services and a shared infrastructure for reducing transaction costs across the economy, for networking and empowering individuals and communities, and for delivering information and services. As such, ICT may be viewed as the enabling cluster for all other clusters and the whole economy.

Taking Account of Synergies and Economies of Scale

The interactions or interdependencies among e-development components are significant in advanced knowledge economies and even greater in developing and emerging economies. Studies in OECD countries indicate a strong link between ICT investment, productivity growth, and competitiveness (OECD, 2004a). Moreover, they show the significance of "interaction effects"—for example, interactions between ICT investment, infrastructure, skill levels, and the policy environment. A critical mass or minimum threshold of ICT deployment can have a significant positive impact on a country's economy. In a network economy, network effects and externalities are substantial. All communication technologies are subject to strong network effects, network externalities, positive feedback, critical mass, and/or economies of scale of ICT supply and demand (Shapiro and Varian, 1999). An integrated approach to e-development should enable policy makers and strategists to tap and harness these synergies and interaction effects.

For developing countries in particular, with multiple "cumulative causations" for information poverty (Myrdal, 1971), the impact of one element of e-development is heavily dependent on, and reinforcing to, progress in others. Investments in ICT must be accompanied by investments in human resources, process innovations, institutional changes, and policy reforms to fully realize the potential benefits. This is consistent with a key lesson of development experience in general, that is, the need for a comprehensive approach to development (Hanna and Picciotto, 2002).

Consider e-government and e-business. Making e-government and e-business services broadly available to citizens and enterprises requires accelerating Internet penetration and affordable connectivity. And the take-up of online services depends critically on the development of digital literacy and an information culture. Education and the policy environment are keys to making technology work. Moreover, when governments tap domestic firms to act as partners in providing e-government solutions, they support private sector development in ways that can broaden e-development and create competitive domestic markets and learning opportunities for developing the local ICT industry.

Consider the links between the IT industry and IT use in government, business, and society at large. By developing the IT industry, more and better IT products and services would be available to businesses, raising their productivity and competitiveness. A competitive IT sector and a large pool of competent IT manpower could also attract leading multinationals—both IT producers and intensive IT users—with increasing prospects for inducing virtuous dynamics and strengthening global innovation networks. A dynamic local IT sector would also facilitate the learning of government transformation and PPPs for e-government services. E-society applications are also easier to seek and exploit when communities and local governments have access to local IT companies and low-cost IT-enabled solutions.

Also consider the virtuous cycle or positive feedback between infrastructure, skills, and content. Digital content is increasingly important part of OECD economies as they shift from manufacturing to high-value intangibles and services. It is becoming the basic creative infrastructure for the knowledge economy. OECD analysis suggests a positive feedback between information infrastructure, e-literacy and skills, and digital content (OECD, 2006). Compelling and relevant digital content is the main driver for investment in broadband infrastructure and associated platforms. This infrastructure can in turn be shared for the delivery of many e-government and e-business services and further diffuse e-literacy and societal applications. By extending access to convergent broadband infrastructure to businesses, government, households, and civil society, the investment costs per consumer falls dramatically.

Governments can play a critical role in guiding all these interactions and creating positive feedback or critical mass of users. One tool for creating critical mass of users is standards setting. Another method for achieving a critical mass is to assemble a group of strategic partners, including customers, complementors, and even competitors. In the United States, where set manufacturers, who have the most to gain from rapid adoption of digital television, are leading the way, the Federal Communications Commission had to induce broadcasters along by offering them free spectrum for digital broadcasts (Shapiro and Varian, 1999, p. 16). Over time e-leadership institutions should be able to identify more and more synergies among applications in e-government, e-business, and e-society and among ICT suppliers and complementors.

Although integration offers many opportunities for tapping synergies among the elements of e-development, an integrated approach to ICT poses a challenge for aid agencies and developing country governments alike. Both face incentives that militate against collaboration and integration. Aid funding and public budgets follow sectoral lines, and it can be hard to get new money for centralized, cross-sectoral initiatives. Whatever the source of funding, ICT efforts—e-government investments, telecommunication reforms, connectivity programs, ICT industry promotion, human resource development, content development, sectoral applications—are typically pursued in isolation. Even within a single element of e-development, such as an e-government program, ICT investments are typically pursued agency by agency or system by system (see Fountain, 2001).

This comprehensive view of ICT for development does not imply addressing all constraints, opportunities, and investment possibilities at once. Instead, it allows designers and implementers to analyze, prioritize, select, and sequence the most critical interdependencies in view of the whole and of the overall resources and capabilities. It helps anticipate and recognize the key interdependencies and manage them over time.

Integrating ICT into Broader Development Strategies

Information technology is not an end in itself, but can be an effective means and entry point to achieve development ends: more transport markets and governments; better educated and healthier population; more productive knowledge workers and entrepreneurs; better natural resources management; more informed and empowered rural population; and greater access to global knowledge and innovation. The ICT sector and its stakeholders are effective entry points to economy-wide transformation. Throughout the world, information and communication technologies appeal to political leaders, entrepreneurs, and the public at large. The sector is led by entrepreneurs exploiting the new technologies and offering substantial opportunities for profit, employment, and export within a relatively short time. But ICT can only serve as an enabling tool if a country has clear strategy to those ends, and the resources, capacity, and commitment to pursue that strategy. It should be put in the service of these broader ends and strategies. Otherwise, it could become an expensive distraction from pressing development problems and needs.

A review of a large number of recent national ICT strategies suggests that their links with overall development strategies tend to be weak, particularly in low-income countries (World Bank, 2006, pp. 87–124). Even when such links are articulated in planning documents, they are often forgotten in practice. The reasons are many: perverse incentives, poor understanding of the links, low awareness and ownership of ICT among public administrators, scarcity of transformational leaders within user sectors, weak involvement of core ministries such as finance and economic planning, and the pursuit of narrow, technology-driven agendas by the ICT ministries or their equivalent. Bridging the gap between national development and ICT strategies requires twin attentions: a focus on the core development priorities, and a broader awareness of how ICT serve as effective tools to address these priorities.

A holistic approach to ICT for development gives primary attention to the organic links between information, communication, and knowledge and the broader national development goals. It articulates the information, communication, and knowledge dimensions of development challenges and priorities of a country and thus the way ICT can help address them. It goes beyond the traditional preoccupation of ICT (and science and technology) ministries with technology, innovation, research. It goes beyond organizational "silos" reflected in ministries' isolated information and communication systems. And it goes beyond aid agencies' common approach of focusing on ad hoc ICT applications in development projects while neglecting shared information infrastructure, systemic constraints, and sustainability.

Creating a knowledge economy or information society requires direction from a national ICT-enabled development strategy. Such a strategy, based on an e-development framework, provides a guide to policies, investments, and implementation mechanisms for developing ICT capability and using it to achieve a country's development objectives.[4] It focuses the actions and resources of different stakeholders—but especially the government—on national priorities for harnessing ICT for development. It taps the interdependencies among these actions and investments over the medium term to realize a shared vision of ICT-enabled development. And it explains how institutions will collaborate and share responsibilities for this development.

E-development is about promoting a new type of development strategy, one adapted to the specific strengths, vulnerabilities, and aspirations of the country, as well as the opportunities and challenges arising from ICT—the general-purpose technology of our times. A national e-development strategy is shaped by the broader goals of national growth and development. It may focus on improving governance and the delivery of public services, bridging economic divides, promoting social inclusion, and drastically cutting transaction costs across the economy. It may seek to exploit new sources of growth and employment by promoting the ICT- and IT-enabled service industries and the use of ICT by small enterprises to network and compete. It may leverage ICT competencies and networking capabilities to position

---

[4]For a review of many national e-strategies, see World Bank (2006, pp. 87–124).

a country to tap global know-how, become a regional service hub and promote smart growth and intelligent society, as has been the case of Singapore (Box 4.1).

Box 4.1 Singapore: Toward an Intelligent Island

Singapore has been a pioneer in developing national ICT plans since 1980. Its successive plans have become more comprehensive over time, covering all elements of e-development. ICT visions and plans remained centrally inspired and driven and closely integrated with the overall growth and competitive strategy of the country. Over time, Singapore's e-leadership institutions have evolved. They have been broadened and deepened. Some of the technical expertise that was developed within the public sector under the National Computer Board and later, the InfoComm Development Agency (IDA), was subsequently transferred to semi-public enterprises like the National Computer Services (NCS) to deliver e-development and e-government advisory services beyond Singapore. More recently, Singapore has been positioning itself to go global, to source talent and partner with others around the Asia region and to leverage its infrastructure and capital to become a hub for the global economy.

IDA was created in December 1999 as a result of the merger between the National Computer Board (NCB) and the Telecommunications Authority of Singapore (TAS). It operates under the Ministry of Information, Communications and the Arts (MITA, formerly the Ministry of Communications and Information Technology—MCIT).[5] The government saw technology as an enabler, providing the country with a sector responsible for economic growth as well as with a means for providing greater socio-economic benefits to the population as a whole. The rationale behind the creation of IDA was therefore to have a single agency for integrated planning, policy formulation, regulation and industry development of the information technology and telecommunication sectors.

IDA has several roles. As a regulating agency, it formulates clear and transparent policies to ensure a fair and balanced competitive environment. As a developer of Singapore's ICT industry, it works closely with the private sector to create a vibrant business environment. As a promoter of Singapore's ICT sector, it works to encourage foreign companies to locate in Singapore and partner with the country's companies, as well as handling the preparation of citizens for living and working in the "new economy." Finally, as the government's CIO office, it drives the implementation of the Singapore e-government

---

[5]IDA web site: http://www.ida.gov.sg/idaweb/aboutida/infopage.jsp?infopagecategory=&<info pageid=I216&versionid=10

action plan and provides the technical expertise for the management of various e-government programs.

IDA does not operate alone; it is closely linked to other key institutions. An e-government office was established in the ministry of finance to champion the e-government. It works closely with the CIO in IDA. The e-Government Policy Committee provides strategic directions and oversight for the program. It is chaired by the head of civil service and composed of permanent secretaries from selected ministries. The committee is assisted by a steering committee composed of CIOs. The permanent secretaries of ministries and CEOs of statutory boards are responsible for the ICT infrastructure and services within their own organization.

Accenture ranks Singapore second (after Canada) for the fourth year in a row in its e-government report.[6] Singapore has adopted a centralized but adaptive information infrastructure. This approach fits well with its size, highly disciplined civil service, and hierarchical managerial culture. After more than a decade of computerization and training in the civil service and heavy investment in broadband communications, Singapore was more than ready for exploiting the Internet and making services available online.

Since 2002, the agency turned its attention to creating relevant content and to promote public usage of e-services, and ensure universal access to e-services. Government agencies were required to conduct surveys of their customers and marketing campaigns were launched to promote the use of e-services through the single window, e-citizen. The Singapore Public Service also puts in place an integrated, one-stop portal to enable e-business. To secure ownership of e-government by civil servants, InfoCom has been empowering public sector officers with training and resources for ICT-enabled innovation and knowledge sharing. The InfoCom Education Program was launched to equip officers with the necessary ICT competencies, and a Knowledge Management Experimentation Program provided seed funding to encourage public sector agencies to jump-start pioneering KM projects to nurture knowledge sharing.

A coherent e-development strategy has other advantages over current practices of governments and aid agencies in developing and applying ICT. By tightly linking national ICT strategies to broader development visions and strategies, it engages policy makers in driving the ICT agenda in response to national development priorities—rather than the other way around. It helps focus the attention of policy makers and program managers on ICT-enabled development results. ICT

---

[6]Accenture. *E-government Leadership: High Performance, Maximum Value.* Accenture Government Executive Series, 2004, p. 94. Canada and Singapore present major contrasts in managerial and political cultures, despite being the two highest ranked countries on e-government achievements.

becomes an enabling force for pursuing policy reforms, transforming institutions, and improving governance and transparency. It can catalyze reforms in education and mobilize knowledge and other resources for social inclusion. Enlightened leaders become engaged in shaping this vision and in using it to build consensus on institutional change and economic transformation.

An e-development strategy is not a mere vision; it operates within institutional and financial constraints. Thus it seeks to optimize the allocation of resources, focusing scarce public resources on the investments with the greatest development impact or those that can produce quick wins with little demand on managerial resources. Investments have to be sequenced and phased in line with these resources and with political demands for tangible and timely results.

By shaping an integrated national program, an e-development strategy also clarifies the comparative advantages of the government, the private sector, civil society, and academia and determines what roles each can best play in designing and implementing programs. In doing so, it helps build partnerships and coordinate work among these stakeholders. Finally, it provides an enabling policy environment for implementation and a healthy ecosystem for the information society.

E-development attempts to balance top-down direction with bottom-up initiative. The balance will vary depending on a country's size, the diversity of its regions, and its tradition of political and administrative centralization. But since ICT is a new dimension of development and a malleable general-purpose technology, the balance should favor mechanisms to empower grassroots organizations, promote local ownership and innovation, ensure local fit and flexibility, and meet the special needs of rural populations. It is at the local level that many of the links between elements of e-development must be sought and built—such as those between connectivity (telecenter development), content development, e-literacy, and the delivery of e-government services. E-development establishes a learning framework that supports pilots and bottom-up innovations while promoting shared learning and the scaling up of successful projects that fit with the overall national strategy.

Each stage of development suggests different priorities within and among these elements, different synergies, and different entry points, sequencing, and phasing. This calls for a holistic, cross-sectoral and coordinated approach, which complicates implementation, but is absolutely crucial for the efficient use of resources and for long-term developmental impact. As acknowledged by several UN ICT task forces, proceeding sector by sector fails to assist countries in identifying cross sectoral linkages or timeframes, or how to prioritize thematic sectors, to determine how to utilize scarce resources (mostly human capacity, finance and infrastructure) across sectors and/or how to create multi-sector/multi-purpose solutions.

e-Development as a Techno-economic Paradigm

As discussed earlier, technological revolutions and the process of installation of each new economic paradigm begins with a battle against the power of the old, established structures and processes. During the installation period, the new technologies do not advance smoothly. They erupt, disturb established fabrics, and help set up new infrastructures, new networks, and new ways of doing things. As the new frameworks and infrastructures are put in place, deployment and widespread diffusion can harness the modernizing power of this techno-economic paradigm and realize vastly superior levels of productivity.

This process of adaptation is not passive and can be accelerated by various enablers and a shared vision of the future. These enablers may include new policies and specialized institutions, regulatory frameworks and institutions, new leadership and managerial capabilities, specialized training and education, standards and architectures, networks and partnerships, financial innovations (such as venture capital). Deep adoption and integration of a techno-economic paradigm is needed to facilitate full diffusion and permit reaping the full benefits of the investments made in infrastructure, training, institutions, and social learning associated with that paradigm. "All this economic and social effort becomes a set of externalities for further investment and wealth creation based on market expansion and compatible innovations. Thus there is a virtuous cycle of self-reinforcement for the widest possible use and diffusion of the available potential" (Perez, 2002, p. 42).

This process of active adaptation and learning is difficult and involves creative destruction in all economic and institutional spheres. Old practices, processes, and regulations become obstacles. Old institutions are inadequate. Skills and infrastructures are found wanting. A new context must be created; a new common sense must emerge and propagate. For diffusion to proceed, this painful adaptation must occur at all levels, institutional, local, and national.

This mutual shaping of society and the new economy is particularly necessary for the ongoing ICT revolution. The world of Internet, instant messages, mobile communications, social networking, online government, e-commerce, flexible production, flexible specialization, global supply chains, and digital transactions has a different logic and different requirements from those that facilitated the spread of the car, highways, and mass production. The processes involved in enacting information and communication technology, leveraging cyberspace, and building the virtual state are not merely technological—they involve substantial organizational and inter-organizational restructuring and learning. As pointed out by Fountain in *Building the Virtual State*, "the use of the Internet for efficiency gains at structural levels deeper than the web interface is difficult, slow, and painstaking political work" (Fountain, 2001, p. 144). Spreading the ICT-based paradigm beyond a single agency or sector demands a broader orchestration across all elements of e-development and deeper investment in policy reforms and institutional transformation.

E-development encompasses the key elements of the ICT-based techno-economic paradigm. It includes investments in the new infrastructures of telecommunications, connectivity, databases, systems, and ICT tools. But it also includes the policies, governance mechanisms, regulatory and socio-institutional frameworks leadership practices, and new skills necessary to enable effective harnessing of technological change and ICT investments. It is about the assimilation of ICT-enabled innovations, process changes, and institutional transformations in the economic and social spheres. It demands an interdisciplinary perspective, as the spread and effective use of ICT is determined not only by investment in science and technology but also by economic, political, institutional, social, and cultural factors.

In adopting e-development as the techno-economic paradigm for the information age, we can have a framework or structure with which to ask questions and address issues of coherence, interdependence, synergy, sequencing, and sustainability. This framework can also help in harnessing the ongoing revolution and in identifying the relevance of ICT for development in a densely connected global economy. It does not provide ready-made recipes. We live through a period requiring intense social learning and institutional creativity. During the early phases of such techno-economic paradigms, the irruption and frenzy phases, there is intense exploration of all the possibilities. Through pilots and experimentation, the potential for using ICT to solve local problems and improve public services is fully discovered. Similarly, through venture capital and diversified trial and error investments, "the potential of the diffusing paradigm for creating new markets and for rejuvenating old industries is fully discovered and firmly installed in the economy and in the mental maps of investors...The process is intensified by the availability of the new infrastructure, which at this time achieves enough coverage to provide clear externalities..." (Perez, 2002, p. 51).

E-development is about seeking coherence and synergy among the technological, economic, and socio-institutional spheres of change, to allow the full spread of the benefits from the ICT revolution. These changing spheres interact and influence each other, with some logical sequencing. The socio-institutional sphere in particular has much greater inertia and resistance to change. This suggests that early engagement and attention be given to leadership and capacity to design appropriate institutions and regulations and other aspects of the enabling environment for diffusion. Overcoming the inertia of vested interests, practical routines, and ingrained practices requires political and institutional leadership, social experimentation, coalition building for reform, and orchestrated change across various spheres.

e-Development as a Shaping Strategy

The proposed e-development framework may serve the role of a "shaping strategy," in the same way as a shaping strategy is used to create competitive ecosystems in various sectors or industries (Hagel et al., 2008). A shaping strategy creates an ecosystem for participants to use the strategy to capture value as they learn from and share risk with one another. Its main elements are to provide a shaping view, a shaping platform, and a set of shaping actions and assets. The shaping view sets the strategic focus and directions for participants, describes the technological forces and economic payoffs of participation, and indicates how concerted actions and shared platforms would reduce the adoption risks that participants would face. The platform may include the set of standards and policies for all participants to share.

The shaper, a leading company or a leading actor like government in the case of e-development, also uses certain acts and asset alignments to provide assurances about the shaper's investment in resources and participants' access to them. Asset alignment signals the shaper's long-term commitment and provides leverage for participants, thereby reducing their risks. It also defines the standards and practices to guide participants and facilitate partnerships or transactions. These elements of a shaping strategy combine to help shapers quickly attract and mobilize a critical mass of participants into a competitive ecosystem. That unleashes powerful network effects.

Shaping strategies are particularly relevant to ICT-enabled development. They have particular value in industries and contexts with a large number of potential participants and widespread uncertainty about the future, usually from technological disruptions. E-development as a shaping strategy would emphasize the development of a shaping view through e-readiness assessment and a well-communicated vision of a desired future. In the case of e-development, the shaper is often more than the government or a single agency: most successful e-development strategies were led by coalitions of political leaders, government agencies, business associations, academic institutions, civil society organizations, think tanks, and public opinion shapers. The shaping platform may include the e-policy and regulatory frameworks for the digital economy, the government-wide information and technology architectures and standards, and more broadly, the alignment of the e-development pillars. Shaping acts and assets may include public–private partnerships, the development of e-leadership cadres and institutions, strategic ICT applications such as public e-procurement and e-customs, investing in innovation funds, and various acts to build credibility and network effects.

e-Development at the City and Regional Levels

In this book we focus on adopting the e-development approach at the national level. But a holistic approach to using ICT for development is as relevant and effective to cities and subnational entities, as it is to national levels. There are a number of reasons for the need to adopt e-development at the regional level, and particularly at the city level.

First, an ICT-enabled urban development fits with the rising role of cities as key players in global competition, as mobilizers of foreign investment, as innovation hubs, and as platforms for global supply chains. Cities and other local entities are growing in economic weight vis-a-vis central governments. They are also acting as global players, networking with other cities, building their information infrastructures, and designing their own strategies to become livable and attractive to global finance and talent. Integrating ICT into the overall development and management of increasingly complex, knowledge-based, and fast growing urban centers is an imperative, not a choice.

A growing number of local governments are emerging as local global players. They are becoming central engines in shaping and spreading globalization. They are called global cities, world cities, knowledge cities, networked cities, digital cities, and e-cities (Lanvin and Lewin, 2006). Cities are now regularly ranked in terms of their e-readiness, information infrastructure, and e-government; national e-readiness indicators often hide major differences between geographic locations. Countries as diverse as Korea, Russia, China, Mexico, Brazil, Morocco, Senegal, and UAE are promoting local champions of innovation hubs and knowledge cities. Most successful are likely to be those who take a coherent and holistic approach to applying ICT to enhance the attractiveness, competitiveness, and sustainability of their urban systems.

Second, an area-focused e-development approach fits well with the decentralization movement in many countries with very diverse socio-economic conditions. E-development is about using ICT in ways that are responsive to local development priorities and tailored to local conditions. This local focus helps in promoting ownership, innovation, and adaption of ICT-enabled solutions. E-development is also about using ICT to leverage local resources and enhance existing comparative advantages. Diverse e-development strategies are likely to emerge, as in the case of AP and other progressive Indian states. Under these conditions, the role of central government becomes one of a catalyst and enabler in support of diverse locally driven e-development strategies.

Government services are increasingly handled at the local levels and subsequently e-government is increasingly developed and managed by local entities. The growing demand for improving urban services to growing and diverse urban populations also makes e-government services and ICT-enabled outsourcing of the production and delivery of such services to the private sector also increasingly attractive. Many city governments are increasingly willing and able to use ICT and outsourcing to serve their citizens. E-government is also used to promote good governance and management, by increasing public access to information about local government decision making. Recent technological advances such as WIFI and WIMAX also favor decentralized solutions. In general, the developments of ICT infrastructure and services tend to reinforce both decentralization and the role of cities in global competitiveness.

Third, urban systems and localities tend to exhibit high degrees of interactions and interdependencies among e-development components. This interaction is manifested in the physical realm by the high volumes of urban transport and urban communication networks. But it is also reflected in terms of diverse electronic and virtual networks. Dynamic urban centers exploit positive feedback from both demand-side and supply-side economies of scale as they accelerate the adoption of new technologies and make them more valuable to a critical mass of users. Content providers and innovators are concentrated in urban areas and intensively interact through dense electronic and human or virtual networks. Local governments can harness these positive interactions and partner with others to promote mutually reinforcing measures to provide shared information infrastructure, develop a critical mass of ICT users, and accelerate learning.

In the knowledge economy, proximity matters, particularly for cooperation and sharing of tacit knowledge. The strengths of local networks also matter. Knowledge flows are facilitated by trust, mobility of employees, and the density of human networks. Transnational corporations must be rooted in the region and engaged in regional networks, so it can act as important disseminator of new information, knowledge, and innovation and for blending global and local knowledge.

Fourth, a differentiated local approach to e-development is needed to tackle issues of social exclusion and digital isolation. The root causes of such exclusions and divides vary depending on local context and local economic resources and opportunities. An integrated e-development approach can maximize the impact of ICT on poverty reduction and social inclusion, provided that such approach is grounded in the local realties of information poverty and limited access to knowledge and local resources.

A final reason for adopting e-development at the city or local levels is that cities or localities can provide entry points for broadening transformation and scaling up. Innovation and transformation into knowledge economy often arise in specific locations (or sectors) following the accumulation of a critical mass of resources, infrastructure, talent, and entrepreneurship. It is often easier to engage the key stakeholders at the local level to coordinate e-development at their level. It is also easier to effect change and reach consensus on reforms at this level. Agility of smaller economic units and the availability of progressive local leadership to seize opportunities in rapidly changing environment can help provide demonstration effects and local best practices.

The successful creation and scaling up of such entry points encourages reforms by convincing skeptics, increasing confidence, and thus overcoming resistance to change. The early successes of the state of Andhra Pradesh in developing a coherent ICT-enabled development strategy—providing e-government services, improving connectivity, and attracting FDI and IT services—provided an attractive model for other Indian states and an impetus for the central government to scale up state or locally initiated e-government programs and homegrown successes. Similarly, China ignited its reform and initiated the bootstrapping process through locally focused reforms, special economic zones, and phased reforms of the local business environment.

Chapter 5
A Vision of e-Transformation

Vision may be the easiest part of the e-development process to understand as a concept, but it is a difficult one to articulate and effectively implement. In fact, many countries have e-development strategies without a vision, which leads to weak stakeholder ownership, shallow engagement, loss of developmental focus. Programs without vision typically waste resources on myriad of uncoordinated projects, driven by powerful but narrow special interests. Other countries have vision statements, but these visions are not clear or not effectively communicated and used as a guide to shaping policies and priorities, re-thinking investment programs or inducing various stakeholders to act and collaborate.

An e-vision should outline e-Transformation in a clear and concise way that motivates and inspires major stakeholders. Both e-strategy design and implementation becomes easier because a clear vision and the strategy's essence can be easily communicated and internalized by stakeholders and implementers. A clear and energizing vision can become the glue that holds stakeholders together on their journey toward shared and transcending goals. Leadership plays a key role in inspiring, articulating, and communicating a vision of e-Transformation, the subject of the next chapter.

A vision is more of a process of engaging stakeholders than a paper statement on a set of goals. To achieve this, it should relate to the roles, needs, aspirations, and performance of various stakeholders. It must tie e-development policies and programs to the overall development priorities and resources of the country. It needs to balance country aspirations for participating in the ICT industry, as innovator and producer, with the need to become an effective user of this general-purpose technology (GPT) for the benefit of the rest of the economy. Finally, it should help tap the potential interdependencies and synergies among various elements and sectors in the e-development process, while providing clear guidance for sequencing and phasing of reforms and investments.

An e-vision should be based on objective analysis of the political, social, and economic contexts and drivers of development process in the country and a strategic choice of the most appropriate focus for ICT-enabled development—a vision that is inspiring yet realistic. Some of the drivers, for example, may be the need for economic diversification, revitalizing, or sustaining areas of competitive advantage, improving the investment climate, promoting social equality, and improving public

N.K. Hanna, *e-Transformation: Enabling New Development Strategies*, Innovation, Technology, and Knowledge Management, DOI 10.1007/978-1-4419-1185-8_5,
© Springer Science+Business Media, LLC 2010

services—that is, the competitiveness and/or public services improvement agendas. These drivers should define the special focus and priorities of e-development in a given country. For example, Malaysia strives to use ICT to secure knowledge-based competitive advantage in the global economy. Early development plans in Malaysia relied heavily on export-oriented labor-intensive manufacturing, but the country started to lose the competitive edge in this field to China. In 1996, Malaysia launched a program called "Vision 2020," which laid out a plan to build a fully developed, knowledge-rich Malaysian society by the year 2020 through the development of the ICT sector.

Best practices to guide the vision development process are to institutionalize stakeholder engagement, articulate ICT options for national development, assess and benchmark, and focus and prioritize.

Institutionalize Stakeholder Engagement

Stakeholder engagement helps to develop holistic vision and adopt balanced approach to the major elements of e-development strategy—such as policy, information infrastructure, human resources, ICT sector development, local content, and applications—for the benefits of society at large. It ensures that the e-strategy is realistic, sustainable, flexible, and responsive to the ever-changing environment and local needs. It also ease the implementation of the e-Transformation by providing opportunities for new partnerships, promoting innovative business models and implementation strategies, mobilizing local resources and communities for change, and strengthening accountability for the efficient use of financial, human, and technology recourses. Last but not the least, engagement of the civil society ensures responsiveness of e-development process to country's social needs and cultural diversity. Visionary and capable leadership, when broadly shared, secures the necessary recourses and government's commitment and ability to deliver on the adopted strategy and necessary reforms. Overall, mobilization of stakeholders, supported by dedicated and institutionalized leadership, builds momentum and continuity for e-development in otherwise fast changing and uncertain environment.

e-Transformation as a techno-economic paradigm, and as a model of interdependent elements, may serve as a shared frame of reference for public leaders, stakeholders, and reformers. To pursue their goals with realistic proposals and consistent actions, stakeholders should understand the characteristics and requirements of the ICT revolution and the relevant ICT-enabled development paradigm. A shared and holistic framework can also facilitate coordination and collaboration among stakeholders from all relevant sectors of ICT and the whole economy.

E-development leaders should engage major stakeholders in framing national ICT agenda and build a broad-based consensus and support for e-development. Most successful countries established some sort of *"Information Society Council,"* a high-level consultative body for development of the overall ICT vision, strategy and policies, action plans, and other ICT-related issues of significant public interest. It consists of all major stakeholders within and outside of the government, including representatives of ministries and agencies, civil society, the private sector, and academia. Such councils usually play an advisory role to the government on major policy issues, but also may perform promotional, benchmarking, monitoring, and evaluation functions.

To succeed, such councils should have high-level political support. For example, the Information Society Commission is an independent advisory body to Government of Ireland. The commission draws on high-level representation from the business community, the social partners, and government itself and reports directly to the prime minister (PM).

This vision should go beyond the confines of the central government and public sector. Most successful countries have used ICT-enabled development as a theme that unified central programs and at the same time promoted bottom-up and locally driven initiatives. An effective vision is developed and shared jointly by leaders from the public sector, private business, civil society, and academia. To the extent this vision is responsive the Millennium Development Goals or a pro-poor growth, it should articulate those areas where ICT can make significant differences such as employment, basic health and education, rural development, or targeted groups.

A nationally shared vision of e-Transformation should be further linked to the development visions various regions or states, to excite and engage local leadership. In large countries like India, China, Brazil, and Russia, it should reflect local priorities, resources, and capabilities. It should help stimulate and engage local leadership in creating its own visions and initiatives of ICT-enabled development, and in linking and adapting national programs to local ICT-enabled development initiatives. In some countries, like Brazil and India, state leadership and vision preceded the articulation of a national vision and the scaling up of connectivity and e-government programs.

Case: Korea's Informatization: Successive Visions and Stakeholder Engagement

Korea presents an excellent example of political will and engagement, combined with national priority setting, stakeholder coordination, and long-term perspective. It also presents rich lessons from its long journey in "informatization" since the 1980s under the leadership of the prime minister, presidential committees, and the relatively autonomous and highly competent National Computerization Agency (NCA). This model was a good fit to Korea's centralized and hierarchical political and institutional culture. Korea invested in e-government through a centrally driven allocation mechanism, after the country first invested heavily in broadband connectivity and ICT user education. It created robust legal and institutional frameworks. A key e-leadership institution was created, the National Computerization Agency, a relatively autonomous agency with special salary structure and incentives to attract a technically competent cadre of staff. It also created a number of high-level policy coordinating committees.

Korea's informatization can be largely described in five phases:

– First phase: National Basic Information System (late 1980s)
– Second phase: Korea Information Infrastructure (KII) Initiative (mid-1990s)

- Third phase: Cyber Korea 21/e-government initiatives (late 1990s to early 2000s)
- Fourth phase: e-Korea Vision 2006/Broadband IT Korea Vision 2007 (mid-2000s)
- Fifth phase: u-Korea or ubiquitous service

The first national IT plan aimed at building basic information systems in key areas such as public administration, finance, and education. Following such initiative, in the early 1990s, building the Korea Information Infrastructure (KII) was regarded as the essential factor for raising national competitiveness. From 1999 to 2002, the focus shifted to the Internet. This was also a time when Korea faced a serious economic crisis. And ICT was used as a strategic tool to emerge from this crisis. Building an advanced information infrastructure, raising national competitiveness, and creating new businesses and jobs were the main activities in the Cyber Korea. This phase also included priority e-government initiatives such as e-service center and e-procurement.

The fourth phase focused mainly on the utilization of infrastructure and technologies already developed. Broadband internet service was launched and e-government services were offered. This phase, characterized by the push for a knowledge-based society, was accompanied by a paradigm shift in 2005 to move forward to the next step: establishing u-Korea, or an intelligence-based society, in which ubiquitous convergence of human, objects, and ICT provide intelligent services and more convenience to all (Box 5.1).

Box 5.1

Multiple stakeholders have been engaged at the top leadership level. The Ministry of Information and Communication is in charge of formulating the country's ICT agenda, with separate branches of the ministry—such as the Informatization Planning Office, the Information and Communication Policy Bureau, and the Telecommunications Policy Bureau—responsible for the e-government and telecommunication fields, respectively. The Ministry of Trade Industry and Energy is responsible for the industrial aspects of ICT and for implementing programs that contribute to its growth. Since 2004, the Ministry of Government Administration and Home Affairs (MOGAHA) has taken the lead on e-government.

An Informatization Promotion Committee (IPC) was established in 1996 and has been chaired by the prime minister, with participation from 24 ministries and agencies. The minister of finance serves as its vice chair. The IPC and its executive committee are advised by an Informatization Promotion Advisory, run by private sector experts from industry, academia, and research institutions. The managerial work for the IPC is done by the Ministry of ICT, and since 2004, e-government managerial work is done by MOGAHA. A national CIO Council, chaired by the minister of MOGAHA, was also created to facilitate discussion among agency CIOs about policies, projects, and performance.

Since January 2001, a special committee for e-government under the presidential commission on government was charged with interagency coordination and oversight over major e-government initiatives. It reported directly to the president and thus enjoys great influence over enforcing horizontal integration. However, apart from political leadership, the core competency and driving force for implementing e-development remains with the National Computerization Agency (NCA). Originally, the NCA reported to the president, then to the Ministry of ICT and since 2004, also to the MOGAHA.

The NCA has been the public sector's IT consulting agency and responsible for the implementation of the country's e-government and the e-literacy and ubiquitous connectivity or u-Korea programs. Created in January 2003, the Korea Agency for Digital Opportunity and Promotion is a public entity created specifically to ensure that ICT services reach all sectors in the population. It targets the disabled, elderly, those with a low income, and sectors of the economy that are less technology-intensive, such as fishing and farming, and works to provide them with free access to information and communication services.

Korea's trailblazing e-government strategy has been centrally driven. It saw ICT as a source of providing a competitive edge in the global economy and e-government as a source of increasing national productivity. As of 2004, it achieved the highest level of broadband connectivity in the world, since it has been managing the shift from building the information infrastructure and promoting the ICT sector to changing the way government does business with ICT-enabled transformation. It has invested heavily in e-government to put the platform for many government to citizen services, present a unified portal to users, encourage departments to digitize content, establish the necessary policies and infrastructures for data sharing and data security, and define the legal status of electronic documents and online transactions.

Despite this rapid advance, particularly in building the information infrastructure and common e-government applications and networks, Korea now faces a number of challenges. A top-down approach proved valuable in making process changes that runs counter to vested interests. But pursued alone, a top-down strategy may not deal effectively with innovation and deep transformation of business processes. Although e-services have been made available, the adoption of those services by citizens and businesses has been lower than anticipated. Low take-up rate implies that citizens do not feel they are at the center of e-government efforts. To move to the next stage of e-government, the focus may need to shift from technology and automation to managerial innovation, public participation, information resource management, and social marketing of e-services.

The government has been developing its next-generation long-term e-government strategy (2007–2030). This strategy gives special attention to the development of an innovation infrastructure for e-government. The shift of e-government portfolio from the Ministry of ICT to Ministry of Government Administration, and thus the reporting of the NCA to the latter, reflects this shift toward managerial innovation and process transformation. The central agency is also giving increasing attention and incentives to encourage local governments to co-invest in common e-government projects.

Articulate ICT Options for National Development

ICT can support a variety of development goals. Fundamentally, it can help developing countries to achieve two overarching development objectives: sustainable growth, driven by increased competitiveness and ability to participate in the global economy; and poverty reduction, facilitated by both broad-based growth and accelerated human development.[1]

Competitiveness is served in two ways: by participating in the fastest growing global industry, ICT, which is also where the highest productivity gains have been possible and by diffusing and effectively using ICT in the public and private sectors and particularly among the large pool of small and medium enterprises (SMEs).

The ICT industry and ICT-enabled services present major opportunities for participation for many developing countries (Box 5.2). Since the 1980s, the ICT industry has witnessed a fundamental restructuring, from the vertically integrated corporations like IBM and DEC, to horizontal industrial structures, with many segments in computer hardware, software, consumer and industrial electronics, telecommunication services, information and media services. Many of these segments, especially software and ICT-enabled services, are not capital intensive and have relatively low entry barriers. The Internet of the 1990s further expanded these segments, diversified points of entry, and encouraged globalization and outsourcing in the industry.

Box 5.2 The East Asia Experience in Targeting the ICT Industry

Many east Asian countries have first targeted the ICT industry, particularly the hardware and electronics segments, for policy and institutional support

---

[1] Some may prefer the term sustainable development, rather than sustainable growth, to emphasize that current patterns of growth are not sustainable and that the aim should be for development that is compatible with the environment.

(Yusuf, 2003; Hanna et al., 1996; Wade, 1990; Amsden, 1989, 1994). In a decade or two, countries such as Korea, Taiwan, Singapore, and Malaysia have managed to increase ICT exports to constitute over 50% of their total export. China has sustained annual gross domestic product growth rates in the 8–10% range for years. By 2006, the Chinese industry had grown dramatically—to $579 billion (Gregory et al., 2009)

Earlier experience suggests the need to balance country aspirations for participating in the ICT industry, as innovator and producer, with the need to become an effective user of this all-purpose technology for the benefit of the rest of the economy. One pitfall is the excessive emphasis put on protecting and promoting the hardware segments of the ICT industry, at the expense of developing the software and ICT-enabled services, as was the case until recently in Japan, Korea, Brazil, Mexico, and India. Another pitfall is the exclusive focus on exports, to the neglect of local applications, local content and language, and local transformation of the majority of the population, as in the case of India. China seems to have combined development of the domestic market with moves into selected segments of the export market for the development of its electronics and information industry (Gregory, et al. 2009; ILO, 2001).

East Asia successes point to some common lessons concerning innovation and technological learning, particularly in the electronics and computer industries. They have given priority to technology policy, R&D incentives, and infrastructure. They committed themselves to high levels of investments in technical education, and financed, or induced the private sector to invest in advanced telecommunications infrastructure. They targeted the most dynamic segments of this industry for promotion and export, and sequenced their entry and systematically upgraded their capabilities toward higher value segment of the global supply chain. Governments acted in partnership with the private sector, promoting incubators, hi-tech cluster development, and knowledge networks. Such networks were linked globally through various means, including trade and FDI. These countries also mobilized their large diaspora for capital, technology, entrepreneurship, and market intelligence.

A second major thrust for competitiveness and broad growth is to *use ICT* in the most critical industries and services of the country, promote ICT diffusion among SMEs, and deploy ICT for modernizing government-to-business transactions.

Although it is up to the private sector to take the lead in leveraging ICT for growth and competitiveness, governments can influence and accelerate this process through various means—establishing the necessary laws and regulations for e-commerce and providing incentives for investments that would alter managerial practices and strengthen supply chains. But SMEs face major constraints to ICT use: awareness, expertise, access and bandwidth, technical support to adoption, relevant content, finance for such intangible investments, and complementary logistics to benefit from e-commerce. Such constraints have been recognized, even among industrial countries (ILO, 2001). Advanced OECD countries have since developed and financed substantial programs to promote ICT or new technology diffusion, particularly among SMEs. Many evaluations have been carried out of these programs, and relevant lessons can be drawn for developing countries (Hanna et al., 1995).

Government-to-business solutions (i.e., e-taxation, e-registration, e-procurement, etc.) increase the transparency and efficiency of both public and private sectors. By one estimate, SMEs spend about 20% of their revenues on transactions with governments, including accessing information and forms, applying for permits, submitting taxes, and complying with a heavy regulatory burden. An effective and transparent government is a critical ingredient in a competitive business climate and an attractive investment environment.

ICT can create new business opportunities and drastically reduce barriers to entry. Information technology application can lower trade and transaction costs by creating digital marketplaces to manage supply chains, automating transactions, allowing local businesses to access global markets, and improving intra- and inter-firm communications. According to Goldman Sachs, estimated cost savings through e-commerce even in "traditional" economy sectors often exceeds 10% (Brookes and Wahhaj, 2000).

In the sphere of reducing poverty and accelerating human development, ICT can assist the government to deliver effective health and education services, facilitate citizen to government transactions, enable public sector reforms, and promote participation and accountability. ICT, as a sector, can create employment opportunities and improve incomes for the poor by targeted programs to support the activities of the poor and increase their productivity, improve their access to market and technical information, and lower the transaction costs of small farmers and traders. ICT can play a major role in helping to monitor food security-related issues (weather, droughts, crop failures, etc.) as well as alerting on natural disasters. ICT is also important in supporting democracy, participation, mobilization, and civil values. Electronic interaction between government and citizens (providing citizens with access to the information and knowledge, consultancy, online voting opportunities, etc.) is also a promising area for e-development (Box 5.3).

Box 5.3 A Growing Array of ICT-Enabled Options for Poverty Reduction

The promise of improving citizen to government transactions (C2G) has inspired many governments to create one-stop services, such as Singapore's e-citizen, and to integrate electronic government into their broader public sector reforms. Even less integrated and more modest bottom-up initiatives such as land record computerization in Karnataka, India, have delivered land certificates in 15 min, instead of 20–30 days, and in the process, reduced transaction costs and corruption, created a viable land market, enhanced the creditworthiness of farmers, and improved the life of the common man.

A major opportunity for using ICT in poverty reduction is to provide information and knowledge to rural populations and to empower local development agents to serve the poor. A variety of informational and connectivity advantages can accrue to the poor through improved operational capacities of the specialized local agencies. One example is Chile's electronic rural information system which connected farmers organizations, rural municipalities, NGOs, and local government extension agencies to the Internet. It was estimated that transmitting information on prices, markets, inputs, weather, social services, and credit facilities cost 40% less than using traditional methods (Balit, 1998). Similar pilots and programs have been applied in Mexico. In Maharashtra, India, a cluster of 70 villages is covered by the "wired village" project, which is modernizing the local cooperatives, and aiming to provide agricultural, medical, and educational information to the facilitation booths in the villages (Bhatnagar and Schware, 2000).

Perhaps the area of most promise but least evidence of successful large-scale application is in the use of ICT to promote broad participation, grassroots innovation, and social learning. Telecenters or community information and communication centers can play several roles: provide affordable public access to ICT tools including the Internet; extend and customize public services, including those offered through e-government; provide access to information in support of local economic activities and learning opportunities; and connect and network people. The last function proved to be the highest priority for many communities who would otherwise have remained isolated. These centers have enabled them to carry out local dialogue, share practical and locally relevant information, and support community problem solving. Given the limited relevance of the vast amount of global Internet content to these communities, the role of these centers in networking and creating local content becomes all the more important. Community centers could also provide women with a medium to participate as producers, consumers–providers–users, counselors–clients. In South Africa, women's organizations are linked to various resource web sites which aim to mobilize women around common concerns. Digital literacy centers in Benin and Ghana have become an important instrument of empowerment of low-income communities, enhancing employability, increasing capabilities, and extending learning opportunities beyond those available in educational institutions (Fontaine, 2001).

Recent emphasis on poverty analysis and on mainstreaming result-oriented development programs has reinforced the need for relevant, reliable, and timely information for policy formulation and program implementation and adaptation. Smart policy and dynamic investment programs rely on access to local and global knowledge and timely information on implementation and impact. Lacking reliable feedback and timely information on implementation, development planners tend to rely on rigid designs, uniform top-down solutions, and limited participation—leading to slow learning and disappointing results (Hanna and Picciotto, 2002).

While options and opportunities for harnessing ICT for development are abundant and growing, local financial resources are not. A key activity of e-development strategy formulation is to articulate and select the strategic options most consistent with the overall development priorities of the country and to synergize among those selected. Engaging stakeholders and coalitions for reforms and broad-based distribution of ICT resources is a key to selecting and balancing those options in favor of equitable development and broad diffusion (Wilson, 2004).

A balanced strategy may be needed, particularly for large poor countries such as India, China, and Brazil. This would reflect the twin development objectives: sustainable growth, driven by increased competitiveness and the ability to participate in the promising fast-growing ICT and ITES industries; and poverty reduction, facilitated by both inclusive growth and accelerated human development through rural connectivity, ICT-enabled public services and SMEs, among others. India presents a case of an imbalanced or narrow vision where ICT options for development have been driven primarily by the ICT industry for over a decade—reinforcing the duality of India's development (Box 5.4).

Box 5.4 India: A Case of Unbalanced Development?

India offers many interesting lessons in e-development. Its rise as an exporter of software services and more recently as a destination of outsourcing services is well known, and many lessons can be drawn from this exceptional performance. These technological capabilities have been developed over time—due in part to early public investments in high-quality technical and business education (the Indian Institutes of Technology, IITs, and the Indian Institutes of Management, IIMs) and in building R&D institutions. Governments at the federal and state levels also financed software and IT parks to bypass their underdeveloped infrastructure and to provide incentives for small Indian enterprises as well as foreign ICT multinationals. Since the late 1990s, the telecommunications sector grew rapidly, spurred by reforms to open markets, introduction of global competition, and abundance of fiber access.

The dramatic success in exporting software services and IT-enabled services, however, has not been matched by the local use and diffusion of the new technologies in support of public agencies, small enterprises, or poverty reduction. This has created two India's—a globally connected knowledge-driven India and a disconnected, poverty-stricken India. The explosive growth of the ICT services (primarily for export) has been concentrated in large urban areas and has yet to bridge the huge gap between these two India's.

India's political leadership is recognizing the challenges and opportunities presented by globalization, persistent inequality and digital divide, the strength of ICT sector, and the emergence of new cost-effective communication technologies. The bursting of the .com bubble in 2000–2001 may have also helped India, as the US market for ICT services slowed down while the Indian market continued to grow. Thus, the Indian ICT industry had an incentive to turn to the local market for expansion and local adaptation. Moreover, there is a growing awareness of the rich grassroots experience arising from experiments to use ICT for poverty reduction and bridging the digital divide, initiated by progressive states, business associations, foundations, and civil society organizations. India has a large and strong NGO base and these grassroots organizations have begun to articulate the information and communication needs of the poor and to create affordable access and content to meet these needs—although most of these innovations are at a pilot scale and face major challenges for scaling up.

The challenge for India is to leverage its strengths, harvest local learning, and replicate local successes. To scale up and maximize the impact of various e-development programs, Indian leaders have to collaborate and coordinate across many ministries, levels of government, sectors of society, and non-government organizations. The low rate of literacy remains a fundamental barrier to broad-based transformation to a knowledge economy. The incentives to promote ICT applications for the domestic economy and to develop local language content are still weak and overshadowed by the export drive. Perhaps most lagging is the use of ICT to increase government efficiency and transform public services. Until now, most of the local pilots remain isolated success stories without structure for scale up and replication.

India has begun to improve its institutional and regulatory environment. Government and business are increasingly aware of the need to enhance the quality and relevance of higher education to ensure educational institutions are dynamic, demand-driven, and quality conscious. Many innovations in ICT training and ICT use in education are driven by private sector and civil society organizations, in partnerships with state governments.

A new governance structure is needed to engage the relevant stakeholders and make this paradigm shift. Inspired by the successful e-service initiatives of the state government of Andhra Pradesh among others and the urgent need to improve governance and the welfare of rural population, the government decided as early as 2003 to support a National e-Governance Action Plan (NeGP) and a Paralel program to create 100,000 Common Service Centers (CSCs). The CSCs are critical channels for the delivery of e-governance services in the rural areas. On the other hand, without e-governance services, the CSCs would not be viable or sustainable. The aim of these programs is for the federal government to partner with state governments and private sector to scale up successes, develop common frameworks and infrastructures for e-government, promote partnership between levels of government, and engage the private sector in the deployment of major e-government projects.

NeGP and the CSC programs are core elements of India's 10th Development Plan. The cost of NeGP is estimated at US $6 billion. The cost of CSCs is expected to be borne by the private sector and NGOs. Although both programs have been conceived in 2003, they had taken some time to gain consensus across government agencies at the central, state, and district levels, and among other stakeholders. As of early 2009, several institutional innovations have been under consideration by the cabinet to secure the requisite competencies, incentives, and partnerships necessary for launching and coordinating these programs. A continuing challenge is to make sure that CSCs and e-governance services come up and support each other, and that CSCs will become viable through a variety of local partnerships and by delivering a combination of government and commercial services.

These elements of e-development also build on earlier reforms and continuing progress in the telecommunication services, ICT education, and the IT industry. Perhaps software services export development and a few e-government initiatives in progressive states as in AP have represented unbalanced developments. But they also provided many of the prerequisites for the current scale up and progress toward more balanced e-development in the future.

Assess and Benchmark

E-strategy should be based on good understanding of local environment, e-readiness, and needs. Tools, methodologies, and indicators for assessing country readiness for the networked world and for participation in information societies and the knowledge economy have mushroomed (by World Economic Forum World Bank Institute; Specialized agencies of United Nations like ITU and UNDP; and OECD, 2000). But these assessments have not been effectively used for or integrated into an e-development strategy process.

Assessment, typically based on both quantitative and qualitative measures of the ICT infrastructure and its accessibility and affordability to the population, is known as "e-readiness." Broadly stated, e-readiness assessments measure a country's ability to exploit ICTs for human, economic, or democratic development. The e-readiness assessment process can help frame realistic projects and identify underlying issues of technical and human capacity that will need to be addressed in order to effectively implement e-government. However, e-readiness assessments cannot substitute for consultation with intended target audiences. Most developing countries have already undergone an e-readiness assessment—some countries have been "assessed" multiple times.

Articulating a vision of ICT-enabled development and formulating a strategy to make it happen must be linked to country e-readiness and country positioning in the global economy. Several methodologies have been developed and used by various organizations to establish rankings for countries, including the Knowledge Economy Index of the World Bank, the e-government rankings of the United Nations, the Growth Competitiveness Index of the World Economic Forum (WEF), and the Networked Readiness Index (NRI) of the WEF and INSEAD (Box 5.5).

Box 5.5 The Networked Readiness Index (NRI): What Does It Measure?

The NRI aims at measuring economies' capacity to fully leverage ICT for increased competitiveness and development, building on a mixture of hard data collected by well-respected international organizations, such as the International Telecommunication Union (ITU), the World Bank, and the United Nations, and survey data from the Executive Opinion Survey, conducted annually by the World Economic Forum in each of the economies covered—127 developed and developing economies in the 2007–2008 survey.

The Networked Readiness Framework, underlying the NRI and relatively unchanged since 2002, assesses

- the presence of an ICT-friendly and conducive environment, by looking at a number of features of the broad business environment, some regulatory aspects, and the soft and hard infrastructure for ICT;
- the level of ICT readiness and preparation to use ICT of the three main national stakeholders—individuals, the business sector, and the government; and
- the actual use of ICT by the above three stakeholders.

These tools and indicators are useful for understanding the initial conditions in the country, for carrying out global analyses and cross-country comparisons, for benchmarking countries against comparators and competitors, and for helping countries monitor progress. But they have been often used as end in themselves, with little connection upstream to the national processes and coalitions that are expected to shape the strategy or more downstream, to specific e-policies and programs. These assessments represent heavy investments in data collection and analyses that should be shaped by the practical needs of local stakeholders who could be mobilized to press for a national strategy. The indicators should also be refined and adapted to help design and implement ICT strategies and integrate them into the overall development process.

At the same time, assessments alone cannot provide guidance for e-strategy development. "The typical e-assessments that countries use in place of a framework function more as a benchmarking tool, pointing to broad areas for 'improvement' rather than providing a structure to develop a strategy." E-assessment cannot "substitute for a holistic framework" (UNDP ICT Taskforce Series 3, 2003). Assessments focus on needs and static analysis of initial conditions. A strategic framework should balance needs and priorities within a constrained environment. It should provide a dynamic and learning framework. It should help engage stakeholders and build coalitions to buy into the vision, to engage in downstream strategy formulation, and to set systems for monitoring progress and evaluating results.

One of the best benchmarking practices in the world has been conducted by the Office of e-Envoy in the United Kingdom. It not only compared the progress of e-strategy in the country versus its peers but also gathered and analyzed best practices and lessons learned from around the world, with heavy emphasis on e-government.

Focus and Prioritize

E-development strategy has to focus efforts, resources, and leadership attention on key priorities to be realistic, produce results, exploit synergies, create momentum, and ensure sustainability. Many countries, however, have vision statements that are "all encompassing in scope without being strategic or actionable" (UNDP ICT Taskforce Series 3, 2003). They avoid prioritizing and instead check all the boxes on the "e-development menu" at once, from "modern ICT-enabled government" to "vibrant and sustainable ICT industry." E-development process without a focused and realistic strategy will be hijacked by special interests and powerful ministries, or spread resources too thinly on many initiatives, falling apart into uncoordinated and unfinished projects.

The vision should provide guidance for the prioritization of e-development projects and programs best tailored for a given country. Yet, some general guidelines are useful.

First, the vision should help articulate priorities for ICT application within each sector and across sectors such as basic public services or thematic areas such as rural development, small and medium enterprise (SME) development. A vision that emphasizes an empowered and productive rural population, for example, would imply giving priority to rural access and connectivity, rural content, multipurpose rural information centers, rural entrepreneurship, and e-government applications at local government levels. Such a vision would also focus attention on the synergies and complementarities among these elements of e-development at all levels.

In promoting e-commerce, the Irish government identified that some segments of the value chain are more relevant than others to Ireland. It initially intended to focus on e-commerce services and utilities, business to business, retail, financial services, and, to a lesser extent, web hosting. For the longer term, it was anticipated that the majority of jobs would come from the infotainment sector, driven by the massive demand for good quality content. Ireland presents a country case that sets clear national priorities and targeted programs and thus launched its success story (Box 5.6).

Box 5.6 Ireland e-Development Strategy

Less than 20 years ago, Ireland was considered a "second world" country in Europe. In the mid-1980s, Ireland opted to focus on creation of export-oriented ICT industry that would work as a locomotive of e-development in the country. Since the country lacked necessary resources at home, the emphasis was on attracting inward investment.

After extensive consultations with the private sector, including multinational ICT corporations, modern information infrastructure was determined as the major pre-requisite. Liberalizing the telecommunications sector and building international connectivity became government's priority number 1. The next most important priority was ICT training and education, with emphasis on school computerization and introduction of ICT-related courses in the higher education system. Other priority measures in the government strategy included the following:

- Creation of favorable ICT-related regulatory environment, for example, common standards for e-commerce.
- Creation of favorable environment for FDI—low corporate taxes, competitive labor rates, a good telecommunications infrastructure, skilled labor and responsive government.
- Very active use of public–private partnerships, especially in areas of R&D, education, and ICT promotion.

Coherent government efforts paid off handsomely. Ireland became a world leader in software export. Inward investment by information technology companies has been one of the keys to Ireland's prosperity, and the country is now attracting large e-commerce and other Internet-related investments. Riding on the wave of booming ICT sector, the Irish government then was able to gradually shift its focus to full utilization of ICT by various sectors in the country, with heavy emphasis on ICT adoption by SME and e-government services. In this dimension Ireland is still not among the world leaders, but has advanced very fast.

Second, an e-development vision should place high priority on common information infrastructure and human resources needs and cross-sectoral interdependencies. It should become the basis for prioritizing, sequencing, and phasing, thus accommodating initial constraints, while exploring potential synergies and virtuous cycles.

For example, government's heavy investment in ICT higher education in India and Ireland allowed for the "production" of a great number of IT graduates; this contributed to favorable conditions for booming software development sector (also promoted by the government), which, in turn, created yet more demand for skilled labor in the country.

Third, an e-development vision should place high priority on projects that promote networking among key players in the information society and are capable of attracting private investments. More than ever before, it is important to explore networking opportunities among public sector, the educational system, the private sector, civil society, and other stakeholders. For example, governments can create favorable conditions for collaboration among business and the educational system. In this case, the private sector supports upgrading of the educational systems—in terms of curriculum development and practice—and the educational system meets the demand of business with qualified professionals.

Fourth, a shared and dynamic national vision should reconcile or seek synergies among competing visions held by various stakeholders and should adapt to major changes in the political context and global environment. In the case of e-Sri Lanka, for example, there were several narrow and competing visions of what ICT may contribute to the development of the country at the start in 2002. It took a deliberate process of engaging various stakeholders to shape a shared vision that attempted to balance the interests of key stakeholders and tap synergies among them. The emerging vision was inclusive and robust enough to survive a major political change in government. To remain relevant it required some adaptation to rebalance vision focus from one of enabling Sri Lanka to become a high-value service hub in a global knowledge economy, to one of delivering basic services to the poor and rural areas through a connected and reengineered government.

Finally, a broadly shared vision should create synergies between top-down initiatives and bottom-up projects and pilots. Such projects are often promoted by NGOs with donor support. These projects or pilots aim to deliver quick results, create local champions, and provide valuable lessons. However, going solely for tempting "low hanging fruit"—easily implementable pilots—often strains resources and diminishes national capacity to deliver on long-term, cross-sectoral, and more strategic projects. Priority should be given to pilots that support the overall e-development strategy and that are replicable, scalable, and sustainable.

Building Foresight Capabilities

In an increasingly globalized and competitive environment, governments, businesses, and communities are challenged to build agility and foresight capabilities. Governments, and more broadly, policy makers, business leaders, and civil society organizations at large often do not have institutional mechanisms to acquire knowledge on new ICT developments and trends and to discuss policy initiatives to respond to these developments. Visions and strategies are not based on a shared understanding of global trends and future possibilities—this understanding remains implicit and untested, typically left to international consultants. Globalization and the profound implications of the ongoing technological revolution lend special urgency to integrating futures research into the process of creating country development visions and strategies.

A number of countries have created foresight units at the national level—although very few have integrated ICT futures research into their foresight. Finland has established a Parliamentary Committee for the Future and conducted foresight forums within the Office of the Prime Minister. This may have enabled the leadership of Finland to anticipate the profound implications of ICT developments on transforming the economy into a knowledge- and innovation-driven economy. Similarly, parliamentary organizations house future strategy units in both Germany and Israel. In the United Kingdom, the PM brought together the performance and innovation units with the forward strategy unit to support strategic decision making of the PM and departmental leadership and identify emerging issues. Japan's unit is chaired by the PM and its members come from business and government. Some developing countries have also instituted this capability at the highest levels, as in Egypt's Center for Future Studies within the cabinet and China's National Development and Reform Commission (Glenn et al., 2008).

Futures research and foresight units for a country may act like a business intelligence function for a company—scan the global and business environments, develop scenarios of the future, use indicators and benchmarks to improve performance, and support and inform strategic decision making. The need for foresight in competing for the future is well established among the best-in-class corporations (Hamel and Prahalad, 1994). National foresight units may network with futures research and strategy units in business, government agencies, and think tanks, integrate and synthesize collective intelligence (using real-time Delphi method, for example), and use these inputs to improve vision creation, strategic coordination, national intelligence, and the public policy-making process. Examining ICT trends and innovation possibilities must be integrated into these units' functions.

Chapter 6
Policies and Institutions for a Knowledge Economy

Introduction

ICT-enabled development must be founded on policies and institutions that are appropriate for knowledge-based, innovation-driven, and networked economy. Development experience shows that the design and functioning of regulatory institutions strongly influence economic performance. Moreover, as experience has repeatedly shown, the long-term efficacy of the regulatory system in telecommunications as in all other areas depends on the avoidance of politicization and industry capture of the regulators, the acquisition and maintenance of high-quality management, and the continuous evolution of the institutions so as to accommodate fast-changing conditions and technological and market innovations (Kay, 2002). We touch only briefly on the regulatory institutions for the telecommunications and other information infrastructures in Chapter 9. We devote this chapter to crosscutting e-development policies and institutions.

Governance of regulatory bodies remains a challenge to both developed and developing countries alike, as demonstrated rather recently by the 2008 crisis of the financial markets. The transparency, accountability, and independence of these bodies must be established and improved upon over time as well as their policy-making and administrative capacities. Institutions, both coordinating and regulatory bodies, are central to the knowledge economy. Lessons are accumulating about the design and functioning of such institutions. Yet institutional and economic development research leaves us with little institutional design recipes. That should not be an excuse for perpetuating the current neglect of institutional analysis and design in designing e-development programs. Learning about institutional models, experimenting with institutional innovations, and evaluating their effectiveness are essential to effectively leading and sustaining e-Transformation.

In this chapter we first outline both the implicit and explicit policies for this new economy and the guiding principles that should shape these policies. Although closely related and interdependent, policies and institutions governing the telecommunications infrastructure are covered later under the information infrastructure. We then define the basic institutional approaches to integrate ICT into development and to govern the e-strategy. We assess the strengths and weaknesses of each model and emerging trends toward certain institutional hybrids and innovations. We

N.K. Hanna, *e-Transformation: Enabling New Development Strategies*, Innovation, Technology, and Knowledge Management, DOI 10.1007/978-1-4419-1185-8_6, © Springer Science+Business Media, LLC 2010

further outline the key design parameters and core competencies needed from central governance mechanisms and e-leadership institutions. Finally, we underline the importance of local governance and the kinds of partnerships needed between local and central e-leadership institutions.

Policy, Legal, and Regulatory Framework

National consensus on policies and plans can create the enabling environment for all components of the e-development process. Many governments have yet to create a dynamic regulatory regime and effective regulatory institutions that can create and sustain competitive markets, protect consumers, promote industry development, and take advantage of the convergence process. They have created detailed investment plans without first or simultaneously making sure that the policies that create incentives or remove the constraints for ICT use and innovation are in place. Lacking the policy and regulatory foundation, this situation often leads to expensive investments, untapped synergies, unsustainable programs, and poor development outcomes.

The type of policies needed for promoting the ICT industry and for stimulating demand for ICT use in the productive sector cover both "implicit" and "explicit" policies. The implicit policies are a subset of good development policy—open trade and investment regimes, and legal and regulatory regimes that promote competition and innovation. The explicit policies are a key extension and adaptation of the traditional development policies to promote and enable working in the new digital environment.

ICT policy development may start with an assessment of the "implicit" policies that create an environment in which the innovation and use of ICT could flourish. These would include trade policies and customs procedures, Foreign direct investment (FDI), credit and financial policies, competition policies, and other policies that promote flexible labor markets and efficient service sectors—especially telecommunications, finance, and distribution (IMF, 2001). These policies are interdependent. They are also similar to those advocated for competitiveness and private sector development in general. Other enabling policies are common to those needed to promote innovation, such as venture capital, entrepreneurship development, tax and other incentives for research and development and for attracting FDI, market-driven R&D institutions, commercialization of publicly financed research, university–industry research linkages, technology parks, and intellectual property rights (IPR). The United States exemplifies a government that focuses on these broad and implicit policies that unleash ICT innovation and diffusion.

In addition, more "explicit" policies are increasingly needed to deal with the special characteristics of this technological revolution and to address specific institutional barriers to ICT financing or adoption. These may include specialized venture capital funds, incentives for investment in intangibles, software technology parks, ICT-enabled service incubators, targeted recruitment of ICT multinationals for local production and training, R&D institutions specialized in ICT, and the promotion of open systems and standards. Silicon Valley, Bangalore and many other ICT innovation clusters point to the critical role of close interactions and specialized infrastructure and support services in promoting innovation in this highly dynamic and learning-intensive sector.

Government can be a leader in demonstrating the use of ICT as well as in setting standards and promoting a competitive domestic market for ICT through its purchasing policies. The public sector is a large part of the "modern" economy in developing countries and can play a leading role in developing the domestic market for ICT through policies and practices governing public procurement, such as outsourcing, competitive bidding, sharing public information resources, promoting open standards and open-source software, and emphasizing quality in procuring software and support services.

Policies and strategies for ICT should also address the special constraints that the public sector faces as an effective user of ICT. First, there is a need for regulations governing citizens' access to government information and services. This is a powerful tool, both a "stick" and a "carrot," to encourage public agencies to go online. Asserting citizens' right to access public information is then necessary through legislation, advocacy, and proactive changes in public sector culture. Second, there is a strong need for setting ICT interoperability standards and transparent ICT procurement guidelines and processes. In many developing countries, substantial and growing investments in ICT systems in government bodies are carried out on an autonomous basis. Aid agencies and ICT multinationals tend to reinforce this fragmentation and technological "lock in," to the detriment of both local suppliers and users. Setting appropriate standards could both advance government-wide service improvement and accelerate the development of the domestic market for a competitive ICT industry.

For the private sector, transactions over the Internet open a host of novel policy and legal issues. These policies span many areas such as privacy protection, certification processes, and regulations to ensure confidentiality and security of electronic transactions and financial data, and enforceability of electronic contracts and digital signatures. Other key legal issues that need to be addressed would cover: encryption (allowing the necessary technologies to provide security for e-commerce), electronic payment systems, computer crimes and electronic fraud, and regulation and liabilities of Internet Service Providers (ISPs) and Internet Content Providers (ICPs). The list of e-policies and e-laws is growing rapidly.

A Multi-layered Enabling Environment

In developing the policy, legal, and regulatory conditions to advance e-development, it may be useful to think in terms of a three-layered approach to the enabling environment and reforms (Guermazi and Satola, 2005). Such environment should enable

- Access to ICT infrastructure and tools
- Access to ICT applications; effective usage; and wide diffusion
- Consumer trust

The most basic layer is policies and regulations to improve access to ICT infrastructure and tools. It is dealt with in more detail in Chapters 9 and 10. Creating a clear and certain policy and legal environment is crucial to attracting investors, particularly foreign direct investment (FDI). Improvements in the enabling investment climate over the last decade have attracted substantial FDI for the telecommunications sector in developing countries, particularly in Latin America and Asia. Attracting such capital remains an extremely competitive endeavor. Meantime, involving community investment in and ownership of local infrastructure through public–private partnerships have proven effective in developing rural telecommunication infrastructure.

A pro-competitive regulatory framework should complement private participation in ICT infrastructure. A poorly planned regulatory reform process would scare away potential investors. Effective competition framework would guard against market abuse by telecommunications incumbents, eliminate barriers to entry, and balance the goals of efficiency and innovation. A future proof regulatory framework would also make it easy to introduce new technologies and services and remain relevant for new technological innovations. Thus, it should support broadband deployment and the convergence of communications, computing, and media, for example, by encouraging market entry by a full range of operators, embracing converged licensing approaches, and minimizing licensing hurdles.

Access to ICT applications, effective usage and wide diffusion requires coherent policies to create the enabling environment. Many countries have not yet moved their legal frameworks from ones designed for physical commercial transactions to ones designed to enable transactions over electronic platforms. Electronic transactions raise legal issues that are unique to the digital or virtual world. These range from acceptance of digital signature to the admissibility of electronic evidence. A holistic approach to regulatory reform should benefit from international best practices and harmonization of international and regional standards, but also adapt these models to local conditions and dynamics.

Building the enabling policy and legal frameworks for Internet-based transactions should be viewed as a dynamic learning process, subject to local adaptation, sequencing, and fine-tuning. This process should reflect the dynamic nature of the ICT industry and infrastructure as well as the fast pace, yet uncertain shape of the digital economy. Among leading countries, policy makers and legislators are giving increasing attention to a new set of policies and laws necessary to enable and promote trust in e-commerce, e-government, e-finance, and other aspects of the emerging "soft" infrastructure. Many of these laws can be adopted quickly, using some borrowed models and international best practices, then monitored and adapted in light of local experience (Box 6.1). Often countries move ahead with pilots (such as in electronic procurement), based on less than optimal or comprehensive laws and then use the experience to guide further improvements of such laws in line with growing local capacity to enforce and benefit from the new practices.

Box 6.1 Model E-commerce Laws

Among the legal areas specified, e-commerce regulation presents a special challenge to policy makers in developing countries. A number of Model Laws and other standards exist in the sphere of e-commerce, among them those prepared by The United Nations Commission on International Trade Law (UNCITRAL): Model Law on Electronic Commerce (1996, amended 1998); and Model Law on Electronic Signatures (2001).

Adoption of Model Laws is aimed to facilitate electronic commerce, adapt existing requirements, provide basic legal validity, and raise legal certainty. UNCITRAL Model Law on Electronic Commerce has been transformed into national law in *a whole or partly* in more than 20 countries, among them—Australia, France, India, Ireland, Republic of Korea, Singapore and Slovenia, Canada and the United States. Legislation based on the UNCITRAL Model Law on Electronic Signatures has been adopted in Thailand and Mexico (2003). EU Standards and regulations can also provide guidance for developing and transition countries (http://europa.eu.int).

Often, the definitions of e-signature and e-commerce *law/legislature* are used interchangeably, which often leads to confusion. E-commerce legislation applies "to any kind of information in the form of data message used in the context of commercial activities" (UNCITRAL Model Law on E-Commerce Preamble). E-signature legislation regulates only one particular aspect of e-commerce, i.e., recognition and effect to electronic signatures. Among other important elements, the law on e-signature should address the issue of contract formation, grant legal status to "electronic documents," cover the full range of transactions between businesses, consumers, and governments (B2B, B2C, C2C, C2G, and G2G) and specify the role of the certifying body. We cannot talk about effective e-commerce development without e-signature legislation.

The third layer is to create the enabling environment for improved consumer confidence and trust. As whole economies move toward increasing reliance on digital transactions, information sharing, and strategic information systems, privacy and security concerns take a prominent position in the enabling environment. The development of a digital economy is predicated on the security of electronic networks and protecting the privacy of users and consumers. Securing the integrity of data and infrastructure is imperative to user confidence.

Key policy issues that determine the trust and confidence in digital networks include network security; consumer protection, cyber-crime, and privacy laws; intellectual property protection (IPR); and dispute revolution (Guermazi and Satola, 2005). Many countries are developing cyber-security policies and local capacity to assess and manage cyber-security risks. This may involve the creation of national Computer Emergency Response Teams and related Computer Incident Response

Teams. To provide emergency alert and response services as well as risk analysis and protection of critical information infrastructure and critical government systems. Data privacy protection frameworks need to strike a balance between protecting privacy of individuals and preserving a government's right to protect the public interest against illegal and criminal use of data. Cyber-crime laws are also needed to protect data, computers, and networks. As the Internet enables low-cost, global dissemination of information, intellectual property becomes more vulnerable to unauthorized use. Finally, dispute resolution mechanisms need to be as speedy as the communication networks they serve.

The economic characteristics of information, knowledge, and digital content raise fundamental issues of public policy concerning IPR and competition (Melody, 2003; and Varian and Shapiro, 1999). The economic characteristics of the relatively high costs of establishing databases and knowledge services and the low costs of extending the markets for services already created provide a powerful tendency toward centralization and monopoly at the national and international levels. Yet, the value of the stock of knowledge in society depends upon how pervasively it is diffused in society. The economics of replicating, using, and sharing knowledge are extremely favorable for its widespread distribution.

This raises a central issue for the knowledge economy governance: how to reconcile maximizing profit in quasi-monopoly information and knowledge markets with the social efficiency of societal distribution at very low marginal costs (Melody in Mansell et al., 2007, pp. 55–72). The current application of IPR in software, publishing, pharmaceuticals, and all digital infotainment is directed to increasing monopoly protection and limiting distribution. Unless appropriate policies are shaped for the knowledge economy and the opportunities being opened by ICT advances, information and knowledge markets will thus continue to function inefficiently. This would lead to increases in gaps between rich and poor, within and between countries.

In this context of liberalized markets, government needs to mark out the domain of the public interest in public information and the digital economy (Melody, in Mansell, 2007). This may include Internet neutrality and universal access to Internet services. In addition, it would be the universal information needs of the public in the knowledge economy. As information and knowledge take on increasing significance, some definable set of information or "public information commons" would be essential to participatory development, inclusive knowledge economy, and effective democracy.

Improving the Policy-Making Process

All these policy frameworks require institutional mechanisms to formulate the frameworks, regulate compliance, and monitor impact. Policy makers must prioritize the development of these policies and regulations and address these issues progressively in line with the growth of their digital networks and capabilities. They should recognize that prevention is at least as important as resolution of dispute or quick recovery from system failure.

Beyond setting the substantive rules of the game, effective implementation of policies requires strong institutional capacity and independent regulatory institutions. A transparent and participatory process guards against regulatory capture. It also acts as a guarantee for private investors. The roles and core competencies of regulatory agencies should be clearly defined.

In leading the policy and regulatory change process, governments should engage the ICT industry, ICT users, and other stakeholders. Laws and regulations that were designed for an earlier and different environment now must be reviewed to ensure that they remained relevant and did not impede the development of new and innovative services for the digital economy. Governments should seek the views, concerns, and expertise of stakeholders, and when needed be guided by international expertise, standards, and best practices. Greater consultation can impact greater stability to sector policy development and at the same time generate confidence in the ability of regulators to act fairly and predictably.

Attention should be extended to the structural weaknesses of ICT policy making. Several factors contribute to these weaknesses. First, there is the low awareness among public leaders and legislators of the potential of ICT and its implications for all types of transactions and economic activities. Second, ICT policy making is not integrated into core public agencies such as the Ministries of Finance and Economy. As a new and fast-changing area, expertise in policy dimensions of ICT is scarce, particularly in the public sector. This is compounded by the lack of engagement of the expertise of the private sector and civil society. International ICT policy making can help by providing model laws, standards and best practices, but international bodies are also often biased by the louder voices and interests of advanced countries and ICT multinationals, as in setting the IPR regimes (MacLean et al., 2002).

Priorities must be set for developing and enforcing these laws—in line with national priorities and in support of the overall e-development strategy. Typically, the ICT industry has a strong local voice in setting ICT policies. NASSCOM of India is a good example. But the complementary and at times countervailing voices of local ICT users are not adequately represented in ICT policy making in most developing countries. Yet, priority should be given to those policies that focus on using ICT to increase productivity of established sectors in which the country has a competitive advantage. Effective ICT policies may not be on those which are directly focused on ICT production, but those which address the complementary factors facilitating use and diffusion. In addition, ICT policies may focus on supporting ICT innovation and local production capacity close to local ICT-using sectors— such as the development of local content, tailored and low-cost software, systems integration, Internet services and local support services.

A broad vision of ICT-enabled development could help build coalitions and energize the process of reforming the laws and regulations necessary to promote access to ICT tools, support electronic transactions, and create the digital economy. In Sri Lanka, for example, the e-development strategy that was initiated in 2002 has mobilized the policy reform process and helped passing into laws many of the e-policies that languished for years prior to the broad sharing of this vision (Hanna, 2007a). Similarly, NASSCOM of India has been a key player in promoting legal and regulatory reforms that improved a range of policies that supports ICT innovation and diffusion. As India's vision of ICT-development has been broadened and deepened, and more stakeholders from civil society and government have participated in shaping this vision, policy reforms have also accelerated and deepened to unleash the innovation potential of India and move it toward a globally integrated knowledge economy.

Institutional Framework

Many developing and transition countries have a history of unsuccessful attempts to deliver on their e-development strategies or initiatives largely because they lack adequate institutional mechanisms for their implementation. The crosscutting nature of ICT requires strategic leadership and strong coordination of e-development activities among key stakeholders and across many sectors.

E-development institutions may span many market institutions—to build a market for ICT production, maintenance, and services; for software and IT-enabled services; for ICT and management consulting services; for institutions to enforce intellectual property rights, etc. It may also depend on business support institutions to facilitate ICT diffusion among SMEs and support institutions to build capacity of NGOs and communities to adopt ICT and make access more affordable to rural communities and other target groups. The institutional framework for e-development would cover the regulatory institutions concerned with telecommunications, broadcasting, and other media. It should cover the institutional mechanisms necessary for coordinating ICT investments across government and the adoption of a whole government approach to an information society. It should certainly cover those institutions concerned with ICT literacy, ICT technical education, and the integration of ICT into all levels of the education sector and life-long learning. It would include partnerships with the R&D and innovation institutions that can facilitate ICT production, adaptation, and diffusion. It may even extend to those cultural institutions that should be involved in building trust in e-government and e-commerce.

But we limit ourselves here to the apex or umbrella institutional mechanisms involved in leading and coordinating the national e-development process rather than specific sector or component of e-development. The primary concern here is what kinds of institutions and instructional mechanisms are necessary to exploit synergies and take account of interdependencies among elements of e-developments, and to insert ICT policies and investments into overall development strategies and programs.

Strategic Issues in Designing e-Development Institutions

Countries have been creating various institutional arrangements to cope with the governance issues and coordination challenges posed by e-development—shifting from one model to another, experimenting with hybrids, and developing entirely new models. Still, countries share the same basic choices and considerations:

- *Integration with development.* What kinds of institutional arrangements are needed to integrate e-development with a country's development strategy and state modernization? What role should central ministries (finance, planning, or economy) play in the process? Which policymakers should decide on e-government investments that are congruent with national development policies and goals?
- *Synergies between e-development components.*[1] What kinds of institutional leadership and networks are needed to tap the synergies among e-government, telecommunications infrastructure, ICT literacy and human resources, ICT as a sector or core competency, and ICT as an enabler or productivity driver for all sectors of the economy?
- *Coordination across e-development components.* How should governments coordinate and balance e-Transformation within government and across the economy? How can the technological imperatives of building a common enterprise architecture be reconciled with the need to empower agencies and ministries to articulate their service priorities, implement their ICT-enabled service transformations, and integrate ICT with their sector strategies? How can public leaders achieve client-centered public services that span agencies and ministries? Beyond coordination, what incentives and institutional frameworks could encourage collaboration? How should e-government programs be sequenced and coordinated with telecommunications, connectivity, digital literacy, and other complementary elements of e-Transformation?
- *Degree of centralization.* How much should governments centralize or decentralize planning and decision making in e-development and e-government investments? What institutional arrangements are needed to promote both bottom-up innovation and top-down reforms and to enable scaling up of successful local e-development initiatives? Which elements of e-development are amenable to central direction and coordination, and which are best left to bottom-up initiatives and decentralized innovation? How can e-development institutions enforce this optimal level?
- *Fit with institutional architecture and capabilities.* How should new e-development institutions and capabilities be designed to fit with—or perhaps transform—a country's political culture and institutional structures? For example, what kinds of institutional arrangements and capabilities would be most conducive to building effective partnerships among government, the private sector, academia, and civil society? What role should be played by the ministry currently responsible for ICT? How much authority and autonomy should be given to a central coordinating ICT agency?

---

[1] For a treatment of e-leadership institutions in the broader context of e-development, see Hanna (2007b).

Institutional Options for Integrating ICT into Development

Institutional and governance frameworks are fundamentally about who makes decisions and who has an input about ICT policies and investments, the ICT specialists or the sector (education, health, public administration, finance, business) specialists. This is an issue that continues to challenge private sector organizations and much can be learned from their experience.

The business literature about IT governance in diversified large enterprises suggests a range of governance styles, ranging from a *business monarchy*, where IT decisions are made by business executives (CxOs), *feudal style*, where decisions are delegated to autonomous business or local units, *federal or duopoly styles*, where governance rights are shared jointly by business and IT executives at the corporate or business unit level, to IT monarchy, where corporate IT professionals hold the decision rights for IT infrastructure, IT architecture, and business applications (Broadbent and Kitzis, 2005).

While no one size fits all, top IT governance performers in the private sector attempt to balance pressures for both the synergies and economies of scale of ICT systems and infrastructures, on the one hand, and the autonomy of business and local units, on the other. They usually bring together senior business and technology executives for joint decision making for overall IT policies, major investments, and prioritization. The mechanisms used to implement governance vary, but they range from IT councils, composed of business and IT executives, executive committees, to IT leadership committees that bring together senior IT executives from across the enterprise. Governance styles should fit business orientation, for example, those enterprises seeking synergies across their businesses may require tight corporate coupling between corporate and IT executives (Broadbent and Kitzis, 2005, pp. 122–127).

Many advanced countries attempt some variations of the federal or duopoly styles, that is, to bring together senior administrators and CIOs or heads of ICT agencies for joint decision making for overall IT policies, major investments, and prioritization. The challenge for integrating IT decisions with business decisions thus goes beyond any specific institutional arrangement and may be sought through the blend of staffing e-leadership institutions with development and sector professionals besides IT specialists, creating policy councils and inter-ministerial committees, and creating a cadre of CIOs within the sectoral ministries. In a sense, all IT decisions are business, sector or development decisions as well.

Shared Responsibility Model

The e-development agenda may be divided among a number of ministries, for example, Ministry of Economy takes care of e-Business promotion, Ministry of Telecommunications develops information infrastructure policies, and the Ministry of the State or Public Services or Administrative Reform focuses on the e-Government agenda, Ministry of Science and Technology or Industry or Trade promotes ICT entrepreneurship and innovation, and the Ministry of Education integrates ICT in education and promotes ICT education and the appropriate skills for an information society.

This model does not challenge the existing responsibilities of ministries and thus is relatively easy and quick to implement. At the same time, lack of coordination and proper monitoring may lead to duplication of efforts and waste of resources. It may also hinder the creation of synergies between the various elements making up a comprehensive e-development strategy—such as e-commerce and e-government—since these would be undertaken separately and independently. Also, common information infrastructure, crosscutting services, and inter-agency projects may be difficult to implement.

Crosscutting Core Ministry Model

A crosscutting powerful ministry may take the overall lead on the e-development agenda. Usually, it is either Ministry of Finance (United States, Israel, Australia) or Planning or Economy (China, Brazil) or a combination such as in Canada, where the e-development agenda is divided between the Treasury Board (e-government) and the Ministry of Industry (e-Business and Infrastructure). In Canada, the Chief Information Officer Branch (CIOB) reports to the Secretary of the Treasury Board and also serves as technology strategist and expert advisor to the Treasury Board Ministers and senior officials across government. It is responsible for determining and implementing a strategy that will accomplish the government's IT goals, including managing the government's IT assets, leading and coordinating the government on-line and service improvement initiatives, and leading the government's IT professionals.

Working out of the Ministry of Finance facilitates proper financing and cost-effectiveness of e-development initiatives. On the downside, finance ministries may lack the necessary technical skills required for developing and implementing the ICT policies and investment programs. It may also focus on ICT applications in support of public finance and resource mobilization, cost-efficiency in government and economic growth more generally—but ignore priorities concerning equity, digital divide, and improved public service delivery.

Lead Ministry Model

Another model is to have a concerned sector ministry to lead coordination of the overall e-development agenda. One common model is the Information and Communication Technology Ministry (South Korea, India, Thailand)—closely associated with the e-development agenda. Working out of the Ministry of Trade or Industry also provides for the availability of competent staff to deal with ICT issues and to involve private sector stakeholders. Where e-government and information society agendas are dominant part of the e-agenda, the Ministry of Public Administration or State or Interior may take the lead in coordinating the agenda. In a growing number of cases, responsibility is shared with ministry of ICT concerned with connectivity and information society agenda and Ministry of Administration concerned with e-government and applications in general (Mexico, Egypt, South Africa). However, any single ministry may be too focused on its "profile area," i.e., Telecom for the Ministry of telecommunications, which creates imbalances in pursuing the broader e-development agenda. Plus, the risk of turf wars with other ministries remains high.

Designated e-Development Agency Model

To mitigate the built-in limitations of the "ministries" models described above, many countries create designated e-development agencies. Such Agency may be in charge of e-government, e-society, e-business/e-commerce, information infrastructure, ICT literacy, and the strengthening of the local ICT industry. The Agency would have a wide range of non-executive functions, such as the formulation of the e-development strategies and policies, the coordination of activities and monitoring the progress and encouraging stakeholders to exchange information, experience, and best practices through focus groups, workshops, seminars, and online tools. At the same time, such agencies increasingly enjoy a degree of executive power, at least in the areas of cross-departmental projects like government networks and joint-up service delivery. Singapore provides an example (Box 6.2).

Box 6.2 Singapore: An Infocomm Development Agency

In Singapore, the Infocomm Development Agency (IDA) operates under the Ministry of Information, Communications and the Arts. It is a single agency for integrated planning, policy formulation, regulation, and overall development of the information technology and telecommunications sectors. As a regulating agency, it formulates clear and transparent policies to ensure a fair and balanced competitive environment. As a developer of Singapore's ICT industry, it works closely with the private sector to create a vibrant business environment. Finally, it drives the implementation of the Singapore e-government action plan.

The e-leadership institutions of Singapore have evolved from separate domains to integrated and networked institutions. Historically, IT, telecommunications, and broadcasting sectors were governed by three sector-specific agencies under the purview of three separate ministries: the National Computer Board (NCB, established in 1981), Telecommunication Authority of Singapore (TAS), and Singapore Broadcasting Authority (SBA). In 1999, the NCB and TAS were merged to form IDA, under the Ministry of Communications and IT, bringing together the regulatory and promotional functions of IT, e-commerce, and telecommunications under a single agency.

IDA has also an investment arm, using equity investments to support IDA's vision and objectives. In 2001, IDA was moved under the purview of an expanded Ministry of Information, Communications and the Arts (MITA). This move set the stage for a more integrated policy approach to managing the converging ICT, broadcasting, and media sectors. In 2003, the SBA was combined with relevant departments of MITA to create the Media Development Authority, under MITA.

A host of support agencies also interact with IDA in support of its developmental role: the Economic Development Board; Agency for Science, Technology and Research; Standards, Productivity, and Innovation Board; and International Enterprise Singapore (promoting Singapore as SME hub and linking them international players). Also various committees have been created to facilitate coordination and technological convergence: the National Internet Advisory Committee, National IT committee, and lately, the National InfoComm Committee—each step moving toward higher level and multi-agency policy-making mandates.

Similarly, strong leadership has been central to the success of e-government in Singapore. All agencies are aligned to the e-government vision, under the e-Government Policy Committee, chaired by the Head of Civil Service, and assisted by the Public service Infocomm Steering Committee (setting directions) and Public Service Infocomm Review Committee (evaluating progress). The Public service Infocomm Steering Committee is also assisted by IDA acting as the Chief Information Officer and Chief Technology Officer, setting frameworks and standards, and managing central ICT infrastructures and projects. Permanent Secretaries of ministries, assisted by their CIOs, are responsible for agency-specific ICT infrastructure and services within their own organizations.

The "umbrella" e-development agencies are actively engaged in promoting universal access to ICT. "Experience from various countries (e.g., Costa-Rica, Estonia, Jamaica, Malaysia, and Thailand) has shown that, rather than giving the responsibility to an existing government office, such as the telecommunications authority, the ministry of science and technology or the ministry of communications, it may be more effective to create an inter-ministerial authority or committee that is directly under the presidency or the office of the head of the state. Such a horizontal body is better placed to address the crosscutting nature of the subject and the far-reaching impact of ICT in the country" (UNCTAD, 2003). A new body is also more likely to be more open to structural and administrative innovations.

To overcome civil service constraints and create agile, partnership-oriented agencies, some countries are experimenting with new models such as creating a specialized public corporation directly under the prime minister or head of state. Sri Lanka is one pioneering example (Box 6.3).

Box 6.3 Sri Lanka: A Public–Private Partnership Agency

A rather innovative approach to e-development agencies can be found in Sri Lanka. It combines private sector participation with the first model. The national Information and Communications Technology Agency (ICTA) functions under the prime minister and is charged with implementing the e-Sri Lanka initiative. Although ICTA is a wholly owned government entity, in effect it is a public–private partnership or corporation. It acts as a business entity and is staffed by experts from both the public and the private sectors and reports to the prime minister via a board composed of stakeholders from government, private sector, and civil society.

The major advantages of this model are that the ICT agency is freed from government bureaucratic requirements and possesses the required flexibility to swiftly react to changing demands. Additionally, it can more easily hire the required professional staff at competitive wages. Lastly, an active participation by the private sector ensures that the agency operates in a responsive and focused fashion and makes best use of scarce resources. On the downside, the lead time between the creation of an agency and its ability to deliver results may be lengthy and may be overtaken by subsequent political developments. Since the agency is officially not part of the government structure, insuring proper level of collaboration from all the government agencies may be difficult, unless reinforced by the prime minister's office and appropriate policy or cabinet-level coordinating committees and CIO's council.

Regardless of which institutional model is adopted, there is always a need for policy coordination at the highest levels across government, and even across all sectors of society, including the private sectors and civil society. To improve collaboration among all concerned government agencies, a *Ministerial Committee for e-development* may be created. It is a Cabinet-level office that provides ministries and agencies a framework for collective decision making on issues of common concern and performs e-development policy formulation and coordination function. The Committee is usually composed of representatives of the key ministers and is chaired by the prime minister. Especially in the smaller countries, such Ministerial Committee also drives the national e-government strategy, including integration of services across organizational boundaries, promoting the use of new online delivery channels, and insuring proper allocation of resources and procurement. In this case, it is comprised of the senior public administration officials most closely concerned with matters related to the modernization of public administration and e-government.

In Ireland, for example, the Information Society Policy Unit (ISPU), under the Department of the Taoiseach (prime minister), has overall responsibility for developing, coordinating, and driving implementation of the Information Society agenda in the country. While the Unit has predominantly a policy development and advisory, monitoring, and co-ordination role, it also has specific functional responsibility for e-government and, in conjunction with the Department of Finance, for submissions to the Information Society Fund. During a very impressive e-development leap in the 1990s, Estonia established the cabinet-level Informatics Centre to be responsible for both the development and the implementation of the country's information policy.

A variation of this institutional model was the Office of the e-Envoy in the United Kingdom. E-envoy reported directly to the prime minister and to two e-ministers: the Secretary of State for Trade and Industry (who is responsible for e-commerce) and the Minister in the Cabinet Office (who is responsible for modernizing government). The Office was charged with setting the overall policy, ensuring coordination across government, and monitoring the progress. It also had some executive powers to manage a number of cross-departmental e-government projects, such as a government intranet and Government Gateway portal. On top of that, the Office of the e-envoy had influence over the Treasury's financing decisions for ICT. To make the e-envoy more effective in advancing the e-government agenda, especially in terms of delivery of joint-up services, it is being transformed into a National CIO Office.

Overall, placing the e-development coordination at the cabinet level provides for high-level political profile to ensure that inter-ministerial rivalries do not threaten the progress of the ICT strategy. On the other hand, such policy coordination may lack direct influence over ministries and stakeholders. They are also rather vulnerable to political pressures and are susceptible to change if government changes. Combination of the direct access to the prime minister and ties to a powerful ministry with budgetary power may help to make the agency's work more stable and also increase its executive power and influence.

Since e-government is a crucially important and arguably involves substantial institutional coordination and transformation, a designated National Chief Information Office (CIO) has emerged in many countries. The idea of the CIO is borrowed from the private sector and is still a relative novelty. Its broadly defined role is to incorporate ICT into government strategic planning and business process reform. Since e-government intertwines with e-Commerce, infrastructure development, and other thematic areas, the National CIO Office has tremendous importance, transcending government boundaries. In some countries, the national CIO may be the chief of the ICT/e-development Agency. In addition to the National CIO office, countries often create CIO positions in major ministries and agencies, allowing them a significant degree of freedom. In countries with federal structures, such as India and Brazil, CIO positions are also created at the state and municipal levels. In this scenario, a special CIO Council under the National CIO Office is created to foster experience and information sharing and a coordinated approach to countrywide e-government solutions.

To balance operational and strategic responsibilities according to the local needs and culture, the exact responsibilities of the CIO vary significantly from country to country and cover roles such as policy and oversight manager, networking specialist, business change agent, operations specialist, interagency coordinator, or any combination thereof. Overall, however, CIOs focus on strategy and policy-related issues, which requires central direction. Their operational and management responsibilities are focused on projects crucial to insure interoperability and to enable seamless integration of ICT systems and services across agencies, leaving agency-specific applications and planning to individual agencies. CIOs are highly involved stake-holders in making policy decisions about the design and use of IT systems across government agencies. Unlike the technology departments, however, CIOs are not necessarily technically oriented. They are more engaged in planning, oversight of the strategic process re-engineering, and change management than with the fine details of particular technology solutions.

The above institutional models, countries that comes close to represent these models, and the advantages and disadvantages of each are summarized in Table 6.1.

Trends in e-Development Institutions

From our review of e-leadership institutions in over 40 countries, we discern some broad trends in the evolution of e-development institutions. First, there is a shift toward direct engagement of the president, prime minister, CEO, or a powerful coor-dinating ministry like finance or economy. This is done, for example, through the placement of e-development unit within the office of the CEO or cabinet secretariat or establishing a policy coordinating committee chaired by the president.

Second, countries have moved from ad hoc responses, informal processes, and temporary relationships to institutionalized structures to respond to the challenges of the knowledge economy and ICT-enabled development. At the outset of the ICT revolution or when national awareness was nascent, governments convened special task forces, commissions, and panels to advise them on the new directions to take. Typically these ad hoc bodies made their recommendations to relevant ministers or heads of state.[2] At that stage, the central message was to raise attention to the enabling role of ICT across the bureaucracy and society. Ad hoc processes were often used to reach out to key leaders and constituencies beyond government and to identify potential e-leaders and stakeholders for the subsequent institutions. Over time, these temporary bodies and ad hoc processes were transformed into permanent institutions and formal coordination mechanisms.

Third, the locus of institutional leadership and coordination responsibility for e-government programs has been shifting from the ministries of ICT to the ministries of public administration or interior. This reflects a shift in emphasis from technology management to institutional change and process innovation management. This shift has the potential of deepening the transformational role of e-government.

Fourth, many countries are opting for creating an independent and strong national ICT agency that reports directly to the head of state. These agencies tend to focus on policy development, governance mechanisms like 'whole of government' enter-prise architecture, and strategic investments that cut across many agencies. They often operate under a special act or civil service framework that allows them to pro-vide competitive compensation and attractive career structure and to operate in a

---

[2]The number of nations who turned to such task forces is notable: Singapore in 1992, The United States in 1993; followed by Japan, Korea, China, among others. See Wilson (2004).

Table 6.1 Models of Governance and Coordination for e-Development

Models	Countries	Advantages	Disadvantages
Shared responsibility model Distributed sectoral responsibility complemented with high-level policy coordination mechanism	Finland, Sweeden, France, Germany	Integrates ICT agenda with relevant sectoral ministries with least disruption to current structures of government	Functions well only in countries with strong traditions of political consensus, collaborative culture, and decentralized government. Does not provide for central push to overcome stovepipe mentality and build common infrastructures
Core ministry model: investment coordination Led by a crosscutting ministry such as Finance, Treasury, Economy, office of Management and Budget, or Planning Commission	Australia, Brazil, Canada (pre-2007), Chile, China, Israel, Japan, Rwanda, the UK, the USA	Has direct access to funding to enable control over funds that are required by other ministries to implement e-government and other e-development programs. Helps integrate e-development with the overall economic management agenda	May lack the necessary focus and technical knowledge/skills required for coordinating e-development and facilitating implementation
Lead ministry model; technical coordination Led by technical sectoral Ministry: Communication and Information Technology Ministry, Science, and technology or Industry	India, Jordan, Kenya, Pakistan, Romania, Ghana, Singapore, Thailand, Vietnam	Ensures that technical staff is available; eases access to non-government stakeholders (firms, NGOs, academia)	Ministry may be too focused on technology, telecommunications, or industry, and disconnected from administrative reform processes

Table 6.1 (continued)

Models	Countries	Advantages	Disadvantages
Administrative and technical coordination			
Led by Ministry of Public Administration, Services, Affairs, Interior, State or Administrative Reform for e-government, and by Ministry of ICT for connectivity and ICT industry development	Bulgaria, Egypt, Mexico, South Africa, Slovenia	Facilitates integration of e-government with administrative simplification and reform, particularly when admin reform is driven by political commitment at high level	May lack technology skills if exclusively led by administrative reform. Needs to share leadership with Ministry of ICT and perhaps others
Designated e-development Agency Model: Holistic Coordination			
Led by autonomous dedicated ICT Agency	South Korea, Singapore, Ireland, Sri Lanka, Canada (2007)	Creates skilled, agile, business-like, and high-performing entity that is relatively free of civil service constraints. Not dominated by the turf of sectorally established ministries	Vulnerable to changes in the authorizing environment and rivalry from the public sector

business-like manner—yet enjoy the legitimacy and authority of top political leadership. The shift to this model is driven by a growing recognition that e-development is a cross-sectoral, cross-hierarchical, and cross-industry process. E-government in particular is a major transformational process that requires political leadership, a holistic view of government, and ability to partner with non-government actors.

Fifth, as e-government programs take hold and mature, countries move beyond concern about the central agency and common information infrastructure to start organize and rationalize at deeper levels of government so as to fully integrate e-government into the governance framework and activity of each sector and agency. In the process, the role of central agencies also change from top-down solutions and common infrastructure issues to playing catalytic roles and leading scale-up processes. The aim is to facilitate e-government innovation at the sectoral, state, and municipality levels, institutionalize innovation and process reengineering, promote collaboration across boundaries, engage more stakeholders, and disseminate best practices.

Finally and more broadly, the components of e-readiness and e-development are changing over time, and e-institutions should evolve accordingly. As the basic level of readiness and information infrastructure is built, the emphasis shifts to innovation, human resource development, business process transformation, public–private partnerships, a holistically supportive environment, bottom-up participation, and other soft factors. E-leadership institutions have to evolve to meet these new balances and requirements.

Lessons of Experience in Designing Institutions

Institutional arrangements should strike an appropriate balance between centralized strategic guidance and policy setting, on the one hand, and decentralized systems and project development with line management ownership, on the other. Strong centrally driven agenda and high-level political support are essential for initiating e-development projects, but implementation of such projects will depend on the level of buy-in from the staff of the participating departments as well as the available project management capacity at different levels. Resistance to change at the mid-level of the government can be especially detrimental to e-government programs aiming at deep change or transformation. Thus, choosing an appropriate degree of decentralization and promoting ownership and commitment are crucial.

Building public–private partnership for e-strategy development is quickly gaining popularity in the developing world. Many transitional and developing countries have established coordinating and advisory committees, whose objective is to smooth out the inherent tensions between ministerial mandates and the crosscutting nature of e-development interventions. These competition and cooperation are typically managed through well-designed committee structures that create bridging and coordinating mechanisms between the players who decide change, create change, and sustain change in the bureaucracy. Such structures provide crosscutting perspective to take full advantage of ICT for service delivery and compensate for the traditional ministry-based approach to policy, investment, and service delivery.

They also allow securing the inputs of potential users of e-services and potential providers of crucial human and financial resources for implementation, e.g., private sector and civil society.

Policy makers should be informed about key institutional options that are needed and available to move from strategy to action, to deliver meaningful results. These archetype models represent options could be adjusted to suit local requirements and existing institutions. There is a distinctive trend, however, toward creation of dedicated e-development and e-government agencies with both policy setting and executive powers. Such offices seem to operate especially well when they have strong ties to an existing powerful ministry, such as Ministry of Finance, but draw on representatives of various key stakeholders and report directly to the prime minister. This model enables a collaborative approach to e-development, insures high-level political support and proper allocation of financial and human resources.

Effective interactions among e-leaders and among e-development institutions are essential to e-development. Social capital and enduring networks that link policy makers, civic leaders, academics, businessmen, and the media are critical to the diffusion of ICT in society and the overall success of e-development—far beyond the soundness of any single e-development agency. Social control of e-development goes beyond government agencies. Studies of ICT policy reforms and institutions suggest that successful countries have created a tight web of e-leaders and e-leadership institutions that cut across public, business, academia, and civil society sectors (Wilson, 2004). Such a web can act to stimulate the demand for sound e-development policy environment, the supply of necessary investments and skills, the coordination of interdependent actions, and the sharing of knowledge for design, implementation, and learning.

Trust, informal norms, and shared expectations are important in shaping this web of learning and governing organizations. Leadership is essential to creating the conditions for trust and developing tight networks that cut across agencies and sectors. During periods of major structural change, the contribution of good leadership is magnified. "Effective leaders provide the psychological and professional bridges between previous period of certainty and later periods of wider agreement."[3] Through their compelling visions, leaders provide meaning and direction in a chaotic world. They bridge boundaries, model risk taking and show others the future.

In sum, there is no single model, no "one size fits all" solution for governments looking to create an institutional framework for their national e-Development agendas. Different solutions have been successful in some countries yet unsuccessful in others. Broadly, however, the institutional setup should be able to address several challenges:

- Engaging key stakeholders to develop and implement a national ICT vision, strategy, and action plans.
- Developing a policy framework, laws, regulations and standards to enable e-government, e-business, and e-society and other applications.

---

[3] Wilson (2004), p. 93.

- Building high-level "executive" ICT function, responsible for the overall e-development process and coordinating multi-level (national, regional, and local) and cross-sectoral strategies and programs.
- Developing effective division of labor and coordination of e-development activities across various government agencies, including inter-departmental framework for collective decision making on policy issues of common concern and development of common ICT standards and guidelines.
- Creating special task-forces and funding arrangements for implementation of high-priority e-development programs that involve various cabinet departments and administration bodies, most notably e-business and e-government.
- Creating mechanisms for monitoring and evaluation of e-development projects across different government bodies and insuring accountability and learning for the whole e-development program.

Mobilizing Demand for e-Leadership Institutions

As a demanding transformational task, e-development requires mobilizing policy-makers to lead policy reforms and institutional changes, and mobilizing potential communities of ICT users to innovate and press for change. Leadership is perhaps the most critical but scarce resource of development. Yet, it should be viewed as a given or immutable constraint. Visions of e-Transformation can persuade and influence leaders. Policies and incentives can engender and empower leaders. Institutions can develop and multiply leaders.

Development experience strongly suggests that local demand and pressure from key stakeholders are necessary to create sustainable institutions (Box 6.4). As a relatively new dimension or option for development, e-Transformation should be institutionalized. But new institutions cannot become effective with adequate demand and pressure from key stakeholders. Strategies to mobilize and sustain this demand are therefore critical to enabling transformation.

Box 6.4 The Need to Build Demand for e-Leadership Institutions

Most successful institutional reforms have occurred when societies have generated strong domestic demand for institutions. In developing countries insufficient demand for institutions is the most important obstacle to institutional development (Fukuyama, 2004).

Effective demand for e-leadership institutions can be created by building business and civil society pressure for improving public services, generating employment, and bridging the digital divide. It can be nurtured by raising awareness among societal leaders and exposing them to international best practices. Citizens should be made owners of e-development programs. They should be engaged—through political leaders and e-government institutions—in shaping the kind of government, information society, and knowledge economy they should have and in realizing their shared vision (Stiglitz et al., 2000). The media can play a critical role here, as it did in the Republic of Korea and several other East Asian countries (Jeong, 2006).

Demand for new institutions or for reforms to existing ones is often time sensitive. When such demand emerges, it is usually the product of crisis or a major change in the political environment that creates more than a brief window for reform. There are serious limitations to the ability of external partners or donors to create demand for institutions and so to transfer knowledge about building new institutions. Thus such windows of opportunities should be anticipated and quickly captured.

e-Leadership Institutions at Local Levels

Strengthening governance and strategic coordination at the local level to promote e-development is on the rise. Subnational economies—particularly cities—are playing a central role in economic growth, competitiveness, and globalization, and hence efforts are increasingly directed at improving institutions and governance of the local knowledge economy. In many cases, local governments and local institutions take the initiative to improve their position in the knowledge economy. They help create shared visions, strategic networks, and integrated policies for knowledge-based or ICT-enabled development. They convene all concerned partners (public and private, internal and external) to jointly generate integrated policies and local initiatives to respond to the challenges of the global knowledge economy. They cooperate to create knowledge clusters, to improve their human resources and knowledge base, to modernize their digital infrastructure, and to build on their comparative advantages. This is increasingly the case among cities or regions within the EU.

Joined-up approaches of national and local/regional governments to e-leadership are also on the rise. Examples include the UK with the "Core Cities" program, the Netherlands with the "Peaks in the Delta" program, and Finland with the regional "Centre of Expertise Programme". Similar joined-up or federated approaches have been recently adopted for e-government programs, as is the case with the National e-Government Program of India.[4]

Leading states and cities have greater agility to pilot e-government services and seize opportunities in rapidly changing environments (Lanvin and Lewin, 2006). Accordingly, e-government program success will depend on institutional arrangements at the state and city levels, where most government services are delivered,

---

[4]India provides an example of the services provided by the central Department of IT at the federal level. The department diffuses and scales up successful priority e-government applications at the state level and adapts and matches central support to local state priorities.

pilots and innovations are conducted, and partnerships with central governments are forged.[5] The movement to decentralize government functions tends to favor the administrative coordination model of e-government, where e-government functions are assigned to the ministry of public administration and local government (or services, affairs, interior, state, or administrative reform). Central e-government institutions then become engaged in disseminating best practices across states and cities, providing matching funds for innovation in local e-government services, addressing common human and infrastructure constraints to local e-government efforts, and leveraging economies of scale across local jurisdictions, among other activities.

---

[5]The same arguments can be made for other knowledge economy institutions (Hanna, 2007c). Much of the experimentation, support services, and partnerships must be forged at the regional, city, and cluster levels where cooperation, competition, and institutional partnerships occur.

Chapter 7
Human Resources for a Learning Society

While ICT provides efficient tools for building a modern, knowledge-based economy, it is the quality of the human capital that will ultimately determine success or failure. Skilled human resources are a necessary condition for leveraging available ICTs and for re-inventing them to get closer to the realities and needs of developing countries. As discussed in Chapter 2, the implications of the ongoing ICT revolution for education and learning are pervasive and profound, both in terms of the demand for new knowledge and skills and the capacity and modes of supplying such knowledge and skills.

Consequences for human resources are not limited to ICT specialists and technology managers or ICT production. Rather they span all specializations and all ICT user sectors. They cover all kinds of economic activities in which innovation, collaboration, competition, and learning are enabled or enhanced by ICT. And the development of information society-related skills has to pervade all channels of education, learning, and knowledge sharing. Yet, surprisingly, e-skills tend to be the missing link in many national ICT strategies.

The emerging global economy and ICT-enabled development strategies will significantly increase the demand for e-skills. These skills will be needed in various ways in both the public and the private sector. They must reach policy makers and corporate leaders as well as knowledge workers and grassroots innovators. They will be of central importance to worker mobility, employability, and inclusion as well as growth, competitiveness, and entrepreneurship. Among advanced economies, the gap is growing between the demands for e-skilled workers and ICT specialists and the ability of educational institutions to supply them. Understanding the projected demand for e-skills, the current and potential channels of supply of such skills, the role of labor policies and markets, and the external factors likely to shape this demand–supply equation is critical to designing the human resource pillar for an ICT-enabled development strategy.

A country e-strategy should address four broad human resources development challenges:

(i) *E-literacy*, that is, developing the capacity of the population at large to apply and use ICT in their roles as knowledge workers and consumers.

N.K. Hanna, *e-Transformation: Enabling New Development Strategies*, Innovation, Technology, and Knowledge Management, DOI 10.1007/978-1-4419-1185-8_7,
© Springer Science+Business Media, LLC 2010

(ii) *E-leadership*, that is, raising the awareness and competencies of policy makers and business executives to set policies and governance mechanisms for ICT deployment in their organizations and the economy at large and to manage the consequent transformation toward networked organizations and economies.

(iii) *ICT education*, that is, strengthening specialized technology management education for ICT practitioners to plan, design, manage, and support ICT systems.

(iv) *ICT in education*, or e-education, that is, promoting the use of ICT to improve the quality of education and lifelong learning. This chapter takes each of these issues in sequence, while recognizing the interdependencies among them and the need to take a holistic view of human resources for ICT-enabled development.

e-Literacy: Public Awareness and User Skills

E-literacy may be viewed in the context of building human capacity for development. This means considering basic e-literacy as a key component of human resources development for the masses and education for all.

Public awareness of ICT potential and the widespread of e-literacy are critical to mobilizing the public's interest in reforming policies and institutions that would support ICT access, diffusion, and education. They help build demand for the country's ICT policies and ICT-enabled development strategies. Promotion and awareness campaigns should utilize a variety of channels such as television, radio, and road shows. Broad basic e-literacy is also essential to creating a critical mass of demand for public and private e-services. It determines the adoption rate and effective use of ICT and the Internet. On the supply side, ICT awareness should help mobilize financial resources and entrepreneurial talents to invest in ICT access, telecenters, ICT ventures, and local content.

This broad-based e-literacy was a core element of Singapore's national IT strategy: to create an "IT culture." A strong IT culture through heavy investment in e-literacy provided for dynamic investment in information infrastructure and advanced applications in government and business, moving the country toward the vision of an intelligent island.

The demand for e-literacy is enormous, particularly for latecomers and large countries. Should e-literacy campaigns focus first on the poor and rural areas where the private sector is unlikely to meet the demand without active policies and incentives? Should public efforts target or extend to the disabled and disadvantaged groups and those unlikely to be exposed to ICT through work or formal education? Should schools or telecenters be used as primary channels to promote e-literacy? Should broadband Internet access be subsidized to mobilize demand and build public awareness? Which popular public services and information needs should be prioritized and delivered online so as to promote broad-based demand for online services? What role should the mass media play?

These are difficult issues and must be addressed so as to prioritize and phase initiatives to build e-awareness and e-literacy quickly and effectively. Fortunately, most developing countries have a large percentage of young people who are quick to adopt ICT tools, to navigate the digital world, and to be part of the Net generation. This target group can also be used to reach the more disadvantaged groups such as rural people, the aged, and women.

Often civil society organizations, grassroots initiatives, business organizations, and other non-government entities are the leaders in experimenting and introducing ICT into decentralized educational systems. These contributions are typically not on a mass scale. But they represent innovative approaches and at times best practices from which governments can draw on for scaling up. The mass media can also play a key role in disseminating best practices and mobilizing resources for scaling up.

While designing awareness-raising and strategic communication activities, it is vital to advertise not ICT per se (a very common mistake) but its ultimate *benefits*. The messages should be about the development ends, not the technological means. For example, in promoting the use of ICT for agro-business or rural enterprise, it is better to frame it not as an "e-agriculture," but as a means to promoting efficient market access for small farms, or to increasing income of entrepreneurs in rural areas by establishing local market information networks. The primary focus should always be on the target users' problems and objectives. While e-literacy can be important in specific IT-enabled services, it is even more important to enhance employability, lifelong learning, and access to knowledge for all economic activities.

Enterprise-based training is increasingly needed for innovation, adaptation, and effective adoption of ICT. Yet, developing country employers tend to underinvest in worker training, and in turn tend to be risk averse and reluctant to adopt new technologies that would demand new skills and practices. These problems are compounded for SMEs as these enterprises are often the lagers in technology adoption. For them, training is unaffordable and training supply not responsive to needs. Broad-based training for ICT diffusion should address these needs and provide adequate incentives and support to broaden the base of users, particularly among the SMEs (Chapter 13).

e-Leadership: ICT Policy and Strategy Leadership

Developing countries need to bridge the gaps that often arise because of the change management issues related to introducing new technologies. First is the gap between ICT specialists and policy makers. Information system developers understand technology but not the realities of governance whereas officials and politicians understand the realities of governance but not the technology. A basic level of awareness and e-literacy is therefore needed for policy makers, legislators, opinion makers, and other public and business leaders. Second, e-development brings massive changes in employment patterns. Thus, preventive measures are needed to ease adjustments and avoid resistance to change, such as re-training and employment assistance. The more innovative and transformative are the uses of ICT, the more critical would be the need for e-leadership. Finally, most e-development programs have long implementation cycle, and policy makers need to balance active promotion of ICT investments with absorptive capacity and re-training programs for managers and impacted workers.

One of the serious problems for e-development in many countries is low awareness of the potential role of ICT in development among public and business leaders. Increasing awareness among the business community is essential to let the private sector play the role of catalyst and accelerator of innovation. The need to increase awareness among political actors is exacerbated by the political nature of ICT interventions. Government authorities and policy makers in a given country are the *porte-parole* of e-development, and their support is crucial in fostering ICT initiatives.

New qualities are required from business and public leaders, in the context of globalization and innovation-driven economies. E-leaders should have deep understanding of the policy, political, organizational, and social impact of ICT and of network-based competiveness. They have to become adept at managing knowledge workers, learning organizations, local and global networks, intellectual assets, and open innovation systems. More collaborative style of leadership will be needed. Change and transformational leadership is in increasing demand.

As e-government and e-business applications continue to diffuse, managerial understanding of ICT potential and governance has to be deepened. Leaders and business executives can shape the enabling environment for ICT diffusion. They also invest in the requisites and complementary investments in skills and process changes are in place to turn ICT investments and innovations into productivity gains. Lack of broad managerial understanding of the potential and prerequisites of the new technologies has been the key reason for failed ICT investments in both public and private organizations. But the problem is particularly acute in the public sector and in developing countries. On the demand side, executives tend to isolate and delegate ICT leadership to technologists and ICT managers and are not aware of the critical role they must play to integrate ICT into their business and development strategies. On the supply side, e-leadership training tends to focus on narrow technological and technical issues, to the neglect of ICT-enabled strategic and institutional change and human resource issues.

A special cadre of e-leaders is the chief information officers (CIOs). These business technology leaders have been recognized in advanced countries as executives in their own right and increasingly on par with other business executives or CXOs. The roles, functions, and profiles of the CIO are becoming increasingly strategic and less technology focused. The public sectors in same countries are catching up in recognizing and advancing the function and profile of these leaders. That is not the case in most developing countries, and particularly in the public sector.

In the business sector in developing countries, CIOs and IT managers are engineers with technical knowledge but without business management experience. They provide technology solutions but are isolated from business or strategic decision making. In the public sector, they are placed further lower down in the decision-making hierarchy, even when they are recognized as a cadre within the civil service.

Attracting ICT leaders to the public sector will require both substantive change in the profile and compensation of this executive function as well as its image and career prospects.

E-leadership requires a blend of core competencies. One broad categorization of e-leadership roles and corresponding competencies is illustrated for the public sector, ranging from the strategic to the technical (Box 7.1). This blend will vary depending on the level of a leader's power and responsibility in the organization. The blend and content will also change in view of the rapidly changing ICT. For e-leadership to be forward looking, current, and flexible, formal education needs to be complemented with lifelong learning and just-in-time peer support.

Box 7.1 Core Competencies for Public e-Leaders

As *top executives and business strategists*, e-leaders should be able to visualize the destination of information society, the results of an ICT-enabled development strategy and/or the possibilities opened by ICT for their agencies and countries. They should be able to build an inspiring vision of how ICT will improve mission performance and build organizational success. They should be able to interact with other executives and stakeholders to shape this ICT-enabled future and then communicate it to the rest of the organization or sector for which they are responsible. They should possess competencies in strategic thinking, strategic communications, and foresight. They should have a broad appreciation and domain knowledge of the business they are in—beyond technology. They should understand the big picture.

Also as business leaders and strategists, e-leaders should define the broad directions for the ICT road map and provide managers and staff with the tools and governance to travel and learn on their way. They should be concerned with mobilizing demand for change and for realizing the developmental results of ICT investments. They should shape and inform expectations for ICT-enabled enterprise. They should also understand the needs of their clients. They should be capable of inventing frameworks and creating environments that bring forth ICT-enabled possibilities in line with business strategy, national aspirations, and/or agency missions.[1] They should strive to bridge the digital divide and to build an inclusive information society.

As *change leaders*, the e-leaders are chief innovation officers of new business processes and new forms of organizations. They are also the chief relationship officers who enable the creating of new networks and work teams within organizations as well as new partnerships and supply chains across organizations. Working with other executives, they lead institutional change and inspire managerial innovation. They should have the competencies to

---

[1] For such leadership qualities, in general, see Zander and Zander (2000).

facilitate the evolution of current hierarchies into agile, adaptive, networked, client-centered, and learning organizations. They should lead process innovation and client-centered service integration and facilitate the corresponding changes in skills, attitudes, and culture. They should be able to create sufficient trust to break silos, build partnerships, and engage process innovators, change agents, and organizational development practitioners. They must have competencies in organizational development, process innovation, team building, network design and management, partnership and coalition building, and culture change management.

A user-focused e-government and seamless joined-up services can be very challenging and costly. Client-focus means changing organizational structures and processes and reallocating resources, and this requires change leadership. It also means changes in attitudes and behavior among civil servants. It can be a great challenge to achieve customer satisfaction while reducing the cost of services and making them affordable. It is up to e-leaders to strike the appropriate balance through process and service innovation and effective change leadership.

As *technology leaders*, CIOs are the suppliers and custodians of ICT resources. This remains an essential role of e-leaders and the traditional domain for chief information officers and chief technology officers. Public service constraints often limit access to technical talent with cutting-edge knowledge of new technologies, project management methodologies, and new approaches to systems development such as rapid prototyping. Also in strong demand are skills to engage policy makers and business leaders in defining systems requirements and process transformation.

Public CIOs are called upon to manage networks of ICT service providers and to engage in increasingly complex partnerships and contractual arrangements that demand current knowledge of the ICT industry and best practices. They should have competencies in outsourcing, portfolio management, project management, business case development, and information resources management. They should have broad understanding of the technological environment—the trends, the new wave of technologies, and the imperatives and the ways and means to secure open standards and avoid the risks of technological lock-ins.

ICT Professionals: Education and Training

A key component of e-strategies is the specialized ICT education and training necessary to build an ICT services industry and to deploy the new technology for improving public services and private sector competitiveness. Skilled human capital is key factor in applying ICT to both public and private sectors, in maintaining and operating ICT infrastructures, and in exploiting the information that ICT makes available. Moreover, education and training in ICT and ICT-enabled services has proven to be a significant generator of employment and economic growth in countries like India, China, Korea, and the Philippines.

International experience shows that heavy investment in engineering, technology management, and ICT-related education helps to create a positive spillover effect on the whole economic system. For example, Ireland's success in reinventing itself to become Celtic Cyber-Tiger has rested heavily on intensive investment in people and considerable emphasis on ICT education. Ireland has succeeded in creating centers of excellence in the domestic educational system that have attracted foreign investors to the ICT industry and supported growth and employment.

In many developing countries, the higher educational system is slow to respond to the ever-changing demands of the knowledge economy, especially in the fields of science, engineering, and technology education. University–industry links and other types of public–private partnerships can be utilized to increase the quality and reach of technical education and training. Blending business management and engineering programs is particularly relevant to technology management and the commercialization of innovation, and to exploiting the potential of ICT as a tool for managerial innovation and institutional transformation.

Continuing education and training of ICT professionals is also essential to e-development. Singapore, for example, provided 70% subsidy against the cost of continuing education of software developers. Government could promote university–industry collaboration in delivering innovative educational programs to meet the special and fast-changing needs of professionals. In Malaysia, the Knowledge-worker Development Initiative (KDI) monitors supply and demand of knowledge workers and partners with the private sector to meet the gaps. KDI is involved in training and internships for undergraduates and existing works and in adapting university curricula to make them relevant to IT sector development. In the process, KDI forms partnerships with companies, academia, and government agencies.

Public–Private Collaboration in Talent Development

Public–private collaboration for ICT skill development is on the rise, in part because of the relatively slow pace of reform of public sector education and training in response to the fast rise and dynamics of the ICT industry. The strategies and motivations of major vendors as suppliers of training should be taken into account in the ICT education component of the e-development strategy. For example, Nokia has helped build ICT training institutes in China and South Africa. Cisco, in partnership with the UNDP, is also active in promoting education as a means of narrowing the digital divide. Major software vendors such as Microsoft and Oracle are providing training around their products throughout the world. Microsoft has increased training output from 30,000 technical professionals 5 years ago to 1.2 million in 2008.

The courses are conducted in commercial classrooms in 1900 independent companies around the world. There are clear advantages to these certified programs, as reflected by the explosion in demand. But if workers do not possess the foundation skills and knowledge, their specific technical skills will become outdated quickly.

Private ICT Education, India: A Franchise Model

The private sector is playing a major role in ICT education and training for all technical levels in India. The National Institute for Information Technology (NIIT) in India offers a broad range of ICT training for individuals and organizations from entry-level e-literacy to advanced courses on state-of-the art technologies centers. It provides on-site, anytime anywhere, on-the-job or project-based training to clients in India through its extensive network of centers. It customizes its training to suit clients, public, or private organizations. It has training programs for individuals, working professionals, colleges, schools, and enterprises.

NIIT provides an interesting model for franchising large-scale, low-cost ICT training. It leverages the relatively low-cost, high-quality ICT education possibilities in India. It has an increasingly global coverage. It has become the "McDonald of ICT training" and Asia's number 1 trainer in IT. It offers learning and knowledge transfer solutions to 5 million students across 32 countries. The IFC and Citibank have invested in NIIT's student loan program. Using Citibank's consumer lending standards, the program is based on student's future earning capacity, thereby making loans affordable to lower income families. Using its established brand, NIIT has also partnered with global players, for example, with SAS to develop talent for emerging business intelligence technologies.[2]

Instruments for Talent Development

Human resource development interventions in ICT education and training should be guided by competitive analysis of the IT sector and its most promising segments. Of particular importance to many developing countries is the IT/ITES offshoring, covering IT/software services, BPO, and knowledge process outsourcing (KPO), and engineering and research and development services (Chapter 8). Interventions should be targeted at the right segments and right groups. For example, if the opportunity is in developing IT services, including R&D, then interventions should target engineers and technical specialists. If the opportunities lie in basic ITES, such as call

[2]NIIT (http://www.niit.com).

centers, and if there is large pool of generalist graduates, then training in languages of export markets and in other industry-specific skills would be opportunistic.

Countries can select and deploy many policy instruments to increase the size and quality of talent pool for offshoring. Expansion of higher education could include specialized IT/ITES institutions, using public–private partnerships. This may be augmented by incentives for international universities to establish local campuses. In the case of Singapore, the Industrial Development Board established training advisory committees involving industry participation and industry-based training schemes. Singapore's InfoComm Development Authority has also promoted global partnerships to develop and upgrade IT skills.

Incentives may be targeted to augment demand for ICT education through government-subsidized student loans. Governments may consider special incentives to encourage investment from local and international ICT training vendors. The talent pool may be augmented by tapping talent in specific areas via simplified visa regulations, as in the case of Malaysia and Singapore. Large countries like India may tap unconventional sources like unemployed graduates or junior college cadres and create bridge schools to provide short programs using targeted curricula for the sector.

Scaling up and expanding the pool over time may require some longer term measures. University curricula could be adapted and augmented by including IT-related and BPO-related skills, and complemented by investments in IT facilities. IT bridge programs would be targeted at the appropriate skill level—for graduates without technical training, it may include final year IT training and internship at software houses. For those with engineering training, a bridge course would improve understanding of software packages and Internet applications and other relevant skills to support consultative selling. Distance learning may leverage available trainable resources. Several states in India have taken some innovative measures, such as Andhra Pradesh's Institute of IT Enabled Services Training. AP has also partnered with GE so as GE would provide content and train-the-trainer support, as well as screening and placement of students, while AP would provide trainers and infrastructure.

The private sector should partner with government in devising and delivering these initiatives and in setting globally benchmarked standards. For example, ICT sector associations should engage their members in defining the skill gaps and communicate these requirements to the government and educational and training organizations. They may fund country-level skill assessment studies. They may also partner with government to fund or facilitate investments in relevant programs in the education sector. In the Philippines, universities partnered with leading standard organizations to maintain quality and align skills with industry requirements.

Targeted interventions can also support research and training to make them better tailored to the needs of local SMEs as users of ICT (Chapter 13). SMEs face special challenges in adopting and mastering ICT, and academic training and research institutions typically neglect these special needs. Many developing countries and their IT enterprises have been attracted to the offshoring opportunities, but neglected the potential of local enterprises, particularly their SMEs. An ICT-enabled development strategy cannot afford to neglect the special human resource needs of SMEs to tap the potential of ICT. Several developing countries have been experimenting with programs to link universities to SMEs and develop the human resources necessary to meet these special needs. Malaysia provides one example (Box 7.2).

Box 7.2 Linking Universities and SMEs for Human Development, Malaysia

Malaysian SMEs experienced difficulties in their research and training activities due to a lack of ICT skilled labor in the country. The Teaching Company Scheme (TCS), a concept introduced in the UK, was employed to tackle the issue. The program creates partnerships in which academics and students join with companies to contribute to the implementation of their strategies on technical or management side. The TCS supplements the SMEs' financial and human capital and allows students to get valuable hands-on experience. It also improves the links between public and private sector in the country—targeted to the needs of SMEs.

Talent development should extend beyond ICT skills to also include middle management talent development, through targeted programs to address ICT-related issues in human resource management, quality assurance, finance, and marketing. On the ground training and internships programs may be also promoted. Such practical training and on the ground observation are even more critical at middle management level. Country ICT associations may organize educational visits leading companies within country, and in leading nations which adhere to standards like Six Sigma.

Measures to secure continuous improvement of the talent pool may include clarifying qualifications, tracking adherence to quality by schools, and providing certification and tracking of ICT and ITES workers. ICT associations may take the lead in promoting common assessment tests for various ICT specialties, such as for ITES-BPO, and for accrediting specialized training institutions. For example, NASSCOM developed a common assessment of competence test for ITES-BPO for India. In the short run, this provides for a common standard for recruitment. In the longer term, it would lead to an alignment between education and employability, help trigger downstream educational and training initiatives to help increase the talent pool, and provide a marketing tool for countries to showcase their skill standards.[3]

Similarly, promoting credible and transparent accreditation mechanisms for ICT and ITES training institutions at the country, regional, or international levels can

---

[3] India's reputation in the software services was similarly helped, among others, by having many of its software houses meet the highest level of CMM quality standards.

ensure that training offered is of a minimum accepted standard. The accreditation framework should include assessment of quality of faculty, current curriculum, pedagogy, infrastructure, and industry linkages. Given the dynamism of this industry, such assessments and accreditation frameworks should be kept up-to-date.

For higher value niches of ITES, such as knowledge process outsourcing (KPO) services, globally benchmarked skills in the knowledge domain are also critical. For example, the Philippines has become an attractive choice for KPO for US financial institutions in part because the universities of the Philippines offer courses in finance and accounting modeled on the US General Accounting Principles. Similarly, Sri Lanka has become an attractive destination for KPO because of its large pool of management accountants certified by Chartered Institute of Management Accountants.

Leveraging the Diaspora

An important issue for ICT strategies is the brain drain and the increasing global competition for software engineers. The brain drain makes it more difficult to retain the very people critical for coping with the ICT revolution. Developing countries must find ways to stem this brain drain, and even reverse the process into "brain gain" by mobilizing the Diaspora for broader national development.

Diasporas can enhance the reputation of the home country and augment or complement the local pool of ICT professionals. In the case of India, Indian ICT professionals in Silicon Valley helped create a sort of branding of Indian software and facilitated various partnerships and outsourcing opportunities. Firms are establishing operations in both the United States—the front office—and India—the manufacturing facility. The worldwide network of Indian ICT professionals has also invested in skill development and has mobilized venture capital for ICT startups at home. The diaspora has had a significant impact as mentors, catalysts for policy change, direct source of returning talent, as well as investors and venture capitalists.

Similarly, the US-based diaspora from Ireland and Israel have been also fundamental to their country's external networking and software export success. Korea and Taiwan had long-standing programs that helped reverse the brain drain and mobilized their diaspora to develop markets and exploit global knowledge. Others like Singapore and Malaysia are aggressively recruiting ICT talent to build innovation-driven economies.

The promising role of the diaspora is particularly pronounced in the case of IT-enabled and outsourced business services for several reasons. First, unlike manufacturing, business services do not require large capital investments in machinery and infrastructure. Much of the investment needed is in the human resources. Second, as a relatively new industry in developing countries, business services face neither entrenched domestic monopolies nor trade unions. India's success is particularly relevant here since the fast export growth in software services began in this sector prior to and as a spur for the broad liberalization of trade and investment in other sectors of the Indian economy.

Governments can play a catalytic role by strengthening the diaspora network infrastructure capturing synergies and leveraging the diaspora talent (Kuznetsov, 2006). Activities include establishing a formal diaspora network, building on existing groups to aggregate this population's talent and capital, promoting partnerships and joint ventures with local SMEs, establishing an innovation fund to promote joint research projects, facilitating short visits and seminars, and involving the diaspora in reviews and reforms of innovation strategies, programs, and institutions. The effectiveness of such diaspora initiatives, however, depends on having the right incentives and an environment of political stability and sound economic management.

e-Education: Leveraging ICT in Education and Learning

There are several rationales for leveraging and mainstreaming ICT in general education and training. The most important is the pedagogical rationale. Information technology offers enormous potential for enhancing access and quality of education and training systems, and tapping this potential for education should be a critical element of any national ICT strategy or education sector strategy. The use of ICT for education can shift the focus from teaching to learning, from teacher-centered education to learner-centered and learner-paced systems. There is also a social or equity rationale, as ICT is becoming increasingly pervasive in everyday life, and integrating ICT in basic education would level the playing field, familiarize young students early on with ICT tools and digital networks and initiate them on a lifelong journey of learning and discovery. The employment and vocational rationale is also important: ICT-based employment skills such as networking skills, IT-enabled services, desktop publishing, etc. Finally, there is the catalytic rationale, as ICT can accelerate reforms in teaching methods as well as in educational management institutions.

The knowledge revolution places further demands on educational institutions, to modernize the curriculum at all levels, to integrate computer and Internet tools into learning and professional development, and to prepare young people for lifelong learning. East Asia has shown that technology orientation and content are as important as resources in improving educational outcomes. ICT tools and skills must be mainstreamed into all levels of education, including professional schools and management education. Industry leaders, business and public managers, and policy makers should understand the organizational and learning requirements to lead this technological transformation. This understanding is essential to educational reforms to integrate ICT tools into learning processes, curricula, and teacher training as well as the management of educational programs and institutions.

Universal primary education and literacy remain a fundamental condition for participating in dynamic and information-intensive economies. Literacy cannot be leapfrogged. Increasingly, this now includes digital literacy. Pilot approaches should be encouraged; comprehensive reforms should be built on what worked.

Countries are experimenting with promising approaches. In Brazil, an NGO is helping communities to develop sustainable "information technology and citizenship schools." Communities who apply and meet sustainability criteria are provided with technical assistance and training for instructors as well as help to procure and install initial donation of hardware. As a result of the NGO work with community associations, more than 35,000 school children in over 200 schools and 30 cities have been trained in basic computer literacy. In Chile, 5000 basic and secondary schools received computers, training, education software, and ongoing support from a technical assistance network of 35 universities organized by the ministry of education. In South Africa, School Net provides Internet services to local schools, including connectivity and technical support. The challenges of scaling up the impact of such pilots are substantial, but a national ICT strategy must build on such experiences and help increase their coverage and effectiveness.

Interest in and use of ICT in education is growing and substantial resources are being invested in this technological transformation. Yet, a growing body of experience in developing countries points to an apparent disconnect between the rationales most often presented to advance the use of ICT and their actual use (Turcano, 2005). The formal rationales are to introduce learning and teaching practices and to foster 21st century thinking and learning skills. Much of the rhetoric is about changing the teaching–learning paradigm: this represents the potential of ICT for transforming educational systems (see Chapter 2). But actual programs of ICT in education are predominantly for use of ICT in computer literacy and dissemination of digital learning materials. In practice, ICT is used to support existing teaching and learning practices (with new and often expensive tools). A key challenge is to bridge this disconnect.

An e-education strategy must be guided by a holistic vision of the priority needs and reforms of the education sector to meet the demands of a competitive knowledge economy and inclusive information society. It is not enough that ICT in education is aligned with the national ICT strategy. It should be also driven by a coherent education sector strategy. It should be driven by clear pedagogical philosophies. Currently, there is tension between traditional and new pedagogies: ICT can serve both traditional, transmission-type pedagogies (more effective in preparation for standardized testing) as well as more learner-centered, constructivist pedagogies, and measures of progress may be linked accordingly.

An ICT-enabled transformation of the education sector demands a holistic and coherent e-education strategy. It calls for a variety of enabling factors and raises important equity issues. Therefore, a holistic approach to educational reforms should be considered where ICT could make a fundamental difference or impact: teacher training, curriculum development, local content, reaching rural and remote areas, lifelong learning, as well as funding, decentralization, and accountability.

But a holistic approach to e-education is challenged by the fact that different parts of government are responsible for ICT in education policies in developing countries, with no effective mechanisms for consultation and coordination. In some countries, ICT in education is the purview of the Ministry of Education, while in others it is handled by the ministry of Science and Technology, Ministry of Communication and Information Technology, etc. Regardless of the locus, problems of coordination among the many stakeholders abound. Yet, successful ICT-enabled transformation of the education sector demands the inputs of many players: Ministries of education, labor, ICT, science and technology, Finance, and rural development, as well as academics institutions, NGOs, civil society, media, and the private sector.

Best practices and lessons learned are emerging, but with a few exceptions, they have not been widely disseminated nor packaged into formats easily accessible for policy makers in developing countries. Little documentation exists about scaling up of pilots and innovative uses of ICT in education. There are many pitfalls involved in e-education strategy implementation. An enduring problem is putting technology before education. A typical bias is toward hardware and connectivity issues and little attention to relevant content and teacher training. Lessons and best practices are emerging and should be systematically sought (Box 7.3).

Box 7.3 Integrating ICT into General Education: Lessons Learned

Lessons of experience and best practices are emerging, suggesting the following guidelines:

- Promote a comprehensive approach. Access alone is not enough to create a cultural shift towards ICT use. All the elements—hardware, software, internet access, teacher incentives and training, improved pedagogy, high quality online content and educational software—have to come together, in the same school at the same time, to be effective.
- Build a critical mass of trained teachers to develop sustainable changes in attitude towards ICT. The challenge of teacher training and support cannot be underestimated. ICT can enable teachers to transform their practices, given a set of enabling conditions. Providing incentives to teachers and administrations are necessary to integrate ICT into learning systems. In Chile, it was found at least 60% of the teachers in the same school have to receive training at the same time to create a cultural shift in the school towards ICT use. Training one teacher per school all over the country as was done in some other countries was a waste of money.
- Train teachers to move to new pedagogical practices and to create more learner-centric pedagogical environment, enabled by ICT. Teacher technical mastery of ICT skills is a necessary but not a sufficient condition for successful integration of ICT into teaching. The development of appropriate pedagogical practices is more important than technical mastery of ICT.
- Expose teachers (on an ongoing basis) to ICT and fast emerging educational applications to be able to remain current and select the most

appropriate resources. Experience indicates that even in the advanced OECD countries, few teachers typically have a comprehensive knowledge of the wide range of ICT tools and resources that are applicable to education.

- Create an unavoidable ICT environment. ICT has to be used in administration functions such that teachers and principal cannot avoid learning the new tools. ICT literacy should be linked to future promotion for teachers.

- Seek cost effective and sustainable solutions for the deployment of ICT. Long term maintenance, operational support and constant upgrading of ICT in the classroom and educational institutions can be costly. Even in developed countries, educational institutions seek private sector funding and in-kind contributions. However, public–private partnerships should be researched and evaluated to enhance their effectiveness and sustainability. Alternatives such as Free and Open Source Software (FOSS) may greatly reduce the cost of software procurement.

- Seek innovative approaches to content development. Digitizing and adapting digital content for access via ICT is a lengthy and expensive process. This is especially true for educational television and video production. This may have equity implications for using minority languages to disseminate content via the Internet. Despite the growing educational resources available on the Internet, experience shows that there is dearth of such resources in a format that is easily accessible and relevant to most teachers and learners in developing countries. Lack of digital educational resources that are directly related to curriculum and assessment of educational outcomes can be an important barrier to ICT use in education.

- Build partnerships with the private sector and academia. Private sector engagement allows for development of effective educational software packages, relevant content and training programs that are well-tailored to the local needs. University-schools partnerships help to improve teachers education and develop network of teacher trainers. Private sector and academia can also promote accountability of government programs to promote ICT use in education by administering an independent Information Literacy Test for teachers.

Source: Turcano (2005).

e-Learning and Lifelong Learning

There are three major formats of e-learning: self-directed, collaboration within a group, and guidance by an instructor. The last format can be further divided into direct e-learning, where computer-assisted networks are used to dissemi-nate knowledge from an instructor to the students, and indirect schemes where computer-assisted networks are used to disseminate knowledge between instructors.

First type of e-learning currently has somewhat limited potential in many of the developing countries because of limited connectivity. Indirect schemes, however, may be applied more easily and have a bigger impact and cost-effectiveness. It can address two interconnected problems that developing countries face. First is a "human capital gap"—shortage of certain skills among the population necessary to build the knowledge economy. Most often developing countries need knowledge transfer in business-related issues—marketing, finance, management, etc. Second problem is that local educational system is often unprepared to fill this gap. There are simply not enough good instructors who can professionally teach these subjects. Indirect e-learning schemes help to quickly build the capacity of the educational system.

Many developing countries have begun to exploit the educational possibili-ties offered by ICT-enabled distance education as a way to expand access and improve quality of educational services and to support adult education and lifelong learning. The Pakistan Virtual University (http://www.vu.edu.pk/) is a relatively recent innovative model that uses various distance education technologies, and partnerships with various "storefront" IT institutes all over Pakistan—some 60 locations. The Virtual University, Pakistan's first university based completely on modern information and communication technologies, was established by the government as a public sector, not-for-profit institution with a clear mission: to provide affordable world-class education to aspiring students all over the country.

Using free-to-air satellite television broadcasts and the Internet, the Virtual University allows students to follow its rigorous programs regardless of their physical locations. It thus aims at alleviating the lack of capacity in the existing universities while simultaneously tackling the acute shortage of qualified professors in the country. By identifying the top professors of the country, regardless of their institutional affiliations, and requesting them to develop and deliver hand-crafted courses, the Virtual University aims at providing the very best courses not only to its own students but also to students of all other universities in the country.

The University opened its virtual doors in 2002 and in a short span of time its outreach has reached over 60 cities of the country with more than a hundred associated institutions providing infrastructure support to the students. Pakistani students residing overseas in several other countries of the region are also enrolled in the University's programs. The Virtual University of Pakistan holds a Federal Charter, making its degrees recognized and accepted all over the country as well as overseas.

Other countries, such as China, Mexico, and Brazil, have been exploiting the educational possibilities offered by ICT-enabled distance education and created mega universities (Box 7.4). The success of such programs, despite the high ini-tial fixed cost investments, can be attributed to the large target population and thus to economies of scale.

Box 7.4 Examples of e-Learning Programs and Mega Universities

Even though comprehensive cost–benefit analysis of e-learning programs in the context of the developing countries is still missing, many countries are investing in this innovation. Particular attention is given to use ICT (including educational television) to improve the quality of mathematics, science, and technology teaching at secondary and higher levels. In China, more than 100,000 students graduate each year using distance learning programs. Mega universities such as China's TV and Turkey's Anadolu universities do not require that students live within national borders. The Open University of the UK had 25,000 international students living in 94 different countries.

The Monterrey Virtual University of Mexico (MTU) represents the new high-tech breed of open universities. It serves about 50,000 students from 10 Latin American countries. Using satellite links, the Internet, Videoconferencing and other technologies, the MTU imports and exports courses from other universities in Latin America, and delver services to diverse clients, including corporations. Mexico's *Telesecundaria* aimed to improve access to secondary education in rural areas, targeting students in 200,000 rural communities with populations of less than 2500. It was started in 1968, and by 1998, the program educated 15% of Mexico's lower secondary students. It uses broadcast satellite to provide a complete package of support to teachers and students in remote rural areas. Its costs are comparable to conventional schools in the more populated urban areas.

In Brazil, the State of São Paulo contracted the educational arm of the Globo Television Network to prepare a new *Telecurso* for its workers. In a joint venture, industrialists and Globo contributed to provide coursework to 500,000 learners at primary, secondary, and tertiary vocational levels (OECD, 2004b).

An open, dynamic, and nationwide lifelong learning system is a key building block for an ICT-enabled development and inclusive information society. Such a system should replace textbook-based rote learning with practices that develop a learner's capacity to learn, create, and apply knowledge. Key policy actions should guide a lifelong learning strategy: ensuring foundation skills for all; improving access to formal education; recognizing all forms of learning; optimizing resource allocation across sectors and over the life cycle; and ensuring collaboration among a wide range of partners (World Bank, 2005b). In addition, this system may adopt a modular approach, to codify and segment knowledge into modules or credit hours so as to favor the earning of qualifications at different stages in life.

Digitization of knowledge, distance learning, and other ICT tools enable lifelong learning systems to function and reach across the country and beyond. A national distance education strategy should be integrated with a lifelong learning strategy.

Youth and ICT

Demographics present unprecedented opportunities and challenges that must be integrated into strategic thinking about ICT for development. As of 2007, about 1.5 billion people are 12–24 years of age worldwide, 1.3 billion of them in developing countries, the most ever in history (World Bank, 2007b). In most developing countries, the number of young people is peaking or will peak in the next decade. These numbers can be a fiscal and economic risk—exerting unprecedented burdens on education and health systems and can be a constraint on growth. They can also be an opportunity as they will constitute fast growth in working-age population and contribute to falling dependency rates in most developing countries—a window of opportunity that may stay open for up to four decades. Investing in this "youth bulge" now is essential to succeed in an increasingly competitive and skill-intensive global economy. Even as countries struggle with basic needs, the global economy is demanding increasingly more technical and problem solving skills and lifelong learning. Investing in youth's e-literacy and knowledge economy skills should build the foundational human capital of the information society.

Young people are the main users of the new ICTs, especially the Internet and more advanced features of mobile phones and participative Internet (social networking). Youth account for 43% of all Internet users ages 15 and older in China, 50% in Armenia, 53 % in Bolivia, 60% in Egypt, and 70% in Indonesia (World Bank, 2007b). The cost of investing in the skills required to learn how to use ICT and to do complex processing tasks is less for youth. Also, long working lives mean that young people have more time to reap the benefits form such investment. With the rapid expansion in ICT and shared access solutions, young people are able to connect to ideas and people outside their communities and traditional channels.

Fortunately, youth use of ICT will increasingly matter for development outcomes and will have wide-ranging effects on youth transitions. ICT offers unprecedented opportunities to youth: harvesting worldwide knowledge, informing and educating inside and outside schools, changing the environment for learning, encouraging peer-to-peer learning, and offering new employment opportunities and second chances. ICT diversifies the opportunities and channels of learning though distance education. Close to 1 million students in higher education are studying online in China. Mexico's Telesecundaria program gives those finishing primary schools in rural areas a way to continue schooling without long travels.

ICT also broadens employment opportunities for youth and provide second chances for work for youth with disabilities. IT-enabled services and business process outsourcing offers considerable scope for future growth in youth employment in developing countries. Offshore employment is estimated at 4 million in 2008, out of 160 million (11% of all worldwide service) jobs that could be carried out remotely (World Bank, 2007b). Such employment acts as an alternative to migration. The average age of a call center employee in India is 23. Youth are also highly represented as Internet café workers, programmers, local language web site developers, and village telephone operators. New ICTs, including mobile phones, also provide information about non-ICT openings to youth. Many ICT jobs do not require mobility, and coupled with possibilities for telecommuting, this opens options for young people with disabilities (ILO, 2001).

Young people are extremely active participants in the global flows of migration. ICT can help migrants to stay connected with their home communities and with one another while abroad. Pre-paid phone cards and voice over Internet protocol (VOIP) calls lower the costs of connecting home.

In formulating a human resource strategy as a key pillar of e-development, governments may adopt specific policies to enhance the development impact of youth use of ICT. Priority may be given to ICT education in schools as well as the promotion and use of multipurpose telecenters for promoting e-literacy among youth. Government regulation can have dramatic effects on the incentives for private entrepreneurs (often youths) to set up telecenters and thus determine youth access. A key priority for governments is to ensure an investment climate that allows the private sector to serve the growing demand for ICT services. This may include easy entry and competition policies. Moreover, governments can reach youth through the media they use and stimulate demand for e-literacy by supporting local content development and providing public service content online. Innovation and experimentation to provide youth with the skills needed to take advantage of the new technologies will be necessary.

A Holistic View of Human Resources

The above discussion underlines the need for a holistic view of the human resource needs and the strategic implications for a national e-Transformation strategy. Human resource development is a key pillar that spans the skills needed to supply a dynamic ICT infrastructure and industry, and those needed to establish effective demand for ICT use and diffusion across all sectors of the economy. Moreover, ICT human resources and skills span all levels of education in increasingly knowledge-intensive and innovation-driven economies. Prioritizing, sequencing, selecting entry points and making other difficult choices concerning human resources will need to be based on the logic and dynamics of educational transformation and overall ICT-enabled development strategy.

For example, in India, ICT-related human resource development focused early and primarily on technical education and specialized ICT training, mainly to exploit ICT potential for exporting software and ICT-enabled services. Until recently, the promotion of e-literacy for digital and knowledge inclusion took a back seat. Similarly, an e-development strategy with a primary focus on an export-driven ICT services industry did not put much emphasis on developing e-leaders or educating potential domestic business users of the new technology for competiveness and globalization. Also only recently did India give much attention to the use of ICT to improve access, quality, and learning at all levels of education, for similar reasons. Rather, IT in education has been primarily focused on preparing the technical skills needed for the ICT industry. The overall logic of an export-driven and an ICT industry-focused e-development strategy provided the rational and entry points for the ICT-related human resources programs. A broad and knowledge-based development strategy or one that promotes social and digital inclusion would have provided a very different set of priorities and choices for human resource development.

Human resource issues interact with other elements of e-development to create either positive or negative cycles, and unless addressed, would reinforce the digital divide among regions within a country. For example, brain drain is a major issue in China as trained and skilled ICT professionals tend to migrate to the urban centers and the more developed eastern regions of China. Successful integration of ICT in development requires a trained and skilled workforce—precisely the types of workers who tend to emigrate. Not only are residents of more developed regions unwilling to work in underdeveloped areas, but few graduates return to rural areas once they get urban residency. One reason for the migration of skilled labor from China's rural areas is low awareness of the significance of ICT for economic development in the underdeveloped areas. Low awareness leads to low investment in ICT infrastructure, impeding further investment in ICT programs. All these factors drive away educated, technologically savvy residents from underdeveloped areas.

A key issue for a human resources strategy for e-development is e-inclusion. As e-skills take center stage in enhancing employability and lifelong learning, so does equal access to acquire such skills. This is a crosscutting issue for an e-skills strategy and should be linked to all key elements of e-development. For example, rural telecenters can play a key role in promoting e-inclusion through special emphasis on e-literacy. Integrating ICT into education, particularly at the basic level, is anther channel to promote equal access to e-skills. Targeted programs to introduce e-skills to women or disadvantaged groups can enhance employability. E-government services primarily targeted to the common man may also stimulate demand for e-skills. Similarly, e-trade, e-customs, e-taxes, and other ICT applications to induce transaction costs between business and government could also be used to induce SMEs to adopt ICT and e-commerce, as was the case with Singapore's introduction of e-Trade Net.

At a more microlevel, ICT-related human resources development investments should be linked and sequenced to support the broad thrusts of ICT applications in government, business, and the economy. Structural changes to public administration and business enterprises should be anticipated to incorporate ICT as a strategic function and enabler of structural transformation. Sectoral priorities may also guide phasing and sequencing of public investments and incentives to develop ICT-related human resources, for example, to promote the use of ICT in education, agriculture, and rural development, social inclusion, or to improve the business environment and promote the export-oriented sectors in the economy.

An e-skills strategy has to be based on sound understanding of the domestic as well as the global market for ICT skills. It requires understanding and monitoring current supply and demand and potential partnerships among public and private sources to bridge current and potential gaps.

Finally, an integrated e-skills strategy requires a multi-stakeholder approach, a shared vision, and a determined leadership. The preceding requirements cut across all sectors and levels of society. They imply many policy and institutional reforms. Educational reforms in particular tend to be demanding and highly contentious, as they engage many stakeholders and vested interests. These are unlikely to be enacted by decree or top-down programs alone. Leadership must be able to engage all major stakeholders around a set of shared objectives and strategic thrusts. Business and civil society must play key and complementary roles. Many ICT multinationals such as Microsoft, Cisco, IBM, HP, Oracle, and Intel are also interested in playing a role in promoting e-skills. The excitement about ICT and its potential to transform educational and learning systems may help accelerate such needed educational reforms, not only to rapidly develop e-skills but also the capacity to learn in a fast-changing information economy.

Chapter 8
ICT Sector for the Innovation Economy

Information and communication technology contribute to development in two ways: (1) as an enabler for the delivery of public and commercial services and a core technological competency for transforming all sectors of the economy; and (2) as an industry, a new source of growth and keystone sector of the knowledge economy in its own right. Chapters 4 and 5 have addressed the potential of applying this technological competency to transform business and promote grassroots innovation. This chapter focuses on the second contribution.

The two roles are interdependent. A competitive domestic ICT services industry is essential to support the country's capacity to fully utilize ICT in accordance with local requirements, reduce technological lock-in and dependency on international suppliers, and become active shapers of content and application. Local ICT capabilities are needed to develop digital content and ICT solutions, particularly for user SMEs, local communities, and the poor. A vibrant local ICT industry is crucial for the successful development of affordable e-government programs. Given the mutual learning and local interactions needed among ICT services suppliers and users, ICT use in business cannot diffuse and deepen to become a major source of differentiation and competitiveness without having competent local ICT services suppliers. These local ICT capabilities have increasingly become a critical ingredient in the development of green technologies and in implementing green development strategies. Meantime, domestic demand for ICT services can build a broad base for growth, learning, and exports, particularly in the ICT services and software applications areas.

This chapter addresses the following issues:

- Why is the promotion of a vibrant and competitive ICT sector a critical element of e-development? Why target IT services as a technology for mastery and innovation?
- What opportunities would the global sourcing of services offer to developing countries? What are the promising entry points?
- How can developing countries benefit from the ICT sector opportunities to achieve sustainable and inclusive growth?

N.K. Hanna, *e-Transformation: Enabling New Development Strategies*, Innovation, Technology, and Knowledge Management, DOI 10.1007/978-1-4419-1185-8_8, © Springer Science+Business Media, LLC 2010

- How can government collaborate with the private sector to create a vibrant ecosystem for the IT services? What are some of the promising tools and practices to promote the ICT sector as a major source of growth and innovation?
- What lessons can we learn from experience with developing incubators, software technology parks, and ICT clusters as platforms for dynamic sector growth?

ICT as a Dynamic Sector

This section reviews some of the specific opportunities and challenges that this sector faces in developing countries. The ICT sector as a whole is a fast growing, high value-added, global industry, with many potential linkages to the rest of the local economy. Both East Asian and OECD country groups have adopted active targeting strategies to promote this sector, and with significant results.

The current structure of the ICT industry allows for diverse entry strategies, depending on matching the strengths and weaknesses of each country to the opportunities and demands of each segment. Different segments (IT manufacturing, IT and software services, software products, IT-enabled services, networking and telecommunications services, content development services) often demand very different specialized skills and infrastructures, hence the need for focused strategies that match country strengths and weaknesses, with the opportunities and barriers presented by each segment. For example, India used its low-cost production of software engineers and large pool of low-wage English-speaking programmers first to do on-site low value-added, customized software services. Then, as it built up reputation and links to user companies, and as it improved its data communications links, it competed for customized software services. Ireland capitalized on its links to Europe and subsidiaries of multinationals to service their needs for software products, localization, and value-added services. China and Korea strengths remain in exporting hardware and embedded software products, which are less dependent on English or cultural proximity to the Western markets.

Despite a first mover advantage for countries like India, the options and possible export niches for many other developing countries have been expanding. The Philippines is leveraging its cultural proximity, high literacy, low-wage English-speaking manpower, and advanced communications to export ICT-enabled business support services. Tunisia is attempting to use its French language and cultural proximity to export animation and other multimedia services to French-speaking markets. East European countries and Russia aim to build on their traditional strengths in science and mathematics to export innovation-driven software products and R&D services. Confronted with the persistent decline of their traditional primary exports, several Caribbean countries like Barbados and Jamaica have targeted the ICT sector, particularly information services, as the source of significant opportunities for export diversification and FDI attraction. Their competitive advantages include high teledensity and low-cost broadband capacity, literate and English-speaking labor force, strengthened ICT education and training, and new institutional arrangements such as investment promotion agencies, industrial parks, and venture capital funds. Not surprisingly, many developing countries have considered promoting the ICT industries as a priority, in view of the size, fast, and potential growth, and the diverse niches and opportunities available to thrive.

Should New Industrial Policies Be Adopted?

What role should the state play in pursuing such polices? Experience with old industrial policy has been mixed, particularly in ICT manufacturing. Early national drives were not always successful, particularly when focused on the local protection of a highly global and dynamic industry such as computer hardware production. In the 1980s and the early 1990s, Brazil and many other developing countries tried to build their computer industries under protection, with mixed results. Similarly, several European countries had selected national champions in the ICT sector, but later abandoned these efforts. Lessons have been learned from such early failures.

However, the most prominent success cases have involved active government support of ICT industry, in partnership with the private sector. Several East Asian countries have produced the "East Asia Miracle," with spectacular growth of exports in electronics and ICT hardware. The World Bank, reflecting mainstream thinking, has chosen to interpret this experience as a triumph of market-friendly or market-conforming industrial policies (Yusuf, 2009). Key to the success of these new industrializers was that these promotion policies and programs were continually tested and adapted by exposure to international competition through liberalizing trade and allowing weak performers to fail. In many cases, the state played an activist role in helping the promising ICT sector to pursue technological learning and acquire a competitive advantage.

More recently, success cases in software, IT services, and ITES have been catalyzed by government policies such as partnering with private sector to develop software incubators, IT parks, and cluster development; enhancing the quality of technical education and telecommunications infrastructure; empowering industry promotion institutions; and developing a host of polices and regulatory reforms to improve the business environment for such dynamic industries.

Much can be learned from the experience of these highly successful industrializers (Rodrik, 2007; Hanna et al., 1996). The hallmark of development is structural change and this process is far from an automatic one. Effective industrial policy is about coordinating actions and resources to stimulate investments and entrepreneurship in new and socially profitable activities. It is a coordination device to leverage

economies of scale and inter-industry linkages. The new industrial policy literature is beginning to bridge the gap by explaining industrial policy as a process to
relax binding constraints and facilitate the experimentation, clustering, learning, and
self-discovery of private sector actors. It focuses on public policies and search networks that are tailored to promote industrial innovation and successively identify
binding constraints and then the actors or institutions that help mitigate these constraints. It is a process of strategic collaboration between the public and private
sectors, with the aim to identify opportunities, linkages, and blockages to new activities, investments, and capabilities and to design appropriate policies in response
(Rodrik, 2007).

East Asia successes point to some common lessons concerning innovation and
technological learning in the ICT industries. East Asian countries have taken the
lead in implementing industrial and innovation policies and ICT strategy processes
which actively targeted segments of the ICT industry for systematic technological deepening, diffusion, and exports (Yusuf, 2003; Hanna et al., 1996). They have
given priority to technology policy, R&D incentives, and infrastructure. They committed themselves to high levels of investments in technical education, and financed,
or induced the private sector to invest in advanced telecommunications infrastructure. They targeted the most dynamic segments of this industry for promotion and
export, sequenced their entry, and systematically upgraded their capabilities toward
higher value segments of the global supply chain. Governments acted in partnership
with the private sector, promoting incubators, hi-tech cluster development, and local
knowledge networks. Such networks were linked globally through various means,
including trade and FDI. These countries also mobilized their large diasporas for
capital, technology, entrepreneurship, and market intelligence. As a result, those
countries with active targeting strategies in this sector had the most outstanding
economic growth (Lall, 2003).

Would this proactive approach mean that the government is "picking winners"?
Not in terms of picking single companies or national champions. But, yes in terms
of targeting this sector (or segments) for its special characteristics and promises, and
where there is a presumption of comparative advantage. Developing countries can
no longer rely on selling generic skills such as low-cost labor as a source of comparative advantage (Porter, 1990). To reduce the risks and improve the impact of
targeting the ICT industry for promotion and focused efforts, governments should
work closely with the private sector to identify target market opportunities, match
specific niches to comparative advantage, systematically assess current constraints,
and jointly devise polices and programs to develop the industry and exploit market
niches. Under such conditions, it is important that such industrial policies would
be pursued with clarity about the merits and impact of IT/ITES offshoring and
the opportunity costs, as well as with flexibility to be quick to revise or reverse
course if the intended results do not materialize. Instruments used to implement
such polices must allow for agility, learning, and continued adaptation in light of
experience.

To further reduce the risks, a proactive approach may start with "no regret" policies that can create positive externalities beyond this sector, such as investing in

technical education and industry–academic partnerships, contributing land as equity for IT or science and technology parks, inducing the development of broadband infrastructure, setting policies to engender trust in digital transactions such as data security and privacy protection, and promoting venture capital industry. These are "no-regret" interventions that could be tailored to context and to the benefit of other sectors of the economy.

The author was a participant in a debate about industrial policy at the World Bank in the early 1990s when he proposed assistance to India, targeted at the IT industry, first in terms of a modest technical assistance to formulate programs to promote software export and later to provide comprehensive assistance to promote the sector and the use of IT in government and business. The first technical assistance was pursued successfully with NASSCOM. It provided much needed visibility for India's nascent IT services capabilities and for policy makers to recognize the size of the opportunity and thus pursue several policy reforms and promotional efforts for the industry. But the follow on proposal for a major assistance program was resisted by management and mainstream economists at the World Bank. At the time, such assistance was denied on the grounds it would amount to encouraging the adoption of industrial policy. Although widely practiced and proved successful in East Asia, this policy posture was then strongly resisted at the Bank. Such a posture has been consistent with the typical risk-averse positions of many aid agencies. Thus, India pursued this opportunity independently and as a result provided an inspiring model for other developing countries in exporting IT/ITES services.

Potential of the Services Offshoring Revolution

Estimates of global onshore and offshore ITES–BPO markets and of country participation vary. An overview of the ITES–BPO industry (Box 8.1) shows the size of both the onshore and the offshore market, and the sizable share taken by India and Philippines. India is by far the global leader in the provision of IT services and ITES. China, Mexico, and the Philippines have also done well and many others are following fast.

Box 8.1 Global ITES–BPO Industry Overview

According to recent industry estimates, the global ITES–BPO market, including both onshore and offshore activity, stood at USD 423 billion[1] in 2006 and is expected to grow at 10 percent to about USD 750 billion[2] by 2012.

---

[1] NASSCOM Strategic Review 2007.

The Americas account for nearly two-thirds of the global spend on BPO. North America individually constitutes the largest market accounting for over 60 percent of the total ITES–BPO industry, growing at nearly 10 percent in 2006.

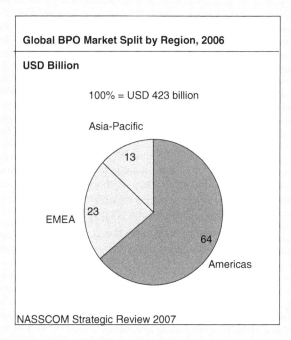

Europe, Middle East and Africa (EMEA) account for about 22 percent market share, with Western Europe accounting for over 95 percent of the regional market. Regional growth for this market as estimated at about 9 percent in 2006.

Asia Pacific, in contrast, represents a relatively nascent market for BPO with a share of about 13 percent; however, it is the fastest growing market with regional growth estimated at over 20 percent in 2006.

Within the global outsourcing opportunity, the global business process offshoring market stood at about USD 28 billion in 2007. Global delivery from multiple locations across regions is a relatively recent trend, gaining prominence overtime.

---

[2]NASSCOM-Everest Study 2008.

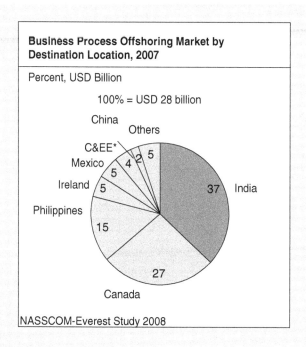

Business Process Offshoring Market by Destination Location, 2007

Percent, USD Billion

100% = USD 28 billion

NASSCOM-Everest Study 2008

There is a significant focus in most developing countries, world over, to encourage the growth of ITES–BPO industry. With a share of 37 percent of the overall business process offshoring market, India has emerged as the leading destination both in terms of breadth and depth within the offshoring related space.

Source: McKinsey (2008)

A number of countries have promoted IT/ITES and this led to substantial exports, job creation, increased income per capita, and increased foreign direct investment. India, the biggest beneficiary of this opportunity, generated export revenues over $40 billion in IT services and ITES in 2007 that contributed about one-quarter of the country's total exports and about half of service exports (World Bank, 2009b, p.7). In addition, India produced $8 billion of domestic software services (Popkin and Iyengar, 2007; Mckinsey, 2008). India employed 1.6 million people directly in its IT and IT-enabled services sector and is expected to create direct employment for 2.3 million by 2010. These jobs employ 50–100% more in indirect jobs than comparable service jobs. With a multiplier of three indirect jobs for every one IT job, an estimated 6.5 million employed people will be engaged in the offshore IT/ITES services by 2010.

Entry Strategies to Global Markets

Countries and enterprises must strategically engage and choose their niches in a very dynamic and globally competitive ICT sector. Many East Asian countries, particularly China, Taiwan, Malaysia, and Korea, have focused on the hardware segments and have dynamically moved up the value chain in the face of fierce global competition.

To illustrate, India, Ireland, and Israel have taken very different paths in developing their software services exports (Tessler et al., 2003). These are major successful exporters of software (Table 8.1). Each of these countries had a different set of goals in developing its software capacity, each started with dramatically different

Table 8.1 Contrasting Early Strategies of Three Major Exporters of Software

	Ireland (started in the early 1970s)	Israel (the early 1980s)	India (late 1980s)
Resources	English-speaking workforce; European location; relatively cheap telecommunications	State-of-the-art technology developed in military R&D projects	Tens of thousands of highly trained, underemployed, English-speaking engineers
Strategic goal	Create jobs in Ireland at all levels. Learn the software industry (low capitalization and environmentally friendly vs. manufacturing jobs)	Commercialize military technology; create export industry; employ tens of thousands of Russian immigrant programmers	Create export industry for job creation, foreign exchange earnings, and technology self-reliance
Opportunity targeted	Flow of United States, Asian technology into the EU. Product localization and support difficulties of MNCs in dealing with multi-lingual market. High telecom costs on European continent	Increasing demand for software technology, especially advanced security technology, in the United States as networking became commonplace	Shortage in United States and Europe of low-level programmers created by demand for ERP installation, Y2K preparations and e-commerce conversion
Key government actions	Offer tax and other incentives to software MNCs to set up shop in Ireland	Create Yozma and other industry investment programs, BIRD alliance programs, technology parks	Combine on-site labor with offshore outsourcing facilities, invest in telecom and computing infrastructure, and quality certification to establish credibility
Segments	Software services and products	Software products and R&D	Software services

National Software Strategies. The result of the variation in their circumstances and goals, and of the opportunities presented at the time, is that each country has a different type of software industry.
Sources: NASSCOM, Enterprise Ireland, and the Israeli Association of Software Houses.

resources, and each capitalized on opportunities in a different part of the software industry at the time. All have moved along the value chain, toward higher value-added activities or more profitable niches, as their cost structure changed. In every case, however, government action was pivotal to the early stages: policy change, investment in human resources and infrastructure, and proactive government promotion programs. Some were more strategic in their approach than others, but all three have had notable success with government partnership with the private sector.

The case of India deserves special attention as a first mover and lead exporter of software services and ITES. In 2004, India was ranked 30th in the World in total exports, but 9th in export of services—with ICT and ITES making major contributions to this growth. The Indian IT market has grown from about 1.7 billion in 1994–1995 to $20 billion in 2003–2004, and its software and ITES export revenues reached $12.5 billion in 2003–2004 and annual growth exceeding 30% (NASSCOM-McKinsey Report, 2005). Starting with the model of sending software engineers to client sites for low skill programming jobs, India has shifted progressively toward exporting offshore services at higher levels of the value chain.

The offshoring revolution has not stopped with software and call center services. India is undertaking innovative work such as management of clients' IT business processes and networks, and increasingly, higher value services, such as IT consulting. India is also diversifying IT-enabled services and call center services to include back-office operations, accounting, insurance claim processing, remote maintenance, medical transcriptions, legal databases, digital content development, online education, travel services, geographic information systems/spatial digitization, human resources services and payroll management, engineering services, and the list is growing. Unlike software services, many of these activities rely on less specialized skills and can have substantial impacts on employment.

Local ICT services capabilities increasingly attracting high-end innovative economic activities to India such as General Electric's R&D center in Bangalore and enabling banks to create new services. Of late, ICT and ITES have become a source of innovation in business practices in the domestic economy. Moreover, the success of the ICT industry is influencing competitiveness in other adopting sectors, such as finance, engineering services, and drug research. It is building confidence in the Indian industry and enhancing the country's brand in the world.

India's IT offshoring evolved from a first phase in the 1970s of investing in technological learning and technical education under a policy of import substitution; to a second in the 1980s, when hardware prices were declining rapidly and demand for software programming were increasing as firms moved from mainframe to client–server computing; to a liberalization and takeoff phase in the 1990s. At the end of this decade, Indian software services were fueled by year 2000 (Y2K) concerns. Since 2000, the industry had to consolidate following the dotcom bust and then, with renewed global growth, India was best positioned to reemerge with large software firms as global players and an ability to move to higher value-added services.[3]

---

[3]In contrast, China software services are fragmented, and this fragmentation exacerbates the Chinese industry's problems of size and expertise needed to capture large international projects—including weak process controls product and project management.

The critical success factors that contributed to this success story have been the subject of research and much debate. Although there is no single blueprint for success in the ICT industry, the Indian experience suggests some key ingredients, given as follows:

- Public–private partnership to push for reforms and create an attractive investment environment, including government championship and a strong industry association.
- Investing in ICT education, including the Indian Institutes of Technology and of Management (IITs and IIMs), IT finishing schools, and English language skills for the offshoring industry.
- Software technology parks.
- Mobilizing a large Indian diaspora in the target export markets, particularly the United States.
- Telecommunications policy and regulatory reforms—since the 1990s.
- Overall economic liberalization—also starting in the 1990s.

No One-Size-Fits-All Export Strategy

As the previous discussion suggests there is no one-size-fits-all set of policies or an off-the-shelf software development strategy for countries with different initial conditions, levels of development, and the relative strength of the different elements of their e-development. Lessons of experience are emerging concerning the main elements of national software strategies and the appropriate roles for government and public policy. But these lessons must be carefully related to local realities, technological capabilities, and potential comparative advantages of each country.

No simple typology can capture the diversity of country conditions and the corresponding policies and strategies in support of software and ITES export and capacity development. But the following provides some pointers:

- For countries with advanced technological capabilities and dynamic national innovation systems, such as Israel and Finland, strategies are likely to focus on high-value and innovative segments of software exports, on commercialization of intellectual property, on joint research and strategic partnership with multinationals, and on working with leading domestic users.
- For countries with less advanced innovative capabilities but a potentially large domestic base of user industries, such as the Philippines, Indonesia, or Vietnam, the focus of national software development may be on targeting those segments that are critical to the competitiveness of key local user industries, and some low value but high growth export niches. Subsequently, these countries may leverage such producer–user linkages to build competitive capabilities for software applications in these segments or verticals where capabilities have been tested and developed with local users. This would equally apply to developing software

and ITES to modernize key service sectors such as finance, as in Brazil, and e-government applications, as is the potential for India.

- Some niche strategies in ITES may leverage specialized skills and knowledge for export. Examples are the niche strategies of Egypt for ITES in technical support to leverage its large pool of engineering graduates, and Sri Lanka's ITES in support of finance and accounting to leverage its large pool of certified accountants.
- Countries with small domestic markets, or small pool of local talent, but large presence of multinationals or their subsidiaries, as in Ireland and Singapore, leveraged this presence to develop software products and services to support these MNCs, first locally, then globally. In advanced stage, same countries may use the presence of multinationals, world-class academic institutions and IT industry subsidiaries to forge global partnerships and attract advanced talent for its IT sector, as both Ireland and Singapore have since done.
- Countries with substantial pools of science and engineering resources with relatively low wages, as India and China, have relied first on relatively low value-added outsourcing opportunities, then moved to higher value-added segments of software services. Indian software companies may partner with Chinese ones to tap the low-cost technical pool of China for software export opportunities. Other countries may leapfrog into selected niche markets of software products, as may be the case for Russia and some East European countries.
- Even the least technologically developed and poorest countries, as most African and Caribbean countries, cannot afford to be left out of the increasingly knowledge-based global economy. Their software capacity development could be focused on those capabilities necessary to support and maintain their national information infrastructure, including public information and services, and trade facilitation systems. They may also promote regional collaboration to develop shared institutions, resources, and capabilities to meet their local user needs and to compete in defined niches globally. They may seek to partner with nearby hubs of ITES for subcontracting or joint-venture opportunities, as the case with several African countries gaining ITES subcontracts from South Africa or Mauritius.
- For many developing countries, localization of existing software, the development of open source applications and the customization of ICT systems for the local business users, community information centers, and multinationals located in the country could constitute an initial entry strategy. Over time, they can probe, learn, and develop capacity in promising high-growth ICT industry segments for export.
- Countries may deploy different software export or outsourcing strategies in response to physical, cultural, and/or temporal distance from their primary markets and these strategies often lead to different software specializations. For example, in early stages, India engaged in low-level design, contract programming, and maintenance as these relatively structured activities demanded less coordination and reduced the need for intensive collaboration in global software

development. Mexico may engage in back-office BPO for US companies since this niche may not need English language proficiency.

• For all countries, regardless of level of development, the fundamentals must be right, that is, public policies that support openness, competition, digital literacy, and private sector-led ICT infrastructure. But to compete and share in the dynamism of this large global industry, countries with potential competitive advantage must move beyond these common prerequisites and build on their own unique strengths.

What About the Domestic Market?

Much of the attention of policy makers and multinational corporations has been focused on the potential of IT/ITES offshoring from developing countries. But IT sector development would be more healthy and sustainable if it were to rely on both the export and domestic markets and to exploit potential synergies among the two. Such balanced development of the sector would contribute to the overall competitiveness of the economy, and further strengthen the virtuous cycles among various elements of e-Transformation (as will be discussed later).

India is a case in point. Until recently, the Indian IT industry has focused on the exports of IT services, with impressive results. But the almost exclusive focus on the export market has distorting effects across India's economy as it focuses local IT firms and the government on incentives and marketing efforts geared to these markets and hampers non-exporting firms to recruit and retain quality staff to address the needs of local users. Indian IT companies focusing on the domestic customers remain small and vulnerable.

Yet, the prospects of the domestic IT market in India are substantial. The domestic IT market is expected to grow at an impressive 25% a year (2005–2009). This may be the highest growth rate in the world. Taking all IT spending (including telecoms, hardware, and software), India's domestic market was estimated at $53.5 billion in 2005 and predicted to grow to $85 billion in 2009 (Jethanandani and Rose, 2005). While neglected by Indian IT companies, this domestic market has already attracted several foreign IT multinationals.

A promising new segment of India's domestic IT market is onshore outsourcing, or domestic BPO market. Large countries such as India, Mexico, and Brazil have seen rapid development of their banking and telecom sectors in recent years. Both these sectors require a high amount of customer service. For example, customer interaction-related services constituted over two-thirds of the domestic Indian BPO market in 2006. Finance and accounting and human resources-related services constituted 13 and 11%, respectively.[4] Box 8.2 Illustrates the magnitude and importance of domestic BPO in India and possible potential as near-shoring for other Asian countries.

---

[4]NASSCOM Strategic Review 2007.

Box 8.2 Role and Prospects of Indian Domestic BPO Market

The Indian domestic BPO market has been growing at 57% annually over 2003–07 (figure), and is expected to reach nearly USD 1.57[5] billion in 2008, presenting a significant potential opportunity for the other South Asian countries. This is particularly so, given the relatively high requirements in terms of the cost advantage and relatively less rigid requirements in terms of English language skills.

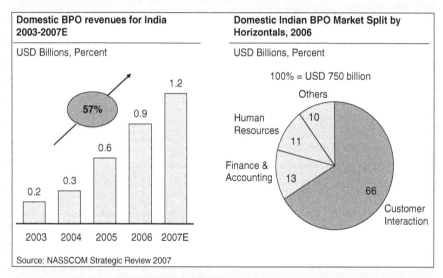

Domestic BPO revenues for India 2003-2007E	Domestic Indian BPO Market Split by Horizontals, 2006
USD Billions, Percent	USD Billions, Percent

Source: NASSCOM Strategic Review 2007

There is a dearth of employable talent for the ITES–BPO industry in India and this has led to a recent war for talent. The average annual attrition rate of the industry is 28 percent[6] This has also led to wage inflation, especially in high-growth sectors such as Banking and Telecom. In such a scenario, companies have begun tapping talent from the interiors of India in order to keep the costs low. There is therefore an opportunity for other countries in the region to either sub-contract work from the Indian companies or to attract recruiters from India since there is a cost differential in running ITES–BPO operations in these countries. Collaboration between outsourcers across countries would help them augment their capabilities and offer a broader range of services to clients and thus tap a larger market.

Source: Ahmed et al., 2009

---

[5] Ibid.
[6] Hewitt's Salary Increase Survey 2007–2008

After operating for decades in a protectionist economy, India's domestic industries were not motivated to invest in IT as a productivity driver. Meantime, Indian IT suppliers were generating substantial profits and growth from offshore markets—tax-exempt and at much higher margins. Economic liberalization over the last decade has spurred global competitors to enter domestic Indian industries. In turn, progressive Indian enterprises are increasingly turning to IT to match their global competitors in productivity, quality, responsiveness, and customer service. They are pursuing catch up strategies after decades of underinvestment in IT. Also, many Indian telecoms are expanding rapidly and likely be offer attractive opportunities for domestic growth in IT applications. Similarly, IT-intensive user multinationals operating in India can provide a promising area for growth for IT services and onshore outsourcing of ITES.

But many challenges remain to broaden this domestic base for IT to cover domestic users, particularly SMEs. Local IT providers underinvest in domestic market education and development. They are reluctant to seek domestic business because greater margins can be earned from global clients. Local CIOs are risk averse and often opt for using well-known or branded IT products and services of multinationals. Barriers facing SMEs are even harder to overcome. Developing domestic demand from SMEs and small grassroots organizations requires significant investment in user education and improved telecommunications.

An exclusive IT export focus also presents future risks by keeping India's sector development as isolated ICT islands or creating a digital chasm and a widening gap between India's cities and rural regions (Popkin and Iyengar, 2007). India's recent successes may be fragile as other countries enter the export market. These countries may build on demanding domestic users and benefit from learning and experimentation in their own dynamic domestic market. An unbalanced development of the sector would also confine India's ICT "miracle" to the elite urban areas and today's digital divide would become a digital chasm. This may lead to dwindling relevance as India would be forced to continue to compete primarily on cost, and forgo the opportunity to become the ICT superpower it is aspiring to become.

China, another giant in IT, provides an interesting contrast. India focused almost exclusively on software and ITES offshoring, but neglected its domestic market. China seems to have combined promotion of the domestic market with moves into selected segments of the export market for the development of its electronics and information industry (Gregory et al., 2009; ILO, 2001). Its success has been in the export of ICT hardware. The linkages between its core competencies for exporting IT and of applying it domestically are emerging slowly, not deliberately. Chinese software and IT services are lagging behind India's in the global market. Government's extensive involvement in the economy, its top-down approach to innovation, and the lack of a strong national trade association to promote the ICT industry present challenges to the future of exporting IT/ITES services.

On the other hand, the rapid expansion of software-using industries boosted domestic growth of the Chinese software products and services. As the overall Chinese economy grew rapidly—averaging 9.6% during 1979–2004—the software industry grew more than three times faster than the overall economy (Gregory et al.,

2009). Substantial investments in infrastructure in general, and in IT infrastructure in particular, and measures to attract multinationals have provided for a platform for faster expansion of the domestic use of IT. The need for adaptation to local conditions provided a ready market for domestic software firms. English language and local practices were significant factors. Even when Chinese software customers could use software products written in English, such products were unsuited for off-the-shelf use because of differences in business practices. Government also provided marketing support by means of their procurement policies which encouraged enterprises to use Chinese software suppliers. China's leaders have been unified in embracing technology as a strategic enabler for national development, and this vision has been critical to the growth of a domestic-based software sector.

Digital Content and the Media Industry

Some developing countries are attempting to extend the success of exporting IT services and ITES to the media industries. In addition to potential exports, the media industry is critical to the domestic market, to developing local content, preserving local culture, and supporting a market economy. In the EU, the content sector—media, publishing, marketing, and advertizing—accounts for 5% of GDP, or 433 billion euros, making it larger than the telecommunications sector and the hardware and software industries (World Bank, 2009b).

In addition, much of the producers of content are small and medium enterprises, contributing to employment generation. India's animation sector alone has a turnover of more than $550 million. Nigeria's film industry is the second largest employer after agriculture.

Global trade in media (mainly audiovisual products) is substantial but asymmetric, mainly from developed to developing countries. Some countries such as the Philippines, Jamaica, and South Africa are increasing these exports. A coherent investment and promotion strategy for the development of a export-oriented multimedia industry holds much promise for some countries aspiring for high-value exports and employment (Box 8.3).

Box 8.3 Malaysia's Multimedia Corridor Strategy

Malaysia presents another example of ICT-driven development strategy, with the aspiration to leapfrog into innovation or knowledge-based economy via the media and content industries. A national ICT framework was developed which comprises targeted investments in human resources, hard and soft infrastructure, and demand-driven applications and content development. Among key measures to achieve this transformation was the setting up of a Multimedia Super Corridor (MSC) to attract world-class companies with cutting-edge technologies to test flagship technologies, such as smart cards. The MSC has been linked by high-speed network to regional and global centers. Another key measure has been the Demonstrator's Application Grant Scheme which aimed to develop, among others, entrepreneurial communities enabled by electronic networks.

No in-depth evaluation of Malaysia's experience has so far proved whether its large investment has reaped the promised benefits. This is a long-term strategy to transform Malaysia to a knowledge-based economy. Malaysia has fully exploited the initial catch up stage, with coherent national strategies aimed at continuous technological upgrading. It has become a leader in many segments of the IT hardware industry. It remains to be seen whether it can replicate its success in the media and content industries.

Success of the current phase will depend on pursuing opportunities opened by globalization, while tailoring policies to local institutional and political realities and the special demands of these new industries for creative human resources and innovation ecosystems. Success will also depend on balancing investments in hard infrastructures with investments in human resources and soft infrastructures tailored to the knowledge industries.

The development of local content is relevant to countries at all levels of development, including African countries. The media is critical for the development of relevant and compelling local digital content in local languages, the promotion of educational software, the wide adoption of IT, and the diffusion of digital literacy. A vibrant local media is also important to educate, inform, and entertain, and to preserve a national culture, enhance governance and democracy, promote inclusive information society, and transition to the digital world. The development impact of media content is related to the relevance and accessibility of this content to the society at large, in formats and languages that diverse groups can understand and use.

There are many encouraging trends that should be relevant to developing countries and should expand the media's role in development. Broadband next generation network (NGN) can deliver TV programs, radio, music, films, games, and publishing interactively and thus provide new, participatory platforms (Chapter 8). Media content is increasingly produced in digital content and becoming the basic creative infrastructure for the knowledge economy. Digitalization of platforms, content, and devices in NGN is expected to converge to deliver all forms of digital content to any device, anytime, anywhere. The digitalization significantly enhances the fluidity and abundant choice of media content.

The developing world, with a younger age structure than industrial countries, may be able to fast adopt the new collaborative technologies and co-create local content, applications, and grassroots innovations. The costs of digital devices and media to capture and produce are falling rapidly and thus diffusing in developing countries. These developments are being complemented by collaborative technologies that help generate user-created content. Mass media and top-down content distribution and their business models are being challenged by user-created content. There is a positive feedback cycle between broadband infrastructure, digital content, and multimedia skills. Countries that are highly ICT-enabled produce more digital content than others. But the ongoing transformation should allow more people and new entrants to participate in knowledge production and dissemination.

It could be argued that the fundamentals for promoting the media industry are very similar to those for IT services and ITES: skilled but low-cost human resources, advanced communications infrastructure, and business-friendly investment climate. Convergence presents a major challenge to regulatory institutions that have been based on line-of-business and line-of-technology. Countries may combine targeted policies for ICT with media content development policies to support specialized education and training, facilitate access to finance, provide shared facilities and business support services to media SMEs, and create appropriate regulatory and investment environment. Promoting the media industry and its SMEs may be also integrated into development strategies and aid programs; their needs may be incorporated into promotion funds, incubators, IT parks, and innovation clusters.

The remaining part of this chapter focuses on policies, instruments, and programs to develop the ICT sector, particularly IT services and ITES. It starts with measures to develop the overall IT sector ecosystem. It then covers specific instruments: competition-based grants or innovation funds, IT incubators, IT parks and cluster development, public–private partnerships for sector development.

Developing the ICT Industry Ecosystem

An ICT industry development strategy should be based on in-depth understanding of the specific constraints facing ICT enterprises. Most software and ITES enterprises in developing countries are SMEs and share the many problems that limit the dynamism of SMEs in developing countries. Among the most common business environment problems for SMEs are unfriendly regulatory framework and investment climate, especially for start ups; limited access to financial resources, especially for new entrants; week incentives to invest in R&D; and underdeveloped networks between education, research, and industry.

In addition, industry-specific constraints to ICT are numerous. First and most important is the adequacy of human resources in each specialized field, combined with lack of specialized training programs for professionals and technicians. Universities and training institutions typically lag in responding to demand for human resources in fast changing fields and must partner with the private sector develop relevant curricula and skills. Meantime, SMEs face severe constraints to investing in their own highly mobile knowledge workers. SMEs also face shortages of high-quality managers, but this is even more critical fro SMEs in dynamic and knowledge-intensive sectors as software and IT services. A common problem is the lack of entrepreneurial skills among IT professionals, given their typically narrow technical education. In the case of ITES, oriented for export to large English-speaking markets, the shortage of English-speaking operators may be an additional constraint for certain segments.

Second, the IT industry is highly dependent on linkages between business, academia, and government. Local companies in most developing countries lack such linkages and thus access to technologies, learning, and global markets. Developing dynamic clusters takes concerted efforts to build missing links and leverage local endowments—advanced human resources, specialized infrastructure, specialized education and research institutions, other supporting industries, certification institutions, and international innovation networks.

Third, poor communications and lack of specialized infrastructure such as IT parks and incubators can be critical constraint. Many developing countries still have underdeveloped telecom infrastructure. In early stages, India bypassed such constraints by establishing software technology parks with advanced infrastructure, communications facilities, and shared services.

Fourth, the IT industry often lacks appropriate financing instruments and channels. This industry, particularly its predominant SME segment, faces greater financing constraints than others. This is due to several factors: intangible assets, intangible products, lack of credit history, high working capital for product development and marketing, and fast growing but poorly understood markets. Financial institutions often lack the knowledge and skills needed to deal with the special needs of this sector. For example, it took India a decade or more for its financial institutions to begin to respond to the special needs of its dynamic but high-risk software industry—a time during which most software SMEs had to rely almost exclusively on self-financing.

Fifth, the legal and regulatory environment has not kept pace with the novel and fast-changing issues arising from the needs of knowledge-based industries like IT and ITES. Laws and regulations for the digital economy are expanding and evolving fast. They cover, among others, laws to protect Intellectual Property Rights (IPR), promote commercialization of R&D, build online trust, and regulate electronic signature. They also involve legal and regulatory policies and mechanisms to enable public–private participation and collaboration—processes for dispute resolution, ability to enforce contracts, effective bankruptcy laws, and laws governing concessions and privatizations.

Finally, an underdeveloped domestic market and poor public sector procurement practices often hinder the development of a dynamic IT services sector and deprive the sector from innovation and learning with local users, public and private. In countries like Brazil and Mexico, governments develop most of their IT systems and services in house or through government-owned enterprises. Yet, experience in many advanced countries suggest that government—as the largest user of IT services—could play an important role in promoting the sector. Similarly, most enterprises in developing economies do not integrate IT into their businesses, despite the potential for productivity and competitiveness. The links between local IT services suppliers and local IT-user enterprises are often weak or even absent. The large, best-in-class IT-user enterprises are most connected to the global economy and can rely on IT multinationals for their access to know-how and cutting edge IT applications.

Responses to IT Sector Development Challenges

Several important and mutually reinforcing measures are needed to create a vibrant IT services industry ecosystem: developing specialized human resources, including managerial and technical resources; strengthening linkages and clusters; developing supporting infrastructure and incubators; promoting appropriate and adequate financing; modernizing the legal and regulatory framework; and developing the local markets, including government outsourcing of its own IT services.

Developing Specialized Human Resources

Several prominent examples of initiatives to develop skilled human resources for the IT/ITES sector include (i) Singapore's recruitment of many IT multinationals with targeted incentives to invest in developing skilled human resources; (ii) Malaysia's Penang Skills Development Center that is based on close linkage with industry; (iii) India's NASSCOM assessment of competency for benchmarking skill gaps on BPO; and (iv) China's initiative to train half a million people for BPO. A common feature of these initiatives is that all these are driven by or involve partnerships with the private sector.

Developing Appropriate Managerial Resources

Management is a key factor of production that should be addressed apart from professional labor or software engineers. They influence labor cost, how complementary inputs are used, lines of business, service quality and reputation, export orientation, local and international alliances, and the firm's culture and business strategy. These managerial processes command special requirements and importance for the software industry, as the industry deals with intangible products and assets, and demands corporate cultures characterized by agility, flexibility, rapid innovation, collaboration, and empowerment of knowledge worker. In new industries for which the optimum managerial culture has not yet been discovered or established locally, national culture can be adapted or appropriate managerial culture can be acquired by close contact with global best practices, through appropriate management training, executive development systems, and international alliances.

Strengthening Linkages and Clusters

Linkages between demand and supply, industry and skill development, financing institutions and IT enterprises, can produce dynamism and externalities, or a "silicon valley" effect. Measures to strengthen knowledge and innovation networks may include support to university–industry research funding for the ICT sector through competitive co-funding of R&D to encourage practical and effective innovations. R&D networking may be strengthened by promoting industry clusters and collaborative research, particularly among SMEs and between them and large private enterprises and multinationals. Tapping into global knowledge is sought through openness to trade and FDI, technical assistance, licensing and public–private technology acquisition funds, knowledge and innovation parks, strategic partnerships, global innovation networks, and mobilizing the diaspora. Chile makes use of global networks to attract investment in high technology. Similarly, Ireland and Singapore provide relevant examples of building linkages between multinationals and local SMEs and using best-in-class organizations and expertise to accelerate learning and skill development.

Developing Infrastructure and Incubators

Measures may include creating centers of information infrastructure excellence, such as specialized IT and software parks, with good international connectivity to attract and promote export-oriented software development, ITES and BPO. Public–private partnerships could be sought to develop technology parks in close proximity to universities and to attract global IT companies and foster linkages between industry and academia for joint R&D development. Incubator programs can reduce the risks confronting start-up enterprises, create new businesses, promote entrepreneurship, and assist the innovative firms by providing specialized infrastructure, business services, and favorable working environment and conditions.

Mobilizing Finance for Innovation and New Ventures

This may include guarantees programs and public-induced venture capital financing of the relatively risky and innovative projects for SMEs in the ICT cluster. It may also include technical assistance to prepare IT companies to be accredited for financing and to prepare financial intermediaries and banks to deal with IT sector financing by developing their capacity to appraise and finance IT companies, as in the case of Mexico's PROSOFT program. Finland provides an excellent example of national mechanisms for innovation financing.

Developing Favorable Legal and Regulatory Framework

Modernizing the IT-enabling legal and regulatory frameworks and putting them into practice is fundamental. To accelerate the reform process, leadership development, strategic communication, awareness campaigns are necessary to generate consensus on reform among legislators, policy makers, private sector, academia, and civil society. Effective implementation of the new laws and regulations also requires training of trial experts, judicial officers, law enforcers, and government officials in interpreting the laws and regulations for the digital products, services, and transactions.

Creating Local Markets

Apart from saving on IT costs and quality and improving overall government performance through e-government, competitive public procurement, subcontracting, and outsourcing of IT services can spur the development of the domestic market for IT and IT services. A competitive local market for software and ICT support services could be created through the strategic use of public procurement for ICT innovation and diffusion, and public–private partnerships for investing in e-government applications. A recent (2006) example of a policy shift to promote public–private partnerships and public sector use of private ICT services is Mexico's federal government mandating that all federal entities to purchase IT services rather than procuring equipment and relying on in-house IT services.

Promotion Funds

Alternative paths to ICT sector development in general and software services and ITES in particular are often the result of a combination of deliberate government policy directions and innovative business strategies that emerge from probing, discovering, and developing market niches. One mechanism that can support such emergent strategies is to create a funding mechanism to support private sector efforts to develop new competencies and market niches through sharing costs and building partnerships. Competition-based grant making and cost-sharing funds can support innovation and probe new and promising market niches. That does not argue for protecting this industry. Neither does it make excessive support necessary. But market failures that abound in the ICT industry—as a result of externalities, coordination failures and information failures—make a strong case for supporting the discovery of markets and the development of new competencies.

To avoid both market and government failures, what is needed is "strategic collaboration between the private sector and the government with the aim of uncovering where the most significant obstacles to restructuring lie and what type of interventions are most likely to remove them" (Rodrik, 2004, p. 3). Private initiative needs to be embedded in a framework of public action that encourages market discovery, diversification, innovation, institutional learning, and technological dynamism. Support should be guided by principles that include setting clear criteria for eligibility and for measuring success, holding beneficiaries accountable for their performance, and identifying and leveraging externalities and shared learning (Rodrik, 2004; Lall 2001).

Innovation funds can be designed to support such strategic collaboration and problem solving for the whole or promising segments of the ICT industry. Countries are experimenting with innovation funds that provide grants or cost-sharing financing based on competitive proposals from the ICT industry. One example is the ICT capacity building and industry promotion fund (ICBF), a mechanism for implementing a broadly defined sector strategy in the context of an integrated e-Sri Lanka development program.[7] The fund, initially established with a US $6 million budget for a 4-year program, aimed at strengthening the ICT industry in Sri Lanka, primarily through private sector-led initiatives. It promotes promising ICT market segments. It develops entrepreneurship for a broad-based growth of the industry. It finances just-in-time training in partnership with the private sector to build new capabilities among local enterprises and to attract foreign investors. It supports measures to promote international competitiveness. It is also designed to increase the capacity of the country's workforce to harness the benefits of ICT for development in selected user sectors, and SMEs in particular.

Incubators: Roles and Models

Incubators can be effective means for creating micro-environments for startups that can encourage innovation and entrepreneurship. Policy measures are addressed at the national level: e-policies, judicious openness to trade and FDI, and promotion of business-support services, among others. These policies can be reinforced and complemented by the networking and sharing of resources that must occur at the incubator and cluster levels.

Incubators represent a mechanism for grassroots-based, demand-driven innovation. They occupy the space between business development services which target a wide range of SMEs, and technology parks, which aim to accelerate relatively mature businesses and are often linked to cluster-driven development strategies.[8] The aim of such incubators is to support innovators by creating an ecosystem for innovation, entrepreneurship, and technological learning.

Incubation plays a crucial role for the ICT industry. A central challenge for national leaders is to create the conditions for startup innovative companies to succeed. The ICT sector in developing countries is predominantly composed of SMEs. Although incubation can apply to young, growth-oriented, technology firms in many sectors of the economy, the focus here is on ICT innovators, both suppliers and user industries. Local SMEs in the ICT sector represent an essential link between the local economy and the global ICT companies. They provide the seeds for homegrown solutions. To perform their functions, however, these small and microenterprises need incubation time and a crucial set of services.

Incubators can act as bottom up mechanisms to influence the policy environment by advocating and demonstrating how to reduce key barriers to ICT innovation and entrepreneurship. For example, enterprises are often stuck in the middle between the types of very small enterprises that microfinance institutions serve and those attractive to large deals from traditional banks. Incubators can help increase the supply of risk capital for promising innovations and new markets. Similarly, incubators

---

[7]For full development of the e-Sri Lanka program, see Hanna (2007a, 2008).

[8]This section draws on the experience of InfoDev: Impact Assessment and Lessons Learned from InfoDev's Global Network of Business Incubators. InfoDev 2008.

can become advocates of policy and legal reforms, advised government partners, or engaged in developing national innovation strategies.

Policy makers, developers, universities, and private sector associations have created incubators with diverse business models and service mix, and with different outcomes for development impact and sustainability (Box 8.4). The InfoDev program for incubators has been supporting a global network of over 70 incubators in over 50 countries, and valuable lessons are emerging. Although this global network supports business incubators in general, most of the incubatees of its most dynamic incubators are either producers of IT services and ITES or intensive and innovative users of IT.

Box 8.4 Incubators Business Models, Service Mix, and Sustainability

In many ways, issues concerning business models, service mix, development impact, and sustainability of incubators resemble those of telecenters (Chapter 7). As with telecenters, business incubators may take a variety of business models to effect ICT-enabled change in distinct complex environments. They may target exclusively high-growth technology firms (e.g., technology business incubation; university-linked business incubation). Alternatively, they may aim at impacting social issues and transforming traditional sectors (e.g., social business incubation, agri-business incubation). Or, they may focus on building a national business or ICT incubation movement (e.g., associations and networks). Each organizational model has strengths and challenges.

Although most incubators are committed to support growth-oriented enterprises at the early high-risk stages, there are no universal models of incubators. They succeed by developing customized service models that adapt to particular weaknesses in their environments. In most developing country environments, there are significant barriers to using ICT as a tool for improving productivity and organizational effectiveness. For ICT incubators this may mean improving access to information technology tools and advanced connectivity, building capacity to leverage ICT, market research, risk financing, brokering relationships between clients and potential investors, and mentoring and networking services. Successful incubators adopt dynamic service models—pushing beyond traditional infrastructure services to offer virtual incubation services. They leverage the use of Internet to provide services ranging from training to advice and best practices resources.

E-development strategies may deploy different models in different contexts in line with country aspirations for promoting the ICT sector as well as using ICT to enable regional and sectoral development strategies. But in similar ways as the telecenters, these incubator models face differing challenges in terms of financial sustainability and must search for the mix of services that balance the need for development impact with the need to generate a sustainable stream of revenue. Strategies range from diversification of services, to selecting a critical mass of clients with high growth potential, to networking to influence the broader environment. Linking the incubator movement to an overall e-development strategy can enhance both the development impact and the sustainability of the incubators as well as strengthen the ICT sector contribution to the overall strategy.

Regardless of the business model, experience suggests that it takes a long time for incubators to achieve financial sustainability—typically 7–10 years. This is particularly the case in developing countries and poor regions. In many countries, developed and developing, central and local governments play a crucial role in financing incubators. Corporate sponsorship and co-financing of incubators can have the added advantage of steering business opportunities and R&D contracts to promising incubatees. University sponsorship also adds the advantage of supplying advisory services, intellectual resources, and other facilities to incubators and incubatees. A franchise model—a management system that provides a set of services and shared resources across many incubators—is a promising way to promote, support, and sustain an expanding network of incubators at the country level and beyond.

Parks and Clusters

IT parks evolved from science and technology (S&T) parks. Advanced countries, particularly the United States, some European countries, and later Japan and Korea, set up S&T parks to promote knowledge and technology-intensive sectors. In the 1970s and 1980s, developing countries started to establish similar parks to promote their IT industry, and later, to promote software services. These parks enabled countries to leapfrog their severe infrastructure limitations and helped create first-world physical, communication, and social infrastructure in third-world countries. Apart from providing such advanced infrastructures, S&T and IT parks help recruit and co-locate IT or knowledge-based firms, provide shared research environment, leverage local knowledge resources, and promote ICT-enabled innovation.

Information technology, software, and ITES parks are specialized parks with a focus on promising segments of the ICT industry and associated services. They typically serve SMEs, beyond incubation. But they also host incubators within their site and help create a cluster of both mature and start up ICT companies. They provide tenants with state-of-the-art infrastructure and shared business development services. They also signal government commitment to the promotion of the

IT or software sector, as has been the case with India's software technology parks, and Egypt's Smart Village, providing a "brand" location and an island of policy and institutional excellence. India's experience with specialized software technology parks suggests that they can be a powerful tool for promoting the software industry.

Clusters represent a new way of thinking about competitiveness and the role of networks and support institutions in creating a habitat of innovation and entrepreneurship (Porter, 1990). The evolution of dynamic and innovative clusters indicates that public policy should focus on designing a coherent set of enabling instruments at the regional or local levels—including the supply of advanced infrastructure and specialized skills and knowledge as well as specialized support institutions that promote entrepreneurship, risk financing, networking, and innovation. Local universities, institutions, and governments must also play complementary roles in cluster formation, so such clusters can become truly dynamic and innovative. Software services and knowledge-based clusters in particular are dependent on collaboration among these actors and on creating synergies among the key elements of e-development at the local level (Chapter 8).

Geographic clustering has been recognized as particularly important in developing the software and other knowledge-intensive industries, because it facilitates the transfer of tacit knowledge. The software industry's reliance on intellectual capital and skilled staff, the value creation that comes from enhanced knowledge sharing and commingling these assets, and the ability to attract supporting business and financial services contribute to the importance of clustering. For example, special economic zones in China have facilitated clustering and the development of its high-tech sectors. The importance of clustering, both for fostering innovation and for enlarging the specialized labor pool, has been noted in particular for Chinese software firms. Over 80% of the Chinese software firms were located in these zones (Gergory et al., 2009). Most of the Chinese software industry is concentrated in the largest cities, and the clustering pattern reflects the concentration of the Chinese universities and research institutes.

Software technology parks (STPs) in India played a similar role, with three STPs early established in 1990. India now has STPs throughout the country, amounting to over 2000, but with natural clustering in urban centers like Bangalore, Chennai Hyderabad, and Pune Early parks relied mainly on government investment and focused mainly on providing high-quality international connectivity, serviced infrastructure, ICT facilities, and basic support services. Over time, services have diversified as well as sources of funding, with private sector participation. Although they came under a single governance structure, STPs adopted diverse ownership structures, including partnerships among central and state government and the private sector, including foreign investors. STPs were effective both in offering clustering advantages and in providing serviced and high-quality infrastructure. Proximity to engineering colleges like the Indian Institutes of Technologies played a key role in creating clusters. Network externalities have also increased with the growing number of software parks in the country. Exports from STPs account for over 95% of India's software exports (STPI web site, 2006).

Bangalore presents a celebrated innovation cluster from which we can learn a great deal.[9] It is named "the Silicon Valley of the south." Like other innovative clusters, it emerged due to a critical mass of skilled labor, proximity of educational and research institutions, presence of specialized suppliers, and evolution of networks among these and local enterprises, mainly small ICT firms. But the presumed links between industry and local educational and research institutions are weaker than those of advanced innovation clusters like Silicon Valley. As it evolved, the focus of the cluster moved rather slowly from production to innovation, and investments by multinational firms remained primarily of an enclave nature with limited technological spin-offs (Box 8.5).

Box 8.5 Bangalore as an Innovative ICT Cluster[10]

Bangalore's success in ICT production and software exports is well known, but its continued dynamism and evolution as an innovation center is constrained by weak links to educational and research institutions and weak networks among the ICT industry and with other local institutions. Key to its competitiveness has been a large pool of engineers and specialists, a critical mass of competitive SMEs and multinationals, and an entrepreneurial culture—all critical ingredients for the ICT services industry. The growth of software exports from Bangalore has been aided by the growth of venture capital. The Indian diaspora in Silicon Valley also played a critical role in supplying venture capital, specialized knowledge, and links to multinationals.

Bangalore's cluster growth has been linear and extensive—rather than nonlinear and intensive. It has been heavily reliant on export to the US market, high-volume low-value projects, and the use of a large pool of programmers and ICT engineers. Over time, it has been moving up the value chain. Some Indian firms are selectively establishing links to universities. Multinationals are establishing R&D centers within the cluster. But these initiatives have been limited in scope or of enclave nature.

Bangalore is at a cross road in its evolution. Bangalore's extensive growth has been beneficial, but is likely to be challenged by competition from other

---

[9]There has been much more research on innovation clusters in industrial countries, and particularly on Silicon Valley. See, for example, The Silicon Valley Edge (2000). Edited by Chong et al., Stanford University Press. It advanced the concept of a habitat in which all resources high-tech entrepreneurial firms need to survive and thrive. This habitat includes skilled and mobile labor force, entrepreneurial firms, major universities and research centers, venture capitalists and financing institutions, and specialized services, and support institutions—and their dense networks and modes of interactions that promote collective learning and flexible adjustment.

[10]Adapted from Dahlman and Utz (2005).

low-cost ICT service producers such as China, Eastern Europe, Russia, and Vietnam. A strategic shift is needed toward innovation-driven growth and higher value-added segments of the ICT industry, driven by investments in innovative capabilities, in advanced infrastructure, and in synergies and networks among academia, industry, and government.

Telecenters for Outsourcing

ITES has emerged as a major user of specialized IT parks, mainly to benefit from broadband connectivity infrastructure. However, ITES holds the potential of diffusion to the poorer regions and rural areas in developing countries, beyond the IT parks. Telecenters with advanced connectivity can become the hubs for outsourced ITES. One interesting example of the potential of ITES to generate growth and employment in rural areas is IIT Madras's company called DesiCrew. IIT Madras has spun off a company, whose aim is to enable employment creation through rural BPO throughout India. The company has initiated its efforts in the state of Tamil Nadu by converting 20 rural kiosks into BPO–ITES centers. Services offered include date entry, computer-aided design, desktop publishing, multimedia works, and localization. The DesiCrew head office is the connecting point between the BPO centers and the world. It procures orders and passes them on to this network of kiosks. This is a compelling example of the potential synergies between telecenters and the promotion of BPO–ITES to create opportunities for growth and rural livelihood (Chapter 10).

Emerging Lessons for Developing Technology Parks

Lessons and good practices are emerging from a decade or two of international experience in establishing and sustaining IT parks.[11] These lessons may be summarized or recast in terms of the following critical success factors: private sector participation and competent park management; effective marketing and anchor recruitment and appropriate product–service mix for the park; leveraging external linkages and partnerships; high-quality physical, communication, and social infrastructures; access to financial and business support services; and enabling national policies, institutions, and strategies for the IT sector.

---

[11] See for example, InfoDev's *International Good Practices for Establishment of Sustainable IT Parks*, 2008. However, evaluation of IT parks continues to be a challenge in view of the different objectives of these parks, the diverse country context, and conditions that influence their performance, and the relatively underdeveloped indicators of performance and development impact, beyond financial sustainability.

Management, Private Sector Participation, and Financing

Both government and private sector have financed the development of IT parks, although the trend in many countries is toward increased participation of the private sector investments in park development and ownership. The extent of government involvement in investing and managing the parks has varied among countries, with Korea, China, and Singapore starting with heavy government involvement then gradually moving to a model where development and management are in private hands, and in some cases as in Korea, including foreign investors. Many of the recent successful parks are developed through public–private partnerships, as in Cyber Towers in Hyderabad state. A common model is for national or state government to provide the land as equity, while the private sector developers assuming management and investing in the on-site facilities.

However, regardless of ownership, private sector management of parks has emerged as an essential ingredient of success to secure operational flexibility, marketing skills and networks, and strong incentives for financial sustainability. Private investors and developers have the necessary incentives and practices in place to reward park management teams for performance. They have the incentives and experience to effectively market and recruit tenants and to service the smaller and startups with know-how in business planning and market assessments. A competent, motivated, and proactive IT park management team is a key asset to secure a dynamic and financially sustainable IT park.

Marketing, Recruitment, and Product–Service Mix

The success of IT parks in attracting IT companies is heavily dependent on the reputation and credibility of the anchor tenant. Hitec City India and Science Park Singapore have been able to market the park based on their reputed anchor tenants such as Oracle, Microsoft. Hence, countries and park developers often go after high-quality, brand name tenants, as AP went the extra mile to attract Microsoft with preferential treatment. It is important, however, that the anchor is not just a "sales office" for a brand name company, but one that can locally conduct innovative activities and locally network with other park tenants and academic institutes. The park investor or developer may also act as anchor tenant and thus early recruiter of other key tenants, as the Indian investor company is expected to act or to bring Indian ITES tenants for Bhutan's IT park.

A key success factor is having the parks focus on products and services in which the countries of operation have a competitive edge and/or where countries are prepared to build competitive advantage. Thus Hitec City of India is focused on IT and BO services and China's ZSP is focused on IT manufacturing and Chinese software. But Cyberjaya in Malaysia has focused on IT services and BPO, in support of diversification and an explicit strategy to move beyond Malaysia's traditional strength of IT manufacturing. S&T and IT parks may also focus on certain technologies or mix of products and services that can facilitate the formation of clusters or centers on technology excellence. Government policies may also link fiscal incentives and subsidies with the identified core competencies and markets of domestic firms. For example, Singapore and Ireland have linked their incentives to R&D spending, while in India and Malaysia, to the export performance of export-oriented IT and ITES firms. These examples highlight the importance of maintaining a fit between national innovation and industrial policies and strategies, and the park's product–service focus and recruitment strategy.

Linkages and Partnerships

Parks as well as incubators of knowledge-intensive industries and innovative enterprises thrive on knowledge and innovation networks and close working relationships with academic and training institutions, research centers, and venture capital institutions, among others. Access to skilled manpower and R&D centers are at least as important as access to first-class infrastructure for attracting innovative enterprises and major tenants. Developing appropriate linkages within and outside the park can make the difference between a developing real estate and creating vibrant knowledge clusters.

The nature and intensity of such linkages will vary in view of the policy objectives and roles of the IT or knowledge parks, and the nature of products and services by anchors or key tenants. These linkages are even encouraged by co-locating prominent academic and R&D institutes with key industry players in the park. For example, Singapore's Science Park has the primary focus on technology innovation in IT products, and this required leveraging specialized R&D infrastructure for basic and applied research and product development. In other cases, technological innovation linkages may not be critical as in IT services and ITES. In these cases, innovation requirements are focused on business practices and service delivery capabilities which are possessed in-house and based on existing IT products. When the objective of such parks is to promote regional development and spinoff effects, the key linkages should extend to local resources, businesses, and development institutions. This would require assessment of the regional resources and institutions as well the potential backward and forward linkages of key tenants to be recruited for the park.

Physical, Communication, and Social Infrastructures

Obviously, infrastructure matters. IT parks often benchmark themselves in terms of availability and cost of land and quality of physical infrastructure and state-of-the-art data and voice connectivity. Yet, many parks failed because they did not attend to the basics. Increasingly, social infrastructure—such as social amenities for recreation, quality schools, and sports and proximity to airports—also matters. An attempt to locate a knowledge-IT park in a city about 1 h from Amman is facing significant hurdles in attracting highly skilled and creative Jordanians who still prefer the amenities of Amman. Recent software parks in India are attempting to recreate the ambience of the campuses of innovative software companies in the United States to attract a highly mobile creative class. Governments are also allowing developers some flexibility in land use, to bundle IT office construction with clubs, recreational centers, shopping complexes, eateries, housing, and other amenities. This flexibility does not only make the project financially attractive but also provide attractive townships and social facilities.

Finance and Business Support Services

Support services may include incubation services, access to market, access to finance and venture capital, business planning, and operational support. IT parks offering incubation services help nurture entrepreneurship and the development of local SMEs, in the process they gain when incubatees scale up to become regular but innovative tenets. Specialized incubator services may help recruit IT professionals in the diaspora to return and invest in start ups, as China has done in its ZSP park. Competitive business support services could also extend to the whole IT park and can be an attractive source of income to park management. Some IT park Management companies like Singapore's Ascendas have contracted organizations specializing in services such as market assessment and business planning and offered these services to tenants.

Venture capital, angel investment, and private equity are key enablers to the development of startups and SMEs, particularly for new and fast-growing sectors like IT. Where the presence of venture capitalists is limited, some IT parks have set up their own venture capital or private equity funds. This is the case of Korea, China, and many others. But like many other measures to support on-site occupants with appropriate and dedicated services, these services are most effective when complemented by national policies to promote venture capital/private equity market and business support services industry at the national level.

Enabling National Policies and Strategies

A supportive and proactive government is a key to successful IT parks program. The role of government has evolved over time in response to the evolution and maturity of the sector. After initial stages of direct involvement, and once the sector attained a critical mass, many governments have shifted to a facilitative role. Yet government policies and strategies for the IT sector and IT parks remain critical. Engaging policy makers in the IT park program, to create islands of excellence for IT and innovation, may open them to further policy and institutional reforms for innovation and private sector development, beyond the parks. A holistic approach to policy development for IT, innovation, and private sector development must be adopted in the context of a national development strategy, as will be discussed in Chapter 8.

Government policies and strategies are critical to successful IT parks programs and their impact on IT sector and business transformation in several ways: policies to encourage the development of IT parks; adopting efficient institutional coordination or single window mechanisms; encouraging private sector participation; aligning policies and incentives with competitive advantage and desired spillover benefits; fostering linkages with the global economy; and adopting appropriate data protection and IPR policies.

Just to illustrate. For large and poor countries like India and China, or middle-income countries with underdeveloped infrastructure like Egypt, Mexico, and Brazil, IT parks can help them provide advanced communications infrastructure and support services in concentrated areas. Focused policies to promote IT park development can jump-start ICT sector and accelerate cluster development. These policies should be consistent across parks and linked to the broad objectives of the IT or S&T park program. Jordan, for example, had developed various parks with different incentives and institutional mechanisms, serving conflicting regional and sector objectives, and leading to conflicting signals to investors.

Good policies alone do not suffice. Even when countries adopt regulations in line with good practice, they often fail in implementation. Most countries have used organizations within government to provide single window service. For example, incentives offered to IT parks and sector in Malaysia are administered by the Multimedia Development Corporation. In India, the single window mechanism for providing requisite approvals is done through the Software Technology Park of India (STPI). The developer of the IT park also requires various clearances for construction. At the state level, in Andhra Pradesh, incentives to IT enterprises are administered through high coordination committee, while the APIIC act as a single point clearance agency for the developer. To expedite adjudication of IPR, India and China have set up dedicated Copyrights Tribunals. Having an industry body specifically to promote IT sector development can further push for policy reforms and institutional coordination.

Encouraging private sector participation in IT park and IT sector development may be extended to other support sectors such as telecommunications, physical infrastructure, financial services, and business support services. The government would continue to play a facilitative role. But it may also continue to play a more prominent role in research and development.

Having the right mix of policies ranging from land use to capital markets can further secure or maximize spillover benefits. The government may also link its incentives and subsidies to the strengths and markets of local companies. For countries aiming to offer offshore ITES, enacting date protection laws would be essential. Similarly, IPR laws are important to a thriving software industry. The challenge for all governments in developing countries is to prioritize this large number of policies and institutional reforms in line with a holistic IT strategy linked to the country's development strategy (Chapter 8). To help prioritize and adapt policies over time for IT sectors and parks, policy makers also need to devise monitoring and evaluation frameworks, linking policies to appropriate development outcome indicators such as contribution to employment, export, innovation, and skill development.

ICT Competencies as Enabler for Broad-Based Development

Why target ICT as a technology for mastery and innovation? Why not rely on the general national innovation systems, policies, and institutions to address ICT innovation needs as well? The following reasons can be advanced.

First, as discussed earlier, ICT is a general purpose technology with very diverse applicability across almost all economic sectors. The bulk of the benefits of the ICT revolution for most countries will come from harnessing these new technologies for wide use throughout their economies. Second, research suggests that targeting technologies with substantial potential and spillovers has greater dynamic benefits (Lall, 2003). Third, technologies differ in terms of their learning requirements. This technology involves substantial learning and localization including the need for corresponding institutional investments and innovations, investing in intangibles, building supplier and customer networks for adaptation and joint learning, and taking account of network effects and externalities. Information technology requires substantial learning from governments as well, as users of the technology to transform the way they do business, as regulators of the telecommunications infrastructure, and as formulators of the enabling e-laws.

Finally, this technology is fast changing and involves complex systems and interdependencies. The ICT sector is innovation-intensive. It relies more on venture capital, research and development, and global knowledge through FDI, than any other sector in most countries. A proactive government policy is essential to help this nascent and dynamic industry address these externalities and coordination challenges.

This technological competency is not developed in the abstract. It should be demand-driven. It should be developed through strategic and innovative application of ICT in various sectors. But the investments required to upgrade information and communication across the whole economy far exceed available resources and implementation capabilities of developing countries. Hence, national strategies may identify leading user sectors and priority areas where ICT could enhance competitiveness or reduce poverty and then fashion the necessary measures to mobilize and optimize local resources and designate appropriate roles for government and other stakeholders. Matching needs with resources through joint efforts, prioritized investments, grassroots innovation are essential for building a dynamic ICT sector and levering its technological capabilities to transform local enterprises, develop a competitive private sector, and enable communities to solve local development problems with the help of ICT.

Advanced development strategies are expected to set priorities and broad directions for the use of ICT in all key sectors of the economy and for programs to diffuse ICT to SMEs and lagging target groups. There are growing digital divides in developing countries among population groups as well as between sectors. While large businesses adopt ICT relatively quickly, SMEs and rural communities lag behind.

Promoting synergies between the local production of ICT goods and services and the domestic use of ICT is a crucial policy area for development strategies. When the domestic sectors start adopting new ICT in their operations they may rely on local ICT expertise to fully realize the potential productivity gains. However, this linkage is not automatic in many developing countries, where local usage is often constrained by local procurement practices that are heavily locked into proprietary technologies or bounded by rules of aid agencies that favor major multinationals over local suppliers. A proactive approach would nurture producer–user networks and local cooperation among ICT companies, universities, and private enterprises, and grassroots organizations. The aim would be to promote local ICT adaptation and diffusion, economic growth, and social inclusion.

Capabilities for both software production and its use tend to reinforce each other. The continuous interaction between suppliers and users of software services is critical to building software capabilities and to adapting software applications to the variety of local needs and the evolving demands of leading users. Many of the lead users became later major leading suppliers. Therefore, a national software promotion policy can be an important thrust of ICT strategies to build a core competency for the knowledge economy and to exploit potential synergies among the production and use of ICT. Ireland's Industrial Development Authority tried to exploit such synergies.

To maximize development impact, it is important to think strategically about the interactions between local ICT sector capabilities and local ICT uses in the economy (Fig. 8.1). When ICT sector capabilities are weak and ICT use is limited among local enterprises, a low-level equilibrium persists (quadrant 1). When the industry is advanced, perhaps through export-led ICT growth strategy, there are increasing opportunities to leverage the accumulated technological capabilities to transform local enterprises in key sectors of the economy (quadrant 2). But IT services and ITES at the low end of skills constitute a footloose industry, particularly when it has no home base for interaction and learning from domestic users. Alternatively, a user-led strategy may target for development those technological capabilities most relevant to the domestic market, without a guarantee for ICT exports (quadrant 3). Striking the right balance to create a vibrant ICT ecosystem among ICT users and producers may be guided by national aspirations and commitment to economic growth and inclusion (quadrant 4).

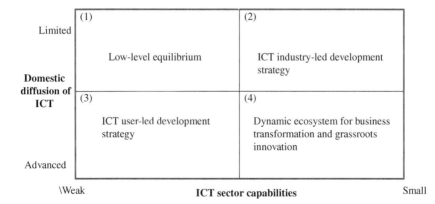

Fig. 8.1 ICT supply capabilities and its use in local enterprises

A special focus of a national private sector development and innovation strategy should be to focus the national innovation system on promoting the ICT diffusion among SMEs. Industries and services in developing countries are predominantly SMEs, and they stand to benefit from the networking and aggregation effect of ICT. But ICT diffusion to SMEs is typically constrained by lack of common infrastructures, low awareness, and weak adoption capabilities, among others (Hanna et al., 1995, 1996). The SMEs also suffer from isolation, low productivity, and limited access to markets, finance, and information. So, the paradox is that these enterprises that have the least access to ICT can benefit the most from ICT deployment and diffusion.

Experience from national ICT diffusion programs suggests that such programs can be effective in accelerating the diffusion process and in linking SMEs to the national and global supply chains (Hanna et al., 1995). Coordination among private sector users is necessary to set cooperative standards for doing business and establish common networks, content, databases, and value-added services. Similarly, governments may work with private sector associations and NGOs to identify priority business segments for promoting ICT diffusion and for partnering to empower communities and grassroots organizations to innovate and solve local development problems with access to knowledge and ICT tools.

Although the focus of developing countries has been on the short-term benefits of export and wealth creation of IT services and ITES, the long-term benefits for the wider economy are likely to be substantial. These industries are providing incentives for governments to improve the overall business environment, thus benefiting all sectors of the economy. Even within the same country, the promise of the industry is promoting competition among states to provide incentives and improve the investment climate for FDI in general, as in the case of India states. These dynamic industries are raising awareness about the importance of education quality and reform, particularly technical and engineering education. They are also presenting models for partnership between educational and business institutions, including ICT multinationals. They are encouraging knowledge transfer of international best practices in IT usage, standards, outsourcing, IT-based businesses, and managerial and business innovation. They have increased the visibility of developing countries like India as a destination for investment and innovation across knowledge-based services and industries, beyond the ICT sector. They have provided opportunities for the diaspora to return to home countries, and augment human and risk capital.

Chapter 9
Dynamic Information Infrastructure

The information infrastructure is the main "hard" component of e-development but its development and dynamism depend on "soft" policies and regulations to induce both supply of and demand for telecommunications. This infrastructure enables the sharing of knowledge and information among various actors in the society. It is the main prerequisite for the introduction of high value-added applications, especially in e-business and e-government as access precedes service rollout. On the other hand, demand drivers, based on content, have to replace the former supply-driven model of "build it and they will come"—to avoid costly public investments. A holistic approach addresses both the demand and supply side at the same time.

The fast advances in communications technology open substantial possibilities to leapfrog old solutions and to leverage new capabilities. For example, most developing countries have high penetrations of televisions, and the introduction of digital television may provide a familiar, cost-effective, and widely used channel for digital communication.[1] The explosive growth of wireless communications also represents a relatively low-cost way to build communications infrastructure quickly. The explosive growth of mobile phones in developing countries has created a new and global platform for delivering old and new services.

Still, there are many challenges to extend the telecommunications infrastructure and provide affordable access to ICT tools. Access to information and communication services remains low and the cost of connecting high, especially in the low-income and rural areas of most developing countries. Proactive government policies and programs are needed. Innovative solutions need to be found to the "last mile" challenges—solutions that can leverage entrepreneurship and private sector investment and provide affordable mass access to ICT tools and communications services.

The technological frontier is a fast moving target in the communications area, and competitive broadband communications services are increasingly a must for many e-business applications and collaborative technologies. As electronic commerce, outsourcing, and networking become ever more ubiquitous in international

---

[1] Brazil and other Latin American countries are exploring this channel of delivery, with the use of inexpensive set-top boxes to convert analog to digital television.

N.K. Hanna, *e-Transformation: Enabling New Development Strategies*, Innovation, Technology, and Knowledge Management, DOI 10.1007/978-1-4419-1185-8_9,
© Springer Science+Business Media, LLC 2010

business, deficient communications networks could reduce global market opportunities and deter foreign direct investment. Quality of access will increasingly matter for an agile networked economy. Difficult tradeoffs will have to be made between investing in high-speed broadband and leapfrogging to frontier technologies, on the one hand, and extending the information infrastructure to poor and marginalized communities and leveraging existing infrastructure to its maximum potential, on the other hand.

A holistic approach could also ensure effective integration of and healthy competition among all forms of access (cable, digital TV, mobile, fixed and wireless, power line solutions, etc.). And in an era when communications (in voice, data, video, and image) are increasingly digitized, the stovepipe model of regulation must be replaced by an open model that allows for inter-platform competition and the increasingly central role of the Internet. Spectrum allocation also assumes increasing importance, not as a source of revenue, but as an enabler of healthy competition, adoption of new communication technologies, and reduced cost to end-users. Switching from analog to digital broadcasting is likely to free spectrum and allow for more individually tailored content. Issues of technical standards also become important to realize economies of scale and the opportunities for ensuring interoperability and information and application sharing across platforms. Regulatory, legislative, and standards-setting institutions must evolve and interact with other e-leadership institutions to create dynamic legal and regulatory frameworks and ensure that reforms are driven by the broader concerns of accelerating growth and overcoming the digital divide.

This chapter does not deal with the host of technical telecommunications and traditional regulator issues, as these are already codified knowledge for which excellent toolkits are available to regulators (see, for example, ITU-*info*Dev, International Telecommunications Union, 2000). Rather it focuses on (1) the basic principles to extend information infrastructure to poor regions; (2) the key global technological forces and market trends shaping the Next-Generation Networks (NGN); (3) the role of regulation in transitioning to the NGN environment and creating future-proof regulatory frameworks; and (4) the policy issues and options concerning rural connectivity and access in support of broad-based e-development programs.

Principles to Extend Communications Services

Here, we only touch on few basic principles, to enable a pro-competitive regulatory framework and extend ICT services beyond the market. First step is to allow the market to work through telecommunications sector reforms and a pro-competitive ICT regulatory framework. Extending services beyond their reach in reformed markets requires systematic identification of the remaining constraints to the functioning of the markets. Policies must address key issues such as opening markets to new entrants—including small local entrepreneurs—rebalancing tariffs and cost-based interconnection regime, securing access to existing infrastructures, and making radio spectrum available (Wellenius, 2006).

Another aspect of pro-competitiveness framework to improve access to ICT is to promote innovation: adoption of new technologies and decentralized supply through wider range of business models. This may mean making more spectrum resource available for shared use. Cost-effective strategies to roll out broadband access to the Internet could be aimed at meeting both private user needs and the requirements of e-government and e-education, for example, through franchising services for rural Internet centers.

Policies to extend access to ICT beyond the market is essentially a political decision, but can also be justified on the basis of broad economic priorities, network externalities, social inclusion, narrowing critical gaps that may otherwise remain. Striking the right balance between enabling the market and providing public support can be difficult. This balance must be addressed within the broader context of ICT-enabled development and in view of tradeoffs among development goals. While public sector support for narrowing gaps in established markets may be compelling and may have dramatic development impact, public sector support for early adoption of advanced ICT services for economic development is less clear. There is a case for selective government support for those advanced Internet-based services for which demand can materialize quickly once service is available. But even here, advanced service is a moving target, so the Internet and related services may increasingly become more and more critical to development services.

In providing public sector support, governments may consider many options. They can stimulate demand by supplying selected services at subsidized prices, by improving customer service and subsidizing Internet access as in Egypt and Morocco, by ensuring access to relevant content, by launching applications of special interest to the public such as land records in some Indian states, and by aggregating the demand of various government branches and providing government commitment to purchase broadband capacity.

Various mechanisms may also jump-start supply (Wellenius, 2006). Cash subsidies may be used to help service suppliers overcome entry barriers or targeted to the desired beneficiaries as output objectives are met, as in Chile and Peru. Good subsidy practice commits service providers to invest and risk their own resources under specified conditions while government subsidies help them meet some investment and start-up costs and reduce access barriers to which low-income groups are especially sensitive. Subsidies should be neutral about competition among service providers, service delivery alternatives, and the technologies deployed.

Specialized telecommunications funds are often used to collect and disburse subsidies. Development funds have a mixed record in financing telecommunications subsidies, and lessons should be drawn from this record to ensure both equity and sustainability. Subsidies are preferably determined and allocated through competition among firms in a transparent process. As mobile services have substantially increased access to voice services, some countries like Colombia, Peru, and Chile have broadened the scope of their funds to develop more advanced communication services and facilities. When well-designed within a credible legal and regulatory environment, competition for subsidies results in lower subsidies, more effective mobilization of private resources, and greater transparency than when investments are funded by traditional public sector means (Wellenius et al., 2004).

Technological Changes and the Next Generation Network

Four trends in the telecommunications industry will have a major impact on the future of the industry and the key stakeholders in e-development: growth of mobile; growth of broadband access; take up of Voice-over-Internet Protocol (VoIP); and growing ICT convergence and access competition. These technological and market forces are mutually reinforcing. They are blurring the lines between traditional telecommunications services and moving many countries to next generation networking that will enable consumers to receive a wide range of services over a single all Internet Protocol (IP)-based network (ITU, 2007). NGN will be associated with Internet access at fast transmission speeds that will facilitate a full range of public services such as e-government, e-health, and e-education.

In wealthy countries, both fixed and mobile networks are being upgraded to offer increasingly higher speed broadband. Many OECD countries are racing to build their broadband infrastructure by providing incentives to operators to proceed with substantial investments at a pace much faster than would otherwise be possible without public partnership. Policy and regulatory measures are included to ensure net neutrality, open networks, non-discrimination and network interconnection obligation. Some governments are also investing directly in the building of such national broadband networks. Advanced countries have developed national strategies for building their broadband infrastructure, including Japan, Korea, Singapore, Finland, Sweden, Denmark, and the United Kingdom.

In i2010, the European Union's vision, widespread broadband access is a key prerequisite for the development of modern economies and is also an important part of the Lisbon Agenda. Accordingly, the European Union has been committed to increase its efforts to promote the use of broadband services and encourage further rollout, particularly in the less developed regions of the Union. In the United States, cognizant of slipping behind advanced countries in building its broadband infrastructure, a broad coalition has emerged to lobby the new Obama administration for a national broadband strategy (Box 9.1).

Box 9.1 A National Broadband Strategy Call to Action in the United States

On December 2, 2008, in an unprecedented display of consensus, a broad and diverse array of groups concerned about America's broadband future released a Call to Action that provides President-elect Obama and the incoming Congress a policy framework for a comprehensive national broadband strategy.

The Coalition includes prominent communications providers, high technology companies, manufacturers, consumers, labor unions, public interest groups, educators, state and local governments, utilities, content creators, foundations, and other stakeholders in America's broadband future. These organizations believe that such a strategy is critical to America's economic vitality, educational opportunity, public safety, energy efficiency, environmental stability, global competitiveness, and a continuing high quality of life.

At the event, representatives of these organizations voiced support for the Call to Action, discussed their shared goals, and announced their intent continue to work together to address key issues and policy priorities. Since then, the membership of the Coalition has more than doubled, and it has now formed six working groups to develop as much agreement as possible on a variety of key issues.

See http://www.bb4us.net/index.html

Fiber backbones coupled with wireless access technologies offer developing countries far richer options of ICT services at lower costs. However, developing countries have largely achieved basic communications through mobile and are likely to develop NGN access networks primarily through wireless. The fixed-to-mobile substitution is most evident in India, China, Russia, and Latin America. In the first quarter of 2007 alone, China and India reported 200 million more mobile subscribers; as of March 2007, China has 480 million mobile (2G) subscribers (ITU, 2007). Almost two-thirds of mobile users are now located in developing countries. The rise of mobile services in developing countries has been fuelled by improved affordability—including cheaper handset prices, prepaid packages, and declining tariffs—and new service options, such as SMS and mobility. The same factors could promote wireless broadband Internet access, as mobile handsets that support both voice and Internet applications become affordable.

Mobile phones now constitute the world's largest digitally based distribution platform. Annual growth of mobile phones averaged 24% between 2000 and 2008. The near ubiquitous use of mobile telephony (with an estimated 4 billion subscribers worldwide and over 70% of world's population covered by mobile networks by the end of 2008) gives this technology the potential to make government and business services more widely accessible to citizens. No technology has spread faster around the world (Economist, 2008). In 2007 alone, the African continent added over 60 million new mobile subscribers and mobile penetration in the region is now close to 30%. Mobiles can reach areas where there are infrastructure constraints for Internet service or where wired phone service is not a viable option.

With the global mass uptake of mobile phones, business players are seeking alternative channels for delivering consumer services and thus reaching new consumer base and enabling new business models. These developments are particularly relevant for developing countries with relatively high mobile penetration, as mobile can become a leapfrogging tool. For example, mobile platforms have been launched to enable the delivery of mobile payment applications and payment-related services in many countries such as the Philippines and South Africa. Financial services allowing mobile subscribers to send cash with a simple SMS have brought people without bank accounts to the world of financial transfer. Such application could potentially reach more than 80% of the populations in developing countries. Mobile operators are also bundling voice with other information services, such as agricultural information services in China and elsewhere (Economist, September 26, 2009).

Unlike the mobile, Internet and broadband access remain low in developing countries: Internet penetration stood at 10%, and broadband at just 3% (in 2006), and concentrated in urban areas. Mobile subscribers are the most evenly distributed and fixed broadband connections the least. As of 2006, broadband penetration has been dominated by the wealthy countries: 70% of broadband subscribers were located in high-income countries, which account for 16% of the world population. China alone accounted for 94% of broadband subscribers in the lower-middle income group of countries. Moreover, developing country subscribers are asked to pay multiple times the rates of developed countries and for relatively low-speed broadband access.

Developing countries aim to increase Internet access as well as improve the quality of access through broadband penetration. The advantages of broadband are becoming clear over time: ubiquitous always on access, high connection speeds, enhanced multimedia applications, enhanced customer relationships for business and government, enhanced security, and enhanced outsourcing. Broadband can also enable the use of content-intensive and socially interactive sites, the development of peer-to-peer communities, better and more diverse access to information, and dynamic approaches to capturing and disseminating knowledge (Qiang et al., 2009). It can thus contribute to accelerated development of human capital for the knowledge economy. Broadband can also play an important role in enabling innovation and collaborative R&D. Telemedicine is another promising area of broadband-enabled application. In many areas without direct access to critically needed medical specialists, broadband networks enable health specialists to use video conference facilities to do rapid diagnosis and treatment, while saving costs and travel time for patients. The information society requires high-quality access to communication and information tools and broadband-enabled services can potentially create many economic and empowerment opportunities.

These benefits are not automatic, however, and the potential of broadband contribution to growth and social development will depend on complementary investments in content, services, applications, human capacity, and institutional adjustments. As diffusion of broadband advances, the number of subscribers increases and applications supported by broadband reach a critical mass, the greater the benefits and network effects. New technologies such as WiMAX promise lower cost broadband services. Taiwan, China, aims to use WiMAX to make wireless broadband service available island-wide for applications such as e-learning and medical services.

Broadband growth is linked to increasing affordability of services and relevant content though a virtuous cycle. As more services become available at higher speeds, prices for usage falls and demand for bandwidth rises. The wider adoption of broadband enables new communication platforms and user-generated content. This is likely to change the way we communicate, in the same way as mobile has been changing the way we communicate. This is one more example of the virtuous cycles linking various elements of e-development.

A third major force that is shaping the NGN is VoIP. Voice-over-Internet-Protocol is fuelled by the demand for lower cost services and is being integrated into new services offered on IP networks such as instant messages and video and music sharing. VoIP challenges incumbent voice revenue streams, leading some countries to ban or limit VoIP. However, VoIP is increasingly used by businesses and individuals all over the world through different regulatory regimes and service plans. Some incumbent operators in developing countries are partnering with others to benefit from VoIP; an Algerian ISP is partnering with a French operator to enable its subscribers to make unlimited calls between France and Algeria. Software companies are expanding into the VoIP market while current VoIP providers are moving into mobile VoIP. Increasingly, operators are launching triple play packages (voice, Broadband Internet, and TV content) where voice is increasingly included in a flat rate package (ITU, 2007).

For developing countries, voice is likely to remain the key source of telecommunication traffic, until broadband is more widely available and capable of supporting multimedia applications. The migration toward NGN will make it increasingly possible to provide voice and Internet at affordable rates. A key to e-development is to create a critical mass of users by adopting business models that enable varied service offerings and make them affordable to poor users. Such models may include prepaid cards, micro-prepaid cards, and phone sharing from providers who can resell ICT services through microcredit. Creating regulatory and policy environments that support such business model innovations is key to enable growth in low-income segments.

Convergence is the fourth and perhaps most profound shaping force. Convergence is the erosion of boundaries among previously separate technologies, networks, services, and practices. It is manifested in the erosion of boundaries among telecommunications, broadcasting, and computing. The digitization of content and communication, IP networking, and the growth of broadband networks are important market enablers of such convergence. By using cheaper IP-based networking and offering multiple services (TV, telephone, broadband services), service providers are able to reduce costs per service and shore up revenues.

Convergence has profound implications for development as it opens up many possibilities for both service providers and ICT users. It can increase network efficiencies, new market entry, and access competition by enabling media, cable, and telecom companies (and other service providers) to enter each other's business, offer multiple services, and cover multiple markets. Network and service convergences can drive price cuts, stimulate business model innovation, improve the utilization of existing infrastructure, increase the reach of ICT and move countries closer to universal service. In turn, these improvements in efficiencies and access can lead to increased demand for content and applications and, in a virtuous cycle, could act as a catalyst for further network growth. Governments may therefore take a pro-convergence stand, seek to respond to and enable convergence, and thus realize the maximum benefits.

The above trends are mutually reinforcing (Fig. 9.1; see also Beardsley et al., 2004). For example, VoIP growth and broadband are mutually reinforcing, as VoIP services are more attractive over broadband access, and in turn, will increase the attractiveness of broadband and stimulate deeper broadband penetration. Also, convergence, mobile growth, and substitution, and broadband growth are mutually reinforcing. They substantially reinforce overall access competition. Convergence can either increase or reduce competition depending on market conditions and policy framework (Raja and Singh, 2009). The digitization of broadcasting could reduce the amount of spectrum required to carry television signals and free excess spectrum for broadband and new wireless services and networks. Comprehensive policies are important to align policy and regulatory responses and harness these interdependencies for maximum impact of ICT for development.

Fig. 9.1 Communication trends, mutually reinforcing

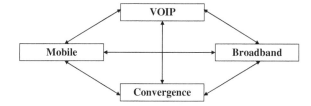

Future-Proof Regulation

These are challenging times for regulators. Regulation plays a key role in determining the pace of the above key trends, the freedom of incumbents to respond to these trends, and the opportunities to exploit the synergies among them. Migration to NGN will take time for most developing countries and may be seen as a continuation of their broadband and convergence policies. Maintaining competitive environment, providing regulatory clarity and certainty, and remaining agile and flexible are necessary conditions to manage these transitions, leapfrog whenever possible, and provide the foundation for an inclusive information society.

Regulatory frameworks need constant updating as technologies, market conditions, and business models change. Regulation should become an agent of change, enabling service providers, and users to harness the full potential of ICT for development. Regulatory inertia can interfere with an efficient evolution of the industry and migration to the NGN. Regulatory frameworks should seek to secure a competitive market and attract the substantial investments needed to ensure that new technologies and services are widely available.

It is beyond the scope of this book to cover such regulatory tools and practices (see ITU-infoDev ICT Regulatory Toolkit, 2000, to be updated). But some key pointers would suffice. It is important that policy makers think strategically about these trends be clear on how to use them for maximum contribution to selected development objectives. This would mean facilitating and even encouraging convergence, while maintaining a competitive environment. Developing countries seeking to build on their advance in mobile services may find that ensuring spectrum for competitive broadband wireless access (BWA) will be as important as adopting local-loop unbundling (requiring incumbents to open the last mile of their legacy networks to competitors) in urban areas to promote fixed line broadband. In the area of licensing, countries have begun to move away from service- and technology-specific licensing toward technology-neutral, more unified licensing or general authorization regimes.

Regulators will need to continue efforts to reduce barriers to market entry and make service provision more cost-effective. This may require renewed thinking about infrastructure sharing. In developing infrastructure-sharing models, regulators may seek to balance the goal of lowering the cost of network deployment with the risk that infrastructure sharing could undercut full competition (ITU, 2007).

Perhaps most important, universal access to affordable ICT should not be ignored in the move toward an NGN environment. On the one hand, developing countries have certain advantages in the migration toward NGN since they have fewer legacy networks and regulatory burdens and can leapfrog to NGN access infrastructure. On the other, the digital divide may grow as the economics of NGN deployment favor initial access network deployment in the urban and more profitable areas. Moreover, the migration to NGN implies that voice traffic will migrate to IP networks thus threatening universal service and access funding models. Creating the enabling environment for NGN deployment should therefore be closely examined and linked with efforts to bridge the digital divide. For example, the scope of universal service programs has begun to go beyond voice telephony. In 2006, India redefined universal access to include mobile and broadband.

Institutional and organizational changes for regulatory authorities are needed to align with these trends and reflect the marketplace. In such a fast changing technological and market environment, establishing independent, competent, and agile regulatory institutions remains as critical as ever. With convergence trends, more countries are moving to multi-sector or converged regulators with responsibilities over telecommunications, broadcasting, and information technology. This model is used in most EU countries as well as Brazil, Australia, Malaysia, South Africa, and several others. Such structures are better equipped to address convergent environments and to facilitate the transition to NGN. With a single government agency as regulator of all converging industry sectors, stakeholders have a one-stop-shop for resolving regulatory issues and consistent regulatory approach and practice. It reduces overlap and turf battles among government agencies. A single regulator would also have a critical mass of expertise and resources and can achieve certain operational efficiencies.

Telecom Policies for Inclusive Society

Telecom sector reform and the consequent migration to the NGN are long-term processes and may take many years to start bringing tangible benefits in terms of better quality of services, higher penetration, and lower Internet costs, particularly in rural areas. Establishing competent regulatory bodies to effectively enforce regulatory and competitive frameworks also takes time. Maintaining independent and effective regulatory bodies has proven to be a difficult and constant challenge in most developing countries.

To alleviate the connectivity problem in the short-to-medium term, countries have been using or experimenting with the following methods: (a) devising special policies and incentives to encourage infrastructure development in rural areas, (b) building subsidized networks for groups of users whose efficient interconnectivity is crucial for economic and social development, i.e., government, academic, R&D, and educational institutions; and (c) promoting shared (community) access to Internet and other ICT tools for disadvantaged and rural areas through telecenters.

Telecom Policies for Rural Areas

Rural areas in developing countries face two gaps: market efficiency and access (Fig. 9.2; Navas-Sabater et al., 2002). The market efficiency gap is the difference between the current level of service penetration and the level achievable in a liberalized market, under an effective regulatory environment. The access gap denotes a continuing gap between urban and rural areas or isolated and poor customers, even under efficient market conditions, since a large proportion of the population cannot afford the market prices at which the service is offered. The market gap can be closed by introducing competition in all service segments and geographic areas, without requiring public transfers. In general, the most effective policies are those aiming to close the market gap through the legal and regulatory framework for effective competition. Reducing the access gap to telecommunication services could be addressed through a variety of legal, supply, and demand mechanisms and funding options (Kunigami and Navas-Sabater, 2009).

Within the access gap, there is a level of penetration that may be called the *sustainability frontier*: it divides those projects that are expected to recover their operational costs and remain profitable, and where public financing works as a "jump-start," from those that would require ongoing subsidies. It is also important to note that all boundaries under this framework are not static. This calls for a continuous review of universal access policies and mechanisms, adapting them to "moving targets" made possible by changing technologies and market conditions.

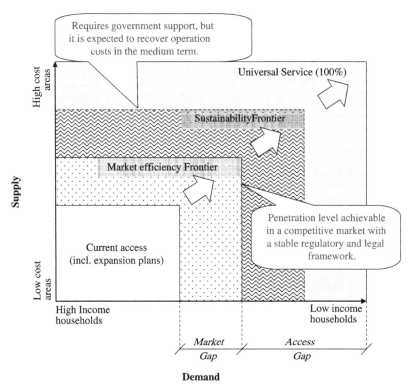

Fig. 9.2 Market gap and access gap model
Source: Navas-Sabater et al. (2002)

To close the access gap, governments need to deploy a mix of approaches, either stimulating supply by providing smart subsidies to reduce the costs (or investments) that operators have to incur in order to serve specific areas or stimulating demand and bottom-up mechanisms by providing direct transfers to end-users (either through cash or coupons) and leveraging new technological trends. These mechanisms are not mutually exclusive, and as in many other elements of e-development, they can be mutually reinforcing. For example, stimulating demand from government institutions as an element in the design of smart subsidies, can reduce demand risks, hence reduce the expected requested subsidy, and at the same time, improve government effectiveness.

Incentives to attract investors to high cost or less profitable areas can be created through universal access policies and public investment subsidy schemes. Under universal access schemes, telecom operators can be required to meet specific quality and connectivity criteria, such as service standards and infrastructure expansion in rural areas, in exchange for the lucrative licenses in urban areas. This approach, although commonly used, has not been effective in many developing countries. A relatively recent and promising alternative has been to devise well-targeted "smart subsidies" that can leverage competitive private investment through competitive tenders, reverse auction, or output-based aid. For example, Chile created a public fund that allocates investment subsidies on a competitive basis to private sector operators who agree to build and operate telecommunication services in commercially unattractive areas. Over a 5-year program, the fund led to dramatic reduction in subsidy per payphone and by 2002, payphones were extended to virtually all Chileans (Box 9.2).

Box 9.2 Rural Telecom Infrastructure Building, Chile

In order to improve telecom infrastructure in rural areas, the Chilean government established a special fund in 1994. The fund was financed by the government budget and managed by a council of the telecommunication minister. Based on geographical proximity and technical solutions, the councils' secretariat, the sector regulatory Subsecretaria de Telecomunicacion (SUBTEL) decided on annual projection, which was publicly announced to telecom companies. Then, through public tender, each project would be awarded to the bidder who asked for the lowest subsidies. Such system greatly contributed to reduction of government subsidies on rural telecom infrastructure development. In 1995, US $2.1 million subsides generated US $40 million of investments and 1285 rural phone lines; for comparison in 1980 s, $30 million subsidies created only 300 lines. The fund supported establishing lines to more than 6000 rural localities with about 2.2 million people between 1995 and 2000; the proportion of Chile's population without access to basic voice communication reduced from 15 to 1% between 1994 and 2002.

Reverse auctions and license obligations have an underlying assumption of economies of scale in telecommunications projects. They are usually designed for big national operators and would be too cumbersome for small rural operators. The new trends concerning convergence, mobile, wireless, broadband, and VoIP may bypass scale requirements or pose limitations on both mechanisms. Mobile services are shifting—albeit slowly—to serve rural and low-income areas with innovative business models such as Nokia's village connection model in India and Celtel's One Network in sub-Saharan Africa. Universal coverage objectives are extended to include broadband connectivity, telephony, and Internet to take advantage of new, lower cost wireless broadband technologies, including Wi-Fi, WiMAX, and GSM. The Last Mile Initiative of USAID is a pilot program that uses such technologies and relies on small local enterprises to sell telephone lines within rural areas in many countries.

The new trends can be leveraged to serve the rural and underserved areas through various mechanisms (Kunigami and Navas-Sabater, 2009). Some mechanisms are primarily legal and regulatory. In order to let small rural access networks provide voice and data services over a broadband network, they need to deliver voice services over Internet protocol (VoIP). Regulation for VoIP services and enforcement of interconnection arrangements are a necessary condition for the attractiveness of local access networks based on broadband connectivity. Flexible use of spectrum could lower entry costs for small local companies in rural areas. Lower costs in spectrum, network, and handsets would allow these companies to provide services to low-income populations as has been done in Brazil. Also, licensing local operators allow specific solutions for small towns and increase their sustainability by allowing revenues from on-net communications. Manufacturers such as Nokia–Siemens are developing solutions for such local-oriented models. Facilities sharing and open access among collaborating companies could extend service coverage toward low-income areas. For example, the Kenyan government is sponsoring a Fiber Optic National Network which in essence will have all existing operators sharing a nation-wide fiber optic network that none would have rolled out alone.

Other mechanisms involve supply-stimulation schemes through bottom-up projects. Successful reverse auctions may be complemented by funding mechanisms to deliver next generation projects involving community participation and innovative business models. By some estimates, only 11% of funds collected for Universal access strategies in Latin America have been committed as of 2005. Implementation of more flexible and fast allocation mechanisms, including bottom-up approaches (that is, projects that stem from communities, operators, or local entrepreneurs), is a way to accelerate delivery of services to beneficiaries. One example is Peru's Telecommunications Investment Fund (FITEL) that included the possibility of financing projects proposed by third parties (they being operators or not).

A final set of mechanisms involve institutional demand stimulation, to exploit economies of scale on the demand side. Such mechanisms can reduce both public transfers to universal access programs and overall government expense in communications. It is critical for these schemes to involve local authorities from the start. Contents and training must be put in place so that local authorities and the general population are able to get the most out of these investments. Coordination issues between multi-sector entities at central and local level may make implementation difficult. A successful example is the KII-G initiative (Korea Information Infrastructure—Government). By committing to become an anchor tenant of a nation-wide fiber optic network and providing soft loans to operators, the government leveraged its investment 19 times and created benefits estimated at $4 billion. Demand was stimulated or secured to serve e-government services, support massive computer literacy programs, and provide broadband connectivity to all schools.

Development of Dedicated Networks

Internet and secure networks to allow exchange of information and use of collaborative applications are essential for the efficient functioning of academic and

R&D institutions. Such academic networks have been emerging all over the world. Besides access to the Internet for institutional and individual members (faculty and students), they generally provide a number of high value-added services, such as e-mail, transferring and sharing of data, programs and documents, access to remote applications, databases or software libraries, and distributing electronic newsletters and forums.

National research and education networks (NRENs) meet high-end users through a dedicated infrastructure. Such users need to share images and large amounts of data for computationally intensive research problems. NRENs integrate scientists into wide research communities and provide easy access to networked resources. Given the dedicated infrastructure, scientists are also assured security for data transfer. They have become an essential part of the R&D infrastructure in 70 countries.[2] NRENs facilitate international innovation and collaboration through sharing data, building databases, conferences, joint experiments, setting of standards, sharing of equipments, solving global problems, and researching new networking technologies.

The high capital investment requirements to establish an NREN implies high risks if the infrastructure is underused (Dutz, 2007). The business model used to own and operate the NREN is critical to success, e.g., business arrangements with partnering telecoms and internal fee structure. Making the NREN affordable in early stages can be an effective way to demonstrate the many uses of high bandwidth. Academic institutions may also need to be subsidized in their information infrastructure investments at the local and campus levels. The culture and incentive regimes in academic and research institutions also need to be addressed to create the institutional conditions that create demand for quality research and NREN use (Box 9.3).

Box 9.3 Academic and Research Network: Hungary, India, and Brazil

About a half of Internet users in the country get free or almost free connection through the Hungarian Academic and Research Network, HungarNet (http://www.hungarnet.hu). It has 900–1000 institutional members—educational and research institutions, libraries, and museums. Institutional members contribute about 10% to the HungarNet's budget, the rest is provided by the Ministry of Culture and Education. As a result, the growth of the Internet in Hungary has been driven mainly by demand in the academic sector. High level of connectivity in the Academia contributes to the increasing quality of research and education in the country.

---

[2]Source: http://internet2.edu.

India is launching a program to upgrade its ICT infrastructure for universities and high-end research institutions. India's NREN will operate as a layered hierarchy of national backbone, state networks, and metropolitan area networks connecting individual campus networks (Dutz, 2007). Many institutional issues are under consideration. Who will manage the network? Who will be the strategic partners? How should India foster a programmatic roll-out, starting with a prototype, aggregating unused infrastructure, and building on it as needed? How should India stimulate demand and manage the risks of large upfront investments?

Brazil established its scientific and academic network (RNP) almost 20 years ago. The Federal Government maintains the RNP, which is managed by a private company. RNP's 2004 initiative created the Community Education and Research Network (called *Redes Comunitárias de Educação e Pesquisa—Redecomep*). It has established new partnerships to expand high-speed Internet access for education purposes, digital inclusion, and to promote Brazil's competitiveness in the knowledge-based global economy. Combined with Brazil's interactive digital television initiative, the impact could be impressive, helping create a more equitable and more competitive Brazil, the two central objectives of Brazil's development strategy (Knight, 2008).

Two aspects of the *Redecomep* are particularly interesting beyond the immediate objective of linking teaching and research institutions with high-speed Internet connections. First, although the *Redecomep* initiative provides funding for network investment from the Ministry of Science and Technology (MCT) through the Financer of Studies and Projects (*Financiadora de Estudos e Projetos*—Finep), it also encourages a wide variety of partnerships for the construction and financing of operating costs. These partnerships have included municipal governments, state governments, and both public and private sector enterprises.

Second, among the enterprises are electric power distribution companies. Most of these—pipeline companies, railroads and other utilities—have fiber optic networks of their own, with a lot of excess capacity given the continual improvements in data transmission technologies for fiber optic cable. By establishing partnerships with such companies, *Redecomep* networks can greatly expand the reach of their networks at very low cost. Likewise, when *Redecomep* invests in its own fiber networks, it can offer excess capacity to other users, thus helping reduce current costs to its own users as well as to its partners.

In many countries, however, such networks are often limited to universities and R&D institutions. The problem is that middle and elementary schools are often partially financed from local or regional budgets and thus ICT investments among educational entities vary significantly, with few institutions in better-off regions investing heavily and others lagging further behind. As a result, the "digital divide" is growing between institutions in the same class as well as between levels of the educational system. The trend will persist as long as educational institutions, and especially middle and elementary schools, continue to rely on their own resources for ICT financing and are not part of any wider support group or network.

Government could either create separate school networks with centralized financing or expand academic networks to cover the entire educational and R&D system, including schools, universities, libraries, research institutions, and archives. The last option, for example, was implemented in Finland. It helped to create major synergistic and spill-over effects that otherwise would not have been possible and that were essential part of a highly successful e-strategy.

To help finance school networks and connectivity, developing countries often opt to develop school-based computer labs into multi-purpose telecenters that provide services to populations after regular school hours and on the weekends. As a general matter, such option is not desirable for businesses due to inconvenient schedule, but suits the general population well. However, schools-based telecenters may not function effectively within the constraints of bureaucratic schools system.

In government, business process automation and modernization of services for citizens and businesses require government-wide data exchange and communications among various agencies. In most developing countries, however, government computerization and networking programs are fragmented along administrative lines and are largely confined to computerization of offices, with limited attention paid even to the Local Access Networks (LAN). One of the major benefits of ICT for public sector—efficient networking and exchange of information—has been largely ignored.

As a general matter, only a handful of government agencies in developing countries have gateways with other organizations (Wide Access Networks, WAN). Networking among the offices of central and regional governments is especially poor. A significant part of government bodies do not even have Internet access. Even the entities that claim to be connected to the Internet often have a very small number of computers that can benefit from this connection because they have limited availability of internal networks.

Aside from lack of financial resources, there are two interrelated reasons for this state of affairs. First, e-government projects are often donor-driven, with limited overall coordination. In this strategic vacuum, some government agencies have disproportionately large number of computers while others have almost none, with networks limited to the organizations supported by a particular donor. Second, there is a persistent misconception that inter-agency networking is a secondary priority—something that governments start to deal with only after all agencies are computerized and internally networked. Millions of dollars are being invested into ICT systems in government bodies on largely autonomous basis. As a result, the country may actually have several incompatible networks that "cannot talk to each other."

Resolving the interoperability issues after the fact may be very costly and time-consuming, severely limiting government's ability to modernize its internal operations and introduce joined-up services to citizens and businesses. Efficient government networking should be a primary thrust of the e-government programs from the very beginning and should include development of interoperability standards and data exchange guidelines. This will allow governments to save significant resources and interconnect various emerging government networks into a national public sector network for the efficient functioning of the whole government.

Information Infrastructure and e-Development

A dynamic information infrastructure and a competitive communication services industry provide the foundation for enabling new development strategies. Recent advances in communication technologies, including broadband and wireless communications, mobile and smart devices, and convergence, further reinforce the need for dynamic and flexible regulatory frameworks. To accelerate ICT adoption and diffusion at affordable costs to developing countries, regulators should promote shared infrastructures, shared capabilities, open networks, and open platforms. They should ensure that new and innovative players can enter the market, interconnect, and compete. They may encourage mobile service providers to standardize so as to enable shared applications and local content development. They may encourage global operators to partner with local ones to accelerate and broaden adoption and promote understanding of local needs.

Defining a national aspiration for broadband should be set in the context of a national e-Transformation strategy: does a world class communications matter for the country and its development strategy? Does the country need to get there sooner rather than later? How should this investment be sequenced with demand for digital content and ICT-enabled public and private services? What is the preferred path to achieve this aspiration? What does the sequence of rollout looks like? How much it would cost? How would the country pay for it? What are the implications for the regulatory framework?

Governments may play a key role in accelerating the rollout of broadband. Many advanced countries and progressive local governments have assumed this role in recognition of the competitive advantage of early adoption of broadband. They can play an influential role in creating a shared broadband backbone infrastructure and in encouraging such sharing at local levels to reach a critical mass at affordable costs. Government can be a lead user, catalyzing the demand for broadband, cloud computing, and Internet-based software services. Governments in poor countries also need to balance investments in advanced broadband infrastructure with concerns for extending connectivity to the rural and poor regions and leveraging the use of existing infrastructure for pro-poor and less-bandwidth demanding applications.

The information infrastructure does not provide development on its own. Correlations between telecommunications penetration (teledensity) and GDP of countries can be misleading, if they were to be interpreted as deterministic or causing development on its own. This infrastructure is mainly an enabler or catalyst of other activities, provided it operates within a healthy local ecosystem of content and solution providers, application developers, capable users, and supportive policies. Demand in developing countries will continue to be driven by level of literacy and the availability of compelling content in local languages. Governments may encourage partnerships among telecom services providers and content and application providers so as to leverage the existing infrastructure for a maximum development impact. They may promote dialogue among operators and providers, and various users, including citizens and business and government agencies so as to identify bottlenecks and opportunities for diffusion. They may provide incentives or competition-based funding for innovative partnerships to develop solutions and applications in mobile banking and microfinance, health surveillance systems, delivery of health services to rural areas, and other priority development programs.

Chapter 10
Shared Access for Inclusive Society

Many developing countries must rely on shared access models to ensure afford-able connectivity and access to ICT tools (UNCTAD, 2003; Fillip and Foote, 2007). Community telecenters (also known as public Internet access points or PIAP, information centers, kiosks, cybercafé, and multi-purpose telecenters) have increasingly become critical components of broader strategies to deliver univer-sal access and extend connectivity to rural, disadvantaged, and remote areas in developing and transitional countries. Even more importantly, telecenters are emerg-ing as vital development and poverty reduction tools. They can serve as means to deliver government services to poor and rural regions, provide vital information and new business opportunities for SMEs, and enable community-driven development through enhancing participation and capacity building at the grassroots level.

The concept of telecenter as a means of connectivity, shared access to Internet and ICT applications, and a variety of value-added services is relatively new. It is a flexible approach to connectivity that can be adapted to a wide range of local needs and circumstances and alternative e-development strategies. It can be viewed as part of the communication infrastructure. But can also be viewed as a microenterprise and a locus of local entrepreneurial development. The concept is evolving. More than just providing shared facilities and services, telecenters can play a major role in developing human capital, social development, and rural development.

There are many types of telecenters based on management style: commercial (cybercafé, mainly offering Internet access), franchise model, NGO-run community telecenter, school-based telecenters, library-based telecenters, local government or municipal-based telecenters, cooperative telecenters (as in Philippines's B2B Price Now and India's Wired Village in Maharashtra), and the multi-purpose telecenter. The range of telecenter types continues to expand to fit into various niches and contexts, with rich lessons to be drawn for sustainability and scaling up.

The record of telecenter development, however, has been mixed. Many telecen-ters, especially donor-supported ones, struggle to financially sustain their operations and demonstrate impact on the development of the target regions. Increasing impact and scaling up from pilot projects for specific locations to national or regional cover-age also proved problematic. Several interrelated challenges need to be addressed if telecenters are truly to become agents of social development and economic growth: developing sustainable business models, providing the right mix of services, and

N.K. Hanna, *e-Transformation: Enabling New Development Strategies*, Innovation,
Technology, and Knowledge Management, DOI 10.1007/978-1-4419-1185-8_10,
© Springer Science+Business Media, LLC 2010

using cost-effective technologies. Emerging lessons are both rich and encouraging. Scaling telecenters for development is emerging as a national and international movement whereby consumers and communities are co-creating the telecenters as institutions that will enable them to pursue their own ICT-enabled development (Fillip and Foote, 2007).

In this chapter, we first outline the need to understand the local context in order to plan for impact, scale, and sustainability of telecenters. Second, we identify the range of organizational options—reflecting various roles for government, private sector, and civil society to match the local context and e-readiness. Third, we examine the mix of services and content needed to be delivered through the telecenters to ensure impact and sustainability. Fourth, technology options are touched on briefly to emphasize the need for affordable and replicable solutions. Fifth, the role of developing national and international networks among telecenters is examined in order to build capacity, share services, and engage other partners. Finally, we conclude this chapter by drawing on lessons learned, view telecenters as part of a bigger ecosystem of e-development, and recommend a strategic approach to scale up and accelerate learning.

Socio-economic Context for Telecenters

A key lesson of past pilots is the need to design telecenter programs based on good understanding of local needs and resources, to engage communities in the process, and to partner with outside organizations such as agricultural extension services and educational institutions. Data on community needs and readiness can help shape decisions regarding types of services and a possible pricing structure. Scaling up telecenters from pilots to national programs requires engaging both local communities and national-level institutions that may become part of the telecenter ecosystem.

A host of methodologies exist to capture rural realities: rapid rural appraisal, participatory rural appraisal (PRA), and market analysis, among others. PRA can be very useful since it involves social mobilization—a cortical success factor in telecenter programs. These methodologies have been adapted from the work of the World Bank with Community-Driven Development (CDD), UNESCO's Community Multimedia Centers, and others. Drishtee, an Indian ICT enterprise, evolved an entrepreneurial network of kiosks, offering a variety of services targeted to local contexts. It adopted a simple rural segmentation methodology that takes account of poverty level (rural economics); population, literacy, and role of local actors (rural dynamics); and state of rural infrastructure.

Scaling up to national programs requires a typology of zones for which telecenter models can be designed. It looks beyond scanning individual communities and toward assessing broader geographic units for potential synergies, for example, to assign larger centers to centrally located communities to serve as hubs for small centers. Local scanning also helps connect local- and national-level institutions—to become clients, service providers, or support agencies.

Business Models and Financial Sustainability

The key factor for success is to understand the local context and overall objectives of the telecenter program to decide on a business model or organizational approach that fits local realities. Is the current context one in which the market is undeveloped? Is there a strong base of NGOs to lead and scale up along a social enterprise model? Can the private sector play a leading role? What kind of an evolutionary path can be taken to move from the present situation to a desired future for the nation, for different geographic regions, and particularly for the underserved and the poor? What institutional resources are available or could be developed and what are the strengths and weaknesses of available candidates? Given the dynamics of information and communication technologies and emerging markets, any telecenter program must be designed to evolve and adapt its business models and services to take advantage of this dynamism.

Sustainability is a key concern about telecenter initiatives. The majority of telecenters that have been launched in the first wave of donor-driven initiatives have not been financially sustainable without continuous outside funding (Stoll, 2003). This many not be a problem in itself if public support is affordable and justifiable in view of other development priorities and if institutional and social sustainability are secured. Telecenters influence social, political, and cultural aspects of comprehensive community development. In this light, they can be viewed as a public good, similar to education, health, water, and transportation systems and may have legitimate claim for continuous government or donor support. Governments can raise money for developing public access centers by creating special universal access funds that channel a percentage of telecommunications operators' income (UNCTAD, 2003). For example, Canada's community access program helped establish 8000 telecenters by mobilizing civil society and awarding grants to individual telecenter initiatives led by NGOs that agree to provide certain levels of service and to "match" grant funding with local resources (Proenza, 2001).

The problem with the "public goods" approach is that it is often used as an excuse for poor management and planning. Lacking financial incentives to perform, telecenter management can become unresponsive to the needs of the community. Subsidized telecenters may also create market distortions and prevent commercial enterprises from entering the field. Thus, many countries have recently opted for increased private sector participation in telecenter development.

In some Latin American countries, for example, the state intervened in closing the access gap by providing so-called "smart subsidies" to the privately owned telecenters through the universal access funds. Since the level of sustained commercial demand for telecenter services in rural and disadvantaged communities is in many circumstances lower than that required for financial sustainability of the telecenter, the smart subsidy concept strives to cover the difference while still encouraging private investment, competition, and entrepreneurship in service provision. In this scenario, government specifies minimum service requirements for a certain period of time and allocates the subsidy to the lowest bidder. Actual disbursement of the subsidy is linked to the pre-specified performance indicators. Smart subsidies have been applied in Chile, Guatemala, Peru, and a number of other Latin American countries. The full evaluation is still pending, but early results are encouraging. Smart subsidies have shown to be a very cost-effective way to encourage the provision of basic ICT services among disadvantaged communities.

The state should provide some capacity building support to the telecenters as many of them lack customer service and marketing experience. It may also provide relevant content and channel its services through the telecenters. It can stimulate the development of Internet content providers. However, the telecenters should be expected to run as commercial enterprises and should be free to change the service package beyond the minimum agreed requirements for the smart subsidy.

The commercial model, however, also has its downside. It focuses on commercial services alone and tends to ignore other services, even if they have a significant social and developmental impact. ICT education and vocational training, e-health and similar services may have low commercial appeal for entrepreneurs in poor countries. One of the biggest challenges for the telecenter movement is to find a management/ownership structure that would combine the benefits of both the worlds: the social impact and development focus of the government or NGO-run telecenter and the flexibility and financial viability of a commercial enterprise.

Grassroots organizations and NGOs are good at reaching the poor, women, and the disabled, at developing community-learning centers and at building social capital. But because they rely on external fund raising, financial sustainability and accountability remain in question. NGO-led models may reflect the current state of low-access and high-connectivity costs which has forced many groups with social development agenda (NGOs) to become providers of shared access in order to deliver their services through telecenters. In the longer term, however, it is likely that most NGOs and local governments will be users of shared ICT infrastructure to deliver their development services and serve their beneficiaries.

Commercial telecenters promise financial sustainability and accountability as they meet a market need, but their development impact and reach may be limited. Telecenter models must adapt to context and target groups. As target population moves from the educated, urban, and young, capacity building and user training become critical and pure commercial models become less feasible. To reach a large mass of low-income people will require social marketing, start-up investment, training, and demand support, at least during the learning stages.

Various approaches appear promising to augment the sustainability of either the commercial or NGO-led model. One scheme is to provide vouchers to stimulate demand from target groups such as women, students, or poor farmers. Another promising approach is the franchise model, especially applied in Asian countries. The umbrella organization or support institution (franchiser) may be a public–private partnership, ensuring developmental focus of the project and setting standards and guidelines for the technology and services. Franchisees—private companies or community organizations running telecenters—comply to those standards as part of the license agreement to obtain government assistance, which may or may not be in a form of smart subsidies, and in exchange of franchiser's continuous support in various forms, such as training, content and service development, technical support, special telecom access rates, revenue-sharing arrangements for provision of e-government and e-business services. Most notably, this approach has been successfully used in a number of Indian states.

Whatever the management structure chosen, evidence from past experience suggests that telecenters are most effective when they are run and managed by local entrepreneurs and communities, as opposed to donor agencies and central state agencies (Proenza, 2001). One variation is to combine NGO or government ownership with the private sector day-to-day management of the telecenters. This organizational structure has been applied for Hungarian telecottages, many of which have the owner as a civil organization, the host as the local government, and the operator as a private company (Wormland and Gaspar, 2003). The primary role of governments and aid organizations should be to help create an enabling policy and institutional environment for various telecenter models to become sustainable.

In the context of scaling up to national programs, covering a broad range of geographic areas with varying e-readiness and market maturity, a flexible approach or multiple models may be needed, as was adopted in the case of e-Sri Lanka and the Gyandoot program (Box 10.1). Many programs are moving to a middle ground between purely commercial and purely subsidized models, or to hybrid organizational models—social enterprise approaches that combine social objectives with a market approach. The social enterprise model tries to balance social needs and economic realities to maximize both sustainability and development impact.

Box 10.1 Organizational Models and Services from Brazil, Egypt, and India

In Brazil, the Committee for Democratization of Information Technology (CDI), an NGO, has pioneered a social franchise approach to provide access to ICT and develop marketable skills and community leaders among poor urban youth. CDI partners with the community to develop information technology and citizenship schools that are managed by community members and focuses on ICT themes important to the community. CDI obtains financial resources from partnerships with government and the private sector. CDI provides schools with necessary start-up resources, but schools must generate resources to sustain their activities through fees. This is in essence a *social franchise* model that targets disadvantaged urban youth. It has proven to be replicable.

In Egypt, the Ministry of Communications and Information Technology (MCIT) has launched the technology club initiative. MCIT partnered with Microsoft and UNDP in 2003 to train the trainers, so IT clubs have qualified trainers and standardized curricula. Focus of clubs is to reach the poor youth, rural areas, and women—thus clubs are often located in schools, youth centers, and universities. Small businesses are also able to use the clubs at designated times for a nominal fee. Currently, MCIT manages the IT clubs and provides the trained managers. This is a *government-led* model with a strong learning component.

In India, the Gyandoot program is a government-to-citizen service delivery portal and multi-purpose telekiosk that brings ICT-enabled services to poor rural areas. It is a *hybrid* model, but involves significant government leadership, local government involvement, and participation of the private sector through local entrepreneurs. There are two organizational models: one led by village committee and the other by a local entrepreneur. In the village model, the committee invests in providing the physical space and hardware. The kiosk operator is selected from three nominees proposed by the community. He is not paid a salary, but gives 10% of his earnings to the village. The district council trains the nominees. In the entrepreneur model, the local entrepreneur registers as owner and assumes all expenses and pay a licensing fee.

The top-down approach used in this model has led to limited fit of the services offered and limited involvement from NGOs and community-based organizations. Services did not attract popular demand among rural poor—leading to sustainability problems.

Drishtee—a private sector-led initiative—is attempting to scale up Gyandoot to the national level, adding and adapting services and transforming this model in the process. *Drishtee* shows encouraging results. The main difference may be the more flexible approach to service provision. *Drishtee* positions itself "not as a rural service provider but as a platform for integrating and delivering a wide range of services to the Indian villager. . . .*Drishtee* would offer its network platform to any service provider who wishes to market its range of services to rural India." (Drishtee.com) Currently, the localized Intranet between villages and a district center provides access to various services, including online land record, registration and applications of income and domicile certificates, market-related information of cereal crops, government health, and education benefits.

Mix of Services, Impact, and Sustainability

Telecenters can significantly enhance their financial viability, as well as their potential for social impact by delivering value-added services that are tailored specifically to the communities' needs and demand. Telecenters can be powerful mediators between users and service providers. Value-added mediation can be simple yet vital and can range from provision of information about how to do it and where to go to get services, to the provision of e-health, e-education, or other e-government services.

The service choice for telecenters can be boiled down to two basic options: to focus on "access to the ICT" (Internet, etc.) or "access to services" (eGov, eBiz, etc.). The first option is simpler, cheaper, and arguably more demand driven. Such "generic" telecenters would provide access just to the medium of interaction—Internet and other basic ICTs such as telephone, fax, computer. Thus, they would stimulate the demand for ICT-based services, but service and content creation would be largely left to the market and/or government. Business-run telecenters often go for this option.

The other approach strives to provide access not so much to the "generic" ICT per se, but to a certain set of ICT-based services believed to have significant overall social and economic impact, such as e-government and e-business services. Such multi-purpose telecenters require more elaborate project design and management schemes. It is often deployed by the government-run telecenters, public–private partnerships, or NGOs.

Telecenters may be thought as composite centers, part technology, center, part community center, part learning center, and part business center. The appropriate mix will vary for different contexts. Services may also increase in diversity and complexity over time, with increased management competency, number of partnerships, and local e-literacy and market maturity. For example, basic communications, some popular information services like land records, and computer training services can be provided on for-profit basis, and then start building demand for more advanced services. Some services may need to be supported initially to build demand for other IT-based services, for example, e-literacy.

The choice between the two options—"simple" or multi-purpose telecenters—very much depends on the local environment. Single-purpose telecenters are simpler to launch and manage at low costs. Many government agencies are motivated to initiate their own telecenters to deliver their own sectoral services. But the rural contexts are very thin markets and a strategy of a series of vertically organized providers of shared access would be costly in the aggregate. Various value-added services potentially increase demand for telecenters. Multi-purpose telecenters ultimately add more value since they can be more directly linked to wider development and poverty reduction efforts. The cost efficiencies of a single, general-purpose center, with government services as part of the mix, are compelling. In the final analysis, telecenters are about empowering people with knowledge and services. Simple access to ICT without relevant local content and services may not be able to provide such empowerment.

Some services cannot be developed without higher level network support, as in e-government and e-learning. A franchise or network may be essential for expansion and diversification into high value-added services. In India and Bangladesh, franchising schemes are attempting to leverage infrastructure and network economies with a large network of franchisees and a comprehensive service package. In India, some states have encouraged commercially driven information kiosks that proved popular in providing access to basic government forms and transactions. Milk cooperative societies have aggregated the demands of small dairy farmers into self-financing multi-service kiosks. They started with simple automating of quality measurement of milk and payment for milk producers, and then they built databases from such information to support producers, developed dairy information services, and then expanded to provide a portal for other valued services and for sharing local innovations. The Grameen Bank has extended the highly successful microcredit for mobile phones to cyber kiosks in rural Bangladesh.

To successfully implement multi-purpose telecenter projects, it is crucial to analyze local needs and service deficiencies and to establish strong partnerships with service and content providers. Experience shows that the biggest gap in developing countries is in local content and government-related services. In remote and rural communities, such services are often missing altogether or delivered very inefficiently. Many telecenter programs have underestimated the challenges of content development and assumed that individual telecenters needed to create content that would be needed in their context. But content development is expensive. Telecenter movements may mobilize other information producers and domain experts to adapt those sources' existing resources through localization. Local and central governments may sign revenue-sharing agreements with telecenter networks on provision of e-government services. Educational institutions can deliver credible course offerings. Telecenters can add considerable value by organizing pointers to relevant content on the web, rather than trying to offer unique local content.

Social services such as education and health are also increasingly popular choice for telecenters. For example, clinical e-health applications (including veterinary services) have the most direct impact on the quality of services to the poor. There is a growing number of success stories with the use of low-cost applications, such as e-mail and simple digital cameras, to diagnose and deliver timely health services.

Public funding may be essential to build demand and ensure equity of access and achieve a balance between telecenters' social and economic goals. Vouchers may be used for a limited time to increase awareness of and demand for services by target groups and to increase the capacity of users to buy other services in the future. Government and aid agencies may finance the delivery of certain extension services and other development programs through the existing telecenters' infrastructure.

One recent trend of service development is financial services (insurance, microcredit, and banking) and business services for rural enterprises as well as agricultural logistics and marketing. Rural information and advisory system and e-business applications help to improve business environment and bridge gaps between market demands and supplies, thus enabling rural enterprises to conquer many inherent disadvantages. E-Choupal is an interesting example of creating a vast network of rural kiosks that currently reaches 3.5 million farmers in 31,000 villages in 6 Indian states. It provides access to agricultural information, aggregates demand for farm inputs, help sell farm produce from the farmer's doorsteps, and reduces transaction costs and wasteful intermediation to farmers, among others.

Overall, the key to substantial developmental impact and long-term sustainability of telecenter programs is flexibility, scalability, and phased development. An e-development strategy should examine various business models and mix of services, pilot them in a few representative locations, and only then expend it to include new geographic and service areas. Value-added services should be piloted and phased and should be part of a continuous process of business development, not a one-shot event or a fully engineered and centrally driven package.

Cost-Effective and Affordable Technologies

To be cost efficient, a telecenter program has to be technology neutral, allowing for a choice in technology solutions, for example, among fixed or wireless technologies. Given the fast change in information and communication technologies, bridging the digital divide will demand remaining flexible and agile to take advantage of new technologies that are most appropriate to rural areas and low-income economies. Latest technological advances show great promise for reducing costs for shared access at the community level. There are growing options for affordable and user-friendly solutions, such as low-cost and open-source software; low-cost, ruggedized, and power-efficient computers; and Wireless Fidelity.[1]

Connectivity is essential for telecenter viability and more importantly for the effective integration with and contribution of the telecenter program to overall e-development. Mutually supportive strategies can speed the process of scaling up broadband connectivity for telecenters. Extending each of networks to rural areas often requires creative combinations of technologies to address the specific needs of diverse areas. Scaling up development impacts will also require attention to appropriate end-user technologies such as providing Internet connectivity to radio stations to extend the reach of Internet to the least literate population. New high-broadband wireless solutions open up significant opportunities to provide affordable broadband access to rural telecenters.

The challenge remains to find cost-effective solutions that are appropriate for different uses, geographies, and socioeconomic environments. A carefully chosen mix of technologies and software is often the most appropriate option for addressing local needs. Appropriate technology should be more easily appropriated. A hybrid approach that mixes old and new technologies, such as broadcasting and Internet technologies, may also provide the most benefit for rural communities. Software with user-friendly interfaces, local language versions, and wide distribution is often the easiest for users to master and to find appropriate training, maintenance, and local support. This again points to the link between telecenters and the healthy

---

[1] For example, in the past, telecenters in rural areas relied either on fixed-line or VSAT technology, which implied significant connectivity costs for these telecenters. Emergence of Wireless Fidelity (Wi-Fi) provided a potentially powerful tool to narrow the digital divide and bolster economic development in rural areas. Wi-Fi provides broadband Internet access to specially outfitted PCs within certain distance from the transmitter. Wi-Fi presents many advantages that make it a suitable solution to support connectivity. Wi-Fi is comparatively cheap (less than US $250 for a small installation), fast and reliable, easy to install, and has low maintenance requirements. With the use of Wi-Fi, it is possible to share the VAST link among several telecenters in a region, thereby achieving economies of scale and reducing cost per telecenter. It operates on unlicensed airwave spectrum, so there are no extra monthly costs on top of the charge for a broadband connection that is shared among the users.

development of a local ICT industry to support cost-effective telecenter technology maintenance, software application, and local adaptation.

Capacity Building to Manage Shared Access

As a mass movement, based on entrepreneurship and new skills, telecenters are dependent on people for success and sustainability. Telecenter managers, local ICT champions, infomediaries play key roles in promoting the effective use of telecenters. But such entrepreneurship and skills are scarce, particularly among rural populations and the poor. Telecenter managers should be first and foremost entrepreneurs, as they are not necessarily the ones with advanced computing skills. They require a mix of business and technical skills and an understanding of the communities in which they serve. The local champion helps make a telecenter project become more locally driven and can play a key role in communication with the community, be an advisor to the initiative, and act as a catalyst to help the initiative introduce innovation (Bridges.org).

Scaling up telecenters to a national program presents special human resource challenges. Such scaling up is risky because of the lead time needed to develop these resources, which are often neglected in favor of investment in hardware and facilities. Innovative methods must be found to accelerate the process of developing and supporting the appropriate cadre of qualified local managers and operators in areas as diverse as business management, technical maintenance, and community development. Networks, associations, telecenter support institutions, and franchise models can provide mentoring, marketing, operational guidelines, and ongoing support to these pioneers. Networks can deliver capacity building programs, work closely with established training and distance education providers, and/or identify and catalogue existing training materials and curricula.

Collaborating for Community and Shared Services

Individual telecenter managers and operators face common challenges but are geographically isolated from their peers. They need national networks or associations to act as a peer support group and gain access to technical support, shared services and content, coaching on management issues, training courses, and economies of scale (Fillip and Foote, 2007). Networks can help monitor and evaluate ongoing initiatives and help synthesize and share lessons across initiatives. They help exploit "network externalities" among the increasing number of telecenter managers and users. They can provide advocacy- and policy-related activities to support and accelerate the development of a national telecenter movement. They thus play an essential role in the telecenter ecosystem by providing the connecting points between telecenters and all other players and partners.

Sustainability cannot be achieved without efficient networking among telecenters. In order for telecenters to share costs, develop local content, achieve economies of scale as well as effectively perform their functions, they need to be organized in overlapping national, regional, and international networks. In the last few years, national-level telecenter networks have emerged in several countries where the telecenter movement has reached a critical mass. In a few cases, the creation of such networks has been explicitly considered at the program design stage, as has been the case in Hungary.

Scaling up telecenters into a national program should explore how to integrate existing telecenters into new networks and leverage past experience for scaling up. Telecenter networking and working on the overall telecenter ecosystem should not be an afterthought. In Sri Lanka, for example, Sri Lanka's largest NGO, Saravodya, drew on its 50 years of community organizing and its shorter but significant experience with NGO-run telecenters to build bridges among different kinds of telecenter managers—including the entrepreneurial and community-run models, temple-based and library-based models, and various NGO models. This helped to build a national telecenter family—encouraging peer learning and knowledge sharing, and increasingly, providing content and marketing support.

Transnational franchises are a new source for scaling up telecenter programs and for transferring know-how in developing business models and social entrepreneurs as franchisees. OneRoof is a pioneering model of such franchise, with a focus on the needs of those at the bottom of the pyramid. It is a not-for-profit organization that is moving a business or for-profit enterprise to secure scale and self-sustainability. It works as an honest broker and collaborates with local partners that have met rigorous criteria for content, local quality, and business integrity. It started in Mexico and now offering telecenter franchise in India and expected to extend to other countries and services. Its role is to help local partners to scale good programs and/or reach more serious impact in changing the way essential services are delivered to the world's rural poor. It develops and shares a delivery platform that provides rural communities with essential services and embeds the telecenter into comprehensive e-strategy and rural development.

Linking Telecenters to e-Development Ecosystem

The development stage for telecenters has changed; they cannot continue to be donor-driven pilots as they have been in the 1990 s. Telecenter programs should become locally driven national movements that can exploit network economies and build a vibrant telecenter ecosystem. A telecenter ecosystem would encompass the local telecenters, the networks, and support institutions that provide technical services and training and the organizations and social enterprises that can provide content and services via the telecenters such as rural health care, e-government, and remittances. It includes the local investors and international NGOs who fund the

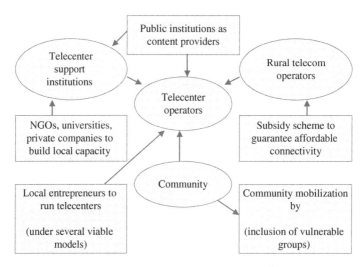

Fig. 10.1   Key institutional roles and links in the telecenter program[2]

centers. A simplified presentation of the ecosystem for telecenters shows some of the key partner institutions that have been engaged in the development and support of telecenters in the e-Sri Lanka program (Fig. 10.1).

Building a vibrant telecenter ecosystem is really about a transformation of the environment within which individual telecenters operate. National policies and public programs for ICT-enabled development do matter for the viability and impact of the telecenters and the creation of a vibrant telecenter ecosystem. They can influence where these telecenters will be located, what they will be used for, and what incentives government agencies face in using this new infrastructure for delivering their own services most effectively.

Policy makers shaping e-development strategies need to help the evolution of a balanced and vibrant telecenter ecosystem. This means influencing a host of stakeholders and institutions: those providing connectivity and access, schools and universities, central agencies concerned with rural and SME development, local governments, private sector associations, technical support institutions, banks and microfinance institutions, among others.

Although there are no blueprints for scaling up or building a vibrant telecenter ecosystem, substantial experience is accumulating within and among countries. Each country has its own history of telecenter development which should influence the path and pace of its development. But a common lesson is to build on what exists, on the experience in building partnerships across stakeholders, on realistic assessment of the country's readiness, and on learning from the pioneers. A phased approach is necessary to link the telecenter program to the e-readiness of

---

[2]Hanna, 2007a.

diverse geographic regions in a country, to the development of other elements of e-development such as the telecommunications infrastructure and e-government, and to other socioeconomic development goals.

Countries have adopted a variety of approaches for scaling up, ranging from an emergent strategy or organic approach, to a deliberate or programmatic approach. The main difference between the two approaches is the degree of deliberate planning and central government leadership. An organic approach was adopted by default by many countries where governments viewed the telecenters as private enterprises, NGOs, or donor-driven initiatives, with limited role for governments. Telecenters were individual initiatives and many were bound to fail. No ecosystem view or coordination was necessary. This approach was viewed as necessary in view of the dependency of telecenters on their microenvironment and the socio-economic conditions of the community they aim to serve. It was an inevitable approach for large and very diverse countries like India and Brazil. But many small and medium countries have also taken this approach by default, leaving the telecenters purely dependent on isolated local initiatives. As a first order of business, the role of government is to create the right enabling environment or the right set of incentives in place for an organic scale up to happen.

A deliberate strategy or programmatic approach aims to accelerate the process of scaling up through government leadership. This leadership goes beyond creating the enabling environment to support capacity building and partnership building. It helps build networks of interested parties. It may also involve smart subsidized schemes for connectivity to rural telecenters, microfinance schemes for telecenter operators, and encouraging government agencies to use the telecenters as a delivery infrastructure for government services. In addition to creating a momentum, this approach takes account of the underdeveloped state of the information and rural markets, and the undersupply of capital. It attempts to address the development and digital divides between the urban and rural areas and to reduce the risk that the private will limit the high margin elite markets in urban areas.

But a purely programmatic strategy carries some risks as government may exert inappropriate top-down controls and politicize the program and thus end up with high-cost, low-impact investment. A programmatic approach where a decisive center asserts prescriptive guidance may be attractive, but it does not guarantee success. Programmatic approaches can be self-defeating if motivated by central government's need to control the process or content. Top-down direction must be complemented by bottom-up initiative and adaptation. Lower levels of government may be close allies to local actors. The grassroot beginnings of the telecenter movement in many countries can be both a catalyst for broader government involvement and the source of creativity and dynamism in a balanced and sustainable program.

Policy makers should also ensure the effective insertion of the telecenter program into the overall national e-development strategy and thus strengthen all elements of the e-development ecosystem. Telecenters constitute a core component of the e-development ecosystem. As indicated above, telecenters can be a key channel for delivering all kinds of e-government and e-business services. They can help the promotion of e-literacy, distance education, and lifelong learning. They can be linked to poverty reduction programs and sector-specific strategies in health, education, and agriculture. On the other hand, e-government services are increasingly seen as a key driver and critical success factor for the sustainability and impact of multi-purpose telecenters. E-policies are a key to enabling telecenters to engage in e-finance and e-commerce services. A dynamic telecommunications infrastructure and an effective regulatory framework can help secure affordable connectivity for telecenters, among other users. In a sense, the telecenters can act as the connecting point for many of the synergies of the e-development program.

A telecenter program is always a risky undertaking and often linked to political imperatives. Its success depends on (a) other critical parts of the e-development program, (b) the extent to which large numbers of people adopt a new technology and learn new skills, (c) major changes in governmental attitudes and the way that public services are delivered, and (d) extensive multi-sector and inter-institutional coordination and collaboration. Because of its visibility and importance, a telecenter program is also visible and susceptible to political interventions that could undermine effectiveness. Caution is warranted during both planning and implementation. Lessons of experience indicate many examples of countries where the telecenters were built and scaled up far ahead of reforming the telecommunications policies to reduce connectivity charges to affordable levels, ahead of the human resources necessary to manage the new telecenters as viable enterprises, ahead of developing networks and institutions to facilitate learning and mutual support, and ahead of the development of relevant content and services to ensure the sustainability and impact of this infrastructure.

Important trends and lessons are accumulating. A general trend is toward moving from purely bottom-up pilots and organic models to the use of programmatic approaches and intermediary institutions for scaling up. These programmatic approaches aim to be flexible and adaptive enough to take account of the diverse local contexts and to leverage the diverse local experiences, models, partnerships, capabilities and resources. Countries are moving from single, government-driven models to public–private partnerships and multiple business models. Countries are learning that different models could serve different contexts and different developmental needs. They are also learning how critical is monitoring and evaluation in the effective selection and use of various business and institutional models so as to adapt or innovate these models to fit changing priorities, changing socio-economic contexts, and changing communication technologies. They are planning and learning to learn.

Section III
Designing e-Development Strategies: Usage

Usage is the most visible dimension of ICT in development. That is where the substantial benefits of the ICT revolution are likely to be and where local capabilities and choices will vary among countries, across sectors, and over time. Harnessing ICT to transform governments, connect businesses, and empower communities is only at early stages of realization, but the journey has begun in most countries. All applications depend on the pillars of e-development: enabling policies and institutions, skilled human resources, dynamic ICT industry and technological capabilities, and communications and connectivity infrastructure. These enabling factors and resources are common foundations for the knowledge economy, but their development, deployment, and mix must be tailored to meet the imperatives of this general-purpose technology.

The next four chapters explore some of the potential uses of ICT in government, business, and community in support of new development strategies. They also identify key tools and concepts to guide the deployment of the new technologies, best practices, and lessons of experience. Effective usage across all sectors depends on common policies, core competencies, shared infrastructures, and the synergies among them. The stakeholders of many applications cut across sectors and development objectives, for example, public e-procurement, serving both public and business sectors, or telecenters, delivering e-government, e-business, and e-society services. These applications offer opportunities to aggregate demand for ICT-enabled services and to exploit supply-side economies of scale. Meantime, strategic technology choices may impact many usages and capabilities, for example, the promotion and adoption of open source software.

These chapters provide many examples of the value of a holistic e-development framework, in securing complementarities, tapping network externalities, promoting cross-sector collaboration, and catalyzing stakeholders to participate in the journey toward a knowledge- and innovation-driven economy.

Chapter 11
Government Transformation: Vision and Journey

E-government is one key area of a broad array of ICT applications with pervasive impact throughout the economy. It also illustrates the profound implications of an ICT-induced institutional transformation. It presents a new techno-economic paradigm for the public sector. For a variety of reasons, public agencies at all levels are pressed to respond to growing challenges. E-government provides powerful tools and new opportunities to address both old and new public sector challenges. The use of ICT can significantly improve the range and quality of public services to citizens and businesses, while making government more efficient, effective, responsive, transparent, and accountable.

E-Government is about effective government, whereby ICT is used to modernize government services and make them accessible, responsive, transparent, and client-centered. It is about transforming relationships within government, and between government and its citizens and the economy at large. A main challenge is to prepare policy makers to take the lead and to influence their thinking on the future role and shape of government. E-government may be viewed as a business strategy to enhance performance, service, and accountability of public institutions. It is less about managing technology, more about promoting service innovation and institutional transformation. It should be integrated with a new vision of government, with outsourcing policies, with decentralization policies, and other efforts to re-define the role of government. Fundamentally, it should support the country's competitiveness and public service reform agendas.

Two contrasting views have emerged of the potential of e-government, reflecting the cyber-optimists and the cyber-pessimists (Norris, 2002, Chapter 6, p. 1). The cyber-optimists believe that the digital technologies will contribute to revitalizing government and promoting communication between citizens and the sate. The pessimists view governments as inherently slow to change and adapt, regardless of technology. From a practitioner perspective, neither view is helpful. I take the position that ICT is disruptive technology, with a major promise for transforming governments. The gap between the possibilities for real transformation and current practices of "window dressing" is large. It suggests that the payoffs are not automatic and change is hard to manage and sustain. But we believe that it is possible to pursue such transformation even in the poorest countries, provided that political

N.K. Hanna, *e-Transformation: Enabling New Development Strategies*, Innovation, Technology, and Knowledge Management, DOI 10.1007/978-1-4419-1185-8_11, © Springer Science+Business Media, LLC 2010

commitment is secured and ICT-enabled change is effectively managed (as will be further developed in Chapter 12).

Technology is increasingly becoming an integral part of transformation efforts in the public sector. While technology alone cannot achieve transformation, increasingly, transformation cannot be achieved without technology. Decades of experience in reforming the public sector and revitalizing the civil service in developing countries have not been encouraging, and the tools available have been blunt. But ICT in general and e-government in particular have been a recent source of inspiration for both developed and developing countries. The promise of ICT can be a trigger for innovation and value creation in government, as in business. The transformative power of ICT has the potential to realign government to a changing context and to reshape government's social technologies in order to remain relevant in a more turbulent, global, interactive, and informational era.

This chapter attempts to answer some key questions: What are the mega-trends and imperative that may drive government role and behavior in the modern economies? What would the government-of-the-future look like? What visions and aspirations may shape government transformation or the demand for e-government? What are the key objectives of public sector reform and what e-government solutions would be most responsive to these objectives? If government transformation is a long journey, then what are the milestones of this journey and what may be the initial steps? The next chapter attempts to answer the questions of the "how" and to draw on lessons learned by early travelers.

I first outline the imperatives for transforming government and changing the role of the state. Governments all over face increasing budgetary pressures, rising expectations, growing inequality, and declining trust. The imperatives of an increasingly integrated and competitive global economy add more demands on local government—to be agile and innovative. Understanding these global forces is useful in shaping the value propositions of e-government.

Next, I present complementary visions of future government. These visions capture the key trends in transforming government, in putting citizens at the center, and in delivering value and service on demand. They also capture the elements of an emerging public sector for the new century: agile, smart, innovative, collaborative, knowledge-based, and competency-driven. These visions are not limited to the central government; they are increasingly critical to cities and local governments. Visions of future government based on the innovation and transformation potential of e-government lie at the heart of national ICT initiatives. Total transformation to such desired states is a challenging journey, to be pursued in phases and sustained over the long term.

I then propose a framework that links the potential uses of ICT in the public sector to key reform and governance objectives. E-government applications are classified and illustrated in terms of enabling public sector reforms and development outcomes: increased efficiency and effective resource management; improved access and quality of public service; improved investment climate and business competitiveness; enhanced governance, transparency, accountability, and citizen participation; and improved policy analysis and knowledge management. The aim is not to provide a comprehensive coverage of e-government applications, but to draw the attention of policy makers to the strategic options available to use e-government to pursue sector reform and development objectives.

This chapter concludes with an overview of the stylized phases of ICT-enabled government transformation process. Policy makers should be aware of the various phases, of the challenges of each phase, and the opportunities for leapfrogging. In all phases, piloting and sequencing are essential before scaling up.

Imperatives Transforming Government

The role and value propositions of e-government must be understood as a response to global forces facing governments. The role of the state is changing, and ongoing public sector reforms and efforts to reinvent governments provide the context and imperatives for ICT-enabled public sector transformation.

Governments all over face a potent combination of challenges: increasing budget pressures and shortfalls; rising public expectations for service and responsiveness; growing inequalities in incomes and in access to information, knowledge, and opportunities; declining legitimacy and trust in government for failing to deliver on promises; and meeting the imperatives of competing in a fast-moving, knowledge-based global economy.

Although governments in developing countries share similar challenges, they differ in severity and initial conditions. E-government must be understood in a developmental context. Much of the literature on e-government is focused on technological imperatives and the challenges facing developed economies. The imperatives for transforming governments in developing countries are additionally driven by severe financial constraints, poor infrastructure and public services, unmet basic needs and expectations, fragile democracies, weak governance, high levels of inequalities, and prevailing information poverty.

Most governments face budget pressures and shortfalls caused by increased demand for services combined with insufficient tax revenues. In higher and middle-income countries, aging populations add a huge burden to health, pension, and other support systems. In poorer developing countries, budget pressures are much higher and caused by additional factors such as fast-growing populations, nascent social protection systems to compensate for the volatility of the global economy, global competition for FDI through tax reductions, and the dwindling of some traditional sources of revenues such as tariffs on international trade. New programs are introduced when economic outlooks look promising, then when cyclical budget shortfalls occurs, politicians are reluctant to cut programs—particularly when faced with a huge backlog of unmet social and popular demands. Many governments face the combination of increasing costs of public services and rising demand for these services. The global financial crisis and economic contraction that started in 2008 just lend more urgency to transforming government and public service delivery.

Governments are also facing rising expectations for demonstrable results and enhanced responsiveness, from citizens and businesses. Their clients and employees understand how business enterprises constantly improve services, and they have come to expect and even demand similar information, services, and support from government. This is particularly the case for middle-income developing countries where e-business has been spreading. Moreover, multinationals are setting the standards for service through their global services, client support, as well as their own service requirements from local governments. Citizens are increasingly mobile and they expect to be connected to government information, services, and assistance anytime and everywhere. These developments make government clients in developing countries even more impatient in dealing with slow and multiple bureaucracies, even for simple services.

There is also the challenge of rising income inequality in access to information, knowledge, and opportunities. In many poor countries, public services are limited to the high and middle class in the major urban areas, if at all. Public services are failing the poor in most countries. Whatever services are provided, they are of poor quality, provided inefficiently at high costs, and a major source for bribes and corruption. As new technologies are implemented, governments face the further challenge of making public services accessible to all citizens through multiple channels. A digital divide may further reinforce the service divide by reducing the pressure from the well-served class for reforming and improving public services across the board. And the digital divide is not only about access to ICT but also to the associated skills to deal with Internet-based information and e-services.

Governments all over but particularly among the poorer developing countries also encounter declining trust and legitimacy, leading to frequent crises and many failed states, as in Africa. New democracies do not avoid these challenges when they fail to deliver basic services and security to large segments of their populations, as in many Latin American countries. The nascent, democratically elected governments are particularly vulnerable to charges of corruption and of failure to deliver basic public services in equitable fashion. Social and political forces are exerting strong pressures for decentralization while economic forces are exerting pressures for integration with the regional and global economies. The current crisis of political institutions and democratic governance in many developing countries can be construed as a unique opportunity to review the framework that inspires and governs how new technologies can assist in designing a holistic reform process of the public sector (Rubino-Hallman and Hanna, 2006).

Imperatives and standards for competing in the global economy are growing. The speed with which capital flows around the world in search of higher returns demands a more agile and innovative government. Globally integrated and demand-responsive supply chains are setting standards for customs, ports, multi-modal logistics, and trade facilitation functions. Governments are pressed to modernize these infrastructures and processes, in partnership with the private sector. Traditional approaches of tariff-based protection for local industries and tax incentives for multinationals become less and less effective in a global knowledge-based economy. Also, the "cost of doing business" is now open for all to examine, and countries are benchmarked annually in the globally competitive race to attract investment (World Bank and International Finance Corporation, 2009). "Business as usual" is no longer a viable strategy for governments to help their industries compete in the global economy. For small business, government overhead and regulatory burden can spell the difference between thriving and not surviving. No wonder business associations are often a strong ally and advocate for government to simplify operations and adopt e-government practices. Growth and economic development are in a significant part determined by how the government can smartly regulate and facilitate business participation in the global economy.

For a growing number of tough economic and social problems in a knowledge society, success increasingly depends on communication, information, and innovation. The more rapid the pace of change, and the more novel the challenges, the greater the need for information and innovation and for knowledge-based learning and adaptive organizations. Increasingly, governments are called upon to manage complex programs requiring complex administrative technologies and partnerships among multiple organizations, at all levels of government, and between public, for profit, and nonprofit sectors. More of the problems facing governments are non-routine, allowing little time to react and involving a high cost of failure, such as SARS, public health, security threats, and disaster management. Policy problems are increasingly interconnected. Responsibility for solving such problems is highly diffused, across organizations, and multi-level, both local and global. Such problems require innovative solutions, drawing on information and communication, on situation-based coordination, network-based approaches, and boundary-spanning performance management (Kettl and Kelman, 2007).

All the above imperatives suggest moving beyond incremental change to transformational change in public sector management. They dramatically increase the stakes associated with the pace of government transformation. They demand painful breakdown or integration of entrenched organizational silos, partnerships with business and civil society, and enabling employees to be part of the change through re-tooling and re-skilling. Transformation of government operations must also occur within very tight financial constraints in most developing countries. Transformational change is demanding and disruptive. But the longer government delays action, the worse the problems become. The world of business is changing fast, to become more responsive, connected, knowledge-based, and globally competitive. Governments have to act with a sense of urgency or run the risk of becoming an economic burden or even irrelevant to their society.

Visions of Future Government

How can the state respond to the forces of globalization and the rising expectations of the information society? How can the state harness the ICT revolution and move toward the government of the future? Visions of the future government should capture cutting-edge practices in reforming government, such as results-based management, putting citizens at the center, and delivering service on demand. They should reflect citizen aspirations for transparent, accountable, and participatory government. Defining the visions of future government should help policy makers and strategists in setting the priorities and defining the uses of e-government, and in marshalling the necessary human and institutional resources for the fundamental changes implied by these visions.

An e-government strategy should be based on a holistic vision of reforming or transforming the public service. An energizing vision of a transformed public service—one that is connected and client centered—can drive and sustain the intensive coordination and collaboration required from the agencies involved in e-government. This vision should be clearly communicated to all stakeholders, including citizens. Broad buy-in from citizens can be the key in countering resistance from organized groups with strong vested interests in the status quo. Moreover, investments in e-government can have the greatest impact when combined with civil service reform: e-government involves not only introducing ICT-enabled process reengineering, but also transforming the skills, incentives, and culture of the civil service to increase professionalism, collaboration, accountability, and transparency. Achieving these changes requires substantial investment in transforming routines, organizations, and power relations—a long-term investment that can be sustained only with a clear and motivating vision.

Transformation is about creating the future, not perfecting the past. However, taking a future-oriented perspective of e-government initiatives does not mean ignoring current performance problems or urgent needs. Neither does it save leaders from facing the challenges of transformation. E-government programs should prepare and enable the government of the future, to solve both current and future challenges in more creative and effective ways than in the past.

The difficulties of transformation cannot be underestimated. They should be anticipated and planned for. How can we avoid automating the status quo? How can we avoid reinforcing the hierarchical, stove-piped, inwardly-focused, routine-based bureaucratic culture of government? How can we reduce the frequent failures or unmet expectations of large e-government projects? We first consider the visions that are motivating government to pursue the challenges of transformation. Later in this chapter, we outline the long journey toward true transformation, and the piloting and sequencing involved. In the next chapter, we take a further step toward understanding the tools and frameworks needed to guide this journey.

Agile, Integrated, Client-Centric Government

This vision responds to the imperatives of meeting rising expectations, redressing service inequities, rebuilding trust in government, and meeting the standards of a demanding global economy, and doing so within growing budgetary constraints. Doing more with less cannot be achieved by only constant reorganizing or sharpening performance management systems. What is needed is a more fundamental change that transcends silos and delivers focused efforts and services through flexible and dynamic networks of agencies or what may be called virtual networked organizations. An agile government will focus on what they can do best, and out-source non-core functions to other partners, private or voluntary organizations, or local governments that may be better suited for these functions. Public agencies will systematically focus on functions where they add the most value and customer satisfaction are high, and intelligently outsource others (Fig. 11.1).

This vision is not without significant risks. Outsourcing public services must be managed effectively. Excessive or premature outsourcing, ahead of built-in infor-mation, measurement, communication, and accountability systems can be costly politically and economically. Many developing countries have a long way to go before striking the right balance and engaging the full innovative capabilities of their partners in the private sector and civil society. Building a virtual networked orga-nization that adapts to changing demands, works closely with other partners, and leverages advanced information and communication systems, is a key to enabling an agile and focused government.

E-government would make it possible to decentralize management structures and virtually integrate together various government agencies. This means moving away from static, silo-based models of public services to a business model that builds vir-tual networked organizations to deliver high public value to the citizen (Abramson et al., 2006). The citizen becomes at the center of the network, a partner in the process. Business processes would be standardized across the networked virtual organization and outside partners so as to simplify, unify, connect and collaborate, and create a virtual network ecosystem. The goal is not to move toward an ideal structure but to create a network infrastructure that adapts continually to chang-ing demands and nurtures a network culture that rewards citizen centricity over a silo mentality. E-government would link organizations through both the front-end systems that interact directly with citizens and the back-end systems that manage

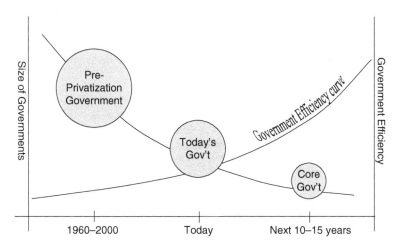

Fig. 11.1 Outsourcing government

common business processes such as finance, procurement, and human resources. A whole-of-government approach may facilitate this drive to integration (Chapter 12).

This is a vision of government that has its business processes integrated end-to-end across the whole enterprise and with key suppliers, partners, and customers, and thus enabled to respond with speed and flexibility (Ramsey, 2004). This is an extended enterprise that aims to increase the productivity of the whole supply chain and uses partners and suppliers to deliver better service and to respond quickly to changing conditions. It extends its basic operating processes to suppliers and clients and contributes to their productivity and effectiveness. According to this vision, business process reengineering in government would extend beyond organizational silos, to transform and integrate agencies, jurisdictions, and/or the public and private partners. Leading governments are piloting and mainstreaming such integrated and client-centric processes in areas such as international trade, health care, and one-stop public services.

Transparent, Accountable, Engaged Government

This vision responds to the rising demands for accountability, clean government, quality service, equal access, and citizen participation. Securing quality of public services has been a major challenge in developing countries, especially those services that are targeted at poor and disadvantaged groups (World Development Report, 2003). Citizens and businesses are users of public services but, unlike in the competitive market, there is no direct accountability of the service provider to the consumer. In theory, the accountability should come through an indirect route: from citizens and businesses (the users) influencing policy makers and, in turn, policy makers influencing public service providers (Fig. 11.2). In reality, however, this scheme often does not work as intended. In many countries, service users have no mechanisms to influence policy makers, while the latter lack incentives and feedback from customers to properly monitor service providers.

Political leaders have three mechanisms that can help provide incentives for public actors to pursue social ends, hold them accountable for results, and restrain corruption and arbitrary action (World Bank, 2000). These mechanisms are (1) rules

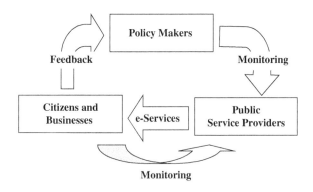

Fig. 11.2 Framework for accountability for public services

and oversight mechanisms within the public sector; (2) mechanisms to promote citizen voice and participation; and (3) mechanisms to promote competition in service delivery. Public sector reform and accountability can be sustained only when government control over public service providers is reinforced by the citizen's willingness and ability to find alternative sources of supply or to exert pressure on the providers to perform.

This vision of a transparent and accountable government may guide the development of e-government strategies in general, and the use of e-government applications to enhance governance and transparency in particular. It is crucial for e-government projects to establish clear standards of performance, feedback, and monitoring channels to ensure openness and accountability. They should also specify and enable the legal, political, and economic means for customers to influence policy makers and providers.

E-government can enable transparent and accountable public service by introducing and supporting broader consumer choices, better information and monitoring systems, and effective participation. E-government introduces new delivery channels for services, thus giving consumers choice and some direct influence over providers. Electronic service delivery also provides users better access to information and feedback channels, such as e-mail, online performance surveys, government information online, and forums to lodge complaints, thus helping to hold both policy makers and service providers accountable. Evaluation-based information is a crucial tool for policy makers to be able to monitor providers and encourage innovation and adaptation of services to needs. Finally, with ICT support, certain services can be subcontracted to private enterprises and NGOs. This enables separating back-end decisions by civil servants about eligibility for service, from front-end service provision by the private sector or NGO, and establishing contractual relationship with rewards and penalties depending on monitored performance of the providers.

The vision of an engaged government is one where the entire political and policy making processes cater to citizens, from the initial agenda setting, to the policy deliberation, to the final decision making—creating a virtuous circle of participation and democracy. Citizens become true partners in the emerging information society. The promise of e-democracy and e-participation goes beyond electronic voting and extends to transformational engagements. Early examples of the possibilities already used in the United States and Europe include webcasting, e-petitioning, e-polling, online consultation, referenda, opinion surveys, negotiated rule making, focus groups, consensus conferences, citizens' juries, and electronic town halls. E-democracy and citizen engagement have even more varied and wider applicability to local government and local issues.

Smart, Innovative, Collaborative Government

A vision of smart and collaborative government would be responsive to the rising expectations, declining public resources, and increasing global competition.

Future government, enabled by ICT tools, will become knowledge-based, intelligence-driven organization. It will increasingly rely on evidence-based policy analysis and formulation. E-government will become a key enabling tool for simplifying and enforcing regulation. Regulations have become more complex and information intensive. In a globally competitive environment, governments are increasingly concerned about regulatory burdens. Yet, in a globally integrated and volatile markets and fragile environments, smart regulation is essential. The skillful and innovative use of technology should lead to new and more effective approaches to regulation (OECD, 2003).

There is also an increasing premium on policy agility. Modern information systems and shared databases will enable policy monitoring and policy agility. Real-time reporting will enable real-time policy making. Reports will become increasingly dynamic. They will draw on broad data assets to add context that would inform and transform policy making. Client-relationship management, case management, document management, and records management would enable rapid, customized, and seamless service delivery as well as provide new capabilities for policy analysis. Seamless, streamlined, and instantaneous reporting would change the context and dynamics of policy development. Information becomes insight, not only informing policy but also shaping the nature of policy options (Fishenden et al., 2006).

Collaborative technologies will further enable timely and robust policy and decision making. They enable task forces to operate across functional boundaries. They enable staff to work together more effectively. Complemented and supported by knowledge management systems, they can empower teams and accelerate organizational learning. The policy-program delivery life cycle—research, design, delivery, reporting, and evaluation—would be transformed when collaborative technologies and interoperable systems would be designed to operate across the whole life cycle (Fishenden et al., 2006).

Governing by networks represent a synthesis of several trends, combining the level of public–private collaboration characteristic of third-party service delivery, with the robust network management capabilities of joined-up government (Glodsmith and Eggers, 2004; Fig. 11.3). Technology is used to connect the network together and give citizens more choices in service delivery options. Facing interrelated and complex problems demanding collaborative innovation, governments are creating extensive networks to join agencies horizontally and to integrate them vertically. The challenge is how to manage such diverse webs of relationships to create public value. This requires thinking strategically about the options for public–private collaboration and correspondingly, the required network management capabilities.

Public services demand innovation not less than business services. Many OECD governments are differentiating the functions of service innovation and design from service delivery. They are beginning to develop a service innovation agenda (OECD, 2005a). Accordingly, governments are exploring opportunities to use ICT not only to improve the delivery of services but also to create new services and reach the

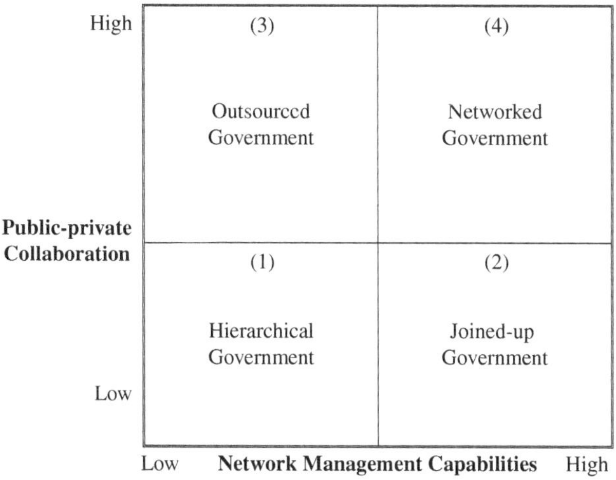

Fig. 11.3 Thinking strategically about collaborative, networked government
Source: Goldsmith and Eggers (2004)

underserved. This service innovation agenda is not viewed as a technology agenda. Rather, it is a management innovation and transformation agenda. It requires public agencies to work together with internal and external stakeholders on priorities for process and service innovation, and on the joint development of existing and new services and delivery channels.

Advances in data-capturing technologies, data storage, and modeling have created opportunities for large-scale analytics (Davenport and Jarvenpaa, 2008). These vastly improved analytical capabilities and business intelligence systems have been tapped by the private sector for fact-based decision making and competitive advantage. Application of analytics and business intelligence, although in its infancy, has significant promise for government to pursue strategic goals in agile and smart ways. For example, it can be used in improving revenue management: revenue analysis, compliance systems, fraud detection, and taxpayer services. It can be applied to supply chain and inventory management in government, to identify and eliminate bottlenecks, and to optimize inventory. Human resource analytics may support forecasting, recruitment, attrition, and strategic staffing functions.

Business intelligence applications and analytics should grow in line with the analytical needs and capabilities required for smart and strategically managed government. While the opportunities from applying analytics in government appear limitless, they do require more than technological innovation. They require dynamic managerial capabilities. Like other visions of the future government, a smart, innovative, and collaborative government can be enabled by analytics and knowledge management systems, but only when accompanied by leadership, managerial innovation, and strategic orientation.

Locally Responsive, Globally Competitive Cities

The leaders and mayors of many cities have been inspired to envision their cities as knowledge, innovation, and intelligent cities; cyber, digital and connected cities; livable and sustainable cities; and global hubs for trade and culture. Every city is potentially an autonomous competitor in a globalizing economy. These visions reflect concerns about competing in a knowledge-based global economy, and opportunities to leverage the role of urbanization in creating innovation economies and information societies. Many cities, such as Singapore and Shanghai, are re-inventing themselves to meet global imperatives and regional challenges.

Competitive cities are increasingly regarding investments in broadband networks as compelling as in transport networks. Increasingly, city governments are stepping as a fundamental partner, stakeholder, and investor for connectivity and city-service applications. They are redefining their role as orchestrators of networked information and knowledge-based services, organized around the needs of their citizens and their role in a global and inclusive information society. A responsive, service-oriented local government, enabled by e-government applications, has become essential to competing for foreign and local investment and for attracting a creative workforce for knowledge-based industries and services.

Singapore envisioned itself as an intelligent island. Some cities, like Stockholm, are turning into a wireless hotspot. Shanghai is creating a knowledge city. Several advanced states in Brazil are competing to develop their broadband-connected, service-oriented digital cities. Several Indian states and cities are competing as choice destinations for innovative businesses and globally distributed corporate research. Dubai is reinventing itself as a trade and knowledge hub for its broader region—envisioning and orchestrating initiatives like the Dubai Internet City, Media City, and Knowledge Village.

Reform-Based and Objective-Driven Uses of e-Government

Development challenges, best practices, and visions of the future should help define the broad objectives of public sector reforms and transformation. In turn, reform objectives should guide the process of transformation and the use of information technology to enable this transformation. Visions are intended to support coalition formation and mobilize demand for reforms. In turn, deriving ICT uses from public sector reform objectives should avoid supply-driven approaches and promote alignment between ICT investments and public sector reform and development objectives.

Traditionally, e-government applications are categorized in terms of users or target clients being served. These categories include improved government services to citizens (G2C); improved transactions between government and business (G2B), leading to improved business environment and a viable SME sector; and improved internal government management through integration and coordination across government agencies (G2G) and informed and empowered employees in the public service (G2E).

In this chapter, we analyze and illustrate the potential uses and impacts of ICT in the public sector, in solving the challenges and realizing the visions of the government of the future. Our aim is not to provide a comprehensive and descriptive coverage of e-government applications, but to draw the attention of policy makers to the linkages between ICT and public management reforms and development visions, and demonstrate the diverse impacts of ICT applications on public sector performance.

We propose a framework that classifies e-government uses and applications in terms of enabling public sector reforms: increased efficiency and effective resource management; improved access and quality of public services; improved investment climate and business sector competitiveness; enhanced governance, transparency, and accountability; and improved policy making, macroeconomic management, and knowledge management.

A framework for e-government that links uses and applications to reform objectives and development outcomes offers several merits as it

- Promotes demand-driven, not technology or supply-driven uses of ICT in government
- Focuses on the broad objectives and common challenges of public sector reform, and thus help mobilize political and social demand for effective use of ICT in government
- Identifies those applications that can potentially support multiple public reform objectives, so as to leverage their uses simultaneously for these objectives (for example, to use e-government procurement, to improve resource management, increase competitiveness, provide transparent pricing, reduce corruption, improve the business environment, and enable participation by large number of local enterprises and SMEs)
- Identifies gaps in current ICT application and support to key reform objectives, and opportunities to expand the possibilities and strategic options of using ICT to deliver new services and higher value added via old and new channels
- Bridges the gap between policy reformers and development practitioners in the field of public sector management, on the one hand, and e-government and ICT specialists, on the other, starting from the common language of development and governance; this should facilitate effective communication among managers of development, business process, and technology, and the alignment of ICT investment with development objectives

Table 11.1 gives an overview of the widely agreed public sector management reform objectives in developing countries and the uses of ICT to enable these reforms. Many e-government applications span across several objectives and uses. These are only illustrative since ICT applications are growing in diversity and their uses are increasingly spanning the fundamental objectives of public sector reforms.

Table 11.1 Reform objectives, ICT uses and common applications

Reform objectives	Uses, impact	Applications, solutions
Improving efficiency and resource management	Focusing and downsizing Reforming civil service human resource management Improving financial resource mobilization Improving expenditure management Reforming public procurement Improving physical resource planning Improving government processes Improving coordination and program management	Outsourcing public services delivery to private sector HR management systems; HRIMS; payroll, talent management system; E-training Systems Tax administration modernization; tax policy analysis Integrated Financial Management Systems (IFMS) E-government procurement; contract management Geographic information systems (GIS) for physical planning and urban management Process simplification; process reengineering Management information systems
Improving access and quality of public services	Improving quality and reach of public services Reducing transaction costs to citizens Providing choice and competition in service delivery	E-services to rural areas and underserved population Issuing online permits, licenses, certificates, visas, grants, land records Social security modernization, e-health, e-education, e-pension, e-employment Providing one-stop service center; single window; e-citizen portals Government call center (311): access to government information, services, assistance Remaining connected to government info and services thru mobile Developing client-focused content for categories of population Customer-service intelligence; analytics; performance metrics

Table 11.1 (continued)

Reform objectives	Uses, impact	Applications, solutions
		Outsourcing services to private sector and NGOs; monitoring service-level agreements
Improving investment climate and business competitiveness	Reducing transaction costs to business Supporting entrepreneurship and small enterprise development Facilitating international trade Meeting global standards Promoting private investment in public infrastructure and delivery service	E-registration E-reporting E-permits E-taxation E-procurement Online business support services Portals for SMEs Portals for microfinance Online land and mortgage Info Online legal and regulatory info E-trade network Port and customs modernizations IPR database Portals for investors, FDI E-finance, credit info database Private investment opportunities in public info infrastructure and services
Increasing transparency, accountability and citizen participation	Making public procurement open and transparent Local budget and financial performance monitoring by citizens Promoting performance management; tracking decisions and outcomes Engaging citizens in policy development and reform Promote effective decentralization Promoting the rule of law	E-procurement E-budget, accessed at local level Results-based management systems; scorecards; performance rating of public agencies E-participation, online discussion forums, public e-mail box, online surveys; e-voting E-cities, e-municipalities; Municipal management systems E-courts; e-justice Legal portals
Improving policy making, governance, and knowledge management	Improving policy formulation and implementation, including macroeconomic management	E-cabinet: document management systems; decision support systems E-parliament

Table 11.1 (continued)

Reform objectives	Uses, impact	Applications, solutions
	Building public sector analytical capabilities Leveraging knowledge resources and sharing best Practices	Modernizing national statistical systems Business intelligence systems; data mining; knowledge management systems; communities of practice networks

To point to e-government possibilities and practices for reformers, the following list illustrates the innovative ways countries are implementing e-government in support of various public reform objectives and the range public services that can be made accessible online.

Improving Efficiency and Resource Management

Reform objectives to improve efficiency and resource management in government are at the forefront of the development and competitiveness agenda of many countries. Pressed by increasing budgetary constraints, rising expectations and demand for services and accountability, and meeting the imperatives of a global economy, governments are seeking to become agile, to promote managerial flexibility, and harness their financial and human resources for an increasingly challenging development agenda. This is an area where ICT has made substantial contributions in the finance and private sectors, and where the potential is vast and relatively untapped for the public sector.

Public reform objectives of improving efficiency and resource management can be enabled by ICT uses and applications that (1) focus and downsize government through systematic outsourcing and partnerships with private sector and civil society; (2) improve public resource mobilization and expenditure management through tax modernization and integrated financial management systems; (3) improve human resource management information and processes and facilitate civil service reforms; (4) increase competitiveness and reduce transaction costs of public procurement with electronic procurement applications; (5) simplify and reengineer government processes; and (6) use management information systems and project management applications to improve coordination, information sharing, and program management.

Most common and advanced applications in support of efficiency and resource management are those concerning financial resource mobilization and expenditure management, including treasury systems, tax and customs administration, and integrated financial management systems (IFMS). Integrated treasury systems, for example, offer significant benefits in managing public resources, including real-time information on the funds available to the state, greater financial control, improved financial transparency and accountability, better reporting at various levels of budget execution, sound planning for future requirements, and better data for budget formulation. Introduction of IFMS can provide the backbone to broad managerial improvement and government transformation. Pressures from the global financial system, aid agencies, and the Ministry of Finance often make IFMS applications an attractive entry point for ICT-enabled policy and institutional reform.[1]

Tax administration, tax policy analysis, and taxpayer services are being transformed under e-government programs. Peru's National Superintendent of Tax Administration initiated an *online tax payment system* in 2003. The social security and health systems of Peru are also part of the system. The system is credited with significantly increasing the efficiency of tax administration. For example, it identifies and automatically rejects incomplete returns, reducing the number of returns that require verification and correction. Argentina also has an *e-tax system* allowing both individuals and businesses to submit tax returns online. More advanced online filing systems, as in Chile, pre-calculate the taxes due and allow the tax payer to just accept the filled-out forms based on payroll deductions and other automated tax payments or to modify as needed. This saves time and avoids filer mistakes.

The challenges and benefits of the use of ICT in tax modernization do not start or end with tax reporting and payment. In fact, much of the benefits come from the quantum leap in administrative reforms and productivity increases that result from transforming back-end processes to enable both within government productivity increases in administering and processing taxes as well as improvements in services and reduction in transaction costs to businesses and citizens. It also has the potential to improve tax policy analysis, compliance, and detection of tax fraud.

Human resource management is a relatively underdeveloped area of public sector management, even though it is essential both to realize substantial gains in productivity, to align incentives and learning to reform goals, and to enable overall change and transformation of government. The integration of human resource management functions such as competency-based training and promotion system is enabled by interlinked ICT applications: HRM System, Learning management system (LMS), learning content management system (LCMS), e-training, etc. Given the poor state of information on the civil service of many developing countries, these applications could offer powerful tools and a quantum leap to government capacity to analyze, reform, and manage a modern civil service.

Another area of increasing attraction and potentially vast efficiency gains is e-procurement by government or e-GP. This is one application that has been successfully implemented in several developing countries, with a wide range of benefits. Experience so far suggests that electronic procurement can save as much as 20% of the costs of publicly procured goods and services. This can amount to half the

---

[1] Including meeting standards prescribed under various international standards and codes, such as the IMF code of Good Practice on fiscal Transparency-Declaration on Principles and the fiduciary standards of the World Bank. Of course, these systems are only enablers and not a substitute for the necessary and accompanying policy and institutional reforms.

annual budget of education or health of Latin America (E-Government Procurement Conference, IDB, 2002). Electronic public procurement can widen competition, reduce prices, lower process and inventory costs, increase transparency, reduce corruption, speed transactions, and support procurement policy analysis and public financial management.

In both Andhra Pradesh of India, and Chile, e-government procurement led to an initial 5% savings in the total public procurement bills—substantial savings in view of the small investment costs involved in establishing these systems. In Andhra Pradesh, the tendering cycle was also shortened from an average of 120 days to 32. No capital costs or project risks were borne by the sate government since the project followed a public–private partnership model where the private sector partner was expected to generate its revenue from transactions fees, in the context of a well-designed service level agreement. In Brazil, an e-procurement system, at $1.6 million cost, enabled savings of $107 million for the state in 2004 alone, and an estimated savings of $35 million for suppliers using the fully automated tendering (Crescia, 2006).

Chile's e-Procurement system is often cited as a success. It is *credited* with making government procurement more transparent, reducing businesses' transaction costs, enhancing cooperation between firms and public agencies, and reducing opportunities for corruption. Under Chile's e-procurement system (*Chilecompra* or Chile buys), companies that wish to do business with the public sector only need to register one time in areas in which they do business. Whenever a public agency needs to purchase goods or services, it will fill out a request in the electronic system, specifying the kind of operation and including all the documentation and information associated with the request. Automatically the system sends an e-mail to all the private companies registered in that area, minimizing response time, and providing an equal opportunity for all firms. At the end of the bidding process, the results are provided online, including details on the participants, the proposals, the economic and technical scores, and the winning contractor.

Although the benefits from e-procurement can be clearly measurable and even dramatic, and thus attractive to private investment or PPP, these benefits are not automatic. Realizing the payoffs depends on, among others, complementary infrastructures, supplier incentives, user capacity building, coalition building, and change management.

For example, despite years of effort and investments since 2001, the use of e-procurement system in Malaysia has been very low and the benefits far below potential, for various reasons (E-gov Magazine, Volume 3, Issue 4, April 2007, pp. 8–13). To become e-procurement enabled, suppliers must pay for smartcard, training software renewal, and other costs that in total may be unaffordable to SMEs. These suppliers face challenges in using advanced systems, including lack of bandwidth support, poor information systems infrastructure, and relevant skills. Traditional small suppliers are slow to change their mindset and embrace new ways of doing business. Although the supplier community is encouraged to be part of the e-procurement community, this requirement has not been made mandatory. More broadly, the e-procurement initiative in Malaysia lacked a holistic vision of procurement reform, a clear strategy for change, and active and continuous promotion and education.

Improving Access and Quality of Public Services

Applications of e-government to improve access and quality of public services are the most politically popular in developing countries. This is understandable in view of rising expectations for better public services, the huge deficits in the delivery of such services in developing countries and the high transaction costs of dealing with unwieldy bureaucracies. Service delivery, particularly when delivered in person, is an expensive part of government work. Governments often face the difficult tradeoff between improving service quality to those who are better off, mainly in the urban areas, and extending access to those with limited or no access, particularly the poor, rural areas, and SMEs. E-government applications can deliver on both quality and access.

There is also the political imperative for public sector leaders to use visible service improvements to build external support for broader government reforms. This support could come from business associations, private groups, or organized citizenry and the middle class. Unlike using e-government for transparency, participatory democracy, and other visions, an initial focus on service improvement is the least threatening to the social and political status quo. An emphasis on service delivery can be a neutral entry point to building longer term political support for performance improvement and government transformation (West, 2005).

This is a rich category with many examples of innovative applications to (1) improve quality and reach of basic public services to rural areas and underserved populations including land titles, permits, licenses, permits, certificates; (2) support health, education, and life long learning; (3) provide choice and competition in service delivery through the use of public–private partnerships; and (4) substantially reduce transaction costs to citizens by providing one-stop service center, single window, and citizen-centric portals, among others.

The range of 'e-Services' applications is broad, given that these applications are online versions of the various transactions citizens or businesses must engage in with central, provincial, local, and municipal governments. The EU identified 20 e-services as common priorities (Table 11.2).

In developing countries, a wide range of basic services is in demand. Examples include *drivers licensing*; *automobile registration*; *land and property registration*; *birth registration*; *procurement*; *invoicing*; *employment*; *education*; *professional training*; *pensions*; *health services*; *tax reporting and payment*; *customs*; and *immigration and border control*. Popular services include school and exam results, health services appointments. In the case of Mexico, the federal government identified high-impact services—those services most important and heavily used. These are classified by themes, based on users' needs and the rule of 80/20—20% of the most relevant information or services are looked up and used by 80% of clients. Examples are passport appointments, job applications, health insurance, driver's licenses, labor

Table 11.2   Public services online in the EU

Government to citizen	Government to business
Income taxes	Social contribution to employees
Job search	Corporate tax
Social security benefits	Value Added Tax
Personal documents	Registry of a new company
Car registration	Submission of data to the statistical office
Application for building permits	Customs declaration
Declaration to the police	Environment-related permits
Public libraries	Public procurement
Birth and marriage certificates	
Enrollment in higher education	
Announcement of moving	
Health related services	

Source: European Commission, Directorate General for the Information Society and Media, "Online Availability of Public Services: How is Europe Progressing" (2005), p. 6.

rights, and information on women's health. In Brazil and South Africa, as in many developing countries, public safety is a major issue, and in response, some of the emerging uses of ICT include online crime reporting, police electronic records, and GIS crime mapping.

In the context of developing countries, many of these services may require significant improvements in back-end processes to provide reliable service and completed transactions. The challenge in developing countries is not only to put services online, but to carry out the internal process transformation and integration necessary to enable complete transactions of such services. This calls for prioritization and sequencing of e-services to ensure that the transformation process is not aborted by limiting e-government to web presence or window dressing.

The *e-Seva* service of the state of Andhra Pradesh in India provides citizens with a wide-spectrum of services ranging from the payment of utility bills to registration of motor vehicles. In Karnataka, India, the *Bhoomi land registry system* has automated 20 million land records since its inception in 1998, yielding *benefits* to farmers, financial institutions, and public officials. Farmers, for example, can quickly get their land records from kiosks and are protected from harassment and extortion. Whereas getting records formerly entailed a delay of up to 30 days, with e-Seva farmers can get their records in less than 2 min. In this as in other e-Government projects, benefits include not only increased efficiency but also reduction in opportunities for corruption. Making government services available to citizens in a transparent and efficient manner can empower citizens to fight corrupt and arbitrary bureaucratic action.

Provincial, local, and municipal governments are also offering localized and specialized government services. India is moving in a big way to support municipal governments to provide services, using a common suite of applications under the National Mission Mode Program for municipalities, and covering birth and death registration and other 40 types of certificates or permits delivered through a single window system, property billing for all services within the jurisdiction of the Urban Development Authority, property taxes, water billing, and complaint monitoring system, among others. Examples of already developed municipal sites include the city of *Bangalore, India, India's Andhra Pradesh* province, and the *Varna district in Bulgaria*. *Peru's 'Public Window' system* gives citizens in three cities the ability to learn how their local governments are structured, to access information on municipal officials, to see how public funds are spent, and to obtain information on procedures for obtaining a birth certificate, restaurant permit, and other official documents. The UK national government has provided *resources* to help local governments create their own e-Government sites.

One of the rare *surveys* of rural users of e-Government in Madhya Pradesh, India, found the following services most in demand: personal documents, including birth, marriage and death certificates, land registry or cadastral services, anti-corruption complaints and other grievances with public services, and transportation-related services, including car registration and purchase of bus and rail passes.

Improving Investment Climate and Business Competitiveness

The imperatives of growing in globally competitive economy are driving govern-ments to improve their business climate and provide effective support services to their SMEs. Public sector reforms to reduce transaction costs to business, to support entrepreneurship and SME development, and to facilitate trade are signif-icantly enabled by e-government applications. Municipalities, as much as central governments, are competing to reduce their regulatory burdens and improve their attractiveness to businesses and investors but they have a long way to go (Box 11.1).

Box 11.1 Municipal Scorecard on Business Climate, and the Role of ICT

IFC, in collaboration with local institutional partners including public, pri-vate, and academic institutions, conducted a pilot to produce the Municipal Scorecard 2007 (www.municipalscorecard.org). The pilot focused on pro-cesses at 65 municipalities in 5 Latin American countries. It focuses on two key processes: operating license and construction permit. Most municipal-ities in Latin America use the operating license to enforce zoning, health, and safety regulations, and to acquire information about economic activities in their jurisdictions, and to improve tax control. Similarly, municipalities use construction permits to ensure that safety requirements are met and that build-ing plans fit with urban development plans and building norms. These are logical and beneficial goals.

Unfortunately, businesses in many municipalities in Latin America report that licensing procedures are slow, expensive, and highly uncertain. Often, business owners cannot find the information they need to complete the process. They wait in long lines and are often asked to come back some other day. They are asked to pay very high fees to obtain a license, and worse, in some municipalities, they are asked for extra payments to speed up the process. To ensure their request is processes, most business owners have to leave their businesses and travel several times to municipal offices. High percentages of these licenses and permits are also rejected, in major part due to poor process management, starting with the poor quality of information that business owners receive requirements and the way in which requests must be presented.

To avoid this burden, uncertainty, and costs, many—particularly micro and small owners—prefer to remain unlicensed, that is, informal. Unfortunately, this means that society is left without adequate protection concerning zoning, health and safety, and municipalities missing out on much needed tax revenues. For these informal businesses, they have less opportunities to grow, get credit, take advantage of businesses to improve their technology, increase productivity, and resist the grip of corruption.

Municipal transactions with business owners and investors can be significantly simplified and made predictable, and the underpinning information more available and reliable with the help of e-government applications. Even just having a portal for business with reliable information about business licensing and permits can go a long way toward improving the business climate. A review of the 2007 scorecards of municipalities on business environment in Latin America indicated that those municipalities with one-stop shop portal scored the highest.

E-government offers many ways to improve the investment climate and business competitiveness. One broad area of application is to use ICT to streamline administrative procedures so as to reduce transaction costs between business and government. Electronic public procurement is an area where results can be demonstrated early and clearly in terms of efficiency, agility, and transparency. Another broad area of e-government applications aims to provide business support services and facilitate access to finance to SMEs. Investment promotion may be supported by applications to provide access to information on polices and regulations for investors. Modernization of customs, ports, logistics, and of trade transactions across the many agencies involved can also facilitate trade and help traders and countries meet the increasingly demanding global imperatives. These applications are illustrated in the chapter on e-business.

Increasing Transparency, Accountability,
and Citizen Participation

All the imperatives for transforming government as outlined early in this chapter motivate reforms to increase transparency, accountability, and citizen participation. Fortunately, some countries are pointing the way by developing their own visions, reforms, and best practices and by using e-government to enable these reforms.

These reforms objectives may be pursued by using ICT in government to (1) make public procurement open and transparent; (2) share information on budgets and financial performance; (3) use performance indicators and performance management systems; track decisions and outcomes; (3) engage citizens in policy development and reform; (4) promote transparent municipalities and facilitate effective decentralization; and (5) enforce the rule of law and modernize the legislative and judicial branches of government.

Apart from its potential as a tool for improving the efficiency of government procurement, as discussed earlier, e-procurement can be a key tool to enable transparency and fight corruption. But it is not a magic bullet or technical fix. E-enabled procurement reform is essentially a political not a technical project. The e-procurement application illustrates the importance of understanding the political economy and demand side for reforms. Many vested interests are at stake. Corrupt practices in public procurement are supported by underlying strong networks of corruption, involving private suppliers and public officials. Procurement reforms—to promote efficiency, transparency, and accountability— may involve building countervailing coalitions including not only reform-mined officials and civil servants from the executive branches of government, but also leaders from the legislation, business, media, supreme audit institutions, and civil society organizations. Political leadership and social control are essential to success.

In the Philippines, a coalition of civil society organizations was essential to enact a new procurement law embodying key reforms and to continue to provide oversight over implementation, using e-procurement to make the process transparent and amenable to monitoring. Chile used e-procurement as a key entry to fight corruption. It used data mining of e-procurement transactions, among other tools, to avoid bid rigging and break up collusive games among suppliers, officials, and procurement officers.

E-participation tools are used to engage citizens and business and seek their views so their interests and needs are better represented in government programs or processes. The goal is to increase the responsiveness of government to citizens and businesses. E-participation includes online surveys and polls, electronic newsletters, e-mail, feedback forms, and web forums where citizens can express their opinions. E-participation tools may supplement public forums or meetings. They may present relevant background information, decisions, and other materials to help citizens and businesses understand certain public policy or regulatory issues. New Zealand has promoted ways for citizens to participate in government in *one site*.

Feedback or citizen comments and complaints may support anti-corruption measures. For example, the Philippine Civil Service Commission (CSC) implemented an *m-government system* that enables citizens to SMS or text in complaints or corruption charges on government officials. Mobile phone users can report grievances against the police using *SMS*.

E-government may be also used to support decentralization processes by increasing the efficiency and transparency of local governments. Many countries are transferring increasing responsibilities and resources to the local level. In this context, OAS and CIDA have partnered to undertake a program aimed at addressing two key issues: the modernization of public services through e-government strategies and the generation of municipal income through the implementation of cadastre information systems for the collection of property taxes. The program is an example of knowledge partnership and collaboration among municipalities, with participation from private sector companies and international financial and aid institutions. Specific actives include municipal portals, e-municipal procurement systems, cadastre and registration systems, online forums, and online training www.swdi.oas.org/ose/english/cpo-munet.asp.

Information technology may be used to improve parliamentary processes in many ways—improving transparency and openness; providing universal access to citizens; improving the mechanisms of accountability of legislators to their electorates; enabling dialogue between the parliament, its members and the citizenry; and facilitating deliberation and legislative decision making.

The World e-Parliament Report of 2008 concludes that there is a significant gap between what is currently possible with ICT and what has actually been accomplished (UN, 2008a). There is increasing pressure on parliaments to be transparent, to ensure that their activities are recorded and accessible to civil society and citizens. As the Internet has become increasingly important for an informed participation of citizens, parliaments must be committed to bridging the digital divide and ensuring that their decisions can be understood and analyzed by their constituents. The crisis of legitimacy of parliaments is ascribed to their inability to safeguard the diversity of the interests of the communities they represent. ICT offers opportunities for parliaments to reach out to the public and provide an accounting of parliament and legislator's actions—attendance, voting records, codes of conduct, performance, and integrity.

In view of a declining involvement of citizens in public affairs, modern technologies have raised the prospects of re-engagement in the democratic process.[2] Traditional practices of parliaments in developing countries, including deliberations and document processing, are highly inefficient and slow and can be significantly enhanced with modern communications and intelligent use of ICT. Moreover, many challenging issues facing parliaments are global problems or have global implications and can benefit from timely access to global knowledge, and the actions taken by other legislative bodies. Finally, as parliaments become more visible through the

---

[2]As in the 2008 US presidential elections.

web, privacy and security become essential to ensure the integrity of parliamentary transparency and the confidentiality of citizen communication.

Improving Policy Making and Knowledge Management

A final broad reform objective is to improve public policy making by harnessing public sector knowledge and experience and empowering its knowledge workers. Many e-government applications can help improve public strategic management, policy making, and the management of knowledge workers and knowledge resources. Rapidly shifting global economic conditions put an increasing premium on timely and reliable information for public policy making and macroeconomic management, as well as information systems in support of sectoral and institutional management and effective supply response.

Information in support of policy making in developing countries is scarce, dated, and unreliable, with serious consequences. Africa's development management, in particular, has been hampered by timely and reliable data on social, demographic, environmental, economic situation. Statistical systems in many developing countries are not oriented to support macroeconomic management and policy analysis, and they have often failed to respond to changing information needs. Both vertical and horizontal communication systems are underdeveloped and highly skewed in favor of the urban elite, further impoverishing the policy making process.

Fortunately, advances in information and communication technologies, packaged applications, remote sensing, and business intelligence systems provide a quantum leap in capturing and analyzing masses of information for policy making and public strategic management. Areas of applications range from e-Cabinet and e-Parliament document management and decision support systems, to modernizing national statistical systems. One of the early decision support systems developed for a cabinet is the one developed by the Information and Decision Support Center for the Egyptian cabinet. One of its early uses was to play "what if" games to assess the impact of various tariff structures on revenue and local employment and to facilitate consensus on reforms (El Sherif and El Sawy, 1988).

Knowledge management is a relatively new and promising area of ICT use in government. Technology-enabled knowledge management solutions build on content technologies and information search tools such as data mining and content management, document management and customer relations management systems; and collaborative or sharing technologies, such as corporate intranets and web 2.0 technologies.

Some developing countries and advanced states have been pursuing knowledge management practices, with mixed results. One example is the state of São Paulo, Brazil (Knight, 2007). A review of the knowledge management and innovation practices of the state of Sao Paulo suggests the embryonic stage and promise of such practices. Its recommendations include putting KM and innovation on the agenda for public managers; treating KM in an integrated manner in the Government;

developing processes for creating, sharing, and using knowledge to improve pub-lic management; and identifying and disseminating initiatives along these areas. São Paulo, like the federal government, could move from isolated examples of good KM practices to the establishment of a comprehensive, government-wide policy to promote KM and innovation in public management.

The Journey to Transformed Government

The visions of future government, enabled by a variety of ICT uses, may present foreseeable destinations, but not the journey. Exploiting the full potential of e-government involves a long journey that requires sequencing and cumulative learning. Understanding this evolutionary, multi-faceted process can be helpful to policy makers in preparing and leading government transformation.

The e-government journey can be viewed as consisting of phases. Several models have been proposed to capture this process. In e-business, the mother of e-government, the "e-business ladder" consists of four stages: informate, auto-mate, integrate, and finally, re-invent (Sawhney and Zabin, 2001). These steps move along the value chain, from organizing information, to process-level automation, to enterprise-level integration to network-level transformation.

A corresponding conceptual model of understanding the e-government journey has been proposed first by Gartner Research, with many variations and adaptations since, by IBM and others (Todd, 2004). Figure 11.4 outlines phases of e-government evolution as it relates to the degree of technological and implementation complex-ity and value delivered to the end users—citizens and businesses. The proposed

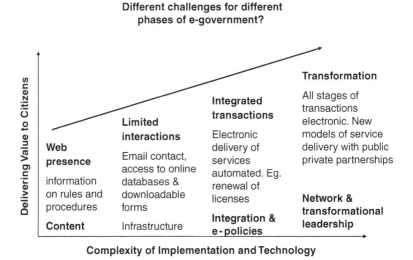

Fig. 11.4 e-Government evolution

model suggests four phases: publish, interact, integrate and transact, and transform. This model is applicable to all levels of government: national, provincial, municipal, and local.

Each phase of e-government has its own challenges and payoffs. These phases are not strictly sequential. Advances on all phases may be possible for different parts of government. Opportunities for leapfrogging several phases are possible for late-comers as technologies advance and lessons of experience accumulate. Advanced phases of integration and transformation are substantially more difficult to reach and are likely to take decades of concerted efforts at the national level.

The web *presence or publish phase* is characterized by putting government information and services online. It provides forms and lists of services online. This is relatively easy since it can be done with little interaction or coordination with other departments.[3] But even this simple step can be a valuable quick win and can make significant difference in the lives of citizens and small businesses who typically suffer from the prevailing scarcity of information about public services and government requirements to access such services. Making such information and services available 24 h a day, 7 days a week, for all year, is a big step forward—particularly given the alternatives of waiting in long lines at inconvenient times and locations at many agencies to seek information or get service. During this phase, few resources are needed to provide direct support to customers and government can reduce the costs of traditional provision of such information. This stage also includes "push" systems that send information to users via e-mail, SMS, or disseminating content to mobile phones or what is called "m-government."

This phase is further advanced as government aggregates content and services in ways that make it easier for users to find information from multiple web sites hosted by different ministries. For example, New Zealand has created a *site* on "things to know when," which provides access to content and services based on activities such as "starting a school" or "having a baby." Australia enables users to browse by *subject*. Even more advanced portal applications provide "personalized" content. For example, Singapore enables users to create their own *my government* web pages, configuring e-government content based on their individual needs and interests (www.egov.infodev.org).

During this phase, government focuses on providing relevant, reliable, timely, and accessible content. The various types of content can be presented through "portals" which aggregate and organize content. Portals and published information, that is, the front-end facing the user, may be supported by back-end systems called content and data management systems. The quality of publish web sites depends on the amount of content, its usefulness, and how often it is updated, as well as navigability, usability, search capacity, accessibility, and download time.

Even at the publish phase, governments can initiate process reform or simplification measures. For example, rather than merely creating electronic versions of existing paper forms, published applications present an opportunity to reexamine

---

[3] Websites may follow a centrally defined format to provide common experience for users.

processes. Process reengineering may eliminate some forms altogether and stream-line the steps in an administrative procedure, thereby simplifying both online and offline processes.

The *interact phase* is when government organizes front-end interactions with clients for better access to services. Users may interact with public officials, such as by commenting on proposed regulations, engaging in e-consultation and e-decision making, or filing corruption complaints. As agencies move services online, a con-fusing array of web sites emerges, making it difficult for potential users to find the right site for particular service. Online presence for various services and agencies is therefore consolidated into portals and organized along life cycles and/or user groups.

In this phase, government focuses on improving the infrastructure to ease access to information and services. The portal acts as an index to help customers navigate to the correct site and becomes a gateway to the increasing sources of information and transaction on the Internet. Portals are designed and optimized to reduce the number of clicks needed to find information or complete multistep transactions—by grouping functions and employing user-friendly terminology, among others. More advanced applications in support of the second phase may include searchable databases, powerful search engines, content management, and knowledge manage-ment systems. The central government of Canada, for example, used customer focus groups to make the portal user friendly in terms of organization and terminology.

Countries may take different routes to front-end integration of information and services. Governments may rely on information intermediaries placed at citizen assistance service centers, as in Bahia, Brazil. In Bahia, each of these centers provide over 500 services from the federal, provincial, and municipal governments—citizens see one face of the three levels of government. This intermediary step may be necessary for some developing countries where individual access to Internet is low, e-literacy is limited, and integration may take a long time to realize.

The first two phases may be characterized as access phase. The challenge of the first phase is providing relevant and timely content, and the second, the infrastruc-ture to organize and make access easier and user friendly. Most governments in developing countries are still building some part of an intelligent infrastructure that improves access as well as the processes to generate relevant, reliable, and timely information. Even in early stages of online presence, there are many steps to achieve sustained improvement.

A recent evaluative study of government web sites in Malaysia show that while the overall e-government is ranked relatively high on the UNPAN's and Accenture's lists (as interactive presence and platform builder, respectively), Malaysian web sites suffer major deficiencies when assessed in terms of currency, reliability, interactiv-ity, privacy, responsiveness to inquiries. They also suffer in terms of quality and functionality of web sites at local government levels, and the availability of local content in local language. They served little and stale information (e-Gov Magazine, Volume II, Issue 3, 2006, pp. 8–12).

The *integrate and transact phase* is when citizens and businesses can com-plete transactions online, such as filing tax returns or applying for government jobs. The focus shifts toward redesigning and integrating back-end processes to provide responsive, customer-centered services. Completing transactions fully online also requires the development of policies for privacy and confidentiality, e-authentication, linkages to legacy systems, business process reengineering, relationship and channel management, and institutional and skill changes, among others.

Applications that involve complete transactions are several steps (and in some cases, a quantum leap) above just providing information or forms to download. Implementation will neither be simple nor cheap. Consequently, transacting such services may require significant changes in back-end processes and government workforce. Success also depends on responding to the needs and capabilities of the intended users.

Internal integration across government agencies may also progresses in steps. Cross-agency virtual integration may start with internal support functions (common business processes, lines of business) like finance, human resources, and public procurement. Later projects may integrate mission critical processes that directly support the customer. Integration may proceed faster among the more advanced agencies or clusters of departments with common clients or needs. Government begins to function as a cohesive unit and employees are in a better position to collaborate.

A "Transact" web site makes government services available at any time from any Internet-connected computer or mobile phone. Traditionally, government services may have required long waits, confrontation with stifling bureaucracy, and the occasional bribe. Innovations such as citizen service kiosks located in shopping centers in Brazil or portable computers that can be carried into rural pockets of India bring e-government directly to the citizens.

The stage of fully integrated and transformed government is more of a vision than a reality of any existing e-government so far. It represents a new and expansive view of e-government, along the visions outlined above. It embraces the power of end-to-end integration in an extended enterprise and the optimization of the whole supply chain. Suppliers, partners, and customers begin to change their own ways of operating and collaborating. Business-process reengineering is extended across the public and private sectors. New applications and services are created, with innovations driven by customer experience. This phase is enabled by open standards, modular IT infrastructure, and modular business processes (Ramsey, 2004).

Challenges and priorities change from one phase to another, demanding higher levels of leadership, institutional coordination, process innovation, and technology management to deliver higher value to customers. Each phase involves several levels or degrees of execution. Some simple solutions can deliver substantial value if they are well targeted and executed. For example, online downloadable official forms decrease the amount of time businesses have to spend in dealing with the government, reducing compliance costs and improving overall business environment.

As government moves to the integration and transformation phases, enabling policies and cultural change become essential, and leadership challenges more demanding. Leaders must take active role in driving change, setting new expectations, and bridging silos within government, then extending outside to all key partners. A transformation map would align culture, human resources, business-process transformation, and IT infrastructure in support of a clear vision of future government. While these later stages are much more difficult to implement than earlier phases, they offer increasingly significant payoffs.

Can this evolutionary process be accelerated? Can a government leapfrog some of the early phases? Yes, with caution. For example, the transact phase usually require more investment in integration and back-end capabilities than the interaction phase, and government may opt for integrating both front-end delivery and back-end processes at the same time. An e-government project may have activities covering more than one phase, ranging from web presence to back-end process reengineering and integration. All four phases may be implemented simultaneously in different parts of the government, depending on the e-readiness and leadership commitment of various concerned agencies. Government may also continue to improve its web presence and deepen its publish applications, even while implementing projects in the transact and transformation phases.

A mix of leapfrogging and evolutionary approaches can accommodate constraints in implementation capacity while promoting results over the short and long term. Few governments in developing countries can afford to leapfrog to full integration of all public services or deep transformation of all agencies. Instead, they may select a few promising entry points—key services with a broad impact—for reengineering and full integration. Fully implementing these, with the corresponding complex systems and back-end process reengineering, will take time. In the meantime, many other services could be improved through an evolutionary process of small steps and incremental quick wins, starting with publishing relevant priority information.

Chapter 12
Government Transformation: Tools and Challenges

In the last chapter, the imperatives for government transformation were introduced. An effective response would involve cutting-edge reforms for future government and visions that embody and motivate these reforms. A variety of e-government uses can support these visions and enable reform objectives. E-government applications should be driven by a unifying vision and overarching reform objectives.

In this chapter I first outline key approaches to guide e-government initiatives: whole of government, customer-centric service, common business processes, multi-channel service delivery, linking central direction to local initiative, and public–private partnership. The aim is to define the guiding principles and frameworks that policy makers and strategists may use to shape e-government programs over time. The main thrust of these approaches is to develop policies to take advantage of economies of scale and scope, promote sharing of infrastructures and services, leverage the comparative advantages of various partners, and reduce costs and maximize value from investments in e-government.

Next I examine a few strategic issues concerning implementation challenges. The proposed tools should facilitate transformation—but will not by any means eliminate the risks, complexities, and challenges. Transformations are poorly understood processes, involving disruptive technologies, creative destruction, and socio-institutional changes. The temptation to limit e-government investments to superficial improvements and window dressing is real. Finally, I conclude with a few lessons that may be kept in mind as policy makers and reformers start along the journey.

Approaches to e-Government

We define here six key approaches or strategic directions for e-government: adopting a whole of government approach; pursuing customer-centric government; developing multi-channel strategy for service delivery; standardizing on common business processes and shared infrastructures and services; balancing central leadership with local initiative, and horizontal enterprise-wide foundations with sectoral ownership; and promoting public–private partnerships.

N.K. Hanna, *e-Transformation: Enabling New Development Strategies*, Innovation, Technology, and Knowledge Management, DOI 10.1007/978-1-4419-1185-8_12, © Springer Science+Business Media, LLC 2010

A Whole of Government Approach

E-government cannot proceed to advanced phases of service innovation and transformation without modernizing and integrating many back-office functions. For example, citizen-centered service delivery involves breaking up silos, integrating across agencies, innovating new ways of doing business, and creating a service-focused culture. Continuing increase in the value and responsiveness of services at the front end, at affordable cost, is not possible without reinventing and consolidating the back-end processes. Consolidation and integration of back-end business processes also frees up resources for additional service innovation. This leads to a better and responsive front end with smaller and smarter back end.[1]

Approaching government as a whole in e-government programs is a profound shift that is easy to grasp conceptually but difficult to practice. It is a paradigm shift toward the vision of a connected, networked, client-centered government. Government agencies share objectives, data, processes, infrastructure, and capabilities across organizational boundaries. They work across boundaries to provide a holistic policy development and implementation, an integrated government response to crises, and a seamless service provision to clients. This shift requires investing in cross-sector capabilities and infrastructures. It also demands transformational leadership, empowered and trained civil servants, and cross-agency coordination mechanisms. This shift may be also driven by external demand, engagement of users as co-producers and co-innovators, and partnerships among public agencies, businesses, and civil society organizations.

Integration and transformation phases also require effective government networking, automated data handling and database management, secure communications, and common data standards and interoperability. Low level of computerization and, especially, networking of government bodies remain a major impediment to the advance of e-government services. To realize the transformational potential of e-government, investment programs should combine front-end service delivery with emphasis on back-office process reengineering and modernization. Such investments should follow an agreed government-wide architecture to ensure interoperability and communication across systems and agencies. Guided by an overall technology and applications architecture, government agencies may adopt a progressive approach whereby units would be allowed to experiment with different services, introducing them gradually.

A whole of government approach is enabled by an enterprise architecture that secures information sharing and integration of information infrastructure across agencies and opens opportunities for innovative methods of partnering with the private sector. Governments need to assess the maturity of their architecture: the front-end and the back-end systems. The point of decision (back end) for a government service always remains within the confines of the government, for it is a statutory function. But the point of delivery (front end) can be the private sector,

---

[1] Jermey Millard. 2007. *ePublic Services in Europe: past, present and future: Research findings and new challenges.*

such as a kiosk or a cable television station. This can happen only if the architecture is sufficiently mature—using a secure network and middleware. Shifting the point of delivery to the private sector has powerful implications for good governance, for it creates multiple options from which citizens can choose and, more important, injects competition into service delivery.

A strategic, "whole of government" approach to e-government offers key advantages. While more demanding than investing in ad hoc, bottom-up initiatives, this approach is likely to economize on investments, reap economies of scope and scale, help citizens deal with government as a single entity, and integrate ICT into the national development strategy. It supports the development of common policy guidelines and frameworks—such as standards for information sharing, interoperability, security, and privacy—that are critical for effective e-government. It clarifies roles and responsibilities within government and with private sector and civil society partners for policy, planning, financing, implementation, and monitoring, and evaluation. It can speed the scaling-up of successful initiatives by addressing systemic constraints and establishing the enabling policies and institutions for replication and diffusion. It can support the sharing of infrastructure and of such business processes as financial management, human resources, and public procurement. And it can lower long-term support and maintenance costs.

Moving toward a whole of government demands the setting of strategic directions and common frameworks. This move requires that all government agencies "own" the government reform and modernization agenda. But this move does not mean wholesale centralization of services and capabilities into one agency. Rather, shared capabilities may be distributed among several centers of excellence. Striking the right balance between setting top-down strategic directions and supporting bottom-up initiatives remains a key issue in designing and implementing e-government programs. The balance may shift over time as common frameworks, governance, architectures, and coordination mechanisms mature and as single agencies and local governments build adequate capabilities and shared understanding for integrated e-government.

Customer-Centric Government

Introducing a customer-centric approach to government is similar to introducing a disruptive technology into a traditional system. It is a paradigm shift in perspective, with the government providing services in ways that make sense from the client's point of view. Indeed, it turns the traditional model of government on its head. It is a shift from inside-out to outside-in, starting from the client, not the agency. The traditional model is centered on the agency providing the service—with service levels, timing, payment mechanisms, and procedures built around the agency. A client-centric government makes the citizen the center of all activity—government services must be available anytime the citizen demands them, anywhere the citizen wants to receive them, and through whatever medium the citizen wants to use. Countries such as Canada, Singapore, the United Kingdom, and the Nordics are adopting this perspective in their e-government programs.

This shift is again easy to conceptualize but difficult to practice. The cyber pessimists are doubtful that governments can make such a paradigm shift and fear that e-government applications may amount to no more than window dressing, a replication of government services practices in the cyber sphere, with mere change in delivery channels through numerous web sites. Yet, governments must develop the necessary understanding, culture, structures, incentives, and capabilities to harness ICT and realize this shift in practice. A variety of mechanisms and practices can be deployed to support and reinforce a customer-centric approach to e-government.

A user-focused government requires an understanding of user needs and the ability to deliver these services according to those needs. By transforming the means of service delivery and the transaction processes involved, user-focused e-government can increase both client satisfaction and government efficiency. Customer-centric e-government strives to improve service attributes such as accessibility, convenience, cost, quality and where relevant, fairness. Service strategies are re-defined so as to start from the perspective of citizens and business. This process starts with defining the target populations that one is trying to serve, their service priorities, and their abilities to use online services or various channels of delivery. For example, in the case of Chile's Business Window Program, the administrative procedures to be "digitized" were selected by entrepreneurs themselves via five focus groups totaling 1200 people and over a 100 of interviews. By 2005, at least 83 processes were put online, incorporating both national and municipal business procedures.

Among developing countries, the poor and those most dependent on public services are among the least able to access and use online services. A user-focused e-government approach would thus require defining the potential users, learning what they want from services, and what they can do (and would be motivated to do) online or through other channels of delivery. Developing countries may have to focus first on those services that have the most impact or value for users and for government. Trade-offs may have to be made between customizing services for diverse populations, and maximizing efficiency gains by e-enabling high-volume, costly services.

Customer-centric e-government demands change in the culture of civil service to make it truly service oriented, and this cultural change can be facilitated by enhanced user feedback and client engagement. Enhanced transparency, feedback and tracking capabilities of service delivery can build the external demand for the cultural shift to customer-focused, service-oriented public sector. Current and potential beneficiaries may be organized to push for user-centric services. Channels to register complaints and feedback on services may be integrated into e-service delivery programs. Service providers can also put in place processes that allow user needs to be expressed, such as user surveys and focus groups. Demand for client-centric services can be measured by analyzing patterns of use. Such analysis should feed into service development and delivery. A customer-centric approach can become a tool for ongoing prioritization for public service improvement within constrained resources.

User-focused perspective will impact not only the design of e-services, but also how public agencies shape their internal operations and structures. The challenges of integrating customers' preferences into existing service delivery and the process and organizational changes required to adapt services and client relationships to meet customers' changing needs should not be underestimated. First and foremost, it demands service-centered leadership and the re-skilling of the civil service. Front-line employees' relationships with users have to change, and their skills and experiences need be managed so as to better understand customers' needs and behaviors and to encourage civil servants to listen to clients and invent client-centered processes and services. As mentioned earlier, reengineering and consolidating back-end processes under a whole-of-government approach can release resources for front-end client-centered service innovation.

Experience from e-government programs in developed countries shows that citizens and businesses strongly prefer joined-up services through single widow or portal organized around their needs or "life events." National entry points, sometimes called "gateways" or portals, aggregate and organize content and services, often with links to web sites of individual ministries or programs. The goal of a portal is to efficiently guide users to the information and services they seek. National portals can represent the face of a country to the world and the face of government to the citizenry. National portals are the most visible expression of a nation's approach to citizen-centered government. Ultimately, national portals can have an impact on government credibility, citizen trust, and public response to e-government. They can influence e-commerce's content quality, technical sophistication, and privacy and security standards.

Pursuing the "single window" approach can be initiated through the Government Services Portal (Box 12.1). This portal can provide the catalytic and integrating framework for e-government implementation first through an effective citizen-centric state portal, and later through other one-stop delivery channels. Such portals aim to package and deliver content and services in ways that directly fit citizens' or businesses' needs. The goal of these portals is to provide "one-stop shopping" so that citizens and businesses no longer need to go to a range of separate ministries, bureaus, or departments to find information on a particular subject or complete a transaction. However, getting multiple government agencies to harmonize the many aspects of user-friendliness (presentation standards, authentication, data quality, access rights, among others) is a major challenge.

Box 12.1 Portals, Single Widows, and Client-Centric Practices

A special one-stop-shop citizen portal can be designed for government services to citizens (G2C). It may include job search assistance, library book search, taxation, civil registration, renewal of driver licenses, change of address notifications, school enrolment, scheduling appointments, marriage certificates, birth certificates and many other public services. E-government would not succeed if citizens were expected to deal with hundreds of websites, each belonging to different agency, and each having different user interface. Serving much more than as a simple gateway, a government portal offers an opportunity to refocus services around the needs of citizens, while reengineering and consolidating back-office processes.

Portals designed around the needs of citizens or businesses are on the rise in many developed and developing countries. South Africa has moved all government departments, government information, and services into a *single e-Government portal*. Its simple, streamlined design, with few data-heavy graphics to download, is well-suited for users with low-bandwidth connections. Singapore's e-Government services and information are effectively combined into one portal, www.gov.sg. *Sweden's Online Public Service Gateway* and the *Canadian Portal for eGov services online (English and French)* are other examples of comprehensive entry points that use a variety of indexing and organizational paths to government information and services. Other examples of user-focused portals include those of *South Africa*, *Singapore*, the *Philippines*, the *United Arab Emirates*, and *Egypt* (Infodev, 2007).

Major advances have been made in portal technology and much experience has been accumulated with the development of such key tools of e-government. There are several excellent examples of single entry government portals, including those of the USA, Canada, Singapore, UK, Australia, Korea, and Germany. In the US, the FirstGov.gov links the government's more than 20,000 websites and 500 millions web pages and makes it possible for citizens to obtain the information and services they need without having to travel or know which agency federal agency controls which function or service. The new generation of portals allow for personalized view of portal contents and for substantial interactivity and connections to both public and private services.

Source: InfoDev Toolkit

A major challenge remains in mobilizing demand and educating users to take advantage of the powerful potential of this portal. Unlocking the potential of e-government depends on high levels of uptake of e-services. In the case of the United Kingdom, for example, a single citizen-centric, all-of-government site is clearly branded and heavily promoted. Consistent navigation is based on user segmentation by audience and topic. High-value services are targeted based on research and analysis of user needs. Similarly, the one-stop business link web site has been developed through cross-agency collaboration in response to feedback from small businesses and changes in business environment. In Germany, the government has set up user councils to support agencies of central and regional government.

A demand-led approach is recommended. Ideally, public service and administrative procedures to be simplified and put online should be selected by entrepreneurs and citizens groups themselves. The portal could start on a pilot basis and involve a limited number of agencies, initially providing only one high value-added service, for example, business registration and obtaining necessary licenses. Selection of services for online delivery should be based on a prioritization framework that takes into account the demand, legal and regulatory framework, policy and economic impact, costs and ease of implementation.

The challenge of mobilizing demand and educating users is particularly relevant to developing countries where there is little awareness among the masses and low ICT literacy. Marketing of people-friendly web sites is necessary. The development of a single e-government brand and a consistent way for navigation with a common look and feel is a best practice, as in Canada and Australia. High uptake is also a consequence of high value services, and these often require collaboration and coordination across agencies. Addressing the need for affordable connectivity should also go hand in hand with investments in online government to build a broad user base and secure the benefits from such investments. Some States such as Andhra Pradesh have figured out a way to build significant user base.

Technical sophistication of such portals should increase gradually. At the first stage, the portal may provide only information services, "how-to" guidance, and downloadable official forms that can be faxed or sent by traditional mail to the agencies involved. Later, the portal would allow submitting and tracking applications electronically. However, even at the initial stages of implementation, the portal has the potential to make government services to businesses and citizens significantly more convenient and transparent.

Delivering joined-up government services to businesses or citizens may seem as a stretch for many developing countries. There are several strong arguments for this approach, however. It is a sensible decision from both administrative and financial points of view. Many countries, such as the United Kingdom, invested heavily into developing e-services divided along administrative lines only to discover that citizens and businesses do not like to use fragmented online services that mirror the administrative complexity of the government. Fixing the situation at later stages requires significant financial investment and process re-engineering. Developing countries have the latecomer advantage to learn from early pioneers and to avoid such costly mistakes. Also, coordinated efforts for upgrading the back-office ICT-enabled business processes of agencies can decrease overall ICT investments and secure shared information and infrastructure.

Multi-channels for Service Delivery

Governments strive for seamless delivery of services across various channels (over the counter, online, mobile, phone, mail).[2] The emergence of mobile as a ubiquitous

---

[2]The role of mobile as a key platform for service delivery is discussed later under governing the technology.

platform represents an exciting opportunity for innovation in service delivery. The growing array of delivery options is creating a drive toward more collaborative models of service delivery. Moving from multiple discrete channels to a networked multi-channel approach demands cooperation across agencies to ensure data, business processes, delivery channels, and ICT infrastructures are interoperable and can be shared or integrated. Such a seamless and networked approach is the ultimate vision of many e-government strategies.

A range of models are being considered in moving toward different levels of integration (OECD, 2005a). The common practice in service delivery is to maintain discrete platforms for delivering services through different channels. Moving toward a more advanced level, another model is to seek vertical integration as well as interoperable delivery platforms. This requires a more collaborative approach, with some sharing of infrastructure and data and a greater focus on standards so as to share platforms for service delivery. The highest level of integration is the model of vertical integration with integrated service delivery platforms. Users experience seamless, user-focused service, working both within and across agencies. This model allows users to gain access to services through different channels, while ensuring that information is consistent across those channels.

A strategy for integrated multi-channel service delivery starts with a common vision and governance measures to achieve this vision. This strategy calls for a single authoritative source of information and data, a technical interoperability framework that maps standards and supports information sharing. It also sets policies for security and authentication, privacy, and stakeholder engagement.

A channel management strategy takes account of the needs, priorities, and capabilities of customers and government. It should balance meeting users' preferences (via a mix of channels) against the economics of service delivery. User preferences should be central to the design of service delivery across channels. Providing the maximum possible range of channels for all services would be prohibitively costly and unsustainable, particularly for developing countries. In making optimal choices, governments need to balance costs and benefits to service users and to government. They should also aim to realize the best public value and make explicit any trade-offs required between equity and efficiency. Assessment of opportunities to reuse or rationalize existing channels is part of the channel development strategy.

Several countries have experimented with a promising service delivery channel, the integrated citizen service centers. One of Brazil's most successful channels for delivering e-government services at state and municipal levels is the integrated citizen service centers or ICSCs (Knight and Annenberg, 2008). These are operated by an increasing number of Brazil's states and some municipal governments. These ICSCs have different names and features, depending on the states in which they are implemented—for example, Citizen Assistance Service Centers (CASC) in Bahia and Timesaver (Poupatempo) in São Paulo. Experimentation with service delivery channels has been a very fertile area of innovation and learning.

Common Business Processes

It is critical to understand the role of common business processes in an e-government strategy. One key tool to realize customer-centered government is to analyze government business processes—to organize and standardize these processes across agencies and around user needs. Common business processes may involve front-office business processes, such as a shared call center for answering questions and providing public information, or a common portal for online contact with enterprises. Or, they may cover shared back-office business processes, such as procurement, financial management, and human resources management (Fig. 12.1).

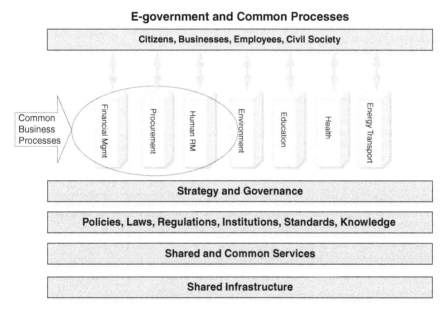

Fig. 12.1 E-government and common processes

Organizing common business processes in government aims to overcome silos of public administration. These silos are even more entrenched in developing countries—duplication and fragmentation are common. Therefore, the benefits of adopting common business processes can be substantial in developing countries. Common business processes can be consolidated or joined up within and across agencies, thus reducing waste and duplication. By reexamining and standardizing common processes, solutions can be created only once then diffused and re-used many times over. This approach can also facilitate information sharing across agencies and reduce user burden of reporting. It can help agencies focus on core activities by providing them with the option of outsourcing standardized processes. Outsourcing common processes help create economies of scale and centers of excellence in performing these core functions. Economies of scale are also captured by consolidating ICT expertise for common business processes. Making elements of service delivery common also raises awareness of overlaps and inconsistencies across programs and creates pressures for alignment and administrative simplification (OECD, 2005).

Countries vary in levels of cooperation among agencies to identify common business processes, develop shared solutions, and realize the benefits. Agencies may agree to limit cooperation to information sharing, and set up a knowledge center to facilitate knowledge exchange on common business processes, or agree on a referential model of standardized processes. Moving up in level of cooperation, agencies may decide among themselves on sharing some common databases and IT systems, and creating a shared service center. At the highest level of coordination of common business processes, this shared service center becomes a separate organization to meet common needs. Approaches to adoption of common business processes vary from top-down control, mandating the use of a common solution, to facilitating approach, using incentives, to a laissez-faire, passive role for the central government. Country factors—ranging from culture, legislation, and politics to public administration traditions—influence these choices.

Most governments persuade agencies to use developed common business processes through incentives that vary from participation in the development of government enterprise architecture to providing agencies with extra funds or budgets for shared processes. In Korea, the special committee for e-government in the President's office analyzes all processes and develops mandatory common solutions at the federal and municipal levels. In Germany, the e-government agency is not empowered to impose mandatory use of common processes. In the United States, e-government office in the OMB uses the federal and the agency enterprise architecture to identify common processes and then uses the budget process to align all major IT investments with this common view and shared solutions.

Implementing common business processes raises many challenges. Involved agencies must be convinced of the benefits of adopting common business processes. Clear communication of advantages and results is critical. It is easier to start small, perhaps in one agency, to show early results, then scale up the usage of the common business processes. Potential users may be allowed to participate early on in development and implementation of common business processes, perhaps through advisory boards or steering committees with representatives of all involved agencies. Cultural change toward collaboration is necessary. Expectations may be managed, recognizing the costs, risks, and long-term benefits. It is also important to agree on mechanisms to share costs and redistribute revenues. Clear implementation responsibilities should be set at the highest levels.

Balancing Top-Down and Bottom-Up

Adoption of a whole-of-government and client-centric approaches, an integrated multi-channel strategy for service delivery, and common, standardized business processes—all call for some top-down directions and coordination mechanisms across the whole government. As depicted in Figure 12.1, these directions provide frameworks for ICT governance, policies for enabling electronic transactions and information sharing, and support for shared services, capabilities, and infrastructures. These "horizontals" provide the foundations on which sectoral applications or "verticals" are established.

But bottom-up initiatives are also critical to ownership, innovation, adaptation, learning, and entrepreneurship. They allow for diversity in line with varying needs and capabilities of agencies and locations. Many e-government applications are sector specific or location specific. Public agencies and city governments want to maintain maximum autonomy to determine their path and pace to ICT adoption and transformation. Some progressive leaders, at the agency or local level, may want to take the initiative and respond to local demands and opportunities, rather than wait for the central government to deliberate on policies and invest in common resources, processes, and institutions. And some agencies are likely to be more e-ready or urgently in need to modernize their operations and services than others.

While countries have followed widely varying paths in planning for e-government, these can be grouped under two fundamentally different approaches:

- An integrated, top-down strategy that is tied to broader economic and development goals. The national government sets policies and provides frameworks and plans for prioritizing investments, implementing projects, and governing, monitoring, and evaluating ICT systems.
- A decentralized, bottom-up strategy that fosters entrepreneurship and allows agencies the independence to launch their own programs. Different agencies or functions of government, including states and city governments, are ICT enabled with relative speed; applications can then be scaled up or spread across other agencies, or hopefully, at the national or federal level.

Each approach has factors that support success as well as risks that may lead to failure. A national strategy directed by government at the executive level, an approach first launched by such countries as Sweden, Singapore, and the Republic of Korea has several advantages. Guided by a shared vision, e-government develops relatively evenly across the government. Integrated platforms are developed, allowing seamless information exchanges and transactions between agencies. The integration of government processes reduces transaction costs to citizens, who can access services from multiple agencies through a single interaction using a smart card or a one-stop shop. Common business processes, open standards, and common guidelines for investment and procurement reduce duplication in spending and allow secure information sharing.

Many governments—and aid agencies—encourage an approach in which efforts to implement e-government target specific sectors, functions, or local initiatives. For example, most of World Bank lending for e-government applications in government follows this approach, mainly through ICT components or pilots in sectoral projects such as education or health. Bilateral and multilateral aid has also focused in pilot ICT applications without much concern about the overall government-wide transformation strategy. This decentralized approach has been politically popular because it has led to small but quick and visible wins. One advantage is that it allows government agencies to embark on their own cutting-edge projects on a sector or service by service. It provides a specific service to a limited target population. It avoids the problems of coordination across agencies. Speed is the decisive element.

Increasingly, countries are experimenting with a hybrid approach that combines features of the top-down and bottom-up strategies. A hybrid approach, for example, might adopt a top-down approach to interoperability standards, architectural frameworks, shared infrastructure, and common services while allowing varying flexibility for bottom-up development of applications and services. This balance often shifts over time. The example of India is one of starting at the state or local levels, as in progressive state like Andhra Pradesh, and then attempted to build upon local experience, scale up successful applications, and develop shared frameworks and infrastructure, starting relatively recently in 2005.

Balancing Sectoral and Cross-sectoral Approaches

The sequencing between sectoral (vertical) and cross-sectoral (horizontal) e-government programs is part of the road map of an e-government transformation process. Should a central agency first set the enabling conditions and shared infrastructure across the government, adopting a whole-of-government approach to transformation? Should the government start with a leading agency or high priority sector through pilots of common business processes, then scale up within the agency then across agencies? Would the focus on such pilots, or sector-specific applications, lead to islands of excellence, duplication in investment, little sharing of date and resources and ultimately, poor agency-centric service? As agencies deepen their own technological learning and further integrate ICT into their business units, would that diminish the role of central ICT agencies and their common frameworks? A national CIO council may help address the sequencing and balancing process.

Governments may adopt some form of a federated approach to e-government program, requiring a continuous balancing act, reflecting the power of central agencies like finance, and the readiness and influence of key sectoral ministries like education and health. Balancing top-down direction and bottom-up initiatives would be reflected in the balance between the horizontal and the vertical integration of e-government or between sectoral approaches and cross-sectoral, whole-of-government approaches. Vertical or sectoral applications would build on and be guided by the shared frameworks, capabilities, and infrastructure. Yet, e-government or e-sector would be organized so as to be fully integrated into the governance and business processes of each sector or public agency (Box 12.2).

Box 12.2 e-Sector Strategies in the Context of e-Transformation

Many of the principles that apply to the national or government-wide levels are also applicable to e-Transformation within and across agencies at the sectoral level. E-sector, the vertical application of ICT at the sector or agency level, is enabled by the building blocks of e-government as treated in this chapter, and by the pillars of e-development, in general.[3] Sectoral leadership and governance are critical. Each sector or agency needs its governing coalition and change agents to initiate and sustain e-Transformation. Leadership must develop and communicate a vision of the transformed sector, enabled by ICT. This vision, together with e-readiness assessment, should guide the design of ICT-enabled sector transformation strategy and the pace and modalities of implementation.

The driver for e-sector transformation is best left to the ministry or agency that owns the business process, to ensure ownership and accountability. The Ministry of ICT may facilitate the process by providing technical assistance and shared resources, but it should not assume the lead in developing or implementing e-health or e-education. Even for common functions or processes such as procurement or human resources management, the lead for e-procurement or e-HR should remain with the national agency that owns this function, that is, the national procurement agency or civil service management agency, together with the participating user agencies.

An e-sector strategy would start with understanding the stakeholders; stakeholder groups vary significantly in influence and support, and across sectors. An e-sector strategy would address sectoral performance priorities, key client services and modes of delivery, and core sectoral functions such as policy analysis, planning and budgeting, monitoring and evaluation, and human resources management. It would examine options for decentralization and networked organization. It would set the stage for establishing priorities for ICT applications within the sector, and for harmonizing and collaborating with other sectors or agencies for shared infrastructures and services.

Each sector agency should take a holistic approach to innovate new ways of doing business and to transform its relationships with its diverse stakeholders. It would deal with its own clients, suppliers, and other stakeholders in developing its own ICT-enabled transformation. These relationships are not binary, but also include potential interactions among the stakeholders. How to unleash the innovative capacity of diverse actors? How to mobilize diverse sources of

---

[3]E-Sector strategies and applications are not covered in detail in this book, except under the e-education section in chapter.

funding for sector transformation? Linkages along the supply chain and new partnerships among government, business, and civil society may be enabled to address sectoral problems and deliver comprehensive services or solutions. For example, in health care, a vision-directed e-health would transform the care delivery across many suppliers and providers, inform and empower the consumer, make costs and quality of health services more transparent to all stakeholders, create better options for promoting health and providing care, promote collaboration and innovation in service delivery, and enable government to coordinate and guide the nation to an equitable and sustainable health system.

Public–Private Partnership[4]

Public–Private Partnerships (PPPs) present alternative ways to obtain goods, services, expertise, and capacity building for the public sector.[5] These partnerships are contractual agreements between public agencies and private companies to supply infrastructure assets or services that traditionally have been provided by governments. Further, in a true PPP, the private sector partner not only stands to profit from a successful project but also assumes some of the risk of failure. In contrast, under ordinary procurement contracts, the private sector vendor is likely to be paid whether the project is successful or not. When first conceived, increasingly, e-government projects have been the subject of PPP initiatives (see, IMF, *Public-Private Partnerships*, March 2004).

The use of ICT in government presents substantial opportunities and options to leverage private sector know-how and resources to accelerate public sector reforms and reinvent government processes and services. E-government initiatives in developing countries are particularly constrained by lack of financial resources, low level of skills and capacity within governments, and the absence of incentive structures for rewarding performance and innovation. Partnership with the private sector to diffuse e-government practices can help overcome many of these constraints, while at the same time increasing opportunities for local private sector development. A frequently cited and early example of an e-government public–private partnership is *e-Seva*, of India (Box 12.3).

---

[4]This section draws on infoDev toolkit (www.egov.infodev.org, 2008), among others.

[5]PPPs were used mainly for physical infrastructure projects, such as power plants. As the need for modern communications systems has increased, PPPs have been developed around access to ICT resources.

Box 12.3 PPP for Government-to-Citizen Service Portal: India's eSeva

e-Seva is an innovative project between the government of India's Andhra Pradesh province and Tata Consulting. e-Seva provides more than one hundred services, ranging from the payment of utility bills to the registration of motor vehicles. In response to access barriers, e-Seva was launched with 43 service centers in the city of Hyderbad, later expanded to 213 towns, and most recently has been extending into rural areas. As a measure of success, e-Seva completes over 1.6 million transactions per month in the city of Hyderbad alone. In this case, Tata Consulting, under the "Build-Own-Operate-Transfer (BOOT)" model, built the e-Seva portal and runs the service, charging normal fees for the various government services and keeping part of the revenue.

e-Seva integrates government-to-citizen with business-to-customer services. It is a key component in implementing the Government of Andhra Pradesh's vision to create a knowledge society by using information technology in all aspects of development and governance. It engages the private sector with a progressive state government in extending public services to all.

Source: www.egov.infodev.org and e-Seva

Partnerships can be built up with the private sector as well as the other stakeholders, including NGOs. Private sector partners who had gained experience in e-commerce may have skills and experience in online service delivery not readily available within the civil service, and they may have greater ability to raise funds necessary for upfront planning and procurement. Through appropriate business models and service level agreements they may also have strong incentives to mobilize demand for the e-service, scale up rapidly, ensure high-quality service, and minimize the costs of systems development, implementation, and operation.

As partners, NGOs can provide complementary resources such as local content and knowledge of target users and the poor. Civil society organizations can also form coalitions to provide oversight and enforce reforms being enabled by e-government, as has been the case in the Philippines with introducing e-procurement in the public sector to promote transparency and fight corruption.

With partnerships, e-government projects and the resulting e-services can be implemented more rapidly at a reduced risk and investment by the government. At the same time, incentives can be provided to the private sector to deliver high-quality electronic services and to scale up adoption. For example, the e-procurement system in Andhra Pradesh, India, was based on PPP, where the private partner put up the capital costs to be paid from adopting users through the transaction fees. This business and revenue model provided strong incentives for the private partners to promote adoption and system success.

Public–Private Partnerships (PPPs) are complex undertakings. They raise critical issues not only of implementation but of legal frameworks, concordance with procurement rules and anti-corruption efforts, principles of selection (including the relative priority given to local and international partners), and methods for assessing public costs and benefits in both the short and the long term. E-government projects raise governance issues that must be thoughtfully addressed.

What is most needed for practitioners in developing countries is a starting point for addressing these opportunities and challenges—where to begin when it comes to PPPs in e-government, and what experiences may be most relevant for their specific conditions and needs. The InfoDev toolkit on e-government (www.egov.infodev.org, 2008) provides a good guide on partnerships with the private sector. A good starting point to start is to understand the various forms of partnerships and their relative merits.

The key to effectiveness for any public–private partnership is to play to the strengths of each partner. The role of government is that of a leader, a catalyst, and, most important, a domain expert who knows "what business it is in." Government alone can resolve legal and procedural problems in implementation, bring together rivals to discuss potential means of competition for the larger public good, decide the terms of competition and regulate them where required, set standards, and provide public infrastructure for the e-government environment. The private sector can provide investments, the latest technology, expertise in delivery and execution, global knowledge, and best practices.

Tools for Leading Government Transformation

This part of the chapter covers a few key analytical tools and processes to complement and translate the conceptual approaches (discussed in the first part) into the practice of planning and managing ICT-enabled government transformation. There is a vast and growing literature on such tools. Policy makers should be aware of tools for stakeholder analysis to gauge resistance to change, mobilize coalitions, and deploy strategic communications. They need to sharpen their human resource management and incentives for change and innovation and develop competencies and CIO networks to lead the change. They should be also able to make the business case for investing in e-government. They need to become aware of the policies and tools necessary to govern and manage the complex technological change as well as the human organization driving government transformation.

Analyzing and Mobilizing Stakeholders

None of public sector reforms will be realized, however, without understanding the stakeholders, communicating across various channels, developing coalitions, and broadening local ownership. Reform programs encounter resistance due to lack of ownership, poor understanding of the impact of reforms on stakeholders, entrenched special interests, weak feedback from stakeholders to decision makers, and inertia, or the need for time to build interest and commitment. More broadly, successful ICT use in government requires attending to governance, political economy, and the social demand side.

But where should we start? What tools we may use? By viewing e-government as a reform process, we may use well-established tools of stakeholder analysis and communications audit to prioritize and phase reforms, mobilize key stakeholders, and promote support for reform (IFC, 2007). This is a smart upfront investment to address the risks and barriers to reform, identify who will help or hinder reform, and use this knowledge as input either to design and sequence the reform program itself or to influence behavior and change the stakeholders landscape in support of reform goals. It can be used to mitigate risks, accelerate reform adoption, and achieve sustainable reform (Box 12.4; Fig. 12.2).

Box 12.4 Stakeholder Analysis

Identifying and analyzing the needs and concerns of different stakeholders is fundamental to shaping and implementing reform. Stakeholder analysis is a structured process to identify, assess, and prioritize the stakeholders and interests that affect the mission and objectives of reform. Stakeholder analysis helps identify the specific interests and characteristics of stakeholders, the capacity of stakeholder groups, relationships among stakeholders to identify potential partners, potential incentives and opportunities to participate, ways to reduce negative impacts on affected stakeholders and mechanisms to improve sustainability.

The process starts with identifying key, primary and secondary stakeholder groups, surveying them for insight and input, analyzing their support and influence and then categorizing these groups along a stakeholder map or matrix (Fig. 12.2). The stakeholder map helps to assess the feasibility of reform and to focus on how to persuade, influence, or empower different stakeholders to advocate for policy changes and promote the reform agenda, together with the enabling e-government application. The stakeholder map is also used to determine the engagement approach for each key stakeholder, who, when and how to engage, depending on the initial location of stakeholders on the map. Options for engaging allies, potential partners, opponents and adversaries can be planned accordingly. For example, potential partners may be informed to enable implementation, motivated to become active supporters, or empowered and organized to lobby for change. For different phases of the e-government application cycle, types of stakeholders would be matched to types of engagement ranging from communications, to consultation, to negotiating for mutually-binding results, to participating in a long term-win-win outcome.

Source: IFC, 2007.

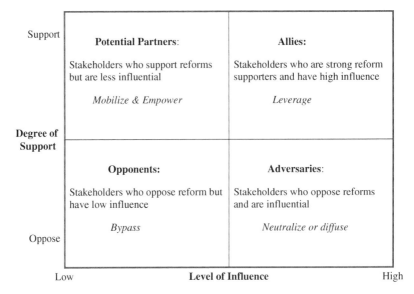

Fig. 12.2 Stakeholder support and influence matrix

Managing for Change and Innovation

Why are change management and innovation critical to successful implementation of e-government programs? How can governments overcome inertia and be able to move from a culture of compliance and risk aversion, to one where innovation is celebrated and change is deemed necessary to superior performance? Can public agencies practice re-engineering and "imagineering" of their processes and services? How to go about evolving a clear change management strategy?

Effective ICT-enabled government transformation requires a holistic or socio-technical approach to change. This should start with a clear vision of the goals and process of transformation, and an explicit strategy that incorporates organizational and cultural change management processes. e-Transformation is often hindered by the poor and different understandings of the goals of e-government and the lack of ownership and widely shared strategy for change.

There cannot be a single change management strategy, since there are many factors that facilitate or inhibit change. Factors include political environment, influence, and support of stakeholders, users or target population, skill level of employees, leadership, degree of resistance, organizational culture, stakes involved in project, time frame for implementation, among others. The changes required range from technology and process level to working habits, skills, and incentives of employees, to organizational level changes in structure and decision-making styles, to legal changes and, at the highest level, to socio-political changes involving policy reforms and empowerment issues.

The biggest challenge for transformational change lies in getting organizational buy-in and dealing with the attendant change management issues. So beyond ensuring a clear political intention, there must be serious assessment of political and administrative mechanisms to ensure that they have the depth and maturity to manage the change that any process of implementing e-government will create. The system must also have the capacity to cope with the hard choices and trade-offs that it will encounter, such as skill change and staff redeployment. Moreover, both the political and the civil service leadership need to understand and accept all the hard trade-offs before they embark on the e-government journey.

Socio-technical change for e-government demands retraining of existing staff, hiring high-quality new staff, updating managerial skills, managing resistance to organizational change, providing incentives for innovation and initiative, partnership and collaborative relationship with the private sector, and working with unions and staff associations. Managerial skills are often more critical than technical skills for managing change, since IT skills can be outsourced. Changing organizational culture may require recruiting new managers from the private sector, as some Mexican agencies did when introducing e-government (OECD, 2005b, p. 106). It may require outside pressures from NGOs, as the Philippines did by engaging civil society organizations to secure government procurement reforms, with e-procurement. Leadership from the top may be combined with a bottom-up approach to help establish common interest, ensure staff buy-in, and deal with specific change requirements and working environments. Finding the right people to build coalitions and lead change in the civil service is a big challenge.

Managing organizational change is critical to overcome resistance to changes in work practices and service delivery. During the pilot and initial rollout stages, it is advisable to retain duplicate delivery channels—the existing manual government counters as well as the online and single-window delivery of multiple services—to reduce resistance to change among both clients and civil servants. But once there is full-scale rollout, phasing out some of the existing government service centers would be preferable: it would lead to big cost savings by reducing the need for physical infrastructure and making better use of government staff, by retraining them to work in other areas.

In developing multi-channel service delivery, governments need to consider the implications for change management and human resources: developing new skills, changing roles, and changing organizational cultures. Apart from technical skills to manage interoperability and enterprise architectures, integrated service delivery channels call for higher levels of skills for coordination and collaboration across organizational boundaries. Changing roles, particularly on the front line, demand staff more familiar with wider range of services offered by a large number of agencies and adept at delivering services through a wider variety of channels. This is part of the shift from being a process workers or bureaucrats to becoming knowledge- and client-centric workers. Coordinated multi-channel service delivery also calls for collaborative management. It calls for devising strategies, incentives, and initiatives to promote innovative and collaborative skills, practices, and cultures.

During later phases of government integration and transformation, e-government programs begin large-scale change management. As more and more manual databases are converted to an electronic format, the government also needs to begin training its vast cadre of employees in the use of e-government systems.[6] Training for public administrators needs to include competencies in change management. Training for middle managers should prepare them for a new culture involving electronic intermediation, information, and knowledge management, and new ways of doing business. Public leaders should be prepared to engage employees and unions throughout all stages of the change process, and particularly in decisions regarding new roles and performance standards. Leaders should hold employees accountable for results rather than mere compliance, introduce incentives for employees to learn and change, and invest in training and re-training. These practices may necessitate civil service policy reforms.

Introduction of e-government services presents a difficult choice for policy makers. On the one hand, there are distinctive benefits in building on existing business process, which can demonstrate significant savings if performed electronically. This is good for quick wins and learning on small projects. Many developing countries, for example, successfully digitized existing processes of renewing various simple business licenses and permits. In essence, nothing changes but the delivery channel. On the other hand, real impact comes from deep process re-engineering rather than with putting existing processes online (Box 12.5). Such projects take time, but ultimately are more rewarding. A national e-government strategy needs to balance the portfolio of quick-win approaches of automating existing administrative procedures without changing them with the more comprehensive approach of reengineering whole functions and core processes with ICT.

Box 12.5 Business Process Reengineering (BPR) and Change Management

Business Process Reengineering (BPR) is a powerful tool for guiding process change and reaping dramatic benefits from ICT in both public and private organizations. Methodologies and practices in BPR have been first applied in business organizations and widely diffused by business consulting firms. BPR is the fundamental rethinking and radical redesign of business processes to achieve dramatic improvements in critical measures of performance such as cost, quality, and speed.

---

[6]Providers of technology packages or solutions often include a training component, but this training needs to be complemented by general information literacy and IT skills.

Applied to the public sector, government process reengineering would start with the question: if a function, service or department were to be designed today, how would it ideally look like, given the status of technology and best practices? Knowledgeable staff, outside experts, and key stakeholders must be involved in the entire BPR exercise. Decisions concerning hardware and software must be guided by the results of BPR. Regardless of whether to buy a standard software package or develop a local solution, BPR is essential, not an add-on exercise. In its widest sense, it is not just about process reforms, but also organizational reforms and increasingly, inter-organizational reforms.

In many developing countries, Business Process Reengineering (BPR) is a new practice even in the private sector, and inexperienced public agencies need much consultation and hand holding to implement process reengineering. Most government agencies manage complex processes that have not been documented or examined for decades. Reengineering these processes often require policy changes and, sometimes, legal changes. Local consultants are often inexperienced in process reengineering and change management, and the time and effort required for these activities are typically underestimated. Integrating processes that span several government agencies multiplies the challenges. All these factors argue for setting realistic expectations and prudent planning for long gestation periods for large, complex e-government applications aiming at higher levels of integration or transformation.

Leading and Organizing to Transform Government

Approaches to leadership and institutional coordination vary among governments, ranging from highly decentralized to centralized (Hanna, 2007b; Hanna and Qiang, 2009). Some hybrid and flexible approaches are emerging, with increasing reliance of Chief Information Officers (CIOs). The position of CIO is vested with institution-wide authority and accountability. For this role to be effective, the center must be able to enforce some key frameworks and standards (to be discussed later). However, decentralized approaches depend more on collegiality, negotiation, persuasion, shared interests, and shared purpose.

Many countries, advanced and developing, are instituting or experimenting with national councils of CIOs, supported by CIOs in ministries and agencies. The role of such councils has become increasingly critical. These councils vary in mandate but often involve addressing common CIO concerns and challenges, such as investment planning, IT procurement practices, IT human resource development, and information security policies.

CIO councils have also been engaged in CIO capacity development by providing inputs into defining core competencies, accrediting CIO education and training programs, and sharing information and best practices among CIOs. Councils are expected to play an increasing role in consensus building, vertical and horizontal communication, team-based problem solving, and knowledge sharing for e-government. When well functioning, they demonstrate the role and power of networks in leading, learning, and innovation to transform governments.

Making the Business Case

E-government is increasingly regarded as fundamental to reform, improvement, modernization, and ultimate transformation of government and the economy. Early in this chapter we discussed the broad objectives of e-government. Put slightly differently, the benefits to be expected from e-government can be categorized into four broad categories: (a) improved efficiency and financial management of public sector agencies and programs; (b) improved delivery of public services, in terms of availability, ease of use, and cost savings to the government, to businesses and to individuals; (c) improved transparency, accountability, and democracy and reduced opportunities for corruption; and (d) broader economic and societal gains, such as improved business environment and empowering communities. Whichever framework is used, the definition of benefits should also inform the process of developing benchmarks for measuring progress.

In early phases of e-government, it is relatively easy to justify investing in major systems for improving efficiency and resource management to enable budget preparation, expenditure management, tax and customs administration, and government procurement. These applications tend to involve relatively large investments in large transaction systems, to implement mandated and fiduciary functions, often driven by the needs of powerful ministries like finance and planning. The benefits are relatively easy to measure in financial terms, particularly in terms of savings or increased revenues to the government. Not surprisingly, these applications tend to be top priorities for government and aid agencies.

Similarly, some early e-government applications such as putting common forms and basic information online (phase one of e-government) for key public services or targeting a few popular or "killer" applications for major target groups can proceed without or costly exercises in appraisal and prioritization or major cost–benefit analyses. Some of the improvements in the quality of services to citizens or business are so dramatic that initiating e-government investments in these services can be easily justified on economic and political grounds. Many examples can be provided in the context of developing countries (Box 12.6). These applications represent "low hanging fruit" and promising entry points for e-government and can help build coalitions for ICT-enabled reform and sustainable e-government transformation programs.

Box 12.6 Making a Difference

Country	Application	Before	After
Brazil	Registration of 29 documents	Several days	20 to 30 min per document, 1 day for business licenses
Chile	Taxes online	25 days	12 h
Guatemala	Banca SAT	30 days	6 h
	E-Procurement	5 hours	On line
China	Online application for 32 business services	2–3 months for business license	10–15 days for business license
		Several visits to multiple offices for filings	Several seconds for routine filing for companies
India, Andhra Pradesh	Valuation of property	Few days	10 min
	Land registration	7–15 days	5 min
India, Karnataka	Updating Land Registration	1–2 years	30 days for approval, request completed on demand
	Obtaining Land Title Certificate	3–30 days	5–30 min
India, Gujarat	Interstate Check Posts for Trucks	30 minutes	2 min
Jamaica	Customs Online	2–3 day for brokers to process entry	3–4 h
Mexico	Access of Public Information	60 days	3 days
Philippines	Customs Online	8 days to release cargo	4 h—2 days to release cargo
Singapore	Issue of Tax assessments	12–18 months	3–5 months
Venezuela	Judicial Case Management System	800 days in debt collection	250 days—initiation to termination
	Speed up commercial cases	400 days in Leasing	150 days

Source: Subhash Bhatnagar and Arsala Deane (World Bank, 2003)

The business case of e-government projects has rarely been monitored and evaluated in its early phases, even in OECD countries, but the need for improvement is acknowledged (OECD, 2003, 2005a). Many OECD countries, and some middle-income developing countries like Chile, are beginning to require that e-government projects or programs make a strong business case. That means incorporating evaluation and monitoring of costs and benefits into e-government investment planning. As e-government initiatives advance and involve services and solutions based on reengineering and joining up of business processes and aim for major transformations of government, it will require more costly investments. Moreover, such investments and transformations are likely to be more risky because of complexity and disruptions to established powers, structures, routines and culture in the public sector. Benefits are also likely to be less measurable in financial terms or the short term for the government.

Because of the above dynamics, the need to clarify the case for ICT-enabled transformation of government and continued investment in e-government is increasing. This includes the need to improve identification and measurement of anticipated costs and benefits, then monitoring and evaluation of post-investment impacts. Making the case is increasingly essential to obtain and sustain public and political support. This will enable decision makers to prioritize e-government investment proposals, hold implementers accountable for managing costs and benefits, and capture opportunities for future improvements.

Governing and Managing the Technology

ICT governance frameworks are essential to guide the evolution of technology architectures and ICT standards across government. We touch on the role of architectural frameworks in providing the set of standards and technologies that provide the foundation for the delivery of ICT-based solutions. We also show some of the emerging technologies most suited to deploying e-government in developing countries. The aim is not to delve into technical details. Technical mastery is not needed from policy makers to effectively harness the technology for development objectives. But it is imperative for policy makers and leaders to understand the trends, benefits, costs, and policy implications of these technological innovations for government transformation.

Tools and technologies relevant to e-government are undergoing intensive development and at times, paradigm shifts, as is the case with mobile phone, open standards, open source software, software as a service (SAAS), collaborative technologies, and utility and cloud computing (computing or common business applications provided as a service over the Internet). These technologies offer substantial possibilities for new service and business innovation models. They offer unprecedented levels of interaction between individuals, communities, and public agencies. They also offer significant opportunities to reduce investments in infrastructures and enhance options for service delivery.

The main policy advice for developing countries is to experiment and learn so as to tap into the new technologies and practices without taking undue risks and costs. Cutting-edge technologies and business models, like cloud computing, present challenges for governance, security, privacy, network reliability, data portability and interoperability, and transition from legacy systems. Developing countries can start experimenting with developing less critical applications and less risky activities first for cloud computing, for example, to start learning and build local capacity to work with the new model. As markets and technologies mature, developing governments can scale up or make full transitions.

For other technologies like mobile, adoption poses less strategic risks, and developing countries may leapfrog to the frontiers. Applications for mobile platforms leverage the benefits of the burgeoning wireless infrastructure that is being deployed in developing countries, forming a basis for m-government projects. Mobile phone may thus be a form of affordable technology for e-government services delivery. Other useful tools and technologies include both proprietary and open source platforms and applications.[7] Extensive sources of information on the specific technologies are available from suppliers, and other neutral sources, such as, the InfoDev Toolkit (2008).

The key challenge for policy makers and strategists is how to manage the growing diversity of information and communication technologies, to balance flexibility and control in a fast-changing and increasingly diverse ICT environment. Should they strive for smooth and robust transitions in technologies? Should they seek to leapfrog to cutting-edge technologies? What kind of frameworks or standards do they need to underpin reliable and cost-effective delivery of e-government services and at the same time maximize flexibility to meet the changing needs of government as quickly and effectively as possible?

Concluding Remarks

The various approaches, frameworks, and tools proposed in this chapter should facilitate implementation of such complex transformation of the public sector—but will not by any means eliminate the risks, complexities, and challenges. Transformation or techno-economic paradigm shifts are poorly understood processes, involving disruptive technologies, creative destruction, and complex political and socio-institutional changes. They also involve equity issues. There are also the real temptation to limit e-government investments to superficial improvements and window dressing, rather than sustainable improvements and real transformation. International experience points to a few lessons that may be kept in mind at policy makers and reformers start along the journey. In the final chapter of this book we sum up the lessons of implementation experience for all aspects of e-development. It may necessary to conclude here with why window dressing is often adopted, rather than sustainable change and deep transformation.

E-government is likely to lead to window dressing or superficial change, unless political and societal leaders choose to use as a tool for reform and transformation. After content analysis of 84 e-government papers, Heeks and Bailur (2006,

---

[7]Many of the tools that governments are adopting were developed originally for commercial use and are available off the shelf or in open source format. These include customer relationship management (CRM) software, enterprise resource management (ERP) tools, and data or content management systems (DMS, CMS).

p. 18) found "A strong theme of overoptimism, even hype, and a consequent lack of balance in considering the impact of e-government." This does not bode well for the future of e-government as its enormous potential for improving the internal processes of government as well as for transforming relationships with clients and providing seamless public service delivery remains largely unrealized.

Another study by the author and Rubino-Hallman of Latin American countries (Rubino-Hallman and Hanna, 2006) concluded that e-government investments in the region have not lived to the potential or promise, limited for the most part to "window dressing" rather than fundamental change in internal processes, external relationships, and service delivery. Despite outstanding exceptions, e-government initiatives throughout the region have focused on front-end service transactions but little on process innovation and institutional transformation. Lack of political will, inadequate budgets, and short time horizons did not permit consistent and cumulative change or true transformation.

The Latin America region is no exception to other developing countries. Recognizing the political economy context and institutional change nature of e-government provides the key to moving e-government beyond "window dressing" and toward realizing the transformational potential of ICTs for governance and public service performance.

E-government can enable reform and accelerate transformation, but it cannot cause them. Key measures to harness ICT potential for reform include informed and committed leadership, national consensus on the priorities and objectives of reforms, incentives for sustained institutional change and process innovation, institutional framework for interagency coordination, partnership and collaborative approaches with business and civil society, and linking the vision of government transformation to implementation mechanisms. Reform, enabled by ICT, requires sustained investments over a long-time horizon to transform and integrate back-end processes. It demands a holistic approach that combines leadership, vision, guiding coalition, managed expectations, and external pressures from organized users, business and civil society.

Using ICT to transform government is inherently a political and managerial leadership function. It demands leadership for change, innovation, and integration. This leadership needs to come from senior executive and legislative officials. Dealing with the challenges of implementing e-government calls for a mandate from the chief executive to support organizational and process change, a managerial culture to promote innovation and client-focused service, and a new cadre of chief information officers and leadership networks to cut across public agencies, private entities, and civil society organizations. To overcome organizational silos, it is often necessary to anchor ownership at the highest levels, in a dynamic, proactive executive leadership team.

A transformative e-government strategy requires widely shared, long-term vision and sustained institutional reform efforts. Coalitions for reform should be developed and nurtured. Change agents, local leaders, and project managers should be empowered with tools and funds to facilitate the necessary changes in roles, processes, and skills that accompany ICT-enabled transformation. These should be complemented by efforts to share successes, manage knowledge about best practices, and secure channels for scaling up. Local and regional successes are more powerful than abstract international best practices. Strategic communications can play an important role in sharing successes and sustaining the reform process.

It is important to manage expectations about e-government programs and their ability to impact the life of ordinary citizens in the short term. Often there are "killer applications" that could have wide and powerful impact such as computerizing and making land records available to the millions of small farmers in Andhra Pradesh. But many investments in e-government will take long gestation periods to show results, and these are often of institutional, infrastructural, and transformational nature. Since e-government will inevitably encounter resistance and doubts, it is important to balance investments between those "low hanging fruits" or quick impact applications, and those investments necessary to build the platforms for wider impact and transformation. Prioritization and phasing of investments should thus take account of the incentives and time horizon of various stakeholders to ensure adequate incentives for a sustained public sector reform process. A compelling long-term vision, one that excites political leaders, civil servants, and citizens is often an essential ingredient to overcoming painful transition costs and temporary setbacks.

Reconnecting e-Government to e-Development

E-government will not achieve its full potential unless ICT is widely adopted, made affordable and accessible. Until usage levels rise significantly, it will remain a major challenge to use technology to spearhead deep transformation in the public sector. Wide citizen adoption of online services is necessary to achieve economies of scale and lower the unit cost of providing these services. This in turn will broaden adoption and help governments realize the potential cost savings and transformation effects hoped for. There are direct connections between lowering the digital divide, e-services usage patterns, budget savings, and ultimately government-wide transformation.

To a significant degree the success of e-government depends on the broader ICT policy and regulatory framework, which can facilitate the development of communications services. In many countries, the legal establishment of a competitive ICT market has been a key factor in expanding the information and communications infrastructures. The reforms include among other policies: the introduction and enforcement of competition and interconnection rules; the establishment of strong, independent regulatory agencies; the elimination or simplification of individual licensing requirements; and the reform of spectrum management to promote wireless Internet access. The legal framework for e-commerce, such as the rules supporting e-payments, laws recognizing the validity of e-documents, and laws covering cybercrime and data protection, also facilitate e-government.

Many policies and practices being adopted by e-government programs concerning information sharing within government and with citizens, as well as e-policies concerning privacy, security, and electronic transactions have wide impact on e-literacy, e-business, the development of the local information services industry and the overall health of information society ecosystem. China is a case in point, where secrecy considerations are high, and the delivery of public information services is heavily dependent on top-down, vertically oriented government agencies— contributing factors to slow development in the information services industry and rural informatization, despite the vast investments in information infrastructure.

Strategic decisions concerning enterprise architecture, interoperability frameworks, and technology standards for e-government have wide impact on the ecosystem of e-development. For example, the adoption of open source as the preferred software standard for e-government systems and applications can have wide ramifications on all other elements of the e-development ecosystem: the competitiveness of the local ICT industry in exporting services, the development of local competency in open source in support of applications beyond government, intellectual property and other e-policies, local content, affordable grassroots applications, e-literacy, and so on.

Investing in civil servants and public managers must move in level and pace with investing in ICT application in the public sector. Many developing countries seeking to harness ICT for public sector transformation face a shortage of policy makers and civil servants familiar with ICT policy and management practices, with e-government potential and requirements, and with their roles in leading and practicing ICT-enabled change and innovation processes. Senior officials are more likely to support e-government initiatives if they understand the role of e-government, and their own roles in leading change. Equally important is for public managers to improve their understanding of the ways ICT can improve government relationship with its clients, what services can be provided online, what best managerial practices may be adopted to implement e-government projects.

Preparing, empowering, and motivating civil servants to engage in major change is critical, but relatively neglected when compared to investing in hardware and basic infrastructure. To adopt and benefit from e-services, users, citizens, and small businesses must be e-literate. Preparing users must be sequenced in line with the rollout of e-services. Investing in human resources in support of e-government is often the weakest link in the chain.

To improve accessibility of e-services on a macrolevel, e-government programs in the countries with poor information infrastructure should be developed in sync with programs to improve public access, for example, through telecenters and/or citizen service centers. Different delivery models should be explored, piloted, and sequenced. In many ways, piloting and scaling up of e-applications should be coordinated and sequenced with that of connectivity solutions and delivery channels. The pillar of communication infrastructure and connectivity is essential to inclusive and sustainable government transformation programs and must be sequenced so as to lead or go in parallel with e-government investments.

E-literacy among citizens, developed around the telecenters, may be also sequenced with the rollout of e-government services. The *Akshaya project* in rural

Kerala, India, provides an interesting example. The project is centered around multi-purpose community technology centers, equipped with high bandwidth wireless connectivity, and run by private entrepreneurs. The centers have a strong e-literacy program, which allows every household to send one member to the local center to acquire training in the basics of computing. By increasing e-literacy among citizens, the project supports the rollout of other services in e-government, e-health, e-commerce, and e-education.

The relationship between e-government and e-development is reciprocal. As shown in preceding examples, effectiveness of e-government programs is heavily dependent on developments in the legal and regulatory environment, e-policies, connectivity, information infrastructure, local ICT industry, relevant content in local language, and the e-literacy of citizens, business, civil servants, and public managers. In short, many of the prerequisites of ICT-enabled government transformation also happened to be necessary conditions for successful e-development strategies more broadly. Reciprocally, e-government information and services may boost interest in all other kinds of ICT-enabled services in a networked economy. They may augment demand for digital content, telecenters services, and broadband connectivity. Investing in the skills and technology necessary to make e-government relevant also build the foundation for an information society.

Timing and sequencing of various elements of e-government (and e-development) are critical. Recurrent themes of this chapter are the need to invest in advanced network infrastructure, the need to develop multi-channel service delivery and standardize on common business processes, the need to reengineer business processes prior to systems deployment, the need to orient organizational culture toward process improvement and client service, and the need to measure and track performance. Net impact of investment in e-government depends on people, policies, processes, and technology. Although this combination may seem to be a simple formula for e-government design and implementation, it could take many variations with significant differences in productivity. As with baking a cake, simply combining butter, sugar, eggs, and flour does not guarantee positive outcome. For example, on average, organizations that re-engineer after the deployment of a network-based application can experience almost 50% smaller improvement in cost containment than organizations that re-engineer prior to ICT deployment (Frosst et al., 2005, p. 33).

Equity issues cannot be addressed effectively without putting e-government in a broader context and working on all elements of e-development. Otherwise, putting public services online may even reinforce the disparities in delivering public services and in making basic services work for everyone. E-government efforts must act on a variety of fronts to overcome barriers facing the poor and disadvantaged groups: secure multiple service delivery channels; secure affordable, sustainable, and widely shared access to the Internet; prioritize services most relevant to the target groups; develop appropriate local content in local languages, invest in digital literacy and awareness campaigns to mobilize demand for e-channels; creatively address disability and gender barriers to access; and engage NGOs in defining and mobilizing demand and in providing feedback on e-government services.

Chapter 13
Enterprise Transformation

In this chapter, I examine the opportunities and challenges of applying ICT in business enterprises. I explore the roles and approaches that governments may take, in partnership with business associations and NGOs, to promote the effective adoption and diffusion of e-business by SMEs or priority user sectors. The aim is to help policy makers and business associations play their key roles in facilitating ICT diffusion among SMEs, and enabling enterprises to deploy ICT for their business innovation and transformation.

Diffusion of e-business is at an early stage, and the drivers and barriers to e-business adoption need to be understood in the context of developing economies. This understanding should guide the design of public policies and technical assistance programs for the adoption of e-business practices in support of competitiveness at the firm, sector, local, and national levels. Moreover, SMEs face special constraints to the adoption of e-business.

The private sector is a key partner and driver of e-Transformation. It is a stakeholder and contributor to the public good, producer of ICT products and services, investor and manager of ICT infrastructure, partner and contractor of e-government applications, beneficiary of government-to-business services and trade facilitation infrastructure, and a leading adopter and intensive user of ICT. These various roles have been explored in the earlier chapters on the ICT sector, information infrastructure, human resources, and e-government. Here, we concern ourselves with the motivations of adopting ICT, and with identifying best practices to accelerate firm- and network-level adoption of e-business. We explore the use of ICT to improve the business environment at the national level.

E-business is a powerful innovation to increase the capacity of companies to connect, grow, and compete. Available evidence shows that electronic markets are more transparent and efficient. Through lower transaction cost and increased reach, they result in up to 15% lower costs to consumers, and up to 20% lower costs in business procurement (ILO, 2001). Among SMEs, e-business can bring about substantial revenue growth by reaching out to new customers and markets as well as serving current customers better and thus inducing more sales and value.

E-business also enables a host of managerial and process innovations and the adoption of modern business practices, as indicated in Chapter 2 and later examined

N.K. Hanna, *e-Transformation: Enabling New Development Strategies*, Innovation, Technology, and Knowledge Management, DOI 10.1007/978-1-4419-1185-8_13, © Springer Science+Business Media, LLC 2010

in this chapter. ICT plays a new role in innovation and competitiveness in the emerging techno-economic paradigm. During the last 2–3 decades of the 20th century, industries have been undergoing a paradigm shift from mass production, economies of scale, and corporate-dominated R&D to an emphasis on economies of scope, flexible and interconnected production, and greater openness and decentralization of research and innovation. E-business plays a central role in facilitating this shift toward flexibility, collaboration, and interconnectedness. E-business diffusion programs emphasize the use of ICT for innovation, knowledge partnerships, cluster development, and local and global connectedness.

This chapter moves from understanding the broad e-business adoption and diffusion patterns, to the specific constraints facing SMEs in developing countries, to lessons of experience in designing e-business programs and options for supporting adoption and improving the business environment. We conclude with identifying some of the interdependencies between e-business and the enabling pillars of e-development. Specifically, this chapter structured to cover the

- emerging patterns of e-business adoption and diffusion in developed countries, and the distinctive differences of developing countries and SMEs;
- designing e-business diffusion programs;
- supporting access to information, finance, and online business services;
- simplifying government-to-business transactions and facilitating trade;
- promoting connectivity for SMEs; and
- taping synergies between e-business and e-development.

Understanding e-Business, Diffusion, Drivers, and Barriers

E-business often suffers from a misconception that it is all about access to Internet or "selling to people online." In fact, the absolute bulk of online commerce involves business-to-business transactions. E-business goes beyond the narrow definition of electronic commerce. It is concerned with improving competitiveness of enterprises by transforming internal processes, advancing marketing and management practices, improving customer service, and accelerating product development and business model innovation. The pervasive impact of e-business had stimulated practically all OECD countries to introduce well-financed promotional programs; e-business is a central pillar of eEurope 2005 Action Plan.

E-business falls into two broad categories:

- Internal ICT applications, providing firms with opportunities to enhance productivity and efficiency. These mainly consist of ICT applications for basic management and operational functions such as office automation and management information systems. It also includes applications within and across the structures of firms such as encouraging email communications internally and externally, including through web sites, with particular emphasis on flexibility, agility, and internal co-ordination.

- E-commerce applications, allowing firms to conduct contractual transactions with other businesses (B2B) as well as individual consumers (B2C), typically over the Internet. E-commerce enables firms to become part of complex integrated networks of players involving various online business processes (such as supply chains) and to contract, buy, and sell online. It enables firms to conduct business-to-government transactions (B2G) and partnerships, as in e-government procurement. The primary benefits or drivers for the adopting firms are to expand markets, enter new businesses, and improve co-ordination with customers and suppliers.

Understanding global trends in e-business diffusion, and the differences between developed and developing countries, should guide the design of national e-business diffusion programs. Similarly, understanding the drivers and barriers at the firm level should guide publically supported programs for SMEs to adopt e-business practices. Surveys of e-business practices are shedding light on the patterns, drivers, and barriers to diffusion (for example, Kraemer et al., 2006).

E-business adoption has been rapid in developed countries, and among the more globally oriented firms or sectors in developing countries, as quick followers. Overall, the impact has so far been more evolutionary than revolutionary. The wide commercial use of the Internet started only since late 1990s. With current advances of broadband and growing network externalities, we may be witnessing the beginning of supply chain-wide transformation.

Global firms engage more extensively in e-business. General Electric engages with 500,000 suppliers and partners in one of the largest supply chains in the world. Procter and Gamble has created a global research network that linked it to more than 1.5 million independent researchers around the globe (Fung et al., 2008, p. 14). Financial institutions, as early adopters of e-commerce, have also been globalizing their back-office business operations, with call centers, software and IT services, and business process outsourcing.

All these globalization practices—in innovation, design, production, marketing, and finance—would not have been possible with e-business adoption. The global firms have become global network orchestrators. Networks compete against networks, not companies (Fung et al., 2008).

Multinational corporations are powerful drivers of diffusion of new technologies and business practices in two ways. They bring resources, including capital, know-how, and own IT-based business practices, to wherever they operate. They also bring competition to local markets and thus pressure on local firms to adopt these technologies and associated business practices. Multinational companies drive e-business diffusion through their co-ordination of global production networks and supply chains. They standardize their operational practices worldwide and push suppliers to align their processes and technologies with them. Global production and supply chains rely on ICT to improve co-ordination and time to market, and to cut inventory and errors.

These practices have major implications for developing countries and SMEs. The openness of the economy to FDI and trade, that is, to global network orchestrators, is a critical factor in e-business diffusion. Integration of countries into global production networks often involves the wide adoption of e-commerce practices as a condition for participation (Ernest, 2003; Dedrick and Kraemer, 2004). Even small local enterprises must be able to remain connected as effective participants in the global supply chain. In Hong Kong alone, at least 50,000 small trading companies manage regional or global supply chains. Fortunately, e-business solutions make it easier for small firms to act globally or join the global supply chains of multinationals. Multinationals may be attracted to co-locate or link with local SMEs, and governments may partner with business to prepare SMEs and support such linkages.

While driven by broad global forces, e-business diffusion is tempered by national environments and firm-level business imperatives (Kraemer et al., 2006). There is a positive relationship between wealth and diffusion of e-commerce. But national factors go beyond wealth. They include competitive pressures, information infrastructure, investment resources, payment mechanisms, and rule of law. Availability of a dynamic and competitive information infrastructure is also a key to wide adoption. Liberalization of telecommunications and financial services is an important driver of e-business diffusion. Policies and regulations concerning privacy and security of electronic transactions can be critical to diffusing e-commerce. All these are key elements of e-development.

Many governments have developed diffusion polices and programs that take account of their special national environments. For example, their e-government procurement may offer incentives to help smaller firms go online and participate in e-government procurement services. While government promotion programs may have not been a key driver of e-commerce diffusion in developed countries, the limited evidence available from nascent diffusion programs suggests that such programs can be influential in developing economies (Kraemer et al., 2006, p. 32). Effectiveness of such programs is enhanced when combined with complementary e-policies and SME support, and effective legal and regulatory environment.

e-Business Diffusion in Developing Countries

The path of business digitization for many developing countries is likely to be different. In most developed countries, e-business adoption started as an in-house process, and only later progressed on to e-commerce and the interconnection of different external actors. In most developing countries the penetration of high-quality in-house ICT applications is very low, especially in the production system, enterprise resource planning (ERP) and supply chain management (ECLAC, 2003). The absence of internal e-business applications is a major obstacle to the adoption of more advanced inter-organizational applications, business-to-business marketplaces, and online transactions. Another barrier is the high costs of world-class ERP software systems.[1] Integrating such systems into the organizational structure requires significant costs for training and overall adjustment in organizational

---

[1] Such as SAP.

functions, as well as institutional flexibility and innovation. Thus, in developing countries, enterprises are pressed to adopt both internal and external e-business applications at the same time.

With the predominance of SMEs in developing economies, governments are also pressed to address the special constraints and market gaps facing local enterprises in adopting e-business. Small enterprises lag far behind large companies in e-business adoption in most developing countries. Yet, SMEs enjoy flexibility as they are not locked into major investments in legacy systems or EDI networks and can rely on open, inexpensive Internet exchanges. Governments are therefore concerned about empowering local SMEs to connect with the digital economy. E-business and ICT policies may be integrated with the SME and innovation policy agendas.

Developing countries face significantly more challenges as governments partner with the private sector to leverage ICT for innovation and competiveness across their economies. Studies of ICT adoption in business in developing countries indicate four broad areas of concern: (1) limited access to affordable and competitive telecommunications infrastructure and services; (2) lack of trust in e-processes and legal protection; (3) perceived uncertain benefits of adoption; and (4) limited absorptive capacity and ICT-skilled labor (UN, 2003; Kraemer et al., 2006; World Bank, 2006, Chapter 4). Insufficient availability, affordability, and poor quality of the existing telecommunication services, particularly of broadband, are often the initial constraints to adoption. Shifting from traditional interactions to electronic transactions also raise many legal and regulatory concerns. Firms fear that the ICT platform is not robust enough to protect online transactions, information privacy, and data integrity.

Most SMEs in developing countries are also not fully aware of ICT-enabled business opportunities and benefits. E-business is a complex and costly undertaking that calls for substantial investments and institutional changes. Adoption is therefore accompanied with uncertainties. These uncertainties are compounded by the limited availability of local advice, locally accepted industry-specific models in practice, and local logistical challenges. Network externalities are limited by the lack of a critical mass of users. Moreover, small firms find it more difficult to absorb ICT costs and risks. Finally, ICT skill shortages and capability failures are a binding constraint, particularly for SMEs. Access to reliable professional advice on integrating ICT into business strategy and processes is both scarce and costly in most developing countries.

As many of the constraints to e-business are typically beyond those of a single sector, ministry, or enterprise, overcoming them would be most effectively done within the broader context of an e-development strategy.

e-Business and Managerial Innovation

In a competitive environment, incentives for ICT adoption in business are naturally stronger than other e-sectors, such as e-government, e-health, or e-learning. With globalization and liberalization of trade and investment, these incentives have grown stronger. There is much to be learned from the experience of developed countries that have started this journey earlier, first to transform the internal processes of enterprises, then to transform relationships across enterprises, suppliers, and customers. These lessons underline the importance of managerial innovation. They point to the need for joint investment in human, organizational, and technological resources to realize the benefits from technological change.[2]

Businesses, particularly in advanced countries, have moved in stages in using ICT in their operations and transactions, from early automation of isolated processes, to re-engineering and integration of various processes and applications, to knowledge management and fundamental transformation of relationships along whole value chains. Moving along these stages was enabled by increasingly proactive leadership and innovative management. Experience has shown that productivity increases were marginal, compared to the costs involved, when ICT investments were limited to automation of administrative processes or front-end online transactions, and when not accompanied by managerial improvement and institutional transformation. Productivity improvements became substantial only when business organizations co-invested in ICT and managerial and institutional innovation.

Usage, involving institutional learning, is a key factor in linking ICT adoption to transformational impact (Hanna et al., 1995; Kraemer et al., 2006). The e-business learning ladder consists of multiple stages from its adoption to its use to manage the impact on the firm's performance. The use of ICT for e-business, beyond the adoption decision to use the Internet to conduct business, refers to the breadth and depth of use. These can be measured by the diffusion of e-commerce across value chain activities, and the intensity or the percentage of value chain activities that is conducted online.

In a similar way to e-government, e-business adoption by companies goes through several overlapping stages of awareness, connectivity, information (web publishing), transactions (interaction), and business integration (transformation) (Fig. 13.1). Most economic benefits come from these later stages of interaction and integration. This is a learning process. E-business needs and solutions will vary among firms depending on where the firm is on the learning curve. A small firm with limited expertise and resources would require a great deal of guidance and support along this journey.

E-business diffusion and enterprise transformation are rarely smooth, linear processes. Some established firms like Cisco, IBM, General Electric, and Wal-Mart as well as others born on the Internet such as eBay and Amazon have shown the potential of e-business. But many others failed to achieve deep usage beyond initial adoption, and thus failed to reap the transformational benefits.

---

[2]As suggested in the last chapter on transforming governments, these lessons are applicable across all sectors.

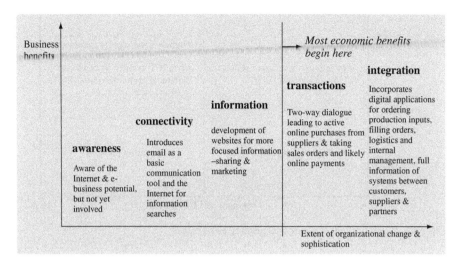

Fig. 13.1 e-Business adoption learning ladder

Managerial understanding influences e-business diffusion and the likely pay-offs from adoption. Managers have to examine the costs and benefits of various uses, ranging from ways to improve productivity and internal efficiency, reduce operational and inventory costs, to ways to improve co-ordination and information sharing with suppliers and business partners, and increase customers service quality. Major payoffs are contingent on integrating e-business with core business processes and/or exploiting e-business to create new approaches to manage value chain activities. Adoption is the start of a learning process, and payoffs are contingent on institutional learning.

Various studies point to the potential role of ICT in improving performance when combined with managerial improvements and institutional reforms(Fig. 13.2).[3] ICT investments alone, without changes in business processes and managerial practices, typically lead to marginal productivity improvements. Improving management practices can lead to significant increases in productivity, even if not accompanied by

---

[3] For example, a study conducted by McKinsey of 100 companies in industrial countries quantified these differences in productivity in France, Germany, the United Kingdom, and the United States found that IT investments have little impact unless they are accompanied by first-rate management practices, which, by contrast, *can* boost productivity on their own. Companies were rated on how well they used three important management practices: lean manufacturing, which cuts waste in the production process; performance management, which sets clear goals and rewards employees who reach them; and talent management, which attracts and develops high-caliber people. The companies that had the highest marks in these areas became more productive, with or without higher spending on IT. Those that combined good management practices with IT investments did best of all.

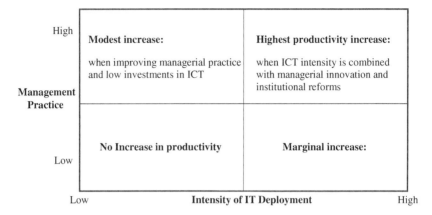

Fig. 13.2 Payoffs from ICT and complementary investments

ICT. But it is when investing in ICT is combined with transformational leadership and managerial innovations that ICT can yield far superior performance and real change. Additional spending on information technology can raise productivity, but only in well-managed companies.

Several managerial and policy implications follow from these e-business diffusion and impact studies.

First, the impact of ICT on productivity of enterprises is significant but conditional on complementary factors and managerial practices. Developing countries need to monitor the evolution of e-business to assess their impact as well as identify barriers for scaling up, and the complementary factors that lead to superior productivity gains in specific sectors and contexts. Public policies and programs may help ensure that local businesses and SMEs be aware of and have access to information about the best practices to deploy ICT to connect and transform business. Policy makers and business leaders need to understand the long-term competitive implications of e-business adoption and what competencies are needed to engage in this new competitive environment.

Second, to drive greater value from e-business, managers may pursue wide uses across the value chain, that is, breadth of use. Which activity should come first is a strategic issue. For firms where operational excellence is strategic, emphasis may be placed on internal operations and value chain co-ordination. For firms where client relationships are strategic, relative emphasis may be placed on customer-facing transactions. For firms where new products and services are strategic, emphasis may range from knowledge sharing, to ICT-enabled innovation, to product development and commercialization.

Third, institutional leadership and managerial innovation are needed to select and sequence these uses, as well as promote deeper usage in each value chain activity. Interactions among business executives and IT managers become more critical and intensive to ensure integration of e-business with their existing technology base, business processes, distribution channels, and corporate culture.

Designing e-Business Diffusion Programs

Lessons may be drawn from these long-standing diffusion programs of OECD countries and their recent evolution for the benefit of developing countries (Hanna et al., 1995). Best practice diffusion programs address incentives, institutions, and capabilities. They start with identifying current local e-business practices and the specific constraints to ICT adoption, particularly those facing SMEs. They promote institutional learning capabilities and engage business leadership and trade and professional associations. Government agencies learn to become catalysts as they work closely with trade associations. Sectoral approach to e-business adoption increases the opportunities to engage the respective sectoral institutions, support the participation of SMEs in the global digital supply chains of their respective sector, and address structural issues facing these sectors as they adopt e-business practices.

OECD experience also suggests that e-business promotion requires close collaboration of public and private sectors. ICT companies, including ICT multinationals, consulting firms, and large companies in traditional industries can be important drivers of e-business adoption. Most of the successful promotional programs have been developed and conducted through private–public partnership.

A few developing countries and emerging markets, such as Korea and Ghana, have initiated their own programs for e-business diffusion. There is a growing variety of approaches to provide such support. Cross-country evaluation is needed to learn to match these approaches to country conditions and stages of e-business adoption. Pending more in-depth cross-country evaluations, we illustrate here some of the promising practices.

I focus on four broad types of support for e-business adoption:

- Information, training, and consultancy services for e-business adoption
- Sectoral support for e-business adoption
- Shared, low-cost, on-demand e-business solutions
- Matching grants for e-business adoption at enterprise, network, or cluster level

Information, Training and Consultancy Services for e-Business Adoption

E-business diffusion programs in developing countries would be expected to target SMEs as they turn out to be the late adopters and need assistance in skill upgrading and understanding the impacts and mechanisms of e-business. Such programs would start with ICT-based business development services for awareness raising, training, and capacity building to help small enterprises make the case for e-business and take the necessary steps to invest in e-business adoption. Among the tools used are

- Self-guided business training materials, tools, information, and databases
- Training programs
- Peer exchange of experience: workshops and seminars
- Benchmarking tools and case studies
- Basic business and technology consultancy
- Support to networking and clustering, supply-chain development
- Simplified business planning and common problem-solving tools
- Online support such as access to existing databases and web site information (on suppliers, price trends, etc.); developing extranets and web sites for business-to-business partnerships

Canada's e-Business Initiative, mentioned earlier, is one example. However, the Canadian program complements online support with direct consultancy services. It would be unlikely for developing countries or economies at early stages of e-business adoption to rely solely on online resources to support e-business adoption and diffusion. However, online tools, appropriately adapted to local conditions, can be cost-effective in raising awareness, complementing, and scaling up assistance for SME adoption of e-business solutions.

Sectoral e-Business Support

Besides "generic" e-business promotion programs, developing countries could benefit from more targeted sectoral interventions, such as e-business in tourism or agri-business. Agriculture remains a very important sector for the vast majority of developing countries. Applications such as rural information and advisory system and e-marketplace can help the farmers to access new markets and achieve sustainable growth by overcoming geographical restrictions, poor technologies, and outdated business techniques. In Chile, for example, the national agricultural extension service created an Internet-based rural information service for farmer groups, rural governments, and NGOs. Transmitting price and market information this way was estimated to cost 40% less than using traditional methods. In addition, the information was more timely, reaching farmers much faster than the printed bulletin that used to take 45 days.

ICT applications, such as online market information systems, e-commerce platforms, and agricultural advisory services could help the farmers to access new markets and achieve sustainable growth by overcoming geographical barriers, inappropriate technologies, outdated business techniques, and lack of relevant market information. One of the most successful interventions to support rural enterprises is e-Choupal in India (Box 13.1). Even though e-Choupal is a privately owned system, it can be adopted as a government-supported solution or a public–private partnership.

Box 13.1 e-Choupal as a Logistics Solution for Fragmented Rural Farmers, India

E-Choupal was designed to make a sustainable efficient supply chain in Indian agriculture through vertical integration of fragmented rural farms. It was established by ITC corporation's International Business Division, which is the largest exporter of agricultural commodities in India. Through its web site, e-Choupal provides various information regarding weather, knowledge of scientific farm practices, and market prices of agricultural commodities in local language. In addition, in order to raise productivity and enlarge capacity of farmer risk management, e-Choupal aggregates demand of inputs for production, and storage and marketing of their products, eliminating involvement of numerous intermediates. Thus, both rural farmers and ITC get a better deal. Rural farmers can access e-Choupal at local kiosks. Since established in June 2000, e-Choupal has created more than 1300 kiosks in 8000 villages across four states.

Another interesting case is use of integrated assistance to improve horticultural supply chains in Ghana. It combines Last Mile Initiative (LMI)[4] and trade and investment initiative to promote competitive non-traditional export crops such as pineapples. This is an example of using supply chain analysis and e-business solutions to enhance farming techniques and post-harvesting logistics and export. The program first analyzed the supply chain for pineapples leading to key European markets and identified key deficiencies in production, precision farming, post-harvesting, and logistics. Working with a network of 17 packinghouses which serves as exporting hubs for the small farmers, the program provided technical assistance to strengthen the capabilities of smaller farmers working in groups.

The LMI complemented this technical assistance in three ways: (1) introduction of electronic data exchange-to-bar code enabled logistics management capability; (2) packinghouse-to-field application built upon telecommunications that is to be subsidized by the universal access fund (UAF); and (3) technical assistance for telecommunications policy and regulatory reform. It helped to develop and implement a packinghouse-to-field application that allowed the farmers to manage and track activity by plot, receive instructions from their packinghouses, and respond with updates and questions regarding pre- and post-harvest activities. These applications enabled the recorded data to meet European traceability requirements

---

[4]The Last Mile Initiative (LMI) is a USAID-funded program which aims to extend access to communications into rural areas. Its objective is to increase productivity and transform the development aspects of farmers, small businesses, new startups, and other organizations in rural areas through voice and data telecommunication networks. (http://www.lastmileinitiative.org).

which improved farm management overall. The application provides farmers easily searchable electronic access to farm extension information that can be updated periodically at the packinghouse using a wireless link. The application has the possibility of future use in ordering inputs such as fertilizer and plantlets, handling the tracking and payment of orders.

Shared, Low-Cost, On-demand e-Business Solutions

Another option to promote the diffusion of e-business solutions is to aggregate low-cost, on-demand solutions such as forming consortia of Application Service Providers (ASPs). Local firms may be encouraged to enter the business application market in segments where smaller organizational units require cost-effective information systems. These user segments may include SMEs, small clinics, and municipalities. Local ICT firms may be in a better position to generate suitable solutions for small agents at low prices. The ASP model presents option for the provision of quality software to small organizational units, by sharing infrastructure service organization and maintenance costs. Implementation costs can be reduced by deploying standard solutions and sharing training resources. Through liability and enforcement assurances, service providers can also guarantee the functionality of the system and provide ongoing updates of applications in a fast-changing technology environment.

The Korean government has taken both top-down and bottom-up approaches in encouraging uptake of e-business solutions. The government invested heavily in rolling-out an affordable and high-capacity broadband nationwide, and in ensuring the supply of low-cost e-business solutions for successful integration of SMEs into increasingly competitive markets. It aggregated existing low-cost, on-demand solution providers through a consortium, and a common online platform (Box 13.2).

Box 13.2 Korea's Consortium for Application Service Providers for SMEs[5]

Recognizing the important economic role played by SMEs, Korea took the initiative to ensure the supply of quality and low-cost on-demand software for SMEs by establishing several consortia of e-business service providers. Application Service Providers (ASP) were chosen as a key element of e-business promotion as they can provide easy-to-use IT services and solutions that are leased on a subscription basis, eliminating the cost burdens to

---

[5]An ASP is a web-based business that provides e-business services to customers over a network. Software offered using an ASP model is also sometimes called on-demand software. The application software resides on the vendor's system and is accessed by users.

implement and own e-business solutions. Demand for ASPs has evolved from the increasing costs of specialized software that have far exceeded the price range of SMEs. Also, the growing complexities of software have led to huge costs in distributing software to end-users. Through ASPs, the complexities and costs of installing, supporting, securing, and upgrading such software can be reduced significantly.

Under the e-business program, the National Computerization Agency[6] selects, through public invitation, a consortium for providing IT services to SMEs. The designated consortium acts independently, attracting SMEs seeking to utilize ASP services. The consortium is composed of broadband ISPs, portal service providers, contents providers, solution providers, who are selected through a competitive process. The government's role is to kick-start the ASP industry cluster and to ensure the cluster can provide quality and low-cost e-business solutions. On the demand side, the program also aggregates SMEs to create a viable market for the ASPs. The government program is expected to last until the ASP market is fully competitive and sustainable.

There are both advantages and disadvantages to using ASPs as a source of e-business solutions. Advantages include low initial cost, low risk, and built-in best practices. Disadvantages include limited customization, security and confidentiality concerns, dependency on quality broadband service, and need for scale to realize economy and sustainability. SMEs may decide to wean off of ASPs as they become more knowledgeable about their e-business needs and are able to afford customized solutions which require higher investment costs.

Matching Grants and Cluster Support

An e-business promotion program can go one step further and include investment support to SMEs and the development of e-business intermediaries and consultants. Eligible areas for matching grant financing would include professional services and training, program fees to help firms assess e-business costs and benefits, prepare and implement e-business plans, and re-engineer business processes and products; web site development, hosting, and security certification; e-Business information services.

Singapore's e-business Industry Development Scheme (eBIDS) is one example. To strengthen the adoption of e-business in Singapore, the Infocomm Development Authority of Singapore (IDA) and Productivity and Standards Board (PSB) put

---

[6]The Korean National Computerization Agency (NCA) is a statutory agency founded by the Framework Act on Informatization Promotion for the purpose of promoting informatization and to support development of related policies for Korean national agencies and local autonomies.

in place a S$30 million incentive program in 2000. Known as the e-Business Industry Development Scheme (eBIDS), the program was initiated by the Ministry for Communications and Information Technology to create a mechanism so that the government could work together with the private sector to implement various strategies to remove barriers and promote opportunities for e-business. The program tailors the amount and type of support services to the position of the enterprise on the e-business learning curve (Box 13.3).

Box 13.3 Singapore: e-Business Development Grants Program

The introduction of eBIDS builds upon a smaller pilot of S$9 million that started in 1998 to jump-start the mass adoption of e-commerce among local enterprises. The objective of eBIDS is to scale-up the LECP effort in assisting greater numbers of local firms and startups in their e-business knowledge acquisition, technology transfer, and e-business value creation. By 2002, the program had increased the overall e-commerce incremental transaction value to S$1 billion.

The program tailor the grant amount and support services to firms, so that firms can have access to the right amount of resources and knowledge required for them to explore their e-business options. Tailored grant programs according to firm size helps distinguish the various SME needs as their capacity for e-business are likely to vary. There are two plans or categories of grant eligibility.

The first plan is an enhanced incentive program modeled after the initial pilot, with an expanded scope to include the use of applications through the Application Service Provider (ASP) model. These applications include customer relationship management, electronic resource planning, and supply-chain management. Under this plan, solution providers will be required to comply with ASP industry best practices. It supports up to 50% of the qualified e-business-related consultancy, subscription fee for up to 12 months, and hardware and software purchases. The incentive is capped at S$20,000 per company.

The second plan focuses on advanced use of e-commerce by firms, e-commerce transactions, and total e-commerce value for Singapore. It targets firms that already have the existing e-commerce capabilities and wish to advance further. It is a performance-based incentive program. Grants are proportionately based on the total e-commerce value created by a firm, up to a maximum of S$500,000. The funding is tied to the actual online transaction value brought about by the proposed project.

A eBIDS-type program represents a public–private sector partnership in which resource allocation and service contracting are made at the market level on a demand-driven basis and without great effort in targeting the various SME groups. The contribution of the client is seen as sufficient to ensure commitment. Experience also suggests that it is useful to include a provision in the design of such programs for a declining value of voucher for subsequent application for assistance.

Some grants programs have promoted e-business adoption at the network or cluster level. Matching grant programs thus target not single companies, but the take up of collaborative e-business by clusters or networks of SMEs. Such programs facilitate the emergence of ICT-enabled alliances and networks for problem solving, competitiveness, and innovation. Information Technology Online in Australia, for example, encourages industry groups to work collaboratively to solve common problems on an industry-wide basis.

Government-to-Business: Information, Transaction, Trade and Connectivity

Governments influence e-business adoption by shaping the overall business environment, using ICT to facilitate government-to-business transactions, modernizing customs and external trade networks, and promoting access to ICT tools for SMEs. These ICT applications may be considered a key component of e-government programs, but it is addressed here from the perspective of business and the need to meet global competition and business standards. Although we focus here on national programs, some progressive municipalities have also used ICT to significantly improve the business environment and support SMEs.

We focus here on four types of support to business, enabled by ICT:

- Supporting access to information, finance, and online business services
- Simplifying government-to-business transactions
- Facilitating trade
- Promoting connectivity for SMEs

Supporting Access to Information, Finance, and Online Business Services

A broad area of e-government applications aims to provide business support services and investment promotion. These applications are designed to improve SMEs access business development information and services, to facilitate access to finance, and to support enterprise development. Key applications include

- Mortgage and Pledge Registry, Credit Information Bureau—to provide information on financial viability of companies
- Online Legal Information Services—to improve SME's access to information on administrative requirements and business-related legal and regulatory framework
- Online Intellectual Property Rights (IPR) Database—to simplify initial search on issues such as trademarks and patents and promote commercialization of R&D
- Online Business Support Services—to provide firm-level support to SMEs such as advisory services and consulting

The banking sector is a leading adopter and enabler of e-business. It is a leading and intensive user in its own right—reaping major productivity gains and service improvements. Internet-based banking or e-banking and e-payments are becoming a main delivery channel as they make it possible to dramatically decrease the unit costs of financial operations at the wholesale and retail levels.

Financial sector adoption of e-business practices also provides significant externalities and further progress of overall e-business and online activities. Secure e-banking transactions can demonstrate the effectiveness of the new e-business tools and create secure transaction systems, standards, trust, and confidence. Trustworthy payment systems can also encourage more advanced online transactions in e-government and other e-sectors.

Small, medium, and microenterprises in developing countries are still largely excluded from formal financial intermediation. This is a long-standing development issue. It is being addressed by introducing e-finance, among others. Making e-banking and e-payments more simple and affordable remains a major challenge, particularly for SMEs and the "unbanked." Relatively new players such as mobile phone operators, e-payment technology vendors, and non-bank transfer operators are developing niches or value-added operations via co-operative arrangements with the main players. Perhaps the most important is the small-scale private financial transfer of migrant remittances. These are increasingly relying on online money transfer systems. However, e-banking and e-payment are still at an early stage in most developing countries (UN, 2008b). They raise new issues of security, cyber-crime, affordability, and credit risk information.

Government actions are needed to promote access to finance with the use of ICT (e-finance). Beyond its role in creating an enabling environment, government can improve the way it shares information like credit-related information. Existing infrastructures like post office networks can also provide access to e-finance services. Smart cards can deliver financial services even with the existing weak infrastructures. Government's role can fundamentally change in areas such as housing finance, insurance, nonblank financial services, storage finance, small- and medium-sized enterprises lending and microlending (Claessens et al., 2001).

For example, central registry of claims, mortgages, and pledges with online access can assist the banks in improving provision of financial services, to SMEs in particular. It could help register the ownership and pledges, properly value the collateral, and ensure transparent and reliable flow of information. The Central Pledge Registry of Bulgaria is an example. It is a central database collecting registered transactions such as pledges, sales, leases, and bankruptcies and is integrated into the optical archive that stores the original filing information. The system allows for web inquircs and legal analysis on this data from financial institutions. The system makes it easier and faster for banks to run enquiries on applicants for loans and financial services while maintaining standards of reliability and certainty of information.

The establishment of online Credit Information Bureau (CIB) can facilitate openness and foster accountability within the private sector. A CIB would allow entrepreneurs and banks to gather information crucial for business decision making, both in terms of partnering and lending. Information will particularly be useful for SMEs or unlisted companies where the disclosure of financial statements is not mandatory or reliability is poor. The establishment of a CIB could also facilitate integration among firms and ease the rigidities of the supply and demand sides of financing. Many countries are introducing such service. For example, Italy's Online Credit Information Service is the portal of a credit information service firm that is widely used. Reportedly, 4000 firms and 300 financial institutions use the service to obtain crucial information on financial viability of companies and individuals crucial to engage in business or financing with these entities. The system provides many services—from information about creditworthiness of companies and individuals to credit ratings. It is fully supported by a functional and user-friendly online system, so that vital business information can be accessed without time and geographical constraints.

To improve access to vital legal information for businesses, a web-based information service can be designed to cover issues of administrative requirements and business-related legal and regulatory framework. This web service could also include sections on important judicial opinions in business-related cases, draft laws and regulations, adopted laws and regulations, government directory/organization chart (with citations to laws), and frequently asked questions. The site could have information in easily accessible form with a problem solving, "how-to" focus. For example, it could explain legal requirements on how to start a business, initiate export/import operations, etc.

To promote R&D activities, national IPR agencies can introduce online databases with functional search capabilities to allow entrepreneurs to quickly conduct initial search on issues such as trademarks and patents. The web site may also provide a comprehensive IPR information service connected to a number of patent databases around the world to obtain integrated IPR information. This can be combined with government expert services that manage and evaluate patents and trademarks to give a picture of the strategic value for companies of a patent or a trademark.

Finally, online government business support services may be introduced to provide firm-level support to local SMEs and address the common issue of limited business and management skills among entrepreneurs. IFC-supported online SME-toolkit may be used as a starting point and/or inspiration for such a portal. It has a number of how-to guides and articles in seven categories: Accounting and Finance, Business Planning, Human Resources, Legal and Insurance, Marketing and Sales,

Operations and Technology. Government Business support agencies can also host online business advisory services provided by various private sector experts. Clients can choose an adviser from among a number of business consultants and other advisers registered with the center. Clients would be able to get a response from the selected expert within a short period of time. Further, in-depth co-operation between the adviser and the company can be conducted on an off-line commercial basis.

One promising example of ICT-enabled business support is Business Edge, an SME management training product, developed and branded by IFC to fill a knowledge gap. SMEs face increasing competitive pressures as a result of globalization and need to improve management skills to meet their full potential. However, the offer of management training in these markets tends to be expensive and often inappropriate for SMEs. Business Edge enables local training providers or corporate financial partners to deliver interactive and practical managerial training tailored to meet local market needs. Since its initial launch in 2001, Business Edge has evolved into an international product with a well-developed methodology for SMEs. To guarantee quality of the training, training workshops are given by certified trainers, and trainers receive training manuals and other capacity building tools. Over time, this program is creating knowledge hubs and virtual networks for training SMEs.

Simplifying Government-to-Business Transactions

One broad area of applications is to use ICT to streamline administrative procedures so as to reduce transaction costs between business and government. Businesses and investors in developing countries are often frustrated by inefficient and bureaucratic public sector, by high barriers to entry because of cumbersome, costly, and lengthy start-up process, and by corruption and red tape. High transaction costs are particularly detrimental to small businesses and small investors with limited resources to pay such costs or to avoid them. Using the business process cycle concept, ICT applications in government of special importance to improving business environment would include

- e-Registration—to reduce time and costs of business registration process, and thus lower barriers to entry
- e-Taxation—to improve revenue collection and enhance the efficiency and transparency of the public tax system
- e-Reporting—to simplify enterprises' business reporting to various government agencies and improve data collection

A key application to expanding business opportunities and enhancing overall competitiveness is e-government procurement. Beyond improving efficiency and transparency of government procurement operations (as discussed in Chapter 11 on e-government), e-procurement can be designed to reduce the transaction costs to business suppliers, promote competition among a larger pool of suppliers, and broaden the participation of SMEs in public procurement. Electronic public procurement is an area where results can be demonstrated early and clearly in terms of efficiency, agility, and transparency. Whenever a public agency needs to purchase goods or contract a service, the system can automatically send an e-mail to all the private companies registered in that selected area, thus minimizing response time and providing an equal opportunity for all the firms (Box 13.4).

Box 13.4 Compranet, a National e-Procurement System, Mexico

E-procurement by Mexico's Federal Government was launched in 2002. Reportedly, the e-procurement system manages 80% of all Federal Government acquisitions. Compranet system has been so far largely successful in cutting administrative costs related to the whole procurement process. Consequently, the following data reveal the great potencies of an e-procurement system:

- Costs for administration of procurement and costs of items procured have been cut, with typical estimates of savings of around 20%.
- Around 25,000 suppliers make use of Compranet, and many state and municipality governments have joined the system.
- Participation costs for business appear to have fallen, and small/medium enterprises from outside the capital region have joined in the procurement process.

Largely as a result of Compranet, a cultural change is underway: a large number of SMEs and public agencies have begun the process of computerization, e-commerce intermediaries have appeared, and overall, ICT is increasingly perceived as an agent of change.

Interactive online business registration system greatly simplifies the application processing and increases the speed of the business registration, which currently can take more then 100 days in many developing countries. Even in the absence of e-signature infrastructure and electronic payment system, investors may be given the possibility of downloading the necessary forms and conducting name searches online. The key is to provide a single platform allowing businesses to retrieve information and/or register with all the relevant public agencies, such as the State Statistical Office, Agency for Payments, the Tax Authorities, and Customs Authorities.

Online taxation system can be introduced to enable taxpayers to submit online tax reports and make secured tax payments. It would bring major changes to the taxation process, relieving taxpayers and tax agencies from heavy workload, and improving the overall efficiency. The system ultimately results in economic and social benefits for all the players involved—taxpayers (enterprises and individuals), tax bureaus, and banks.

To simplify and speed up the business reporting for companies, internal information flow among government agencies can be improved to offer single-entrance-point service. Once the enterprise has submitted the required information to one dedicated web site, the service transmits it to all the relevant government bodies. For example, the Center of Formalities of the Companies in France (CFC) is a portal that gathers required information from enterprises for various government agencies, such as the local trade register, the taxation office, the administrations in charge of social security and pensions, and the statistical office. Once the enterprise has given the required information to the CFC, the service transmits this information to the other relevant administrations to simplify and speed up the administrative procedures.

Municipalities play a key role in shaping the business environment through business process simplification, particularly for SMEs. Lessons should be drawn from using ICT to accelerate and sustain such reforms at the local level. Reviews of municipal business process simplification projects in Peru and Ecuador show that administrative simplification requires implementation of ICT tools to make processes more cost-effective (Franco-Temple, 2008).

Simplification projects should address ICT issues early in the design process to avoid risks of delays and budget overruns and ensure that ICT tools are tailored to actual client capabilities and resources. Otherwise, such projects could suffer long delays or not fulfill their client requirements. Experience also indicates that it is advisable to include all necessary ICT support issues in suppliers' contracts, such as training, maintenance, and IPR concerning access to software source codes. These concerns should also cover issues of sustainability of systems and reforms, despite changes in staff and regulations.

Facilitating Trade

The effective use of ICT has been contributing to the expansion of trade by enabling significantly more efficient and speedy trade management practices. Trade efficiency measures covers a broad array of instruments ranging from trade facilitation, customs modernization, computer-based cargo tracking systems, and logistics optimization to ICT-facilitated financing and insurance systems. With the rapid advances in ICT and growing imperatives of global trade and global supply chains, countries are making significant investments in their infrastructure for managing cross-border trade transactions.

Although trade liberalization can generate many benefits, these potential benefits may be constrained or completely lost if excessive delays and costs hinder trade transactions and undermine export competitiveness. Conversely, customs modernization and trade facilitation could be advanced with ICT-enabled process re-engineering and online invoicing/export declaration services that would benefit both the private and public sectors. These applications aim to simplify and speed up compliance with legal and administrative requirements for exporting and importing goods. They facilitate documentation and transactions across large numbers of agencies, including customs, ports, banks, and traders. The business community benefits from faster and cheaper processes to comply with legal and administrative requirements for international trade. Firms also gain from enhanced competitiveness in national and international markets due to reduction in delays, uncertainties, and costs that are achieved with predictable and efficient movement of goods across borders.[7]

Several developing countries have deployed ICT for trade facilitation and customs modernization. Ghana, in 2003, introduced GCNet customs system to foster trade facilitation and mobilization of customs revenues. GCNet, a public–private partnership, linked customs, excise, preventive services department, and GCNet office, among others, enabling quick online processing of customs clearance and facilitating clearance of goods through ports. Within its first 18 months, GCNet increased customs revenues by 49%, substantially reduced clearance times, and increased the reliability and transparency of the clearance process.

Singapore started in the early 1990s with TradeNet, using EDI facilities, then more recently leveraged SingaporeOne, in 2007, to enhance port operations and allow real-time data-intensive communications among ships, their customers, and business partners. The Tunisia Trade Net provides another example of the broad impact of such applications on e-business and the country's overall competitiveness (Box 13.5).

Box 13.5 Tunisia Trade Net System

Tunisia Trade Net System (TTN) provides a good example of stakeholders coming together to simplify procedures and automate trade documentation and customs requirements with the use of ICT. A key initiative was the creation of a semi-public agency TTN in February 2000 to create and operate a value-added network that would provide electronic data interchange for stakeholders and to expedite flows and processing of trade documents. TTN shareholders include 10 government agencies, among which are the national port authority and Tunis Air, and 18 private sector units, among which are

---

[7]Public administrations also benefit from a more efficient system to enhance controls, collect revenues, and improve data collection and analysis.

several banks and the Tunisian Internet Agency. The steering committee and a technical committee were set to involve key stakeholders at the early stages of the process. Not only were these committees instrumental for the design of the initiatives but also in implementation. The initiative was supported at the highest level of the government.

The system interfaces with all agencies involved in international trade procedures, including the Tunisian Customs, Ministry of Commerce, technical control agencies, Central Bank, ports, as well as the private sector traders, agents, freight forwarders, customs brokers, and banks. Documents are processed through the TTN system. In addition, the system processes on-line tariff payments.

There is evidence that the investments made in trade facilitation are dramatically reducing import and export processing times. For example, the imported goods can now be cleared in an average of 2 days, compared to an average of 7 days a few years ago. Manifest processing after the completion of vessel operations used to take up to 4 days; electronic processing has cut that time to one day. The time needed to prepare and process customs declarations has dropped to 15 minutes, down from as long as 3 days. Trade document processing using the Tunisia Trade Net has also generated savings for the maritime cargo handling operator and demonstrated the payoffs of adopting other e-government and e-business applications in the country.

A key success factor was the commitment at the highest levels of government. This was essential since a large number of government ministries and agencies are involved in the trade transactions and clearance, and reforms and process reengineering must be coordinated across all these agencies. Another success factor was the involvement of private sector stakeholders at all stages of the reform process. A public-private implementing body was created from the outset to develop an improved overall design which was assimilated into various systems relatively rapidly. Stakeholders came together, through a steering committee and a technical committee composed of key public and private sector stakeholders, to simplify trade procedures and automate documentation and customs requirements. Successful implementation was also based on a phased approach to allow enable quick wins and demonstration effect to show impact and generate further interest in reform. International trade standards such as UNEDIFACT were also adopted to enable easy exchange of required information with trading partners and authorities. Implementation was also guided by user feedback to fine tune systems development and ensure the emerging net would be responsive to private sector needs. Another success factor is sequencing, first to simplify and eliminate some procedures, then standardize information that responds to needs of different operators, then facilitate exchange of information. A final success factor is extending electronic processing to all agencies involved in trade transactions, not only customs, and developing or reengineering their back office systems to seamlessly handle these transactions electronically (Alavi, 2008).

Promoting trade may be also pursued at the regional level for small and medium enterprises through one-stop online information and trading resource. One interesting example is USAID-supported central Asia trade promotion program to enhance the competitiveness of SMEs in the region. Companies in the region can place information about their products and services in both Russian and English, making it possible for companies from all over the world to use the portal to access such services. The program provides opportunities to register companies in business directory and/or marketplace with www.smetrade-center.net and use all the tools of e-commerce. The program also delivers assistance from trade specialists who assess trade opportunities and help establish relationships with potential partners.

Launched in 2002, the portal was first supported by USAID, then in 2006, was privatized and now headed by a trade promotion company. Over its first 3 years, the regional trade network has facilitated about $110 million of SME trade. The Market place has over 2 million visits from 104 countries. Among the key lessons learned are the need to raise awareness of SMEs of the benefits, to use real stories of success to inspire SMEs of the possibility of portal-facilitated trade, to extend the network by finding partners and beneficiaries, and aim for commercialization and long-term sustainability of regional trade promotion services.

Promoting Connectivity for SMEs

New channels for providing affordable ICT-enabled services to SMEs are promising. One such relevant channel that has not yet been fully leveraged is the telecenters. For example, a growing share of the income for telecenters in Latin America comes from such business support services, particularly for micro- and small businesses. The India Shop, an initiative of the Foundation of Occupational Development (FOOD India), is an e-commerce site driven by e-marketers to promote the sale of local handicrafts.[8] Telecenters such as those developed under the Partnership for e-prosperity for the poor in Indonesia are providing farmers with access to valuable farming knowledge to improve breeding techniques and combat pests.

While most telecenters are concentrating on efforts to provide shared and affordable access to the Internet and ICT tools, and on developing basic computer literacy, an increasing number of telecenters are providing applied training in how to use ICT for tapping economic opportunities. Examples include e-business training,

---

[8]Chin, S. Y. "e-Marketers of South India". IDRC. 2002.

business-related services, employment-related information, sector-specific business information and communication, and to a lesser extent, e-finance. A relatively novel use of telecenters for employment generation is what is termed "social outsourcing," that is, the outsourcing of IT services and ITES to social enterprises located in poor communities (www.gk3onlineinteractions.net/en/node/79).

The potential for using telecenters to support rural enterprise and livelihood is still largely untapped. Realizing this potential depends on the quality of the general infrastructure and business conditions. But they can also be advanced with the development of local content, user-generated content, help desks, and infomediaries. For example, in Indonesia, each telecenter has an infomobilizer—a person who uses and promotes the use of information for community development and works with the village to identify its needs for improving livelihoods. To support economic activities, provide value-added services, and broaden their impact, telecenter networks may collaborate with business supporting institutions, microcredit institutions, professional associations, and social and educational institutions.

Mobile phones, being the main communication tools for small entrepreneurs in developing countries, have great potential for e-business applications. Mobile telephony is also likely to be the primary tool for connecting the vast majority of low-income population to business and information society, at least in short to medium term. For example, SMEs that export agricultural products may be alerted to business opportunities and receive timely price information for their products. Mobile commerce, mobile banking and payments (m-commerce, m-banking, m-payment), and mobile content are spreading in most developing countries. The potential is great, provided there is an enabling regulatory environment. In many countries, prepaid mobile services are used to provide mobile public payphones, and this improves accessibility in rural areas. As mobile handsets grow in sophistication and add new functionalities, such as digital photography and multimedia messaging and other utilities, they will provide a gateway to digital literacy.

The Philippines provides an interesting example of leveraging mobile phones for e-commerce by farmers. With very low penetration of Internet, the government tapped into the culture of SMS to provide two mobile applications, one, for farmers to post prices of their products, and the other, for mobile users to compare price of the top most traded products in a province. The program works with co-operatives to provide a level playing field and by giving players access to a common source of reliable and online market prices are helping farmers maximize their selling prices (Box 13.6).

Box 13.6 The Philippines: e-Commerce for Farmers Through SMS, Co-operatives and Partnerships

Farmers in the Philippines have relied on traders or slow government agencies to act as intermediaries and providers of market information. The result is outdated prices and lack of a standard pricing mechanism throughout the Philippines' 7107 islands. Further, there has never been a mechanism that allows farmers and co-operatives to trade directly with buyers and sellers from distant islands without a face-to-face encounter.

B2Bpricenow.com was conceived as a platform on which farmers could market and trade their products more efficiently and at the most competitive prices. It is an Internet-based agricultural e-marketplace where farmers can access prevailing market prices for free by visiting a local Internet cafe and having their own personal page where they can put up their preferred buyers and sellers.

The Philippines' Internet penetration is still extremely low, but it is the short messaging system (SMS) capital of the world with an average of 20 million SMS messages sent per day.

B2Bpricenow.com has tapped into this culture by providing two mobile applications. One, for the member to canvass and post the prices of their products of interest, and two, for any mobile phone user to compare price indications of the top 10 most traded products in a particular province. The cost to access price information via mobile phones using SMS is USD 0.05 or a dime per download or upload of price information.

The program works with farmers' co-operatives, which have more resources and better access to technology than individuals. It hopes to level the playing field among large, medium, and small players by giving players access to a common source of reliable and online market prices, helping farmers maximize their selling prices. By working with co-operatives, it hopes to increase the bargaining power of co-operatives vs. institutional buyers of produce and fuel intra-co-operative trade. The program educates co-operatives to own and manage business centers in their municipality and aims to establish 1500 B2B centers nation wide. By targeting co-operatives, B2Bpricenow.com aims benefits the microfarmers since individually their volume of trade will not merit any bargaining power in a big market.

The key to the development of B2Bpricenow.com lies in the partnerships it has forged with the stakeholders that share the same goal and have the greatest interest in seeing the project succeed. Just a few examples of partnership. In exchange for 5% ownership of B2Bpricenow.com, Unisys Philippines has undertaken the responsibility for the web and payment gateway design and programming, as well as the upgrading, scaling, administration, and maintenance of the site. The online payment gateway completes the e-marketplace and enables seamless and end-to-end electronic trading transactions. A premier TV and radio program in the Philippines also has 5% ownership and in turn provides free advertising spots and radio shows for the next 3 years.

The Philippine Rural Reconstruction Movement is the NGO partner responsible for implementing a training program for co-operatives and farmers on e-commerce.

Another interesting feature is the use of the SMS (short message service) facility to handle the following transactions: (1) check prevailing market prices for commodities, (2) change prices of items posted, and (3) canvass prices of suki (Filipino term for a supplier or buyer with a special relationship due to regularity and volume of transactions between each other, normally resulting in preferential treatment such as special discounts or faster delivery and payment).

For developed countries, the impact of broadband on business has been fairly documented in terms of reducing costs, increasing revenues, and expanding markets—but the evidence of broadband impact on business is still fairly thin among developing countries, even at the firm level (Qiang et al., 2009). The experience of developed countries is therefore critical to guide broadband and e-business diffusion and impact in developing countries. A study of broadband deployment in business in several Latin American countries showed that deployment was associated with considerable improvements in business organization, including knowledge diffusion within organizations, and speed of business reengineering and network integration (Momentum Research Group, 2005). Broadband may also help firms in specializing in core activities and outsource the rest. Broadband may also help in building distinctive capabilities by allocating activities more efficiently between workers tackling complex and creative tasks and more transactional workers (Johnson et al., 2005).

The highest productivity gains appear in firms that commit to integrate broadband, and IT in general, with reengineered business processes. Organizations that align their investments in network infrastructure, network-based applications, business processes, and organizational behavior experience greater increases in business outcomes than organizations that disproportionately focus on one or more of these elements.

In some industries, broadband is transforming the whole sector or supply chain—removing the need for proximity to customers, facilitating extreme differentiation of customers and choice, and enabling marketing strategies of niche products (so-called long tail strategies, see Allaire and Austin, 2005). Broadband has considerable impact on information-intensive service sectors such as insurance, finance, accounting, consulting, marketing, real-estate, travel, tourism, advertising, and engineering and graphic design. Export-oriented firms also benefit considerably from broadband use. So do entertainment, publishing and animation industries and those enabling direct involvement by users in creating digital content. And in the case of developing countries in particular, broadband-enabled IT services hold significant promise, as demonstrated so far by the case of India's software and ITES exports.

e-Business and e-Development

Effective and efficient e-business promotion strategies mirror and depend on comprehensive e-development strategies. Supporting SMEs through their journey from adoption to transformation requires diagnosis of SME e-business needs and capabilities, and well-timed and co-ordinated investments, in information infrastructure, human capital, and applications to match these needs. More advanced levels of e-business usage, to enable enterprise transformation, depend on holistic support and advances on the broader agenda of e-development.

E-business diffusion will not go very far without adequate attention to other elements of e-development. In particular, the e-business promotion program should proceed in sequence with promoting affordable Internet and telecommunication access in the country. Easing bottlenecks in the telecommunications infrastructure is a precondition for wide adoption of e-business.

The diffusion of e-business depends on the quality of the Internet such as bandwidth and spectrum capacity. Provision of shared technology infrastructure for technology-oriented SMEs can bring down the capital costs for such firms. Hong Kong, for example, has established an Information Communication Development Center and a Photonics Center offering shared facilities for companies locating in the Hong Kong Science and Technology Park. Vietnam established software parks to overcome its communications constraints and foster electronically enabled business environments for its SMEs. Apart from facilitating connectivity and provision of bandwidth, provision of open access, low-cost backbone infrastructure could help lower the investment threshold and business risks for ICT-oriented SMEs to offer value-added services at the edges of the network.

E-business and e-commerce can be also facilitated through appropriate development of legal and regulatory frameworks to foster trust and confidence in B2B electronic transactions, and through the standardization of e-business practices. A wide range of e-policies impacts the adoption of e-business such as those pertaining to e-security, data protection, consumer privacy, forming contracts online, intellectual property, copyright, cross-border e-invoicing, and digital signatures. Many national ICT strategies now articulate an e-business vision in the national ICT strategy, and use this vision to guide the development of the enabling environment to fulfill existing and future e-business demands.

E-business diffusion programs may incorporate or be complemented by training and awareness-building activities for SMEs to adopt e-business practices. Such activities could extend to employee training, training the trainers, and creating a pool of managerial talent that understands e-business issues pertaining to SMEs. In addition, the sharing of best practices is important to guide SMEs in their uptake of e-business.

Demand mobilization is also a key to take advantage of network externalities. Policy measures can encourage trade associations and others to provide awareness raising and consultation services. The promotion of FOSS adoption through government deployment of infrastructure and services can provide SMEs with a viable alternative to expensive, overdesigned, and non-localized proprietary software.

Governments as model users can also act as standard setters for ICT adoption by firms, as firms adjust to maintain interoperability with online government services.

Many of the e-government applications concerning public e-procurement, trade and customs applications, and government-to-business services (covered in Chapter 12) can further promote trust and security in online transaction and increase the return on ICT investments by firms. They help create the right environment for use of e-business by SMEs. E-business would also need electronic payment and funds transfer systems which would need to be facilitated by governments.

With government accounting for a substantial proportion of the economy, typically 35% of national economies, the speed of take-up of technology by the economy will be significantly influenced by the rate of public sector adoption of e-government. It is also for this reason that the e-commerce model and standards adopted by government carry greater weight than the immediate applications intended within government. A strategic approach to ICT by government could enhance interoperability and connectivity throughout the economy, business and community, with potential gains in productivity and competitiveness.

An e-business support program may be incorporated into wider government efforts to improve the competitiveness of private enterprises, promote export, and innovation. E-business may be integrated into sectoral programs. E-business issues may be considered as a fundamental element of private sector and enterprise development programs.

Public policies aimed at the diffusion and effective use of ICT in business should recognize and exploit the dynamic relationship between ICT and innovation. These links are becoming stronger and a number of countries have placed the use of ICT by enterprises (e-business) and innovation policies within the same institutional and policy framework. National innovation systems may be adapted to tap the synergies between ICT use and innovation-led competitiveness and reinforce the complementarities between ICT and innovation policies, particularly those aimed at SMEs. Business associations and SME partners need to understand the competitive implications of ICT adoption and the skills and complementary investments needed to engage in process and product innovation. Again, public policy can accelerate this technological learning.

Chapter 14
Empowering Poor Communities

One of the most promising usages of ICT for development is to reduce poverty and promote broad participation, grassroots innovation, social learning, and social inclusion. This chapter calls ICT applications that are targeted for poor communities and poverty reduction, e-society or grassroots innovation. Much of these empowered local initiatives and innovations are about building the local capabilities to appropriate the new technologies to solve local needs and priorities. They are also about developing local markets, building local innovation and learning networks, creating a critical mass of users among poor communities, and developing local content.

Efforts to bring ICT to the forefront of thinking about social development and poverty reduction are still very nascent and recent. The early debate of the 1990s about choosing between ICT and other pressing development imperatives has evolved but not resolved. The Millennium Development Goals (MDGs) cover ICT targets, but mainly in terms of access to telephony and Internet connectivity. Much of the early innovations and demonstration projects are initiated by NGOs and external donors but seldom integrated into poverty-reduction strategies, ICT-enabled development strategies, or priority social and human development programs.

However, there is increasing awareness of the crucial potential role of ICT for expanding choice, empowering communities, reducing poverty, and building an information society. Some of these efforts are beginning to bear fruit at the policy and strategic level. There is growing consensus that the digital divide is less about ICT equipment and connectivity than about relevant content, social applications, and the ability of local communities to create and derive value from ICT use. Digital inclusion is about using ICT to increase the efficiency with which development communities will pursue all the MDGs through social, economic, and political empowerment. An ICT-enabled development strategy cannot leave this link to chance.

A perquisite of successful appropriation of ICT for socio-economic development is that stakeholders be aware of the possibilities that ICT offers in all development sectors: education, health, environment, etc. ICT can also address poverty reduction through off-farm employment, small enterprise development, microfinance, and other means to leverage the resources and improve livelihood opportunities.

ICT has the potential of bringing ideas, information, and knowledge to even the most isolated, opening them to the world outside their village. Much of the relevant

N.K. Hanna, *e-Transformation: Enabling New Development Strategies*, Innovation, Technology, and Knowledge Management, DOI 10.1007/978-1-4419-1185-8_14,
© Springer Science+Business Media, LLC 2010

development experience, best practices, and practical innovations reside locally, but seldom shared within the country or even within a community. ICT allows people to share their experience with the rest of the country, if not the world. It also empowers citizens and communities to participate in political institutions and policy making of their communities and to aggregate their voices at the national level.

A strategic thrust in using ICT in development programs for poverty reduction requires a new view of the poor, both as producers and consumers. Information poverty is pervasive in developing countries and the poor suffer the most from the lack of access to local content, relevant services, and local networks. The poor often pay more for their basic needs and receive less for their produce than their more the informed producers and consumers. The poor are also potential adaptors, innovators, and problem solvers, particularly of issues most central to their livelihood. Digital technologies can draw on the capacities of the 80% of the world population to solve global poverty. Information is power, and ICT is generating new tools and novel ways to reach, mobilize, and empower the poor to help themselves. With increasing affordability, portability, miniaturization, and user-friendliness of ICT tools, it becomes easier to share information and develop relevant applications for and with the poor. E-society aims to design programs around the poor's specific needs, resources, capacities, and livelihood.

In this chapter, I first examine the promise of demand-driven, ICT-enabled development, and the significant size of the market (including that of ICT) at the base of the economic pyramid. Second, I explore new approaches to innovation and the new ICT tools now available to support these new approaches: the collaborative and user-led innovation approaches and the promise of the participative web and collaborative technologies. Third, I deal with promising mechanisms to explore and promote innovative ways to apply ICT for poverty reduction and social development. Finally, I suggest a balanced approach between bottom-up, specialized mechanisms to promote pro-poor innovation and application of ICT, and top-down approaches to integrate ICT into social development and poverty eradication programs.

Demand-Driven ICT-Enabled Development

ICT is a new and general-purpose technology that must be "re-discovered," enacted and adapted to different social contexts.[1] Despite substantial anecdotal literature on ICT for development, there is little practical and codified knowledge available about how to effectively use ICT for poverty reduction and economic growth. Investment in local learning and experimentation is needed for this practical knowledge to be accessible and relevant the local level. Financing grassroots innovation and adaptation at the local level can help fill this gap and empower NGOs and communities to initiate such innovation and learning about the uses of ICT for development.

Mainstreaming ICT in development assistance requires subordinating the technology to more fundamental development objectives. National ICT strategies must

---

[1] McNemara (2003) and Fountain (2001).

be integrally linked to comprehensive development strategies. Similarly, ICT components in development projects must be in support of the broader objectives of these projects. A major barrier and source of failures of ICT for poverty reduction stems from the dominant techno-centric approach to ICT projects in developing countries. Much of the emphasis has been on advances in the technology and the next new "new" thing, and much less on leveraging existing infrastructures and tools through relevant content and applications. Mechanisms should be developed to reflect the voice and priorities of potential users, particularly the poor in developing countries. Development practitioners may also blend with ICT specialists in multi-disciplinary teams to provide a broader view of possibilities and constraints.

Meaningful integration of ICT into local development requires local capabilities to link ICT potential to local resources and development priorities, that is, for local institutions to "discover" ICT potential and harness this potential to address specific local conditions and challenges. The potential contribution of ICT cannot be identified and realized through sole reliance on top-down mechanisms. Financing mechanisms should aim to build awareness, knowledge, and capabilities at the grassroots levels to use ICT for empowerment and social development.

Institutional and policy support for pro-poor innovations is urgently needed to complement market-based approaches and reach the very poor. ICT markets are highly imperfect, particularly in responding to the needs of the poor. The incentives for ICT multi-nationals to meet information and communication needs of the bottom of the pyramid are relatively weak—although many large companies are learning to reach down to the relatively poor (see below). Innovation and adaptation are highly constrained by the lack of resources and partners. Scaling up and diffusion of innovations relevant to the poor and rural areas are similarly constrained. Financing of innovations for ICT use for poverty reduction must empower users and local NGOs to address these constraints and market failures.

Public funding for R&D in the ICT sector in developing countries has been primarily driven by the priorities of the ICT industry—by the suppliers and exporters of ICT. Yet, most developing countries stand to benefit more from the effective use and wide diffusion of ICT among its key sectors than from mere production and export of ICT products.[2] R&D efforts and resources should be re-directed to maximize the exploitation of ICT as enabler for the whole economy. Public funds for R&D in ICT should be driven by local adaptation needs in the user sectors of most promise or importance to national development. They should also empower local users and communities to enact and adapt the new technologies to meet their local priorities for development.

Taking advantage of ICT applications and realizing the potential benefits are not automatic. They require substantial R&D for adaptation, experimentation, and localization. Mainstream ICT systems have been designed almost wholly for the OECD markets, which are better endowed with physical capital and educated human capital than in developing countries. These designs do not generally reflect the capital mix of lower income groups in such markets and so present major barriers to adoption of

---

[2]See, for example, Hanna (2003). World Bank.

such applications as e-business for small enterprises and local NGOs. R&D can play a critical role in lowering the ICT complexity barrier and increases affordability and sustainability of ICT uses for SMEs, educational institutions, local governments, NGOs, and community-based organizations. Such adaptive R&D is also essential for improving access and use by the poor and rural population.

The conventional approach to technology diffusion is built around infrastructure provision. In contrast, a demand-driven pro-poor approach to technological diffusion and adaptation would start with creating the capacity to demand the needed services from a given infrastructure. Accordingly, innovations, content development, and demand-creating and aggregating measures would come first, followed by infrastructure, followed by the remaining elements of the process.

There are also strong arguments for subsidies to encourage digital inclusion and bridge the digital divide. One is pump priming—there appear to be positive returns to scale for early investments in ICT infrastructure and ICT applications, so that the initial returns are less than the average returns over time. Subsidies for start-up costs can speed the initial learning phases of the institutionalization process. It is also the case that many applications of ICT benefiting the poor help meet basic human needs more fully and more efficiently, and equity concerns suggest subsidies are appropriate for such applications. There are strong externalities for the pilot and demonstration projects, as the beneficiaries of the lessons learned through such projects are not only the direct beneficiaries of the project, but the beneficiaries of other projects improved by the findings. Grant-funded, relatively small projects, therefore, have a potentially important role in promoting ICT diffusion and applications for the poor.

Incremental innovation—continuous improvement of products and processes—is critical to national competitiveness. The cumulative and pervasive impact of incremental innovation in ICT use and adaptation is likely to outweigh major "disruptive" innovations or ICT inventions. Although disruptive innovation stimulates demand for the highest engineering skills and world-class talent, it is risky and costly for most developing countries. It may divert scarce research resources and talents away from the challenges of ICT adaptation that address the pressing needs of the majority of population. Government role should be primarily aimed at incremental innovations to adapt ICT to local needs.

Bottom-up and demand-driven approaches to ICT application are particularly suited for developing local content. The web is World Wide, but the evidence suggests that people are primarily interested to access locally relevant information. Content and networking remain highly local or context-specific, particularly in rural areas and in countries whose population does not master other languages but native. As developing local content is expensive, innovative mechanisms are needed to develop specifically tailored content for farmers, small and medium enterprises, and rural populations. Beneficiaries may be mobilized and organized to develop and update content, thus reducing costs, and ensuring relevance and sustainability. Information and communication needs assessments may be carried out, with the help of sociologists and rural development specialists to set priorities for funding, and to empower intermediaries and local partnerships to provide such content.

The Next 4 Billion—A Market Approach

A majority of the world's population—4 billion low-income people—constitute the base of the economic pyramid (BOP). New empirical measures of their aggregate purchasing power suggest significant opportunities for market-based approaches to meet their needs and improve their productivity and incomes.[3] It is the entire BOP and not just the very poor who constitute the low-income market. Most BOP population segments are not integrated into or benefit from the global market economy. They have significant unmet needs. They lack access to markets and depend on subsistence livelihood. They pay higher prices for basic goods and services than wealthier consumers. These needs and the entire low-income market should be analyzed and addressed for opportunities for market-based solutions to be realized.

A market-based approach focuses on people as consumers and producers and on solutions that make markets more competitive, efficient, and inclusive—so that the BOP can benefit. Such solutions may involve market development, consumer education, consumer finance, microloans, cross-subsidies among different income groups. They may also involve partnerships with NGOs and public sector, and franchise and local agent strategies that create jobs and incomes. Yet, these solutions are ultimately market oriented and demand driven. Most important, these solutions emphasize sustainability as key to meet the needs of 4 billion people.

The information and communication market represents a major BOP market. It was estimated at US $51 billion in 2006, but probably more than twice that in 2009 because of rapid growth of this market, mainly due to mobile phone (IFC and WRI, 2007). Except in the very lowest income segment of the BOP, ICT spending per household exceeds spending on water. In the upper BOP segments, ICT spending sometimes exceeds spending on health. Continuing rapid growth in the ICT sector in developing countries, the decline in ICT cost/performance ratio, and the emergence of new business models that enhance affordability—all suggest ample untapped demand. Business models in ICT services have been adapted to serve the BOP population and make ICT affordable in developing countries: recent approaches of pre-paid mobile telephony in small units, Internet access by the quarter hour in cybercafés, etc.

The biggest challenge to serve the BOP population is to develop business models that bridge the urban–rural divide in developing countries. For example, in Brazil, the BOP market for ICT is 97% urban and average annual spending by urban BOP households is seven times that by rural households. However, despite the general lower levels of ICT spending in rural areas, the size of the rural population in some countries still aggregates the demand into a sizable market. For example, Thailand rural BOP market for ICT is $1.5 billion and India's is $3.8 billion. Clearly, some forms of shared access to ICT are necessary to aggregate demand and increase

---

[3]For an excellent treatment of this topic, see International Finance Corporation and World Resource Institute. 2007. *The Next 4 Billion: Market Size and Business Strategy at the Base of the Pyramid.* World Resource Institute: Washington, DC.

affordability to the BOP in rural areas. Mobile phones also present a new platform most particularly suitable for delivering services via the Internet to the BOP populations in the rural areas.

The lack of access to ICT services in rural areas can be a significant penalty for BOP population—one that keeps rural people disconnected from markets and broader information resources and thus reinforces rural isolation and poverty. ICT represents a general purpose enabler to meeting many other needs of the BOP population. Not only are the poor deprived of access to ICT, but they also lack ICT products, services, and applications suited to their needs and to empower them to meet many non-ICT needs such as access to microfinance, learning opportunities, agricultural extension, market information, and remittance transfers (Chapter 2).

There are many pilot projects that demonstrate the utility of ICT in many fields. But more concerted efforts and effective mechanisms are needed to innovate new ICT tools, apply them to diverse socio-economic contexts and problems, and create relevant digital content to meet social needs. Equally important is to seek sustainable solutions to scale up and diffuse such applications more widely.

Strategies to Serve the Base of the Pyramid

Promoting ICT use and adaptation to address development and poverty challenges can draw on the emerging literature and practice in serving the potentially huge market of poor populations in developing countries. Prahalad (2005) presents a leading example of business thinkers and strategists who are exploring ways to partner with the poor to innovate and market products that effectively serve the needs of the majority of populations in developing countries. This literature challenges the dominant business logic of multi-nationals that the four billion people at the bottom of the pyramid do not constitute an attractive market for their products and services. Serving this large market, however, requires different modalities for product creation, marketing, distribution, and after-sales support.

The emerging business strategies to serve these populations provide many Paralels and lessons for developing and applying ICT for development and poverty reduction. These strategies include focusing on the BOP by adapting or re-inventing products and services to enable access or make such services affordable and suitable to BOP needs; localizing value creation through franchising and agent strategies that involve building local ecosystems of suppliers or vendors, or by treating the community as the customer; and building diverse partnerships. The spread of wireless devices among the poor through such schemes as prepaid cards and the Grameen phone is one example. The use of telecenters such as e-Choupal allowed farmers to check prices and improve their margins. Innovative micro-financing and purchasing schemes have expanded the capacity of the poor to consume. These innovations required substantial experimentation and engagement of the poor and their representative organizations.

Many of the guiding principles of innovation for the bottom of the pyramid can be transferred and adapted to promote community-driven ICT application and adaptation for poverty reduction.[4] Large producers can engage NGOs and local community-based organizations to co-create new products and services. Serving this market requires focus on price performance. It requires hybrid solutions—blending advanced technologies with existing traditional ones. To serve large markets of poor populations solutions must be scalable, adaptable, and transferable. Innovations must conserve on resources and build on local advantages. They must take account of skill levels, poor infrastructure, and access to service. Investing in educating consumers on product usage is also important.

The User Innovation Revolution

Recent business experience points to a user innovation revolution (Leadbeater, 2006). There is a rising recognition of the role of customers in product innovation and adaptation. Traditionally, consumers are viewed as the final link in the value chain; they can choose between products but have little say over their design or creation. Innovation is assumed to come only from companies. Recent literature suggests changes in consumer and company behaviors. Once passive, consumers are becoming adaptors, inventors, and innovators. They are contributing to the way products and services are developed and produced. Companies are learning to identify and work with groups of lead users, to remove barriers to user-innovation, provide user-innovators with easy-to-use tools and incentives to innovate, build user capacity to adapt and innovate, create settings for prototypes to be tested, and create supporting communities for user-innovators to share ideas.

This experience is particularly relevant to community-driven application and adaptation of ICT in developing countries. ICT producers and suppliers have yet to understand the special communication and information needs of the poor and rural communities in developing countries. Mechanisms to engage these target groups as co-producers and co-inventors in ICT application are needed to overcome the cultural, institutional, and skill barriers to realize the potential of this user innovation revolution. These mechanisms must start with respect to the poor as co-creators. The process of co-creation treats local NGOs and poor communities as equally important partners and joint problem solvers.

A new innovation paradigm is needed—a pro-poor user-driven innovation paradigm that democratizes innovation.[5] Innovation funds, research institutions, and national innovation systems have primarily focused on advancing the technology, not understanding user needs, and particularly the poor and small enterprises. The ICT revolution open promises similar to those delivered by the green revolution for the poor and small farmers. Like agricultural technology, information technology must be adapted to the many and varied ecological and social contexts of

---

[4]These guiding principles are adapted from Prahalad (2005).

[5]Eric Von Hippel (2005). *Democratizing Innovation*. MIT Press.

application. Partnerships are needed among government, business, academic institutions, and community organizations to co-create value and services to the poor.

User-engagement and innovation lessons can be extended to the design and delivery of e-government services. Advanced e-government programs have learned to engage the leading users in co-designing new e-services and providing continuous feedback on these services. Moreover, the adoption of online services is critically dependent on the widespread of e-literacy and the creation of information culture. E-government programs are thus dependent on Paralel advance in promoting digital awareness and literacy among a large segment of the population.

Social Knowledge Creation and Participation

E-society programs can promote bottom-up knowledge creation and content development through community involvement and social interactions, facilitated by small grants or co-financing. Small grants to communities and NGOs may also finance social and network infrastructure to facilitate social knowledge creation. New knowledge is increasingly created through interactions among members in a network. It is enhanced socially as people build on each other's contributions. This approach may take advantage of the social networking and collaborative tools (web 2.0) as well as partnerships between community organizations, local governments, small businesses, and NGOs.

E-society programs can also finance platforms and content for sharing municipality, community, or neighborhood knowledge. A pioneering example, Neighborhood Knowledge California (NKCA), is empowering residents to improve their communities (Tapscott and Williams, 2006). It provides easy access to web-based tools to transform raw public data into formats that are useful to community residents and local-government policy makers. Among others, it integrates data from all levels of government and private sector (e.g., investment, toxic release notices) activities that can be tracked at the local level to develop an interactive monitoring system. Such grassroots projects show how platforms for participation that empower and involve people in identifying and resolving problems in their communities can improve public sector governance and enrich democracy. Such interactive platforms can track information on issues such as employment and public health.

Promising approaches are also emerging to engage local stakeholders and communities to develop local content and to localize global best practices in relevant fields of knowledge. These approaches blend the traditional methods of community development with the use of technology to build community portals and to capture local and global knowledge in ways that would support livelihood and income generation. These approaches integrate content development with access to a comprehensive web portal and targeted training. These initiatives also develop methodologies and tools to help communities build capacity to develop local content and localize global knowledge in areas deemed most relevant to the community and thus help scale up community-driven effort to blend and access global and local knowledge. When combined with community-driven development (CDD) approaches, community-driven portals and ICT-enabled networks could scale up access to relevant knowledge and best practices, procurement of inputs, and markets for local products. One Economy (www.one-economy.com) is a promising example of a non-profit organization that is creating community-driven approaches to content development and access in an expanding number of countries (Box 14.1).

Box 14.1 One Economy: Building capacity for community-driven portals and content

One Economy (www.one-economy.com), a non-profit organization, adopts such a promising approach. Its cornerstone is a comprehensive web portal (www.thebeehive.org) that provides information on topics that matter most to the poor: jobs, money, health, and education. One Economy engages communities and community-based NGOs in developing community portals to provide contextually and culturally relevant and user-friendly content written in local languages. It engages stakeholders in a participatory process to design and implement community portals. The community portals serve three functions: increasing livelihood and income generation for low-income individuals, building capacity of NGOs, and fostering private sector investment in low-income communities.

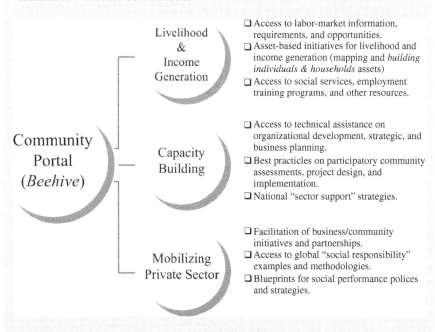

In an effort to scale up, reduce costs, and shorten time-to-market of community portals, One Economy has developed a toolkit that utilizes a global content system which contains all of One Economy's universally applicable content; stakeholders engagement tools to engage partners in providing specific content; a site-building wizard to allow partners to create their own site more easily; and a comprehensive training manual to support partners with examples to create their own site. In partnership with others, such as CISCO and Teachers without Borders, One Economy is also developing a curriculum for young people and for telecenter managers that will equip them with the tools to help them serve their communities and make sustainable IT solutions a reality.

Inclusive and Grassroots Innovation

Crosscutting strategies are typically needed to make the country's innovation system responsive to the needs of the poor and common people and to open up the national innovation system to mobilize and tap poor people's innovative abilities and assets. As a general purpose technology, ICT is particularly suited to access many of the problems of poor people: isolation, information poverty, insufficiently developed skills, and inability to access markets and assets on fair terms.

Harnessing this new technology for social inclusion can be pursued through bottom-up grassroots initiatives as well as formal, centrally directed programs to diffuse promising ICT-enabled solutions, much like the extension programs of the green revolution. We first illustrate the bottom-up approach with the grassroots innovation networks and grassroots innovation funds. Later, we illustrate the programmatic approach to diffuse and mainstream ICT into thematic development programs for poverty reduction and social inclusion.

How can we harness and scale up grassroots pro-poor innovations? One approach is to develop grassroots networks that support innovative products and mobilize local knowledge at the individual and community level. These networks would focus on innovation and adaptation—largely initiated at the grassroots level, and based on community knowledge and practices. Because such grassroots innovations are simple, low cost and easy to apply and replicate, such products have large social impacts on the livelihood of the marginalized. While such networks are not limited to ICT innovations, they are typically about ICT-enabled innovation, information sharing, and knowledge capturing. They may involve documentation and dissemination of traditional knowledge and innovations.

Known examples from India include the Honey Bee Network and Society for Sustainable Technologies and Institutions—two largest non-government programs. The two largest India Government network programs are the Grassroots Innovation Augmentation Network and the National Innovation Foundation. These networks attempt to capture and document knowledge from informal innovators (individuals, farmers, and entrepreneurs) who accumulated such knowledge from years of trial and error or incremental innovations embedded in tools and agricultural practices. They connect innovators to academics, NGOs, and policy makers. They seek to protect the intellectual property rights of knowledge holders and provide financial and institutional backing. The Society for Sustainable Technologies has also organized international scouting contexts with awards given to grassroots innovators form China, Vietnam, and India. Major products with successful value addition from this network include botanical pesticides and growth promoters, and health-healing treatments.

There has not been much assessment of how such programs have contributed to improving the livelihood of the people. Grassroots innovations face several challenges in India and elsewhere but these challenges can be systematically addressed (Dutz, 2007). High transaction costs of scouting and documentation are inevitable in programs that support a large number of scattered innovators. Most grassroots innovations require much more analysis and testing to improve the value of the innovation. Diffusion and dissemination efforts are also required for commercialization and a fund may be needed to acquire rights to such innovations. Even for innovations sufficiently developed to be commercialized, their scaling up and distribution need financing. These networks can therefore be complemented by, and in turn support grassroots innovation funds.

Grassroots Innovation Funds

A very powerful tool for promoting development of local content and applications is the so-called e-Society or Grassroots Innovation Funds. They are specially created to support rollout of innovative ICT applications and pilot projects to develop real-life skills and knowledge, promote grass-root innovation and participation. Small grants and cost-sharing finance are based on bottom-up proposals from NGOs, communities, and small enterprises with potentially broad replication and high impact on poverty reduction. Several countries have initiated such innovation funds, such as Malaysia, India, and Sri Lanka. Malaysia has established a demonstrator Application Grant Scheme to stimulate innovative use of ICT (Box 14.2).

Box 14.2 Malaysia—Demonstrator Application Grant Scheme

The National IT Council introduced the Demonstrator Application Grant Scheme, which provides funding support to projects that facilitate the social and economic progress of Malaysians through the innovative use of ICT. It also promotes closer co-operation and collaboration between public agencies, private corporations, and non-profit organizations through joint ventures and institutional linkages.

Demonstrator Applications (DAs) projects are small and focused projects with clearly defined objectives and a short implementation cycle of less then 12 months. They emphasize community inclusion and local content creation, providing a model of sustainable development. This scheme provides grant support of up to seventy percent of the total project cost. There are three types of DAs:

- *Perdana DA* has the key aim of enhancing cooperation between companies or consortia of companies, or joint ventures between the public and private sectors, and community-based organizations for the development of national-level projects of strategic importance for realizing the national ICT strategy. To be accredited as Perdana DAs, projects have to be scalable to national-level, with strategic importance, and can be undertaken by companies or joint ventures between public and community-based organizations.
- *Public Sector DA* refers to value creation projects supported by federal ministries or state governments, with the joint participation of the private sector, institutes of higher learning, and non-profit organizations. Encourage the active involvement and participation of society in the creation of an efficient public service.
- *People DA* aims to grant opportunities to individuals, societies, the private sector, non-governmental, and non-profit organizations to create ICT projects that can re-engineer and provide solutions to problems specific to a society. People DAs are "smart solutions" to age-old problems.

Source: Government of Malaysia.

Many lessons have emerged from e-Society funds designed to promote grassroots innovation in applying ICT. Such funds should focus on ICT and innovation not as an end but as a means—a tool that can transform the capabilities of communities, the performance of institutions, the functioning of markets, the potential for partnerships, and the livelihoods of the poor. With appropriate governance and transparency mechanisms, grassroots innovation funding can become an effective, sustainable institution for innovation and empowerment. They are also relevant to national initiatives aimed at adapting ICT to community needs, local conditions, and national development priorities.

Mechanisms to fund grassroots initiatives can be a good complement to centrally led national programs. A grassroots-innovation fund can provide inputs to the centrally led national program, supporting grassroots initiatives that are developing local content, local capacity e-government adoption, regional connectivity, and telecenter networks. It can build awareness and capacity at the user's end, including community capacity to partner with local and national institutions and to make effective use of e-services, when made available. And it captures promising innovations that may spontaneously arise, for adaptation and scaling-up.

Generating truly innovative proposals from relatively unsophisticated rural and vulnerable communities requires mutual, cumulative learning by the innovation grant program providers and recipients. The innovation process needs to be interactive—engaging those who know about local social conditions and capabilities with those who know about the potential of new technologies. Such funds can tap the grassroots presence of the community-based organizations and their understanding of the communities themselves.

Taking ICT to the rural people and disadvantaged members of society—who are among those least likely to be familiar with the new technologies—presents many challenges. Strategic communication and social marketing are needed to familiarize target communities and stakeholders with the fund. Other means of mobilizing demand may involve engaging international and local NGOs active at the grassroots and using a process consultant to facilitate communication and work with community-based organizations.

Effective use and diffusion of ICT for development is essentially a social learning process. It requires a knowledge management system to capture, augment, and complement the tacit local knowledge being mobilized. Sharing the lessons of experience is perhaps both the greatest challenge for innovation funds and the biggest determinant of their development impact.

Grassroots innovation funds are, by design, demand driven. Demand-driven innovation mechanisms that support grassroots initiatives can complement and help reorient the national innovation system. Research institutions in many developing countries focus on complex technology applications, serve large enterprises, or pursue the interests of their own scientists. E-society innovation funds can fill a critical gap in this national innovation system, creating an enabling institutional mechanism for grassroots application of ICT. The fund may also help show how to reorient these institutions to promote demand-driven incremental innovation and adaptation, particularly to serve rural people and the poor.

Mainstreaming ICT for Poverty Reduction

Piloting ICT use for poverty reduction or creating e-society innovation funds would not stand alone as an effective approach to ICT-enabled development. Some development practitioners have argued for the exclusive reliance on grassroots initiatives to ensure ICT can address the social and economic divides—in response to frequent and major failures of large-scale ICT projects, excessive reliance on imported and centrally driven solutions, promising pilots and performance of local NGOs, and the often poor understanding of and responsiveness to poor communities by large and distant government and business bureaucracies. While these are understandable reactions to the disappointing results from exclusive reliance on top–down approaches to ICT for development programs, such arguments are misleading. They could deprive ICT-enabled development from creating the enabling policy environment, the tools, the resources, and the partnerships needed to scale up grassroots innovations and have major impact on poverty reduction.

Centrally directed national programs would involve harnessing and directing ICT research, development, application, and diffusion to better meet the needs of rural population, the disadvantaged, and the poor. The high-yield variety or green revolution in food grains provides an inspiring example of such programs. Over the past four decades, a set of integrated packages, inputs, and practices were developed and diffused through an extensive network of agricultural R&D and extension institutions. This revolution has significantly improved food security and reduced rural poverty in many parts of the world, in Asia in particular. While new challenges are precipitating a recent food crisis in several developing countries, much can be learned from these early technology development and diffusion programs. In this current phase, ICT is likely to play a key role in increasing agricultural productivity and improving value chains and increasing incomes in the rural areas.

The most critical lesson from the green revolution is the need to create incentives for pro-poor early-stage technology development and commercialization by the formal sector. This would include reorienting the incentives in public R&D and universities to develop and adapt technology for the service of the poor and harnessing the research capacity of the private sector to work on the technological and developmental problems of the poor. Sectoral ministries and national agencies play a key role in mainstreaming and diffusing the new technologies. In the case of the green revolution, this involved partnerships among ministries of agriculture and their research institutions, private sector, local government and at times, community organizations like the irrigation associations. Traditional, supply-driven public extension systems in agriculture have been changing or replaced by more flexible, market-responsive support mechanisms, involving public–private partnerships, and farmer organizations. In the case of ICT , its diffusion should involve even more stakeholders as ICT cuts across all economic sectors, requires a flexible package of services and not just a fixed technology solution, and is relevant to both rural and urban areas.

Lessons learned from financing social funds over the last decade add more insights into the role of grassroots innovation networks and funds in development and the need to align them with sectoral programs (World Bank, Operations Evaluation Department, 2002). Such funds channel resources to local communities for small-scale subprojects proposed by stakeholders and screened for eligibility criteria. These funds were initially set up as emergency response mechanisms, but have increasingly shifted focus to longer term development impact and institutional development. They were often created and operated as attractive alternatives to overly centralized and slow government sectoral agencies and as a vehicle to decentralize development and empower communities. Although social fund projects proved effective in delivering small-scale infrastructure projects and reaching the relatively poor, they were limited in supporting new sectors or applying technologies not familiar to traditional and isolated rural communities, such as ICT. Sustainability of the new assets required engagement of local governments and alignment of these initiatives with decentralization and fund coordination with relevant line ministries. Similarly, fund impact on institutional development depended on alignment of these bottom-up mechanisms with national programs. The key lesson is to integrate social funds into the country's sectoral and overall development strategies.

Mechanisms for financing grassroots initiatives to apply ICT to socio-economic problems can complement and help adapt centrally driven national initiatives to meet diverse local socio-economic conditions. E-society and other similar innovation funds can fill a critical gap in creating an enabling institutional mechanism for grassroots innovation, adaptation, and learning. The fund may also promote demand-driven incremental innovation and adaptation, particularly to serve rural people and the poor. National e-leadership institutions are then expected to focus on the policy environment, lumpy infrastructure investments, complex technology applications, and serving government enterprise-wide needs. National e-development programs and institutions can also tap promising grassroots innovations and ICT applications for scaling up. Various government agencies and ministries can also integrate the new ICT applications, local contents, home-grown best practices, and local capabilities into their ICT-enabled services and sector-wide development programs.

Striking a balance between top-down mechanisms for mainstreaming ICT in development and bottom-up mechanism to seek innovative applications and adaptations is a key strategic decision in designing e-development programs. This balance must take account of central and local capabilities, the scale and diversity of socio-economic conditions in the country, the existing e-readiness at the national and regional levels, and the existing level of fiscal and administrative decentralization, among others. Mechanisms to promote grassroots initiatives must be a key component of a balanced and inclusive e-development. Equally important is for national e-leadership institutions to create the enabling conditions and broad capabilities for grassroots adoption and adaptation of ICT to solve local development issues.

e-Society and e-Development

E-society is a key component that interacts and mutually reinforces other elements of e-development. It could be argued that it is in applying ICT to the problems of poverty at the local or community level where all elements of e-development must be integrated and synchronized. Successes in applying ICT to solve social problems and enabling the poor and local communities to derive social and economic value are dependent on many complementary factors and investments and must address key mutually reinforcing constraints to sustainable local development. Bottom-up initiatives, enabled by e-society innovation funds, can systematically test the local market and local communities in terms of potential demand, constraints, and capacity to use ICT for solving local development problems before any mainstreaming such applications or adoption of complementary investments in a scaled-up program. They can also help test, tailor, and integrate ICT-enabled services to meet the unarticulated needs of the poor and underdeveloped regions.

E-society calls for holistic e-development at the grassroots level. This implies a key role for strategic partnerships to provide integrated solutions to local socio-economic problems. In the case of Sri Lanka, for example, the fund has financed local initiatives to catalyze local knowledge and digitize relevant content for delivery through locally owned telecenters. Meanwhile, telecenter operators trained in content development and management under the e-Sri Lanka program have partnered in seeking e-society partnership grants to jointly develop local content and services. Innovative proposals are also seeking to promote e-literacy and popularize ICT for development, in collaboration with universities and NGOs. All these grassroots initiatives are filling gaps in local capacity, services, and content development for the telecenters and e-government programs. Another initiative funded through a partnership grant is e-curriculum development, designed to enable rural children grades 6–11 to access school curriculum in local languages through the telecenters. This partnership involved the Ministry of Education, the e-Society fund, and NGOs.

E-society programs can complement national and regional public service broadcasting by developing content for community-level broadcasting. Community broadcasting provides bottom-up information on development most relevant to communities as well as lateral communications of shared interests such as farmers, women, or children. Community radio is very cost-effective: in the Philippines, the cost of community radio per 1000 audience members is $1.6–3.1 compared with $86.7 for local print and $32.8 for television (Lucas, 1999). Community broadcasting has also proved effective in supporting behavioral changes necessary for community-driven development projects. The recent combination of Internet access and community broadcasting facilities is further transforming their relevance and reach as demand-responsive knowledge banks. But in many developing countries, the absence of enabling legislation has been a major obstacle to community broadcasting, including in Sri Lanka.

E-society, combined with the new social networking tools, may engage citizens as co-producers of the public good and further the evolution of e-government. As discussed earlier, user-driven innovation and user-created content turn formerly passive customers into active participants in the co-creation of contents and services. This new model of innovation can be adopted for e-government, and citizens or communities would do more to customize or personalize government services. Financing local content development and the innovation of locally relevant services can be designed to reinforce and facilitate centrally produced e-government services.

Innovating and appropriating ICT for social use can be facilitated by building local capacity and communities to adopt open-source software and practices. The potential of "open-source" software to provide low-cost tools for generating local content and innovation is substantial and should be promoted and integrated into e-development strategies. Open source is a fast growing movement, especially in e-education, e-government, and e-society. However, contrary to the popular belief, it is not about getting something for no charge. The idea is to allow free redistribution and modification of the software for it to successfully evolve and adapt to various specific conditions and uses. Financial and developmental benefits for the end user are significant and therefore building local capabilities for open-source software may be linked to e-society programs.

Telecenters or community information centers can play important roles: provide access to ICT tools including the Internet; extend and customize public services, including those offered through e-government; provide access to information in support of local economic activities and learning opportunities; and connect and network people. Telecenters may be used to open channels for villagers to submit grievances about government services and abuses and thus improve accountability and provide feedback to government agencies on performance problems and opportunities for service innovation. Community centers can also promote gender equality by providing women with a medium to participate as producers, consumers, and counselors-clients. In South Africa, women's organizations are linked to various resource web sites that aim to mobilize women around common concerns (Fontiane, 2000). Government can provide support and incentives for partnerships between universities to develop innovative social applications and relevant local content and to disseminate them through telecenters and other delivery channels.

The involvement of civil society and local communities in e-development via e-society funds and grassroots innovation programs can have broader impact beyond specific e-society applications. It can provide a countervailing force to those forces that contribute to the growing social and digital divides. It can mobilize a key constituency in support of greater resource allocation of ICT as a means of achieving broad economic and social development objectives. It can also generate a continuous feedback on current e-government services. It can promote syndications and partnerships to integrate and customize public, private, and civil society services for various target groups.

Finally, progress in using ICT to fight poverty and inequality should be measured within the context of ICT-enabled development strategies. This requires frameworks, scorecards, indicators, and methodologies to measure the efforts and estimate the effects of higher investments in ICT for poverty reduction. Scorecards should help trace the missing links or conditions to realizing the benefits of ICT investments in poverty reduction: as a general-purpose technology ICT is an enabling technology that opens up new opportunities rather than offer complete solutions. Feedback mechanisms should help reward and scale up public and private sector efforts to promote ICT for social development.

Section IV
Implementing e-Development Strategies

The key to explaining why some countries have made significant achievements in ICT-enabled development lies in the effective execution of national e-strategies. Beyond stable political leadership and national consensus on development, success factors in implementation included dynamic governance; clearly articulated institutional mechanisms; a competent cadre of e-leaders; strategic partnerships among public and business sectors and civil society; incentives for change and innovation; monitoring, evaluation, and learning systems; and effective mechanisms for participation and consultations throughout the e-development process.

This section focuses on a few key factors that influence implementation of e-development strategies and lessons learned from their implementation in emerging economies. Chapter 15 covers ways and means for managing e-strategy implementation and the associated risks. It first examines the sources of current gap between visions and realities of ICT in development. This requires tailoring strategies to the country's initial conditions. It also suggests an evolving role for government and development partners. In fast-changing technological and institutional environments, e-strategies also face many risks. We conclude with an overview of the role of monitoring, evaluation, and learning systems in the effective implementation and continuous adaptation of e-development strategies.

In the last chapter, I identify key lessons of experience in designing and implementing e-strategies and suggest future directions for both developing countries and aid agencies.

Ten broad lessons are suggested for e-Transformation strategies: integrating ICT as the enabler of new development strategies; pursuing a holistic approach; leveraging synergies and scale; pursuing quick-wins within long-term perspectives; engaging stakeholders and forming reform coalitions, attending to the soft aspects of institutions, leadership, and culture; building strategic partnerships; balancing strategic direction with local initiative; building capabilities for an adaptive learning process; adopting integrated approaches to e-inclusion; and promoting regional and global collaboration.

Chapter 15
Managing Implementation and Risks

This chapter first examines the sources of current gap between visions and realities of ICT in development. I suggest a schema for tailoring strategies to the country's initial conditions (strategic fit with levels of development). I also suggest an evolving role for government and other partners, including the sequencing or phasing of investments so as to increase the role of private sector over time, as may be appropriate. Attention should be given to the development of dynamic governance, clearly articulated institutional mechanisms, and a competent cadre of e-leaders. The changing and complementary roles of various actors or stakeholders should be reflected in new strategic partnerships among public and business sectors and civil society. Incentives for change and innovation are also essential.

In fast-changing technological and institutional environments, e-strategies also face many risks. These risks cover all elements of e-development. We only illustrate such risks in implementing e-government programs. To reduce these risks and maximize the developmental outcomes of e-strategies, effective mechanisms should be developed for participation and consultations throughout the e-development process. The chapter concludes with an overview of the role of monitoring, evaluation, and learning systems in e-development strategy implementation and adaptation over time.

Sources of Vision-Implementation Gap

Many countries have developed national ICT strategies or e-development strategies. But few have been successful in following through with effective implementation (Heeks, 2006). Visions and aspirations often result in ambitious e-development strategies. But there is a growing gap between strategy statements and implementation and results. Excessive optimism is often followed by excessive pessimism. What is at the heart of this implementation crisis? Several factors tend to contribute to this gap.

First factor is weak ownership. As developing countries and aid agencies have given increasing attention to preparing national and regional e-development strategies, strategies were often developed by outside consultants, with little local

N.K. Hanna, *e-Transformation: Enabling New Development Strategies*, Innovation, Technology, and Knowledge Management, DOI 10.1007/978-1-4419-1185-8_15, © Springer Science+Business Media, LLC 2010

ownership or local capacity to implement. This implementation gap is especially felt when aid agencies work with countries to finance e-development programs. Yet, a locally driven and owned process is critical to develop a shared vision, build coalitions for reform, and secure the authorizing environment for effective use of ICT throughout government and the economy. A locally owned process would also commit the necessary human and financial resources and continually learn and test implementation constraints. It is also more likely to appreciate the local constraints to implementation, and thus set more realistic expectations for pace of transformation.

The second factor is scarce e-leadership. A key missing capacity in securing successful e-strategies is e-leadership. The common failure to scale up successful pilots is typically due to scarce e-leadership. Replicability and sustainability of local and donor initiatives demand substantial e-leadership resources, not blueprints. E-leadership is needed at all levels to integrate ICT as a crosscutting enabler for overall development strategies, to promote the ICT as a sector, to create appropriate e-policies and institutions, to set investment priorities for access and e-government services, to lead bottom-up initiatives and innovations, and to learn and scale up.

The gap between the *demand* for leaders able to think and act strategically about the deployment of ICT and the *supply* of such individuals may be increasing. This gap is not only quantitative, but also involves qualitative improvements in capacities to think beyond the technology, to include political and managerial skills. It is also attitudinal, as leadership for transformation calls for openness to innovation, collaboration, and learning.

A third source of implementation problems is the failure to focus and prioritize. This often leads to overly complex projects, with high risks of failure, and of tackling investments that are all long-gestating, with little quick wins to sustain political commitment. Implementing organizations are often faced with a long laundry list of ambitious projects, far beyond the human and financial resources likely to be available.

A fourth factor is weak articulation of program implementation tools and processes such as the annual national budget, monitoring, and evaluation. E-strategies should be designed for implementability. E-government programs in particular should be developed within a medium-term framework and integrated into the country's medium-term expenditure framework.

A review of current e-strategies of many developing countries confirms that monitoring and evaluation functions are often missing. Yet, a key tool for implementation and for further improvement in designing future e-strategies is monitoring and evaluation. Given the fast pace of technological change and the novelty of ICT applications in developing countries, adaptive planning and learning-oriented strategy processes are essential. Monitoring and evaluation systems are needed to learn quickly from pilots and from early phases of implementation. Focusing on results and indicators of progress is also important to continuously negotiate reforms and build coalitions for implementation.

A final contributor to the vision-reality gap is technological change far outpacing institutional capacity for change. The "lead time to implementation" is increasing as technological change leaps far ahead of capacity development and institutional adjustment. At times, slow and cumbersome procurement practices of aid agencies cause considerable lags. But the most binding constraint to keep pace with technological change and take advantage of continually advanced technological capabilities is usually the slow pace of change of skills and institutions.

Tailoring e-Development Strategy to Country Conditions

E-development interventions should fit with and respond to the needs, national goals, and social and economic conditions of each country. E-development cannot be based on a "one-fits-all" approach. At the same time, e-development framework allows for some degree of generalization based on countries' size and level of economic development. A typology such as in Box 15.1 is neither all-encompassing nor operationally detailed, but it illustrates the kind of broad guidance and priorities for overall e-strategy development.

Box 15.1 Country Typologies and Generic Priorities

Newly industrializing and transitional economies

Countries in this category are best positioned to promote the most comprehensive approach to ICT, balancing two overarching development objectives: (i) sustainable economic growth, driven by competitive ICT sector and ICT-enabled "traditional" industries and (ii) poverty reduction though accelerating broad-based growth and accelerated human development. Priority objectives include

- Promoting the software industry for both domestic use and niche export, stimulating local market for IT-related services
- Developing a comprehensive e-government program with significant emphasis on front-office applications
- Promoting outsourcing of government IT operations and services
- Developing national information infrastructure
- Supporting key industries and SME clusters in ICT adoption
- Promoting ICT literacy and education

Small and island economies

Such countries have to be very selective in setting their national priorities and allocating scarce recourses. They may benefit from putting strong emphasis on

using ICT to integrate with and gain competitive advantage in the global economy. ICT may also enhance the collaboration and the pooling of resources on
a regional basis. Priority objectives include

- Developing national information infrastructure through privatizing and
  liberalizing telecomm sector, improving international connectivity
- Promoting clusters of information technology industry with strong export
  potential, creating favorable conditions for FDI into the sector
- Developing information-intensive services and multimedia
- Supporting ICT adoption by key export-oriented industries, such as
  tourism and agriculture
- Reducing the high costs of government services and harnessing regional
  and global expertise through outsourcing of government functions and
  pooling of expertise

Low-income, large economies

The countries in this category would benefit most from creating conditions
for wide ICT diffusion in government, economy, and society with focus on
overall economic growth and poverty reduction. Priority objectives include

- Developing national information infrastructure, with emphasis on universal
  access in rural and disadvantaged communities
- Promoting links between the information technology sector and local
  industries
- Developing e-government with active participation of end users, with
  particular emphasis on G2B applications
- Providing information on domestic and foreign markets
- Financial and capacity building support to e-business adoption especially for rural and agricultural enterprises, developing rural market
  information systems and ICT-based business development services
- Promoting universal ICT literacy

Examples from the group of small states suggest that the profound impact of
that can be realized from enhancing their connectivity with the rest of the world.
There are about 50 small states (with populations of less than 2 million), of which
about 30 are islands. These states spend 1% of their GDP more than do larger
states on telecommunications services, mainly due to non-competitive monopoly
market structures (Favaro, 2008). Such high costs are especially damaging for isolated small states. A small domestic market limits capacity to diversify risk, adapt to
volatile international trade, and exploit economies of scale in production and service
delivery. Good ICT policies, institutions, and regulations are needed to exploit international trade opportunities, location, and other sources of competition and growth.

Some small states have pioneered ICT-enabled ways to improve the quality and reduce the costs of public sources through outsourcing of government functions to regional bodies the remote delivery of services. Caribbean and West and Central Africa have delegated traditional functions of central banks to regional bodies. The East Caribbean governments outsource regulation of telecommunications and civil aviation to regional bodies, and thus facilitate reform, pool scarce expertise and resources to build centers of knowledge and expertise (Favaro, 2008). Sustaining a high-quality cadre of civil servants in each small country in isolation would have been very costly. The World Bank is also financing common communication and e-government institutions and facilities for these countries. In the Pacific and East Caribbean, states also cooperate in providing higher education, and ICT is opening opportunities to share knowledge and educate future leaders. With ICT, they also cooperate to monitor and handle disruptions like natural disasters. Some small countries and islands also started to participate in the outsourcing revolution, like call centers in the Caribbean, thus diversifying their economies. The potential dividends from ICT are enormous for these small countries, yet to be fully exploited with coherent ICT policies and holistic strategies.

Sequencing the Role of Government

For better management of the e-development process, it may be divided into successive stages, with the government playing three distinctively different roles: initiator, enabler, and driver. Actions taken at the each stage vary significantly depending on the national development priorities; the tables below provide general directions based on lessons learned. This sequencing reflects the need for effective use of scarce financial and human resources and prioritizes key actions such as developing access ahead of e-services. It also acknowledges the notion that, realistically, the government can become an effective and committed promoter of ICT in other sectors only after a certain threshold of ICT adoption and literacy in the government itself.

At the first stage, government leadership focuses on initiation of a broad-based e-development process, starting with the essential ingredients, such as promoting stakeholder engagement and collaboration, and improving information infrastructure. This is largely a pre-investment stage (Table 15.1).

At the second stage, the government crystallizes its long-term e-development strategy and vision, supported by a short-term action plan focusing on building its own ICT capacity (technological and institutional) and creating enabling environment for participation of other sectors and stakeholders (Table 15.2).

Finally, the government takes a proactive role in advancing ICT use across all sectors of the economy and society, shifting its focus from enabling policies to direct investment and capacity building support through partnerships with other relevant stakeholders (Table 15.3).

The e-development strategy is divided into separate interventions in the table for illustrative purposes only. Countries should avoid fragmentation of

Table 15.1   Government role as initiator

Initiator	
Leadership, policy, institutions	• Engaging major stakeholders—private and public sectors, academia, and civil society—into constructive dialogue and formulation of national e-development vision and priorities
	• Creating permanent advisory institution
	• Designating cabinet level or independent e-development agency
	• Insuring clear division of labor and collaboration mechanisms among existing ministries and agencies for design and delivery of ICT-related projects
	• Developing general government IT interoperability standards and guidelines (technology and application architectures)
Information infrastructure	• Improving access to ICT. Telecom sector liberalization—multiple and competing providers of services—in fixed networks, mobile services, ISP, etc.
	• If fixed-line teledensity is very low and special programs to promote shared access are needed, then support piloting of telecenters based on different models
	• Investing in government local area networks
Human resources	• Promoting use of ICT in tertiary education
	• Piloting programs for universal IT literacy, starting with IT literacy in schools
	• Ensuring supply of software development specialists through education and training programs
ICT sector development	• Introducing competitive and transparent procurement of ICT services in public institutions
	• Supporting the development of local ICT industry associations
Applications and content	• Learning through independent initiatives and piloting (along some prioritization scheme, exploiting opportunities for "quick wins" and complying to the extent possible with the common IT interoperability standards and guidelines)

e-development strategy and strive for an integrated approach no matter what stage of development they are at. Comprehensive e-development strategy is not a "luxury" for developed countries only. It is a development paradigm that makes ICT-enabled development effective. The synergies created by a comprehensive approach are even more relevant to resource-constrained developing countries than developed ones.

The role of government in creating the knowledge economy is also evolving and shifting, from a diminishing role as major producer to increasing role as facilitator, partner, strategist, and leader (Fig. 15.1; Lanvin, 2003). Governments are taking leading roles in providing society-wide vision of ICT-enabled development, addressing the digital divide, and creating the enabling environment, as well as user and innovator in applying ICT to public services. Governments are also assuming a strong facilitating role in promoting overall societal e-readiness through education policy and e-education.

Table 15.2 Government role as enabler

Enabler	
Leadership, policy, institutions	• E-development action plan focusing on improving efficiency of government operations and adoption of ICT by various sectors • Designated e-government body with executive powers and formation of appropriate institutional mechanisms such as National CIO Office and CIO Council • Full range of e-laws and regulations. Public key infrastructure
Information infrastructure	• Creation of a universal access fund to channel part of the telecom's revenues and possibly government subsidies into improving access in remote and disadvantaged communities • Scale up successful telecenter models into national program • E-government networks at national, regional, and local levels
Human resources	• Focus on universal IT literacy—introducing ICT education in primary and high schools • ICT awareness for public sector leaders and academia • Ensuring sufficient supply of software and communications specialists
ICT sector development	• Laws to protect intellectual property rights and promote commercialization of R&D • Favorable legal environment for industry–university collaboration • Promote partnerships among local ICT providers and links with international service providers • Transparent IT procurement and outsourcing guidelines for government
Applications and content	• Strategic e-administration applications such as integrated financial management systems, customs administration, e-trade networks, tax administration, and social security systems • Piloting selected joined-up e-services, often with focus on G2B applications

Developing e-Leadership

Leadership—political, institutional, and technical—is essential to development, including ICT-enabled development. Stable and informed political leadership is especially important to the quality of e-development implementation and to adopting long-term solutions and sustainable policies essential for economic and social transformation. The quality of leadership that resides in all the institutions of governance is equally important. Leaders should be also the agents of change. They should anticipate and be aware of the potential of ICT for change and be equipped to lead this ICT-enabled change and transformation.

In Singapore, leadership has been essential to the high quality of implementation and success of e-development. The Singaporean public sector plays a key role. Public sector leaders have been pragmatic, yet willing to invent, change, and set long-term visions. Potential leaders are selected and groomed in meritocratic ways. Their compensation is competitive with the private sector. They "anticipate,

Table 15.3 Government role as driver

Driver	
Leadership, policy, institutions	• E-development action plan focused on the diffusion of ICT across all sectors of the economy and on creating favorable conditions for ICT sector development
	• Public–private partnership for e-business promotion
	• Policies and regulations to promote and regulate joined-up e-services for citizens and businesses, including private sector participation in investing in and operating e-services
	• Policies to promote local content industry
	• Active outsourcing of government IT services
Information infrastructure	• Creation of academic, R&D, and school networks
	• Broadband development and improving international connectivity
	• Diversify telecenter services to support SMEs and priority national programs
Human resources	• ICT awareness and promotion for late adopters
	• ICT vocational training
	• Supporting university–industry collaboration for ICT skill development and centers of education excellence in selected competencies or sectors of ICT industry
	• Mainstreaming ICT-enabled learning at all levels of education and lifelong learning
ICT sector development	• Funding and capacity building support to university–industry research-funding ICT programs
	• Investment in incubators and technology parks
	• Venture capital support
	• Where competitive advantage is likely, support marketing, quality assurance, and other measures to promote the export of software and IT-enabled services
Applications and content	• Comprehensive e-business support program
	• Special fund to promote innovative solutions for the use of ICT in societal applications
	• One-stop-shop e-government portal with electronic transactions capabilities, such as e-taxation and e-procurement, to promote use of ICT by enterprises and citizens
	• Promoting synergies between various e-development program components, such as telecenters and e-business promotion

change, and stay relevant," thus ensuring that their decisions are creative and forward looking. Working as a team across government agencies, and in partnership with businesses, unions, and communities, helps sustain policy coherence and mutually reinforcing programs. At the institutional to technical levels, the government invests in building a cadre of CIOs. To stay ahead of the technology adoption curve, these leaders collaborate with the industry and use the proof-of-concept lab as a test bed for government to assess new technologies for government transformation.

Leaders are needed for each sector or component of e-development and for orchestrating the overall e-development process. These leaders play different roles

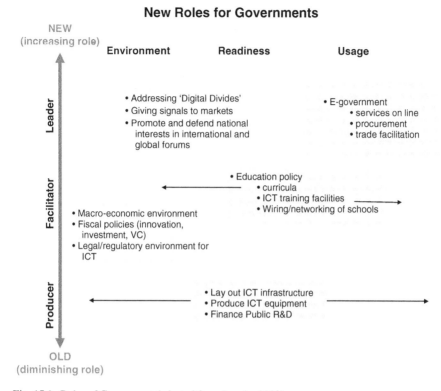

Fig. 15.1 Roles of Government (adapted from Lanvin, 2003)

that range from developing national e-policies and government-wide ICT governance to engaging local communities and grassroots organizations in defining local information and communication needs and experimenting with new ICT applications.

E-leaders should possess *core competencies* that range from awareness of ICT potential and trends to developing their own general leadership skills. Competencies to communicate in the language of development strategies and development results are essential to be understood by policy makers, business leaders, and mainstream development strategists. These are urgently needed to bridge the current divide between ICT specialists and development practitioners. E-leaders strive to understand the political process, gain the support and confidence of the political and business leadership, and mobilize the stakeholders of the e-development process.

E-leadership calls for new competencies to secure a balanced e-development process and tap synergies across all components of e-development. E-government leaders, for example, cannot take for granted the existence of adequate content, connectivity, and user competencies to make e-government investments worthwhile. E-leaders have to concern themselves with the whole of the e-development process; this process is dynamic and involves substantial learning and adaptation.

Therefore, e-leaders ought to master the tools of agile e-development: measuring and benchmarking e-readiness, establishing and enforcing ICT governance frameworks, designing public–private partnership schemes, carrying out stakeholder analysis, building coalitions for necessary legal and regulatory reforms, and practicing participatory monitoring and evaluation.

E-leaders develop competencies in designing and managing partnerships and in leveraging ICT to build and facilitate networks of public services providers. They are expected to devise e-services that span the boundaries of single agencies, covering private suppliers, civil society organizations, and several public agencies in order to provide integrated, client-focused services. They govern by networks. They leverage ICT to build and manage their networks to deliver maximum public value.

E-leaders need to operate at three levels with distinct but complementary competencies:

- As business executives and strategists of public agencies and programs
- As business process architects and institutional change leaders
- As technology resource managers

As *top executives and business strategists*, e-leaders are able to visualize the destination of information society, the results of an ICT-enabled development strategy, and the possibilities opened by ICT for their agencies and countries. They should be able to build an inspiring vision of how ICT will build organizational success. They interact with other executives and stakeholders to shape this ICT-enabled future and then communicate it to the rest of the organization or sector for which they are responsible. They possess competencies in strategic thinking, strategic communications, and foresight. They have a broad appreciation and domain knowledge of the business they are in—beyond technology. They understand the big picture.

Also as business leaders and strategists, e-leaders define the broad directions for the ICT road map and provide managers and staff with the tools and governance to travel and learn on their way. They are concerned with mobilizing demand for change and for realizing the developmental results of ICT investments. They shape and inform expectations for ICT-enabled enterprise. They understand the needs of their clients. They are capable of inventing frameworks and creating environments that bring forth ICT-enabled possibilities in line with business strategy, national aspirations, and/or agency missions.[1] They strive to bridge the digital divide and to build an inclusive information society.

As *change leaders*, the new e-leaders are the industrial engineers and chief innovation officers of new business processes and new forms of organizations. They are also the chief relationship officers who enable the creation of new networks and work teams within organizations as well as new partnerships and supply chains across organizations. Working with other executives, they lead institutional change and inspire managerial innovation. They facilitate the evolution of current

---

[1] For such leadership qualities, in general, see Zander and Benjamin (2000). *The Art of Possibility.* New York: Penguin Books.

hierarchies into agile, adaptive, networked, client-centered, and learning organizations. They lead process innovation and client-centered service integration and facilitate the corresponding changes in skills, attitudes, and culture. They create sufficient trust and winning coalitions to break silos and engage process innovators, change agents and organizational development practitioners. They must have competencies in organizational development, process innovation, team building, network design and management, partnership and coalition building, and culture change management.

A user-focused e-government and seamless joined-up services can be very challenging and costly. Client focus means changing organizational structures and processes and reallocating resources. It requires change leadership. It means changes in attitudes and behavior among civil servants. It can be a great challenge to achieve customer satisfaction while reducing the cost of services and making them affordable. It is up to policy makers and e-leaders to strike the appropriate balance between efficiency and improved services. With creative leadership, both objectives are often achieved through process and service innovation.

As *technology leaders*, CIOs are the suppliers and custodians of ICT resources. This remains an essential role of e-leaders and the traditional domain for CIOs and CTOs. Public service constraints often limit access to technical talent with current knowledge of project management methodologies, business continuity and security management, and new approaches to systems development.[2] Also in strong demand are skills to engage policy makers and business leaders in defining systems requirements and re-inventing administrative processes.

Public CIOs are called upon to manage networks of ICT service providers and to engage in increasingly complex partnerships and contractual arrangements that demand current knowledge of the ICT industry and best practices in outsourcing. They can benchmark and hold accountable their outsourcers, build business cases for IT investments, manage a portfolio of projects, and help capture and share the information resources throughout their sectors or organizations. They have broad understanding of the technological environment—the trends and the imperatives and the ways and means to secure open standards and avoid the risks of technological lock-ins.

Multi-level and Multi-skilled Leaders

The span of skills required by such new e-development executives is thus enormous. On the domestic front, they conceptualize national strategies that move millions of public sector employees, contractors, and citizens forward to electronically connected government. They leverage IT so that government services are delivered effectively both offline and online. They popularize IT so that communities even in remote rural areas can have access to virtual libraries, critical knowledge, and timely information.

---

[2]Such as rapid prototyping.

On the international front, these leaders should thoroughly understand global IT dynamics and imperatives and be able to define investments in infrastructure, human capital formation, and industrial promotion incentives to attract multinational business in software, IT processing services, and other digital goods. They negotiate with local and global IT suppliers on behalf of their agencies and nations. Accordingly, they benchmark outsourcers, manage service level agreements, and negotiate with fully informed global players. More broadly, they should be able to assess the potential impact of IT on various local industries and their implications for the competitive positioning of their countries, cities, and enterprises.

These skill requirements go far beyond the traditional role of chief information officers in the public and private sectors. These skills cover public policy, business strategy, institutional change, and technology management. They span leadership, partnership, and integration skills. Such imperatives point to the urgent need for a wholly new type of executive that can be equally conversant in building coalitions for reform, designing national IT-enabled strategy, leading IT-enabled institutional change processes, creating new service delivery channels, and building critical infrastructural systems.

Managing the Risks of Program Implementation

Implementation of e-Transformation is fraught with risk and uncertainty. Learning to manage these risks and uncertainties is essential to sustainable transformation. This applies to all elements of e-development. E-government is a good example.

E-government projects and programs are inevitably political. The developmental promise of e-government and the concurrent administrative reforms and institutional changes needed to deliver on this promise have become a part of high-level national politics and an important political currency (World Public Sector Report, 2003, UN). The modernity that ICT represents has its public and political appeal. But it also calls for political support to bring about difficult changes. It brings about a focus on customers and empowers them with information. It shifts power within public administration through flatter structures, possible outsourcing of public services to private business and NGOs, possible elimination of intermediary level of management, and information sharing across departments.

As governments move to deploy ICT in all their activities, they must also define the new ways and manners by which their customers (citizens, businesses) will be served. The new value propositions will be different for different agencies, depending on the services they offer and segments of customers they serve. Moreover, implementation of e-government programs requires the engagement of private participants, including businesses and civil society organizations, and this raises many political issues concerning transparency and public–private roles.

The high profile of e-government programs and the implied shifts in power within government and with clients often lead to important consequences (UN, 2003). First, e-government programs tend to adopt ambitious goals. This is not entirely negative as this could lead to greater attention to much needed administrative reforms and public service improvements. Thinking big may be needed to initiate innovation and reforms of significant magnitude. But the common danger is that it leads to sweeping initiatives and overly complex and large projects, and complex projects often fail, particularly in developing countries. According to OECD, "Public sector budgeting systems can encourage the funding of large and highly visible projects. ...Very large projects, i.e., expensive, long term and complex initiatives, often fail."[3] Some analysts estimate the rate of failure of e-government projects in developing countries to be as high as 60–60% (particularly for Africa).[4] While outsourcing may reduce the risks of government failure, it should not be viewed as a magic bullet, as failure rates of PPPs are also high.

Second, there is the risk of short time horizon and unrealistic expectations. Many of the early declared successes and failures of e-government (and telecenter) projects proved to be premature. Successful results are often a function of the time horizon taken for evaluation. It takes significant durations to embed and appropriate the technology within organizations and communities to prepare the ground, build local capacity, and meet the enabling conditions. Adopting short time horizons for evaluating results and impacts tend to miss out on social and organizational learning and in the transformative processes being triggered by the new technologies. The pressure for quick results militates against sustainable improvements and investments in capacity development and organizational capital, and leads to early and premature declarations of success.

Third, e-government programs often fail to build the necessary systems to pursue results and measure impact. It is rare to find e-government programs developed within a transparent monitoring and evaluation framework. The political sensitivity of failure in these high visibility programs often lead to suppression of data from pilots and lessons to be learned from failures.

Fourth, there is the risk of limited demand for e-government services. Many factors are involved in demand for e-services, including affordable connectivity and the availability and actual transaction costs of alternative channels for public service delivery. A key demand factor is trust in government and government information. Other factors include awareness, ICT, or Internet literacy, and the reliability and security of e-government channels. Many countries have rushed to deploy government online services without adequate demand mobilization, or due consideration of securing timely and relevant content and the management and maintenance of the facilities.

Finally, government agencies are less flexible to change, compared with the private sector. As government and aid agencies are inspired by the possibilities and lessons learned from e-business, the specificity of the public sector is often ignored or underestimated. Government agencies are typically averse to risk and information sharing. Public organizations are likely to adapt to new processes and models at

---

[3]"Information Technology as an Instrument of Public Management Reform: A Study of Five OECD Countries," PUMA (98) 14, December 4, 1998, p. 14.

[4]UN (2003); Heeks (2002).

slower pace than private organizations. In many developing countries, it is not only the consumer of digital content (students, patients, citizens) who feels uncomfortable with ICT, but also the provider (teacher, physician, public official) (Hilbert and Katz, 2003). Re-engineering government and moving it online involve uncertainties, discontinuities, and profound changes in roles, skills, and daily routines. There are few incentive mechanisms and training opportunities to foster the integration of ICTs into the daily routine of teachers, physicians, lawyers, or other civil servants (ECLAC, 2003).

Fortunately, tools and frameworks have been developed to reduce the risks and manage the change process. Chapter 12 examined some of these tools, such as stakeholder analysis and engagement, user engagement and feedback, and strategic communications. These tools are applicable across all elements of e-development. In the following we further examine the role of consultation and participation in facilitating effective implementation of e-development.

Consultative and Participatory e-Transformation

Consultative and participatory processes are critical to all stages of e-development to

- Create a shared, inclusive, and energizing vision of ICT-enabled development
- Generate shared understanding of initial conditions and e-readiness, including the key stakeholders and their concerns
- Build consensus and coalitions for policy and institutional reforms that are essential to ICT industry and infrastructure development as well as ICT use and diffusion
- Agree on priorities and secure governance of ICT investment strategies and action plans
- Guide bottom-up initiatives and innovations and build partnerships for scaling up and diffusion
- Promote participatory monitoring and evaluation and societal learning

Visioning and future scenario building are first steps in strategic thinking and planning for e-development. These can be engaging and energizing exercises. Although such exercises are common in the corporate world, they are not adequately used at the national level or in situations where large numbers of people are or should be involved. Yet visioning exercises can be effective communication and mobilization tools. Thinking about the future, particularly a desirable future, can captivate people's imagination, help shape a shared vision, and secure support for its implementation.

E-readiness assessment methodologies suffer major limitations when carried out in isolation from effective people-centered, participatory, and consultative processes. They are designed for ranking countries in terms of access and use of ICT. They prescribe a given state compared to what exits in developed countries. They are post facto analysis, with limited concern about the needs of most people for information and communication. As they reflect aggregate indicators of e-readiness at the national level, they rarely capture the digital divides among regions within countries or consider the role of ICT in poor and rural areas.

E-readiness methodologies could be strengthened to be more inclusive. At the national level, assessments of e-readiness can be a helpful source of information for brainstorming about ICT-enabled futures, especially if they are focused on people rather than documents. They need to be adapted or complemented by selective in-depth market analyses, digital divide analyses, and local or community-level assessments (http://www.bridges.org). National e-strategies may draw on a blend of assessments at the national, regional, and community levels to capture diversity, regional disparities, and the needs of special populations. But perhaps most important is to adapt these methodologies so as to use e-readiness assessments as part of change management processes to raise awareness, engage stakeholders, and form coalitions for reform.

Consultative and participatory processes are also necessary to build consensus and coalitions for policy and institutional reforms and to agree on priorities and secure governance for ICT investment strategies and action plans. Policy reforms and laws by themselves are not sufficient to bring about changes, particularly those changes most critical to transform government and business practices. Technocratic design of e-strategies is unlikely to induce innovation or overcome resistance to the massive changes that accompany these strategies. Rather, strategies and action plans may be viewed, among others, as marketing tools to be used to communicate the intentions of national leaders and reformers. Stakeholders need to be involved in developing policies, in setting priorities, and in governing and coordinating ICT investment programs. Strategic communication and ongoing consultation with stakeholders are essential to the effective implementation of e-policies, and the use of ICT to enable role changes, power shifts, and process transformations. Consultation should be representative so as to include the marginalized groups such as women, youth, and rural and poor populations.

Participatory methodologies and consultative processes should be also deployed to guide bottom-up initiatives and innovations and build partnerships for scaling up and diffusion. "Letting a thousand flowers bloom" may be adequate for local learning and local innovation, but not a viable or sufficient strategy for sustainability or scaling up development impact. Governments may draw on trade and professional associations, community-based organizations, and other non-government organizations to engage in grassroots innovations, to diffuse best practices and to form partnerships for scaling up successes.

Consultation, participation, and communication plans should be anticipatory and integral to the process of e-development policy planning and strategy implementation (Labelle, 2005). Typically, public consultations are not undertaken on an ongoing basis, and there are no institutional mechanisms that build consultation into the process. Often, technocratic leadership first develops fully detailed strategies and then engages in selling them to constituents, or only after such strategies encounter implementation crises. Alternatively, political leadership engage in selling grandiose visions and vague ideas of investing in ICT, then turn to the technocrats to make this happen in isolation of the stakeholders. Neither approach is adequate. An institutionalized process should build various forms of consultation into all stages of e-strategy development and implementation.

These consultations may range from focus group meetings, town hall meetings, and national search conferences to online consultations, the use of media and the participation of representatives of stakeholders in the governance of various agencies responsible for strategy implementation. Furthermore, different components of e-development may require different approaches for participation and communication. For example, in the e-Sri Lanka program, raising awareness about and mobilizing demand for telecenters and for e-society applications included activities ranging from engaging community-based NGOs and SMEs to conducting street dramas in the rural areas and using media to communicate in simple and local languages.

Strategic and Flexible Approaches to Funding

A variety of funding mechanisms are likely to be needed to finance various elements of e-development, combining both strategic and flexible approaches to financing, innovating, and scaling up. Some elements of e-development require upfront and sizeable investments as in telecommunications infrastructure. Others require long-term view and vision of resources necessary for e-development as in human resources. Other elements require intensive coordination among government agencies, as in e-government. Others demand venturing, innovation, and experimentation before scaling up as in telecenters, e-society, and programs to diffuse ICT among SMEs. Some aspects of e-development are more attractive than others for the private sector to finance, as in telecommunications, while others require diverse financing partnerships as in specialized human resources development, community information centers, and societal applications.

Several e-development areas, such as ICT industry promotion and ICT diffusion in business and communities, are less amenable to centrally driven financing and discretely defined medium-term investments. These areas require cost sharing from the private sector and/or civil society organizations. They rely primarily on bottom-up initiatives. Central funding through innovation funds can provide a flexibly, demand-driven mechanism to support industry associations, NGOs, and other grassroots organizations through competitive bidding and cost sharing. Chapter 8 on the ICT sector (industry promotion) and Chapter 12 on networking business (ICT diffusion among SMEs) show some of these flexible funding mechanisms. The development of human resources for ICT production and use (Chapter 7) many also be financed through competitive cost-sharing mechanisms, to induce reform and innovation among educational institutions, and to promote partnerships among educational institutions and the ICT industry.

The telecommunications infrastructure has been attractive to private investors, particularly mobile telecommunications, and most recently, the broadband.

Removing regulatory obstacles to competition can harness private sector and FDI to help meet public policy objectives of extending access. Market-based approaches have proven effective for leveraging the financial resources and operational expertise of the private sector to meet public policy goals of growth and universal access. However, in many rural and remote areas, market forces are not adequate to meet economic and social goals, and public financing may be used to provide competitive subsidies or form PPPs. Chapter 9 shows some approaches to developing and financing a dynamic and inclusive information infrastructure. The design and implementation of PPPs and competitive subsidies will require innovative approaches to tailor the solutions to the context and needs.

In Chapter 10 on inclusive access, we touched on some of the innovative means of financing deliberate national strategies for telecenter programs. Many telecenters were developed through organic means or pilots, one at a time, with financial help from foreign donors, aid agencies, foundations, and/or NGOs. Many faced sustainability problems. Experience with telecenters shows that financial sustainability is essential to scaling up and is most likely when partnerships among public, private, and civil society sectors are formed and used to leverage their relevant financial and non-financial resources. Universal service funds are being leveraged for rural community access. Franchise business models are incorporating key replicable elements: business and financial planning templates that can be adapted to local conditions, a set of proven technology solutions, a common marketing package, and packaged training for rural entrepreneurs and for customers (Chapter 10). The telecenter development movement is still young, and experimentation with business models, financing and PPPs is warranted to extend access, expand the range of value-added content and services, and enhance the livelihood of rural populations.

Developing countries are sensitive and vulnerable to world-wide economic downturns and financial cycles and these can have disastrous effects on FDI flows, venture capital, private participation in infrastructure, and investments in telecommunications, and e-Transformation. But some e-development programs require more upfront investment and steady and predictable funding over the medium term, as in e-government programs. Government budgetary practices are inflexible and tend to reinforce the silo mentality of sectoral ministries—not amenable to capturing the synergies among investments or crosscutting dimensions of e-Transformation. Financing mechanisms have to be created for the integration of ICT into the different sectors and socio-economic structures.

As discussed in Chapter 12, for example, financing e-government investments is particularly challenging for developing countries, given the scarce local resources and pressing and competing development priorities. Time horizons are particularly short, in view of political and economic uncertainties. Accordingly, governments often rely on ad hoc injections of public funding or donor support to launch e-government initiatives.

The relative scarcity or abundance of budget support makes a large difference to the ability of the government to innovate and transform. Finding appropriate ways to transfer this upfront development costs to the private sector, through public–private partnerships, is one way to reduce the burden on taxpayers. Some governments have engaged in PPPs, for example, for their portals, particularly at the state and local levels.

The budget remains a powerful tool for implementation of coordination, innovation, and integration of new technologies in the public sector. Budgeting for ICT and e-development more broadly, should be institutionalized and adapted to technological requirements. Even though institutions play a decisive role in designing, funding, and implementing e-development strategies and programs, they are often treated as an afterthought. Some countries have ignored the need to create umbrella agencies to coordinate highly interdependent e-development investments. Others have lacked a clear division of responsibilities between various government agencies and other partners, creating political and bureaucratic obstacles for e-development implementation, and inhibiting the proper allocation of resources and policy coordination across stakeholders. Yet others have over-centralized e-development and e-government investments under single agencies or ministries, contributing to a separation between ICT investment decisions and mainstream development issues.

Governments, supported by donors, have often resorted to creating project implementation units to control new investment programs, including e-government and other elements of e-development. The underlying assumption is that e-development development is a one-off project or a blueprint that can be designed by international consultants, and subsequently implemented by a temporary project implementation unit created specifically to follow the accountability and governance requirements of the donor. Lacking a vision of the leadership and institutional capabilities required for sustainable development, such project implementation units often suck capacity out of or crowd out (rather than complement) weak state capacity (Fukuyama, 2004). The new entities may also duplicate the functions of existing donors. Different aid agencies may work with different ministries and place their funding and project implementation units within those ministries—reinforcing isolation, fragmentation, and duplication of information infrastructures and e-government applications. To reinforce a perception of control and accountability, aid agencies have also sought to design e-development programs in details, very much as a straightjacket or blueprint to be implemented by the newly created project implementation units.

But e-Transformation is a process, not a one-time event or a rigid blueprint. It is a continuous process of policy development, investment planning, innovation, learning, and change management (Fountain 2001; Ramsey 2004). This process must fit with and respond to a dynamic development strategy that supports evolving national goals and creates sustained institutional reforms and public service improvements. The challenge is to build effective governance and institutional frameworks for ICT-enabled modernization and make the new competencies part of the country's human and institutional resources. Rather than seeking agreements on rigid plans and multi-year investments in separate systems and infrastructures, the focus may shift to institutionalizing budgetary process improvements and financing frameworks. E-development funding would be integrated into the medium-term budgetary framework of the public sector. A funding strategy for e-Transformation would also integrate other sources of funding from the private sector, NGOs, and aid agencies.

The World Bank-aided e-Sri Lanka program is an example of a flexible, programmatic approach to financing e-development (Hanna 2007a, 2008). In general, the Bank and other aid agencies prefer a rigid blueprint plan for investment projects, particularly for new areas of lending (Hanna and Picciotto, 2002). Upfront detailed design is considered an effective way to reduce risks and secure control and accountability for the funding agency. However, in this case, resistance to programmatic flexibility in financing e-development was overcome, in recognition of the many unknowns and uncertainties in upfront-design of investment programs in new and dynamic areas. In e-Sri Lanka, e-government is financed on a programmatic basis, not upfront-defined systems. Similarly, with the telecenters, they are financed as a program, not single centers. Innovation or competitive funds have been also created to stimulate innovations, partnerships, and grassroots initiatives for promoting software services and ITES and societal applications. These initiatives are generated on demand and throughout the life of the program. Emphasis was put on building the capacity of local institutions, local participation, and the creation of a national ICT agency to secure continuous investment planning and adaptation.

Korea shows another example for strategic, yet flexible, funding for e-Transformation. It deployed a central fund to move relatively quickly toward e-Transformation (Box 15.2). The informatization promotion fund is a special vehicle to overcome the rigidities of the annual budget and promote multi-year, cross-agencies e-government programs. It included both public and private financing.

Box 15.2 Korea's Flexible Financing for e-Development Initiatives

The promotion of ICT adoption in government and overall economy requires large-scale and long-term investments and cooperation across government agencies. So, it is difficult to carry out these projects within the general budget of Korea. The Informatization Promotion Fund (IPF) was established in 1996 as a special vehicle to overcome the budgetary rigidities and promote e-government projects across agencies. This provided a flexible financing mechanism for e-development initiatives.

The goals of the IPF are to roll out broadband networks, promote e-government projects, educate workers, and support R&D and standardization in ICT in a holistic approach to government and economic transformation. The fund, based on government budgetary and private sector contributions, promotes the use of profits from ICT fields to be rechanneled into the ICT sector. From 1993 to 2002, the IPF reached US $7.8 billion, with 40% coming from the government budget. A total of US $5.3 billion was invested in between 1994- 2003. The fund is managed by the Ministry of Information and Communication (overall), the Institute of Information Technology Assessment (specific project management), and the Fund Management Council (evaluation). The chair of the council is the vice minister of the MIC, and its members are members and directors general of related ministries.

The IPF played a key role in the balanced and flexible promotion of e-development (informatization) policy to create demand for ICT and to promote supply through the ICT industry.

Source: Adapted from Suh and Chen, 2007. p. 92.

Managing for Results Through Monitoring, Evaluation, and Learning

A review of e-strategies suggests that countries at all income levels and regions perform poorly in their use of M&E (World Bank, 2006). The majority of these strategies say little about institutions or processes to monitor and evaluate progress and secure timely learning and adjustments. Even among those with specific M&E plans, fewer provide plans for financing these M&E activities. And among those providing budgetary details for M&E, most are dependent on one-off funding from aid agencies.

Given the fast change in ICT and in the innovations needed to exploit them, traditional monitoring and evaluation systems will not be adequate for the task. National strategies should develop more agile learning systems to assess progress and adapt programs in time. Such learning systems should address the needs of all stakeholders at all levels, including intended beneficiaries. They should not be driven by donors' demands for accountability and data-intensive methodologies. Given the lag in producing development outcomes, participatory and continuous evaluation will be necessary. Measuring impact in the rural areas may include rapid rural appraisal and participatory rural appraisal and other related rapid assessment methodologies designed to listen and learn from stakeholders and beneficiaries at the local level (Blackburn et al., 2002).

Monitoring and evaluation of e-development programs should go beyond measuring progress in connectivity or roll out of technology. E-readiness assessments, ICT statistics and monitoring, and performance indicators have been too focused on ICT inputs than development outcomes. The benefits of the new technologies are the result of not only increased connectivity and access to ICT tools, but more importantly the facilitation of new types of development solutions and economic opportunities that ICT makes possible. Benefits come from a number of interrelated factors: human capacity, business-friendly environment, locally relevant content, and accountable institutions.

A focus on development outcomes or Millennium Development Goals (MDGs) needs to be reflected in the monitoring and evaluation processes of national e-strategies. This means increased focus of M&E systems on measuring development impact and progress on using ICT as enabler to realize these outcomes, not just as a sector. This will pose methodological challenges to evaluators, since it would cover the impact on almost every sector, as well as the role of ICT in strengthening the enabling conditions to achieve the MDGs such as transparency, partnership, and broad participation. As many upstream linkages between ICT and development outcomes are either conditional on several factors or poorly understood, M&E frameworks may benefit from theory-based evaluation methods, that is, making explicit the causal chains then testing them empirically through comprehensive monitoring and evaluation. This approach can play a crucial role in educating policy makers about the potential role of ICT. It can also enhance international support for ICT role in development. This is one way for monitoring and evaluation practices to support learning and speed up the journey of e-Transformation toward a truly global information society.

M&E indicators should reflect the sequencing of strategy objectives, starting upstream from policy objectives like diversifying the economy or improving educational outcomes to downstream specific outcomes of e-strategy initiatives and actions (Fig. 15.2; World Bank, 2005a, pp 47–63). The World Bank has launched a toolkit to integrate M&E indicators into a logical framework. At the top level of the logframe are the development impacts of policy goals of the country, and this in turn should determine the outcome indicators for the strategic priorities of e-strategy (second level). The third level considers output indicators of key initiatives,

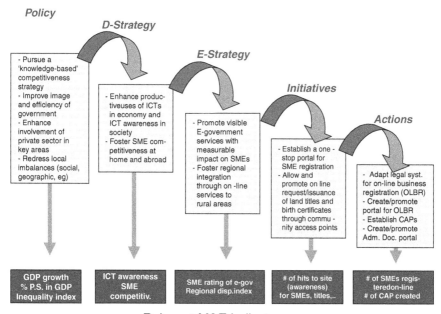

Fig. 15.2 Integrating M&E into e-Development process (adapted from Lanvin, in World Bank, 2005a)

the fourth level considers deliverables of key actions, and the base level considers inputs and resources required to implement e-strategy. Such conceptual frameworks could be helpful in systematizing and improving M&E indicators and practices. But advance will be conditional on country commitment to adapt such frameworks to their local conditions, clarifying causal links within specific local contexts, and to provide concrete examples of using such frameworks for strategic choice and learning.

A possible pitfall is to overdesign M&E systems and generate massive and expensive data collections and surveys that remain unutilized. Several factors may contribute to this. Current national statistical systems do not capture much information of the ICT sector or e-readiness indictors, let alone possible linkages to development outcomes and impacts. Traditional enterprise and household surveys, among others, do little to cover ICT inputs or to inform the design of e-strategies. Many e-strategies initiatives have little precedent to go by, making it difficult for stakeholders to agree on indicators or to grasp the scale of required inputs and resources. All these factors argue for massive efforts to improve M&E systems for e-strategies. They may be further reinforced by the concerns of aid agencies to provide evidence of ICT impact and secure accountability for the increasing resources being allocated to ICT investments within development projects and for free-standing ICT projects.

The pitfall of premature introduction of overly complex M&E systems can be costly as it would divert resources away from more practical and timely learning that comes from simple, homegrown, locally owned solutions. It can also delay the design and introduction of M&E at early stages of the design or implementation of e-strategies. Alternative approaches should leverage the capacity of established M&E agencies and networks, including those of ICT-using sectors. They may also introduce e-strategy and ICT-related indicators into ongoing household and enterprise surveys and others being conducted by the National Statistical Offices. M&E instruments for e-strategies should be made as compatible as possible with existing M&E instruments for the whole development strategy of the country so as to reinforce linkages with national development objectives and avoid perception of ICT as a fad or a distraction from development. Simple and transparent M&E systems are also more comprehensible and useable by local stakeholders (including government agencies, NGOs, and academia) as well as external partners (investors, donors).

One strategic choice in institutionalizing monitoring and evaluation is whether to embed this capacity into the implementation structures for e-development, or to locate it at the highest policy levels, independent of the implementing agencies. A common pitfall is taking an either/or choice. Monitoring and evaluation capabilities are needed at many levels of e-development strategy development and implementation. Embedding M&E into implementation structures is important to leverage existing capacity, access to data, ownership and learning. Having M&E capacity at the highest and independent levels is important to secure oversight and accountability, authority and influence to make course corrections, and perhaps promote more focus on development outcomes. A balance may be established between self-evaluation (internal to implementing agencies) and independent (external) evaluation systems. This should take account of the prevailing governance mechanisms, political culture, and best practices in the country.

Two African countries present contrasting examples of M&E structures. Mozambique has created projects that focus on data gathering and analysis as standalone initiatives of its e-strategy. In contrast, Rwanda's e-strategy laid out the institutional responsibilities for M&E and how M&E activities would be integrated in all levels of the implementation machinery. The Rwanda model combines implementation-level ownership of M&E—the Rwanda International and Technology Authority and various Plan Execution and Coordination Committees—with executive level oversight—the National Information Technology Commission, headed by the President, the national ICT champion (Adamali et al., 2006).

Monitoring and evaluation systems should be viewed as strategic tools for the design, implementation, and adaptation of e-Transformation strategies. To do so, monitoring and evaluation should be designed and incorporated into e-development thinking at the earliest stages. They should evolve over time in line with local capacity and the level of ICT advance and usage in the economy. Viewed accordingly, they can become powerful instruments for learning and adaptation and can make e-strategies more meaningful to all stakeholders.

Chapter 16
Lessons and Future Directions

e-Transformation is a long-term challenge for all developing countries—a profound reform and change process that countries must undergo to both exploit the new opportunities arising from the ongoing technological revolution and cope with the imperatives of competing in an increasingly fast-paced, innovation-driven global economy. All countries are still at early stages of mastering this new techno-economic paradigm. Emerging experience in the design and implementation of national e-strategies shows that the development impact of ICT investments has varied as a function of many factors, and these factors should guide future directions.

The focus of this concluding chapter is on emerging lessons concerning e-Transformation. In earlier chapters, I have identified some of the key issues and lessons concerning each element of e-development, and some of the links or inter-dependencies between each element and the overall e-development process. Each component of e-development can thrive and be effective only when its ecosystem is also made viable and sustainable. For example, telecenters are effective and sustainable only when complemented with content, e-government services, affordable communication infrastructure, supportive e-policies. Similarly, examples of ITES and e-government were shown to be dependent on complementary e-development initiatives.[1] The focus here, however, has to be selective and focused on those lessons most relevant to the holistic approach to ICT in development that I have advocated throughout this book. The aim is to maximize the developmental and transformational impact of ICT.

I thus conclude with the 10 broad lessons that should guide future thrusts for e-Transformation strategies:

1. Integrating ICT as the enabler of new development strategies
2. Pursuing a holistic approach: leveraging synergies and scale

---

[1]Research has focused on the complementary relationships between ICT and organizational investments to bring about productivity growth and e-Transformation at the organization level (for example, Brynolfsson, 2009); this book focuses on the relationships among all elements of e-development to bring about e-Transformation at the country or regional level (see Chapter 4 for the holistic e-development framework).

N.K. Hanna, *e-Transformation: Enabling New Development Strategies*, Innovation, Technology, and Knowledge Management, DOI 10.1007/978-1-4419-1185-8_16, © Springer Science+Business Media, LLC 2010

3. Pursuing quick wins within long-term perspectives: focusing, prioritizing, and managing portfolios
4. Understanding the political economy: engaging stakeholders, building coalitions, managing expectations
5. Addressing the soft aspects of transformation: shaping institutions, leadership and culture
6. Building strategic partnerships
7. Balancing strategic direction with local initiative and innovation
8. Building local capabilities for an adaptive learning process
9. Adopting integrated and tailored approaches to equity
10. Promoting regional and global collaboration

This chapter briefly covers these broad lessons and directions. It concludes with some issues concerning the role of aid agencies in adopting e-Transformation and moving ICT into mainstream thinking and practice of economic development.

Integrating ICT as the Enabler of New Development Strategies

It is urgent to begin thinking strategically about the links between ICT and development, with an accent on development opportunities. National ICT strategies are evolving from an exclusive focus on ICT infrastructure- or industry-centered approaches to one that enables the transformation of the economy by deploying ICT across all key sectors. A telecom or ICT-led approach often leaves other actors in passive roles and runs the risk of being supply driven. Most of the potential benefits of ICT come from its diffusion and effective use throughout the economy.

e-Transformation is no longer the domain of few countries with advanced ICT industry or knowledge-intensive economy. By harnessing ICT with complementary investments in institutional change and human capital—to build on their comparative advantages and pursue their development goals—all countries can participate in this techno-economic paradigm and position themselves for a transformed global economy.

E-development is about transformation. But, transformation for what or to what aim? Countries may answer this question in two ways: in terms of preparing and positioning themselves for a changing global economy, where increasing premium is put on agility, innovation, and knowledge-based competition; and in terms of using ICT to transform institutions and development programs in ways that would enable them to realize development goals most effectively.

This transformation should be guided by clear national development goals and informed public debate. Much of the characteristics and ultimate impacts of this transformation process are uncertain or unknown at present, same as past transformational impacts of electricity and modern transport were not fully understood upfront. In the case of ICT, the pace and scope of change have been unprecedented, and the possible paths and options for transformation are likely to be very broad. For some countries, this debate may consider broader options than strategies for economic competitiveness. It may involve issues of open information society, participatory development, and national identity, or what kind of a society would be possible and desirable in a globally networked economy.

E-development assumes that the use of technology in society and economy is a development policy issue, not a pure technology issue. It is not just about a technology-determined environment, but about economically, socially, politically, and culturally constructed one. Policy makers and ICT ministers should jointly ask Internet for what? E-government for what? A tool for freedom or control? An economy for the few or the many? They need to start from a desired future state: a competitive market-based economy? An inclusive, self-organizing information society? An open and transparent governance? Answers to these questions should guide ICT policy and investment interventions.

e-Transformation strategies should thus be deeply rooted into overall national development objectives and priorities to bring about their desirable impact. Increasingly, the global economy requires companies and countries to focus and specialize in their areas of core competencies or comparative advantage. For developing countries, ICT deployment should begin by identifying areas where e-Transformation would have a critical impact on development goals and on creating new competencies or dynamic competitive advantages. Chile may be a relatively successful case of thinking through this integration (Box 16.1).

Box 16.1 Integrating ICT into the Chilean Strategy for Development

The inception of the Internet and the constellation of innovations that accompanies it have been perceived by the Chilean Government as a great opportunity to advance its strategic agenda for development. New technologies are not granted magical capability in development. Rather, the Government aims to integrate ICT into the development agenda and allow technology to find its way in different sectors of society. The Government views the future challenge is to determine how ICT introduces threats to national competitiveness, but especially to open up opportunities.

The focal points of ICT integration into the development agenda included:

- An efficient state oriented to address citizens' needs (e-services, e-procurement, e-taxes)
- An economy integrated into the world (e-trade, e-customs, G2B services, R&D)
- A highly dynamic services sector (offshoring)
- An equitable nation (e-schools)
- A nation prepared for the future (e-policies, telecom policy, university network)

In year 2000, a new president gave a major impulse to digital issues, drawing on a presidential commission representing all relevant sectors of society: government, parliament, civilians and academic world and the involvement of more than 100 experts in a 7-months debate. He also headed a public–private mission to Silicon Valley and created the Ministerial Committee on ICT to promote policies and initiatives for human resources, information development, e-commerce, e-government, ICT and content industry, and inclusive Internet access; and to accelerate the social learning process associated with the use of networks, and the digital diffusion of education and culture. The digital agenda was further deepened and institutionalized in 2003 so as to achieve:

- Widely available access, including community broadband access at schools, Info-centers, and Cyber-cafes, using the private sector, with the government subsidizing remote and rural areas, low-income communities and microenterprises.
- Integration of ICT in education and training, beyond just connectivity, using digital technologies as a learning resource for the curriculum and the classroom, and investing in digital content, advanced teacher training, and spread of better practices.
- Evenly transformed government, beyond to online services, to transform back office processes, integrate services, accelerate digital development at local government levels, integrate the public sector with broadband networks, and improve security of transactions.
- Digital development for business, with e-trade, government to business applications, and the wide use of private and public e-marketplace.
- Dynamic ICT industry, by promoting quality standards and collaboration among companies, universities and research centers.
- Advanced legal framework for the digital economy.

The government continues to broaden and deepen the integration agenda, as new challenges arise:

- In the human resource development, internationalization of services calls for a major change in the education of professionals. A key challenge is to increase the flexibility of education modalities and the dynamism of educational institutions, and the availability of digital content in Spanish language and the lack of international collaboration here.
- In international competitiveness, Chilean enterprises in the services in general and ICT in particular are small and being challenged by globalization. A key challenge is to promote standards and international partnerships.
- In government, there is still a huge potential for public value generation by integrating ICT for back office process transformation. Several

> challenges face current e-government programs: rigidities in labor reg-
> ulations, use of outsourcing mechanisms, and balancing the need for
> innovation at the agency level to maximize public value, with the need
> for demand consolidation, systems integration and standardization to
> exploit economies of scale.
>
> For Chile, ICT is a set of instruments to realize a national development
> strategy, to promote growth, equality and democracy.
>
> Source: Alvarez, 2006.

Accordingly, ICT strategy would not be an "add-on" to development thinking, to be determined after a national development strategy has been already designed. Rather, ICT would be jointly explored with other fundamental factors of development and systematically integrated into all promising sectors and programs. This integration process may go beyond exploiting opportunities to automate or increase the efficiency of ongoing programs, and toward changing the very business models or core processes of these sectors and programs. This integration may also deepen the goals of development, to empower individuals and expand substantive freedoms (Sen, 2000).

But how can governments at all levels insert ICT into their thinking and designing of their overall development strategies? This is a common challenge with no standard answer. Some insights may come from private sector experience with integrating ICT into corporate or business strategy. This integration has enabled some business leaders to use ICT to innovate new business models. In similar ways, effective integration of ICT and development strategies promises to create new development models.

Much has been learned about integrating ICT into corporate or business strategies and bridging the gap between business and technology leaders. Accordingly, ICT strategy and governance flow from strategic intent and competitive stance (or in the case of not-for-profit sector, the mission and positioning of services). The ICT strategy is also guided by the corporate approach to governance and to coordination among its business units, and the type of human resource capabilities necessary for the business strategy. Many enterprises have been developing clear ICT governance mechanisms to synchronize ICT strategy and business strategy, and their corresponding investments. These governance mechanisms define the various ICT domains in which decisions need to be made, who makes decisions and has input in each ICT domain, and the institutional mechanisms or committees used to implement these joint ICT–business decisions (Broadbent and Kitzis, 2005, pp. 111–127).

Private sector experience also shows that ICT–business integration will not be a one-time transformation event or a blueprint action plan. Rather, public leaders will need to shape expectations and set the governance mechanisms (through budgets,

ICT investment decision rights) to continuously weave ICT strategies into development processes. In Korea and Singapore, for example, the head of government, the
ministry of finance, and all key sectoral ministries are fully engaged in the shaping of the knowledge economy and e-development strategy. Similarly, the national
ICT agency or its equivalent should be engaged with other agencies in formulating
poverty reduction and growth strategies, and with the various sectoral ministries in
shaping their sectoral transformation or e-sector strategies.

At times, this integration process may be carried out in sequence, first to develop
the overall development or sector strategy, then to draw implications for a supportive e-development or e-sector strategy. A more fundamental approach would
consider both strategic development options and the possibilities now opened with
ICT in a joint and interactive manner so as to imagine and pursue new development
paths and transformation possibilities. This approach requires technology-aware,
savvy, and committed leadership. I also require enhanced domain knowledge from
ICT leaders—knowledge of development paths, growth opportunities, and reform
options. This calls for deliberate co-evolution of ICT and development strategies
(Chapter 1).

Integrating ICT into development at the national and local levels is a process
of social learning and transformation, and thus requires intensive communication of vision-shared, progress-made, development outcomes realized and lessons
learned—to broad and varied audiences. Unfortunately, reviews of e-strategies
show that communication processes are often neglected in e-strategy development
and implementation. Awareness building and communication campaigns among all
concerned stakeholders are essential to organic mainstreaming and decentralized
integration of ICT into development activities. They are also necessary to develop
the competencies of development agents to appropriate the new technologies and do
their own ICT-enabled transformation of their own roles and functions, as managers,
teachers, or civil servants.

Promising practices include preparing leaders at all levels to communicate the
e-Transformation vision, the use of multimedia campaigns, and the engagement of
many stakeholders through various working groups in shaping the vision and programs. In Chapter 12 we discussed stakeholder analysis and communication audit
as tools to mobilize and communicate with diverse stakeholders for government
transformation. These tools are equally applicable to the whole e-Transformation
process.

Community-driven development and experiences with participatory development
also point to ways for integrating ICT into local development. Such integration
should be easier to carry out at the local level, where bureaucratic silos can be
bridged and practical needs of information and communication can be made more
concrete and specific. The challenge here is that most communities do not yet
have familiarity or the experiential knowledge with the possibilities of the new
technology. Policies, institutions, innovation funds, and other e-development mechanisms should allow for sufficient flexibility, experimentation, social learning, and
socio-technical adaptation at the local to facilitate ICT-enabled, locally driven
development. New breeds of barefoot infomediaries, local e-champions, telecenter

managers, and ICT-savvy NGOs will also need to be integrated into the local development leadership teams.

Adopting a Holistic Approach: Leveraging Synergies and Scale

E-development is about thinking and acting holistically to take account of critical interdependencies to maximize development impact and sustainability, yet investing selectively, to focus resources, leverage strategic entry points, and move up the learning ladder. Orchestrating the key elements of e-development over time can bring about a powerful and sustainable development dynamics.

Integrated approaches are needed to exploit the systems and network effects by partnering among stakeholders and co-investing in complementary resources. Holistic approaches would also address the necessary institutional and regulatory adjustments to realize ICT benefits. Proceeding with ICT applications in isolation fails to assist countries to set priorities, identify cross-sectoral linkages, reuse modules across government agencies, share multipurpose access centers, and sequence interdependent investments. They also miss on developing and utilizing scarce human, financial, and infrastructural resources across sectors.

As argued throughout this book, elements of e-development are interdependent. Content providers cannot operate without infrastructure suppliers. E-government cannot be inclusive and sustainable without a critical mass of users, and in turn, unless e-literacy, relevant content, affordable connectivity, and delivery channels are developed at the same time. Programs that manage to orchestrate various elements of e-development and bring together partners with diverse and complementary competences can deliver significant and sustainable developmental impact. Synergies create virtuous cycles in which initial government and private investments attract significant investments by other interested parties.

Each element of e-development is effective and sustainable only when a healthy ecosystem or critical success factors are secured. For example, the ICT services industry is only possible to thrive when several appropriate ingredients are combined such as enabling environment, human resources, communication infrastructure (Chapter 8). Accordingly, industrial policy that promotes that ICT industry would be viewed as a process of strategic collaboration between the public and private sectors, with the aim to identify synergies, linkages, and blockages to new activities and capabilities and to design appropriate policies in response. Similarly, improving rural access attracts content developers and service providers, which, in turn, increases the demand for infrastructure solutions and helps secure the financial sustainability of rural telecenters (Chapter 10).

Understanding of the economies of scale on the supply and demand side is essential to practicing a holistic approach to e-Transformation. Economies of scale on the supply side are better understood as they have been a major driver of the industrial economy. They will continue to play a key role in building the pillars of e-Transformation. They offer opportunities to share information infrastructure (including broadband) and access to ICT, consolidate data centers, share information systems development, develop a critical mass of skilled human resources, and expand local capacity to produce and adapt ICT products and services.

However, the new information economy is also increasingly driven by demand-side economies of scale or network economics (Shapiro and Varian, 1999). The value of connecting to a network depends on the number of people already connected to it. This fundamental value proposition goes under many names: network effects, network externalities, positive feedback, and demand-side economies of scale. Technologies subject to strong network effects tend to exhibit long lead times followed by explosive growth: as the installed base of users grows, the benefit for the users increases, and more and more users find adoption worthwhile. Once a critical mass of customer base is achieved, the market builds on itself with positive feedback and demonstration effects. Such adoption dynamics point to the importance of pooling demand, forming demand alliances, promoting open networks and standards, and investing in e-literacy to create critical mass and significant positive feedback as early as possible.

There are many examples where supply-side and demand-side economies of scale combine to make positive feedback in network economy and e-Transformation especially strong. Aggregation of delivery channels or integration of services can augment demand for broadband infrastructure, last mile connectivity, and content development to offer a broader range of value-added services to clients (Chapter 9). Telecenters can become multipurpose, aggregating demand for e-government and e-business services and e-society literacy and capacity building programs (Chapter 10). Collaboration across government agencies could also help realize economies of scale in ICT procurement and skills development and augment demand for local ICT industry services (Chapter 12). Government e-procurement, e-trade networks, and customs modernization can be designed in such ways as to promote broad adoption of ICT-enabled business practices, among SMEs, and thus create pools of skills and core competencies for a networked economy (Chapter 13).

The e-Transformation of each sector of government, business, and community depends on the four pillars discussed in Section II: enabling public policies, appropriately developed human resources, competitive ICT sector, and dynamic and inclusive information infrastructure. For example, the health and education sectors are potential targets for reform and transformation in most developing countries. But progress in each sector critically depends on appropriate balancing and sequencing of these pillars.

Unfortunately, holistic approaches do not come naturally to governments, politicians, policy makers, or business actors. E-development creates significant coordination challenges. Short-term political cycles and government budgetary practices tend to reinforce the short term and thus miss the synergies and interdependencies whose impact become evident only over the longer term. Turf and silo mentality often dominates the behavior of public bureaucracies. Policy makers' awareness and understanding of system-wide interactions and of opportunities to realize supply- and demand-side economies of scale are also low. Leadership, policies, and institutions to bring about integration are missing, especially for new and crosscutting dimensions of development as e-Transformation.

How can countries discover and manage these interdependencies among various elements of e-development over time? How can they tap synergies? How can they overcome local barriers to coordination and integration? What are the promising practices?

Some promising approaches may include developing leadership, shared vision, and coordinating institutions; engaging stakeholders, forming coalitions, and promoting cross-sectoral collaboration; using the budget, M&E systems, and other incentives to manage key interdependencies among investments in e-Transformation; having major users such as government become lead users and drivers of e-Transformation; and/or pursuing integrated e-development at the local level.

Leaders and e-leadership institutions are essential to integrating and orchestrating the various elements of e-Transformation (Box 16.2). As discussed in Chapter 6 on institutions, most advanced e-Transformation programs have been initiated by presidential commissions led by central cross-sectoral ministries such as finance, planning or economy, or powerful coordination agencies for ICT and information society. Public–private councils and CIO councils provide a critical link in integrating ICT across sectors and sharing best practices on a continuous basis.

Box 16.2 Role of Vision, Leadership, and Institutions in Managing Interdependencies

A holistic and energizing vision, owned and communicated by policy makers, and widely shared and pursued by e-leadership institutions is perhaps the most powerful tool to discovering synergies and managing interdependencies across the e-development system. Through their compelling visions, leaders provide meaning and direction in a chaotic and fast changing world. They bridge boundaries, promote collaboration, model risk, and help others discover and shape the future (Hanna, 2007b).

Leadership and coordination mechanisms must be institutionalized to capture emerging interdependencies and tap synergistic opportunities on a continuing basis. Some interdependencies can be anticipated, planned for, and leveraged upfront in well-integrated polices and investment programs. Others cannot be anticipated and would emerge or be discovered and tapped over time. The quality and competency of these leaders, institutions, and networks determine the capacity to leverage synergies and manage interdependencies for e-Transformation over time.

E-leaders and e-Transformation institutions may also engage the stakeholders in the process of discovering and harnessing these synergies and complementarities. Capturing interdependencies and opportunities to realize economies of scale is not purely an analytical process or the product of a comprehensive program design. This is as much a product of engendering a shared vision of a new paradigm of development, appreciating the size of opportunity to be realized, signaling mutual commitments for transformation, and engaging all stakeholders in identifying appropriate policies and processes that can help them achieve their collective goals.

Political, public, and business leaders may engage stakeholders in the process of forming partnerships and leveraging their complementary assets and competencies to further compete in the global knowledge economy and bridge the digital divide. Government may signal its commitment to a holistic vision of e-Transformation, prime the pump with its demand as lead user of ICT, and invite stakeholders to co-invest in national information infrastructures and human resources, and other pillars of e-development. Various agencies may collaborate on developing common strategies for shared information infrastructures, integrated citizen services channels, common training programs and certification standards, and frameworks for interoperability. Industry, government, and academic institutions may collaborate to broaden the talent pool for both ICT suppliers and users. This is a social learning process. Some countries are more predisposed to collaboration than others. But most can learn to partner more effectively.

Government budgetary practices can be a powerful tool for promoting integration and collaboration. In countries like Mexico, budget inflexibility and the lack of mechanisms for joint funding across organizations were considered an important barrier to collaboration (OECD, 2005b). Other OECD governments have created budgetary mechanisms and other incentives for collaboration. These incentives include the use of collaboration as a measure for performance, and the provision of special funds for cross-agency projects.

Feedback, monitoring, and evaluation mechanisms are important means to detect gaps and assess complementarities during the implementation of e-Transformation strategies. Monitoring and evaluation systems of ICT programs typically focus on each element of e-development in isolation. Following a holistic approach, they should extend their coverage to capture the potential linkages among these elements and thus exploit supply- and demand-side economies of scale. Focusing on results and developing channels for feedback from various stakeholders can improve understanding of these linkages. They can be designed to capture key ingredients for thriving ecosystems, detect lagging sectors, and guide the search for synergies. Discovering and experiencing various modes of integration can also become a part of institutional and social learning.

The government can play a lead role as a strategic user and driver of e-Transformation. Development of common government–citizen–business portals, for example, can create advanced forms of coordination and identify gaps and duplications in existing information and services. By setting standards and adopting service-oriented architectures and common platforms, government also develops ecosystems and opportunities for collaboration among suppliers and public agencies.

The above challenges in managing complementarities and taping synergies within an integrated view of e-development suggest it may be easier to pursue a holistic approach at the local levels. Some good examples of advanced coordination and integrated e-development are emerging, as in some states of India and Brazil. This decentralized approach to e-Transformation can lend itself to local ownership and effective integration with ongoing local development programs. It can also provide successful models for integration for other states and for scaling up to the federal level. In large and diverse countries, however, holistic approaches can and should be pursued at many levels.

Focusing, Prioritizing, and Managing Portfolios: Pursuing Quick Wins Within Long-Term Perspectives

A holistic approach to ICT-enabled development does not mean attempting to transform all regions and sectors of a country at the same time. A mutually supporting advance in ICT integration across a broad range of sectors can produce balanced development and a critical mass of users. However, a uniform and even advance across sectors is not always possible, as public and private actors will adapt to the new roles and processes at different pace. Change and innovation often arise in specific clusters, locations, or sectors, enabled by a critical mass of leadership, talent, partnerships, and resources. A comprehensive e-Transformation program, applied evenly and rigidly across all sectors, may thus risk holding back initiatives and progress among the leaders, reformers, pioneers, and innovators, while prematurely push for costly change among the lagers. Alternatively, an adaptive, holistic approach would constitute a shaping and enabling strategy to support local efforts and pioneering agencies. The role of national leadership, public, and private is to support agents of change, leverage entry points, scale up success, and diffuse best practices.

Holistic approaches need to be flexible and adaptable in light of experience. They need to tailor the ingredients of e-development to sectoral and institutional contexts. Sectors such as health and education are often resistant to change. Special attention to the attitudes and incentives of physicians, teachers, and civil servants would be important to integrate ICT into their daily routines. Advance is likely to be relatively slow in such sectors, and targeting them for transformation will depend on clear national development priorities.

Focusing scarce resources on exploiting ICT for national priorities usually means selectivity. For example, an e-development strategy may address the special needs and dynamics of promising segments of the ICT industry for export and economy-wide competitiveness. The promotion of the ICT sector to export IT-enabled services has been a popular entry point to more comprehensive e-development. At the same time, e-development may aim to re-orient the national innovation system to meet the substantial and cumulative technological learning requirements of ICT as a general-purpose technology. It may also attract and channel foreign investment into high value-added sectors where ICT is produced or intensively used is a key enabler. ICT in education has also been a common sectoral entry point to IT usage in many countries, reflecting the popular belief that e-literacy and e-education offer significant opportunities for the emerging knowledge economy.

Some sectors may be selected as leading ICT users and then targeted for a holistic e-sector transformation strategy. The logic for such selectivity and sequencing should be explicit. The selected sector may used to stimulate the rest of the economy with the help of forward and backward linkages. In this case, it would be important to demonstrate and secure these forward and backward linkages to the rest of the economy. Alternatively, the selected sectors may be more advanced in terms of e-readiness and sector leadership, and can thus be used for demonstrating early wins and building political support for wider government transformation. National consensus and political commitment on reforming certain sectors may make such sectors good candidates for e-Transformation. Alternatively, global imperatives to meet certain standards of performance that rely on intensive use of ICT may be the driver of e-Transformation in certain sectors or functions of the economy, as is the case in banking, customs, and trade facilitation. The challenge for policy makers and e-Transformation strategists is to sequence, link, and leverage these entry points or leading sectors for learning, diffusion, and network effects, to the benefit of other sectors of the economy.

e-Transformation demands balancing progress for the near term—tapping windows of opportunities and quick wins—with a steady but often not easily visible advance toward long-term fundamental objectives—requiring clear focus and consistent strategic intent. e-Transformation is for the long haul, and developing countries have limited human and financial resources available to meet growing challenges and competing needs. National e-development action plans should therefore focus and prioritize interventions to tap synergies and deliver maximum developmental results within constrained resources.

Early learning and demonstration effects of quick wins can help build commitment and capacity for policy reforms and institutional change. Quick wins can build confidence and momentum, while small projects allow organizational learning at low cost and risk. For example, giving early priority to public services with the largest number of potential users and beneficiaries can help sustain commitment to and demand for continual improvement. Funding a variety of grassroots initiatives can further provide demonstration effects and tangible benefits and thus build and sustain coalitions for reform. But major fast-track projects should be pursued within a holistic and sustainable e-development strategy.

A portfolio combining quick wins and foundational investments for e-Transformation should strike a balance between short- and long-term priorities, pursued within political, financial, and human resources constraints. For example, within e-government programs, some quick-win proposals could be attractive because they promise to expose civil servants or the public to new technologies and information-sharing practices—and thus to mobilize demand and change the climate for participation and empowerment. Yet by design, an e-government strategy should also give due attention to major foundational projects as priorities for funding—projects focused on establishing the common infrastructure and architecture for the entire program. Foundational projects take long gestation periods to develop and implement—including the lead time to build relationships with and capabilities of the owners of the new information systems, to map and reengineer business processes, to analyze systems requirements, to design these systems, and to manage the change process.

Prioritization means that "something has got to give," which can make e-development a politically charged process. Governments may put a premium on creating voluntary stakeholder forums, with high-level political support, to build consensus on primary e-development objectives. Ultimately, all the major stakeholders—government institutions, private sector, academia, and civil society—must reach and sustain consensus on these priorities.

Inclusive and consultative approaches to e-development strategy formulation run the risk of producing long wish lists with no priorities attached. Well-intentioned attempts to seek quick wins and make a difference can also absorb scarce institutional and implementation capacities and work against coherent programming and priority setting. Political pressures also support pet projects and reinforce the tendency to add, rather than prioritize (ICT Task Force, 2003). Donors can further frustrate the prioritization process by adding their own priorities. ICT industry suppliers and vendors, local and global, can inform other stakeholders, or alternatively, distort and diffuse national priorities in deploying ICT for development.

To reduce such risks, stakeholders may be engaged in prioritization through participatory budgeting. They may be involved not only in identifying priorities but also in negotiating among priorities and trade-offs within hard budgetary constraints. They may also be engaged in developing solutions to mobilize additional resources. A well-designed and phased program conforming to these priorities would thus encourage new partnerships and mobilize new sources of investments. Consultation may also move beyond obtaining support for stand-alone initiatives and toward enhanced collaboration and partnerships to implement nationally prioritized programs, and shared infrastructures and capabilities. Better understanding of demand and of beneficiary responses to already piloted services should also inform the prioritization and consultation processes.

Understanding the Political Economy: Stakeholders, Coalitions, Expectations

Understanding the political economy is essential to improve governance, policies, and institutions and to enable broad transformation to an inclusive knowledge economy and information society. This means understanding local stakeholders, power structures, and the socio-political context, to set the enabling policy reforms and institutional conditions to sustain transformation. The political orientation of the government is critical in determining the role of the state, the role of other actors, and the scope for reforms and ICT-enabled development.

To illustrate, telecommunication and media reforms are particularly visible and politically demanding (Chapter 9). Designing independent and effective regulatory institutions for telecommunications and broadcasting requires balancing the interests of consumers and suppliers, among others. Creating ecosystems for a vibrant ICT services industry (Chapter 8), sustainable telecenters (Chapter 10), effective e-business diffusion (Chapter 13), and innovative applications for community empowerment (Chapter 14)—all require understanding of the key stakeholders and the political economy. Implementation of e-government strategies is conditioned by the willingness of powerful leaders to share information and knowledge with their populations, the political culture of the country, and social demand for accountability and clean government. Specific applications, such as e-procurement, are essentially about enabling public reforms, increased transparency, and the adoption of new relationships and practices, and thus also demand understanding the political economy (Chapter 12).

Stakeholder analysis should move beyond understanding, toward shaping the design of e-development and influencing stakeholders throughout strategy design and implementation (Chapter 12 and Figure 12.2). It should provide a basis for action—influencing stakeholders, institutionalizing stakeholders' engagement, signaling commitment for reform, building broad ownership, and expanding opportunities for ICT investment. E-development should be policy-setting, action-oriented, shaping strategy. It involves forming and sustaining coalitions. These coalitions may be inclusive of the diverse interests of all the key stakeholders. Alternatively, it may involve organizing potential beneficiaries and building new coalitions to counter powerful anti-reform lobbies, for example, encouraging ICT users among businesses and consumers to form lobbies to counter those representing primary telecommunication carriers and promote competitiveness and innovation.

E-development-enabled reforms may have a noticeable impact in a relatively short time, but their full effect often require consistent and sustained action across all pillars of ICT policies, infrastructure, human resources, and technological learning. For example, putting public services online or via community access centers may significantly alter the relationships between citizens and public service providers. But this reform can be shallow and short lived if not politically sustained to reengineer and integrate core business processes across government agencies. To sustain and deepen such reforms, e-Transformation should be based on understanding the political economy of the country as a whole and on building cross-sector coalitions and national consensus on fundamental change. Reforms can still be pursued incrementally, sequentially, and dynamically, over time, building on success and evidence of impact, and in pace with the emerging national consensus, as has been the cases in China and India.

Occasionally, ICT-enabled development initiatives are spurred by a national economic crisis. Finland's transformation was spurred by such a crisis in 1991 and Korea's in 1997. Both Finland and Korea are examples of concerted consensus building efforts that used institutional mechanisms in place to manage the transition from economic crisis to ICT-enabled knowledge economies. Mobilizing coalitions for e-Transformation can be difficult in the absence of a sense of a crisis.[2] Raising awareness about the increasing demands for competing in global economy may help spur e-Transformation, in the absence of an immediate crisis. This would require engaging different kinds of stakeholders, with an emphasis on vision, opportunities, and sources of growth. Chile has been an interesting example of adopting a future-oriented and opportunity-seeking e-Transformation strategy that built on recent successes and prepared the nation for an unpredictable future with increased global competition.

In many developing countries, coalitions exist in favor of a sector-focused approach. These sectoral or agency-based coalitions are typically reinforced by sector-organized and turf-conscious aid agencies. However, these coalitions could be informed and harnessed in support of the broad diffusion of ICT as enabler of all stakeholders. Moreover, horizontal coalitions should be developed to complement these sectoral coalitions. A shared vision of the role of ICT as enabler of development should help in mobilizing these cross-sectoral coalitions. User-centered coalitions (of farmers, SMEs, women, students, etc.) are typically weak, as they cut across sectors and are seldom organized. They need to be mobilized and linked into coalitions in support of broad-based e-Transformation.

Effective networking and empowerment of such weak but potential important stakeholders are essential to implement e-Transformation. This involves raising their awareness, augmenting their resources, and engendering their commitment to action. It also involves mobilizing coalitions to promote policy and institutional reforms, enabling institutional innovation, and providing opportunities for mutual learning and support for e-leaders. To promote equity and social inclusion, mobilization and networking among marginalized groups of ICT users would be important. Of similar significance would be building such networks and coalitions across sectors and among complementary elements of e-development.

A national e-Transformation strategy should manage expectations about what is possible in using ICT to enable accelerated development. ICT is not a substitute for painful but necessary policy and institutional reforms. Rather, it is a catalyst. The promise of the technology and the enthusiasm it generates can be channeled into reform and action. An e-development strategy should be grounded in objective analysis of needs and constraints, systematic benchmarking, assessments of e-readiness and skills, and learning from past initiatives. It should help set realistic targets and programs within likely resource availabilities within a medium-term expenditure framework.

Changing political contexts is expected to influence priorities across all elements of e-Transformation. E-development programs cannot be disconnected from political horizons or election cycles in the hope of allowing stable priorities and efficient resource management. For example, changes in the governments of Sri Lanka and

---

[2]The current (2008–2009) global financial crisis may provide a spur for economy-wide e-Transformation in the United States and OECD countries, and hopefully in developing countries.

Andhra Pradesh (AP), India, following elections in 2004 led to a new emphasis on rural development and social inclusion. Consequently, ongoing e-development programs had to shift their resources to support accelerated development of rural telecenters in Sri Lanka and rural content and connectivity in AP.

Portfolio management of ICT investment projects is not a purely financial and technical resource management issue—it has political economy dimensions. Lacking immediate and tangible results from foundational projects, political leaders would press for visible quick wins. The need for quick wins is typically reinforced by the political imperatives of weak and embattled governments. Meanwhile, rising expectations and demands are likely to come from communities and agencies to initiate their own new e-government projects and score some quick wins. Aid agencies and other sources of funding may further reinforce local demand for visible and quick wins.

Such demands and opportunities cannot be ignored. Empowering potential reformers and innovators and newly appointed CIOs to act on local initiatives is important. Quick impact projects are necessary to build momentum and sustain political support for a new e-Transformation program. In e-government, for example, these quick wins may include high-priority e-services that are technically simple, have high transaction volume, and involve a large clientele. Response to political pressures for quick results, however, should be gauged so as to avoid diverting substantial financial and technical resources away from fundamental but long-gestating projects.

A political economy perspective is also helpful to develop effective ICT governance and to sustain transformation at the sectoral and specific application levels. Introducing e-procurement into government involves a host of stakeholders, with winners and losers. Deploying ICT to help transform the education and health sectors usually encounters powerful resistance from strong interest groups that currently benefit from poor transparency and accountability. Strategic communications and awareness campaigns through the mass media and other measures to mobilize popular demand are therefore essential ingredients of e-Transformation.

Addressing Soft Aspects of Transformation: Policies, Institutions, Leadership

The ICT revolution is raising many novel policy and governance issues. These range from security and privacy in the digital world to regulation of a converging digital communication infrastructure, to managing new and systemic risks emerging from ICT-enabled financial products and services, such as swap and hedge products and mobile banking (Chapters 2 and 6). Enabling e-Transformation in the health sector, for example, requires establishing new policies or modernizing current policies concerning information sharing of the electronic records of patients. The potential benefits from such sharing are substantial, but polices governing privacy, security, and sharing are essential determinant of success or failure to initiate this transformation and realize the potential benefits.

Similarly, e-finance is creating substantial benefits and returns from new and complex financial products and transactions in highly integrated global markets. Yet, these possibilities could be undermined if the corresponding regulations and governing institutions did not keep pace with the transforming financial sectors, locally and globally. Policies concerning privacy and access may make the difference between the Internet as a tool of bureaucratic control or personal empowerment, a conduit of corporate profits or communal needs (Chapter 2).

e-Transformation is essentially about change and innovation; to bring them about, energizing vision, enabling policy environment, transformational leadership, new institutions and incentives for innovation are needed. New types of policies, institutions, leadership, and cultural practices are needed to build an enabling ecosystem, realize the potential benefits, and sustain the diffusion of transformation processes. Effective use and diffusion of ICT involves a techno-economic paradigm shift that demands profound changes to the socio-institutional context and optimizing the technical and social–institutional aspects of transformation at the same time.

Unfortunately, many national ICT strategies adopt metaphors and models of change that convey technological determinism. The concept of an information "highway" is one. In some countries this has meant giving exclusive attention to heavy investment in telecommunications at the enabler of transformation. The risk of taking this approach, however, is overinvesting in one element of e-development, with the presumption that it is the key binding constraint to e-Transformation. The bias for investing in technological infrastructure is always present in ICT for development programs—as if e-Transformation were an engineering program, determined only by technology. The risk is that, once the connectivity infrastructure is developed far ahead of demand, government may view the infrastructure as a totally built information environment, and the process of transformation to an information society as completed, and may thus cease to address other key diverse and complementary measures of change.

E-government programs as well as business enterprises often adopt technologically deterministic models and exhibit a bias toward under-investing in the soft but critical factors necessary for transformation. Yet, the overwhelming evidence from the successful transformation of leading enterprises and the frequent failures of e-government projects shows that payoffs from ICT investments are significantly higher and sustainable when integrated with soft but critical ingredients of change: investing in policy change, new skills, organizational capital, and managerial and process innovation. Private sector experience in the United States indicates that, to realize highest productivity payoffs, investments in intangible assets and organizational capital typically dwarfs investments in ICT (75% in intangibles vs. 25% in ICT; Brynolfsson, 2009).

Sequencing the soft and hard investments also matters. Developing new information and communication systems may be relatively fast, but the time needed for institutions and people to embrace this change cannot be compressed drastically. Payoffs are higher when investments in these soft factors are done ahead of major investments in physical ICT assets. Visions, incentives, and strategic communication have also proven to be influential in shaping the culture and shared values necessary to support client-centered service. Early investments in the soft aspects and in preparing the grounds for transformation can secure and accelerate the institutional and social learning necessary for e-Transformation.

Although ICT is potentially a revolutionary, all-purpose enabling technology, it cannot operate in a vacuum. To realize its promised benefits, ICT must be accompanied by complementary policy reforms, organizational change, and capability development. Fast changes in ICT enable nations to leapfrog generations of technologies, but countries are unlikely to leapfrog basic education, institutional change, or social learning. Like the new seeds of the green revolution, ICT must be part of an integrated package of complementary ingredients.[3]

Whatever the national development objectives may be, a successful e-strategy will depend on effective leadership. Leadership is a key to manage change, mobilize key stakeholders, make strategies actionable and dynamic, and integrate ICT into various development domains. Adopting the right roles and attitudes is as critical as building the appropriate knowledge and skills among these leaders (Box 16.3).

Box 16.3 Roles and Attitudes for Leading e-Transformation

Experience with e-development shows that transformation demand leadership at many levels. E-development solutions often demand difficult policy changes, and sustained efforts and investments over time, thus requiring considerable political will. Effective e-Transformation strategies are about reforming polices and institutions, building new competencies, shifting power structures, coordinating investments, and changing roles and ways of doing business. Significant change management in public and private organizations alike requires informed change leadership at several levels. Such leaders should envision the possibilities of ICT applications, and consistently provide the support, drive and adaptation required throughout implementation. E-leadership is responsible for aligning the goals, incentives and roles of diverse stakeholders, and providing the space to negotiate tradeoffs and capture win-win opportunities.

But effective e-leaders, chief information officers (CIOs), and institutional change agents are scarce human resources, particularly in the public sector. Several leading nations are beginning to address this gap. In the United States, core competencies for CIOs have been identified, core curricula designed, and leading schools encouraged to provide certified educational programs to build this new cadre within the public sector. In many developing countries, such

---

[3]The best examples of World Bank-aided projects have been those where ICT was intentionally used to induce broader institutional and policy changes and capacity development, and where investments in skills, process reengineering, organizational learning, and other complementary ingredients were phased and secured early on in ICT for development programs.

cadre does not exist, or exist only in name in the civil service. E-leadership should also be developed at the highest business management and policy-making levels to engage organizational and business leaders in leveraging ICT for transforming their business and service models. The possibilities for harnessing transformational power of ICT cannot be left alone to the ICT specialists.

A key factor in realizing the potential benefits from ICT in the economy is the attitude of senior public and business managers who should learn to integrate ICT into their development or business strategies. It has been suggested that four postures are typically adopted by senior officials toward ICT in public sector reforms: ignore the potential role of ICT in such reforms; isolate ICT from mainstream management and delegate the function to the experts; idolize and focus on ICT while giving little attention to the broader reform; and integrate ICT into the development process (Heeks, 2000). The first three postures are most common, although there is a distinct shift among many from ignoring to idolizing ICT. The only viable approach to success-fully realize ICT potential for economic and social transformation is the last option, that is, to view ICT as an enabler and to integrate the technology into the overall strategy, planning, and management functions of each sector and organization.

Cultural factors also play a significant role in ICT adoption. There is a widespread understanding among policy makers of the crucial role that educa-tion and skills play in the e-development process. But they often fail to recognize the importance of cultural and human factors, such as acceptance of change in local culture, local business practices, and people's attitude toward government. Yet, e-development often involves cultural change. For example, in many Arab, Asian, and African countries, where women are effectively excluded from indepen-dent economic and social activities, special measures—technological, political, and social—will be necessary to ensure gender equality in access to ICT opportunities.

A common human factor that often impedes e-development is public distrust in government and excessive reliance on personal contacts rather than formal processes in conducting business operations. Even if the population is rather well educated and technologically savvy, as in Russia and eastern Europe, these factors have slowed the adoption of e-business and e-government practices. Focused efforts and public policies to build trust in electronic transactions and ensure their security will be paramount.

Building Strategic Partnerships

e-Transformation places a premium on partnership to exploit comparative advan-tages, create user–producer ecosystems, and promote open innovation and mutual learning among ICT suppliers and users. It also exploits demand-side economies of scale through cross-sectoral collaboration measures to share common infrastructures and capabilities, tap synergies and economies of scale, and harness network effects. Central to a successful implementation of e-Transformation is the capacity to create and sustain cross-sector partnerships among government, private sector, civil society, education, and research organizations (Wilson, 2004). To avoid falling behind in capacity to adjust policies and practices to the pace of technological changes, public leaders must seek innovative public–private partnerships. These partnerships can inject business know-how and innovation practices into ICT adoption in the public sphere.

Partnerships may cover all elements of e-Transformation. The potential is enormous and remain relatively unexploited. These partnerships often involve interested parties within a sector, but should be expanded across sectors. All pillars of e-development may be built through such partnerships (Chapters 7–10). The ICT industry and its associations are collaborating with academia and the government in building new competencies and developing an ecosystem for a dynamic and innovative ICT service sector (Chapter 8). Governments are partnering with private investors to induce investment in broadband and last mile connectivity (Chapter 9). The telecenter movement embodies many such partnerships (Chapter 10). Many e-government programs are moving toward new forms of co-investments that involve public–private partnerships (Chapters 11 and 12). Programs to diffuse ICT among SMEs and rural communities are also increasingly dependent on building cross-sectoral partnerships (Chapters 13 and 14).

Success in using strategic partnerships to implement e-development strategies relies on tapping the best elements of each partner and weaving them into a cogent strategy. The Indian state of Andhra Pradesh has shown how these ingredients work together. Its e-development initiative was driven by a few empowered civil servants under a dynamic political leadership and implemented in strategic partnership with the private sector. This partnership has adopted on a broad front; it extended beyond isolated projects to cover many aspects of e-development across the state (Box 16.4).

Box 16.4 Partnering with the Private Sector for e-Development in Andhra Pradesh

The Indian state of Andhra Pradesh has emerged as a regional leader in e-government. Its e-government initiative—which also included creating a technology cluster aimed at boosting the competitiveness of its economy—was driven largely by a handful of members of the elite Indian administrative service under the leadership of the state's then chief minister, Chandrababu Naidu.

What set this initiative apart from similar ones was its clear focus on strategy and implementation for key complementary elements of e-development. State planners thought through each project in great detail, considering service maturity and delivery, return on investment, options for financing through private partnerships, the dovetailing of projects to ensure internal consistency, and brand building and management. Among the key achievements:

Andhra Pradesh was the first Indian state to create a statewide area network. Created in partnership with a leading telecommunications service provider, on a build-own-operate basis, the network connects all 25 major cities and 1,122 mandals (the next level of administration) with fiber. The network is used for videoconferencing to ensure rapid implementation of development schemes and projects.

Andhra Pradesh was the first state to create a citizen database—76 million records, each with 110 fields. This database, along with a land hub—12 million records on a GIS-based platform—forms the state's master database, housed in a supercomputer in the state's secretariat.

Andhra Pradesh was the first state to offer remote citizen services, through its eSeva centers. This project provides citizens integrated services from 20 departments across a single counter.

Andhra Pradesh has rolled out a "digital nervous system" for the state—the secretariat knowledge and information management system (SKIMS). This enormous project, which involved automating all file movements and document management in the secretariat, was carried out in partnership with leading private sector players.

Andhra Pradesh has created a high-tech corridor and the "AP Inc. brand" and marketed itself through global forums. It is now home to software development and back-office centers for such leading companies as Microsoft, Oracle, GE, HSBC, Motorola, Infosys, TCS, and Satyam.

Source: Gupta et al., 2004.

New thinking about public–private collaboration is needed for e-Transformation. Best practices of leading nations indicate that it is essential to engage and take advantage of the financial resources and competencies of private participants in all aspects of e-development. The participation of private enterprises and NGOs can augment implementation capabilities of government as a user of ICT and as a catalyst in promoting e-business, e-learning, and e-society. Furthermore, business and NGO participation would speed up the transformation process in government, draw on more advanced e-business experiences, draw on local and user knowledge, and open up the government to outside parties and thus make it more inclusive and transparent.

New models of public–private partnerships (PPPs) are growing, and they are opening options for developing countries to leapfrog in e-government services without committing substantial investments and risks. But such PPPs must be restructured carefully and managed effectively to ensure accountability, quality, and reliability of services (Chapter 12). And capacity to partner has to be built over time, through experimentation and practice.

Partnership building and strategic outsourcing may also be pursued to avoid excessive centralization within government. New national ICT agencies are typically borne with very limited internal capacity and external authority to fulfill their extensive mandates. They quickly learn the limits of their formal authority to impose top-down blueprint plans—despite their formal location under the heads of government or their equivalent. They also ultimately recognize the importance of ownership by the sectoral agencies involved in implementation. For example, rather than imposing a centrally driven e-government program, countries may opt for developing the necessary incentives and culture to promote resource sharing and collaboration across e-sectors. Countries all over are seeking an optimal level of centralization that is consistent with effective adoption of the technology, the need to secure complementarities among investments, and the prevailing sociopolitical culture.[4]

Striking the right balance in decentralization and outsourcing will require differentiating among partners and developing partnership frameworks that match the uneven capabilities and commitments of the implementing agencies. Partnership frameworks also need to be guided by the level of centralization each country has to set for itself. Through mutual understanding, the central ICT Agency may place ultimate responsibility for the success of a project on the sectoral or owner agency and offers support and resources conditional on its partner's complying with clearly specified obligations.

Balancing Strategic Direction with Local Initiative and Innovation

Local initiative and innovation are essential to e-Transformation for several reasons including the versatility of ICT and uncertainties of the new digital world, the context-specific complementary inputs, and the importance of localization of knowledge. Bottom-up initiatives and multi-sectoral participatory approaches remain essential to generate local solutions, innovation, and learning, and thus unlock the transformative power of ICT.

We are entering a new world we cannot fully anticipate, much like the transition from the "pre-electric" world to that of electric utility and ubiquitous grid—those at the beginning of that transition could not anticipate how electricity and the electric light would transform their life and their economies (Carr, 2008). e-Transformation is a complex phenomenon being pursued in a fast changing global and technological environment. It is still new and in flux, with no easy answers or codified strategies. As a general-purpose technology, ICT will come to be used in ways that cannot be fully foretold at the present.

---

[4]For detailed treatment of such issues, see Hanna (2007b).

The versatility of ICT has to be matched by a willingness to understand the social and institutional contexts within which the technology is applied. e-Transformation is essentially about ICT enabled process and institutional innovation. It involves joint investments in complementary factors. It deals with intangibles such as knowledge, innovation, learning, software, and organizational change. e-Transformation is also linked to issues of communications, language, identity, control, and empowerment. Much of these intangibles and complementary factors are context specific and subject to local understanding and decisions. e-Transformation cannot be under the exclusive power of a central agency. Neither it can be bought as a blueprint plan or turnkey solution.

Localization of knowledge and content is essential to e-development. Technology-driven visions of downloading global knowledge are misleading (Stiglitz, 1999b). The vast variety of human societies requires the localization of knowledge. Practical know-how is largely tacit knowledge, to be acquired through apprenticeship and social interactions. Each society and community should therefore take an active role in the local learning process and in the creation of local content and indigenous knowledge. The growth of community access to the Internet, community networks, digital literacy, and social networking tools should help this locally driven social production, adaptation, and application of information and knowledge.

Developing countries thus need to develop the capabilities to acquire, adapt, maintain, customize, and re-invent existing "ICT solutions" to meet their needs and specific requirements under very diverse local conditions. Development experience shows that *dirigist* central planning fails in diverse and pluralistic environments. Not only is local initiative essential to effective appropriation and integration of ICT into development activities but also ICT can be a powerful enabler of decentralized and grassroots development across all sectors (Chapter 14).

So, what should be the role of national strategies? Experience in many developing countries shows that a national strategy, backed by international best practices and donor financing for key immediate elements, can facilitate consensus, engender ownership, promote shared understanding, induce policy reforms, enforce priorities, and mobilize resources. It may be used to bring endless debate to closure on investment priorities in the face of pent-up demand and large service delivery gaps. It can provide an objective and transparent process for prioritizing services across government.[5] It can generate a list of e-government services that arguably reflect local priorities and the differing states of e-readiness among agencies.[6] Moreover, it can empower a nascent central ICT Agency with an authoritative tool for enforcing shared frameworks and priorities in line with economy-wide needs. In short,

---

[5] Many prioritization schemes, designed for use in developed countries, involve high levels of quantification and sophistication. Care should be taken to use methodologies that are consistent with local conditions, including capabilities and the availability of demand data.

[6] For example, the European Union's standard list does not include foreign employment, a major source of income, employment, and remittances for Sri Lanka.

strategic planning exercises are not only about formulating a prioritized investment program but also about engendering consensus at the national level, and thus
facilitating initial action and implementation.

Yet, formulating a national strategy through a top-down process has its risks
and limitations. Pressures to produce a plan may not allow adequate time for data
collection, healthy public debate, and broad local participation. Without enough
robust data and research on users' needs, preferences, priorities, and capabilities,
the planning exercise inevitably starts with many assumptions. Rather than emphasizing an iterative and adaptive process, top-down strategic exercises risk rarifying
the final planning document and glossing over the original assumptions, and thus
undermining continued learning, strategic thinking, local initiative, and grassroots
innovation.

These risks are magnified when aid agencies and poor countries end up hiring
international consultants to carry out pro-forma strategic planning exercises and
end up buying standard recipes, or national ICT strategy documents that are not
grounded in local diagnosis or linked to local initiatives and aspirations.[7] Local
e-leadership institutions would end up being bypassed or left highly centralized and
underdeveloped (Box 16.5).

Box 16.5 Role of Multi-level and Cross-Sector Leadership Institutions

The role of central agencies as providers of strategic directions and budgetary
resources should be complemented with their role as enablers, facilitators,
and aggregators as well as inducers of local experimentation, innovation, and
collaboration. Strategic directions are expected to be set by policy makers
and e-leadership institutions at the national level. However, central institutions
cannot provide all the answers and should not attempt to impose top-down,
rigid, and uniform solutions.

e-Transformation is a national development process that draws on leaders
and change agents at all levels, links central resources with bottom-up initiatives, and creates the policy environment and space for a range of actors
to participate in the development and implementation of the strategy. This
process is necessary to build ownership, develop local content and capabilities, mobilize local knowledge and creativity, and address the specific needs
of varied regions. This process would create the enabling environment and
incentives for organizational learning and participatory planning. The process
would include mechanisms for sharing lessons and scaling up successes. It
would promote learning from within and from other countries. Incentives for

---

[7]Similar arguments are made against adopting a standard recipe for growth strategies and
institutions (in Rodrik 2007).

change and innovation would be systematically examined and secured for all elements of e-development. The task for policy makers, the business community, and civil society representatives and institutions is to create conditions for building the knowledge base and participation channels in ways that maximize the benefits and reduce the risks of ICT.

For large countries like India and Brazil, state and local governments are often better positioned than central governments to lead many elements of the national e-Transformation strategy. State- and locally led e-Transformation programs could lead to healthy competition among the states and local governments in attracting ICT investors, promoting technical education, and demonstrating best practices in areas such as e-government. The Indian state of Andhra Pradesh provided such a promising model that other Indian states have begun to emulate. The AP state used a statewide computerization program covering all levels of administration to redefine its relationship with citizens. In contrast, until recently the state Karnataka lagged behind in domestic applications, even though it has been the home of the premier software services export cluster, Bangalore. The ongoing federal government initiative to scale up local successes to a National e-Government Program (NeGP, as described in Chapter 11) builds on such local initiative and innovation.

Given the cross-sectoral nature of ICT-enabled development, it is necessary to involve the relevant ministries, local governments, private sector, and civil society in this national effort. Countries have created a variety of partnership and coordination mechanisms to address policy reforms, infrastructural problems, and investment mobilization (Chapter 6). They deployed inter-ministerial councils, taskforces, working groups, and other mechanisms to facilitate horizontal coordination. Some countries have relied on a leading ministry such as the Ministry of Economy or a newly constituted Ministry for Information and Communication Technology. Others created a special body. There is no single institutional recipe for leading across levels or sectors that can be suitable for all circumstances. But it has proven to be promising to rely on visible leadership at senior government and business levels, combined with light but effective coordination mechanisms for overall strategic guidance and knowledge sharing. This institutional setup should be complemented by devolution of authority and responsibility to relatively autonomous organizational structures to oversee different aspects or elements of the national ICT strategy.

Orchestrating top-down and bottom-up initiatives can create powerful and sustainable e-development dynamics. Top-down initiatives would set the overall vision, create awareness, build coalitions, assess e-readiness, establish e-leadership institutions, invest in shared infrastructures and capabilities, and evaluate progress toward development outcomes (as detailed in Chapters 5–10). Grassroots innovation funds may be used to provide matching grants in support of bottom-up proposals for ICT-enabled community innovations, digital local content, local capacity building, local partnerships, e-literacy, digital inclusion, and last mile connectivity initiatives (Chapter 14). A combination of bottom-up and top-down processes would develop mechanisms to support pilots and rapid-results projects and to scale up successful pilots into a critical mass of projects and national initiatives. This combination would then lead to the adoption of deeper institutional changes, medium-term budgetary priorities, long-term reform agenda, institutionalized monitoring and evaluation, and a second generation of pilots, policies, and programs.

Balancing top-down direction with bottom-up initiative is a continuing challenge and depends on many factors, including initial conditions, degree of ICT diffusion, and maturity of e-Transformation. In some countries, such as India, for example, e-development initiatives, and e-government in particular, started in isolation at few incubators, agencies, or localities. The aim was to respond to local pressures or to experiment, innovate, and gain some quick wins and visible (often, front-end) improvements in specific services. As these initiatives have gained visibility and built some experiential base for scaling up, these countries began to face the challenge of searching for economies of scale and scope. This demanded new top-down directions to consolidate demand, integrate systems, standardize data, and share infrastructures and solutions (Chapter 12).

Striking the right balance also depends on political and administrative culture of the country. Countries with more plural and decentralized traditions, and active and informed civil society, such as Canada and India, are likely to adopt more flexible national e-development programs that are informed and influenced by local initiatives, put resources and capabilities at the local level, and support local experimentation and innovation. In other countries, such as Korea, the initial push for e-development has been top-down with clearly defined goals and foundational investments, and only later came the search for stimulating innovation and deeper transformation in processes and services. No one-size-fits-all optimal balance is likely for societies with diverse initial conditions and political cultures.

But the trend is clear. As countries advance toward more connected governments, networked enterprises, and Internet-literate communities, e-Transformation programs have to become more flexible, pluralistic, community based, and locally driven. Countries that started with some central plans like China, Vietnam, Indonesia, and the Philippines have since moved—or in the phase of experimentation—toward more decentralized ICT investment programs, enabled by selective and strategic central investments.

Building Local Capabilities for an Adaptive Learning Process

Experience with e-development shows that successful programs give special attention to building local capabilities and institutions and adopting a learning process approach to implementation. An inspiring vision is essential to give people hope about the potential of ICT to change their lives. Yet, e-strategies should convince people that the proposed programs are achievable and in line with their capabilities and resources. Many e-strategies have been "all encompassing in scope without being strategic or actionable" (ICT Task Force, 2003). Many governments have developed ambitious strategies only to falter during implementation.

Attention to implementation has been the hallmark of successful e-strategies in countries like Singapore and Korea. This implies matching expectations to available resources, particularly human resources and implementation capacity. It also points to the need to mobilize local resources and build distributed capabilities. Also, national programs must have built-in flexibility to mach local capabilities and learning processes.

e-Transformation is an adaptive, learning process. Designing e-Transformation is about strategizing and thinking throughout implementation processes, not developing rigid, detailed blueprints. Much of the details of e-Transformation strategy will have to emerge from a learning process approach to strategy design and implementation.

Process approaches mobilize and integrate local capacity building for learning and adaptation during strategy design and implementation, rather than rely on extensive upfront analysis and centralized planning. Process approaches start small, with a bias to action and learning. A learning process approach is flexible, evolutionary, participatory, and result oriented. e-Transformation strategies should therefore build on local learning and adaptation capabilities, as they combine top-down strategic approaches with vibrant and diverse bottom-up local initiatives (Hanna and Picciotto, 2002).

A learning process approach to strategy development would give due attention to institutional experimentation and development. These e-institutions would make strategic choices, prioritize investments, manage continual change, learn from pilots, and sustain transformation through difficult times (Chapter 6). The focus would be on building adaptive institutions and learning capabilities, especially at the local level. Institutional mechanisms for developing and implementing strategies would be worked out with the stakeholders and with oversight and political commitment at the highest levels. e-Transformation programs would rely on result-oriented monitoring and evaluation systems to provide for timely adjustment, user feedback, and adaptive planning (Chapter 15). They would require relentless pursuit of citizen feedback about e-services so as to drive further government transformation. Learning would be a key tool to reducing and managing resistance to change.

Most essential to the success of a learning process approach is to build capabilities and access to resources to enable participation, appropriation, and adaptation of information and communication technologies at the local levels. This approach should be based on an understanding of how people gain the confidence and knowledge to appropriate ICT for their own use. It would emphasize early investment in areas such as e-literacy programs, shared access centers, social innovation funds, and an ecology of collaboration. It would emphasize building capacity at the provincial and municipal levels to support community-driven, ICT-enabled solutions.

Building capabilities for adaption and learning equally applies to business enterprises and public agencies. e-Transformation for business has become an imperative for survival, if not for thriving and growth. But it can be a traumatic and risky proposition, particularly for SMEs. Many of the lessons for strategizing, organizing, and managing for general innovation in business can apply to ICT-enabled innovation and enterprise transformation (Chapter 13). Incentives for ICT adoption, technical assistance and capacity building for SMEs, the promotion of incubators and clusters, and various other means are designed to enable such learning and adaptation throughout the journey of e-Transformation.

Adopting Integrated and Tailored Approaches to Equity

The ICT revolution is unleashing powerful forces that will shape income distribution and employment opportunities throughout the world. In Chapter 2, I outlined some of the major risks and concerns about concentrating wealth and increasing income inequalities within many countries that can be attributed to technological change and globalization. Further unfolding of ICT revolution, including the emergence of universal computing grid, may end up automating much of information processing work, eroding the middle class, and widening the income divide. In the same chapter, I show the potential of the ICT revolution for generating tremendous opportunities for new sources of growth and economic diversification and for extending public services and information to rural areas and the poor. In Chapter 14, I drew on the experience of national programs, innovation funds, and NGO-corporate partnerships to suggest some ways to promote pro-poor innovation, localization and adaptation of ICT in order to reduce poverty, transform the bottom of the pyramid, and promote inclusive information societies.

No e-Transformation strategy can ignore these issues. Developing grassroots initiatives and pro-poor innovation mechanisms could be integral to a national e-Transformation strategy. But these initiatives, by themselves, are unlikely to provide an adequate response to the powerful forces driving concentration and inequalities. The mutually reinforcing and interdependent elements of e-development can generate virtuous cycles that support broad-based transformation and social inclusion. But these interdependencies also constitute multiple barriers to digital inclusion, and if not addressed in a coherent ways at the local and national levels, could lead to vicious cycles, rising inequality, and entrapment in poverty.

An inclusive national e-Transformation strategy has to take a more integrated and tailored approach to promote equity. This approach would promote access to knowledge, e-services, and IT-enabled employment opportunities. It will also have implications for each element of e-development and for promoting integration among these elements into coherent packages and local strategies for poverty reduction.

Many policy makers have equated digital and social inclusion processes with supporting shared and affordable access to ICT and the Internet through schools, libraries, and community centers. Digital inclusion is viewed as a time-bound problem of access to technology or a ramp to the information highway. Even in some of the most connected nations like Canada, the move from access to inclusion has been difficult, particularly for the rural and isolated communities.

In most developing countries this inclusion process will have to address multiple barriers: competency, connectivity, and content. It raises public policy issues concerning the role of government in complementing the market and addressing these barriers in partnership with the private sector and local organizations. For example, developing local content and relevant applications can be costly, and thus requires upfront strategy, incentives, foundational support, training, and collaboration with sources of knowledge at the local and national levels. What policies and incentives would enable low-cost development of content and local innovation of applications, and consequently encourage innovation sharing and scaling up? How could pro-poor applications be encouraged to leverage widely shared platforms like mobiles?

Experience suggests that advancing ICT-enabled social inclusion requires both integration and localization of e-development. Integration and adaptation can be pursued at two levels: national and local.

At the national level, it would include creating the enabling policies and partnering with, and making resources available to local institutions. National programs should secure complementary investments to enable local agents to use ICT as a tool for empowerment, social inclusion, and the delivery of basic services. National programs may provide mass e-literacy and help build the skills of participants to shape their own local solutions. These programs could include special measure to reach the poor, disabled, and disadvantaged groups. They may also seek to identify local, home-grown, low-cost solutions for potential knowledge sharing and scaling up to national levels. Advocacy and the use of the media are necessary to change attitudes and practices and prepare stakeholders to integrate ICT as enabler into various sectoral strategies and programs to improve rural livelihoods.

Government may also engage the private sector and research institutions in working with the base of the pyramid, to customize existing products for the poor. Government may help aggregate potential demand for new ICT products and services that are most relevant to the poor. Government may seek various ways to make markets work for the poor. This role is most relevant when dealing with new technologies and markets such as innovating and diffusing ICT applications most relevant to the livelihood of the poor. For example, government may support and complement market forces by promoting low-cost access devices and open source and societal applications through cost sharing in product development and commercialization (Chapter 14).

Technology blending and integration should be tested and tailored to meet the special needs and capabilities of the poor. Older technologies and infrastructures such as radio and television may be blended with the new such as Internet and mobile phone for a variety of simple but relevant applications. Community radio still holds much promise for allowing community input and relevant content. At times, the latest technologies may be the most user friendly and least demanding in terms of technical or literacy capabilities as has been the case with mobile phones.

Much of the integration and adaptation will inevitably be carried out on a smaller scale at the local level through local partnerships, continuous adaptation, and incremental innovation (Box 16.6). E-development programs may work with NGOs and local institutions that are particularly focused on helping poor communities, so they would collaborate and integrate ICT into local problem solving and learning. They may seek multiple channels to promote equity, for example, by enabling access to government information and services of particular importance to the poor, networking rural and small enterprises, and promoting grassroots innovation and appropriation of ICT solutions. Multi-purpose telecenters, appropriately supported and networked into associations, can become focal points for integrating and tailoring solutions at community levels (Chapter 10). Special attention may be given to creating local content, participatory video, and community-based networks.

Box 16.6 Partnerships to Enhance the Livelihoods of the Poor

Enabling the livelihood of the rural poor with ICT needs to overcome multiple challenges: little understanding of the needs and livelihood strategies of the rural poor; weak collaboration among local stakeholders and local institutions; limited capacity at the service delivery level; and service affordability and sustainability. These challenges are interdependent, as weak partnerships affect the demand, value added, and the sustainability of services, among others.

Organizations with extension networks like the Ministries of Agriculture and Rural Development may use ICT to leverage these networks for more effective and less costly extension or service delivery. Their field workers and relevant community-based organizations may be trained in developing and using digital materials and enabled by ICT infrastructure such as community-based knowledge centers, IT-based microcredit systems, and mobile phone-based messaging market information updates. They may also be engaged in reviewing ICT interventions to ensure they meet the requirements of potential users and poor communities. Organizations without networks available for livelihoods development need to collaborate with intermediaries with extension networks.

Promoting rural enterprise can also be advanced through partnerships among business development service (BDS) providers and other institutions that are directly involved in providing ICT services such as the ICT industry, telecenters, and universities. Such partnerships could provide market support, market information and intelligence, linkages between buyers and suppliers, and assistance with product promotion and marketing. They could also supply MSMEs with information on available options for financial support schemes. They could promote networking across the supply chain and build communities of practice among BDS and ICT service providers, infomediaries, and other stakeholders.

Promoting Regional and Global Collaboration

Collaboration at the regional and global levels to harness the ICT revolution can serve several purposes: accelerate learning from each other; provide forums for coordination and joint actions; complement individual country efforts through shared infrastructures and resource development; and address global problems, commons, and governance issues.

Most economies are at early phases of e-Transformation. Countries can be co-learners. Those open to learning from others as well as from within—with a mindset of openness and pragmatism—have been the adept movers or fast followers. Much can be learned from leading countries that have set their development processes on the ICT-enabled growth and innovation track—even if their e-strategies were implicit or given other names such as knowledge or innovation economy or information society. These include high-income economies such as Finland, Ireland, Korea, Singapore, and Taiwan; middle-income ones such as Chile and Costa Rica; transitional economies such as the Baltic countries; and low-income countries such as India and China. These countries have been active learners—with vision, openness, pragmatism, and determination. They have a lot to learn from each other and to share with the developing world.

Countries learn most from regional models. For example, India's success in outsourcing services has inspired e-Sri Lanka's program as well as most of south Asian countries. Korea's, Singapore's, and Taiwan's successes in ICT hardware were inspiring models for many other east Asian countries, including China. The Baltic countries are exchanging lessons among themselves as well as with other EU countries. EU institutions have established various platforms and forums for shared visions, common policies, joint research and action, and exchange of experience. Rivalry and emulation among Middle Eastern countries are evident among Dubai, Jordan, Tunisia, Egypt, and others, despite disparities in income. African and Latin American countries are also searching for local and regional models to emulate. In Latin America, some of this collaboration occurs among cities and municipalities, with the support of regional institutions like OAS and regional banks like IADB.

Many promising examples of regional and global cooperation on ICT for development are emerging and lessons many be drawn from them to ensure their effectiveness (Box 16.7).

Box 16.7 Examples of Regional and Global Cooperation on ICT for Development

Regional and international cooperation can complement country-level efforts to learn from others. One example is the Global Knowledge Partnership (GKP), a large network of NGOs and co-learners in support of developing inclusive information societies and knowledge economies. A host of global and regional forums have emerged since the two World Summits on Information Society of 2003 and 2005, sponsored by UN organizations in partnership with the private sector, including UNICT Task Forces. InfoDev, an ongoing and evolving multi-donor program hosted at the World Bank, supports knowledge sharing on ICT for development. It also funds a global ICT-enabled innovation network that provides financing and technical assistance to over 160 incubators and 9000 small and microenterprises in more than 75 countries.

An e-development thematic group was established in 2003 to support learning within the World Bank and with other aid agencies and client countries. Since, this group has been evolving and expanding to thousands of stakeholders in over 80 countries. As of 2009, the World Bank has initiated new global forums and global dialogues on various elements of e-development, in support of peer learning, knowledge sharing, and other forms of collaboration. Some studies are also examining more action-oriented collaboration mechanisms to promote, for example, IT services and ITES in south Asia, building on the success of India. A process to develop and measure ICT indicators and benchmark progress for over 150 countries has also started, with partnership among the World Bank, ITU, and several UN organizations (World Bank, 2009b).

Many global forums and initiatives involve private support. Microsoft's Government Leadership Forum is one example of supporting regional forums for raising awareness and sharing experience among policy makers on the ICT and the knowledge economy. To take an example of action-oriented initiative, Cisco Systems, through the World Economic Forum's Global Education Initiative and other initiatives, has teamed with governments, school administrators, local and global companies, and NGOs around the world to develop curricula, train teachers, and provide IT infrastructure to schools in poor regions. Some of these privately supported ICT for development projects are covered in the Donor Guide accompanying the infoDev Toolkit on e-government.

The picture is changing rapidly and these in no mechanism to keep abreast of the regional and global forums for cooperation and knowledge sharing. Perhaps most important, there is no independent reviews or assessments of the development effectiveness of these various efforts. While regional and global collaboration remain necessary, and may be scaled up, timely and frequent assessment of various forums and mechanisms for collaboration remain necessary to reduce fragmentation of efforts and make them more effective and complementary to individual country efforts for e-Transformation.

Most important in learning from global and regional "best practices" is to learn to differentiate between "me too strategies" or following a standard recipe, and active experimentation and learning based on more thoughtful understanding of the fundamental enablers of success and their transferability and adaptability to local context. A strategy for e-Transformation must learn from others, but must not overemphasize best practices as blueprints at the expense of experimentation and local experi-ence.[8] Building local capacity for understanding recent experience and monitoring regional and global trends and for learning from others is a key to informed and agile learning. Participatory strategy development and implementation is a most effective means for processing and aggregating local knowledge and learning.

Regional and global collaboration can help complement individual country efforts through pooling resources and sharing infrastructures. Africa presents a good example. Most African countries have small populations and very limited pool of human resources to compete in IT services or IT-enabled services, but they potentially compete in exporting such services, if they can pool their human resource development efforts and complement some of their skill gaps (Chapter 8). Similarly, a World Bank–IFC partnership with 22 African countries and ICT multi-nationals is already underway to invest in a regional backbone infrastructure project across the periphery of the continent. Similarly, collaboration among countries in the Caribbean region had made it be possible to attract private–public partnerships to invest an advanced backbone infrastructure.

Global collaboration on e-Transformation is also necessary to address global problems, commons, and governance issues. Rising levels of trade and human mobility, immigration, security, environmental and global health systems are reinforcing interdependencies among countries. From a global perspective, e-government can be viewed as a key dimension of the world's capacity to respond collectively—in terms of information, learning, and shared capacities for action (United Nations, 2008). These challenges are rendering e-government as much a global as a national imperative. A meaningful response is to promote regional and global collaboration and leverage the lessons learned from advanced countries in harnessing ICT to transform government for the widest possible number of commu-nities and countries. Global collaboration can also accelerate the development and sharing of knowledge and other global development commons.

Similarly, global collaboration is called for to ensure that Internet governance reflects the interest of the majority of mankind. As the importance of the Internet as a shared global infrastructure grows, decisions about its governance, and its structure and protocols, will take on greater weight. Also, as the new computing grid spans the world, it would become the dominant medium for communication, commerce, and perhaps culture. This will have profound national and global implications. Coming to grips with these manifold ramifications demands global collaboration mechanisms.

Issues for Aid Agencies

Aid can play a key role in advancing e-Transformation through financial and techni-cal assistance programs and in supporting regional and global collaboration to help countries contribute and tap into global commons. Many aid agencies have begun

---

[8]Rodril (2007) makes similar arguments against imposing best practice recipes in designing growth policies and institutions.

to address the challenges arising from the ICT revolution for the way they do business, for acquiring new competencies to provide advisory services, and for building client capacity to harness ICT for development. These initiatives have raised awareness about the relevance of ICT for development and poverty reduction. But they have not made a major impact on overall mainstream development thinking and practice.

The World Summits of Information Society of 2003 and 2005, sponsored by the UN and particularly ITU, have raised awareness about the opportunities and risks of the ongoing technological revolution for development. The challenge remains to translate this raised awareness into pragmatic and effective approaches to integrate ICT into national development strategies, aid programs, and global governance.

The growing number of donor-funded initiatives, partnerships, and conferences in the sector may have created the illusion of action. Inward-oriented knowledge management initiatives in the World Bank and other aid agencies may have overshadowed the urgent need to build country capacity to access global and local knowledge and to master the use of ICT for poverty reduction and sustainable growth. The USAID has been sponsoring a Last Mile Initiative to fund shared access to ICT and Internet connectivity in small towns and rural areas in collaboration with ICT multinationals. The ILO has been helping with pilot projects and partnerships to mentor young entrepreneurs to start their ICT-related enterprises and facilitate access of young people to business networks. The UNDP is piloting the use of ICT in improving governance. The list is growing, but the potential is hardly tapped and the lessons are not widely shared. Efforts by UN organizations remain fragmented, underfunded, and technology driven.

A World Bank strategy addressed issues of assistance to the information infrastructure, but did not address issues concerning the integration of ICT into development strategies (World Bank, 2002). As of 2008, the bank has a portfolio of over US $7 billion in ICT components under implementation in its investment program. Several reviews of World Bank lending suggest that ICT applications are pervasive and significantly present in 60–80% of all bank-funded projects. These components are growing in coverage, complexity, and pervasiveness, but these remain add-on components, with little integration, quality control, or systematic evaluation (Hanna and Boyson, 1993; and more recently reports by the Quality Assurance Group in 2008, and by the International Department in 1996, among others). The World Bank is slowly responding to some of these findings.

Information technology has yet to be mainstreamed into the core business of aid at the country, sector, and project levels. A key issue facing such integration is whether to build a critical mass of core competencies in ICT in a central location to serve all sectors or to decentralize and integrate such competencies in each sector. A related issue is whether to develop hybrids of leaders and experts who would have domain knowledge of development (of a specific sector, such as education) and of ICT as a general-purpose technology.[9] Developing such hybrids is not easy.

---

[9]The experience from successful business organizations and IT projects indicates that such organizations and projects are best led by hybrids who span the technical and business domains.

This is not typically supported by existing human resource management systems and incentives. Similar issues of integration arise at the country and regional levels, where ICT may provide a new lens for re-thinking development options and country assistance strategies.

Within aid agencies, some development practitioners view ICT as a threat to established sectors and ways of doing business, and thus exert subtle but pervasive resistance to the required changes to mainstream ICT into development. Sectoral turfs and the poor fit of ICT into sector-oriented organization perpetuates the isolation of ICT from the development agenda and sectoral strategies of aid agencies. A minority view this fundamental technological change as an opportunity for developing countries to address old age development problems and create new means to achieve development goals in the context of new global realities. Regardless of the view one holds, evidence supports the school of thought that developing a national ICT strategy has become increasingly vital to a country's economic development. A more bold view, advocated in this book, is to view the ongoing ICT revolution as a new techno-economic paradigm with profound implications for our search for new and advanced development strategies and for including deep transformation in all priority sectors.

Current aid practices constrain the adoption of an integrated approach to ICT for development or a holistic e-Transformation. For example, aid-financed projects typically focus on a single sector or agency, without the sharing of resources, capabilities, and other factors essential to sustainability of ICT applications. Pursuing e-government programs project by project can exacerbate problems of coordination and institutionalization. A donor bias toward isolated ICT applications can be a key obstacle to government adherence to common frameworks for prioritizing investments, adopting open standards, and sharing infrastructures and capabilities. Aid agencies need to think strategically about their role in developing integrative approaches, innovative business models, and budget processes that take into account the whole of government as well as other actors, including other aid agencies, the private sector, and civil society.

Aid agencies are currently struggling to catch up and integrate this technological revolution into their core businesses. They are challenged to develop their core competencies and to build the external partnerships necessary to help their clients capture the opportunities and address the options opened by the ongoing revolution. This is a major area where global knowledge and best practices are evolving rapidly. The risks of slow learning and ad hoc response are quite high to both developing countries and aid agencies.

Aid agencies could help governments set appropriate public policies and programs for e-Transformation. They could take a strategic and holistic view of ICT, beyond ad hoc assistance to ICT components in investment projects or stand-alone telecommunication operations. Aid agencies could work with governments and local stakeholders to build local capabilities and develop home-grown strategic responses that take account of the emerging techno-economic paradigm. They could alert policy makers to the opportunities to mainstream ICT in the fight against poverty and to the need to get the enabling environment right. Aid agencies could also alert them to the pitfalls of viewing ICT as a magic bullet, in isolation of complementary investments and reforms. They could show respect to local realities and capabilities by emphasizing local experimentation and adaption. In doing so effectively, aid agencies must be at the cutting edge of a fast evolving practice and need to scan the global environment and draw on global knowledge and emerging best practices. They must be equally engaged in partnerships and learning experiments with their client countries to mobilize local know-how and resources, adapt and tailor global best practices, and facilitate local innovation and learning.

In sum, aid agencies have an important role in helping developing countries formulate policies and strategies for using ICT in development—taking full account of the potential of this technological revolution. They should help countries integrate ICT fully into their development strategies. This does not mean pushing ICT at the expense of broader development priorities. Rather, it means having the integrative processes and institutional commitment to harness the potential and manage the risks of this revolution. It also means that aid agencies and developing countries should engage in strategic dialogue on holistic approaches to ICT in development. It means that aid agencies should find ways to direct resources to e-Transformation programs as well as strategically selected ICT components within development projects.

Since the promises, pitfalls, and critical success factors of ICT are not yet fully understood, aid agencies must engage in knowledge partnerships among themselves and with their client countries to embark on the journey of e-Transformation. The ICT revolution raises unprecedented challenges and provides a sense of hope and excitement, particularly for developing countries. The world is in the midst of a major multiple financial, food, water, energy, and environmental crisis, making the need for inclusive, innovative, and sustainable solutions greater and more urgent than ever before. In this search for solutions, the developing world cannot afford to forgo the promise of e-Transformation. It cannot afford but deploy the most transformative, general-purpose technology of our time.

I hope this book could serve as a guide for an exciting journey of e-Transformation to a better future for mankind.

Bibliography

Abramovitz, M., and David, P. A. 1999. *American Macroeconomic Growth in the Era of Knowledge Based Progress: The Long Run Perspective*. Stanford Institute for Economic Policy Research, Discussion Paper Series, No. 99-3, Stanford University, 180 pp.

Abramson, M., Breul, J., and Kamensky, J. 2006. *Six Trends Transforming Government*. IBM Center for the Business of Government.

Agranoff, R. 2003. *Leveraging Networks: A Guide for Public Managers Working Across Organizations*. IBM Center for the Business of Government.

Alavi, H. 2008. *Trading Up: How Tunisia Used ICT to Facilitate Trade*. IFC Smart Lessons. Washington, DC: IFC.

Allaire, J., and Austin, R.D. 2005. Broadband and collaboration. In: Austin R.D., and Bradley, S.P. (eds.). *The Broadband Explosion*. Cambridge, MA: Harvard Business School Press.

Alvarez, C. 2006. ICT as part of the Chilean Strategy for Development: Present and Challenges. In: Castells, M., and Cardoso, G. (eds.). *The Networked Society: From Knowledge to Policy*. Washington, DC: Johns Hopkins Center for Transatlantic Relations.

Amsden, A. H. .1989. *Asia's next Giant: South Korea and Late Industrialization*. New York: Oxford University Press.

Amsden, A. H. 1994. Why isn't the Whole World Experimenting with the East Asian Model to Develop? Review of the East Asian Miracle. *World Dev* 22(4):627–633.

Anderson, C. 2006. *The Long Tail*. UK: Random House.

Atkinson, R., and Castro, D. 2008. *Digital Quality of Life: Understanding the Personal and Social Benefits of the Information Technology Revolution*. Washington, DC: The Information Technology and Innovation Foundation.

Badshah, A., Khan, S., Garrido, M. (eds.). 2003. *Connected for Development. Information Kiosks and Sustainability*. New York: UN ICT Task Force.

Balit, S. 1998. Listening to farmers: Communication for participation and change in Latin America. Retrieved August 2, 2004 from: http://www.fao.org/WAICENT/FAOINFO/SSTDEV/CDdirect/Cdan0018.htm.

Beardsley, S., Moregenstern, I. B., and Verbeke, W. 2004. Towards a New Regulatory Compact. In: *The Global Information Technology Report 2003-04*. New York: Oxford University Press, pp. 71–86.

Beckhard, R., and Harris, R. 1987. *Organizational Transactions*. Reading, MA: Addison-Wesley.

Bell, D. 1973. *The Coming of Post-Industrial Society*. Harmondsworth, Middlesex: Peregrine/Penguin.

Benkler, Y. 2006. *The Wealth of Networks*. New Haven: Yale University Press.

Best, M. 1990. *The New Competition: Institutions of Industrial Restructuring*, Cambridge: Polity Press

Bhatnagar, S. and Schware, R. (eds.). 2000. *Information and Communication Technology in Rural Areas*. Washington, DC: World Bank Institute.

N.K. Hanna, *e-Transformation: Enabling New Development Strategies*, Innovation, 419
Technology, and Knowledge Management, DOI 10.1007/978-1-4419-1185-8,
© Springer Science+Business Media, LLC 2010

Blackburn, C., Chambers, R., and Gaventa, J. 2002. Mainstreaming Participation in Development. In: Nagy, H., and Robert, P. *Making Development Work*, pp 61–82.

Boyson, S., Harrington, L., and Corsi, T. 2004. *In Real Time: Managing the New Supply Chain*. Westport, CT: Praeger.

Bresnahan, T. F., and Trajtenberg, M. 1995. General Purpose Technologies: engines of Growth?. *J Econom* 65:83–108.

Bressand, F., et al., 2007. *Curbing Global Energy Demand Growth: The Energy Productivity Opportunity*. California: McKinsey Global Institute.

Broadbent, M., and Kitzis, E. S. 2005. *The New CIO Leader*. Boston, MA: Harvard Business School Press.

Brookes, M., Wahhai, Z. 2000. The 'New' Global Economy—Part II: B2B and the Internet, *Global Economic Commentary*, Goldman Sachs.

Bryan, L., and Joyce, C. 2007. *Mobilizing Minds*. New York: McGraw-Hill.

Brynjolfsson, E. 2003 Presentation. *Transforming Enterprise*. The First International Conference on the Economic and Social Implications of Information Technology, held at the US Commerce Department in January 2003.

Brynjolfsson, E. 2009. Presentation. *IT and Organizational Productivity*. World Bank Conference on Enabling Development, held January 26–29, 2009, Washington, DC.

Brynjolfsson, E., and Hitt, L. M. 2000. Beyond Computation: Informational Technology, Organizational Transformation and Business Performance. *J Econ Persp* 14(4): 23–48.

Brynjolfsson, E., and Saunders, A. 2009. *Wired for Innovation: How Information Technology is Reshaping the Economy*. Boston, Mass: MIT Press

Carayannis, E., and Sipp, C. 2006. *e-Development Toward the Knowledge Economy: Leveraging Technology, Innovation and Entrepreneurship for "Smart" Development*. London: Palgrave Macmillan.

Carr, N. 2008. *Big Switch: Rewiring the World, From Edison to Google*. Boston: Harvard Business School Press.

Castells, M. (1996). *The Information Age: Economy, Society and Culture. Volume I. The Rise of the Network Society*. Malden and Oxford: Blackwell.

Castells, M., and Cardoso, G. (eds.). 2006. *The Networked Society: From Knowledge to Policy*. Washington, DC: Johns Hopkins Center for Transatlantic Relations.

Chandler, A.D. 2001. *Inventing the Electronic Century*. New York: Free Press

Change, A.-M., and Kannan, P. K. 2008. *Leveraging Web 2.0 in Government*. Washington, DC: IBM Center for the Business of Government.

Chesbrough, H. 2006. *Open Business Models*. Boston, MA: Harvard Business School Press.

Ciborra, C. 2000. *From Control to Drift: The Dynamics of Corporate Information Infrastructure*. Oxford: Oxford University Press

Claessens, G., and Kingbiel, 2001. *E-Finance in Emerging Markets: Is Leapfrogging Possible?* World Bank.

Colony, G., Radjou, N., and Howard, E. 2002. The X Internet: Leveling the Playing Field for Businesses in Developing Nations, The Global Information Technology Report-Readiness for the Networked World, 2001–2002. New York: Oxford University Press.

Council of Economic Advisors. 2001. Economic Report to the President, U.S. Government, Washington, DC.

Crescia, E. 2006. What is the Impact of e-Government Services: The Experience of Sao Paulo Brazil. Presentation made to the E-Development Thematic Group at the World Bank, Washington, DC: February 9, 2006.

Dahlman, C. J., and Aubert, J.-E. 2001. *China and Knowledge Economy: Seizing the 21st Century*. Washington, DC: World Bank.

Dahlman, R., and Yla-Anttila, P. 2006. *Finland as a Knowledge Economy*. Washington, DC: World Bank

Dahlman, C., and Utz, A. 2005. *India and the Knowledge Economy*. Washington, DC: World Bank.

Ferranti, De., Guasch, M., and Schady, S.-P. 2002 *From Natural Resources to Knowledge Economy*. World Bank.

David P. A. 1990. The Dynamo and the Computer: A Historical Perspective on the Modern Productivity Paradox. *Am Econ Rev* 80(2):355–361.

David, P. A. 2000. Understanding Digital Technology's Evolution and the Path of Measured Productivity Growth: Present and Future in the Mirror of the Past. In: *Understanding the Digital Economy*. Brynolfsson, E., and Kahin, B. (eds.). Cambridge, MA: MIT Press, pp 49–95.

Davila, T., Epstein, M. J., and Shelton, R. 2006. *Making Innovation Work*. New Jersey: Wharton School Publishing.

Dedrick, J., and Kraemer, K. 2004. *Impacts of Information Technology on the Organization of Economic Activities*. Irvine, CA: University of California.

Devenport, T., Jarvenpaa, S. 2008. *Strateigc Use of Analytics in Government*. Washington, DC: IBM Center for the Business of Government.

Dongier, P., and Sudan, R. 2009. Exports of IT Services and IT-Enabled Services: Market Opportunities, Development Impact and Policy Options. World Bank. 2009. *Information and Communications for Development 2009. Extending Reach and Increasing Impact*. Washington, DC: World Bank.

Dosi, G., et al. (eds.) 1988. *Technical Change and Economic Theory*. London: Pinter and New York: Columbia University Press

Drishtee Village Information Kiosks (2003). In Badshah, A., Khan, S., Garrido, M. (eds.). *Connected for Development. Information Kiosks and Sustainability*. New York: UN ICT Task Force, pp. 149–157.

Drishtee, P. Retrieved July 15, 2004 from: http://drishtee.com.

Drucker, P. 1993. *The Post Capitalist Society*. Oxford: Butterworth Heineman.

Dutta, S., and Lopez-Claros, A. (eds.). 2005. *The Global Information Technology Report 2004–05*. New York: Palgrave Macmillan.

Dutta, S., and Mia, I. (eds.). 2008. *The Global Information Technology Report 2007–08*: Fostering Innovation Through Networked Readiness. New York: Palgrave MacMillan.

Dutta, S., Lanvin, B., Paua, F. (eds.) 2003. *The Global Information Technology Report 2002–2003*. New York: Oxford University Press.

Dutta, S., Lanvin, B., and Paua, F. (eds.). 2004. *The Global Information Technology Report 2003–04*. New York: Oxford University Press.

Dutz, M. A. (ed.). 2007. Unleashing India's Innovation. Washington, DC: World Bank.

Economic Commission for Latin America and the Caribbean (ECLAC), United Nation (2003). *Road maps towards an information society in Latin America and the Caribbean*. Santiago, Chile: United Nations.

Economist, September 26, 2009. Mobile Marvels: A Special Report of Telecoms in Emerging Markets. London: The Economist

Eggers, W. *Government 2.0*. 2005. New York: Rowman & Littlefield.

Eggers, W., and Singh, S. 2009. *The Public Innovator's Playbook: Nurturing bold ideas in government*. Deloitte Research and Ash Institute.

Eggleston, J., and Zekhauser. 2002 Information and Communication Technologies, Markets and Economic Development. In: *The Global Information Technology Report—Readiness for the Networked World*, World Economic Forum, 2001–2002.

Einstein, E. 1979. *The Printing Press as an Agent of Change*. Cambridge: Cambridge University Press.

El Sherif, H., and El Sawy, O. A. 1988. Issue-Based Decision Support System for Egyptian Cabinet. *MIS Q* 12(4).

Ellerman, D. 2002. Helping People Help Themselves: Autonomy-Compatible Assistance. In: Hanna, N.K., and Picciotto, R. *Making Development Work*. pp 105–133.

Ernest, D. 2003. *The New Mobility of Knowledge: Digital Information Systems and Global Flagship Networks*. Working Paper, Honolulu: East-West Center.

European Commission (EU). 2007. Information Society and Media. 2007. *i2010 Annual Information Society Report 2007*. European Communities.

Favaro, E. M. (ed.) 2008. *Small States, Smart Solutions*. Washington, DC: World Bank.

Fine, C.H. 1998. *Clock Speed: Winning Industry Control in the Age of Temporary Advantage*. Reading, Mass: Perseus Books

Fishenden, J., et al. 2006. The New World of Government Work. Microsoft Public Services and eGovernment Strategy: Discussion Paper Series.

Florida, R. 2004. *The Rise of the Creative Class*. New York: Basic Books.

Florida, R. 2005. *Cities and the Creative Class*. New York: Routledge.

Fontiane, M. 2000. High Tech Grass Roots Education: Community Learning Centers (CLCs) for skill building. In: *Techknowlogia*, July/August 2000.

Fountain, J. E. 2001. *Building the Virtual State*. Washington, DC: Brookings Institution.

Franco-Temple, E. 2008. Why and How to Integrate Information Technology in the Business Process Reform. IFC Smart Lessons. June 2008. Washington, DC: IFC.

Freedman, T. L. 2005. *The World is Flat: A brief History of the Twenty-first Century*. New York: Farrar, Straus, and Giroux.

Freeman, C., and Louca, F. 2001. *As Time Goes by: From the Industrial Revolution to the Information Revolution*. Oxford: Oxford University Press.

Freeman, C., and Soete, L. 1997. *The Economics of Industrial Innovation*. London: Pinter.

Freire, P. 1970. Pedagogy for the Oppressed. New York: Continuum.

Frosst,D., Brown, S., and Elder, A. 2005. Net-Impact: European e-Government. pp29–42, In *The Global Information Technology Report 2004–05: Efficiency in an Increasingly Connected World.*, edited by Dutta, S., and Lopez-Claros, A. New York: Palgrave Macmillan, pp. 29–42.

Fukuyama, F. 2004. *State-Building: Governance and World Order in the 21st Century*. Ithaca, NY: Cornell University Press.

Fundap/Fundação Instituto de Administração – FIA (2006). *Avaliação de Gestão do Conhecimento e da Inovação Governo do Estado de São Paulo*. São Paulo: Fundap.

Fung, V. K., Fung, W. K., and Wind, Y. 2008. *Competing in A Flat World*. New Jersey: Wharton School Publishing.

Glenn, J., Gordon, T., and Florescu, E. 2008. *State of the Future*. Washington, DC: 2008 Millennium Project, WFUNA.

Goldin and Katz 1998. The Origins of Technology-Skill Complementarity. Q J Econ August: 693–732.

Goldsmith, S., and Eggers, W.D. 2004. Washignton, DC: Brookings Institution Press.

Gordon, R. J. 2000a. Does the new economy measure up the great inventions of the past? J Econ Perspect 14(4):49–75.

Gordon, R. J. 2000b. Interpreting the one big wave in US long term productivity growth. In *Productivity, Technology, and Economic Growth* 2000. Van Ark, B., Kuipers, S., and Kuper, G. (eds). Kluwer Academic Publications: The Netherlands.

Grace J., Kenny, C., Qiang, C., Liu J., Reynolds, T. 2001. Information and communication technologies and broad-based development: A partial review of the evidence. Retrieved, August 16, 2004, from: http://www.tessproject.com/guide/pubs/telecom/ICT_&Broad_Based_Development.pdf.

Gregory, N., Nollen, S., and Tenev, S. 2009. *New Industries from New Places*. Washington, DC: World Bank.

Grubler, A. 1990. *The Rise and Fall of Infrastructure, Dynamics of Evolution and Technological Change in Transport*. New York: Verlag.

Guermazi, B., and Satola, D. 2005. *Creating the "Right" Enalbing Environment for ICT. In e-development: From Excitement to Efectiveness*. Wshignton, DC: World Bank.

Gupta, P. M., Kumar, P., and Bhattacharya, J. 2004. *Government Online: Opportunities and Challenges*. New Delhi: Tata McGraw-Hill.

Hagel, J. III, Brown, J. S., and Davidson, L. 2008. Shaping Strategy in a World of Constant Disruptions. In: *Harvard Business Review*. pp. 81–89. Boston, MA: Harvard Business Publishing.

Hamel, G. 2007. *The Future of Management*. Boston, MA: Harvard Business School Press.

Hamel, G., and Prahalad, C. K. 1994. *Competing for the Future*. Boston, MA: Harvard Business School Press.

Hanna, N. K. 1974. Hearings before US House of Representatives, Subcommittee on International Cooperation in Science and Space. Ninety-Third Congress, Second Session (May 21–23, 1974) on International Science and Technology Transfer Act of 1974. Washington, DC: U.S. Government Printing Office. (Statement of Nagy K. Hanna, pp. 83–87).

Hanna, N. K. 1985a. *Indonesia Management Development*. Washington, DC: World Bank (3 volume report).

Hanna, N. K. 1985b. *Strategic Planning and Management*. World Bank Working Papers, Number 751, Washington. DC.

Hanna, N. K. 1991. Informatics and the Developing World. In: Finance and Development, Vol. 28/Number 4. A Quarterly publication of the International Monetary Fund and the World Bank, Washington, DC.

Hanna, N. K. 1991. *The Information Technology Revolution and Economic Development*. World Bank Discussion paper 120, Washington, DC.

Hanna, N. K. 1994. *Exploiting of Information Technology for Development: A Case Study of India*. World Bank Discussion Paper, Number 246, Washington, DC.

Hanna, N. K. 1999. A Proposed role for Aid Agencies in Helping Developing Countries to Design National Information Technology Strategies. In: Technology Management: Strategies and Applications, Overseas Publishers Association.

Hanna, N. K. 2000. *Annual Review of Development Effectiveness, 1999*. Operations Evaluation Department. Washington, DC: World Bank.

Hanna, N. K. 2003. *Why national strategies are needed for ICT-enabled development*. World Bank Staff Paper. Washington, DC: World Bank.

Hanna, N. K. 2007a. *From Envisioning to Designing e-Development: The Experience of Sri Lanka*. Washington, DC: World Bank.

Hanna, N. K. 2007b. *e-Leadership Institutions for the Knowledge Economy*. World Bank Institute Working Paper. Washington, DC: World Bank.

Hanna, N. K. 2008a. *Transforming Government and Empowering Communities: The Experience of Sri Lanka*. Washington, DC: World Bank.

Hanna, N. K. 2008b. Why a holistic e-development framework? *Information Technology and International Development Journal*. Cambridge, MA: MIT Press, Vol. 4, Number 4, Fall/Winter 2008, pp. 1–7.

Hanna, N. K, and Qiang, C. 2009. Trends in National E-Government Institutions. In: *Information and Communications for Development 2009: Extending Reach and Increasing Impact*. Washington, DC: World Bank.

Hanna, N. K., and Qiang, C. China's Informatization Strategy. In: *International Experience in e-Development*. (forthcoming).

Hanna, N. K., and Robert, P. 2002. *Making Development Work: Development Learning in a world of wealth and poverty*, New Jersey: Transactions Publications.

Hanna, N. K., and Sandor B. 1993. *Information Technology in World Bank Lending*. World Bank Discussion Paper, Number 206, Washington, DC.

Hanna, N. K., Boyson, S., and Shakuntala, G. 1996. *The East Asia Miracle and Information Technology*. Washington, DC: World Bank.

Hanna, N. K., Ken G., and Erik A. 1995. *Information Technology Diffusion: Experience of Industrial Countries and Lessons for Developing Countries*. World Bank Staff Working Paper. Washington, DC: The World Bank.

Heeks, R. 2000. The Approach of Senior Public Officials to Information Technology Related Reform: lessons from India. In: *Public Administration and Development*, 20:197–205.

Heeks, R. 2002. Failure, success and improvisation of information systems projects in developing countries. Institute for Development Policy and Management, University of Manchester. Retrieved Aug. 16, 2004, from: http://idpm.man.ac.uk/publications/wp/di/di_wp11.shtml,http://www1.worldbank.org/publicsector/bnpp/Gyandoot.PDF.

Heeks, R. 2006. *Implementing and Managing e-Government*. London: Sage Publication.

Heeks, R., and Bailur, S. 2006. *Analysing eGovernment Reasearch: Perspectives, Philosophies, Theories, Methods and Practice*. Manchester, UK: University of Manchester, Institute for Development Policy and Management (IDPM), Development Informatics Group, e-Government Working Paper Series, Paper No. 16,

Heeks, R. 2008. ITC4D 2.0: The Next Phase of Applying ICT for International Development. In: June 2008 issue of IEEE Computer Society, pp. 26–33.

Helpman, E. (ed.). 1998. *General Purpose Technologies and Economic Growth*. Cambridge, MA: MIT Press.

Hilbert, M., and Jorge, K. 2003. Building an Information Society: Latin American and Caribbean Perspective. Santiago, Chile: ECLAC.

Hirschman, A. 1958. *The Strategy for Economic Development*. New Haven, CT: Yale University Press.

Hirschman, A. 1970. *Exit, Voice and Loyalty*. Cambridge, MA: Harvard University Press.

Hirschman, A. 1995. *A Propensity to Self-Subversion*. Cambridge, MA: Harvard University Press.

Hobday, M. 1994. Export led Technology Development in the Four Dragons: The Case of Electronics. *Development and Change* 25(2):333–361.

Hobday, M. 1995. Innovation in East Asia: the Challenge to Japan. Aldershot: Elgar Press.

Huston, I., and Sakkab, N. 2006 Connect and Develop: Inside P&G's New Model for Innovation. Harvard Business Review. March 2006. Boston, MA: Harvard Business Publishing.

ICA-IT (International Council for Information Technology in Government Administration). 2006a. "Country Reports – Australia" presented at the ICA 40th Conference in September 2006 in Jaslico, Mexico. [http://www.ica-it.org/conf40/docs/Conf40_country_report_Australia.pdf].

ICA-IT. 2006b. "Country Reports – Singapore" presented at the ICA 40th Conference in September 2006 in Jaslico, Mexico. [http://www.ica-it.org/conf40/docs/Conf40_country_report_Singapore pdf].

Indian Institute of Management. 2003. An Evaluation of Gyandoot. By Center for Electronic Governance. Indian Institute of Management, Ahmedabad, India.

Infocomm Development Authority of Singapore (IDA Singapore). 2005. *Report on Singapore e-Government*. [http://www.igov.gov.sg/NR/rdonlyres/C586E52F-176A-44B6-B21E-2DB7E4 FA45D1/11228/2005ReportonSporeeGov.pdf].

International Finance Corporation (IFC) and World Resource Institute (WRI). 2007. *The Next 4 Billion: Market Size and Business Strategy at the Base of the Pyramid*. Washington, DC: World Resource Institute.

International Labor Organization (ILO). 2001. *World Employment Report*. Geneva: International Labor Organization (2001). Also retrieved August, 16, 2004, from: http://www.ilo.org/public/english/support/publ/wer/index2.htm.

International Monetary Fund (IMF). 2001. World Economic Outlook. The Information Technology Revolution. Washington, DC: IMF.

International Telecommunications Union (ITU). 2007. *Trends in Telecommunications Reform 2007: The Road to Next Generation Networks*. Geneva, Switzerland: ITU.

Ithiel de Sola, P. 1983. Technologies of Freedom. Boston, MA: Harvard University Press.

ITU-InfoDev. 2000. *Telecommunications Regulation Toolkit*. Washington, DC: InfoDev.

Jensen, A., and Trenholm, S. 2007 *Interpersonal Communication*. London: Oxford University Press.

Jeong, K.-H. 2006. *E-Government: The Road to Innovation: Principles and Experiences in Korea*. Seoul: Gil-Job-E Media.

Jethanandani, J., and Rose, E. 2005. Gartner Dataquest Market Databook Asia/Pacific October 2005. G00136901, Gartner Research.

Johnson, B., Manyika, J. M., and Yee, I.A. 2005. The Next Revolution in Interaction. *McKinsey Quarterly* 4:20–33.

Jorgensen, D. W., and Stiroh, K. 2000. Raising the Speed Limit: U.S. Economic Growth in the Information Age. Brookings Papers on Economic Activity, pp. 125–235.

Kamarck, E., and Nye, J. (eds.). 2002 *Governance.com: Democracy in the Information Age.* Brookings Institution Press.

Kamensky, J., and Burlin, T. (eds.). 2005. *Collaboration: Using Networks and Partnerships.* Rowman & Littlefield Publishers.

Kamensky, J., and Morales, A. (eds.). 2006. *Competition, Choice, and Incentives in Government Programs.* Rowman & Littlefield Publishers.

Kasvio, A. 2000. Information Society As a National Project – Analyzing the Case of Finland. Retrieved July 20, 2004, from University of Tampere, Finland, Information Society Research Centre Web site: http://www.uta.fi/~ttanka/Finland220500.html.

Kay, J. 2002. The Balance Sheet. *Prospect Magazine* 76(July):22–28.

Kenny, C., and Motta, M. 2002. The ICT Framework in Chile. Washington, DC: World Bank, Processed.

Kettl, D. 2002. Managing Indirect Government. In: *The Tools of Government: A guide to the New Governance*, edited by Lester Salamon. Oxford: Oxford University Press.

Kettl, D., and Kelman, S. 2007. *Reflections on 21st Century of Government Management.* IBM Center for the Business of Government.

Kirkman, C., Cornelius, P., Sachs, S., and Schwab, K. 2002. *The Global Information Technology Report 2001–2002: Readiness for the Networked World,* New York: Oxford University Press.

Knight, P. T. 1998. The Half-Life of Knowledge and Structural Reform of the Educational Sector. In: Claudio de Moura Castro (ed.), *Education in the Information Age: What Works and What Doesn't.* Washington, DC: Inter-American Development Bank, pp. 48–57.

Knight, P. T. 2007. Knowledge Management and e-Government in Brazil. Paper prepared for the Workshop on Managing Knowledge to Build Trust in Government, 7th Global Forum on Reinventing Government, 26–29 June, Vienna, Austria. Available online at http://unpan1.un.org/intradoc/groups/public/documents/unpan/unpan025989.pdf.

Knight, P. T. 2008a. *Smart Grid* – Redes elétricas inteligentes, *Banco Hoje*, November (2008) p. 10.

Knight, P. T. 2008b. Teaching, research and community networks in Brazil, *Connect World*, Latin American Edition, 2008, pp 7–9. Available at http://www.connect-world.com/PDFs/magazines/2008/LA_2008.pdf.

Knight, P. T., and Annenberg, D. 2008. Brazil's Experience with Integrated Citizen Service Centers. PowerPoint Presentation at Zelenograd Prefecture, Moscow, Russian Federation, 28 May.

Kotter, J. P. 1996. *Leading Change.* Boston, MA: Harvard Business School.

Kraemer, K., and Dedrick, J. 1997. Computing in Public Organizations. *Public Admin Res Theory* 7(1):89–112.

Kraemer, K., and King, J. L. 2005. Information Technology and Administrative Reform: Will E-Government Be Different. Memio, University of California, Irvine.

Kraemer, K., Dedrick, J., Melville, N., and Zhu, K. (eds.). 2006. *Global E-Commerce: Impacts of National Environment and Policy.* Cambridge: Cambridge University Press.

Krugman, P. 1994. The Myth of Asia's Miracle. *Foreign Affairs* 73(6):62–78.

Krugman, P. 1995. *Development, Geography and Economic Theory,* Cambridge, MA: MIT Press.

Krugman, P. 1996. Making sense of competitiveness debate, *Oxf Rev Econ Policy* 12(3):17–25.

Kuhn, T. 1962. *The Structure of Scientific Revolutions.* Chicago: University of Chicago Press.

Kunigami, A. M., and Naves-Sabater, J. 2009. Alternative Options to Increase Access to Telecommunications Services in Rural and Low-Income Areas. In: *2009 Information and Communications for Development: Global Trends and Policies.* Washington, DC: World Bank.

Kuznetsov, Y. (ed.). 2006. *Diaspora Networks and the International Migration of Skills.* World Bank: Washington, DC.

Labelle, R. 2005. *ICT Policy Formulation and e-Strategy Development.* UNDP-APDIP Asia Pacific Development Information Programme. New Delhi: Elsevier India.

Laitner, J. A., and Ehrhardt-Martinez, K. 2008. *Information and Communication Technologies: The Power of Productivity.* Washington, DC: American Council for an Energy-Efficient Economy.

Lall, S. 1999. *Competing with Labour: Skills and Competitiveness in Developing Countries.* Geneva: ILO, Issues in Development Discussion Paper 31.

Lall, S. 2001 *Competitiveness, Technology and Skills,* Cheltenham, UK: Edward Elgar.

Lall, S. 2003. Foreign direct investment, technology development and competitiveness: issues and evidence. In: *Technology Development in East Asia: Lessons for Other Developing Countries,* World Bank Institute.

Lanvin, B. 2003. Leaders and Facilitators: The New Roles of Governments in Digital Economies. In: *The Global Information Technology Report 2002–03.* World Economic Forum. Oxford: Oxford University Press.

Lanvin, B., and Anat L. 2006. The Next Frontiers of E-Government: Local Governments May Hold the Key to Global Competitiveness. In: *The Global Information Technology Report 2006–07.* New York: Palgrave.

Leadbeater, C. 2006. *The User Innovation Revolution.* London: National Consumer Council.

Lee, C.-M., Miller, W. F., Hancock, M., and Rowen, H. S. 2000. *The Silicon Valley Edge: A Habitat for Innovation and Entrepreneurship.* Stanford, CA: Stanford University Press.

Lei, D., and Kingsley E. H. 2004. The Role of Telecommunications Infrastructure in Regional Economic Growth of China. Paper presented at the Telecommunications Policy Research Conference, Washington, DC.

Levy, F., and Murnane, R. 1996. With What Skills are Computers a Complement? American Economic Review 86(2):258–262.

Li, Z. 2003. The Impact of ICT and E-business on Developing Country Trade and Growth. Presented at OECD-APEC Global Forum: Policy Frameworks for the Digital Economy, January 15, Honolulu. HI. http://www.oecd.org/dataoecd/20/9/2492709.pdf.

Lindbeck, A., and Snower, D. 2000. Multitask Learning and the Reorganization of Work: From Tailoristic to Holistic Organization. J Labor Econ 18(3):353–376.

Lindblom, C. 1959. The Science of Muddling Through. *Public Admin Rev* 29:79–88.

Litan, R. E., and Alice M. R. 2000. The Economy and the Internet: What lies Ahead? Brookings Conference Report No. 4, Brookings Institution.

Lucas, Fr., and Francis, B. 1999. Posted at: http://www.fao.org./sd/CDdirect/CDan0026.htm.

Lundvall, B. A. 1996. Information Technology in the Learning Economy: challenges for Development Strategies. Background paper for the UNCSTD Working Group on IT and Development.

MacLean, D., Deane, J., Souter, D., and Lilly, S. 2002. *Louder Voices: Strengthening Developing Country Participation in International ICT Decision-Making.* Commonwealth Telecommunications Organization and Panos, London for UK Department for International Development, London, UK.

Mann, C. 2002 Electronic Commerce, Networked Readiness, and Trade Competitiveness. In: *The Global Information Technology Report-Readiness for the Networked World,* World Economic Forum, 2001–2002.

Mansell, R., and Nordenstreng. 2007. Great Media and Communication Debates: WSIS and MacBride Report. In: *Information Technologies and International Development.* Vol. 3, Number 4, Summer 2006, pp. 15–36. Boston, MA: MIT Press.

Mansell, R., and When, U. (eds.). 1998. *Knowledge Societies: Information Technology for Sustainable Development.* Oxford, Oxford University Press.

Mansell, R., Chrisanthi, A., Danny, Q., and Roger S. (eds.). 2007. *The Oxford Handbook of Information and Communications Technologies.* Oxford, UK: Oxford University Press.

Mas, I. 2008. Realizing the Potential for Branchless Banking: Challenges Ahead. Focus Note 50. Washington, DC: CGAP.

Mas, I., and Kabir, K. 2008. Banking on Mobiles: Why, Who and for Whom? Focus Note 48. Washington, DC: CGAP.

McKinsey & Company. 2008. Development of IT and ITES Industries – Impact, Trends, Opportunities, and Lessons Learned for Developing Countries. Presentation to the World Bank in June.

Meier, G. M. 2005. *Biography of a Subject: An Evolution of Development Economics.* New York: Oxford University Press.

Melody, W. H. 2003. Policy Iimplications of the new information economy. In Tool, M., and Bush, P. (eds.). *Institutional Analysis and Economic Policy.* Dordrecht, NL: Kluwer, pp. 411–432.

Millard, B., and Provan, K. 2006. *A Manager's Guide to Choosing and Using Collaborative Networks.* IBM Center for the Business of Government.

Mintzberg, H., Ahlstrand, B., and Lampel, J. 1998. *Strategy Safari.* New York: Free Press.

Momentum Research Group. 2005. Net Impact Latin America: From Connectivity to Productivity. Austin. TX. http://www.netimpactstudy.com/nila/pdf/netimpact_la_full_report_t.pdf.

Nambisan, S. 2008. *Transforming Government Through Collaborative Innovation.* IBM Center for the Business of Government.

Nambisan, S., and Sawhney, M. 2008. *The Global Brain.* New Jersey: Wharton School Publishing.

NASSCOM-McKinsey Report 2005. Extending India's Leadership of the Global IT and BPO Industries. New Delhi, India: NASSCOM

Navas-Sabater, J., Dymond A., and Juntunen N. 2002 *Telecommunications and Information Services for the Poor.* Toward a Strategy for Universal Access. World Bank Discussion Paper. Washington, DC: World Bank.

Nelson, R. R. 2000. National Innovation Systems. In: Zoltan, J. Acs, (ed.) *Regional Innovation, Knowledge, and Global Change*. London: Printer, A Cassell Imprint.

Norris, P. 2002. *Digital Divide: Civic Engagement, Information Poverty, and the Internet Worldwide.* Cambridge: Cambridge University Press.

OECD (Organization for Economic Cooperation and Development). 1998. Information Technology as an Instrument of Public Management Reform: A Study of Five OECD Countries, PUMA 14(98):14.

OECD. 2000. *Measuring the ICT Sector.* Paris: OECD.

OECD. 2001. *Information Technology Outlook: ICTs, E-Commerce and the Information Economy.* Paris: OECD.

OECD 2002. *Survey of knowledge management practices in ministries/departments/agencies of central government.* Paris: OECD. Available in pdf at http://www.oecd.org/dataoecd/59/18/1946891.pdf.

OECD. 2003a. The Learning Government: Introduction and Draft Results of the Survey of Knowledge Management Practices in Ministries/Departments/Agencies of Central Government. Document of 27th Session of the Public Management Committee at 3–4 April 2003. Paris: OECD. Word Document available from http://www.oecd.org/LongAbstract/0,2546,en_2649_201185_33709749_1_1_1_1,00.html.

OECD. 2003b. From Red Tape to Smart Tape: Administrative Simplification in OECD Countries. Paris: OECD.

OECD. 2004a. *ICTs and Economic Growth in Developing Countries.* DAC Network on Poverty Reduction. Paris: OECD.

OECD. 2004b. Lifelong Learning. OECD Policy Brief, Paris.

OECD. 2005a. *e-Government for Better Government.* OECD e-Government Studies, Paris.

OECD. 2005b. *Mexico.* OECD e-Government Studies, Paris.

OECD. 2006. *Digital Broadband Content.* Paris: OECD.

OECD. 2007. *Participative Web and User-Created Content: Web 2.0, Wikis, and Social Networking.* Paris: OECD.

OECD. 2008. *OECD Information Technology Outlook 2008.* Paris: OECD.

Oliner, S. D., and Sichel, D. E. 2000. The Resurgence of Growth in the Late 1990s: Is Information Technology the Story? J Econ Perspect 14(4):3–22.

Paul, S. 1991. Accountability in Public Services: Exit, Voice and Capture. Washington, DC: World Bank.

Perez, C. 2001. *Technological Change and Opportunities for Development as a Moving Target.* Maastricht: UNU.

Perez, C. 2002. *Technological Revolutions and Financial Capital.* Cheltenham, UK: Edward Elgar.

Perez, C., and Soete, L. 1988. Catching up in Technology: Entry Barriers and Windows in Technology. In: Dosi, G. et al. (eds.). *Technical Change and Economic Theory.* London and New York: Pinter Publishers. pp. 458–479.

Popkin, J. M., and Iyengar, P. (Gartner, Inc.). 2007. *IT and the East.* Boston, MA: Harvard Business School Press.

Porter, M. E. 1980. *Competitive Strategy.* New York: The Free Press.

Porter, M. E. 1990. *The Competitive Advantage of Nations.* New York: The Free Press.

Prahalad, C. K. 2005. *The Fortune at the Bottom of the Pyramid.* New Jersey: Wharton School Publishing.

Proenza, D. J. 2001. Telecenter Sustainability – Myths and Opportunities. In: Dixon, W. (ed.), *Bridging the rural knowledge gap: Information systems for improved livelihoods.* Rome: FAO. Retrieved July 15, 2004 from: http://www.fao.org/Waicent/FAOINFO/AGRICULT/ags/Agsp/pdf/ProenzaTelecenter.pdf.

Proenza, D. J. 2003a. ICT-enabled networks, public sector performance and the development of ICTs. In: Badshah, A., Khan, S., Garrido, M. (eds.). *Connected for Development. Information Kiosks and Sustainability.* New York: UN ICT Task Force. pp. 15–24.

Proenza, D. J. 2003b. A public sector Support Strategy for telecenter development: Emerging lessons from Latin America and the Carribean. In: Badshah, A., Khan, S., Garrido, M. (eds.). *Connected for Development. Information Kiosks and Sustainability.* New York: UN ICT Task Force. pp. 9–14.

Qiang, C. Z., and Rosotto, C. 2009. Economic Impact of Broadband. In: *2009 Information and Communication for Development: Extending Reach and Increasing Impact.* Washington, DC: World Bank.

Quinn, J. B. 1992. *Intelligent Enterprise.* New York: Free Press.

Radwan, I., and Eskinazi, R. 2006. *Offshore to India,* Washington, DC: World Bank.

Raja, S., and Singh, R. 2009. Nothing endures but change: Thinking Strategically about ICT Convergence. In: *2009 Information and Communications for Development: Extending Reach and Increasing Impact.* Washington, DC: World Bank.

Ramsey, T. 2004. *On Demand Government: Continuing the E-government Journey.* Indiana: IBM Press.

Resnick, M. 1998. Technologies for Lifelong Kindergarten. Educ Technol Res Dev 46:4.

Resnick, M. 2002. Rethinking Learning in the Digital Age. In: *The Global Information Technology Report-Readiness for the Networked World,* World Economic Forum, Kirkman, Cornelius, Sachs, Schwab.

Rodriguez, A. 2008. *Knowledge and Innovation for Competitiveness in Brazil.* Washington, DC: World Bank.

Rodrik, D. 2004. Getting Institutions Right. *CESifo DICE Report.* University of Munich, Center for Economic Studies, and Ifo Institute for Economic Research.

Rodrik, D. 2007. *One Economics, Many Recipes.* Princeton, NJ: Princeton University Press.

Rodrik, D. 2008. *Second-Best Institutions.* CEPR Discussion Paper 6764. London: Centre for Economic Policy Research.

Rubino-Hallman, S., and Nagy K. H.. 2006. New Technologies for Public Sector Transformation: A Critical Analysis of e-Government Initiatives in Latin America and the Caribbean. *J e-Gov*3(3):3–39.

Sachs, J. D. 2005. *The End of Poverty: Economic Possibilities for Our Time.* New York, NY: Penguin Group.

Sanchez, S., et al. 2001 Constrained Global Integration: A Note on Microenterprise in Latin America. Washington, DC: World Bank.

Schon, D. 1983. *The Reflective Practitioner: How Professionals Think in Action.* New York: Basic Books.

Schumaker, E. F. 1973. *Small is Beautiful: Economics as if People Mattered.* New York: Harper and Row.

Schumpeter, J. A. 1942. *Capitalism, Socialism and Democracy.* New York: Harper & Row (original publication).

Scott, A. J. 2000. Global City-Regions and the New World System. In: Yusuf, S., Wu, W., and Evenett, S. (eds.). *Local Dynamics in an Era of Globalization.* Washington, DC: World Bank, pp. 84–91

Sen, A. 2000. *Development as Freedom.* New York: Anchor Book.

Shapiro, C., and Varian, H. R. 1999. *Information Rules: A strategic Guide to the Network Economy.* Boston, MA: Harvard Business School Press.

Snyder, W., and Briggs, X. 2003. *Communities of Practice: A New Tool for Government Managers.* IBM Center for the Business of Government.

Soete, L. 2000. Towards the Digital Economy: Scenarios for Business. *Telemat Inf*17:199–212.

Solow, R. 1987. We'd Better Watch Out. Book Review No. 36. *The New York Times*, 12 July.

Song, G., and Conford, T. 2006. Mobile Government: Towards a Service Paradigm. In: *The proceedings of the 2nd International Conference on e-Government.* University of Pittsburg, USA, pp. 208–218.

Stiglitz, J. 1996. Some lessons from the East Asian miracle. World Bank Res Observer11(2): 151–177.

Stiglitz, J. 1998. Towards a New Paradigm for Development: Strategies, Policies, and Processes. Ninth Raul Prebisch Lecture, United Nations Conference on Trade and Development, delivered at the Palais des Nations, Geneva. October 19.

Stiglitz, J. 1999a. Knowledge for Development: Economic Science Policy, and Economic Advice. In: *Annual World Bank Conference on Development Economics.* 1998, Boris, P., and Joseph, S. (eds.) Washington, DC: World Bank, pp. 9–58.

Stiglitz, J. 1999b. Scan Globally, Reinvent Locally: Knowledge Infrastructure and the Localization of Knowledge. *Keynote Address, First Global Development Network Conference*, Bonn, Germany.

Stiglitz, J., Peter, R. O., and Jonathan, M. O. 2000. The Role of Government in a Digital Age. Study commissioned by the Computer and Communications Industry Association. Washington, DC [http://unpan1.un.org/intradoc/groups/public/documents/APCITY/UNPAN002055.pdf].

Stoll, K. 2003. Basic principles of community Public Internet Access Point's sustainability. In: Badshah, A., Khan, S., Garrido, M. (eds.). *Connected for Development. Information Kiosks and Sustainability.* New York: UN ICT Task Force, 99. 61–66.

Suan, B. H. 2003. Making e-Governance happen – a practitioner's perspective. In: James, S. L. Y. (ed.). *E-Government in Asia.* Singapore: Times Edition, pp. 366–391.

Swahney, M., and Zabin, J. 2001. *The Seven Steps to Nirvana*: Strategic Insights into Ebusiness Transformation. New York: McGraw-Hill, Inc.

Talero, E. 1997. National Information Infrastructure in Developing Countries. In: *National Information Infrastructure,* Brian, K., and Ernest, W. (eds.). MIT Press.

Tapscott, D., and Williams, A. D. 2006. *Wikinomics: How Mass Collaboration Changes Everything.* New York: Penguin Group.

Tapscott, D., Williams, A., and Herman, D. 2008. *Government 2.0: Transforming Government and Governance for the Twenty-First Century.* New Paradigm White Paper.

Tessler, B. A., and Hanna, N. 2003 Role of Software. In: *Electronic Journal on Information Systems in Developing Countries,* Erran, C (ed.), special issue on the Emergence of Software Exporting Industries in Developing and Emerging Economies.

The Economist. 2008. Halfway there: How to promote the spread of mobile technologies among the world poorest. http://www.economist.com/business/displaystory.cfm?story_id=11465558.

Toffler, A. 1990. *Power Shift: Knowledge, Wealth and Violence at the Edge of the 21st Century.* New York: Bantam Books.

Tuohy, B. 1999. E-Commerce – the Irish perspective. Retrieved August 15, 2004, from http://www.dcmnr.gov.ie/display.asp/pg=766.

Turcano, M. 2005. *Knowledge Maps: ICT in Education*. Washington, DC: infoDev /World Bank.

UNCTAD. 2003. E-Commerce and Development Report 2003. New York and Geneva: United Nations.

UNDP. 2003. The Role of Information and Communication Technologies in Global Development. ICT Task Force Series 3.

UNDP. 2007. e-Government Interoperability: Overview. Bangkok, Thailand: UNDP.

UNESCO. 2005. *Media and Good Governance*. Paris: UNESCO.

United Nations. 1998. *Knowledge societies: Information technology for sustainable development*. Oxford: Oxford University Press.

United Nations. 2008a. World e-Parliament Report 2008. New York: UN. ISBN: 978-92-1-023067-4.

United Nations Development Program. 2001. *Human Development Report2001: Making Technologies work for Human Development*. New York: UNDP.

Van Widen, W., and Van Den Berg, L. 2004. Cities in the Knowledge Economy: New Governance Challenges. Rotterdam, The Netherlands: European Institute for Comparative Urban Research.

Vijayaditya, N. 2000 Wired Village: The Warana Experiment. In: Bhatnagar, S., and Schware, R. (eds.) *Information and Communication Technology In Rural Areas*. Washington, DC: World Bank Institute.

Vincent, S. W., and Vickery, G. 2008. The Participative Web: Innovation and Collaboration. In: Dutta, S., and Mia, I. (eds.). 2008. *The Global Information Technology Report 2007–08*. World Economic Forum. pp. 109–118.

Von Hippel, E. 2005. *Democratizing Innovation*. MIT Press.

Wade, R. 1990. *Governing the Market: Economic Theory and the Role of Government in East Asian Industrialization,* Princeton, NJ: Princeton University Press.

Wade, R. 2002 Bridging the Digital Divide: The Route to Development or a new form of Dependency? *Global Govern J*.

Waterman, R., Peters, T., and Phillips, J. 1980. Structure Is not Organization. *Business Horizon*, pp. 14–26.

Weill, P., and Jeanne, W. R. 2004. *IT Governance: How Top Performers Manage IT*. Cambridge, MA: Harvard Business School.

Wellenius, B. 2006. Extending Communications and Information Services: Principles and Practical Solutions. In: *2006 Information and Communications for Development. Global Trends and Policies*. Washington, DC: World Bank, pp. 41–55.

Wellenius, B., Forster, V., and Calvo, C. M. 2004. Private Provision of Rural Infrastructure Services: Competing for Subsidies. Policy Research Working Paper 3365. Washington, DC: World Bank.

West, D. M. 2005. *Digital Government: Technology and Public Sector Performance*. Princeton, NJ: Princeton University Press.

Wildavsky, A. 1984. *The Politics of the Budgetary Process*, 4th ed. Boston: Little, Brown, and Co.

Wilson, E. J., III. 2004. *The Information Revolution and Developing Countries*. Cambridge, MA: MIT Press.

World Bank. 1997. *The State in a Changing World. World Development Report 1997*. Washington, DC: World Bank.

World Bank. 1999. *Knowledge for Development, World Development Report 1998–99*. Washington, DC: World Bank.

World Bank. 2000. *Reforming Public Institutions and Strengthening Governance: A World Bank Strategy*. Washington, DC: World Bank.

World Bank. 2002. *Building Institutions for Markets. World Development Report 2002*. Washington, DC: World Bank.

World Bank. 2003. *Making Services Work for Poor People. World Development Report 2003*. Washington, DC: World Bank and Oxford University Press.

World Bank. 2005a. *E-development: From Excitement to Effectiveness.* Washington, DC: World Bank. Global Information and Communication Technologies Department.

World Bank. 2005b. *Expanding Opportunities and Building Competencies for Young People: A New Agenda for Secondary Education.* Washington, DC: World Bank.

World Bank. 2005c. *A Better Investment Climate for Everyone. World Development Report 2005.* Washington, DC: World Bank.

World Bank 2006. *Information and Communications for Development 2006. Global Trends and Policies.* Washington, DC: World Bank.

World Bank. 2007a. *To Give People Voice: Media and Broadcasting Development.* Washington, DC: World Bank.

World Bank. 2007b. *Development and the Next Generation. World Development Report 2007.* Washington, DC: World Bank.

World Bank. 2008. Mexico Project Appraisal Document. Washington, DC: World Bank.

World Bank. 2009a. *Reshaping Economic Geography. World Development Report 2009.* Washington, DC: World Bank.

World Bank. 2009b. *Information and Communications for Development 2009. Extending Reach and Increasing Impact.* Washington, DC: World Bank.

World Bank, Operations Evaluation Department. 2001. *Information Infrastructure: The World Bank Group's Experience.* Washington, DC: World Bank.

World Bank, Operations Evaluation Department. 2002. *Social Funds: Assessing Effectiveness.* Washington, DC: World Bank.

Wormland, T., Gaspar, M. 2003. Hungarian Telecottages. In: Badshah, A., Khan, S., Garrido, M. (eds.). *Connected for Development. Information Kiosks and Sustainability.* New York: UN ICT Task Force, pp. 191–198.

Yong, J. S. L. 2005. *e-Government in Asia.* Singapore: Times Media Publishing.

Yusuf, S. 2003. *Innovative East Asia: The Future of Growth.* Washington, DC: World Bank.

Yusuf, S. 2009. *Development Economics Through the Decades.* Washington, DC: World Bank.

Yusuf, S., Wu, W., and Evenett, S. (eds.). 2000. *Local Dynamics in an Era of Globalization.* Washington, DC: World Bank.

Zander, R., and Benjamin, Z. 2000. *The Art of Possibility.* New York: Penguin Books.

Index

CPSIA information can be obtained
at www.ICGtesting.com
Printed in the USA
LVHW081207200420
654119LV00011B/931